The Post-Falklands Dinner, 1982.

Front row from left to right: Sir Anthony Parsons (UK Rep to UN), Adm Sir 'Sandy' Woodward (Task Force Comd), Adm Sir John Fieldhouse (CinC Fleet), Gen Sir Edwin Bramall (CGS), Cecil Parkinson (War Cabinet), William Whitelaw (War Cabinet), Adm Sir Terence Lewin (CDS), The Prime Minister, The Lord Mayor of London, John Nott (SofS Defence), Sir Michael Havers (Attorney-General), Adm Sir Henry Leech (First Sea Lord), ACM Sir Michael Beetham (CAS), Maj Gen Jeremy Moore (Land Force Comd), Sir Nicholas Henderson (UK Ambassador to USA).

The Chiefs

The Story of the United Kingdom Chiefs of Staff

by
General Sir William Jackson GBE KCB MC MA
and
Field Marshal Lord Bramall KG GCB OBE MC JP

BRASSEY'S (UK)

(A Member of the Maxwell Macmillan Group)
LONDON · WASHINGTON · NEW YORK

First edition 1992

UK editorial offices: Brassey's, 50 Fetter Lane, London EC4A 1AA
orders: Purnell Distribution Centre, Paulton, Bristol BS18 5LQ

USA editorial offices: Brassey's, 8000 Westpark Drive, First Floor, McLean, Virginia 22102
orders: Macmillan Publishing Company, Front and Brown Streets, Riverside, NJ 08075

Distributed in North America to booksellers and wholesalers by the Macmillan Publishing Company, N.Y., N.Y.

Library of Congress Cataloging-in-Publication Data
available

British Library Cataloguing in Publication Data
available

ISBN 0-08-040370 0 Hardcover

Typeset by Florencetype Ltd, Kewstoke, Avon
Printed in Great Britain by B.P.C.C. Wheatons Ltd., Exeter

To the real 'Chiefs' –
our wives, Joan and Avril

Contents

Acknowledgements

We wish to thank and acknowledge the help we have received from Professor Brian Bond of King's College, London, Major General Tony Trythall of Brassey's and Robin Brodhurst of Pangbourne College for their help with the historical background to the Chiefs' work; from John Andrews, the Ministry of Defence's Chief Librarian and his team – Michael Chapman, Judith Blacklaw, Mavis Simpson and Richard Tubb – for their great help in providing reference material; and from the Imperial War Museum and the Ministry of Defence for the photographs of the Chiefs throughout their existence.

We wish to thank also, for permission to use photographs the Hulton Picture Company, the National Portrait Gallery, the Mary Evans Picture Library, the RAF Museum and the National Army Museum, and Lord Mulley to reproduce Mac's 1978 cartoon of the Chiefs 'doing Jankers'. The Crown copyright photographs in this publication are reproduced with the permission of the Controller of Her Majesty's Stationery Office.

We are grateful to the following for permission to reproduce substantial extracts from material to which they hold the copyright:

Her Majesty's Stationery Office: The British Official History Series of the Second World War; and *Defence White Papers*.
Allen & Unwin: *Supreme Command*, Lord Hankey. *The Birth of Independent Air Power*, M Cooper.
Bodley Head: *Vanguard to Trident*, Eric Grove.
Cassell: *The Second World War*, Winston Churchill.
Collins: *The Turn of the Tide*, Arthur Bryant. *Triumph in the West*, Arthur Bryant. *Trenchard*, A Boyle. *Alanbrooke*, David Fraser. *Mountbatten*, Philip Ziegler.
Constable: *The Ironside Diaries*, Roderick Macleod & Denis Kelly.
Hamish Hamilton: *Monty*, Nigel Hamilton.

Harvard University Press: *The Politics of Grand Strategy*, S R
   Williamson.
Heinemann: *The Memoirs of Lord Chatfield*, Chatfield. *The Memoirs of
   Lord Ismay*, Ismay.
H.M.S.O.: *Grand Strategy Series*, and all Government documents
   quoted.
Hodder & Stoughton: *Right of the Line*, John Terraine.
Hutchinson: *Out of Step*, Michael Carver.
Macmillan: *The Tides of Fortune*, Harold Macmillan.
Michael Joseph: *The Time of My Life*, Denis Healey.
Michael Russel: *Turning Points*, Harold Watkinson.
Oxford University Press: *From Dreadnought to Scapa Flow*, Arthur
   Marder.
Royal United Services Institution: *The Central Organisation of Defence*,
   Michael Howard.

List of Plates

DEFENCE REORGANISATION, 1964
41. Admiral of the Fleet Earl Mountbatten, Peter Thorneycroft, Sir Henry Hardman (PUS) and Air Marshal Sir John Lapsley (Secretary).

MOUNTBATTEN'S FAREWELL, 1965
42. Field Marshal Sir Richard Hull, Admiral Sir David Luce, General Sir James Cassels and Air Chief Marshal Sir Charles Elworthy.

THE CHIEFS AT THE CORONATION, 1953
43. Air Chief Marshal Sir William Dickson, Admiral Sir Rhoderick McGrigor and General Sir John Harding.

THE FIFTIETH ANNIVERSARY OF THE CHIEFS
44. The Chiefs of Staff Committee in 1973: Admiral Sir Michael Pollock, Air Chief Marshal Sir Dennis Spotswood, Admiral of the Fleet Sir Peter Hill-Norton, General Sir Michael Carver, Sir James Dunnett and Sir Michael Carey.

SOME CHIEFS OF DEFENCE STAFF IN THE 1970s
45. Marshal of the Royal Air Force Lord Elworthy.
46. Admiral of the Fleet Lord Hill-Norton.
47. Field Marshal Lord Carver.
48. Marshal of the Royal Air Force Lord Cameron.

THE CHIEFS IN POLITICAL DISFAVOUR
49. Mac's 1978 cartoon of the Chiefs 'doing Jankers'.

THE FALKLANDS TEAM, 1982
50. Admiral of the Fleet Sir Terence Lewin, Admiral Sir Henry Leach, Air Chief Marshal Sir Michael Beetham, General Sir Edwin Bramall and Sir Frank Cooper.

CDSs OF THE 1980s
51. Admiral of the Fleet Lord Lewin.
52. Field Marshal Lord Bramall.
53. Admiral of the Fleet Lord Fieldhouse.
54. Marshal of the Royal Air Force Lord Craig.

Cover Illustrations
Front: Thatcher's Falkland's Chiefs.
Back: Churchill's Wartime Chiefs.

List of Acronyms

ANF	Atlantic Nuclear Force
ANZAC	Australian and New Zealand Forces (from Australian and New Zealand Army Corps in the First World War)
AOC-in-C	Air Office Commanding-in-Chief
ASW	Anti-Submarine Warfare
BAFF	British Air Forces in France (1939–40)
BEF	British Expeditionary Force
CAS	Chief of Air Staff
CCS	Combined Chiefs of Staff
CCS 94	Combined Chiefs of Staff strategy paper of July 1942 agreeing Operation Torch
CDS	Chief of Defence Staff
CENTO	Central Treaty Organisation
CGS	Chief of General Staff
CID	Committee of Imperial Defence
CIGS	Chief of the Imperial General Staff
C-in-C	Commander-in-Chief
CND	Campaign for Nuclear Disarmament
CNS	Chief of Naval Staff
COS	Chiefs of Staff
CSA	Chief Scientific Adviser
DMO	Director of Military Operations
DRC	Defence Requirements Committee
EEC	European Economic Community
EOKA	Greek terrorist organisation in Cyprus seeking reunion with Greece
ETOUSA	European Theater of Operations United States Army
GDP	Gross Domestic Product

GHQ	General Headquarters
GOC-in-C	General Officer Commanding-in-Chief
IMF	International Monetary Fund
IRA	Irish Republican Army
JCS	Joint Chiefs of Staff (United States)
JPS	Joint Planning Staff
LTC	Long Term Costings
MINIS	Management Information Service
MLF	Multilateral Nuclear Force
MRCA	Multi-Role Combat Aircraft
NATO	North Atlantic Treaty Organisation
OKW	*Oberkommando der Wehrmacht*
PUS	Permanent Under Secretary of State
QMG	Quartermaster General
RAF	Royal Air Force
RFC	Royal Flying Corps
RN	Royal Navy
RNAS	Royal Naval Air Service
SACEUR	Supreme Allied Commander Europe (NATO)
SALT	Strategic Arms Limitations Talks
SAS	Special Air Service
SEATO	South East Asia Treaty Organisation
S of S	Secretary of State
SSN	Nuclear Powered Attack Submarine
TA	Territorial Army
TA & VR	Territorial Army and Volunteer Reserve
TEZ	Total Exclusion Zone
TG	Task Group
TUC	Trade Union Congress
UDI	Unilateral Declaration of Independence (Rhodesia)
VCAS	Vice Chief of Air Staff
VCDS	Vice Chief of Defence Staff
VCIGS	Vice Chief of the Imperial General Staff
VCNS	Vice Chief of Naval Staff
WW1	COS strategy paper for the Arcadia Conference

PROLOGUE
Who are the Chiefs?

'*Each of the three Chiefs of Staff will have an individual and collective responsibility for advising on defence policy as a whole, the three constituting, as it were, a Super-Chief of a War Staff in Commission.*'

Salisbury Commission's Report of 1923,
setting up the Chiefs of Staff Committee.

On the 5th Floor of the Ministry of Defence's Main Building on the south side of Whitehall, directly opposite Downing Street, there is a well lit but heavily curtained conference room. It measures 40' × 20' – the size of a modest drawing-room – with a low ceiling, and is entered through a small waiting-room. It is simple, modern and clearly designed for functional purposes, and its colour scheme and furnishings are businesslike: beige walls, brown carpeting, mahogany woodwork and black upholstery.

At the near end of the room, where you enter, there is a large projection screen set into the wall. In front of the screen there is a low dais or platform with an adjustable lectern on it for briefing and presentations. On the left-hand side of the room, opposite three windows on the right-hand side, you see a large illuminated wall-map of the world with several clocks above it, showing the different times in selected places around the globe, and beyond it is a long thin desk evidently placed there for secretaries. At the far end of the room, there is another low platform with two rows of chairs, looking a bit like cinema seats, which are for those who have come to listen rather than participate, and are in consequence called the 'one and nine-pennies'. And round the room, just above head height, there are several television monitors.

The most striking feature of the room, however, is the very large and heavy coffin-shaped table, made of light Burma teak, which takes up most of the room in front of the film projector screen. It is very broad at the screen end, and it does not start to taper until about halfway down its length. Then it narrows gently towards the far end, where it is just wide enough for the chairman to sit in ample comfort. Around it are twelve black swivel chairs, whose occupants can see and be seen by the chairman, and all have an uninterrupted view of the screens as well.

It is at this table that, on at least one afternoon a week, and more frequently during emergencies, a dozen or so men, mostly in their middle fifties and usually in civilian clothes, gather to discuss, courteously and deliberately but always emphatically and sometimes heatedly, military matters of importance not only to the Armed Forces but also to the nation as a whole. These are the Chiefs of Staff in Committee, together with their most immediate colleagues and advisers from amongst the senior military, civilian and scientific staffs of the unified Ministry of Defence and from other interested ministries in Whitehall, like the Foreign and Commonwealth Office.

At the narrower end of the table, in a slightly higher backed chair, with the emblem and motto of the Order of the Garter emblazoned upon it – a reminder, like the Burma teak of the table, that it was Earl Mountbatten of Burma who first brought the room into use – sits the Chief of Defence Staff (CDS for short). He is the head of the Chiefs of Staff in the sense that he is the chairman of their Committee, the principal military adviser to Her Majestry's Government on all aspects of Defence Policy, and the man who, in peacetime crisis management and in limited war outside NATO, is in overall charge, under Cabinet direction, of any military operations undertaken by British Forces, and to whom the Central Defence Staff report.

On CDS's right, by tradition, sits the Chief of the General Staff (CGS) – a full general, who is the professional head of the Army. On his left, sits his Naval equivalent – a full Admiral with the dual title of First Sea Lord and Chief of the Naval Staff (CNS). The Chief of Air Staff (CAS), an Air Chief Marshal, sits alongside CNS; and the Permanent Under-Secretary (PUS) is next to CGS. The latter is the civilian official head of the Ministry in its role as a Department of State, as opposed to a military headquarters, and is the Secretary of State's adviser on financial, political and parliamentary matters. The PUS, as he is known, is a valued participant in the Chiefs of Staff discussions, although, constitutionally, he is a co-opted rather than a full member of the Committee. Next to the PUS sits the Vice-Chief of Defence Staff (VCDS), who became the fifth full member of the Committee in the Heseltine reforms of 1985. He acts as the Chief of

Staff to the CDS across the whole spectrum of policy work undertaken by the Central Defence Staff.

The remaining seats on the right-hand side are taken up by representatives of the Foreign and Commonwealth Office, the Defence Scientific Staff and the Defence Policy Staff; and opposite them sit the Secretary of the Chiefs of Staff Committee (a Captain RN, Colonel or Group Captain) and a number of other senior staff advisers, who attend as required, depending on the subjects listed on the agenda.

Most of the weekly meetings are formal ones, involving the circulation of discussion papers on which each Chief of Staff will have been fully briefed by his own departmental staff before the meeting. The agenda will probably engage the Committee for two to three hours, and the minutes taken by the Secretary and his team of assistant secretaries will invariably be on the desks of those who attended the meeting by early next morning. Sometimes, when a particularly sensitive subject is to be discussed, the meeting is held informally, either in the same room or in CDS's office with only the Chiefs of Staff and their Secretary present and with no papers circulated beforehand.

The responsibilities of the Committee have varied in emphasis over the seven decades of its existence. Today, they are to advise the CDS, and, through him, the Government of the day on the capabilities and current activities of each of the Armed Services, and on the military aspects of Defence policy as a whole. This is so that sound, realistic and practical military judgements can be made; activities within and between the three Services can be co-ordinated; and military advice to Ministers and the Government can be assembled and clarified. The current Defence effort involves half a million Servicemen, reserves and civilians; a £20 billion budget, which is somewhere near 5 per cent of the Gross Domestic Product and 11 per cent of all government expenditure; and a wide ranging strategy both within and far beyond the boundaries of Europe.

The professional advice given by the Committee is based upon not only the background and personal views of the three single-Service Chiefs of Staff, but, more importantly, upon the vast accumulated experience of the Navy, Army and Air Force of which they are the professional heads, and for whose morale, operational efficiency and well-being they are individually responsible in peace and war. In this way, power to offer advice is tempered by responsibility for executing the resultant decisions; for it must never be forgotten that when it comes to war it is men's lives that are at stake. The Chiefs' advice also has to take into account political direction given by ministers accountable to Parliament, and financial realities over resources which, historically, never quite match up to perceived commitments.

Such is the growing complexity and interlocking nature of the three Services that formulation of Defence policy has become increasingly centralised while their management has had to be devolved to the Admiralty, Army and Air Force Boards. These are chaired by a Minister of State with their Chiefs of Staff sitting as the senior military member or chief executive. Thus policy and management are linked through the single-Service Chiefs of Staff as members of both the policy-forming Chiefs of Staff Committee and the management-orientated Service Boards. The non-political and detailed day to day management of each Service is carried forward by the Executive Committee of each Service Board, chaired by its Chief of Staff; hence his personal responsibility, which, in effect, puts him over all his Service's Commanders-in-Chief and Commanders in terms of authority.

With such responsibilities, it is hardly surprising that the Chiefs of Staff Committee has, in slightly different guises over the years, played a little publicised but crucial part in the higher machinery of government. It has helped governments to handle innumerable crises and small wars; played a major part in the successful conduct of the Second World War; master-minded victory over the Argentinians in the South Atlantic; and, more recently, has been at the heart of the crisis management in the Gulf conflict.

The 'Chiefs' collectively have therefore a special niche in public life which is fully recognised. As individuals, however, they are rarely seen as public figures, and, if they are, then it is usually due to wartime involvement. Some, like Jellicoe, Beatty, Robertson and Trenchard in the First World War, and Brooke, Pound, Cunningham and Portal in the Second, did become national figures. But, as government officials – for that is what they really are – it is not their responsibility to present the Defence case in public or to court the limelight: that is for ministers to accomplish. Yet the esteem in which the Chiefs are held as a corporate body was well illustrated not long ago by one of the Anglican Bishops saying that the Chiefs of Staff were the only people in our society of the calibre that he would expect. He then went on to make the surprising admission that, if he were in trouble, which God forbid, it would be to them that he would turn for help rather than to his fellow bishops!

Although this unsolicited accolade from such a surprising quarter can be construed more as a reflection on his clerical colleagues than as an accurate indication of the calibre and character of the Chiefs themselves, there is an underlying recognition that the Chiefs do represent national continuity, high standards and integrity; and that however much their powers may be constitutionally constrained by political control, out of fear of a latter-day Cromwell emerging, they are a force in the land, which no government can afford to ignore on matters of strategy, military organisation, weapon policies and national security generally.

Nor can this view be entirely discounted. Resignation by the Chiefs of Staff is, very properly, seldom even threatened let alone resorted to. However, in certain circumstances, and particularly if submitted as a body, it could provoke a crisis which the Parliamentary Opposition and the media would not be slow to exploit. 'Will the Right Honourable Gentleman confirm that his plan has the support of the Chiefs of Staff?', a Secretary of Defence may well be asked in a Commons debate; or 'Will the Secretary of State for Defence say what advice the Chiefs of Staff have given him on this matter?', another questioner may inquire. If the answer to the first question is 'Yes', ministers are likely to make political capital from it; whereas if the answers were to be 'No' to both, the questions would not be answered directly and ministers would probably take evasive action behind the principle that it is neither proper nor appropriate to divulge the advice given by public servants!

But despite the importance of their role in national affairs, the public at large know very little about the work the Chiefs do individually or as a team. In normal years, most people would find it hard to name any of the Chiefs, whereas the names of major trades union leaders tend to spring to mind quite easily – or at least they used to. This can be attributed partly to the security aspect of the work of the Chiefs, but more importantly to the conventions that politicians are the spokesmen for government policy, and that they have a duty to guard the position and reputation of the Chiefs, who, as loyal public servants, cannot reply if and when attacked. Indeed, in contrast to Victorian and Edwardian times, the Chiefs are positively discouraged from engaging in public debate and from any form of public relations activities, even when this might prove helpful to their leadership. It is feared that they might draw the limelight away from ministers or perhaps embarrass the Government and jeopardise their non-political public service role.

As far as the media are concerned, the Chiefs tend to be lumped together under the more depreciatory title 'Top Brass', with the implication that they represent forces of reaction, thwarting progressive ministers and others in their attempts to modernise the Armed Forces, and always bickering amongst themselves. Lowe's 'Colonel Blimp' is far from dead amongst popular journalists, and this is a cross that the Chiefs have to bear without reply.

So in this book, we will be telling the story of the Chiefs, tracing their origins and their development through many reorganisations and changes of emphasis from the formation of the Committee of Imperial Defence in 1904 to the collapse of the Communist threat to Europe and the beginnings of a new military epoch in 1989. We will be recounting their successes and failures in managing the Services through the two World Wars, the Korean War, Suez, the withdrawal from Empire, and finally the Falklands Campaign, conducted 8,000 miles from home – the last providing a model for the way in which political, strategic, tactical and logistic considerations can be moulded together by this uniquely British institution into one coherent whole with dynamic direction driven right down to the fighting sailors, soldiers and airmen, however distant the operational theatre.

We will also be introducing the varied characters and personalities who have held the appointments of Chief of the Naval, General and Air Staff in their capacities as the professional heads of their own Service, and of the Chiefs of Defence Staff, who , for the last 35 years, have led them in their collective capacity as the Chiefs of Staff Committee. It is a story of evolutionary progress, punctuated with periods of revolutionary reform, always leading to greater unity of effort in handling the Armed Forces of the Crown, and justifying the motto emblazoned on the British Army officers' epaulette stars for historic, religious and not military reasons: **'Tria juncta in uno'**.

Chronology
FOR CHAPTER ONE

1854–6	Crimean War.
1856	Duke of Cambridge becomes C-in-C of the Army.
1857–8	Second Opium War.
	Indian Mutiny.
1861–65	American Civil War.
1866	Austro-Prussian War.
1867	Dominion status for Canada.
1868–74	First Gladstone Liberal Government.
1868–74	Cardwell Reforms.
1869	Suez Canal opened.
1870	Franco-Prussian War.
1874–80	Second Disraeli Unionist Government.
1874	Ashanti Campaign.
1877	Russo-Turkish Balkans War.
1878–9	First Colonial Defence Committee.
1879	Zulu War (Isandhlwana and Ulundi).
1879–80	Second Afghan War.
1879–82	Carnarvon Commission.
1880–5	Second Gladstone Liberal Government.
1880–1	First Boer War.
1882	British occupation of Egypt: Bombardment of Alexandria and Battle of Tel-el-Kebir.
1884–5	Nile Campaign and the death of Gordon.
1885	First Salisbury Unionist Government.
1886	Second Salisbury Unionist Government.
	Second Colonial Defence Committee.
	Naval Intelligence Division formed.
	War Office Intelligence Directorate formed.
1887	First Colonial Conference (Golden Jubilee).

1888–90	Hartington Commission.
1889	Naval Defence Act (Two Power Standard).
	Joint Naval and Military Official Committee formed.
1890	Dismissal of Bismarck.
1892–5	Last Gladstone Liberal Government.
1895	Third Salisbury Unionist Government.
	Cabinet Defence Committee formed.
	Induced retirement of the Duke of Cambridge.
	War Office Council formed.
1896	The Jameson Raid in South Africa.
1897	Second Colonial Conference (Diamond Jubilee).
1898	Battle of Omdurman.
	Fashoda crisis with France.
	German Naval building programme begins.
1899–1902	Second Boer War.

1
THE QUEST FOR MILITARY EFFICIENCY WITHOUT LOSS OF POLITICAL CONTROL
Cardwell, Carnarvon and Hartington: 1868–1899

'There might be some advantage in the formation of a Naval and Military Council, which would probably be presided over by the Prime Minister, and consist of the Parliamentary Heads of the two Services, and their principal professional advisers.'

Hartington Commission Report of 1890.[1]

The appointment of professional heads of the Army and Navy can be traced back to the latter half of the 17th Century: the Army's to the Restoration of the Stuart Monarchy in 1660; and the Navy's to the 'Glorious Revolution' of 1688, when William of Orange was invited to ascend the throne as a constitutional monarch responsive to the supremacy of Parliament.

Prior to William's accession, the Sovereign alone was charged with the defence of the country and its overseas interests. Despite the Parliamentary victory in the Civil War, the Act of 1661, dealing with Charles II's Royal prerogatives, affirmed that:

> Forasmuch as within all His Majesty's realms and dominions the sole supreme government, command and dispositions of the militia and of all forces by sea and land, and all forts and places of strength, is, and by the law of England ever was, the undoubted right of His Majesty. . . .[2]

After the Revolution, responsibility for the defence of the realm was split between Crown and Parliament. It took most of the 18th Century to evolve the workable, though administratively inefficient, system of naval and military management that served the country tolerably well throughout the Marlburian and Napoleonic Wars.

The Captain-General and Commander-in-Chief (C-in-C) of the first standing army ever allowed by Parliament in peacetime was the all-powerful commander of the Commonwealth Army, who engineered Charles II's return to the throne, General George Monck, later Duke of Albemarle. He is perhaps best known today as the Colonel of Monck's Foot, which became the 2nd Foot Guards, the Coldstream. He was the unchallenged and unchallengeable professional head of the Army from 1660 until his death ten years later.

Thereafter, the post remained unfilled until it was revived in 1773 at the beginning of the Great American Rebellion, or the War of American Independence, as the Americans prefer to call it. The 'Grand Old Duke of York' of nursery-rhyme fame became C-in-C in 1795, and remained in office until 1825 with an unfortunate break of two years between 1809 and 1811, when he was forced to resign over the scandal of his mistress, Mary Anne Clarke, trafficking in military commissions!

The Navy's first professional head emerged three decades later. Since medieval times the Navy had been managed on behalf of the Sovereign by a political appointee, the Lord High Admiral of England. When Charles II was restored to the throne in 1660, he appointed his brother, the Duke of York, later James II, to the post, which he handled with the zest and efficiency that he displayed in his sexual pursuits. He was aided in his naval activities by the indefatigable Samuel Pepys, who was the powerful Secretary of the Admiralty.

The Duke was forced to resign in 1673 after Parliament passed the Test Act, barring Catholics from high offices of state. The post was then 'Placed in Commission', its duties being performed by six Lords Commissioner of the Board of Admiralty, who might be politicians or professional sea officers. The First Lord was the principal political appointee and acted as Secretary of State for the Navy, although he was quite often a very senior admiral; while the Second Lord, who adopted the unofficial title of Senior Naval Lord, was invariably a serving naval officer.

The title of 'Senior Naval Lord' appears officially amongst the Lords Commissioner of the Admiralty for the first time in 1689, but the holder often found himself a cypher, particularly when the First Lord was also the sea-going C-in-C of the Fleet during the frequent naval wars of the 18th Century. The resulting muddles and squabbles as to who was the professional head of the Navy did not end until the death in 1762 of Lord Anson, the last First Lord to command afloat in time of war. The Second Lord was re-named 'First Naval Lord' in 1771, and much later in 1899 'First Sea Lord' to make it abundantly clear who was, indeed, the Navy's professional head.

No one could foresee in 1688 how the unique Anglo-Saxon compromise of a constitutional monarchy would work out in practice. Demarcation lines between the Crown's prerogatives and Parliament's responsibilities were ill-defined, and, like most English compromises, were fudged. Time and pressure of events were needed for practicable working arrangements to evolve that would balance the contradictory requirements of diffuse parliamentary government and decisive military command.

Finding ways of handling the split responsibilities for national security proved one of the most intractable political problems of the 18th Century. New mechanisms were sought to enable political laymen to control the naval and military professionals without endangering the defence of the realm. Their efforts were complicated by the armed forces' traditional attitudes of loyalty to the Crown, and by the electorate's view of the two services. The curse of Cromwell – the fear that the major-generals might once again intervene in internal politics – cast its shadow over the Army; while the Navy, being less of an internal political threat, was held in higher esteem as the country's first line of defence. But both Services suffered the reluctance of Parliament to pay more than the minimum for their maintenance – economic management regrettably being prized above military efficiency.

Political control of navies and armies did prove reasonably practicable up to the beginning of the 19th Century. Mastery of the principles of war was still within the capabilities of able ministers. But as Britain's power grew after the Napoleonic Wars, and as revolutions in weapon technology began to tumble over each other in the 19th Century, efficient political control of military policy became more and more problematical. New ways of maintaining the principle of political control, despite ministers' inadequate knowledge of military affairs and technological possibilities, had to be found. The disasters of the Crimean War (1854–6) set in train the debates and evolutionary processes that were eventually to lead, a century later, to the British and American Chiefs of Staff Committee systems of the Second World War, and then on to the unified British Ministry of Defence and United States Defense Department of today.

The Royal Navy won Trafalgar and the Army beat Napoleon at Waterloo, priding themselves on their independence, and with little need and not much desire to help one another except during relatively small, though quite frequent, amphibious operations, and in the shipment of smallish bodies of troops around the world as

Britain's imperial commitments required. Such co-ordination as was needed between them was provided by discussion between the responsible ministers in Cabinet, where, in those days, no minutes were taken. The only record of what took place was preserved in the Prime Minister's reports to the Sovereign. War plans were carried in the heads of the Prime Minister and his Cabinet colleagues, who directed their departments according to their understanding – or misunderstanding – of what had been decided. The commanders, afloat and on land, acted upon the broadest of directives, often sent to them straight from the Cabinet rather than through the First Lord of the Admiralty or Secretary at War, whose responsibilities were administrative rather than operational.

At the speed at which operations could be conducted at the beginning of the 19th Century, with sail at sea, horses on land and visual telegraph systems for communication, there was ample time for co-ordination by consultation both in Whitehall and between the responsible men on the spot. Indeed, as late as 1906, the First Sea Lord, Admiral Sir John Fisher, had to confess that the only naval war plans that existed were locked in his head.

In the four decades of European peace that stretched from Waterloo to the Crimean War, the two Services went their separate ways. With Napoleon safely put away on St Helena, public interest in the Navy and Army faded and turned instead to the arguments about electoral reform, the abolition of slavery and the perennial problem of Ireland. Financial retrenchment, belief amongst the victorious naval and military establishments that they knew all that there was to know about war, and lack of any tangible threat to the country's security, made naval and military reform hard to achieve.

In the first five years of peace, the Navy was run down from 98 to 13 ships of the line, and from some 130,000 to about 20,000 men – a process not dissimilar to the 20th Century run-down from the great fleets of the two World Wars to the 50 frigate Royal Navy of the 1980s[3]. With no threat to the British Isles to guard against – the Navy's primary *raison d'être* – the Admiralty concentrated its efforts, more by corporate instinct than conscious planning, upon the best sea training it could find: protection of British seaborne trade, exploration and hydrography in the oceans of the world. It also reflected the growing confidence of the British people in their apparent God-sent mission to bring enlightenment and good government to the benighted inhabitants of the globe. Naval frigates ran up the Union Flag whenever and wherever it seemed practicable, profitable and morally right to do so. Trade, administrators and missionaries followed the flag until the sun never set on Queen Victoria's Empire.

While the Navy carried out its civilising role with relatively little fighting, the Army too returned to its role of extending and consolidating the Indian Empire, and garrisoning many of the outposts seized by the Royal Navy as victualling and, later, coaling stations. It lost any pretensions it had of maintaining the military balance of power in Europe. Indeed, it was no longer taken seriously by the major European powers, who were moving towards the massed conscript armies that were to tear their continent apart in the 20th Century. The Army's regimental system, bequeathed to it by Cromwell's New Model Army, and so successful in the 18th Century wars, remained prized and unreformed to meet the needs of future European warfare. Further British military involvement on the Continent seemed impracticable and unnecessary to both major political parties in Britain when Victoria ascended the throne in 1837. There was no pressing need or desire for change amongst the Duke of Wellington's surviving battle-hardened commanders and long service professional soldiers; nor did anyone doubt the correctness of Britain's traditional strategic policy of depending upon naval superiority, backed by a small regular army organised primarily for overseas garrison duty.

In the British way of life, three things – two unpredictable and the third constant – bring about military change: the imperatives of defeat, the pressures of public opinion, and the ever present Parliamentary quest for economies in military expenditure. When change does come, it is more often than not the result of an accumulation and interaction of all three over a decade or so. Near defeat and maladministration in the Crimean War of 1854–6; the shock of the Indian Mutiny of 1857–8; the changing face of battle displayed in the American Civil War of 1861–5; and the emergence of the triumphant German Great General Staff, headed by Helmuth von Moltke, in the Austro-Prussian and Franco-Prussian Campaigns of 1866 and 1870, all combined belatedly to create the pressures for military change which owed more to public outcry than governmental inclination.

The Army was the first to come under 19th Century political scrutiny when Gladstone's first Liberal Government, with its anti-imperialist tendencies and fear that the Army could be used to suppress popular liberties, came to power in 1868. Edward Cardwell became Secretary of State for War and set alight the fires of reform

that had been smouldering since the Crimea. He was backed by a
cabal of reformers: progressive soldiers, who wanted to modernise the
Army and assume a greater measure of control of military policy in
view of the growing complexity of war; professional civil servants,
who were keen to face military reality and yet were determined to
maintain the strict political and financial control of Parliament over
the Army; and a few high-minded Victorian statesmen with an interest in sound government and a fascination for military issues.

The Army, since the Restoration, had owed its loyalty to the
Crown and not to Parliament, and it was officered by gentlemen of
sufficient wealth to purchase their commissions. It was managed on a
two tier system: command vested in the Commander-in-Chief – in
Gladstone's day the Queen's cousin, the Duke of Cambridge – with a
military staff at the Horse Guards in Whitehall; and its administrative support, which had proved so chaotic during the Crimean War,
handled by no less than thirteen different government departments,
mostly civilian, under the loose direction of the Secretary at War – a
politically appointed official directly responsible to Parliament for
Army finance. Unlike the continental armies of the United States
and Europe, all its men were still long service regulars (12 years
engagement with the option of extension to 21 years for a pension),
who could withstand the rigours of imperial policing in unhealthy
climates around the world. It would hardly have been sensible in the
days of sail to man overseas garrisons with conscripts. They would
barely have become acclimatised before starting their journey home
for discharge into the reserve.

The Cardwell reforms did five crucial things: four were driven
forward by political and military opinion, and the fifth, as usual, by
Treasury pressure for economies. First of all, the C-in-C was made
subordinate to the Secretary of State for War[4], and the staff of the
Horse Guards was co-located with that of the War Office, then
situated in the Duke of Cumberland's former residence in Pall Mall,
which stood where the Royal Automobile Club is today. Nothing was
done to weaken the Army's loyalty to the Crown, because that
loyalty reflected the political impartiality of the constitutional
monarchy, and was a means of keeping the Army politically neutral.
Further diminution of the Royal prerogative in military affairs was
also rigorously opposed by the Queen, the Duke of Cambridge, who
always claimed that he disapproved of all change on principle, and
the conservative majority amongst the generals of the Army.
Command of the Army remained, for the time being, the responsibi-

lity of the C-in-C and included training, discipline and the patronage of appointments and promotions.

Cardwell's second set of reforms, for which he is best known, was the introduction of the system of linked infantry battalions within regiments, one of which was stationed abroad at full strength, while the other acted as the regimental recruiting and training depot at home, as well as being available for Home Defence. Each regiment was also made responsible for administering two or more militia battalions and any other volunteer units belonging to its county.

Cardwell saw no point in introducing conscription on Continental lines since there was no obvious threat to the British Isles and conscripts would be useless for imperial defence. His third measure, however, took some notice of the need to build up trained reserves in case a threat did emerge. The traditional long service engagements were reduced to seven years with the colours and seven in the reserve. This proved an unfortunate compromise: it did not create a large enough reserve for continental warfare, and yet it weakened battalions abroad by filling them with too many immature youngsters.

Cardwell's fourth measure perhaps did most to start pulling the Army out of the 18th Century and preparing it for the 20th. The time-honoured system of purchase of most commissions in the cavalry and infantry was abolished, enabling men of military ability but modest financial means to make the Army their career. The impact was not immediately evident because like still followed like into the Army. However, from 1870 onwards, able men such as Field Marshal Sir William Robertson, who entered the Army as a trooper and held every rank including sergeant-major, could, and in his case did, become its professional head.

And his fifth and least well known measure, which flowed from Treasury demands for economies, was to complete the progressive withdrawal of Army garrisons from self-governing colonies as they advanced towards Dominion status. Colonial governments grumbled almost as much as the American colonists had done a century earlier: while they welcomed greater self-government, they were much less keen on becoming responsible for their landward defences and paying for them. Still shielded by British sea-power, they displayed an obstinate reluctance to replace British units as they were withdrawn, and instead began to exert pressure for the development of a strategic plan for Imperial Defence. Their demands did much to induce the birth of the Committee of Imperial Defence at the turn of the

Century – the forerunner of the Chiefs of Staff Committee.

One thing that Cardwell did not do was to emulate the creation of the German Great General Staff. Advanced strategic and operational planning remained unexplored territory that attracted little interest in the *laissez faire* attitudes of the mid-Victorian era. Indeed, the very idea of allowing military planning was anathema to the politicians of the day: the Curse of Cromwell still cast shadows across the politico-military scene, surprising though it may seem today.

The Cardwell Reforms did much to modernise the Army, but it still lagged a long way behind the Navy in public esteem and in the minds of the few Victorians, who thought and felt deeply about the security of the Realm and Empire. Like the Army, the Navy had been managed on a two tier system: political control and naval command vested in the politically appointed Civil and Naval Lords Commissioner of the Admiralty in Whitehall; and administration lying in the hand's of officials – both civil and naval – of the Navy Board at the Navy Office in Somerset House. Under the Admiralty Act of 1832 the two tiers were merged, each Lord Commissioner being made responsible for a department of the combined Admiralty Office. The basis for a balanced mix of political, naval, and technological control was thus established for the Navy much earlier than for the Army, which had to wait until the retirement of the Duke of Cambridge in 1895 for the formation of a War Office Council on similar lines.

The Navy had other advantages. It was accepted as Britain's first line of defence, and under the Articles of War was given precedence over the Army. It did not suffer from the Curse of Cromwell; nor was it hampered by Royal influence, or plagued by undue squabbling amongst its leaders. It kept in the closest touch with the armament and ship-building industries, and its patronage was sought by many of the leading scientists and technologists of the day. And, most important of all, it was better and more realistically trained and equipped than the Army.

There was, of course, a reverse side to the naval coin. Its was an aging force with new ship construction under-funded, and the abilities of its officers declining through age and lack of recent battle-experience: the average age of full admirals in 1843 was seventy-six; there were three hundred captains over sixty; and there had been no major fleet actions since Trafalgar[5]. Moreover, the Naval Service was riven by technological uncertainties and dilemmas. Its corporate judgements, at times, caused public concern and some disloyalty among the more technically minded officers. There was a long period of 'belt and braces' policy as steam ousted sail. As late as 1881, Britain's latest battleship, *Inflexible*, was completed with masts and sails to supplement her engines[6]. There was similar controversy over breach-loading versus muzzle-loading guns and electrical fire control, and over the merits of introducing mines, torpedos, destroyers and submarines. Boiler design too caused as much steam and as many explosions in the Admiralty boardroom as it did at sea!

Nevertheless, the Admiralty Board system did develop into a well balanced mechanism that not only gave adequate political control without endangering naval efficiency, but could also handle the technological turbulence of the times. In stark contrast, the Army's management system, even after the Cardwell reforms, was at least thirty years behind. Its stumbling block was the continued existence of the post of C-in-C and its overstrong links to the Crown, which inhibited greater political control. Moreover, the civil servants and military officers within the War Office were like oil and water, with little desire to co-operate. The soldiers believed, with some justification, that the civilians represented the dead hand of financially inspired bureaucracy and were devoid of sound military judgement; and the civilians accused the soldiers, with equal justification, of narrow-minded bigotry and inconsistency. General Charles Gordon resigned an appointment in the War Office, declaring that it was easier to find his way around Africa than through the Pall Mall labyrinth.[7]

But the greatest weakness in both the Admiralty and War Office, only dimly perceived when Cardwell left office in 1874 on the fall of Gladstone's first Liberal Administration, lay in the absence of any form of planning staff to do their strategic thinking, to examine options and to develop war plans. Nor was there any recognised system of inter-Service co-operation, or of co-ordination of policy with the other ministries in Whitehall concerned with national and imperial defence – the Home, Foreign, and Colonial Offices. With the country secure behind its sea walls, and with no intention of intervening on the Continent, pressures for strategic thinking and inter-departmental collaboration were minimal.

In the mid-1870s, there should have been growing unease about imperial defence. The threats posed by French colonial rivalry, Russian expansionism and the rise of Bismarck's Germany, could not be ignored. And yet the debates in Westminster and Whitehall were centred not on the need for strategic planning but on the evolution of

a less expensive system of defence, and on the constitutional relationship between the colonies and mother country. The Russo-Turkish
War of 1877, which caused near panic in London because it seemed
to threaten British commercial interests in the Middle East, led to a
first hesitant and very modest step forward. Disraeli set up a departmental Colonial Defence Committee, composed of officials from the
Admiralty, War Office, Colonial Office and Treasury '*to consider what
steps could be taken at short notice to provide some measure of security for
Colonial Ports*'.[8]

In its first incarnation, the Colonial Defence Committee only
lasted a year. It was at too low a level to make any real impact on
Whitehall thinking other than to trigger the establishment in 1879 of
the Carnarvon Commission to study longer term imperial defence
planning. Lord Carnarvon was Colonial Secretary in Disraeli's
second Unionist Administration (1874–80), and responsible for colonial defence policy. The Commission worked for three years, but
only extracts from its three reports were ever published, largely
because Gladstone ousted Disraeli a year after its work began, and
his anti-imperialist sentiments inhibited much of its work.

Carnarvon recommended more coaling stations to help the Navy
protect British trade; he highlighted the danger of sudden, unexpected attack upon the United Kingdom; and he stressed the need for
self-governing colonies to take over the upkeep of naval stations
and harbour defences in their territories, while the fleet itself
remained the powerful instrument of external defence firmly held in
the hands of the mother country. But he failed to grasp the nettles of
inter-Service co-ordination in war; of standardisation of colonial
forces' organisation, training and equipment; and of establishing
Cabinet-level machinery to formulate imperial strategy.

World events came crowding in upon Whitehall ministries during
the five years of Gladstone's second Liberal Administration (1880–
85), and the public became more and more alarmed about the
French and Russian threats to British imperial interests. The usual
harbinger of change in Whitehall – the setting up of a inter-
departmental committee to grapple with some new problem –
emerged with the rebirth of the Colonial Defence Committee in 1885
under the chairmanship of the Permanent Under-Secretary of the
Colonial Office and with Colonel George Sydenham Clarke as its
secretary – a Royal Engineer officer, who had served with Wolseley
in Egypt and was to make a considerable impact upon the gestation
of the Chiefs of Staff system.

George Clarke (later Lord Sydenham of Combe) developed a system whereby plans, drawn up by colonial governments for the defence of overseas territories and bases, were called for and examined by the Colonial Defence Committee and then returned to the territory concerned, with recommendations for changes considered necessary by Whitehall ministries. In this way, an early version of the Government War Book, which was to become an important feature of British mobilisation planning, was brought into existence, but only in the context of colonial and not national defence.

During the first seven years of the Committee's life, it authorised some sixty colonial defence plans, but it had neither the staff nor the remit to develop a comprehensive imperial defence plan. Its most useful work was done in providing the briefs for the First Colonial Conference that took place in 1887 during Queen Victoria's Golden Jubilee celebrations. The Prime Minister, Lord Salisbury, in his opening address, urged greater co-operation in colonial defence, but he took no initiative to bring it about, hoping to generate a demand from the colonial leaders themselves to which he could respond without giving the impression of foisting fresh military burdens upon them. The colonial leaders did not rise to the bait, and instead held tenaciously to their view that it was Britain's duty to run the Empire and to defend it.

It was not only the colonial leaders who were dissatisfied with Salisbury's failure to take any initiative to establish coherent imperial defence planning and inter-Service co-ordination. Demands both in Westminster and in the press for naval and military expansion were growing in step with the obvious French and Russian threats to the Empire, though not, as yet, to counter the German threat in Europe. The public had been particularly alarmed in 1884 by articles in the influential *Pall Mall Gazette*, entitled *The Truth about the Navy* by W T Stead, revealing the un-prepared state of the Fleet and its decline relative to the Russian and French navies.

Much of the information in Stead's articles had been leaked to him by Captain Jackie Fisher, later Lord Fisher of Kilverstone, who was to become one of the most memorable First Sea Lords and an Admiral of the Fleet. Jackie was the *enfant terrible* of the Navy: a powerful, wilful and controversial character, who was either worshipped or loathed by his naval contemporaries, but who was acknowledged as one of its most technically competent officers as well as being an outstanding operational commander. The thrust of his criticism was aimed at the dangerous under-funding of the Navy, and his main demand was an accelerated warship-building programme to bring the Fleet up to the famous Two Power Standard, making it superior to the combined strength of the French and Russian fleets, eventually sanctioned in the Naval Defence Act of 1889.

The Army was not far behind in the battle for public opinion and funds, though less successful in putting its case due to internal divisions within its leadership. Its *enfant terrible* was General Sir Garnet Wolseley, the leader of the military reformers in the War Office, who had supported Cardwell against the ultra-conservative elements loyal to the Duke of Cambridge. Appointed to command the Ashanti Expedition in 1874, he had selected a team of like-minded subordinates, including Evelyn Wood, Redvers Buller, Frederick Maurice and Henry Brackenbury, all of whom were to achieve fame in one way or another before the century was out. Known as the 'Ashanti Group' in the continuing and bitterly fought battles in Whitehall for further Army reform, their aim was not only to match the battle-winning techniques of von Moltke's Prussians, but also to expand the Army to meet its growing imperial commitments.

The Army's case for expansion was unimpeachable, though it was less charismatic and less ruthlessly presented to the electorate than the Navy's case for the Two Power Standard. The Cardwell system of linked battalions had, in fact, broken down soon after its inception. Extra battalions, over and above those planned by Cardwell for overseas service, were sent to southern Africa to meet the crisis of the First Boer War of 1881; more had to be left to occupy Egypt after the battle of Tel-el-Kebir in 1882; and the Sudan had to be evacuated – leading to Gordon's death – to provide extra troops needed to meet further Russian incursions into Afghanistan in 1885. Some fifteen battalions that should have been in their depots at home, providing drafts for their overseas battalions, were themselves sent overseas. The Empire had outgrown the Regular Army, which was seriously overstretched, as it was to remain for the next hundred years!

The large increases in naval and military expenditure asked for by the Admiralty and War Office, and supported by public opinion were – as was the usual practice – presented separately to Parliament. Lord Randolph Churchill, who had resigned the previous year as Chancellor of the Exchequer, because he believed that the Britain's military expenditure could be pruned if a lower profile in foreign policy were to be adopted, led an influential group of politicians in both Houses, including Sir Charles Dilke, Admiral

Lord Charles Beresford, General Lord Wolseley, Spenser Wilkinson and the Colomb brothers, in demanding that the estimates should be presented in a unified form and be based upon national and imperial defence requirements rather than the narrowly calculated and separate needs of the Admiralty and War Office.

In winding up the debate, these Parliamentary rebels moved that the Government should state:

> . . . the general principles of defence which have determined the gross amounts proposed . . . and indicate the main lines of the general plan or programme of British defence, to which the Admiralty and the War Office . . . are respectively to conform.[9]

Such was the pressure of public opinion that the Salisbury Administration agreed, against its better judgement, to set up a Royal Commission under Lord Hartington. Its terms of reference disappointed the critics. Instead of being directed to examine ways of developing a strategic plan for national and imperial defence, upon which Naval and Army estimates could be sensibly based, the Commission was commanded by Royal Warrant,

> . . .to inquire into the Civil and Professional Administration of the Naval and Military Departments, and the relation to each other and to the Treasury. . . .[10]

The need for better co-ordination between departments in administration was thus acknowledged, but there was no acceptance of the parallel requirement for strategic planning. In truth, the Salisbury Government, as is the case with most British governments to this day, continued to see improved economic management as more important than naval and military efficiency. It is always claimed that the economies imposed will not in any way weaken the Services' ability to fulfil their primary roles, but this is rarely the case.

Today, at the end of the 20th Century, it is difficult to appreciate the fears generated amongst British politicians in the late 19th Century of the introduction of military planning staffs to match von Moltke's creation. The introduction of a General or a Naval Staff on Prussian lines seemed to suggest surrender of an unwelcome degree of political control over the country's military policy to professional Service officers, and the abrogation of Cabinet responsibility for national naval and military strategy. A General Staff's work must inevitably be secret and could be directed, unknown to the Government, to military intervention in internal as well as external affairs. The whole idea smacked of latent military dictatorship.

The most that either the Tory or Liberal Governments would accept in the way of military planning staffs was the establishment of small Intelligence departments in both the Admiralty and War Office, but without any formal arrangement for a flow of information between them or with the Colonial and Foreign Offices. The Naval Intelligence Division of the Admiralty was founded in 1886. It was the covert intention of the First Naval Lord to use it as the nucleus of a future Naval Staff. In the same year, General Sir Henry Brackenbury, one of the 'Ashantis', was appointed Director of Military Intelligence in the War Office with his new department based upon the existing, but mundane, Topographical and Statistical Department. He was made responsible to the Adjutant General and not to the C-in-C. The former was responsible for mobilization and was, therefore, considered to be the right person to provide appointed force commanders with intelligence.

The Hartington Commission's report, unlike Carnarvon's, was published in 1890, but it could not be fully implemented before its findings were overtaken by events. Moreover, much of the evidence presented to it was suppressed to avoid offending Royal sensitivities. Nevertheless, it forms the true starting point of the story of the creation of the Chiefs of Staff. Spencer Cavendish, Marquis of Hartington and later 8th Duke of Devonshire, emerges from the debates of the late 1880s as one of the founding-fathers – or perhaps more accurately, founding-grandfathers of the 'Chiefs'.

Hartington had been Secretary of State for War briefly in 1866 before the Cardwell reforms, and again from 1882 to 1885, during the British occupation of Egypt. He was a strong supporter of Wolseley's 'Ashanti' group, although he was an equally ardent advocate of maintaining political control over military policy, however complex war might become. He had seen the results of the lack of Admiralty/ War Office co-ordination in the useless destruction of much of Alexandria by naval bombardment in July 1882, carried out without Army support and a good six weeks before Wolseley's expeditionary force could reach Egyptian waters. The crassness of the naval action, in which many of its shells failed to explode, due to faulty fusing, was masked from public scrutiny by Wolseley's successul landing at Ismailia in August, his victory at Tel-el-Kebir and occupation of Cairo in September. Hartington had also experienced the lack of foresight and the dithering of Gladstone's Cabinet over Wolseley's Nile Campaign that led to Gordon's death at Khartoum three years later in 1885.

George Clarke, the immensely hard-working and articulate Secretary of the Colonial Defence Committee, was appointed Joint

Secretary to the Hartington Commission, the membership of which included Lord Randolph Churchill, Henry Campbell-Bannerman, Admiral Sir Frederick Richards, and General Sir Henry Brackenbury. Clarke was a prolific contributor to newspapers and journals on defence questions, and could be described as the midwife in the birth of the 'Chiefs'. After a spell as Governor of Victoria at the turn of the century, he returned to London to become a member of the Esher Committee at the end of 1903, and the first Secretary of the Committee of Imperial Defence in 1904. His influence was to be felt until he over-reached himself in 1907 in challenging Jackie Fisher's *Dreadnought* programme, and was packed off to India as Governor of Bombay.

The other Joint Secretary, Reginald Brett, Viscount Esher, was to have even greater influence upon the development of machinery for strategic planning and inter-Service co-ordination. He was private secretary to Lord Hartington at the time his Commission was sitting, and was to become one of the dynamic forces in the formation of the Committee of Imperial Defence in 1904.

Hartington's report first castigated the existing, or rather non-existent, arrangements for co-operation between the Admiralty and War Office:

> . . . little or no attempt has ever been made to establish settled and regular inter-communication or relations between them, . . .[11]
>
> It has been stated in evidence before us that no combined plan of operations for the defence of the Empire in any given contingency has ever been worked out or decided upon by the two Departments. . . .[12]

The Commissioners then laid three stepping stones in the river of 19th Century strategic mismanagement, leading towards the Chiefs of Staff system. The most politically and militarily controversial of these stones was the recommendation that the post of C-in-C of the Army should be abolished. A Chief of General Staff would be appointed as *primus inter pares* on a War Office Council, and would head a newly created department of the General Staff. He would be the Secretary of State's principal adviser on Army policy, intelligence, war plans and operations, and act as the channel of communication with the Admiralty, other government departments and the Army commands.

Recommending the abolition of the post of C-in-C brought Hartington into collision with the Queen, who saw his report as 'really abominable', and the Duke of Cambridge, who damned it as a 'catastrophe' that threatened both the Crown and the Army.[13]

Wolseley felt that Hartington had gone too far, and so did the
conservative majority of the Army's general officers. Political tradi-
tionalists on the Commission like Sir Henry Campbell-Bannerman,
the future Secretary of State for War and Prime Minister, also
objected vehemently to this further diminution of the Royal prerogative in the Army's affairs. Campbell-Bannerman, while supporting
the general thrust of the Commissions report, also reserved his position on the creation of a General Staff in a closely argued addendum.
He expressed the main objection as follows:

> It is true that in continental countries there exists such a department as is here
> described. But those countries differ fundamentally from Great Britain. . . .
> They are constantly, and necessarily, concerned in watching the military con-
> dition of their neighbours, in detecting points of weakness and strength, and in
> planning possible operations in possible wars against them. But in this country
> there is in truth no room for 'general military policy' in this larger and more
> ambitious sense of the phrase. We have no designs against our European
> neighbours. Indian 'military policy' will be settled in India itself, and not in
> Pall Mall. In any of the smaller troubles . . . the plan of campaign . . . would be
> left (I presume and hope) to be determined by the officer appointed to direct
> operations . . . I am, therefore at a loss to know where . . . the new Department
> could find an adequate field in the circumstances of this country.[14]

Opposition to the abolition of the post of C-in-C was so strong that
an unworkable compromise was reached whereby the Duke of
Cambridge would remain C-in-C and carry out the functions of a
Chief of Staff to the Secretary of State, but without the benefits of a
General Staff to help him! He was eventually manoeuvred into retiring with the Queen's reluctant consent in 1895 at the age of 76. Even
then the opportunity was not taken, as Hartington had intended, of
establishing the post of Chief of General Staff. Wolseley took over as
C-in-C, with responsibility limited to general supervision of the military departments, but with his military colleagues on the newly
formed War Office Council – Adjutant General, Quartermaster
General, Director of Artillery, and Inspector General of Fortifica-
tions – being directly responsible to the Secretary of State for the
work of their departments. The disasters of the Boer War were to be
needed before the Army's 'Chief' could be properly established and
authority given for the creation of a General Staff.

The second stepping-stone was the firming up of the First Naval
Lord's responsibility '*as Chief Adviser of the First Lord in all great
questions of Naval Policy*', with the suggestion that he should be freed
from administrative duties to enable him to become *de facto* Chief of
Staff to the First Lord of the Admiralty. There was, however, no

mention of the need to establish a Naval Staff to support him in operational planning.[15] Nevertheless, the idea of the First Naval Lord becoming the Naval 'Chief' was gaining ground. (The title of First Naval Lord was not changed to First Sea Lord until the turn of the century.)

The third stepping-stone was the tentative proposal to set up a Naval and Military Council, preferably presided over by the Prime Minister, consisting of *'the Parliamentary Heads of the two Services, and their principal professional advisers'*.[16] The Council might also include one or two officers of great reputation or experience, who were not holding official positions at the time. The Council's task would be to screen the annual Service financial estimates before they were submitted to the Cabinet, and *'to consider and authoritatively decide upon unsettled questions between the two departments . . .'*.[17] Although there was again no mention of strategic planning, and no mechanism for co-operation with the Foreign and Colonial Offices in imperial defence, there was at least an acknowledgement of the need for inter-Service co-ordination of naval and military policy.

Wolseley, in his evidence to the Commission, had proposed the appointment of a Minister of Defence to oversee the two Service departments, and his plea had some support in the Commission. It was turned down for reasons that were to be repeated many times over the next seventy or so years.

> The difficulty which they [the Secretaries of State] must find at present in mastering the detail of one of these departments would be doubled in the case of a Minister of Defence made responsible for both. Moreover, the existing tendency towards centralisation would be greatly aggravated, and in the result, the Minister of Defence would be involved in a complex mass of work with which no one man could adequately deal.[18]

The Navy added the strange but heartfelt objection that Army influence in the joint ministry would be so great as to prejudice the interests of the Navy – strange, because the Navy's prestige in the eyes of the public was so high that the boot was likely to be on the other foot!

Lord Randolph Churchill, who believed that war had become too complex for politicians, proposed an ingenious solution, which placed the Admiralty and War Office under professional instead of political heads: the former titled the Lord High Admiral, and the latter, the Captain General, both of whom would be appointed for five years and would have seats in the Lords. A civilian Minister of high Cabinet rank, with a seat in the Commons, would provide a link between the two, and would be responsible to Parliament for annual expenditure and audit.

Lord Randolph's proposal failed because it was seen to weaken political control over the Services. Moreover, the Commission rightly feared that the Commons would come to hold the Minister responsible for all Defence matters, and he would thus become Wolseley's proposed Minister of Defence, an appointment which they had already turned down as too difficult for one man to handle. The Commission stuck to their own tentative proposal for a Naval and Military Council.

There was a gamut of reasons why the Commission's proposal never took political root. It was presented in such a tentative way that it looked and was half-hearted; it aroused political fears of a strengthened military authority; it incurred opposition from vested Admiralty and War Office interests; it angered the Queen, who was not keen to see such a council giving directions to the Duke of Cambridge, as C-in-C of *her* Army; international tensions had eased momentarily; and there were few electoral votes to be gained by pursuing it at a time when Home Rule for Ireland was dominating the political landscape. It withered and seemed to die when Salisbury temporarily lost power to the last Gladstone Administration of 1892–95.

The proposed Naval and Military Council, however, was not as dead as it seemed to politicians and the public at the time. In Whitehall, there is a recognised procedure for backing 'ministerial' committees with 'official' committees, composed of officials who do the spadework of gathering facts and drafting papers on which the 'ministerial' committee can base its deliberations and decisions. In anticipation of the establishment of a Ministerial Naval and Military Council, senior Admiralty and War Office officials had set up a Joint Naval and Military Official Committee in 1889, which did some useful work, but, lacking a Ministerial committee above it, had no political clout.

By the time Salisbury was back in power in 1895, with Arthur Balfour as First Lord of the Treasury and Leader of the House of Commons, and with Joseph Chamberlain, the Imperialist, as his Colonial Secretary, the threats to British interests world wide had become so obvious that a bi-partisan consensus began to form within Parliament, in the Press and amongst the military intellectuals, that cast doubt on the adequacy of intermittent Cabinet discussion on the security of the country and its empire.

The military situation faced by Salisbury was, indeed, fraught. The European scramble for Africa was at its height; Anglo-French colonial rivalry was intense; Anglo-Russian relations were deteriorating, particularly in the Far East; and the German threat, heralded by dismissal of Bismarck in 1890, was beginning to emerge. Salisbury turned to Hartington, who by then had succeeded to the title of the Duke of Devonshire, and asked him to form and chair a Cabinet Defence Committee.

The First Lord of the Admiralty, George Goschen, recommended turning the existing Joint Naval and Military Official Committee into the Cabinet Defence Committee by adding the responsible ministers to it. Lord Lansdowne, the Secretary of State for War, would have none of it: he disliked any idea of politicians and officials conferring at the same table, however eminent the officials might be! And so began the two-tier system for the higher direction of the defence of the realm that is still in use today. The Cabinet Defence Committee was at Ministerial level, and was backed by the Naval and Military Committee at official level. Today's equivalents are the Cabinet Defence and Overseas Policy Committee, backed by the Chiefs of Staff Committee.

This first venture at making the formulation of Defence policy the responsibility of a Cabinet committee was not a great success. Devonshire's Defence Committee suffered from a number of debilitating flaws. Salisbury was not sufficiently interested in problems of national and imperial defence ever to take the chair himself. Although Devonshire was Lord President of the Council and a respected political personality, he did not have the authority to decide major defence issues, as the Prime Minister would have been able to do. Furthermore, the Committee had no permanent secretary, and there was the usual resistance from vested interests within Whitehall who were only prepared to make use of it, if and when it was clearly in their interests to do so.

One issue that the Defence Committee did try to tackle, and which was to bring out fundamental arguments about power and responsibility that would recur time and again in the development of the Chiefs of Staff system, was the unsatisfactory compromise over the status and responsibilities of the Army's C-in-C after the induced retirement of the Duke of Cambridge in 1895. The principles of political control, and the need to vest military command in one man, are well nigh incompatible, and can only be resolved by balanced compromise and good will. In the 19th Century there was scant good will between politicians and their professional military advisers, just as little between civil servants and military staffs, and even less between the two Services.

From Lansdowne's point of view, as Secretary of State for War, he needed the widest possible spectrum of advice during the formulation of policy, and yet the counsel of one experienced and generally respected military figure when it came to executive action. The Hartington Commission proposal to replace the C-in-C with a Chief of Staff, who would be *primus inter pares* amongst the military members on the War Office Council, was nicely balanced and owed much to the Admiralty system, which was generally acknowledged to be working well. During the formulation of policy, all voices on the Council would have equal weighting, but, when it came to decision-making, the views of the Chief of Staff, as principal military adviser to the Secretary of State, would carry greatest weight. The Chief of Staff would be able, when he deemed it necessary, to establish an agreed military position at a preliminary meeting with his military colleagues on the Army Board, which was the 'official' committee supporting the War Office Council.

Wolseley, when he took over from the Duke of Cambridge, saw things differently. As C-in-C, he quite reasonably expected all the military members on the War Office Council to be subordinate to him, and that he should be the sole military adviser to the Secretary of State. If, as the Order-in-Council of 1895 laid down, he was only to be responsible for the 'general supervision' of the military members, he would be, in his words, 'the fifth wheel of the coach' – neither C-in-C nor Chief of Staff.[19] Commenting on a paper setting out his duties as C-in-C, he said:

> According to my notion of an army, whether in the field or on a peace establishment, his (the C-in-C's) first duty to the Queen and country is, that the army under his command should always be a thoroughly efficient fighting machine. This responsibility he cannot divide or share with any Adjutant General or any one else.[20]

In any case, as long as he was titled C-in-C, he would over-awe his theoretically co-equal colleagues, military discipline being what it is. The idea that each military member of the Council was responsible direct to the Secretary of State for the business of his department, and yet was expected to consult the C-in-C before advising the Secretary of State on major policy matters, was to Wolseley's way of thinking a formula for indecision, confusion, misunderstanding and disaster.

What was not generally understood in the run-up to the 20th Century was the impracticability of combining the roles of C-in-C and Chief of Staff. Decisive military command by one man could only be exercised, and, indeed, was only practicable in Army Commands and Fleets at sea. In Whitehall, the need was for careful development of policies through informed debate, tapping all the best military, technological and financial advice, and assessing relevant information and intelligence from a wide variety of sources. That was the task of a Chief of Staff, supported by a highly trained and motivated General Staff such as von Moltke had created. But, in the 1890s, the creation of a General Staff still had few supporters in Westminster and Whitehall, and so the Cabinet Defence Committee found no solution to the Army's management problem.

Regrettably, it took further military disasters to make General and Naval Staffs acceptable to Britain's political establishment. Those disasters were just round the corner. The Jameson Raid had taken place over the New Year period of 1895/6. The Kaiser had sent his telegram of congratulations to President Kruger upon the capture of Jameson's force at Doornkop, encouraging Boer resistance to British domination of southern Africa. At the same time, there was a threat of war with the United States over what the Americans saw as a British infringement of the Monroe Doctrine in the Venezuelan boundary dispute. Then, as Kitchener was avenging Gordon's death at Omdurman in September 1898, war seemed equally likely with France over the Fashoda incident; and the German Naval building plan began adding a further dimension to the Salisbury Administration's strategic problems. To cap it all, on 12 October 1899, the Boers invaded Cape Colony and Natal. The Second Boer War had begun. Never was a sound Chiefs of Staff system more necessary, but still so far away.

The Second Colonial Conference had taken place during Queen Victoria's Diamond Jubilee celebrations in 1897. Salisbury had put forward his famous proposal for a 'Great Council of Empire' to the visiting prime ministers, but such was the rising force of colonial nationalism that his grand design, which might have led to high level imperial defence planning, gathered little support. Kipling reflected the mood of the Conference and, indeed, of the Jubilee itself with his *Recessional*:

> God of our fathers, known of old,
> Lord of our far-flung battle line,
> Beneath whose awful hand we hold

Dominion over palm and pine –
Lord God of Hosts, be with us yet,
Lest we forget – lest we forget!

Britain still depended more upon her ability to muddle through rather than upon any mechanism for military planning.

Chronology
FOR CHAPTER TWO

1902	Anglo-Japanese Alliance.
	Balfour's Unionist Government formed.
	Elgin Commission on Boer War.
	Re-establishment of Cabinet Defence Committee.
1903	Esher War Office (Reconstitution) Committee.
1904	Esher Report Part I.
	Formation of the Army Council and the General Staff.
	Russo-Japanese War begins.
	Kaiser's visit to Tangiers.
	Anglo-French 'Entente Cordiale' formalized.
	Establishment of Committee of Imperial Defence (CID).
1905	Battle of Tsushima.
	Campbell-Bannerman's Liberal Government formed.
	Moroccan Crisis and Algeciras Conference.
	Anglo-French secret military staff talks start.
1907	Haldane Army Reforms initiated.
	Clarke replaced by Ottley as Secretary of the CID.
	Anglo-Russian Entente.
1908	Asquith's Liberal Government formed.
1909	Imperial Conference: Imperial General Staff set up.
1911	Agadir Crisis.
	'Two Wilson' CID meeting.
1912	Creation of Naval Staff at the Admiralty.
	Haldane's Anglo-German Naval talks begin.
	Hankey succeeds Ottley as Secretary of the CID.
	Royal Flying Corps formed.
1912–13	Balkan Wars.
1914	Ulster Crisis (Curragh Mutiny).

2
THE RISE AND FALL
OF THE COMMITTEE
OF IMPERIAL DEFENCE
Elgin, Esher, Haldane and Churchill: 1899–1914

First Sea Lords		Chiefs of General Staff	
Lord Walter Kerr	1899	Sir Neville Lyttelton	1904
Sir John Fisher	1904	Sir William Nicholson*	1908
Sir Arthur Wilson	1910		
Sir Francis Bridgeman	1911	**Chiefs of the**	
Prince Louis of Battenberg	1912	**Imperial General Staff**	
		Sir John French	1911
		Sir Charles Douglas	April 1914

'The object is to secure for the British Empire, with least possible derangement of existing machinery, the immense advantages which the General Staff has conferred upon Germany.'
Esher Report (Part I), page 3.[1]

Before the Boer War there had been, as we have seen, a growing demand in Westminster and Whitehall, though not amongst the public at large, for better ways of managing the country's naval and military affairs. 'Black Week' in December 1899, when successive defeats at Colenso, the Modder River and Stormberg left Ladysmith, Kimberley and Mafeking under Boer siege, shocked the nation and added the pressure of public opinion to the political momentum for change.

Why, it was asked, were adequate numbers of troops not deployed to southern Africa before war broke out, and why were they so woefully ill-prepared when they did arrive? Why was there no properly developed war plan ready before the Government risked goading

* Nicholson's title was changed from CGS to CIGS in 1910 after the Imperial Conference of 1909.

the Boers into military action? And why had there been no British
von Moltke, with a General Staff, to think through the consequences
of confrontation with the Boer Republics?

Coupled with these military worries, there were doubts about the
handling of Britain's foreign policy. Her 'splendid isolation' – a
phrase coined by Lord Goschen in 1896 – was beginning to look
much less splendid by the end of the Boer War. As Salisbury's grip
on foreign affairs slackened, his successor at the Foreign Office, Lord
Lansdowne, began a quest for alliances and understandings with
other powers to give Britain useful allies. First came the Anglo-
Japanese Alliance of 1902; then the *Entente Cordiale* with France in
1903/4; and finally the Anglo-Russian *Entente* in 1907. All three had
politico-military connotations, but there still was no recognisable
machinery in Whitehall for the co-ordination of strategic policy below Cabinet level.

In the many post-mortems carried out between the beginning and
end of the Boer War (1899–1902), the politicians and soldiers blamed
each other for operational and administrative disasters inflicted on
the Army by the Boers. Matters were brought to a head by the
Queen asking Wolseley, as C-in-C of the Army, to draw up a memorandum stating the military side of the argument. His paper, which
recommended the appointment of one supreme military commander,
concluded:

> It is a military axiom, accepted universally except at our own War Office, that,
> for an army to be efficient, its staff administration and its command should go
> together. These two are now separated by us . . . administration rests with
> officers subordinate to the apparent and nominal head of the Army, and the
> command has passed to a Minister who, however able and conscientious, can of
> necessity have at best but a surface acquaintance with things military.[2]

Lord Lansdowne, at that time Secretary of State for War, responded
by charging Wolseley with failure to work the Hartington reforms of
1895 in good faith. He accused him of interfering with the work of the
other military members of the War Office Council instead of planning and preparing for military contingencies. Wolseley, in
Lansdowne's view, did not appreciate the limitations which parliamentary government imposed on civilians and military alike.

Salisbury, supporting his Minister, brought the argument temporarily to a close declaring, *'any attempt to take the opinion of the expert above
the opinion of the politician must, in view of all the circumstances of our
Constitution, inevitably fail.*[3] Nevertheless, he did recognise the need to
placate public opinion, and so set up the Clinton Dawkins

Committee at the end of 1900 to look into Wolseley's complaints. With the memories of 'Black Week' still fresh in the Committee's minds, and with further mismanagement in South Africa reinforcing his case, Wolseley regained some of the military ground lost in the Hartington reforms. The Committee recommended that the authority of the C-in-C should be increased by bringing the Adjutant General with the Directors of Mobilisation and Intelligence under his control, thus creating an embryo General Staff.

Once the Boer War was over, the Wolseley/Lansdowne controversy burst into flames again. Arthur Balfour, who took over as Prime Minister from Salisbury in July 1902, set up a Royal Commission under Lord Elgin *'to inquire into the military preparations and other matters connected with the war in South Africa'*.[4] Its terms of reference made it a fact-finding body, although Lord Esher, who was one of its members, insisted upon it making recommendations.

Elgin found that the Intelligence staffs had given ample warning of the Boer's hostile intentions, but that Wolseley, as C-in-C, had failed to make the necessary preparations for war. Nevertheless, it exonerated him and placed the blame firmly on the shoulders of the Government in that the Cabinet had not kept the War Office informed of its negotiations with President Kruger; it had refused requests made by Wolseley for the precautionary dispatch of reinforcements because it had not wanted to provoke the Boers, and because it had not been prepared to incur the expense; and it had misjudged the Boers, believing that a show of force was all that would be needed to bring them to heel.

Elgin's view was that the principal fault lay in inter-departmental communication: the Foreign and Colonial Offices failing to keep the Service Ministries informed of their policies and objectives; and the Admiralty and War Office staffs thus being unable to warn the political departments of military limitations to their plans. Much of the wind, however, was taken out of the Commission's sails by Balfour re-establishing the Cabinet Defence Committee seven months before Elgin reported in July 1903.

The cause of Balfour 'jumping the gun', and setting up a new Cabinet Defence Committee, was a forthright memorandum from the First Lord of the Admiralty, Lord Selborne, and the Secretary of State for War, St John Brodrick, later Lord Middleton, demanding its reconstitution. They were not prepared to stay in office unless there was some means of surveying the Empire's naval and military needs, and of ensuring inter-departmental co-operation within

Whitehall. There had to be some way of overcoming the absurdly embarrassing lack of strategic co-ordination displayed at the 1902 Colonial Conference when the Admiralty and War Office gave widely differing versions of imperial defence policies.

Since Queen Anne's day, two opposing schools of thought – Maritime and Continental – have vied with each other in determining British strategy. The Tories and, quite naturally, the Navy belonged to the Maritime school. They believed that naval supremacy would ensure the security of the British Isles, and would pay for itself indirectly by purloining other countries' colonies and seaborne trade in time of war. All that was needed, therefore, was a strong Royal Navy and a balanced fleet. The Whigs and some, but not all, Army officers belonged to the Continental school. They held that the security and prosperity of the country depended upon maintaining the balance of power in Europe, and that expenditure on the size of army needed for that purpose was money well spent.

After the Napoleonic Wars, the Maritime or 'Blue Water' strategy became national policy, and naval supremacy an article of faith. The Army was generally content with its supporting role of providing the backbone of the Indian Army, the imperial garrisons, and a small central reserve of regular troops in Britain for the reinforcement of the North West Frontier of India and the support of colonial policies.

By the turn of the 19th Century, views of the Navy's capabilities, and of the Army's responsibilities, had begun to change. The Continental strategists had already experienced something of a revival under the title of the 'Bolt from the Blue' school during the invasion scares of the 1880s and 1890s, when doubts were cast on the Navy's ability to guarantee the country's security against invasion. The Army began to realise, perhaps subconsciously at first, that a new and independent role was emerging for it in the aftermath of the Prussian Army's startling successes in Europe, and in the light of its own inadequacies as a modern fighting organisation displayed in South Africa. Could British interests in Western Europe still be protected by diplomacy and naval power; or was a continental style army not needed as well; and, if so, should the Army not be given greater financial backing?

The first steps taken by the War Office to gain a larger role in national defence were faltering and unrealistic. St John Brodrick, when he became Secretary of State for War in 1900, had proposed an over-ambitious scheme for creating a force of six army corps in England, three of which, amounting to 120,000 men, were to be ready for overseas operations. He proposed to achieve this by a combination of bringing troops home from overseas garrisons and recruiting more soldiers. He received little support from his professional advisers, who were all too well aware of the Treasury's propensity for cutting uncommitted reserves during periods of retrenchment. They preferred to hold onto their overseas garrisons as secure commitment 'pegs', on which to hang the Army's order of battle, but they were prepared to argue for a larger reserve in the United Kingdom on the grounds that they doubted the Navy's continuing ability to guarantee the defence of the Empire.

The Army's doubts were well founded. The Navy's world supremacy had declined, both in numerical and qualitative terms, with the rise of the more modern American, Japanese and German fleets. The 'Bolt from the Blue' school, which included Field Marshal Lord Roberts, who succeeded Wolseley as the Army's C-in-C, and St John Brodrick, argued that technological advances in naval warfare gave the advantage to ruthless aggressors. The fleet could easily be lured away from home waters, leaving the country vulnerable to invasion by the powerful conscript armies that had been created on the Continent. The Admiralty, using the colourful language of Jackie Fisher, who was then Second Sea Lord, countered by pointing out that, if naval supremacy was lost, any army of the size that Britain could afford and could recruit, would be too small to defend the country and its world-wide imperial interests. There should be no deviation from the well tried policy of dependence upon naval supremacy with the Army in a supporting role.

Arthur Balfour accepted the Selborne/Brodrick demand for governmental machinery to resolve strategic arguments so that sensible decisions could be taken on the annual Naval and Army financial estimates. In re-establishing the Cabinet Defence Committee in December 1902, he took a number of steps to make it more effective than it had been under Salisbury, whose lack of interest in its deliberations had left it toothless.

He gave it political power by chairing it himself, and, indeed, attended over sixty of its meetings before he left office in December 1905. Membership was in his personal gift, and he broke with tradition by inviting the professional heads of the two Services and their directors of Intelligence to attend meetings, thus increasing the naval and military credibility of the Committee. But he also stressed its advisory nature, emphasising that its existence in no way infringed the collective responsibility of the Cabinet for Defence policy.

Placing membership of the Defence Committee in the Prime Minister's personal gift had another advantage. It enabled him to invite Dominion statesmen to attend meetings when questions of their concern were on the agenda. The first to do so was Canada's Prime Minister, Sir Frederick Borden, in 1903.

There were two important things that he did not do. He did not include the Chancellor of the Exchequer, believing that the Committee's work should not be unduly inhibited by financial considerations, which were better dealt with later in Cabinet once the strategic options had been clarified. And he did not provide the Committee with a secretariat of its own. A Foreign Office clerk took the minutes and acted as the Prime Minister's 'Remembrancer'.

In the first debates of this newly reconstituted Cabinet Defence Committee, the Admiralty team was united in its determination to entrench the Maritime strategy, and to impose it on the Army. The Admiralty team – William Palmer, Earl of Selborne, the First Lord; Lord Walter Kerr, the First Sea Lord; and Prince Louis of Battenberg, the Director of Naval Intelligence – were a formidable trio with public and parliamentary support behind them. By contrast, the War Office representatives were divided and uncertain as to the best policy to pursue in the Committee.

There were a number of causes for the War Office's disarray. Its political and professional heads saw a European style role opening up in front of them, but there was no agreement as to how it should be exploited. Brodrick continued to advocate his ludicrously expensive six corps concept; and Lord Roberts was for ever beating his drum for the introduction of conscription to provide a counter-invasion force. The only man with his feet firmly on the ground was General Sir William Nicholson, the Director-General of Mobilisation and Intelligence, who appreciated that the Army's future lay in convincing Balfour's Committee that there was a real threat of invasion. Very few policy-makers in Westminster and Whitehall in 1903 were envisaging intervention by the British Army on the Continent in some future conflict.

The Admiralty case was elegant in its simplicity. Until the Navy lost command of the sea, invasion would be difficult, if not impossible; and afterwards it would be superfluous. The soldiers were unimpressed, stressing the overcommitment of naval resources, which had been the very basis of the naval demands for increased warship construction. A home based army was essential to protect the country, if, by some mischance, the Fleet met with disaster. It would also be available for imperial reinforcement, and for delivering the *coup de grâce* to an enemy trounced at sea.

The naval riposte, which helped to clinch the argument, was that it would be cheaper, more effective and more acceptable to the electorate, to provide a second fleet instead of a large continental style army, which could only be raised by conscription – anathema to both major political parties. Balfour was certainly impressed with the Navy's case and, in his summing up in July 1903, came down in favour of maintaining the Maritime strategy.

The Army's discomfiture was compounded almost immediately by the publication of the Elgin Report, which, although it placed responsibility for lack of preparation for the campaign in South Africa squarely upon the shoulders of the Salisbury Administration, pilloried the War Office for incompetent management. It did not recommend the abolition of the post of C-in-C, but insisted that he should be kept better informed of government policy. Lord Esher, however, in an annex to the report, disagreed and advocated the reconstruction of the War Office on admiralty lines. The C-in-C should, he said, be replaced by a Chief of General Staff with duties analogous to those of the First Sea Lord.

Balfour could not leave the criticisms of the Army's management in the Elgin Report to go unanswered. Its publication had coincided with a Cabinet reshuffle caused by internal disagreement over free trade and protectionism. Brodrick was moved to the India Office. Balfour asked Esher to take over as Secretary of State for War, but he refused the offer, and so Hugh Arnold-Forster, a junior minister in the Admiralty and another well known critic of the Army, was appointed instead.

Unable to make use of Esher's long experience in Army affairs, dating back to the days of the Hartington Commission in the 1890s, Balfour asked him to head a three man committee to decide what executive action should be taken to put the War Office to rights. After some difficult negotiations, which involved King Edward VII, Balfour appointed Jackie Fisher, then C-in-C Portsmouth and First Sea Lord (Designate), and Colonel Sir George Clarke, the former Secretary of the Colonial Defence Committee, to be the second and third members of Esher's committee, which was styled 'The War Office (Reconstitution) Committee'.

No one could be in any doubt about the Esher Commission's intentions. Its three members belonged to the Maritime school and each had, on many occasions, declared the view that the War Office should be rebuilt on Admiralty lines. This was Balfour's view as well, and it was supported by the new Secretary of State for War, Arnold-Forster. With the political tide flowing so strongly in the Maritime direction, the Committee could and did ride rough-shod over the conservative elements in the War Office that had resisted change for so long.

The 'Triumvirate', as Esher, Fisher, and Clarke were soon nick-named, were an interesting team. Esher was essentially a courtier or *éminence grise*, who enjoyed power but avoided responsibility, and enhanced that power by making himself the confidant of Edward VII on naval and military affairs. His father, the first Viscount Esher, had been highly successful at the Bar. Esher inherited his analytical brain, shrewdness and persuasive powers, but preferred to use them in the corridors of power rather than in the law courts. His fasci-nation with defence policy had begun when he was private secretary to Hartington in the 1880s, but despite, or perhaps because of, his early familiarity with the War Office, he was a determined advocate of Maritime strategy. He bore no allegiance to either political party, serving the country to the best of his remarkable abilities, according to his own view of its best interests.

The ebullient Fisher had the pugnacity of and some resemblance to Winston Churchill. He was a dynamic, if erratic, exponent of the naval arts, who saw everything in the starkest shades of black and white. He would rarely compromise, preferring to turn friends who disagreed with him into enemies. His creed embraced his three 'Rs' – Ruthless, Relentless, Remorseless – and he lived up to them. But he was a man, for all his faults, who could make both Whitehall and the Navy react to his flashes of genius. Friends advised him not to serve on Esher's committee because of the damage it could do to his relations with the Army when he became First Sea Lord, but he believed that he had a mission to preserve the nation's traditional Maritime strategy in the face of Britain's growing involvement in the European political cauldron. He saw that being a member of Esher's committee would help him to impose his vision of what was needed for the country's security upon ambitious continentalists in the Army.

Esher, when speaking to Balfour about the composition of his committee, remarked, '*Clarke is excellent. All on the right lines – and fat and comfortable.*'[5] Clarke came from that Royal Engineer stable of great staff officers, who were to serve the Committee of Imperial Defence and the Chiefs of Staff Committee so well in the years to come. His versatility, width of vision and co-ordinating abilities, enabled him to lubricate the evolution of national strategy in much the same way as Esher, but, unlike Esher, he was prepared to accept responsibility as he showed when Governor of Victoria and of Bombay. He did not suffer fools gladly, and could be tactless and overbearing. His years as Secretary of the Colonial Defence Committee made him an acknowledged imperial strategist, and he was a persistent advocate of the German General Staff system.

There was one other character of importance in the story of the Esher Committee, not for any great skills, but because he did not support his own team. Arnold-Forster, the new Secretary of State for War, was *persona non grata* in the War Office. He had been a constant critic of the military management since he was elected to Parliament as the member for West Belfast in 1892. He thought nothing of the Cardwell system, and wished to replace it with a pet scheme of his own of dividing the Army into two classes – long service men for overseas garrison duty and three year men for home defence. It was not the unsoundness of his scheme, which would have reduced operational flexibility, that brought him into conflict with the War Office Council so much as his dogmatic self-assertiveness, rigidity of outlook and refusal to listen to his advisers. To make matters worse, he did little to disguise his preference for the Admiralty system and his coolness to the growing realisation in the Army that an independent continental role was becoming a possibility.

The Committee started its work in November 1903 at Admiralty House Portsmouth, Fisher's official residence, because he was too involved in the reorganisation of the Fleet to go up to London. George Clarke was still on his way back from Australia and contributed little to the Triumvirate's early work. By contrast, Fisher is said to have arrived at the first meeting with a draft of the committee's final report in his pocket! This may well have been so. Esher and he were great friends; they thought along the same lines; and had no difficulty in playing the duet expected of them by informed opinion.

They started from the premise that the War Office was organised for peacetime administration, unlike the Admiralty, which was established primarily for war. They then took up the Elgin Committee's conclusion that the real fault lay with the Cabinet having no firmly established mechanism for developing sound strategic policies. They decided not to look at the War Office in detail until they had cleared their minds on the best way of overcoming this fundamental weakness in governmental machinery.[6]

The Committee looked once more at the possibility of establishing a Ministry of Defence, first suggested by Wolseley to the Hartington Commission in 1889. They rejected the idea again, finding Hartington's reasons for doing so '*to be unimpeachable*'.[7]

They turned instead to the Cabinet Defence Committee. While tactfully commending its work on questions of national defence since its reconstitution by Balfour, they went on to say:

> Valuable as is the work which this Committee has accomplished, the fact remains that there is no one charged with the duty of making a continuous study of the questions [of Defence]; of exercising due foresight in regard to the changing conditions produced by external developments; and of drawing from the several departments of State, and arranging in convenient form for the use of the Cabinet such information as may at any time be required. . . . The object should be to secure for the British Empire, with least possible derangement of existing machinery, the immense advantages which the General Staff has conferred upon Germany.[8]

Thus, the proposal was made that led to the creation of the Committee of Imperial Defence. On 11th January 1904, the Triumvirate recommended that the Cabinet Defence Committee should be given a permanent nucleus consisting of:

> I.　A permanent Secretary who should be appointed for five years renewable at pleasure.
> II.　Under this official, two naval officers, selected by the Admiralty, two military officers chosen by the War Office, and two Indian Officers, nominated by the Viceroy, with, if possible, one or more representatives of the Colonies.

This nucleus was to undertake five specific duties: consideration of all questions of Imperial Defence; obtaining and collating data from all government departments; preparing papers in anticipation of the needs of the Prime Minister and the Defence Committee; furnishing advice on Defence questions involving more than one government department; and keeping records for the use of the Cabinet of the day and of its successors.

Esher and Clarke viewed the nucleus as the foundation on which might be built a future British Great General Staff, or, in modern parlance, a Defence Policy Staff. Fisher was not so sure. He had always been an advocate of a General Staff for the War Office, and, when Second Sea Lord, for the Admiralty as well, but now that he was approaching his promotion to First Sea Lord, he began to have doubts about a Naval War Staff. He preferred the Admiralty system of the Director of Naval Intelligence advising the First Sea Lord on potential naval threats, and for the recently established Naval War

College at Greenwich to develop operational concepts to counter them.

It was Balfour, however, who was the most reluctant to accept the idea of a permanent nucleus that the Triumvirate put to him in their covering letter as:

> ... a 'Department', to use a well-understood term, for the Defence Committee containing elements of a permanent character. . . . located in close proximity to the residence of the Prime Minister, and under his exclusive control.[9]

The proposal seemed unconstitutional in that it could lead to the usurpation by naval and military professionals of the Cabinet's collective political responsibility for the defence of the realm. He insisted that the advisory nature of Cabinet Defence Committee must be preserved, and the permanent nucleus should be a 'Secretariat', as opposed to a nascent Imperial Great General Staff. The proposed Secretariat was also pruned down to a Secretary and two assistant secretaries, one from each Service to start with. The idea of inviting Dominion ministers to attend meetings, when matters of their concern were discussed, was retained, and gave substance to the Committee's new title, the Committee of Imperial Defence (CID).

As soon as the Triumvirate had the Prime Minister's agreement in principle to the Cabinet level organisation, they tackled the War Office problem with a ruthlessness that had not been possible for earlier commissions, which had not enjoyed such a flood-tide of political support. They recommended that the post of C-in-C be abolished; the Admiralty Board system be imposed; and a General Staff be created. The Army Council, with the Secretary of State for War at its head, was to have four military and two civilian members: Chief of General Staff, Adjutant General, Quartermaster General, Master General of the Ordnance, Permanent Under Secretary of State, and Financial Secretary – an organisation that has stood the test of time and still exists today under the title of the Army Board.[10]

Realising that a determined counter-offensive would be mounted by their opponents, the Triumvirate sent Part I of their report to the Prime Minister on 11th January 1904, hoping to win Cabinet agreement quickly enough to pre-empt opposition when Parliament returned after the Christmas recess. With Fisher living up to his 'Three Rs', they requested the immediate removal of all the incumbent military members of the War Office Council so that their successors would be ready to implement the reconstitution of their ministry on lines set out in Parts II and III of the Committee's report to be published on 23rd February and 9th March respectively.

'New measures,' they said, 'demand new men, and we therefore attach special importance to the immediate appointment of Military Members who have not hitherto been closely connected with existing methods. . . . Failing this action we see no hope that the reconstitution of the War Office will be a reality.'[11]

Opposition did emerge, but failed to hold back the axe. Salisbury, Lansdowne and Brodrick all took exception to the implied criticism of their stewardship. Campbell-Bannerman, Leader of the Opposition in the Commons, likened the Esher Triumvirate to a new 'Committee of Public Safety'; and one political wag asked what else could be expected from:

> a financial courtier;
> a Times leader-writer;
> and a Cingalese sailor![12]
> (Fisher's mother was a 'native' of Ceylon.)

But Esher and Fisher had taken the precaution of ensuring Edward VII's support for their proposals, neutralising any opposition that might emerge from the C-in-C, Lord Roberts, or from his military colleagues on the War Office Council.

The sacking of the Victorian folk hero Lord 'Bobs' of Kandahar and victor of Paardeburg would have been a formidable undertaking had Esher and Clarke not known that they would meet less opposition from him than from other more orthodox members of the War Office Council. He had always favoured the introduction of a General Staff system, and he had felt, when taking over as C-in-C from Wolseley, that he was likely to be the last holder of the appointment. He was not prepared to resist changes that his instincts told him were for the good of the Army, although they brought to an end the traditional post of C-in-C or Captain-General with its greater loyalty to the Crown than to Parliament.

But 'Bobs' had every reason to depreciate the manner of his going. Arriving in his office one morning, he found that his staff, without prior notice, had been evicted, bag and baggage, to make way for the new General Staff!

Arnold -Forster had sided with the Triumvirate against his predecessors and his military advisers. The Letters Patent creating the new Army Council were published on 6th February 1904, enabling him to go ahead with the wholesale sacking of his opponents in the military hierarchy. He would have liked to have retained General Sir William Nicholson as the first Chief of General Staff (CGS), but the Triumvirate were adamant that there must be no exceptions.

General Sir Neville Lyttelton, a general officer better known for his outstanding abilities as a tennis player than as a profound military thinker, was appointed instead of Nicholson. He was the first of five Riflemen to hold the post in the next 85 years, and he was the only one not to be made a field marshal. When he retired, he became Commandant of the Royal Hospital, Chelsea, where he stayed on for an inordinately long time, rebuffing pointed suggestions that it was high time he left.

Three months later, the famous Treasury Minute of 4th May 1904 was signed formally bringing the Committee of Imperial Defence into being with a permanent secretariat.[13] Sir George Clarke was appointed as its first Secretary, and Balfour invited Esher to become one of its permanent members.

The Admiralty hoped that it had created an effective Whitehall mechanism for the continued subordination of military to naval strategic policy. And so it had, but only in the short term. With Fisher as First Sea Lord from October 1904, Esher on the Committee, and Clarke its Secretary, it could not have been otherwise. The War Office was in no position in the immediate aftermath of its reconstitution to mount effective opposition to the strong Admiralty team.

Much to Arnold-Forster's chagrin, the military members of the new Army Council were no more amenable to him personally or to his ideas professionally than their predecessors. Balfour had chosen Lyttelton as the Army Council's First Military Member and Chief of General Staff on Esher's advice because he thought that he would be malleable and co-operative. Esher was to be proved right. Lyttelton did not have the drive or strength of personality to win back ground already lost to and firmly secured by Fisher on behalf of the Admiralty. Moreover, an effective General Staff could not be created overnight. Within the War Office, the Chief of General Staff's Department was given three Directorates – Military Operations, Staff Duties and Military Training – with Intelligence forming part of the Military Operations Directorate. The new General Staff directors needed time to settle in and to establish properly considered policies; and so the War Office lacked a mainspring as the CID Secretariat picked up the reins of the agreed national Maritime strategy.

During the earliest debates in the CID, the relative positions of the two Service ministries remained unaffected, as yet, by the shifts in the world balances of power that had been going on while the Esher Committee had been dictating the way ahead. The general consensus of opinion in Whitehall strongly favoured the Admiralty. The Army could make little headway in carving out an independent role for itself by insisting on the need for a strong central reserve for three purposes: to meet imperial emergencies like the Boer War; to reinforce the Indian Army; and to guard against any attempted invasion of the United Kingdom. Balfour and the CID remained unimpressed by the Army's demands for an increased share of the national budget, whereas Fisher's programmes for *Dreadnought* class battleship and *Invincible* class battle-cruiser construction – later on to be supported by the public jingoism of 'We want Eight, and we won't wait' – were accepted, despite shrill Treasury objections to their cost.

Three major events in 1905 were to bring about the total reversal of Admiralty and War Office fortunes in the CID and their attitudes towards it. The first was the dramatic end to the Russo-Japanese war with the sinking of the Russian Baltic Fleet at Tsushima in May 1905, and the Russian Army's defeats in Manchuria. The former, coupled with the *Entente Cordiale* of 1903/4, removed the Franco-Russian challenge to British naval supremacy; and the latter reduced the Russian threat to India.

The second event was the Moroccan crisis of 1905/6, which illuminated German hostility to France and Russia on land, and to Britain at sea. And the third event was the fall of Balfour's government, which brought the Liberal Campbell-Bannerman into Downing Street as Prime Minister and led to the appointment of Richard Haldane as Secretary of State for War – a man with the intellectual abilities to mastermind the changes that would be necessary to meet the challenges on the Continent or elsewhere, while Fisher grappled with the Kaiser's ambitions at sea.

In the last months of the Balfour Administration, it was the Admiralty that was first to react to the changing strategic scene. The centre of gravity of the fleet was already being shifted under Fisher's direction from the central Mediterranean to Gibraltar, and its units in the Channel and North Sea were being reinforced in response to the growing strength of the German Navy. The Naval War Courses at Greenwich had begun to consider the practicability of amphibious operations against European objectives instead of within more usual colonial scenarios.

Captain Charles Ottley, who had taken over as Director of Naval Intelligence from Battenberg, recommended to Fisher that the CID Secretariat should examine the possibility of launching amphibious operations against the German North Sea and Baltic coasts in the event of a European war. Clark leapt at the suggestion when it was put to him, seeing it as an opportunity to develop the strategic planning organ of government, envisaged by the Esher Committee. Balfour agreed that a Combined Operations Sub-Committee of the CID should be set up:

> to arrive at certain definite plans for combined Naval and Military action in certain contingencies, and to work out these plans to the actual stage of giving effect to them.[14]

The War Office was not far behind in appreciating the implications of the Moroccan crisis. The new Director of Military Operations (DMO), Major General Grierson (later General Sir James), had run a wargame at the Staff College, Camberley, at the beginning of 1905 to study the problems of British military intervention on the Continent in the event of another Franco-German conflict. The general conclusion was that the Army's most likely tasks were the support of Belgium, whose neutrality Britain had guaranteed, coupled with the prolongation of the northern flank of the French Army on the Franco-German frontier.

In the preliminary discussions setting up the Combined Operations Sub-Committee, the Admiralty presented Fisher's pet plan for landings in Schleswig-Holstein to cut the Kiel Canal, as well as other naval concepts such as the seizure of some of the Friesian Islands as advanced bases for blockading destroyers, or attacks on the main German North Sea naval bases. The War Office turned down all these proposals as militarily unsound. Such landings might have been possible in the 19th Century, but with the development of railways and electric telegraph communications, the Germans could concentrate their forces over land quicker than the Royal Navy could move fully equipped troops by sea.

It also transpired that the Admiralty were not prepared to launch any amphibious operations until command of the sea had been won. By that time, in the War Office view, the decisive land battles might well have been fought and probably lost by the French in the absence of substantial British military help. The mobilisation of the Russian Army would be too slow to affect the issue.

The War Office had logic on its side, but amphibious operations were not the actual issue at stake. Fisher wanted a re-affirmation of the national Maritime strategy before the demise of the Balfour Administration in order to protect the naval construction programmes at the Army's expense. This was fully appreciated by members of the new General Staff, like Colonel William Robertson (later

Field Marshal and CIGS), who were determined to abort the Sub-Committee by the simple expedient of refusing to collaborate with the CID Secretariat in developing plans for amphibious operations, which they deemed to be militarily impracticable.

War Office prevarication kept the issues undecided until Balfour's Unionist Administration had been replaced by Campbell-Bannerman's Liberals in December 1905. The Sub-Committee died without ever holding a formal meeting. The first chance that the Triumvirate had of creating a Defence Policy Staff died with it.

The new Government was deeply divided on Defence policy. The Liberal imperialists in the Cabinet were opposed by the radicals, who were pacifists at heart and inclined towards appeasement of Germany rather than a deterrent alliance with France. In consequence, Campbell-Bannerman, and Asquith, his successor, were inhibited from using the CID to its full potential by this fundamental disagreement on Foreign and Defence policy within their Cabinets. Without the Prime Minister's full support, the Secretariat could but deal with issues presented to it by the Admiralty, War Office or Foreign Office. And each of these powerful departments of state were only prepared to use the CID to further their own interests or to baulk those of the others' policies which it disliked.

The chasm between Admiralty and War Office that the CID was intended to bridge started to widen further early in 1906. The French ambassador, Paul Cambon, decided that he should probe the new British Government's loyalty to the *Entente*. At his first interview with the new Foreign Secretary, Sir Edward Grey, who was one of the Liberal imperialists and a supporter of the *Entente*, he suggested the possibility, already mooted by Colonel Repington, the *Times* military correspondent, and Major Victor Huguet, the French Military Attaché, of secret and deniable staff talks to establish the outlines of naval and military support that Britain might be able and willing to give France if she were attacked by Germany. A few days later, the DMO, James Grierson, met Huguet, as if by chance, riding in Hyde Park. The military staff talks, which flowed from that meeting, and which were conducted intermittently from 1906 onwards on a contingency basis without political commitment on the British side, were to lead in the end to the dispatch of the British Expeditionary Force (BEF) to France in 1914.

While the War Office took the German threat to British interests extremely seriously, it also saw the opportunity afforded by these staff talks to establish a continental role for the Army. Fisher, who was offered similar naval talks, refused to reveal any of the Admiralty war plans to the French, and did his utmost to obstruct the General Staff's intervention planning by refusing to authorise Admiralty staff co-operation in working out shipping schedules for the hypothetical movement of the BEF to France. In his view, the creation of an independent continental role for the Army was not in keeping with the agreed Maritime strategy – as, indeed, it was not – and henceforth he became the opponent rather than the friend of Clarke and his CID Secretariat.

Fisher had been the dominant personality in the Balfour era, but he met his match in Haldane, who took over the War Office in January 1906. The vain, rotund and forensically skilled Scottish lawyer won the loyalties of the Army Council as few other Secretaries of State for War had ever done before; and he made the War Office voice in the CID as powerful as the Admiralty's had been.

In the short period of one year, Haldane fought through the reorganisation of the Army, devised by the General Staff, which was to turn it into a force to be reckoned with seven years later – 'contemptible', maybe, in the Kaiser's eyes, but the best equipped and trained land force that Britain has ever sent into the field at the outbreak of a war. Maintaining the Cardwell system, he created an Expeditionary Force of six regular infantry divisions and a cavalry division. And he wrapped up the plethora of existing Militia, Yeomanry and Volunteer units into the Territorial Army of fourteen divisions for Home Defence and for possible expansion of the Expeditionary Force after six months collective training when mobilised.

When Haldane proposed the formation of the BEF, he did not, in fact, envisage its use solely on the Continent in support of France as the General Staff were already tending to do. He was a convinced supporter of Britain's traditional maritime strategy, and saw his creation as the Empire's central military reserve for use in support of Britain's sea power. In his and the CID's view, the BEF was more likely to be used to deal with some new Indian or colonial crisis than to be deployed on the Continent where it would be out of scale in a European conflict.

George Clarke appreciated that the combination of Fisher's defection from the CID, the Army's determination to pursue an independent continental strategy, and the Prime Minister's inability to use the CID for its true purpose, would negate his and Esher's efforts to create a Defence Policy Staff. He lobbied for and was given the governorship of Bombay in July 1907. Fisher made certain that Clarke's successor was a 'navalist'. Ottley, by then Rear Admiral Sir Charles, his Director of Naval Intelligence, was appointed. He was not as strong a character. Under his stewardship, the Secretariat grew in size, like all bureaucracies, but not in power. The War Office made most use of it to win acceptance of a role for itself in Europe, and the Admiralty largely ignored its recommendations, as opinion in Whitehall swung hesitantly towards a continental strategy.

Ottley's chances of succeeding where Clarke had failed in developing a Defence Policy Staff were further diminished by the change of Prime Ministers. Asquith, who replaced Campbell-Bannerman in April 1908, was a Liberal imperialist at heart. He found that the easiest way to neutralize the most critical radicals in his Cabinet was to invite them to join the CID. By so doing, he hoped to convince them that the *Entente* was not being converted into a formal alliance, and that there were no plans to go to war with Germany. This practice weakened the CID in two ways: it made it less manageable, due to its size and diversity of opinion; and it became necessary to confine knowledge of the progress of the secret military staff talks to a few key Liberal imperialists on a need-to-know basis.

During Ottley's period as Secretary, the War Office was able to exploit the CID to justify the size of BEF that Haldane was creating, and to fend off the efforts of Lord Roberts and the National Service League's campaigns for the introduction of conscription. The Admiralty, under Fisher's guidance, either cold-shouldered or obstructed CID inquiries by two specially appointed sub-committees to look into the military requirements of empire, and into the likelihood and possible scale of invasion of the United Kingdom. The recommendations of both sub-committees supported Haldane's re-organisation of the Army and gave little comfort to Fisher, who feared for the funding of the Admiralty's programmes.

The CID momentarily came into its own during the Agadir crisis of 1911. Several new personalities had emerged in the strategic debates in Whitehall: Reginald McKenna, a navalist but with radical tendencies, had become First Lord of the Admiralty in 1908; General Sir William Nicholson had returned to the War Office in the same year to take over from Lyttelton as Chief of General Staff and, perhaps surprisingly, proved just as ineffectual; Admiral Sir Arthur Wilson, an inflexibly orthodox sailor, had replaced Fisher as First Sea Lord in 1910, though Fisher remained a member of the CID; and the dynamically controversial Major-General Henry Wilson (later

Field Marshal Sir Henry) had taken over as Director of Military Operations in 1910 as well.

Of these, only Henry Wilson was to make a positive impact upon national affairs. His influence was to be decisive in modifying Britain's maritime strategy to accommodate intervention on land in support of France. He has been described as '*lanky, horse-faced, arrogant, at forty-six with a reputation for insubordination, intrigue, and strongly held opinions*'[15]. He was an Anglo-Irishman, who supported Lord Roberts on the conscription issue and Ulstermen opposed to Home Rule for Ireland. Despite these apparent political handicaps and his unguardedly caustic tongue, he survived as DMO through his generally acknowledged competence as a General Staff Officer and a professionalism that was hard to fault.

On assuming office as DMO, Wilson found the BEF far from ready to move to France if war broke out with Germany. There were no rail and road movement plans worked out; the Admiralty was still refusing to have anything to do with shipping schedules; there was a shortage of essential guns and ammunition; and there was a crippling lack of reserve horses. With little support from Nicholson and the other members of the Army Council, he set about the twin tasks of getting the BEF ready for a Franco-German war, and of planning its deployment on the French northern flank. In doing this, he made full use of friendships that he had already established within the French High Command when he had been Commandant at the Staff College, Camberley, immediately prior to becoming DMO, and his ability to speak fluent French.

The new Moroccan crisis of 1911 was brought to a head by the appearance of the German gunboat *Panther* off Agadir ostensibly to protect Berlin's interests, but, in fact, to challenge French influence in Morocco. The First Sea Lord, Admiral Sir Arthur Wilson, refused to believe that war was a possibility and was in Scotland shooting. His soldier namesake, Henry, who was in close touch with military opinion in Paris through Huguet (by then a Colonel, and still French Military Attaché in London), thought very differently, as did Haldane, Esher, Ottley and Winston Churchill. Churchill was Home Secretary at the time and, although he had no official standing in CID affairs, was an active Defence lobbyist. As the direct result of pressure from General Henry Wilson and Churchill, Ottley called a special CID meeting for 23rd August with invitations restricted to those who were aware of the staff talks. Churchill was amongst those invited to attend.

The 23rd August meeting, which became known as the battle of the two Wilsons, marked a critical watershed in the development of British strategy and in the development of the CID. The soldier Wilson, speaking as Director of Military Operations, gave a brilliant exposition of the military situation on the continent. He showed convincingly that the French armies might well be defeated in the West before slow Russian mobilisation in the East and the effects of the British naval blockade could bite unless the BEF was dispatched to the Continent in time to tip the military balance in France's favour. Whether the BEF went to help the Belgians or formed a reserve behind the French Army's northern flank, it would have to be shipped to French ports west of the Straits of Dover for protection against German naval attack. It would then be assembled in a concentration area west of Maubeuge, from where it could either advance into Belgium or support the French flank.

It was then the sailor Wilson's turn to put the naval alternatives. He and McKenna, the First Lord, had already elicited Fisher's views on the crisis. Writing from holiday in Lucerne, Fisher had damned the War Office intervention plans saying:

> . . . if the government land a single British soldier in France, there will be an upheaval in England that will cast them out of office. . . . The whole single object is compulsory service and an increase of the Army Estimates and military influence; I much fear the Prime Minister may be 'nobbled' by Napoleon B [Haldane].[16]

Admiral Wilson did little to help the naval case by giving the meeting a pathetically inept presentation of sketchy naval plans for amphibious landings on the German coast aimed at drawing troops away from the Western front. Nevertheless, the meeting broke up without Asquith taking the obvious course of instructing the Secretariat to put in hand an examination in depth of the two opposing strategies. As was his wont, Asquith ducked the issue and gave no rulings on the lines on which action was to be taken, if the Agadir crisis did lead to war. British strategic policy in the run-up to the First World War was thus to be based upon one brilliantly partisan exposition by Henry Wilson and a superficial and badly presented alternative set out by Arthur Wilson. The second real chance of developing a Defence Policy Staff to undertake the essential task of evaluating strategic options on an impartial national basis was lost.

Asquith tended to side with the radicals in his Cabinet in their dislike of any commitment to intervene on the Continent, and he hoped, as he wrote to Haldane after the 23rd August meeting, *'that we may not have again to consider the contingency'*[17].

Although Asquith did not act, others did. Churchill, an imperialist and navalist at heart, reversed his position as a result of the 23rd August meeting. He became a forceful advocate of the Army's intervention policy, and set his sights on taking over the Admiralty, which had shown itself to be as inefficient as the War Office had been before the Esher reforms. It would be going too far to say that he had become a member of the Continental school, but both he and Haldane accepted that the decisive point in another Franco-German war would be on land, although the sea would become increasingly important if the conflict was prolonged.

Soon after that fateful meeting, Churchill joined Haldane in an attack on the Admiralty's lack of a Naval War Staff capable of working with the General Staff in developing co-ordinated operational plans. They succeeded in persuading Asquith to make changes in the Admiralty hierarchy, but, much to Haldane's consternation, he was not given the Admiralty. Churchill's aspirations were fulfilled instead. He changed places with McKenna, who went to the Home Office with ill grace, having sought and received Asquith's assurance that the Government had no intention of implementing the War Office scheme for deploying the BEF on the Continent.

Haldane magnanimously offered and, indeed, gave Churchill his full support in reshaping the Admiralty. In doing so he ensured that henceforth there would be the fullest collaboration between the two ministries in war-planning. Churchill took immediate steps to change the First Sea Lord, and to set up a Naval War Staff. He replaced Arthur Wilson with Admiral Sir Francis Bridgeman, a surprisingly colourless man, whose judgement was trusted in the Navy, but who lacked the personality needed for success in Whitehall; and he gave the task of establishing the Naval War Staff to Admiral Sir Ernest Troubridge, who was of comparable seniority to the First Sea Lord, but was not seated as a member of the Admiralty Board. Churchill tended to use the retired Fisher as unofficial First Sea Lord; and it was not until 1917 that the posts of First Sea Lord and Chief of Naval War Staff were combined as they are today.

The closer and more genuine co-operation between the Admiralty and War Office further weakened the CID in that the two ministries could develop their own war plans in collaboration with each other without the help of a third party. Ottley retired in March 1912 to take up a lucrative appointment in Vickers shipbuilding on the Tyne. He was succeeded by his principal Assistant Secretary, Captain Maurice Hankey, a Royal Marine Officer ideally suited to the CID at that time. When he took over, he was essentially a secretary with the ability to handle committee business rather than developing strategy. Nonetheless, he had a deep understanding of the issues involved and this enabled him to steer the Committee's pre-war business with a remarkable sureness of touch for a man still in his early thirties.

As Hankey matured, he became, as we will see, the confidant of seven successive prime ministers as Secretary of the various Cabinet committees directing the war effort during the First World War, and as the Cabinet Secretary in the inter-war years, until he retired as Lord Hankey in 1938. He was a man with an overwhelming desire and ability to serve his country constructively and yet anonymously; and he had a thoroughness in attention to detail that made him unrivalled in the speedy and accurate implementation of Cabinet business. Like Esher, he enjoyed discreet power behind the scenes, and he maintained political and inter-Service impartiality, which made him *persona grata* to ministers of all parties and to the Service Chiefs throughout his long career.

Under Hankey's guidance, the number of CID sub-committees grew and the Secretariat staff multiplied as he grasped all the loose ends of war planning that needed pulling together at national level. His two greatest achievements, while Secretary of the pre-war CID, were the creation of the War Book, which laid down the actions to be taken by all ministries at the various stages of alert in the run-up to war; and the work of the Air Defence Standing Sub-Committee, which led to the formation in April 1912 of the Royal Flying Corps with Naval and Military Wings.

At the 1911 Imperial Conference, formal agreement was reached that Dominion Prime Ministers or their representatives, could be invited to attend CID meetings when matters of their Dominion's concern were to be discussed. Although they were unable to commit their Dominions without reference back to their governments, an immensely valuable liaison system was established, which was to pay dividends in 1914, enabling the Empire to rush forces to Britain's assistance much quicker than would otherwise have been possible.

The main strategic controversy in 1912 and 1913 was centred not on North-West Europe but in the Mediterranean. The radicals in the Cabinet became increasingly restive about the dangers, as they saw them, of Britain's close links with France at the expense of Anglo-German relations. Their anxiety was increased by the German announcement of a supplementary naval building programme, the *Novelle*, calling for three extra dreadnoughts, a third naval squadron, and an increase in naval personnel. Largely to placate the radicals, as well as to avoid the financial drain of a renewed naval armaments race, Haldane was asked by Asquith to travel secretly to Berlin to propose the scrapping of the *Novelle* in return for British help in assuaging Germany's colonial ambitions. Haldane's mission failed, and Churchill, at the Admiralty, was faced with the problem of increasing the strength of the Home Fleet to counter the potential increase of German naval strength in the North Sea.

The new Naval War Staff proposed the withdrawal of the six remaining battleships from the Mediterranean, leaving only cruisers based on Malta to protect British lines of communication to Suez. They recommended that the *Entente* should be invoked: the French navy should concentrate in the Mediterranean to deter the Austrian and Italian fleets, while the Royal Navy should oppose the Germans in northern waters. This proposal, which was accepted by Churchill, brought to the surface the distrust of France, which has always been endemic in British minds, and presented the Government with an awkward dilemma. The Naval War Staff's proposed policy would only be acceptable if there was a formal Anglo-French alliance and not just an *Entente*; but an alliance would certainly be opposed by the Cabinet's radicals. The alternative, which the Admiralty naturally favoured, but thought equally impracticable politically, was the addition of an extra three or four million pounds to Naval votes to pay for ten more battleships, of which three might be built and paid for by Canada.

The Press on both sides of the Channel started debating the issue. In London, the suggestion of an alliance was seen as equating to the introduction of conscription to provide France with adequate military support. The alternative of more ships was preferred since the political and financial costs would be less – it was estimated that conscription would add eight million pounds annually to the Army estimates – and Britain would retain her freedom of action. The Paris press saw France's acceptance of responsibility for the Mediterranean as equating to an alliance, and demanded a *quid pro quo* in the form of a firm British commitment to help in the defence of the Franco-German frontier.

Churchill proposed that the CID should meet in Malta so that

Kitchener could come from Egypt to help resolve the issue. Asquith, Churchill and Kitchener did confer there, but not as the CID, which eventually met in London on 4th July 1912. Such was the opposition from the radicals and some imperialists, like Esher, to a formal alliance with France, that the cost of some extra ships was accepted to maintain the British naval presence in the Mediterranean at a 'one power' standard – sufficient to defeat the Austrian or Italian fleets, but needing French help if the two ever combined. Unfortunately, the Canadian Prime Minister, Sir Frederick Borden, failed to convince the Parliament in Ottawa of the need to acquire the three battleships that he had hoped to purchase.

This essentially naval debate swung public opinion away from intervention in Europe and back to maritime isolationism. The chain of events in 1913 was to have an equal and opposite effect.

There had been another changing of the guard in both the Admiralty and War Office during 1912. Prince Louis of Battenberg took over from the ineffectual Bridgeman as First Sea Lord, and complemented Churchill's drive to get the Navy ready for war without trying to force naval theories up on the Army. Haldane, who had become increasingly opposed to the use of the BEF on the Continent, left the War Office to become Lord Chancellor. In his place came the accident prone Colonel Jack Seely, who could never master his brief properly in parliamentary debates.

In the War Office itself, Seely was no match for the forceful Henry Wilson, and was dragged along on the DMO's coat tails into the interventionist and conscription lobbies. General Sir John French, who had been commanding at Aldershot and was deeply involved with Wilson in shaping the BEF for war on the Continent, relieved Nicholson as Chief of the Imperial General Staff (the 'Imperial' had been added to the title of the Army's 'Chief' after the 1909 Imperial Conference, when it was agreed that Dominion and Colonial military forces should be standardised on British Army organisation and equipment, and staff officers should be exchanged). 'Johnnie' French too was no match for Wilson, who saw the new CIGS as a soldier 'pure and simple', and wished he had 'more brains and knowledge'.

Enough had leaked out in Parliament and the press about the secret Anglo-French staff talks and the training of the BEF to cause public debate about the need to support France and the adequacy of the BEF for that purpose. Surprisingly, the CID's efforts were waylaid by yet another invasion inquiry that lasted until May 1914. Throughout 1913, Esher tried repeatedly to persuade his colleagues on the CID to review the insidious drift towards a continental strategy caused by the General Staff's over-intimate association with their French colleagues. The Cabinet had never formally acknowledged the swing away from the maritime strategy caused by the Army's quest for a satisfying independent role, and by General Wilson's single-minded determination to see the BEF alongside the French Army if war did break out. In a memorandum for the CID dated 7th November 1913, Esher warned that the British Army existed for garrison duty, overseas reinforcement, and for use as an auxiliary of the Royal Navy. Given the conditions of modern continental warfare, with massed conscript armies, the BEF had no business on the Continent.[18]

The CID's ability to carry out the review of strategy demanded by Esher had already been eroded by its inflated membership; by the deep divisions in the Cabinet most of whom were never informed of the very detailed staff talks that had been going on between the two general staffs; and by Asquith's personal determination to avoid war. Esher's pleas fell on very deaf ears. While the decision to go to war lay entirely in the hands of the Government, the momentum created by the staff talks rather than the deliberations of the CID led to Britain's ill-considered and unstated adoption of a continental strategy.

So unmanageable had the CID become that an informal working group called the 'High-Level Brigade' was formed consisting of Churchill, Seely, French, and Battenberg with Hankey as secretary to co-ordinate Admiralty and War Office policy. The smooth transition of both the Navy and the Army from peace to war in August 1914 was directed by this group, though Seely and French were forced to resign in March 1914 over the Curragh 'mutiny', when fifty-eight officers of the Dublin garrison asked to resign their commissions rather than take part in any military coercion of Ulster. Asquith took over the War Office portfolio temporarily; General Sir Charles Douglas became CIGS; and French was appointed C-in-C (Designate) of the BEF. The DMO, General Wilson, although an Ulsterman and sympathetic to the 'mutineers', avoided resignation and continued his task of ensuring that the BEF would reach Maubeuge in good order and in time to stop a repetition of 1870.

Right up to the eleventh hour, there was no certainty that the BEF would be deployed to the Continent. On 1 August 1914, when French mobilisation began, Wilson recorded in his diary that Asquith wrote to the new CIGS, General Douglas, saying :

training was not to be suspended, and 'putting on record' the fact that the
Government had never promised the French an Expeditionary Force.[19]

Later that day, the Cabinet reaffirmed its opposition to continental
involvement. Britain would give only naval aid to France. By 5
August, intense lobbying by the French Ambassador and those in
favour of dispatching the BEF to France, had reversed the position.
At the hastily organised first War Council meeting that day, the War
Office team presented such a united front that the decision was taken
to despatch a four division BEF at once with the other two divisions
to follow later if the danger of invasion receded. The CID took no
part in these decisions and died in all but name, spawning, like a
Pacific salmon, the various governmental mechanisms that directed
Britain's war effort from 1914 to 1918.

THE FOUNDING FATHERS

1. Spencer Cavendish, Marquis of Hartington and later the 8th Duke of Devonshire. *(Hulton Picture Company)*

2. Reginald Brett, Viscount Esher. *(Hulton Picture Company)*

3. Colonel George Clarke, later Lord Sydenham. *(National Portrait Gallery)*

4. Colonel Maurice Hankey, later Lord Hankey. *(IWM)*

SOME 'FROCKS' IN THE ASQUITH ERA

5. Herbert Henry Asquith. *(IWM)*

6. Richard Burdon, Viscount Haldane. *(Mary Evans Picture Library)*

7. Winston Churchill. *(IWM)*

8. David Lloyd George. *(IWM)*

SOME 'BRASS HATS' OF THE ASQUITH ERA

9. Field Marshal Earl Kitchener. *(IWM)*

10. Field Marshal Earl French. *(IWM)*

11. Admiral of the Fleet Lord Fisher.
(IWM)

12. Admiral of the Fleet Prince Louis
of Battenberg. *(IWM)*

LLOYD GEORGE'S CHIEFS

13. Admiral of the Fleet Earl Jellicoe.
(IWM)

14. Admiral of the Fleet Lord Wester Wemyss. *(IWM)*

15. Field Marshal Sir Henry Wilson.
(IWM)

16. Field Marshal Sir William Robertson. *(IWM)*

Chronology
FOR CHAPTER THREE

1914
22 Aug	Mons.
26 Aug	Tannenberg.
15 Sep	Massurian Lakes.
10 Oct	Fall of Antwerp.
19 Oct–22 Nov	First Ypres.
1 Nov	Turkey declares war on the *Entente*.
25 Nov	War Council replaced CID.

1915
24 Jan	Dogger Bank.
19 Feb	Dardanelles outer forts bombarded.
10 March	Neuve Chapelle.
18 March	Naval attack on Dardanelles narrows fails.
22 Apr	Second Ypres – gas used for first time.
25 Apr	First Gallipoli landings (Helles & Anzac).
2 May	Gorlice-Tarnov offensive begins.
9 May	Aubers Ridge.
15 May	Festurbert.
15 May	Resignation of Admiral Fisher.
23 May	Italy declares war on Austro-Hungary.
25 May	First Coalition Government formed.
6 Aug	Second Gallipoli landings (Suvla).
15 Aug	National Registration Act.
22 Sep	Bulgaria declares war on the *Entente*.
25 Sep	Loos.
5 Oct	Anglo-French landing at Salonika.
4–30 Nov	Kitchener's visit to Gallipoli.
19 Dec	Haig in command of the BEF.

| 19–20 Dec | Suvla and Anzac beachheads evacuated. |
| 23 Dec | Robertson becomes CIGS. |

1916

8–9 Jan	Evacuation of Helles.
27 Jan	Military Service Act.
21 Feb	Verdun battles begin.
29 Apr	Fall of Kut-el-Amara.
11 May	Air Board set up.
25 May	Conscription introduced.
31 May	Jutland.
5 June	Kitchener's death.
1 July	Battle of the Somme begins.
3 Dec	Jellicoe becomes First Sea Lord.
7 Dec	Lloyd George becomes Prime Minister.

3
EASTERNER 'FROCKS'
VERSUS
WESTERNER 'BRASS'
Asquith, Kitchener and Churchill:
1914–1916

First Sea Lords		Chiefs of the Imperial General Staff	
Prince Louis of Battenberg	to Oct 1914	Sir Charles Douglas died	Oct 1914
Lord Fisher	Oct 1914	Sir James Wolfe-Murray	Oct 1914
Sir Henry Jackson	May 1915	Sir Archibald Murray	Sept 1915
		Sir William Robertson	Dec 1915

'The remarkable deadlock which has occurred in the western theatre of war invites consideration of the question whether some other outlet can be found for effective employment of the great forces of which we shall be able to dispose in a few months' time.'
Hankey's Boxing Day Memorandum of December 1914.[1]

In the last weeks before war was declared in 1914, Esher and his 'Triumvirate' could look back with some pride at the first decade of the 20th Century. Through their work as the Esher Committee they had established a governmental mechanism that could, if used properly, achieve three out of four of the essential requirements of Parliamentary control of naval and military affairs without unduly impeding operational efficiency. First of all, the CID, which they had created, was providing a forum for the co-ordination of Imperial Defence policies, and of inter-departmental preparations for war through Hankey's War Book.

Secondly, they had succeeded in dragging the War Office into the 20th Century by forcing it to adopt the Admiralty's board system. The War Office Council with its Secretary of State for War and five Military and two Civilian Members was working effectively. Indeed, by 1914, they could claim that the War Office was developing military policy more positively than the Admiralty.

And thirdly, they had established the General Staff in 1904, which had become the Imperial General Staff with the willing co-operation of the Dominions in 1909; and belatedly, thanks to Haldane and Churchill, they had forced a Naval War Staff upon the reluctant Admiralty in 1912.

But they knew that they had failed to establish a Great General Staff for the development of national Defence policy and for war planning. After Clarke had left the CID in a disillusioned frame of mind for his governorship of Bombay, Esher had maintained pressure for the creation of such a staff as each international crisis occurred, but to no avail. The vested interests of the five great departments of state – Admiralty, War Office, Foreign Office, Colonial Office and India Office – stood in his way; and Asquith and his Liberal Administration were insufficiently interested in the establishment of a body of naval and military professionals dedicated to preparation for war – the very thing that, as a political party, they were pledged to avoid.

There were, regrettably, three other grave weaknesses in the pre-war Defence policy-making machinery, which neither the Esher Triumvirate or anyone else, other than Kitchener, had perceived, but which war was soon to reveal.

There was no plan to establish a British Supreme Command, let alone an *Entente* Supreme Command. Maurice Hankey records in his autobiography of the war years, *The Supreme Command 1914–18*, that both Ottley and he had raised the question, but had met 'with a frigid reception' from Asquith.[2] The strongly held belief in the collective responsibility of the Cabinet to Parliament for the defence of the realm blocked any such proposals; and the shadow of Cromwell's Protectorate chilled Liberal minds when they contemplated the need for a *Supremo*.

Nor had there been any deep thought given to the control of manpower if Britain entered a Continental conflict. There had been endless political debates and no less than three CID sub-committee inquiries into the need to introduce conscription for home defence, but never for the purpose of raising and sustaining an army on a Continental scale, because this was not within the bounds of the nation's accepted maritime philosophy.

The voluntary system of manning Britain's Armed Services was maintained for traditional reasons, but, more importantly, because informed opinion thought that the rapid advances in weapon technology would make long wars, like the American Civil War, impossible in Europe. Any clash on the Continent would either be short and decisive with an aggressor catching his victim off guard; or, if he failed to do so, then the two sides would soon come to terms to avoid the ruination of their economies. At all levels in British society, men rushed to enlist when war was declared in August 1914 so as not to miss the action. The speedy arrival of the BEF in France was expected to tip the balance decisively in the *Entente*'s favour. 'The boys will be home by Christmas' – or so most people thought.

A similar train of thought led to the third deficiency in the CID's pre-war preparatory work. Nothing had been done to plan the mobilisation of British industry for war production; and equipment and ammunition scales were more appropriate to a Boer War type campaign than a continental conflict for very good Whitehallesque reasons: larger scales could not be justified within the recognised scenarios of the maritime strategy, nor in the Treasury's perceived view of the duration of any foreseeable conflict.

The Army's scales of equipment were based upon the findings of a War Office committee under Sir Francis Mowatt, which sat in 1901. It assumed a force of seven divisions fighting a campaign anywhere in the world at Boer War scales of intensity. Its findings were approved in 1904. British infantry battalions were given two machine-guns each, compared with the sixteen in German battalions; out of the BEF's 500 guns only 24 were medium calibre and none were heavy; and there were only one million rounds of field gun ammunition available in reserve stocks, allowing for just 21 days operations at modest battle-expenditure rates until war production could be put in hand. Even then, there were no plans for letting contracts outside Royal Ordnance Factories and established commercial munitions firms, and no purchases were envisaged from abroad.[3]

But above all, old habits die hard. By 6 August 1914, two days after the declaration of war, the whole of Esher's carefully structured edifice for developing a sound war policy collapsed like a pack of cards, and proved itself to have had no firm roots in the British body politic. Asquith acted as if nothing had happened since Hartington's Royal Commission in the late 1880s. He began to direct the war from the Cabinet, much as William Pitt had done during the Napoleonic Wars.

The CID was the first part of the structure to collapse. It was relegated to completing the War Book measures, and to helping in the co-ordination of the efforts of the Admiralty, India Office and the

Colonial Office to clear the seas of German commerce raiders and merchant shipping, and to purloin all Germany's colonial possessions. Admiral Sir Henry Jackson, whom we will be meeting later as First Sea Lord and who had been Chief of Naval War Staff immediately prior to the outbreak of war, presided over a CID subcommittee 'on overseas attack', which carried out these operations very successfully. He was a modest, able man with a marked technological bent, who had pioneered wireless telegraphy for the Navy. He was never to command a fleet at sea , which is perhaps just as well, as he was the quintessence of a 'Whitehall warrior', and lacked the fire of inspirational leadership.

The General Staff at the War Office lost credibility almost at once, and the Naval War Staff was eclipsed within a few weeks of the outbreak of war. The former's problems were partly caused by the short war syndrome. Most of its key members had been given mobilisation postings to Sir John French's GHQ staff on the assumption that the war would be too short for the development of new policies in the War Office; and that those officers of the General Staff who had been instrumental in planning the BEF's commitment on the continent, were the best men to take it to war. Sir John's principal staff officers were: Sir Archibald Murray, Chief of General Staff with Henry Wilson – the formidable, but devious DMO – as his deputy; Sir Neville McCready, Adjutant General; and Sir William Robertson, Quartermaster General. They were replaced in Whitehall by a second eleven composed largely of retired officers brought back from the Reserve of Officers. They did not have the standing to face up to the first eleven at GHQ, which became the dominant military power-base in the early days of the war.

A more potent reason for the semi-demise of the General Staff at the War Office was the appointment of Kitchener as Secretary of State for War. He did not need a General Staff and had little idea of how to use one. In all his victorious campaigns, he had worked in aloof isolation, acting as his own chief of staff, and depending upon a small group of trusted subordinates to carry out his instructions. He had been used to acting as a Supremo in undisputed military and often political command in the Sudan, South Africa, India and most recently in Egypt; and he wore on his belt the scalps of not only the Mahdi and the Boer's President Kruger, but also of a Viceroy of India, Lord Curzon, whose resignation he forced over the arguments about the powers of the C-in-C, India. He was too old to change his ways on entering the War Office for the first time at the age of 64.

The War Office General Staff was also just 'plain unlucky'. General Sir Charles Douglas, the CIGS at the outbreak of war, was a sick man, and died in office in October 1914. He was succeeded by General Sir James Wolfe-Murray, an incompetent sycophant, who was scared of his illustrious Secretary of State and was aptly nicknamed 'sheep' Murray by Winston Churchill. Kitchener treated him as little more than a Military Assistant – a post usually occupied by a young and up-and-coming lieutenant colonel! His excuse for accepting Wolfe-Murray as CIGS was that he did not wish to deprive Sir John French of a better man from the first eleven.

The troubles of the Naval War Staff were of a different order. The First Sea Lord, Prince Louis of Battenberg, was driven from office, ostensibly by popular outcry about his German ancestry. Ill-wishers in the press saw the failure of the Mediterranean Fleet to stop the escape of the German cruisers *Goeben* and *Breslau* through the Dardanelles to sanctuary at Constantinople in August; the sinking of the three British '*Crécy*' class cruisers by a submarine off the Dutch coast in September; and the mining of the battleship *Audacious* off Scotland in October, as the work of a German spy in high places. Gossip in the London Clubs and Fleet Street, together with a stream of anonymous letters, made Prince Louis of Battenberg's life intolerable, but these were only symptoms and not the real cause of his resignation at the end of October 1914.

It was not just the gossip columnists who had lost confidence in Prince Louis after the string of relatively minor disasters that plagued the fleet as it settled down to prosecute the war at sea. The naval establishment had done so as well, but for quite different reasons. Prince Louis was seen as too weak to stand up to the thrusting young First Lord, Winston Churchill. In Fisher's opinion, he 'was a cypher and Winston's facile dupe'. And worse still, he was generally considered to be lacking in vigour and imagination, due to ill health. Fisher added the comment '*Our directing Sea Lord is played out*'. This was confirmed by Esher, who believed that a change was badly needed.[4]

Churchill chose his old friend and confidant, Lord Fisher, as Prince Louis's successor. He was blithely confident that he could work in tandem with '*the septuagenarian sea-dog*' as Asquith called him. Indeed, Churchill threatened to resign if Fisher was not brought back.

Fisher was 74 and well past his prime when he returned to his old office. His mind had set in the mould of his thinking when he was last on the Admiralty Board. He had two dominant obsessions: one credible and the other far-fetched. The former was his determination to bring the German High Seas Fleet to a decisive action; and the latter was his hankering after his old schemes for major amphibious landings in the Baltic. His Schleswig-Holstein plans had been supplemented by ideas for landings on the Pomeranian coast within 90 miles of Berlin. He would certainly have brought on a fleet action by trying to force an entry into the Baltic, but the speed with which German troops could have been concentrated by rail to oppose landings in Pomerania, made the notion utterly impracticable as the General Staff were at constant pains to point out.

Fisher and Churchill had too many similarities in their characters and the age-gap of three decades was far too wide for the warmth of their initial relationship to last. Politico-professional relationships in naval and military policy-making can be difficult at the best of times, but the old adage 'if youth only knew and old age only could' certainly applied to the Churchill-Fisher combination. At first, Fisher tried his best to work in harmony with his young minister, who had fought so hard to bring him back to run his beloved Navy, but, as a dedicated professional, he very soon found that Churchill's '*pictorial mind, brimming with ideas*', as Asquith described it, was more than he could tolerate. The Admiralty soon became disunited as the schism developed between First Lord and First Sea Lord.

To make matters worse, Fisher had no time for the Naval War Staff, which was headed by Vice-Admiral Sir Doveton Sturdee – a man who was convinced that he was the only naval officer who knew anything about war. His time as Chief of War Staff was not a success. Admiral Thursfield, who served in the Operations Division at the time wrote:

> Neither the Chief of War Staff, nor the Director of Operations Division seemed to have any particular idea of what the War Staff was supposed to be doing, or how they should make use of it; they had been brought up in the tradition that the conduct of the operations of the fleet was a matter for the admiral alone, and that he needed no assistance. . . . Consequently the dozen or so commanders – of whom I was one – were set to the task of recording the movements of ships which were not engaged on any thing of great importance at the moment; for, if they were, it was considered so secret that it was not even allowed to be marked up on the chart in the War Room.[5]

The War Staff slumbered under Sturdee. For all Fisher's dislike of staffs, even he could see that Sturdee was a disaster in the post. He replaced him with the First Lord's Naval Secretary, Rear Admiral

Henry Oliver (later Admiral of the Fleet Sir Henry). Oliver was a 'workaholic' and not an inspiring leader, but full of down-to-earth commonsense – a good seaman and a very wise old owl. He looked and was imperturbable; never used two words when one would do; and had the reputation of being the worst-dressed officer in the Navy. He gathered all the Admiralty operational reins in his hands, and gradually restored the status and usefulness of the Naval War Staff as the months went by.

For the first four and a half months, Asquith ran the war from the Cabinet, which met every day with some twenty-one ministers present. It was far too cumbersome a body for wartime decision-making, and it was hampered by the constitutional custom of there being no agenda and no minutes. Crises were dealt with as they arose by informal gatherings of two or three key ministers, often without professional advisers present. Kitchener and Churchill were the dominant voices with the opportunist Lloyd George, the Chancellor of the Exchequer, contributing his own compelling individualism in Cabinet debate.

It was almost by chance that Kitchener had become Secretary of State for War on 5 August. He had returned on leave from Egypt in July and was in London as the final crisis developed. Asquith was still acting as Secretary of State for War, which he had been doing since Jack Seely's resignation after the Curragh 'Mutiny' in March. It was obvious that this arrangement could not continue. With few exceptions, members of the Liberal Government, with their anti-military prejudices, had no wish to bow to the intense public and private lobbying which arose for Kitchener to take over the War Office, and he himself had no wish to do so. One of the exceptions in the Cabinet was Churchill, who, with the help of Haldane and the Press, convinced Asquith that Kitchener was, indeed, the right man for the job.

Kitchener was on his way back to Egypt when the Prime Minister's summons reached him. He had himself been lobbying during his leave for the Viceroyalty of India, and was far from keen to take over the War Office. He had served abroad for practically all his distinguished military career; he knew nothing about English politics; and was renowned for his taciturn dictatorial methods. Asquith appreciated that to bring Kitchener into the Cabinet could pose a threat to his own leadership, but he also sensed the mood of the country and its demand for Kitchener to play a leading role in the supreme direction of the war. Kitchener as Secretary of State for War would strengthen the Cabinet's unwarlike image, but as

Asquith noted in his diary: '*It is a hazardous experiment, but the best in the circumstances I think.*[6]'

In accepting Asquith's offer, Kitchener stipulated that he would serve as a soldier without allegiance to any political party, and that he wished to return to Egypt or India when the war was over. And so he became the first soldier Secretary of State for War since General George Monck in Charles II's reign. The carefully devised post-Restoration division of powers between the ministers responsible to Parliament and the professional Chiefs was temporarily abandoned in the case of the Army.

Kitchener's greatest contribution to the war effort was his early prediction of a long war, and his single-minded determination to recruit and equip his New Armies to a continental scale of seventy divisions. He worked inhumanly long hours with the Adjutant-General, General Sir Henry Sclater, to recruit the men; with General Sir John Cowans, the Quartermaster General to house and supply them; and with the Master General of the Ordnance, General Sir Stanley von Donop, to equip and provide the ammunition for them. He was acting virtually as C-in-C of the Army, CIGS, Minister of Labour and Minister of Munitions as well as being Secretary of State for War, responsible in Cabinet and to Parliament for the military conduct of the war.

One of his early decisions was and still is criticised. He refused to use Haldane's Territorial Army as the foundation for his New Armies. He saw the TA as a mob of playboys, who would contaminate the morale of the new regular units, and he distrusted the County TA Associations as sources of unhealthy nepotism. He based his views on his own studies of militias during the American Civil War, the Franco-Prussian War and his own campaigns in the Sudan and South Africa. At the time, he was also bitterly criticised by General Headquarters (GHQ) in France for taking away experienced officers and NCOs from the BEF for his New Army divisions instead of reinforcing the existing regular divisions and letting them give birth to the new formations. Henry Wilson, writing to his wife on 15 September 1914, reflects the general cynicism of GHQ:

> K's 'Shadow Armies', for shadow campaigns, at unknown and distant dates, prevent a lot of good officers, NCOs and men from coming out. It is a scandalous thing. . . . What we want, and what we must have, is for our little force out here to be kept up to full strength with the very best of everything. Nothing else is any good.[7]

By mid-November, Asquith had begun to realise that using the peacetime Cabinet system was a poor way to run a war. He turned to Maurice Hankey, who had carved out a job for himself temporarily as the Prime Minister's personal briefer on naval and military affairs. Hankey was given the task of setting up the first War Council with himself as its Secretary and its secretariat drawn from the remains of the CID's staff. Amongst the ten original members of Asquith's War Council were Lloyd George, Grey, Churchill, Kitchener, Balfour and Haldane. Asquith turned back the clock to pre-CID days by making the two Chiefs, Fisher and Wolfe-Murray, advisers and not full members of the War Council in their own right, with unfortunate results, as we will see.

By then Germany's Schlieffen plan had failed. France had not been defeated before the German High Command had been forced to switch forces to the Eastern Front. In the West, the Retreat from Mons had taken place; the Battle of the Marne had been won; and the Race to the Sea had ended in the German failure to break through in the 1st Battle of Ypres. In the East, the Battles of Tannenberg and the Massurian Lakes had been won by the remarkable Hindenburg/Ludendorff command team. In the Eastern Mediterranean, Turkey had just entered the war on the side of the Central Powers. And on all fronts and at sea, the approach of winter was beginning to slow down operations. The War Council had been established just in time for a fundamental reappraisal of strategy.

In the War Council's debates over the Christmas and New Year period, Churchill, Lloyd George and Hankey came quite independently to much the same conclusions about strategic policy for 1915. They saw that stalemate had been reached on the Western Front, and that there was unlikely to be a decision there until the resources of the Central Powers had been brought nearer to exhaustion, or some new technical solution had been found to defeat the lethal combination of machine-gun, trenches and barbed wire. It was time, all three agreed, to look elsewhere for Germany's Achilles heel.

Churchill and Hankey advocated diversionary operations in the Eastern Mediterranean to protect Egypt and to induce as many Balkan states as possible to side with the *Entente*. Breaking through the Dardanelles to take Constantinople was only one of several possibilities at this early stage in the debate on strategy for 1915. Many of the arguments used were to be repeated in 1942/3 when Churchill advocated the offensive against the 'Soft Under-Belly of Europe' rather than mounting the cross-Channel invasion of North West

Europe before the German ability to resist had been fatally weakened.

In their papers, which became known as the 'Boxing Day Memoranda', Churchill and Hankey also advocated research into the possible use of armoured tractors to break the tactical stalemate in the West. It was their enthusiasm for the idea of land-battleships that was to lead to the appearance of the first tanks on the Western Front in small numbers in the autumn of 1916.

Lloyd George's theory was significantly different. He advocated stretching German resources by lengthening the frontline eastwards from France through Italy and the Balkans to the Middle East, so that the *Entente's* seapower and superior manpower (taking Russia's masses into account) could be used to best effect by attacking the weaker sections of the extended front. The Istrian Peninsula, the Dalmation coast, Salonika, the Dardanelles, and the Levant coast were all possible targets for the extension of the front, but he tended to favour a landing at Salonika to help Serbia as the most profitable venture.

None of these ideas appealed very much to the military professionals, like Kitchener and the GHQ staff in France, who had been trained to honour the First Principle of War – concentration of force at the decisive point. They had three main criticisms to these lay ideas for the conduct of the war. The first and cardinal objection was that while it might not be possible to win the war on the Western Front in the short term, it could be easily lost there if the Germans chose to go onto the defensive in the East to launch a decisive offensive in the West. The British line had only just held in the First Battle of Ypres, in which the original BEF had been all but destroyed. Every available soldier was needed to reinforce the line before spring weather returned.

Their second objection was to the very idea that the German front could not be broken in France. Once the British and French armies had enough ammunition, it seemed inconceivable to them that holes could not be blasted through the Western Front, provided that the Russian armies played a significant role in the East, holding down the Austro-German forces opposing them in Poland and Galicia.

And their third objection was strategically fundamental, and had been raised time and again by the General Staff when opposing Fisher's plans for amphibious operations in the Baltic. The Central Powers were operating on interior lines and could shift reserves more quickly by rail across Europe and supply them more easily than the *Entente* could do by sea.

These debates in January 1915 highlighted two new and opposing versions of the maritime and continental schools of strategic thought, which were to bedevil British and French military planning for the rest of the war. The politicians, who had to justify any heavy loss of life to Parliament and the nation, tended to favour the diversionary operations advocated by Churchill and Lloyd George. They became the 'Easterners' with a maritime ring to their creed. The more ortho-dox senior commanders and staff officers, who believed that the only way to defeat the Germans was through concentration of effort at the decisive point – the North Sea and Western Front – became the 'Westerners'. In the popular press and the public imagination, the Easterners were cartooned as the 'Frock Coats', and the Westerners became the 'Brass Hats'.

Looked at in terms of a contest between these two schools of strategic thought, the First World War became a four round contest after stalemate had engulfed the Western Front at the end of 1914. The Easterners lost the first round when the Gallipoli Peninsula was evacuated at the end of 1915. In the second round the Westerners' punches at the Somme and at Jutland failed to achieve a knock-out. The third round was lost by the Westerners in the mud of Passchendaele in 1917. And in the last round, both sides could claim a share in victory, but the knock-out blow came as, indeed, both schools always accepted that it would, with decisive blows on the Western Front.

With no Great General Staff to help in the formulation of a war strategy, the Cabinet was swayed as much by the random coincidence of events as by the collective thinking of its War Council. The whole sorry saga of the disastrous Dardanelles Campaign started with a cable from the Grand Duke Nicholas, the C-in-C of the Russian Armies, asking for a diversionary attack to relieve Turkish pressure in the Caucasus – pressure that ironically was already being dissipated by Russian successes in Armenia, although this was not known at the time.

Kitchener's New Armies were only just forming, and no troops could be spared from the Western Front, where tell-tale signs of a renewed German offensive at Ypres were causing anxiety. Churchill, however, had been closely involved with the Naval Brigade's attempt to help the Belgians hold Antwerp in September 1914, and had witnessed the destruction of the outer forts by modern German heavy artillery. He believed that the old axiom that ships should not challenge well served land batteries was no longer valid, and that the guns of modern British Dreadnoughts were powerful enough to destroy the relatively antiquated Turkish forts that defended the passage through the Dardanelles.

An attempt to force the Dardanelles and to threaten Constantinople quickly gained credibility in the War Council. It was attractive to Edward Grey at the Foreign Office as a means of encouraging the Balkan states to join the *Entente*, and of helping Russia. The poor performance of the Turks in the recent Balkan Wars suggested that they might bow to *force majeure* displayed by a British fleet reaching the Sea of Marmara. And Churchill was able to announce that Fisher was enthusiastic about the idea without, however, pointing out that the old admiral was proposing a combined operation, using old battleships not needed in the North Sea and supported by Indian troops, whom he suggested should be withdrawn from the Western Front where they were not really suited to the conditions prevailing there.

Two preliminary consultative steps were taken. Kitchener sought Sir John French's views on the diversion of troops to the Eastern Mediterranean, and received the predictable reply that he and Joffre would oppose any weakening of the decisive front. Moreover, Sir John wished to mount an offensive in conjunction with the Navy to re-take Ostend and Zeebrugge to prevent the Germans using them as submarine and torpedo-boat bases from which to threaten cross-Channel traffic. He would need all the troops that he had been promised, including the last available regular formation, the 29th Division, the deployment of which was to become the weathercock of the War Council's constantly veering intentions over the next three months.

Churchill cabled Admiral Carden, commanding the naval squadron watching the Dardanelles, asking:

> Do you think that it is a practicable operation to force the Dardanelles by the use of ships alone?

Carden replied on 5 January 1915:

> I do not think that the Dardanelles can be rushed, but they might be forced by extended operations with a large number of ships.[8]

A week later Carden's outline plan was on Churchill's desk. He proposed to reduce the Turkish forts systematically, one by one, with naval gun-fire while mine-sweepers swept a passage through the Strait. He estimated that the operation would take about a month to complete. Fisher accepted the plan and enhanced it by agreeing to add the new fast battleship, *Queen Elizabeth*, and two quasi-Dreadnoughts to the proposed bombarding force of older battleships.

Regrettably, neither Churchill nor Fisher seems to have considered the capabilities of the man whose plan they were espousing. Carden had been Superintendent of Malta Dockyard, having been passed over for promotion before the war, but had been given command of the Dardanelles squadron by one of those accidents of mobilisation postings at the outbreak of war. General Birdwood sized him up in a report to Kitchener in March: '*Very second-rate – no go in him, or ideas, or initiative.*'[9]

Churchill brought Carden's plan to the War Council on 13th January. Kitchener reiterated that he had no troops available to send to the Eastern Mediterranean, but agreed that the operation was worth trying because it could always be broken off at any stage if Carden's estimates proved too sanguine. This was a major error of judgement for a man so steeped in the political sensitivities of the Moslem world. To break off an operation so clearly aimed at the heart of the Ottoman Empire would do great damage to British prestige in the Middle East and India. Fisher, who attended the meeting, did not object when the Council decided:

> That the Admiralty should prepare for a naval expedition in February to bombard and take the Gallipoli Peninsula with Constantinople as its objective.[10]

It was, after all, only a planning directive at that stage, and he believed that it was not his place to argue against the headstrong young First Sea Lord in the War Council, at which he was only his professional adviser and not an actual member.

Before the plan was brought back for Cabinet approval, Fisher had second thoughts, influenced by the C-in-C of the Grand Fleet, Sir John Jellicoe, who, like Sir John French, wished to see no diminution of strength in the decisive theatre. The Dardanelles force was 'growing like Topsy' as forces tend to do when detailed planning starts and unforeseen problems begin to arise. It had reached 15 battleships, three modern battle-cruisers and 32 other warships, to which Churchill had persuaded the French to add a squadron. Fisher and Jellicoe had every reason to be nervous about the diversion of naval effort from the North Sea.

So averse did Fisher become to the operation that he asked not to attend the War Council on 28 January. Churchill could not overcome his objections, and insisted that he should put them to Asquith at a private meeting just before the War Council met. Three things bothered Fisher: the resources allocated to the Dardanelles could be better used elsewhere – possibly in the Baltic; the Grand Fleet's margin of superiority over the German High Seas Fleet would be narrowed significantly if the Dardanelles operation became prolonged; and it was technically unsound for the Navy to go it alone. Churchill rebutted the first two points successfully, and Fisher did not press the third. The weakening of the Grand Fleet's reserves of ships became Fisher's main concern in the weeks ahead and not the absence of Army support.

No record has been published of exactly what was said during the Asquith-Churchill-Fisher preliminary meeting. It seems Asquith was in one of his temporising moods. Churchill believed that he had the Prime Minister's backing to go ahead, while Fisher thought the matter was still open for further consideration and that it would not be discussed at the War Council. To Fisher's fury, Churchill opened the subject as soon as the War Council meeting started. Fisher got up to leave the room and to write out his resignation, but Kitchener jumped up too and persuaded him return to his seat. Fisher did so, saying to himself, '*Well, we can withdraw the ships at any moment, so long as the military don't land*'.[11]

The meeting approved Churchill's proposals with acclamation. Kitchener supported it warmly; for Balfour '*it was difficult to imagine a more helpful operation*'; and Grey liked it because it would '*finally settle the attitude of Bulgaria and the whole of the Balkans*'. Fisher sat sullenly silent. Mid-February was set as the target date for the operation.[12]

As is usual, turning what had so far been a hypothetical concept into reality concentrated many minds. But there was no Great General Staff to ask such pertinent questions as what was to happen when the Fleet broke through into the Sea of Marmara and could threaten Constantinople? How could the line of communication through the Strait behind the Fleet be kept open? Some troops surely would be required for occupation duties? And if the Turks did not surrender, as was so confidently expected, would the Gallipoli Peninsula not have to be assaulted and occupied?

The answers to some of these questions lay in Foreign Office negotiations with the Balkan states. There was every hope that the Greeks, Bulgarians and Russians could be persuaded to provide troops if an equitable agreement could be reached on the division of spoils when Constantinople was in *Entente* hands. Nevertheless, it became generally recognised that some British troops would be needed to follow-up behind the Fleet to provide a British military presence, and perhaps to secure the passage through the Dardanelles for unarmoured supply ships, if Turkey tried to stay in the war.

As pressure grew in Whitehall for the provision of troops for follow-up purposes, Joffre vetoed French's plan for the attack towards Ostend and Zeebrugge, making it easier for Kitchener to divert the 29th Division to the Mediterranean; the Turks were ignominiously defeated on the Suez Canal, thus reducing the threat to Egypt; and the ANZAC Corps would have completed its training in Egypt by the end of February and so would be available for operations in the Eastern Mediterranean. Kitchener could no longer maintain that there were no troops available to support the naval attack.

At the War Council Meeting on 16 February, Kitchener did agree to send the 29th to the Mediterranean, but no sooner had he done so than he was assailed by French and Joffre. They pointed to the continuing Russian failures on the Eastern Front, and to intelligence assessments warning of the growing possibility of the Germans switching their main effort to the West in the spring. They needed every available regular formation to defend the Western Front. Kitchener bowed to their objections and cancelled the move of the 29th Division without telling Churchill!

It may seem that, as Churchill argued, the Westerners were exaggerating the impact which the last uncommitted British regular division could have upon the balance of forces on the Continent. But it was not just the 29th Division that was at stake. It had become a symbol in the minds of the French Government of Britain's continuing commitment to the defence of France; and to the staff of GHQ, its diversion to the Mediterranean was the thin end of the wedge that could lead to a progressive weakening of the BEF. General Sir William Robertson, who, at the turn of the year, had taken over as French's Chief of Staff from an over-tired and aloof Sir Archibald Murray, to whom Joffre's staff had taken a marked dislike, wrote:

> To force the Dardanelles, dominate Constantinople, and open up the Bosphorus, was a task that might well call for the services of many divisions . . . [Kitchener's] error, if he made one, was not so much in temporarily holding back the 29th Division, as in departing from his first, simple, and accurate instinct that sufficient troops for the new venture could not be found.[13]

Carden's naval bombardment of the forts at the entrance to the

Dardanelles began on 19 February and was initially relatively successful. The first forts to be attacked were silenced, and Royal Marine landing parties completed their destruction without much opposition. As the days went by, however, the Turks recovered and began to oppose the landing parties. And they brought up mobile artillery batteries, which made mine-sweeping hazardous. The need for troops to follow-up on land became increasingly obvious.

Without an effective General Staff in the War Office, no studies had been carried out to assess the implications of the dispatch of troops to the Dardanelles or how they should be employed. Churchill was still envisaging the Greeks clearing the Gallipoli Peninsula as soon as Carden reached the Sea of Marmara, but in the first week of March, the Russians made it clear that they would not countenance any Greek participation in the occupation of Constantinople. Greece fell back into a hesitant neutrality. Kitchener then agreed once more and most reluctantly to send out the 29th Division, but without even an outline plan available for its future employment. To make matters worse, it was loaded non-tactically and so would have to be reloaded after it reached the Mediterranean and a plan had been made.[14]

Kitchener appointed General Sir Ian Hamilton, his former Chief of Staff in South Africa, to command the land forces. His first words to Hamilton were '*We are sending a military force to support the Fleet now at the Dardanelles, and you are to have command*'.[15] Giving evidence later to the Dardanelles Commission, Hamilton explained '*We soldiers were clearly to understand that we were string Number 2. The sailors said they could force the Dardanelles on their own, and we were not to chip in unless the Admiral definitely chucked in the sponge*'.[16]

Hamilton reached the Fleet base in Mudros Bay at Lemnos Island at the entrance to the Dardanelles the night before the major naval attempt to force the Narrows was launched on 18 March. He had no staff and no plan. And he found that Carden had gone sick and his second-in-command, Admiral de Robeck, was in charge. General Sir William Birdwood, who commanded the ANZACs at Gallipoli, described de Robeck as '*a fine fellow – worth a dozen of Carden*'.[17]

The naval assault came within a hair's breadth of success, though this was not known until after the war. By late afternoon the forts had been subdued. Then one French and two old British battleships were sunk by undetected mines, and three others were seriously damaged; and de Robeck called off the action. In the view of Enver Pasha, the Turkish Commander, a fresh attack within the next week would have broken through. The larger Turkish guns were almost out of high explosive shell capable of doing damage to armoured ships, and there were no fresh supplies nearer than Germany.

De Robeck had, perhaps understandably, lost confidence in the Navy's ability to break through without unacceptable losses. At a conference in the *Queen Elizabeth* on 22 March, Hamilton agreed with de Robeck that no fresh attempt on the narrows should be made until the Army was ready to occupy the Peninsula, and that would not be until the last week of April at the earliest, as the 29th Division had to be reloaded tactically at Alexandria. Moreover, a detailed assault-landing plan had still to be prepared and the troops trained for the operation.

The month-long hiatus gave General Liman von Sanders, who took over the Turkish defence on 26 March, ample time to prepare for Hamilton's assault, which, though well planned and courageously executed, ended in failure to establish more than two precarious toe holds on the Gallipoli Peninsula. Had it not been for the extraordinarily fine leadership of Mustafa Kemal (later Kemal Ataturk, President of Turkey), commanding the 17th Turkish Division, the story might have been different, but machine-guns and wire favoured the defender just as much on the rock strewn Mediterranean hillsides as they did in the mud of Flanders. The same depressing stalemate set in at Gallipoli after the Turkish counter-attacks had been successfully repulsed.

In France, Sir John French was endeavouring to support Joffre's offensives in Artois and Champagne with attacks on the German lines opposite the BEF. At Neuve Chapelle, Haig's First Army came near enough to success on 10 March to confirm the GHQ view that, given enough ammunition, a break-through on the Western Front was practicable. In the Second Battle of Ypres, fought at the time of the Gallipoli landings, Smith-Dorien's Second Army just managed to defeat the German counter-offensive, in which gas was used for the first time. Then on 9 May, Sir John tried once more to show that it was possible to break the stalemate in the West with another attack by Haig's First Army on Aubers Ridge. The attack cost almost 12,000 British lives and led to the great Munitions Crisis of 1915, which contributed to the fall of Asquith's Liberal Government and to its replacement by the first National Government under his premiership.

Success breeds success, but, in a democracy, failure brings a struggle for power: the failure to break through the Dardanelles; the stalemate on the Gallipoli Peninsula; and the losses on the Western

Front, all weakened the credibility of Asquith's Cabinet. Three men triggered the Cabinet showdown: Sir John French, Lloyd George, and Lord Fisher.

French had made his reputation in South Africa as a dashing cavalry leader. He had risen in the Army through his prowess in small wars, but he had reached his ceiling commanding a force of the size of the original BEF. His mind moved slowly, and he took time to appreciate the impact of events. Impulsive and short tempered, his frequent moods alternated between extremes of optimism and pessimism, and he was too easily swayed by gossip, especially when it emanated from Henry Wilson, who had become his Chief Liaison Officer with Joffre in January 1915, and who was no respecter of Kitchener.

Sir John French was childishly jealous of Kitchener, and resented him acting both as Secretary of State for War and as a Field Marshal. The two men had first clashed during the retreat from Mons when Kitchener had travelled to France in uniform to countermand Sir John's intention to withdraw the BEF behind the Seine and out of the Battle of the Marne. Their relationship steadily deteriorated over what French saw as Kitchener's failure to provide the BEF with the men, guns and ammunition needed for success on the Western Front. The combination of dispatch of the 29th Division and large stocks of ammunition to Gallipoli, and French's failures at Neuve Chapelle and Aubers Ridge, brought their mutual antagonism to a head.

But French was not alone in his dislike of Kitchener. Lloyd George, with his acute awareness of political opportunity and with his urge to conquer new fields as stepping-stones in his path to greater political power, saw that he could exploit the growing volume of complaints emanating from GHQ about ammunition shortages, which were seen as the main cause of the heavy loss of life in France. He was joined by Lord Northcliffe, the proprietor of the *Times* and *Daily Mail*, who had crossed swords with Kitchener over the treatment of his reporters, particularly the influential, but devious, Colonel Repington, a close friend of Sir John French.

Northcliffe had become convinced that one of the greatest services that he could render the country was to get rid of Kitchener. He chose the ammunition issue; sided with Lloyd George in anti-Kitchener lobbying inside and outside Parliament; and was fed with the information for his attacks by Sir John French via Repington. Five days after the failure on Aubers Ridge, the *Times* was demanding more ammunition with detail that could only have come from GHQ; and a week later the *Daily Mail* carried an article under the banner headline *'Shell Scandal: Lord Kitchener's Tragic Blunder'*, demanding his dismissal.[18]

The attack backfired. Kitchener's reputation in the country was too high even for the powerful Lord Northcliffe to scale. Copies of the *Daily Mail* were burnt on the floor of the Stock Exchange and its circulation fell by 200,000 copies. All might have been well had not Fisher decided to resign at this moment, when the country was reeling under so many failures.

Fisher's relationship with Churchill had, like French's with Kitchener, been deteriorating ever since the Dardanelles decision had been taken in January, and for much the same reason – the diversion of resources from the decisive point in the war at sea – the North Sea. The last straw for Fisher came in bitter arguments with Kitchener over Fisher's demand for the withdrawal of the powerful *Queen Elizabeth* from the Dardanelles, which Kitchener saw as the Navy letting down the Army after it had come to the Navy's rescue and was suffering heavy losses ashore; and with Churchill over sending out further naval reinforcements to the Eastern Mediterranean. Fisher resigned in a huff – the ninth time he had threatened to do so – but this time he was in deadly earnest.

Pressure soon mounted to persuade him to remain at his post. Asquith, concerned about the stability of his Government, sent him the terse message:

> In the King's name, I order you to remain at your post.[19]

In the Admiralty and at sea, he had the support of all the Sea Lords and of the Fleet in his deadly joust with Churchill. Jellicoe summed up the feeling of the Fleet when writing to the Second Sea Lord:

> Lord Fisher had many enemies, more enemies than friends, in the Service, but even his enemies have been saying that his presence at the Admiralty was essential, as he was the only person who could tackle the 1st Lord. . . . Winston Churchill is a public danger to the Empire . . .[20]

As news of his resignation leaked out to the Press, there was a surge of headlines such as *'Lord Fisher Must Not Go!'* An article in the *Globe* hit the nail on the head, posing the questions: *'Lord Fisher or Mr Churchill? Expert or amateur?'* And several papers, including the *Times*, suggested that Fisher should become First Lord so that the war would be prosecuted at sea and on land by politico-professional Chiefs – Fisher wielding supreme power at the Admiralty as Kitchener was doing at the War Office.

Unfortunately Fisher became over-confident of his ability to unseat Churchill, and of his own indispensability to the Asquith Government and the country. He sent Asquith a letter setting outrageous terms for withdrawing his resignation: Winston must go; he would not serve under Balfour who was an Easterner; a new Board of Admiralty of his choosing must be appointed; he should have untrammelled and sole command of all naval forces; the First Lord must be restricted to policy and parliamentary business; and he, Fisher, must have complete charge of naval construction. No Prime Minister could accept such an ultimatum; and so Fisher's long and brilliant career came sadly to its end, Asquith remarking to the King that Fisher's letter *'indicated signs of mental aberration'*.[21]

The Government crisis that followed Fisher's resignation resulted in the formation of the first National Coalition Government under Asquith. Lloyd George had seen that if he brought Asquith down over the munitions crisis and Dardanelles failure, he would lose office himself, since Bonar Law was most unlikely to offer him a portfolio in a successor Unionist administration.

In the horse trading that went on in the formation of the new Liberal-Unionist cabinet team, Lloyd George tried to oust Kitchener and to take his place. The King, however, was determined that he should not succeed. The Palace view was that Kitchener should become C-in-C of all Imperial forces as well as holding the War Office portfolio, thus clarifying his position vis-a-vis Sir John French. Esher also urged Kitchener to combine the two posts, quoting Wolseley's view of the paramount need to concentrate political and military control in one hand during war.

Kitchener did survive, but with responsibility for production of munitions taken away from the War Office. Lloyd George was hoist with his own petard. He was made responsible for forming the new Ministry of Munitions instead of inheriting the War Office portfolio. Balfour, on Churchill's recommendation, took over as First Lord. The obvious successor to Fisher was Sir Arthur Wilson, but he declined to serve under anyone other than Churchill. Jellicoe would have been a strong contender, if there had been an obvious candidate to take over the Grand Fleet. Beatty was as yet unproven as a potential C-in-C, and was considered to lack administrative ability. And so Admiral Sir Henry Jackson, the experienced Whitehall warrior, electrician and engineer, who was most people's second choice, inherited Fisher's mantle. There could hardly have been two First Sea Lords with such contrasting styles: Fisher noisy, intuitive and aggressive; Jackson quiet, intellectual and self-effacing. Churchill had to content himself with a seat in the Cabinet in the sinecure of the Duchy of Lancaster.

The change of ministers did not cauterise the problems facing the new Cabinet. On the Eastern Front, the Austro-German forces had launched their highly successful Gorlice-Tarnov offensive on 2 May, which was to carry them to Warsaw by the beginning of August and to the Russian frontier at Brest-Litovsk by the end of that month. On the Western Front, Sir John French had conformed to Joffre's policy of attritional attacks in preparation for a major offensive in September. Haig had attacked at Festubert after three days preparatory artillery bombardment with the declared intention of wearing down German resistance. The battle, which lasted from 15th to 27 May, cost the British 16,000 casualties for a gain of about a thousand yards on a two mile front. The Germans lost only 5,000 men! At sea, Jellicoe was still trying to draw the German High Seas Fleet out to battle. And in the Mediterranean, Italy had joined the *Entente* on 23 May, opening the first of twelve costly battles of the Isonzo; and there was stalemate at Gallipoli.

As is the normal practice in Whitehall, the Cabinet sub-committees of the previous administration lapsed. Asquith replaced the War Council with the Dardanelles Committee, which had all the weaknesses of its predecessor: it was too large; it had a good secretariat under Hankey, but no Great General Staff; and all major policy decisions had still to be debated twice – in the Committee and again in full Cabinet.

Kitchener was the dominant personality on the Dardanelles Committee, but it was to be for the last time that he could dictate military policy without bothering to justify his decisions to his Cabinet colleagues. Churchill put his finger on the reasons for the slump in Kitchener's influence in the new government – it never declined in the country at large – when he wrote that without an effective General Staff at the War Office:

> . . . Lord Kitchener himself was left to face the rushing, swirling torrent of events with no rock of clear, well-thought-out doctrine and calculations at his back.
>
> In consequence he gave decisions now in this direction, now in that, which were markedly influenced by the daily impressions he sustained, which im-

pressions were often of a fleeting nature. As a result his decisions were sometimes contradictory.[22]

Faced with the forensic skills of men like Sir Edward Carson, and
the quick witted emotionalism of Lloyd George, Kitchener found it
increasingly difficult to carry conviction in Cabinet. He was clear in
his own mind that the *Entente's* strategic policy should be defensive in
the West during 1915 while his New Armies were being equipped,
trained and gradually given operational experience; and that in the
meantime Turkey should be forced out of the war with forces that
could be spared temporarily from the decisive front. He was also
clear that there could be no withdrawal from Gallipoli without
undermining British prestige in the Moslem world.

Having asked Ian Hamilton how many troops he needed to defeat
the Turks at Gallipoli, he persuaded the Dardanelles Committee,
despite strong opposition from the Westerners, to despatch five extra
divisions to the Mediterranean. But events and his Cabinet colleagues conspired against him.

The new landings on the Gallipoli Peninsula on 6 August were a
disaster. Stalemate returned to Gallipoli; Bulgaria was encouraged to
join the Central Powers; German successes on the Eastern Front
enabled von Falkenhayn to despatch troops to co-operate with the
Bulgarians in crushing Serbia; and on 25th September the Battle of
Loos began, resulting in another 60,000 British casualties for no
worthwhile gains. With the stench of muddle and failure pervading
the corridors of power in Whitehall, Asquith demanded the creation
of what amounted to a Great General Staff to guide and advise the
Cabinet and its Committees, but since the war on land was so
predominant in ministers' minds, he felt that this need could be
satisfied by a strengthened General Staff at the War Office.

At Asquith's behest, the useless Wolfe-Murray was replaced as
CIGS by his namesake Sir Archibald Murray, who had been Deputy
CIGS with special responsibility for the training of the New Armies
since leaving the BEF at the end of 1914. Kitchener acquiesced
because he knew that Archibald Murray – a handsome man with a
facade of professionalism – would not stand up to him, and his
control over military strategy would be unimpaired. He was right
about Archibald Murray, but wrong about his own control of
national military strategy continuing. Dissatisfaction with his dictatorial methods grew as failures multiplied.

Matters came to a head at the Dardanelles Committee on 9th
October. Lloyd George asked Kitchener whether anything had been

heard of the expected German attack on Serbia. Kitchener said nothing had come in before he left the War Office for the meeting, but was immediately proved wrong. When the cable reporting the German crossing of the Danube was read to the Committee, Carson passed a note to Lloyd George saying:

> K does not read the telegrams – and we don't see them – it is intolerable.[23]

Carson then cross-examined Kitchener on Gallipoli as if he were a hostile witness. Kitchener's secretiveness, lack of candour and reluctance to explain his intentions exasperated his Cabinet colleagues, who were never on the best of terms with one another, let alone with a Secretary of State for War who owed allegiance to neither political party and depended for his power base upon public esteem.

The desperate plight of the Serbs gave the anti-Kitchener clique in the Cabinet an opportunity to get rid of him. The rape of Serbia had inflamed French popular opinion in much the same way as the British public had been swayed by the invasion of Belgium in 1914. An Anglo-French force had landed at Salonika on 5 October and was competing for resources with Gallipoli. The obvious man to go out to the Eastern Mediterranean to sort out priorities was Kitchener, but he realised that, if he went, he might find Lloyd George in his place when he returned.

Lloyd George did, indeed, bring matters to a head with a letter to Asquith at the end of October, threatening to resign if Kitchener was not removed from the War Office. Asquith knew that his shaky coalition would not survive Kitchener's dismissal, and so he offered him a number of prestigious posts: C-in-C of all British forces not in the BEF; C-in-C Home Forces; or even Viceroy of India, which he had long coveted. But Kitchener was no longer interested, believing that he could not leave the conduct of the war to self-seeking politicians, and that he had still much to give the country as its War Lord.

After making sure that Asquith would take over the War Office temporarily while he was away, Kitchener agreed to go out to the Eastern Mediterranean to review the situation. When he left on 4 November, he pointedly took his seals of office with him, but this did not prevent his detractors attempting to strip him of much of his power while he was away. Goaded by Lloyd George and Carson, Asquith decided to reorganise his government's machinery for conducting the war. He replaced the cumbersome Dardanelles Committee with a smaller War Committee, which, like its predecessors, stayed small for only a few weeks. French's failure at Loos, and his blatant attempts to shift the blame onto Haig, led to his own dismissal and supersession by Haig. And Lloyd George set himself up as the self-declared heir apparent to Kitchener at the War Office, if, as he hoped, Kitchener could be persuaded to stay in the Eastern Mediterranean as British pro-consul.

But Kitchener would have none of Lloyd George's scheming. When he made it clear that he would be returning by the end of November, his opponents tried to make his position untenable by insisting that advice to the Government on military strategy should be the sole responsibility of the CIGS. Realising that Archibald Murray would not stand up to Kitchener even if he were to be given greater powers, Asquith approached Sir William Robertson, the BEF's Chief of Staff and a determined Westerner, to undertake the task of providing the consistent military advice to the Cabinet, which Kitchener had so singularly failed to do. Robertson, however, would only accept the appointment if he could come to a firm understanding with Kitchener on a clear division of their respective responsibilities.

Robertson drove a hard bargain before accepting. In setting out his terms as Asquith asked him to do, he proposed that the CIGS should be the sole authoritative channel through which the War Committee received advice on military operations; and that all operational orders should be signed by the CIGS on the authority of the War Committee, and not on that of the Army Council presided over by the Secretary of State for War. Kitchener, tired and dispirited by personal attacks on his political and professional judgement, advised Asquith to accept these changes, but to appoint Lord Derby as Secretary of State for War in his place. He could not, he said, remain Secretary of State for War with his responsibilities reduced to feeding and clothing the Army.[24]

Esher once more flits briefly across the pages of the history of the Chiefs. Robertson was most upset when he heard that his terms might result in the resignation of Kitchener. Writing to the King's private secretary, he remarked that it was *far more necessary that K should remain S of S than I should become CIGS*.[25] He wanted Kitchener to remain at the War Office, but was equally determined to have his own way in the conduct of business. Esher, as always, had the King's ear and decided to mediate. Kitchener explained to him that, as Esher knew all too well, the Secretary of State was constitutionally responsible to Parliament for the actions of the General Staff. This would no longer be so if the CIGS signed orders on the authority of the War Committee. Robertson took the point when it was put to him. He reversed his position and agreed that all orders signed by the CIGS would be on the authority of the Secretary of State for War instead of the War Committee.[26]

Few people expected the Kitchener-Robertson team to last very long. Surprisingly, it developed into a constructively happy partnership, short though it was to prove to be. Kitchener was used to getting his own way; 'Wully' Robertson – forceful, shrewd, tenacious, and blunt but likeable – was equally determined to have things his way. The common bond between the two men was their professionalism, which made them both Westerners almost by definition. Committed though Kitchener was to winning the Gallipoli campaign, because of his fear of the consequences for British prestige in the East, he had always seen it as a stop-gap until his New Armies were fully ready for operations in Flanders. He had no difficulty in accepting Robertson's extreme Western views.

Whether Asquith foresaw the changes in strategic policy that his autumn reorganisation would bring about is doubtful. The Westerners were now in power; Lloyd George had failed to unseat Kitchener; and, for the time being, his advocacy of a campaign based on Salonika was discredited. Suvla and ANZAC Cove were evacuated successfully without loss on 19–20 December. The War Committee then agreed on 28 December that Haig should be authorised to prepare for a major offensive on the Western Front during 1916, at a date to be decided later. And to make this possible, all 'side shows' were to be cut back. The last toe-hold on the Gallipoli Peninsula was given up on 8–9 January when Helles was evacuated. Henceforth, the first principle of war was to be applied by concentrating all available resources on the Western Front and in the North Sea; and the second principle of war, economy of effort, was to be applied elsewhere.

In 1915, the high hopes of the Easterners had been dashed: in 1916, the Westerners were to be just as badly disappointed. The year can be summed up in three words: Verdun, Jutland and the Somme.

With Robertson's arrival as CIGS, the war on land was brought under firm military control. This was not the case at sea. The Balfour-Jackson team lacked the dynamism to drive naval policy forward. A feeling of lack of direction began to permeate the Admiralty, which Fisher, watching from the Lords, was not slow to exploit. A movement for his return to power started in the drawing-room of his admirer, the beautiful wife of the 13th Duke of Hamilton.

The main plank in his case for return to the Admiralty was the generally agreed need to dispel the lethargy that had engulfed naval affairs since his resignation; and his specific attack was aimed at the serious delays that were occurring in the battle-cruiser and destroyer building programmes, which he had initiated early in the war.

The Admiralty's inability to keep its construction programmes on schedule stemmed from the Unions' reluctance to accept dilution of skilled labour; from the energy and drive of Lloyd George, who was syphoning off dockyard workers into his ammunition factories; and from Asquith's hesitancy in introducing conscription and direction of labour. Asquith, as a committed Liberal – and strongly supported by Kitchener and opposed equally strongly by Lloyd George – had been determined to avoid undermining the voluntary system for as long as possible. The National Registration Act had been passed in August 1915 as a preliminary measure, but the Military Service Act itself was not in place until the following January, and conscription was not actually introduced until May 1916.

Lieutenant Colonel Winston Churchill, back from active service in Flanders on special leave to speak in the March debate on naval estimates, condemned the Balfour-Jackson team in a brilliant speech which articulated the causes of the widespread disquiet about their administration of the Navy. His Parthian shot was a call for Fisher's reinstatement as First Sea Lord. But Churchill's attack, though justified by later events, was premature: Balfour won the debate, and Fisher did not return, but disquiet about the direction of the war at sea did not abate.

The Germans had pre-empted the *Entente's* plans for 1916 by opening their own attritional offensive at Verdun on 21 February with the deliberate intention of bringing about the collapse of the French Government by bleeding the French Army to death. The first major Anglo-German clash of the year occurred at sea towards the end of May, when the new German Naval C-in-C, Admiral von Scheer, took the High Seas Fleet into the North Sea. The Battle of Jutland was not the Trafalgar for which Jellicoe had hoped and planned. Losses on both sides were comparable, but the German High Seas Fleet never challenged the Royal Navy's command of the North Sea again. The war at sea became a struggle to defeat the German U-Boats.

Within a week of Jutland, the sea claimed Kitchener when the *Hampshire* was mined off the Scottish coast. Despite intense lobbying by Robertson, who had no desire to see a leading Easterner in the

War Office, Lloyd George became Secretary of State for War, just one step away from his ambition of taking over the conduct of the war from Asquith.

With the benefit of hindsight, it is possible to see that Haig's offensive on the Somme should have been delayed until 1917, when tanks would have been available in large numbers. At the time, however, the consensus of military opinion was that with the vast quantities of shell by then available, and with Kitchener's New Armies ready for action, there was no reason to believe that the German defences could not be torn apart. Moreover, if Brusilov, the Russian commander on the Eastern Front, had not been so successful in June, and if Haig had not attacked on the Somme at the beginning of July, Verdun might have fallen and France might well have sought a separate peace. The shattering British losses on the Somme – 60,000 on the first day and 420,000 all told – saved France, but discredited Robertson, Haig and the General Staff. By the beginning of November, when the fighting died away on both fronts with the approach of the third winter of the war, the policies of the Westerners lay open to counter-attack.

The summer's failures also heralded another winter of Cabinet discontent as had happened in December 1915. Fisher's resignation was parallelled by the enforced resignation of Sir Henry Jackson, in whom both the Board of Admiralty and the Fleet had lost confidence over his lacklustre handling of the anti-U Boat campaign. Jellicoe replaced him as First Sea Lord on 3 December, and Beatty took over the Grand Fleet. Bulgaria's entry into the war was parallelled by Roumania's belated declaration of war and almost immediate collapse, and gave the Easterners good reason to attack the Cabinet's mishandling of its Balkans policy. And the minister, who brought the crisis of confidence to a head, was once again Lloyd George!

Lloyd George had spent the summer in the War Office surrounded by Westerners and brooding over his inability to overturn the general consensus of opinion that favoured concentration of effort on the Western Front. His relations with Robertson were cool from the outset, and were turned to ice by his disloyalty in discussing the faults of British senior officers with Foch behind their backs during a visit to France in September. His mind was still set upon a major campaign in the Balkans, based upon the Anglo-French foothold at Salonika. The failure of the Somme offensive, coupled with the Roumanian débâcle, gave him the opportunity to attack the Westerner bias in Asquith's management of the war.

On 1 December 1916, Lloyd George presented Asquith with an ultimatum, threatening to resign if the War Committee was not reconstituted as a committee of three under his own chairmanship. He also demanded a seat in Cabinet for his ally, Carson, and the removal of his rival, Balfour, from the Admiralty. Asquith tried as usual to find a compromise that would enable his coalition to survive its internal disorder, but this time he failed. On 5 December, Lloyd George resigned, making failure to give timely support to Roumania his reason for doing so. Asquith realised that he could no longer command enough support to carry on and resigned too. On 7 December Lloyd George became Prime Minister. The Easterners were once again in the ascendant.

One issue which lay outside the mainstream of events in 1916, but was to make a fundamental impact on the Chiefs in the years to come, was the creation of the Air Board – the forerunner of the Air Ministry. In the early years of the war, the operations of the naval and military wings of the Royal Flying Corps did not overlap. The only real need for co-ordination was in the development and purchase of aircraft. By early 1916, however, the defence of the Home Counties against Zeppelin raids had brought the need for operational co-operation to the fore, and cut-throat inter-Service competition for aircraft production had become a scandal.

The first attempt to co-ordinate Naval and Army air policy was a total failure. A Joint War Air Committee was set up under Hankey's auspices with Lord Derby as chairman. Neither the Admiralty nor the War Office would co-operate with it. Hankey tried again, and this time an Air Board was formed under Lord Curzon, who saw its establishment as a first step towards the formation of an Air Ministry. The Admiralty, however, still refused to co-operate, arguing that all facets of naval warfare must be under their direct control. They continued to order their own aircraft and aeronautical equipment often without reference to the Air Board. Controversy over the Air Board's powers raged between Curzon and Balfour throughout the summer and autumn of 1916 and had not been resolved when the Asquith Coalition Government fell in December.

Chronology
FOR CHAPTER FOUR

1917

1 Feb	Unrestricted U-Boat War declared by Germany.
8 March	Russian Revolution begins.
11 March	Baghdad taken.
6 April	US declares War.
6 April	German withdrawal to the Hindenburg Line.
9 April	Arras and Vimy Ridge.
16 April	Nivelle's offensive on the Aisne begins.
17–30 April	'Black Fortnight' in the U-Boat War.
29 April	First Convoy sailed.
2 May	Posts of First Sea Lord and Chief of Naval Staff combined.
15 May	Nivelle replaced by Pétain.
21 May	Messines.
8 June	War Policy Committee formed.
13 June	First Gotha raids on London.
20 July	Geddes becomes First Lord.
31 July	Third Battle of Ypres and Passchendaele begins.
17 Aug	Smuts' Report on an independent air service.
24 Oct	Caporetto.
– Nov	The Air Force (Constitution) Bill passed.
31 Oct	Third Battle of Gaza.
7 Nov	Lenin and Trotsky seize power (25 October on old calendar).
7 Nov	Supreme War Council set up.
10 Nov	Passchendaele ends.
20 Nov	Cambrai.
3 Dec	Russo-German cease-fire on Eastern Front.
9 Dec	Fall of Jerusalem to Allenby.

27 Dec   Jellicoe replaced by Wemyss.

1918
 2 Feb   Executive War Board formed.
 9 Feb   First Treaty of Brest-Litovsk signed.
16 Feb   Robertson resigns; Henry Wilson becomes CIGS.
21 March   German counter-offensive in the West begins.
26 March   Foch becomes Generalissimo.
 1 April   Formation of the RAF.
13 April   Dismissal of Trenchard.
23–25 April Last German High Seas Fleet sortie aborted.
15 July   Last German attacks in the West fail.
 8 Aug   Amiens (The Black Day for the German Army).
19 Sep   Megiddo.
30 Sep   Bulgaria accepts armistice.
23 Oct   Vittorio Veneto.
29 Oct   German naval mutinies.
11 Nov   War ends.

4
POLITICAL DICTATORSHIP VERSUS PROFESSIONAL JUDGEMENT
Lloyd George, Jellicoe and Robertson: 1917–1918

First Sea Lords		Chiefs of the Imperial General Staff	
Sir John Jellicoe	Dec 1916	Sir William Robertson	Dec 1915
Sir Rosslyn Wemyss	Dec 1917	Sir Henry Wilson	Feb 1918

Chiefs of Air Staff	
Sir Hugh Trenchard	Dec 1917
Sir Frederick Sykes	April 1918

'Can the Army win the war before the Navy loses it?'

Letter from Fisher to Hankey
in April 1917.[1]

Asquith bequeathed to Lloyd George two highly professional, much respected, but politically antipathetic Chiefs: Jellicoe as First Sea Lord and Robertson as CIGS. They were supported by two Cs-in-C, who had the complete confidence of their Services and of the general public: Beatty with the Grand Fleet at Scapa Flow, and Haig with the BEF in France. Lloyd George also inherited the growing menace of the German U-Boats at sea; and an *Entente* strategic policy, agreed at Chantilly in November 1916, that sought to exploit German exhaustion at Verdun and on the Somme by maintaining pressure on the Western Front throughout the winter in preparation for the resumption of offensives on all land fronts in the spring.

Lloyd George saw Asquith's weaknesses as indecisive management of the British war effort; subservience to the Westerners of the General Staff; and acceptance of an apparent lack of offensive spirit on the part of the Naval War Staff. His first action on becoming

Prime Minister was to create a 'Dictatorship in Commission', as Hankey has described it – a political hegemony within constitutional proprieties, shared with a handful of close colleagues, and responsive to the will of Parliament and the Electorate, but a supremacist system nevertheless.

The new Prime Minister dispensed with the Cabinet as such and the cumbersome War Committee, and in their place he established a small War Cabinet of five members, of whom only the Prime Minister and the Chancellor of the Exchequer, Bonar Law, held actual administrative responsibility. The other members – Lord Curzon, Lord Milner, and Arthur Henderson (representing the growing Labour Party) – were without portfolios. Departmental ministers were accorded Cabinet status, but only attended War Cabinet meetings when items of their concern were to be discussed. Thus the principal war ministers – Sir Edward Carson, who took over the Admiralty, and Lord Derby, who succeeded Lloyd George at the War Office – had no permanent places in the British Supreme Command; nor had the two Chiefs, although they, or their deputies, briefed the War Cabinet on the latest operational events at the beginning of meetings, which took place almost every morning. They were expected to withdraw as soon as they had answered any questions put to them. They did not return to the Cabinet Room unless required to support their ministers on specific items of Admiralty or War Office concern.

This new War Cabinet system had obvious advantages. The need for the Cabinet to re-debate War Committee decisions in order to maintain the principle of Cabinet collective responsibility was eliminated. Departmental ministers could concentrate on running their departments rather than spending most of their time in Cabinet and War Committee meetings; and the full War Cabinet members could focus all their energies on winning the war. Thanks to Lloyd George's grip on his Administration, the War Cabinet was never allowed to expand in the way that all its predecessors had done.

Perhaps the most important innovation put in hand by Lloyd George at the beginning of his time as Prime Minister was the dropping of the time-honoured custom of having no agenda or minutes for Cabinet meetings. Hankey was authorised to convert his War Committee staff into the War Cabinet Secretariat. The Cabinet Office, as we know it today, was born with this decision.

On the debit side, the War Cabinet suffered from the weaknesses of a quasi-dictatorship even though 'in commission'. It reflected

Lloyd George's strengths and weaknesses; the normal checks and balances of orthodox Cabinet government were weakened; and his political intuition was often brought too directly into conflict with the considered policies of his professional advisers.

Lloyd George had three obsessions: his Easterner bias; his distrust of the Naval and Military hierarchies; and his belief in unity of command at national and international level. The grim toll taken by Haig's offensive on the Somme strengthened his determination to pursue his Easterner inclinations, which he had first enunciated, along with Churchill and Hankey, in 1914 in the 'Boxing Day' memoranda. He sought less costly ways of defeating Germany by 'knocking out her props' with offensives in the Middle East, Balkans and Italy, rather than attacking German strength on the Western Front.

His distrust of the professionals was not caused only by the failures at the Dardanelles, Jutland and the Somme. As he wrote in his *War Memoirs*, a man from the rank and file, who had never been to one of the older universities or to a staff college, was now Prime Minister.[2] By upbringing and class, he was suspicious of the establishment and, in particular, of 'Brass' like Jellicoe and Robertson, even though the latter had risen from the ranks as he had done. And as a born politician, he sought advice as much from independent and often politically motivated sources and from junior Service officers as he did from his professional advisers, making his methods anathema to the Naval and General Staffs.

In creating his War Cabinet, Lloyd George had established unity of command to his own satisfaction at national level. He neglected no opportunity to persuade the *Entente* to establish a supreme command, not only as a means of improving the co-ordination of Allied war effort, but, more deviously, to bring the British Chiefs, whom he so distrusted, to heel by placing them under the French, whom he believed were somehow better served by their senior military officers.

Paradoxically, although Lloyd George did establish a system verging on dictatorship, he was acutely aware of his vulnerability in national debate on military policy. Much as he would have liked to discard the advice of Jellicoe and Robertson, he knew that he could only do so if he had the undivided support of his Government colleagues and the backing of the Press barons. Within the War Cabinet, he could criticise military proposals with impunity; he could insist on their re-justification; but he knew that there were great political risks in being seen by Parliament or the public to overrule the professional advice of the First Sea Lord, the CIGS and, towards the end of the war, the newly created Chief of Air Staff.

Throughout 1917 and the first two months of 1918, attitudes in the British Supreme Command were polarised at the extremes of the politico-military spectrum. Lloyd George had the acutest of political antennae, but little understanding of naval and military policy; Jellicoe and Robertson, on the other hand, were dedicated professionals with a contempt for political methods. The War Cabinet was composed of articulate men, who enjoyed the cut and thrust of political debate; both Chiefs were mentally slower and better on paper than in presenting their views in committee. It was no coincidence that Jellicoe, Robertson and Trenchard (the first Chief of Air Staff) did not survive; and were replaced in the winter of 1917–18 by more politically aware Chiefs – Admiral Sir Rosslyn Wemyss, General Sir Henry Wilson and Major-General Sir Frederick Sykes. But this is anticipating events to which we must now return.

*   *   *

Like all new brooms, Lloyd George was soon reviewing the *Entente*'s strategy for 1917, concentrating on the possibility of knocking out one or more of Germany's 'props' – Turkey, Bulgaria or Austria. As was to occur in the Second World War, he soon found that shipping was one of the principal limitations in pursing his Easterner policies. Jellicoe accepted the need to provide ships to maintain the forces already in Egypt, in order to clear the Turks away from the Suez Canal, but he allied himself with Robertson in opposing any further development of the Salonika campaign against Bulgaria as an unsupportable drain on British merchant shipping in the face of growing U-Boat successes.

Shortage of shipping, however, would not limit an offensive against Austria on the Isonzo front in north-east Italy, but Robertson was quick to point out the almost insuperable difficulties of fighting through the Julian Alps to reach any worthwhile Austrian targets. The boot was, indeed, on the other foot in Italy. The real danger was the collapse of the inadequately equipped and trained Italian Army if it were attacked by an Austro-German force freed from the Eastern Front. Anglo-French reinforcements were more likely to be needed to shore up Italy rather than to knock out Germany's Austrian 'prop'.

Unannounced, Lloyd George tried to outflank his own Naval and General Staffs by persuading the other *Entente* governments at a conference in Rome early in January 1917 that they should adopt a defensive policy temporarily on the Western Front in order to attack the Austrians in Italy. He failed to win either French or Italian support due, in some measure, to Robertson's lobbying behind the scenes. From that moment onwards, his relationship with the CIGS, which had never been cordial, began on its fateful downward spiral.

It was only a matter of days before that relationship took another turn for the worse. In December 1916, the French had replaced the imperturbable 'Papa' Joffre as C-in-C of the French Army with the up-and-coming General Nivelle, who had become a French military Messiah by recovering most of the ground lost at Verdun. He had used orthodox artillery preparation, followed by the newly devised creeping barrage, to carry his assaulting infantry onto their objectives. His remarkable success, achieved on a relatively small scale, suggested that he might have found the formula for breaking the stalemate on the Western Front.

Lloyd George, ever looking for quick and easy panaceas, was attracted, despite his Easterner inclinations, by Nivelle's proposals for a war-winning offensive on the Aisne, accompanied by a diversionary attack by the BEF in the Arras sector, timed for early April 1917. Neither Robertson or Haig, or, indeed, many French generals and politicians, believed in Nivelle's scheme. Lloyd George not only accepted it with enthusiasm but also tried to place Haig under Nivelle's command.

The story of Haig's subordination to Nivelle is one of unforgivable duplicity on the part of Lloyd George. Lord Derby, Secretary of State for War, and Robertson were advised that they need not attend the War Cabinet meeting held just before the British delegation left for Calais to discuss Nivelle's plan, because there was no item of War Office concern on its agenda. When the Calais conference opened, however, Lloyd George, much to Derby's and Robertson's consternation, drew Nivelle, who had been tipped off beforehand through political channels, into proposing unity of command with Haig subordinate to himself. Unbeknown to them, the War Cabinet had discussed and agreed this command structure behind their backs at the meeting which they had been told they need not attend!

Lloyd George's motives reflected both his obsession with the creation of an *Entente* supreme command and his distrust of his professional advisers. The record of a conversation between Lord Stamfordham, the King's private secretary, and Lord Curzon, explaining the War Cabinet's determination to ensure unity of command under Nivelle, gives the damning War Cabinet assessment of the Army's High Command:

> Independent opinion shows that without question the French Generals and Staffs are immeasurably superior to British Generals and Staffs, not from the point of fighting but from that of generalship, and of the knowledge of the art of war.
>
> The War Cabinet did not consider Haig a clever man. Nivelle made a much greater impression on the members of the War Cabinet – of the two in the existing circumstances Nivelle was the right man to have supreme command.[3]

Robertson and Haig fought back, not eschewing the support of friends in the Press like Lord Northcliffe with the *Times* and *Daily Mail* under his direction. Their case was simple and compelling. Nivelle was only answerable to the French Government. Did the War Cabinet, and hence the British Parliament, really wish to abrogate control over the major part of the British Army? If so, should not the country be told?

Lloyd George considered sacking Haig or forcing his resignation over the issue, but realised that he would lose Derby and Robertson as well. Hankey, rightly, advised him that such a course would bring down his Coalition Government.

Robertson did succeed in having the unity of command proposals watered down and limited to the Nivelle offensive. But then Nivelle's tactlessness in dealing with Haig, and the disastrous failure of his offensive killed, for the time being at least, Lloyd George's first attempt to establish an Allied Supreme Command.

Part of the compromise command arrangements agreed by Robertson sowed the seeds of his own resignation that were to mature almost exactly a year later. A British Military Mission was established at the French C-in-C's Headquarters at Chantilly. At Nivelle's insistence, the francophile Henry Wilson was made Head of Mission. As there was no love lost between Robertson and Haig on the one hand and the politically articulate Wilson on the other, the appointment could not but lead to trouble sooner or later.

Robertson's relations with the Prime Minister never recovered from these distasteful episodes. Lloyd George would have liked to have forced his resignation, but knew that he would not survive himself if he did so. And so, on land, Haig was allowed to go on preparing his summer offensive in Flanders, aimed indirectly at clearing the Belgian coast to help the Navy in its struggle with the U-Boats.

The problems of the General Staff during the first three months of

1917 were well matched by the difficulties facing Carson, Jellicoe and the Naval War Staff at the Admiralty. Carson and Jellicoe made a well balanced team, in which the great political and forensic skills of the former were coupled with the naval professionalism of the latter. But neither was proof against Lloyd George's lack of confidence in Admiralty policy. Jutland had been a national disappointment, and shipping losses from U-Boat attacks were mounting at an alarming rate, suggesting that the Navy's anti-submarine tactics were not working. Pressure began to mount in the Press and Parliament for the introduction of the traditional Convoy system, which had been the Navy's method of protecting shipping in the days of sail, but which Jellicoe and the Naval War Staff had rejected as impractical in the face of submarines attacking with torpedos. Their naval instincts told them that the solution should lie in offensive action against the U-Boats and their bases rather than in defensive convoys.

On 1 February 1917, the German High Command took the risk of bringing the United States into the war by declaring unrestricted U-Boat warfare, hoping to starve the United Kingdom into submission before the Americans could mobilise their resources. It was a decision that nearly won the war for the Central Powers. Shipping losses rose dramatically, but Jellicoe resisted pressures to introduce a convoy system on the grounds that he could not provide the necessary number of escorts without denuding the Grand Fleet of its protective screen; that the value of superior surface ship speed to the submerged speed of submarines would be lost as convoys had to sail at the speed of the slowest ship; that the majority of merchant ship captains could not keep station in convoy, particularly in fog or bad weather at night; that ports could not handle such concentrations of shipping without protracted delays in turning ships round; and that, if a submarine did locate a convoy, it would make a lucrative killing.

Lloyd George, advised by Hankey, began his usual tactic of seeking advice from junior officers and all those who felt that the 'establishment' was misguided. Lieutenant Commander Kenworthy (later 10th Baron Strabolgi), and Captain Richmond (later Admiral Sir Herbert), kept him *au courant* with the opinion of the 'Young Turks' in the Navy, but it was Commander Henderson (later Admiral Sir Reginald, who became Third Sea Lord and Controller just before the Second World War), who provided the evidence from within the Naval War Staff, which undermined Jellicoe's position.

All great departments of state like the Admiralty tend to accept

figures without overcritical examination if they support policies to
which they are wedded. The Naval War Staff's claim that there were
not enough escorts to implement a convoy system was based upon a
figure of 300 arrivals and departures from British ports per week.
Henderson found that the actual figure was nearer 120, which would
make provision of escorts more practicable. Moreover, he saw that
while convoys did present large targets, they could also be used as
bait for U-Boats, which could be detected and attacked more successfully near a convoy than in the vast open expanses of sea in
inaccurately predicted U-Boat patrol areas.

Henderson's views cut no ice with his superiors, but by the middle
of February he had convinced Hankey, and hence Lloyd George, that
convoys were at least worth trying. The tonnage of shipping lost was
mounting alarmingly: January, 368,521; February, 540,006; March,
593,841; and April 881,027 tons, 400,000 of which were lost in 'Black
Fortnight' – 17–30 April.[4] At the War Cabinet on 23 April, Jellicoe
would only admit that the introduction of convoys 'was under consideration'. With no apparent sign of a change in Naval anti-
submarine policy, Lloyd George secured the approval of the War
Cabinet two days later to take the unprecedented step of visiting
the Admiralty *with a view to investigating all means at present in use in
regard to anti-submarine warfare*.[5] As Churchill put it later, the Prime
Minister had signalled to the Board of Admiralty, *'Act or Go'*.[6]

Three days before the Prime Minister's visit, Jellicoe approved a
first trial convoy, which was to be sailed from Gibraltar. Lloyd
George prided himself in his *War Memoirs* that his threatened visit
created the Admiralty change of heart. The sinkings in 'Black
Fortnight' and Henderson's figures of the smaller numbers of ships to
be escorted, in truth, made a much greater impact upon Admiral
Duff (later Sir Alexander), the highly competent, six foot two,
Director of the Anti-Submarine Warfare Division of the Naval War
Staff, and persuaded him to recommend the trial to Jellicoe.

Lloyd George's visit, however, was only the tip of a planned
investigatory iceberg. Once more, at Hankey's and the naval 'Young
Turks' instigation, he used the visit to start probing the widespread
criticism of the Admiralty's disappointing performance in the war at
sea. It was at this time that Fisher wrote the lines quoted at the head
of this chapter.

The Prime Minister suspected that part of the fault lay with
Jellicoe, and part with Admiralty organisation. Jellicoe, like many
senior naval officers, brought up in the tradition of the captain being

solely responsible for everything that happens to and within his ship, found de-centralisation difficult. He was taking his responsibilities as First Sea Lord too personally; was grossly overworked; and had too little time to think about strategic policy. Remembering the same fault in Kitchener, that had led to the 1915 ammunition crisis, the Prime Minister decided that one way of lightening Jellicoe's burden was to take away from him the responsibility for overseeing naval construction by bringing back the pre-war post of Controller of the Navy and Third Sea Lord. He appointed Sir Eric Geddes, a railway engineer by training, who had made his name sorting out the railways behind the BEF in France where he has been granted the temporary rank of major general.

Geddes was a masterful Scot in his early forties with the gift of going to the root of problems and getting things done. He was reluctant to take on the job, but did so when assured of Jellicoe's and Carson's genuine support. Others on the Admiralty Board were less willing to accept a civilian in the guise of a major general being given the honorary rank of vice admiral and wearing naval uniform! The last time such a thing had happened was when Cromwell placed Generals Blake and Monck in charge of the Commonwealth's fleets. In the Admiralty, Geddes was soon known as 'Goddis' for his dictatorial manner!

Lloyd George then turned to ensuring that the First Sea Lord concentrated upon operational policy rather than administration. He insisted upon the Admiralty adopting the War Office General Staff system with which he had become familiar when he was Secretary of State for War. Since its inception in 1912, the Naval War Staff had been an advisory body to the Admiralty Board. Under Lloyd George's reorganisation, it became the executive operational and planning staff of the First Sea Lord, who, on 2 May 1917, became Chief of Naval Staff, although retaining the traditional title of First Sea Lord.

These changes brought the Admiralty back full circle to the pre-1832 organisation when the old Navy Office, which used to administer the Navy, was absorbed by the Admiralty. The Admiralty Board in 1917 was divided into two again: operational policy under the First Sea Lord and Chief of Naval Staff, and administration under the Controller. The First Lord held overall political responsibility for both and was Naval spokesman in Parliament. The Naval Staff was also sub-divided into two: responsibility for the Operations, Mobilisation, Intelligence and Signals Divisions, was given to Oliver, who became Deputy Chief of Naval Staff; and the Trade, Anti-Submarine, Minesweeping and Convoy Divisions were placed under Duff as Assistant Chief of Naval Staff. Due to Jellicoe's initial opposition, a Planning Section was not added to the Operations Division of the Naval Staff until mid-July when Captain Dudley Pound – later to become the Navy's Chief in the Second World War – was appointed as its head.

Reorganisation alone could not cure naval malaise. Jellicoe was becoming more and more pessimistic about the war at sea, and depressed by his unsatisfactory relations with the Prime Minister. This was noticed by the King, Beatty, Robertson and Haig as well as by Lloyd George. Matters came to a head at the War Cabinet on 20 June 1917 when Haig's proposals for his Flanders offensive were discussed. Jellicoe stated that, due to the unabated U-Boat successes, Britain could not continue the war into 1918. Haig's diary records him as saying:

> There is no good discussing plans for next Spring – we cannot go on.[7]

This outburst made Lloyd George look for a pretext for getting rid of Jellicoe. He did not feel himself politically secure enough to sack him personally, although he did bring Churchill back into the Government as Minister of Munitions despite violent Unionist opposition. He hoped that Carson would wield the axe, but Carson stayed steadfastly loyal to Jellicoe and would not do so. And so Carson was pushed upstairs to the War Cabinet, and Geddes was promoted from Controller to First Lord on 20 July with a brief to remove Jellicoe if the conduct of the war at sea did not improve. One disgruntled admiral, who disliked Geddes, wrote at the time:

> We have the great Enrico Geddes now as First Lord of the Admiralty – the other day assistant manager of a Railway – a bullet headed sort of cove who anyway looks you straight in the face, which is more than those confounded politicians will do.[8]

While these changes in the Admiralty had been taking place, Lloyd George had set up a special War Policy Committee, consisting of himself, Curzon, Milner and General Jan Smuts, to decide what operations should be undertaken on land. Smuts had been the South African representative at the Imperial War Cabinet of 1917, and had been invited by the Prime Minister to stay on as a Dominions' representative on the actual War Cabinet. Smuts developed a penchant for helping Hankey to carry out special investigations for the Secretariat.

Lloyd George and his political colleagues on the War Policy Committee argued once again for an offensive in Italy, but Robertson and Jellicoe had a strong case to resist any diversion of resources away from the decisive theatre. Russia had collapsed in revolution in March and, though her armies did not cease fire, was unlikely to exert much pressure on the Eastern Front; the French Army had suffered a series of well concealed but nevertheless crippling mutinies after the failure of Nivelle's offensive; and shipping losses, though showing the first signs of decline due to the introduction of the convoy system, were still running above a sustainable level. In their professional judgement, the two Chiefs advised against any diversion of resources from the Western Front and home waters. It was tempting to go over onto the defensive in France until the Americans, who had declared war in April 1917, could arrive in sufficient strength to tip the balance in the *Entente's* favour. But by then the Navy might well have lost the war if the Army could not capture the U-Boat bases at Ostend and Zeebrugge.

Haig explained to the War Cabinet that his proposed Flanders offensive towards the two ports would be mounted in a series of limited attacks similar to his very successful seizure of Messines ridge in May. No attack would be allowed to continue if losses mounted without compensating gains. The War Cabinet, however, had its doubts and only authorised the opening of Haig's offensive on 31 July 1917 with the greatest reluctance. The Third Battle of Ypres, as it is known, led through many frustrations to the horrors of Passchendaele that autumn.

Until June 1917, the war in the air had not been politically controversial. Asquith had set up the Air Board under Curzon's chairmanship in 1916 to grapple with the lack of co-ordination and rivalry between the Admiralty and War Office, and Lord Cowdray had succeeded him in Lloyd George's Government. The Zeppelins had been an irritant in 1915, but the successful shooting down of six in the autumn of 1916 by fighters, using the newly developed incendiary bullets, ended their potentially serious threat to civilian morale. On 13 June and 7 July 1917, however, the first fixed-wing bomber attacks on London were carried out by twin engined *Gotha* bombers. The *Gotha* raids were only marginally more impressive than those of the Zeppelins, but the general public saw them as the shape of things to come. There was an immediate outcry for retaliatory action against German cities that led almost directly to the formation of the RAF as the world's first independent air force.

In the air war, a struggle had been going on behind the scenes between those who believed that aircraft were just new weapons for use in naval and land battles, and those who foresaw the totality of air power. The Navy had been the first to try using bombers on strategic missions to hit German Zeppelin and naval installations from bases in France. Ironically, Major General Hugh Trenchard, Haig's air commander and the accepted father of the RAF, had objected to naval long range bombing of such strategic targets from 'his' territory, and had won the Air Board's tacit agreement to his definition that '*the Army is responsible for land operations and the Navy only for work with the fleet*'.[8] Responsibility for strategic bombing was, in consequence, transferred to the Royal Flying Corps, but Trenchard still viewed the use of longer range bombers as part and parcel of Haig's battles on the Western Front, and was reluctant to expend bomber effort on attacking industrial targets or centres of population in Germany.

The *Gotha* raids on London were rarely carried out by more than 40 aircraft, and only 120 tons of bombs all told were dropped between June 1917 and May 1918 when the raids came to an end. As was to happen in 1940, daylight raids soon proved too expensive and were replaced by night attacks. The German High Command saw this air effort as a harassing adjunct to the U-Boat campaign, and not as a major attempt to break British civilian morale or to dislocate the seat of government as the British press, public, and, indeed, the War Cabinet thought at the time.

The British way of dealing with unexpected crises is to assemble a high level committee to examine short and longer term counter-measures. Lloyd George appointed a two man committee comprised of himself and General Smuts to look into:

1. The defence arrangements for Home Defence against air raids.
2. The air organisation generally and the direction of aerial operations.[9]

Smuts did most of the work, and completed two reports in little more than a month. The first dealt with short-term air defence measures and was generally welcomed and implemented. The second, completed on 17 August 1917, was more controversial. He set himself to find acceptable answers to three questions:

Should the Air Board be turned into an Air Ministry?
Should the two air services, the RNAS and RFC, be amalgamated to form a unified Air Service with its own Air Staff?

How should the new Air Service discharge its functions of supporting the Navy at sea and the Army on land?

The door to the creation of the Air Ministry had already been pushed open by Curzon and Cowdray, as successive chairmen of the Air Board, and was generally accepted as sensible. The decision on unification depended upon two interconnected factors: was there an independent role for an air force beyond the horizons of the Navy and Army; and would enough bomber aircraft be available for strategic bombing after the priority needs of the sea and land battles had been met?

The example of the *Gotha* raids, and the public's demand for retaliation, showed conclusively that there were strategic long range tasks, which would best be undertaken by an independent force. Evidence given to Smuts by Cowdray was that the rate of bomber production would provide a fleet of 400 aircraft surplus to Naval and Army requirements by the turn of the year, and that production was expected to treble by the spring of 1918. An independent bomber force was, therefore, a practical proposition. Smuts was able to articulate the first successful and prescient case for independent air power:

> Unlike artillery, an airfleet can conduct extensive operations far from, and independently of, both Army and Navy. As far as can at present be foreseen, there is absolutely no limit to the scale of its future independent war use. And the day may not be far off when aerial operations with their devastation of enemy lands and destruction of industrial and population centres on a vast scale may become the principal operation of war, to which the older forms of military and naval operations may become secondary and subordinate. . . . In our opinion there is no reason why the Air Board should any longer continue in its present form as practically no more than a conference room between the older services, and there is every reason why it should be raised to the status of an independent Ministry in control of its own war services.[10]

The War Cabinet accepted in principle Smuts' answers to his first two questions – establishment of an Air Ministry and a unified air force – and gave him the task of working out how the RNAS and RFC should be amalgamated without weakening air support to the Navy and Army. The Air Force (Constitution) Bill passed through Parliament in November 1917, and the vesting date for the Royal Air Force was set for 1 April 1918. We need not go into the in-fighting that went on in Whitehall over the actual creation of the RAF, but the selections of the first Secretary of State for Air and the first Chief of Air Staff are important in the story of the Chiefs.

Lloyd George, characteristically, approached the appointment of the new Secretary of State from the point of view of political usefulness to himself rather than finding the right man to develop a sound Air policy. Asquith, as leader of the Liberal Party, had the Liberal press to support him; Bonar Law, as leader of the Unionists, had the Tory press; but Lloyd George had no press barons at his beck and call. Lord Northcliffe, whom he had tried to suborn by sending him on a prestigious mission to the United States, was on his way home and was his first choice as Secretary of State for Air, but Northcliffe declined the offer in an offensively contemptuous letter published in the *Times*. Lloyd George then turned to Northcliffe's younger brother, Lord Rothermere, who accepted the portfolio and soon proved himself entirely unsuited to the job. Brought up in the cut-throat world of Fleet Street, he was incapable of working in committee, and tried to treat his senior professional Air advisers as pliant newspaper editors.

The choice of Chief of Air Staff was not easy either. The obvious candidate for the post was Major-General Sir David Henderson, who had been Director-General of Military Aeronautics at the War Office for most of the war, but he was worn out, in ill health, and was deemed to have lost his fire. Trenchard was second choice, but he did not wish to give up commanding the air component of the BEF, which he had built up and led with great success since September 1915. Moreover, ironically, he at first opposed the idea of a unified air force on the grounds that it would diminish close support for the Army. Initially, Haig was only prepared to let Trenchard go if the posts of Chief of Air Staff and command of the BEF's air component could be combined. This was clearly impracticable, and so he bowed to political pressure and persuaded Trenchard to become the first CAS in December 1917. Major General John Salmond, a future Chief of Air Staff and Trenchard's eventual successor in the post, took over from him in the BEF.

The autumn of 1917 was as depressing as those of 1914, 1915 and 1916 had been. Defeat and recrimination filled the air. On 24 October, the Italian Army had collapsed at Caporetto; the Kerensky Government's efforts to keep the Russian armies fighting on the Eastern Front had been brought to an end by Lenin's and Trotsky's seizure of power on 7 November (25 October, Julian calendar), freeing large numbers of German divisions for employment in the West in 1918; Haig's Flanders offensive ended on 10 November, sunk in the mud of Passchendaele; losses at sea were still running at about

160 ships, or 400,000 tons a month; both shipbuilding and aircraft manufacturing programmes were far behind schedule due to labour disputes; French manpower resources were running out and Britain's were in steep decline.

The only bright spots in the otherwise depressing scene were in the Middle East where Maude had retaken Kut-el-Amara and entered Baghdad in March 1917, and Allenby had won the Third Battle of Gaza at the end of October, entering Jerusalem in early December. Fortunately for him, Haig had won his startling success with tanks at Cambrai on 20 November, making his recall after his failures in Flanders less easy for Lloyd George to justify.

There was, however, one great difference between the autumn of 1917 and the previous years, when recrimination had led to the collapse of successive Asquith governments. This time it was Lloyd George who was under pressure, and he had no intention of being made a scapegoat, nor of allowing any of his political colleagues to be cast in that role. He felt that events during the year had supported his contention that the fault lay with the naval and military establishments, and he now had ample justification for getting rid of Jellicoe and Robertson if not Haig, provided he played his cards with finesse.

Jellicoe was the first to fall. When giving Geddes the Admiralty portfolio, Lloyd George had stipulated that Jellicoe should not be removed unless Geddes found that he could not work with him, because the Fleet had complete confidence him. Friction between the two men started almost immediately over Smuts's air proposals, which Geddes considered eminently sound. Jellicoe and the Naval Staff thought just the opposite: air operations at sea, in their view, could only be conducted satisfactorily under naval command. Even if naval aircraft were procured by some centralised organisation, the crews should be trained by the Navy and be part of it. Beatty, much to Jellicoe's dismay, did not oppose the Smuts' proposals as strongly as he hoped and expected. As C-in-C of the Grand Fleet, Beatty believed that the Admiralty was being too parochial and should be seeking to improve the Smut's proposals from the naval point of view rather than swimming against the tide of informed opinion.

Then came what the Naval Historian Arthur Marder, has called the 'Tale of Woe in Home waters': the sinking of two convoys between Scotland and Norway by German light cruisers in October and December; the unsatisfactory cruiser action in the Heligoland Bight in November; and the controversy over the apparent failure of the anti-submarine barrage in the Straits of Dover, which led to Geddes's sacking of Admiral Bacon of the famous Dover Patrol, despite Jellicoe's objections.

By Christmas 1917, Lloyd George was satisfied that there was a strong case and enough support amongst his Cabinet colleagues to get rid of the First Sea Lord without jeopardising his Government. Jellicoe was given a peerage and his deputy, Admiral Sir Rosslyn Wemyss, was appointed in his stead.

Wemyss was almost unknown to the general public, and in the Navy had the reputation of being a 'court sailor', who was 'politically aware'. Beatty had a high regard for him, saying in a letter to Jellicoe *'What experience Wemyss has to run the complex and great machine I do not know but I do not fear for the future'.*[11] Indeed, Wemyss possessed many valuable assets for the post of First Sea Lord. To begin with, he was one of the most popular Flag Officers in the Navy. He had a tall, imposing presence – monocle and all – and a natural charm and buoyancy that made him a good mixer. Unlike most of his contemporaries, he knew how to delegate responsibility and refused to immerse himself in detail. For all his jovial casualness, he had clear ideas on naval policy and the moral courage to assume responsibility, which enabled him to get the best out of subordinates and to handle the complexities of Whitehall.

'Rosy', as Wemyss was known in the Navy, had another important asset. He had a much wider vision of the world than most of his predecessors. Brought up at Wemyss Castle in Fife, he was one of George V's oldest and most trusted friends; and he could deal on equal terms with eminent political figures at home and abroad, and with chiefs of staff of foreign states. He spoke fluent French, and was *persona grata* with the Italians as well as the French, which made him unusually suited to the post of First Sea Lord in the period of international supreme command that was dawning in the autumn of 1917.

Indeed, it was the creation of the *Entente's* Supreme War Council that gave Lloyd George the opportunity that he had sought for so long to get rid of Robertson. Throughout the summer months, the Prime Minister had been developing ideas for such a council, organised on the same lines as his own War Cabinet with an Inter-Allied General Staff and Secretariat to back it. Suspecting that he would get no support from Robertson for this proposal, he went behind his back yet again, and asked Field Marshal Lord French and General Sir Henry Wilson to let him have papers setting out their views on the conduct of the war. The papers of both men were critical of the Flanders offensive; and they both supported the idea of a Supreme War Council, though for quite different reasons. French had become a bitter and twisted enemy of his former subordinates, Robertson and Haig, and saw this as an opportunity to undermine them just as Lloyd George intended. Wilson, the political opportunist, wished to ingratiate himself with the Prime Minister. Still a convinced Westerner, his paper stressed what he knew Lloyd George wanted to hear; that the establishment of a Supreme Allied War Council was essential to the successful conclusion of the war.

As French and Wilson were not his official military advisers, Lloyd George proposed to summon a War Council as Asquith had done at the outbreak of war. Its task would be to advise him on alternative military strategies for 1918, and so it would be legitimate to invite them to express their views officially at the Council. Had it not been for the intervention of Hankey, Derby and Robertson would have resigned as soon as they heard of the Prime Minister's intention. This way of conducting business would have shown a blatant lack of confidence in them as the Government's constitutional military advisers. Balfour, Curzon, Carson and Robert Cecil would have followed them, bringing about the collapse of the Coalition Government. Lloyd George pulled back from the brink just in time, and was rescued a fortnight later by the Italian disaster at Caporetto, which made the case for an Allied Supreme War Council for him without the need to call a War Council of his own.

At the inter-Allied conference summoned hastily at Rapallo early in November to agree ways of stemming the Italian collapse, Lloyd George got his way at last. It was agreed that a Council should be set up at Versailles with an advisory international General Staff composed of Permanent National Military Representatives with supporting staffs. At Lloyd George's insistence, his latest military favourite, Henry Wilson, was appointed British Military Representative! The French military team was led by Foch, and the Italian by Cardona. Robertson, although antagonistic to the whole idea of the Supreme War Council, because it would diminish British – and his – control over strategy, realised that the political currents were flowing too strongly against him to make further resistance practicable. The final collapse of the Russian armies on 3 December 1917 made it certain that Lloyd George would win any confrontation with him over the issue. Closer inter-allied collaboration was seen on all sides to be vital in the new and dangerous situation.

The Russo-German cease-fire, which was to lead to the first Treaty of Brest Litovsk in February 1918, would enable Ludendorff to transfer some 70 battle-hardened divisions to the Western Front. The critical problem facing the new Supreme War Council was how to meet the German onslaught in the West that everyone knew would come in the spring. The Permanent Military Representatives were tasked to review *Entente* strategy for 1918 in the light of the new situation.

The Permanent Military Representatives, much to Lloyd George's delight and Robertson's chagrin, recommended defensive action on the Western Front in 1918 until the German onslaught had spent itself, and while American forces were being built up and trained for a decisive counter-offensive in 1919. In the meantime, offensive action should be taken against Turkey in Palestine as Lloyd George had been advocating. After a long and difficult debate, this strategy was accepted by the Supreme War Council at the beginning of February. Robertson, mindful of Fisher's silence during the fatal Dardanelles debate in 1915, decided that he must make it clear before the Council gave its formal approval that he was opposed to this strategy. Speaking with the great deliberation and gravity, which was his style, he said:

> It is not for me to approve or oppose any resolution of the Council as I am not a member of it, but as I have been summoned to attend I feel compelled to submit, in view of the Entente's resources, especially in men and shipping, and of possible events on the Western Front this year, that the Council ought to adopt a defensive policy in all secondary theatres, and keep no more troops there than are necessary for that purpose. I am also of the opinion that to undertake the campaign in Palestine as recommended by the 'technical advisers' [the Permanent Military Representatives] is not a practical plan, and to attempt it will be very dangerous and detrimental to winning the war.[12]

This outburst by his principal adviser at an international conference was more than Lloyd George could tolerate. Although Robertson apologised afterwards, pointing to Lloyd George's own criticism of Fisher for staying silent, the Prime Minister angrily swept the precedent aside, saying that, as he was well aware of the General Staff views, there was no need to repeat them in the Council. Not surprisingly, a search for his successor began at once.

The final breach with Robertson had been long in the making. Both men were extremists in their different ways, mirroring the characteristics of the Celtic and Anglo-Saxon races: Lloyd George mercurial, imaginative and restless, always seeking new political paths to success; and Robertson steady, unimaginatively orthodox, and dedicated to following properly considered courses of action. Their disagreement was rooted in Robertson's determination to pursue sound military policies and to eschew the politically attractive sideshows favoured by Lloyd George; and in Lloyd George's mistrust of standardised military thinking of the Camberley-trained officers of the General Staff.

Lloyd George considered sending Robertson to India as C-in-C, and then offered him Wilson's job at Versailles or continuing as CIGS with his powers reduced by his subordination to the Supreme War Council. He declined both. The post of CIGS was then offered to General Sir Herbert Plumer, the Commander of Second Army in the BEF, victor of the battle of Messines and commander of the British troops sent to help the Italians to stabilise their front on the Piave after Caporetto. Plumer declined too, making it clear in his cable refusing the appointment that he supported Robertson in his objections to the Versailles policy. Lloyd George was not well at the time, and for a few days it looked as if the refusal of two of Britain's most senior and respected generals to accept the post of senior military adviser to him, which would entail implementing that policy, would bring his Government down.

Henry Wilson was waiting in the wings. As he had been one of the authors of the Versailles policy, he had no compunction in accepting the post when it was offered to him by the Prime Minister on 16 February 1918. Lloyd George now had two more pliable Chiefs at the Admiralty and War Office. Robertson' resignation was assumed rather than offered since he never deigned to send a letter of resignation. Unlike Jellicoe, he did not accept a peerage. It was not to be long before Trenchard's short reign as first Chief of Air Staff was brought to an end as well.

Trenchard was certainly not the type of man to be put into joint harness with Rothermere, who had no understanding of the need for team work and compromise in setting up the new Air Ministry and Air Staff. Trenchard was a military professional drawn from the same stables as Robertson and Haig. He was as inarticulate in political debate as they were, but, unlike them, was not good on paper either. He was essentially a commander with the gift of leadership and a powerful personality with a firm grasp of broad policy, but without any claim to intellectual perception. By early February, it was clear that Trenchard and Rothermere made an awkward and unmanageable team. They were both dictators, and Rothermere followed Lloyd George's practice of seeking advice from wherever he chose. By 18 March 1918, Trenchard had had enough. He wrote to Rothermere:

> I am far from denying that you have a perfect right to see whom you like, but at the same time if you have not sufficient confidence in me even to tell me what is happening in the branches of my own department I consider, and I feel sure that you will agree with me, that the situation created is an impossible one.[13]

Rothermere's reply:

> I cannot regard the advice of any of the members of the Air Council as pontifical . . . and it is impossible in the early days of a new service, for a Secretary of State to accept the advice of any professional adviser entirely without demur.[14]

led to Trenchard tendering his resignation on 19 March, but the German breakthrough on the Western Front two days later, and the RAF's vesting day of 1 April, put the matter into abeyance until 13 April, when Rothermere at last accepted it. The press soon linked Trenchard's departure to command the newly formed Independent Air Force, responsible for strategic bombing operations, with the sacking of Jellicoe and Robertson. The Northcliffe's *Daily Mail* thundered:

> The list is steadily growing of acknowledged masters of their craft for whose services in the crisis of our fate the Government has no serious use.[15]

Rothermere did not survive the Press campaign against him. He was replaced by Sir William Weir, a successful industrialist, who had been Controller of Aeronautical Supplies in the Ministry of Munitions. He was given a peerage to enable him to speak as Secretary of State for Air in the Lords.

Trenchard's successor, Frederick Sykes, paralleled Wemyss and Wilson in being able to handle politicians and political issues with greater assurance than his predecessor. He had been commissioned originally into a fashionable cavalry regiment, the 15th Hussars, and was politically well connected through his marriage to Bonar Law's daughter. He had, however, become *persona non grata* in the RFC, because he was reputed to have tried to unseat Henderson when the latter was commanding the BEF's air component in 1915. He had been seconded to the Royal Marines and sent to command the naval air detachment at the Dardanelles. He fought his way back into favour with some help from his political connections. Nevertheless, he had established a good claim to a leading role in the newly formed RAF as an ardent believer and strong advocate of Smuts's vision of a separate strategic bombing force, free from the parochial control of the Admiralty and War Office.

Weir and Sykes made a good team as they both believed in the need for an independent air force, but, in this belief, they were both ahead of their time in two respects. In the first place, most of their colleagues on the Air Council stayed mentally attuned to serving either the Navy or Army, and had grave doubts about the soundness of the reasoning behind the creation of a third fighting service. Their doubts were reinforced by failures in the bomber production programmes, which never reached the output figures on which Smuts's proposals had been based. In consequence, there were far too few aircraft for successful independent bomber operations.

And in the second place, the bomber aircraft that were available in 1918 did not have the payload or range to do much damage to strategic targets, the primary reason for the RAF's birth. In the last raid of the war, on Saarbrücken, the total bombload was less than that carried by one four-engined bomber in the Second World War. Trenchard was very clear about the inadequacy of his Independent Force, which became the Inter-Allied Independent Air Force in the last months of the war. Writing his diary for 11 November 1918 he recorded:

> Thus the Independent Force comes to an end. A more gigantic waste of effort and personnel there has never been in any war.[16]

The story of the fight for the RAF's survival, however, belongs to the next chapter.

The now three new Chiefs – Wemyss, Wilson and Sykes – were faced initially with the consequences of the dramatic events of 21 March 1918 when Ludendorff launched the *Kaiserschlacht* offensive (the Emperor Battle) on the Western Front. The German divisions, brought over from the Eastern Front during the winter, broke through Gough's Fifth Army on the Somme, and threatened to break through to the French Channel ports. While on the Eastern Front, Ludendorff had discovered one half of the formula for defeating the combination of machine-gun, trenches and wire. He had developed the concept of élite storm battalions, which the Germans used to infiltrate, unhinge and dislocate an enemy's defences ahead of the main assault by standard infantry divisions. In the early morning fog of 21 March, the German storm battalions were highly successful in opening up the British front. But Ludendorff had not solved the other half of the problem – how to maintain momentum. By mid-July the final German effort was spent, and the weight of the American Army was beginning to tell in the *Entente's* favour.

The complementary effort by the German High Seas Fleet with its sortie into the North Sea on 23 April ended in fiasco for both sides: Scheer failed to reach his convoy target, due to faulty intelligence, and Beatty was equally unsuccessful in intercepting him. And in the U-Boat war, Allied losses had been almost halved by June and were continuing to fall, while sinkings of U-Boats steadily rose and Allied shipbuilding, at last, began to exceed sinkings.

The great crisis in Allied affairs, caused by Ludendorff's last desperate attempt to snatch victory from defeat, did lead to the realisation of Lloyd George's dream of a Supreme Command under Foch, which might not have been possible if Robertson had still been in power. Wilson with his understanding of the French political scene and his intimacy with the French commanders and staffs, eased British acceptance of French command. Indeed, it was he who drafted the formula that made it possible:

> General Foch is charged by the British, French, and American Governments with the co-ordination of the action of the Allied Armies on the Western Front. To this end all powers necessary to secure effective realization are conferred on him. The British, French and American Governments for this purpose entrust to General Foch the strategic direction of military operations. The Commanders-in-Chief of the British, French and American Armies have full control of the tactical employment of their forces. Each Commander-in-Chief will have the right of appeal to his Government if in his opinion the safety of his Army is compromised by any order received from General Foch.[17]

It was a formula that was to provide the precedent for Eisenhower's assumption of Supreme Command in Europe in the Second World War.

As the tide turned in the *Entente's* favour, the bitterness went out of the struggle between Lloyd George's quasi-political dictatorship and his professional advisers. There was nothing left to fight about. On 8 August, Haig demonstrated the other half of the solution to trench warfare: the tanks came into their own during the battle of Amiens that day, which Ludendorff called the 'Black Day for the German Army'. The German line was thereafter pressed steadily back towards the German frontier during September and October, although it never broke or lost cohesion.

In Italy and at Salonika, two personalities of importance to this story of the Chiefs were emerging amongst the successful commanders of the First World War. The first was the Earl of Cavan, who had commanded the British 14th Corps when it was sent to help the Italians after Caporetto, and was later asked for by the Italian Government to lead the Italian Tenth Army in their final offensive across the Piave in October. In the battle of Vittorio Veneto, of which the Italians are so inordinately proud, only the British 14th Corps succeeded in establishing a bridgehead over the wide Piave in the first phase of the battle. It was then Cavan's Tenth Army that widened the breach and broke through. The Austro-Hungarian Army collapsed as its different ethnic contingents deserted and made for home in order to play their part in re-establishing their own nation states as the Dual Monarchy fell apart.

The second was General George Milne, known as 'Uncle George' to the men of the British force at Salonika, whom he commanded from the initial landings in 1915 when it was only 27th Division, then 26th Corps and finally the British Salonika Army in its final successful offensive in September 1918, which helped to persuade Bulgaria to seek an armistice. He then led them in the advance into Turkey and the occupation of Constantinople on 27 November 1918.

'Props', as Lloyd George called Germany's allies, fell away one by one, but not through anything to do with his Easterner proclivities. It was Germany that was collapsing and taking them with her, undermined by the unglamorous but remorseless blockade by the Royal Navy which had been sustained since the first month of the war; by the costly but equally intense pressure exerted by the British and French armies of the Western Front; and by the political infection spread by the Russian Revolution, which brought about the German naval mutinies in October 1918, and then the final overthrow of the Second Reich.

We shall never know whether the changes in the British Chiefs that took place during the winter of 1917/18 and brought more politically astute men into office, would have eased the friction between the Government and its military advisers if it had taken place earlier when the tide of events was still flowing against the *Entente*. Success stills argument and breeds its own success. But it is worth recalling von Clausewitz's dictum about war being a continuation of politics by other means. The First World War showed that political and military strategy were, in fact, indivisible. The successful direction of the national war effort has two facets: the need for military understanding on the part of the politicians, and corresponding political awareness amongst the military. With Lloyd George in power there was nothing but antagonism between the two sides: total distrust and disloyalty on Lloyd George's part, and intense loathing of politicians by Jellicoe, Robertson and Trenchard.

A third facet in the requirements of supreme command emerged with the advent of air power and tanks as potential battle-winning factors. Technological awareness started to become an essential ingredient of political and military leadership, but this would not be fully understood until the crash rearmament programmes of the 1930s forced its acceptance upon the British and French politico-military policy makers. The Germans were already proving themselves quicker in exploiting advances in technology; and the Americans, with their ingrained mechanical aptitudes, understood the requirement from the everyday needs of their way of life.

Regrettably, Britain ended the war still without the equivalent of the German Great General Staff for the development of strategic policy and tri-Service co-ordination. The Committee of Imperial Defence, which had been allowed to lapse at the outbreak of war, had not been strong enough to resolve the great strategic dilemma facing the country before 1914: could Britain continue to rely on sea power for her security, or would she have to intervene with land forces on the Continent? She had intervened at very great cost and had emerged on the winning side, but the dilemma remained unresolved and had been given a third dimension with the advent of air power. The three Chiefs remained the heads of independent sovereign Services with opposing views upon future national strategy and as bitter rivals in the post-war struggle for resources in the chill financial climate of the 1920s. Some new co-ordinating machinery was seen to be needed, but what shape it should take had to be left until the dust of victory had settled.

Chronology
FOR CHAPTER FIVE

1918
Nov   Armistice signed.
           Haldane Report on Machinery of Government.
Dec   Lloyd George wins 'Coupon' General Election'.

1919
Feb   Trenchard succeeds Sykes as CAS.
June   Treaty of Versailles signed.
Aug   Ten Year Rule introduced.
Nov   War Cabinet disbanded.
           Beatty succeeds Wemyss as First Sea Lord.

1920
Mar   Return to One-Power naval standard.
Dec   Bonar Law Committee on Battleship Replacement.

1921
March   Cairo Conference leading to RAF command in Iraq.
Aug   Geddes Committee on National Expenditure starts
           work.
Nov   Washington Disarmament Conference.
Dec   Four Power Pacific Treaty signed.
           Washington Naval Treaty (5:5:3 ratio) signed.
           Anglo-Irish Treaty establishes the Irish Free State.

1922
Jan   Churchill Committee evaluates Geddes Report.
Feb   Cavan succeeds Wilson as CIGS.
Sep   The Chanak Crisis.

Oct   Lloyd George resigns; Bonar Law becomes PM.

1923
Jan   French occupy the Ruhr.
Mar   Salisbury Committee on National and Imperial
               Defence.
               RAF's successful Kurdistan Campaign starts.
May   Baldwin succeeds Bonar Law.
June   Home Defence Air Force of 52 squadrons announced.
July   Balfour report on RN/RAF responsibilities.
               Chiefs of Staff Committee's 1st Meeting.
Aug   Treaty of Lausanne ends Turkish threat to Iraq.
Nov   Hitler-Ludendorff Munich Putsch.

1924
Jan   Ramsay Macdonald's First Labour Government.
Apr   Hindenburg becomes German President.
Nov   Baldwin returned as PM; Churchill as Chancellor of
               the Exchequer.

1925
Oct   Treaty of Locarno.
               Colwyn Committee on Expenditure.

1926
Feb   Baldwin reaffirms integrity of the RAF.
               Milne succeeds Cavan as CIGS.
May   General Strike.

1927
July   Madden succeeds Beatty as First Sea Lord.
Sep   Breakdown of Geneva Naval Conference (Cruisers).

1928
July   Ten Year Rule made a rolling assumption.
Aug   Kellogg-Briand Pact.

1929
June   Ramsay Macdonald's Second Labour Government.
Oct   Wall Street crash.
Dec   John Salmond succeeds Trenchard as CAS.

1930
Apr   London Naval Treaty.
Jul   Field succeeds Madden as First Sea Lord.

1931
Aug   Ramsay Macdonald's National Government.
Sep   Japanese invasion of Manchuria.
                Invergordon Naval Mutiny.

1932
Feb   Geneva Disarmament Conference.
Mar   Ten Year Rule ended.
May   Air Plan for Singapore finally rejected by CID.

1933
Jan   Hitler becomes German Chancellor.
                Chatfield succeeds Field as First Sea Lord.
Feb   Montgomery-Massingberd succeeds Milne as CIGS.
Mar   Geoffrey Salmond succeeds John Salmond as CAS.
                Japan leaves the League of Nations.
May   Ellington becomes CAS on death of Geoffrey Salmond.
July   Germany leaves the Disarmament Conference.
Oct   Germany leaves the League of Nations.
Nov   Chiefs of Staff examine Britain's readiness for war.

5
THE BIRTH OF THE CHIEFS OF STAFF COMMITTEE
The Ten Year Rule and Disarmament: 1919–1933

First Sea Lords		Chiefs of the Imperial General Staff	
Sir Rosslyn Wemyss			
Earl Beatty	1919	Sir Henry Wilson	
Sir Charles Madden	1927	The Earl of Cavan	1922
Sir Frederick Field	1930	Sir George Milne	1926
Sir Ernle Chatfield	1933	Sir Archibald Montgomery-Massingberd	1933

Chiefs of Air Staff	
Sir Frederick Sykes	
Sir Hugh Trenchard	1919
Sir John Salmond	1930
Sir Geoffrey Salmond*	April 1933
Sir Edward Ellington	1933

'. . . for the first time in our history, we had recognised machinery for close and continuous consultation between the Fighting Services, for tendering of collective advice to the Cabinet on defence problems as a whole, for the preparation of long-term plans in time of peace; and, in event of war, for acting as a battle headquarters.'

Lord Ismay.[1]

As the euphoria of victory faded in 1919, the three wartime Chiefs – Wemyss, Wilson and Sykes – were faced with the harsh realities of an economically and morally exhausted country. Britain was still one of the Great Powers, but had lost her former will to govern, and had gained an idealist craving for peace at almost any price.

At home, the 'Upstairs, Downstairs' syndrome was being swept away in a wave of egalitarianism, which may have been making Britain 'a place fit for heroes' in the longer term, but was certainly

---

* Died after only three weeks in office.

creating immediate social and industrial unrest. Abroad, the theme of 'the war to end all wars' was being translated into blind faith in the League of Nations and world disarmament, both of which were themselves flawed by the self-interest and ambitions of the other Great Powers – the United States, France and Japan. And in the corridors of power in Whitehall, the dominant theme was financial retrenchment with little thought for the future, or for the require- ments of any longer term strategy. The Treasury was demanding a cut in Defence Expenditure from £604m in 1919 to £103m for 1922.

The three Chiefs were men whose personalities and abilities were well suited to grappling with the Armistice's immediate aftermath – peace conferences, crash demobilisation, occupation of the Rhine- land, and anti-communist intervention in Russia. But they had not been great wartime commanders, and though well cast as Chiefs of Staff in this period of politico-military bargaining, they were in the uncomfortable position of having national heroes like Beatty, Haig and Trenchard looking over their shoulders.

Sykes was the first to be replaced in February 1919. Churchill had become Secretary of State for War and Air after the General Election of December 1918. Lloyd George had combined the two portfolios because he intended to save money by getting rid of the Air Ministry and the RAF, and because he was short of competent ministers for his new coalition government. However, he chose the wrong man to act as the RAF's executioner. Churchill, strongly influenced by his predecessor, Lord Weir, and mindful no doubt of his friend Smuts's far-sighted and supportive report two years earlier, decided that he would fight for the RAF's reprieve. Weir, however, advised him that he would need a stronger and less devious Chief of Air Staff with a mind of his own if the RAF was, indeed, to survive. He recom- mended 'Boom' Trenchard as a man who could make bricks with the minimum of straw – a very necessary attribute in the chill economic climate of 1919 – and had the reputation and strength of character to fight successfully for the survival of the RAF in political jungles of Whitehall.

Inarticulate though Trenchard may have been, he had the good sense to surround himself with what he called his 'English Merchants', who shaped his ideas into presentational form and ena- bled him to force the acceptance of his arguments through sheer weight of personality and massive integrity. He once said to his staff, whom he kept on their toes by pressing all the bells on his desk at once, 'I can't write what I mean; I can't say what I mean; but I expect you to know what I mean.'[2] Strong, stern, touched with eccentricity, selflessly kind and humane, he was loved by all who worked for him.

Trenchard was at first reluctant to return to the post from which he had resigned in 1918, but pressure exerted by his former colleagues for him to do so for the good of the RAF was decisive in his acceptance of Churchill's offer. Soon after he reassumed the duties as the RAF's Chief, he fell victim to the 1919 flu' epidemic that was sweeping the country. He tried to keep going, but acute pneumonia set in. He was nursed back to health by Katherine Boyle, the widow of a colleague who had been killed at Mons. Despite being an apparently confirmed bachelor, he proposed to her when he was getting back on his feet, but was laughingly refused. The setback did not deter him. They were married in July 1919.

By October 1919, Churchill and Trenchard were ready to put their case for the RAF's continued existence to the Cabinet. They proposed three alternative schemes: 'A', 40 operational and 42 training squadrons for £23m; 'B', 34 and 21 squadrons for £17m; and 'C', 27 and 18 squadrons for £15m. Lloyd George forced a hard bargain. He saw that 'A' was the right answer but insisted that it should be carried out with the 'B' scheme's cash. Trenchard said 'Snap', realising that Lloyd George had by implication accepted the continued existence of the RAF for the time being at least. He had won the first round of what was to prove a very long, relentless contest with the Admiralty and War Office that was not to be finally won until 1926.

Wemyss was the next to go. He was no match for the arrogant, ambitious Beatty, whom the Northcliffe press championed as his successor. Wemyss came out of the unedifying struggle for succession with more personal credit than Beatty, but then showed that he was not free from vanity himself by resigning when he was offered a barony instead of a viscountcy for his wartime services. Beatty became First Sea Lord and Chief of Naval Staff on 1 November 1919.

Admiral the Earl Beatty was an Anglo-Irishman and proud of it. Handsome and debonair, his dash and courage in battle at sea matched his love of hunting on fast horses on land. The *panache* of his tilted cap, and the eccentricities of his life style, all created an aura of a latter day Prince Rupert, but they also masked his true abilities. The quality of his leadership of the Battle Cruiser Fleet, and later of the Grand Fleet, was there for all to see, but far less was known of his outstanding abilities as a naval policy-maker. Unlike Trenchard, to whom he was invariably and implacably opposed, he could assimi-

late every detail of an intricate subject and present a case with all the
lucid clarity of an accomplished lawyer. He could hold his own in
political debate, even with the ebullient Churchill. Hankey paid him
the compliment of saying, '*You are the only First Sea Lord I have known in
my twenty-six years' experience who could really talk on equal terms to the
highest Cabinet Ministers and stand up to them in argument*'.[3] Moreover, he
managed to maintain a remarkably good relationship with politicians
of all parties and with the civil servants, despite their outlooks and
purposes often contrasting so sharply with his own consistently hawkish approach.

Beatty's private life was a help, hindrance and eventually a burden
to him. He had married an extremely wealthy, but, as he learned
later, mentally unstable American divorcee, Ethel Tree in 1901. Her
wealth brought him the enjoyment of large houses, a private yacht,
and a string of fine hunters, but little real happiness. She was spoilt
by her wealth, iron willed, unreasoningly possessive as far as Beatty
was concerned and yet promiscuous. While he found solace with his
mistress, Eugenie Godfrey-Faussett, he never failed to give Ethel
unremitting care as her bouts of nervous depression increased in
depth and frequency. He carried the heavy burden of her illness
throughout his time as First Sea Lord. She died in July 1931.

Wilson was the only Chief not to lose his job in 1919. He still had
Lloyd George's confidence at that time; and unlike Sykes and
Wemyss, there was no obvious candidate standing in the wings to
replace him as CIGS. Haig and Robertson were *personae non gratae* to
the Government; Allenby was holding the important proconsular
post of British High Commissioner for Egypt and the Sudan; and
Rawlinson, the highly respected commander of the 4th Army and
victor of the Battle of Amiens on 8 August 1918 (Ludendorff's 'Black
Day for the German Army), was about to take up the post of C-in-C
India. With no pressure for change at the War Office, Wilson was
able to serve out his full four year tenure as CIGS, although he
became increasingly alienated from Lloyd George over policies for
dealing with Irish and Indian nationalism abroad and industrial
unrest at home.

Incidentally, Robertson, who had succeeded French as C-in-C
Home Forces in May 1918, was offered the Irish Command by
Churchill. Wilson opposed the appointment not because of his antipathy for his predecessor, but because, knowing Ireland as well as he
did, he considered Robertson too inflexible for the subtleties of Irish
politics. Lloyd George turned down Churchill's proposal, and

Robertson changed places with Haig in April 1919, taking over the British Army of the Rhine while Haig became C-in-C Home Forces. Wilson's views on Ireland, which were to place him on a collision course with the Prime Minister, were already crystallising. Writing to Robertson in June 1919, he said:

> Ireland goes from bad to worse and it seems to me that we cannot get out of it, and ought not to get out of it now, without a little blood letting . . .[4]

Beatty, Wilson and Trenchard were thus the three Chiefs who were to grapple with Defence policy in the early 1920s; but the old adage 'Two's company, three's none' soon proved to be an apt description of their relationships. The two older Services tended to gang up on the brash newcomer, whom they had failed to strangle at birth and were determined to dismember at the first opportunity; and all three were turned into bitter rivals in the struggle for re-sources forced upon them by post-war financial stringency. Many influential politicians and journalists became convinced once more that 'Chiefly' harmony would only be achieved by the creation of a Ministry of Defence with a very senior minister at its head. Churchill, indeed, saw himself as that minister, and was encouraged in this ambition by his appointment as joint Secretary of State for War and Air. Having been First Lord already, it seemed but a short step to become master of the three Services. Giving the wayward Churchill such power was, however, politically unthinkable.

The formation of a Ministry of Defence had, in fact, been recently examined by Lord Haldane, who had been tasked in July 1917 to look into the post-war Machinery of Government. His committee reported in November 1918, recommending, *inter alia*, that Hankey's Cabinet Secretariat should become a permanent feature of the Whitehall bureaucracy; and that, instead of creating a Ministry of Defence, the Committee of Imperial Defence should be resuscitated. There was, regrettably, still no suggestion that the CID should be supported by some sort of Great General Staff to develop national defence policy.[5] Hankey, as usual, kept the reins of power in his own hands by ensuring that the CID's Secretariat remained under his direction and formed part of the Cabinet Office in Whitehall.

Lloyd George retained his War Cabinet system until November 1919, so there was little reason to refer matters of Defence policy to the full CID until 1920. Its Co-ordination Sub-Committee, however, was set the immediate task of rewriting the War Book, and its Historical Section started the preparation of the British Official

History of the Great War, which eventually ran to some fifty volumes.

Until the Chanak crisis in 1922 induced the birth of the Chiefs of Staff Committee, the three Chiefs went their own ways, much as they had done in pre-war days, with no responsibility for tendering corporate advice to the Government. They faced in different directions, each grappling with the intractable post-war problems of his own Service. Beatty was immersed in capital ship replacement, world naval disarmament, Anglo-American rivalry at sea, and his struggle with Trenchard to wrest aircraft operating with the Fleet from Air Ministry control. Wilson was trying to persuade Churchill to end his futile attempts to reverse the Russian Revolution, and Lloyd George to reduce British military commitments in the Middle East and in Europe so that sufficient troops could be concentrated in the United Kingdom to deal effectively with the Irish problem and to ensure that industrial unrest did not lead to a British Revolution. And Trenchard was concentrating on creating the RAF on as economic a basis as possible, while fending off attacks from many different quarters.

Despite this diversity of interest, the policies of the three Chiefs were dominated throughout the 1920s by two things: the notorious Ten Year Rule, and the Air Staff's determination to demonstrate the growing importance of Air-Power.

The Ten Year Rule was formulated by the War Cabinet on 15 August 1919, in response to an Admiralty request for guidance in drawing up the Naval Estimates for 1920/21. It read:

> It should be assumed for framing revised estimates, that the British Empire will not be engaged in any great war during the next ten years, and that no Expeditionary Force is required for this purpose.[6]

Although intended as an assumption for that year's estimates only, and as such reasonable enough, it was invariably renewed each year until, in 1928, Churchill, of all people, as Chancellor of the Exchequer, made it a permanent rolling assumption – tomorrow never comes! Indeed, it was not finally laid to rest until 1933 when the Disarmament Conference collapsed and Germany and Japan left the League of Nations. It gave the Treasury an unchallengeable grip on Defence expenditure throughout the 1920s and early 1930s.

There was one less obvious facet of the Ten Year Rule. It gave the Air Staff a useful weapon in arguing their case for substitution air-power to discharge former naval and army commitments on the grounds of greater cost-effectiveness. Much to the chagrin of the

Naval and General Staffs, they were not slow in exploiting these arguments, but they were held in check by the difficulty of proving the Air's future potential. It was too easy for cynics to portray the Air Staff as impractical visionaries or extremists.

Between 1920 to 1923, the Chiefs were at loggerheads over three major policy issues, all of which hinged upon their conflicting views on the effectiveness of air power: the future of the battleship, the use of air power in Imperial policing, and the reconstitution of the Royal Naval Air Service. The Naval and General Staffs, and many in Parliament and the Press, challenged the words enshrined in the White Paper on Air Policy of December 1919:

> The principle to be kept in mind in forming the framework of the Royal Air Force is that in future the main portion of it will consist of an Independent Force, together with service personnel required in carrying out aeronautical research. In addition there will be a small part of it specially trained for work with the navy, and a small part of it specially trained for work with the Army, these two small portions probably becoming, in the future, an arm of the older service. It may be that the main portion, the Independent Air Force, will grow larger and larger and become more and more the predominating factor in all types of war . . .[7]

While the Navy and Army noted the sop thrown to them of the possibility of their air arms returning to them at some future and unspecified date, they resented bitterly the final sentence, suggesting a future primacy for the RAF, and they do so to this day whenever such claims are made. Beatty was personally affronted and became locked in a never ending struggle with Trenchard to curb the ambitions of the RAF and to recover Naval Aviation. Wilson and the Earl of Cavan, who succeeded him as CIGS in February 1922, generally supported Beatty in his endeavours but never went to the extremes that he and the Naval Staff did in declaring the controversy 'a fight to the finish' – a fight that was to flare up once more in 1937 over the re-establishment of the Fleet Air Arm, and yet again in the carrier debates during Denis Healey's time as Secretary of State for Defence in the mid-1960s.

The battleship controversy began in November 1920 when the First Lord of the Admiralty placed Beatty's proposals before the Cabinet for restarting capital shipbuilding in 1921, to ensure continuing naval supremacy on the accepted 'One Power Standard' with the US Navy as the relevant yardstick. The Royal Navy had ended the War with the most powerful fleet in the world, but its ships were ageing. It had only one post-Jutland capital ship in commission, the battle-cruiser *Hood*, and this would still be the position in 1925, if replacements were not laid down at once. If the Americans completed their 1916 building programme, which was aimed at giving them 'a fleet second to none', they would have sixteen new post-Jutland capital ships by 1925. Japan would have eight by 1925 and sixteen by 1928. Beatty proposed laying down four new ships a year from 1921 onwards.

Beatty's programme was leaked, and caused an immediate storm in Parliament and the Press. The Disarmament and Air lobbies came together to oppose it publicly: the former on the grounds that Britain should be setting an example to the world by scrapping and not building battleships; and the latter because, in its view, battleships had lost credibility in the new age of air-power. And the Treasury opposed it behind the scenes as a breach of the Ten Year Rule, and as an insupportable burden on the country's impoverished economy. Austen Chamberlain, Chancellor of the Exchequer, assured the House that 'an exhaustive investigation' would be undertaken by the CID before any further decisions were taken.

Bonar Law, the Lord Privy Seal, headed the sub-committee of the CID tasked to look into 'Naval Ship-building'. Trenchard and the pro-Air witnesses pointed to the growing vulnerability of surface ships to bomb and torpedo attack, which had recently been demonstrated in trials by the United States Navy, when the ex-German Battleship *Ostfriesland* was sunk by bombs. The countering Naval evidence was divided. Beatty drew on the conclusions of an Admiralty committee under Admiral Sir Richard Phillimore and argued that '*the latest type of capital ship is so well protected that she can be hit by a considerable number of the most effective torpedoes now existing without being sunk*'[8]. He and his contemporaries were all 'big gun' men, who maintained that the '*capital ship is and will remain a necessity for naval warfare*'[9]. More junior naval witnesses such as Rear Admiral de Bartolome, a former Third Sea Lord, and Rear Admiral Richmond, President of the Royal Naval College, expressed doubts.

The Committee itself was divided on the issue. The uncommitted members were not convinced by the Admiralty case, and yet they were not entirely persuaded by the Air evidence that the battleship had had its day. Churchill laid aside his mantle of Secretary of State for War and Air and swung back to his former naval allegiance. He came out strongly in favour of the Admiralty Board's position, arguing powerfully for the battleship in principle and for the immediate implementation of Beatty's shipbuilding programme. The split report of the Committee enabled the Treasury to block any new construction until the outcome of the Washington Naval Disarmament Conference of November 1921 was known.

The Washington Naval Treaty and the Four Power Pacific Treaties signed in December 1921, which limited the United States, British and Japanese capital ships to the 5:5:3 ratio, and fixed upper limits for their displacements, stopped the threatened and cripplingly expensive naval armaments race. Furthermore, it delighted the enthusiasts for disarmament since it enabled the three powers to scrap two million tons of outdated warships. The British acceptance of the one power standard seemed reasonable at the time in view of the unlikelihood of war with the United States. It would provide a forty per cent superiority over the Japanese, but not if Britain was facing a hostile European naval power at the same time. Such a contingency, however, had to be discounted in 1921 for financial reasons.

It is interesting to note that similar arguments were going on in the American naval hierarchy, which was divided between Anglophiles and Anglophobes, and between 'big gun' men and aviation enthusiasts. During the 1920s, the Anglophobes led by men like Admiral William Benson, the wartime Chief of Naval Operations, pressed for a continuation of the 'Second to None' policy, aimed at wresting naval supremacy from the British. Like their British rivals, they were mostly 'big gun' men, and demanded the continuation of battleship building rather than aircraft carrier construction.

There was, however, amongst their middle ranking admirals a man of genius – Rear Admiral William Moffett – who established the Naval Bureau of Aeronautics in 1921 and remained at its head until he was killed in the crash of the naval airship *Akron* in 1933. Thanks to Moffett, the United States Navy began to exploit the potential of air power much earlier than the Royal Navy. He was helped by the counter-productive antics and excesses of the principal American advocate of a unified air service on RAF lines, Brigadier General William Mitchell. Not only did Moffett manage to swing United States naval thinking towards the aircraft carrier at the expense of the battleship, but he won the battle to retain naval aviation as an integral part of the United States Navy. While the British Admiralty was concentrating on recovering the Royal Naval Air Service from the RAF, Moffett was developing the concept of the fast carrier task forces which were to play such a crucial part in the Pacific during the Second World War.

The difference in attitudes of the two navies to air power is reflected in the priorities that they gave to gunnery spotters in naval aircraft development. The British priorities were gunnery spotters, fighters, torpedo bombers, long range reconnaissance aircraft. The Americans' choice was bombers and torpedo bombers, fighters, gunnery spotters, long range reconnaissance. In the 1930s, Admirals like Ernest King and William Halsey had come to appreciate that naval actions would probably be fought out of the range of the battleship's big guns. 250 carrier-borne aircraft took part in the American naval exercises of 1929: the Royal Navy had a total of only about 150 aircraft all told at that time!

The controversy over the use of the RAF for Imperial policing began in February 1921, when Churchill became Secretary of State for the Colonies. He remembered Trenchard briefing him when he was Secretary of State for War and Air on the great economies that could be made by adopting a policy of air control in undeveloped areas like the North West Frontier of India. Aircraft could reach and overawe hostile tribesmen in difficult terrain far more easily and much more cheaply than using the traditional, cumbersome punitive expeditions mounted by the Army. Dangerously exposed British outposts could be replaced by British officered local levies working with political officers, who could call for air support when trouble was brewing, and could be reinforced by air with British regular troops from centrally positioned reserves if need be.

The Air Ministry maintained that such techniques had already proved workable in a small way in ending the long standing rebellion of the Mad Mullah in British Somaliland in 1920. There was no one in Whitehall at the time to refute the myth that the RAF had achieved in twenty-one days what the Army had been struggling to do for twenty-one years. Major 'Pug' Ismay (later Lord Ismay, Churchill's wartime Chief Staff Officer), who was commanding the Somaliland Camel Corps during the campaign, gives a very different picture in his *Memoirs*. He says that the few bombing attacks carried out by the RAF detachment of six DH 9s made no significant contribution to the campaign. However, he comments that although the Air's claims were ill-founded, they were *'justified a hundredfold if they did anything to strengthen the case for the independent Air Force'*. He shuddered to think *'what would have happened in the Second World War if the Admiralty and War Office had had their way and the Air Arm had become a mere auxiliary of the older services.'*[10]

The Air Ministry's claims were soon to be put to the test. One of the most troublesome colonial-type problems inherited by Churchill was the establishment of stable regimes in the British mandated territories in the Middle East – Iraq, Transjordan and Palestine – the former under the India Office and the other two under the Foreign Office. Iraq had been in a state of rebellion throughout 1919 and was still expensively garrisoned by 190,000 British and Indian troops under the temperamental General Sir Aylmer Haldane, a cousin of Lord Haldane. Churchill with his usual vigour persuaded the Cabinet to bring all three territories under the Colonial Office, and to allow him to try out Trenchard's scheme of Air Control to reduce the cost of maintaining the mandates.

Wilson, the CIGS, found himself in an embarrassing position. He had been pressing Lloyd George to reduce military commitments in the Middle East, and so he was in a weak position to oppose the Churchill/Trenchard scheme, though he and the General Staff were sceptical of its practicability. He had expressed his feelings about the RAF's ambitions to take over part of the Army's Imperial policing duties in a speech to the Staff College, Camberley, when he described the Air Force as:

> Coming from God knows where, dropping its bombs on God knows what, and going off to God knows where.[11]

Churchill went out to Cairo in March 1921, accompanied by Trenchard, to impose his policies upon the reluctant resident High Commissioners and Generals, who did not believe that the RAF could do more than frighten rebellious tribesmen into momentary submission. Bayonets on the ground, particularly in the major cities, would still be needed to maintain political stability. Trenchard, a trained soldier, of course, appreciated this. His case was based on the Air's ability to speed up operations and reduce, but not eliminate, the need for soldiers in Imperial policing. Where he was on less secure ground was in demanding that responsibility for internal security in the three mandates should be handed over to an RAF commander instead of developing his system in support of the Army. He was lucky in having the two Salmond brothers – Geoffrey and John – both trained soldiers, to inaugurate the RAF Command in Iraq, John succeeding Geoffrey in October 1922.

Churchill returned to London with an outline plan for the run-down of the Army in Iraq from 33 battalions in April 1921 to a mere three battalions a year later, and for the transfer of responsibility for internal and external security from the War Office to the Air Ministry. Fleshing out the plan in London and the hand-over be-

tween ministries was far from amicable. The War Office took its lead
from Wilson and was as obstructive as it could be in an endeavour to
demonstrate the operational and administrative unsoundness of the
whole scheme. Trenchard was even forced to use Air Force funds to
build armoured cars in RAF workshops in England and Egypt for his
RAF officered local Levies because the War Office refused to provide
any! The real trial by fire was not to come for another year.

By the end of March 1921, the country was beginning to lose faith
in Lloyd George, who had become an Olympian figure, preoccupied
with increasingly unpopular international peace conferences, aloof
from Parliament, and careless in his own financial and sexual activities. Unemployment was rising alarmingly, the miners' strike of April
all but turned into a General Strike; IRA atrocities in Ireland were
not abating, despite the draconian efforts of the 'Black and Tans';
and in the Press and Parliament there was a growing demand for
cuts in Government expenditure, particularly in Defence spending.
Bonar Law articulated the country's mood when he said that Britain
was refusing to act any more as 'the policeman of the world'. As part
of his ploy to re-establish his government's credibility, Lloyd George
set up the inquisitorial Geddes Committee on National Expenditure
– the Geddes Axe – which started taking evidence in August 1921.

Beatty and Wilson saw the Geddes Committee as a God-sent
opportunity to get rid of the Air Ministry and to dismember the
RAF. Their case was simplistic: the economists on the Committee,
they believed, should be able to see that large savings in overheads
would accrue if the third Service were to be scrapped. They harped
back to the pre-Smuts' Report division of responsibilities and argued
that naval aviation should be brought back under the Admiralty,
while all air operations over land, including strategic bombing,
should be returned to the War Office. They reinforced their case by
pointing out that the United States, France and Japan had refused to
follow Britain's lead in establishing independent air forces.

They misjudged Trenchard, who counter-attacked with two bar-
rels. His first was aimed at the Naval and Army overheads. He
ordered his staff to co-operate fully with Geddes, opening all the Air
Staff books and allowing a thorough inspection of all Air Ministry
establishments. He was confident that no fat would be found on the
body of the RAF, which had started from scratch and had only been
able to afford the leanest of administrative structures, whereas the
two older Services were still carrying grossly uneconomic overheads
due to war time expansion which Geddes soon uncovered.

Trenchard's second barrel was aimed at the operational responsibilities. He drew on papers that he had been showering upon the CID that summer, suggesting that air power should not be treated as an 'addition' to naval and army capabilities but as more efficient and economic 'substitution' for some of their existing functions. His primary target was the hallowed assumption that the security of the United Kingdom still rested upon naval supremacy. He presented a strong case for transfer of that responsibility to the RAF, which would discharge it by creating a bomber force able to deter and, if need be, attack the bases of hostile air and naval forces, rather than depend upon relatively short range naval guns. Even if there was some doubt about the battleship's vulnerability to air attack, the bomb was more powerful, weight for weight, than the shell; its range was 200 miles rather than the shell's 20 miles; and capital and running costs of a single battleship would fund a far more cost-effective number of bomber squadrons.

Geddes rejected Beatty's and Wilson's case for the dismemberment of the RAF, but other sections of his report engendered such opposition on the grounds of inaccuracy and misapprehension of Service requirements that Lloyd George gave Churchill the task of reviewing the validity of his recommendations on behalf of the Cabinet.

Churchill strongly supported Geddes's recommendation for the retention of the RAF, and this was given formal approval in Parliament on 16 March 1922. He then tried to devise a formula for naval aviation that would satisfy Beatty and Trenchard. He proposed that while the Air Ministry should remain responsible for the overall development and control of British air power, 'the Admiralty should ask Parliament for the money to pay for the aircraft they require, and should have full and unfettered control over the said aircraft while employed for naval purposes'.[12]

Beatty was prepared to accept Churchill's plan since it meant that the Admiralty would then be able to decide how much it was prepared to spend on naval aviation in relation to the rest of the Navy's budget. As long as the Air Ministry held the purse strings, the sailors would always suspect that their requirements were at the bottom of the Air Ministry's priority list. Churchill's formula solved this problem, but Trenchard would have none of it. He was myopically wedded to his thesis of the unity of air power. With the future of the RAF already assured by the statement in the House on 16 March, many historians believe that he was unwise not to have accepted the compromise, at least as a basis for further negotiation. He refused to do so, and so the Naval Aviation controversy remained unresolved when the Chanak crisis (see page 127) pushed the problem into the Government's pending tray.

Amongst his other recommendations, Geddes proposed, yet again, the creation of a Ministry of Defence. The Cabinet went as far as accepting that this might be an ultimate solution, and then set up the Mond/Weir Committee to see whether there could be some amalgamation of common administrative services. It concluded that this would only be practicable if the Services were themselves amalgamated, since a separate Service must be in a position to decide expenditure priorities within its own budget. The most that could be done without amalgamation, which was seen to be impractical, was to seek economies through co-ordination of common services by inter-departmental committees. These arguments were to be advanced time and again over the next forty years.

By the time Henry Wilson retired at the end of his tenure as CIGS in February 1922, he had so alienated Lloyd George by opposing the creation of the Irish Free State in December 1921 that he was not consulted about his own replacement. He first heard that the Earl of Cavan was to succeed him from Cavan himself! Wilson's choice would have been Allenby, but Lloyd George, with Kitchener in mind, had no desire to be saddled with another praetorial figure from the East! Cavan's political unobtrusiveness probably told in his favour, in spite of his apparent inexperience for a job with such a high political and staff content.

On his retirement, Wilson was elected MP for North Down, but within four months was shot and killed on the steps of his house in Eaton Square by two Irish Nationalists connected with the IRA. It was a tragic end to a brilliant though controversial career.

Wilson himself described Cavan as 'ignorant, pompous, vain and narrow, but a nice man and a fine fighting soldier'.[13] Commissioned into the Grenadier Guards, he was shortish by their standards, but robustly built and with a rather over-large head. As the Italian Campaign showed, he was able to inspire men in battle. However, he had no pretensions of being a gifted staff officer. He had no previous experience of Whitehall, had never been to the Staff College and always prided himself on being an ordinary semi-educated country gentleman first and a professional soldier second. There is every indication that he followed Field Marshal Lord Byng's advice to sit tight and say as little as possible until he knew his job, but, in fact, he made minimal impact on national and military affairs during the whole of his four years as CIGS. The quip by 'Boney' Fuller (Major-General J F C Fuller), one of the Army's Young Turks of the inter-war years, can hardly be bettered: '*As CIGS in the War Office he was as much out of place as a nun in a night club*'.[14] Beatty was left to wage his continuing battles with Trenchard bereft of Army support.

During the summer of 1922, war clouds started to billow up over the Dardanelles again as the Chanak crisis with Turkey developed. Faced with the unexpected possibility of war with Kemal's Turkish nationalists, Lloyd George sought strategic advice from the three Chiefs. Much to his disgust and annoyance, Beatty, Cavan and Trenchard presented contradictory plans, which lacked any semblance of co-ordination and showed clearly how little things had changed in the years since the disastrous Gallipoli landings in 1915. His instinctive dislike for professional military advisers welled up as he said in effect:

> Gentlemen, I am tired of these squabbles. We all know the navy has to protect the Straits, the army has to reinforce Chanak, and the air force to cover both. It's your job to tell us how. Come back when you have an agreed plan.[15]

An agreed plan did emerge in a remarkably short time, but it was the ever alert Hankey, who saw the opportunity for establishing the equivalent of the Great General Staff with which Esher and Clarke had wanted to equip the CID as far back as 1904. Throughout the Chanak crisis, which lasted until the middle of October 1922, Churchill, as Colonial Secretary responsible for the Middle East, chaired daily meetings of an *ad hoc* Chiefs of Staff Committee. Kemal backed off from attacking General Sir Charles Harington's British troops holding the eastern side of the Dardanelles at Chanak, and the crisis ended with his acceptance of the Pact of Mudania.

Lloyd George's handling of the Chanak, although in the end successful, persuaded the Conservative members of his administration to part company with him. Accumulated dissatisfaction with coalition government; the 'Surrender to the Irish'; the high taxation, which created economic stagnation at home without compensatory benefits abroad; and the alleged trafficking in honours, finally brought Lloyd George's 'Dictatorship in Commission' to an end. Bonar Law succeeded him towards the end of October after the Conservative revolt at the famous Carlton Club meeting.

Bonar Law, when he took over as Prime Minister, was faced with a pile of unresolved policy issues in the Defence field. Beatty had returned to the attack upon Air Force ambitions; many of the Geddes recommendations were still being challenged; and Hankey was pressing for the regularisation of the *ad hoc* Chiefs of Staff Committee. Bonar Law, therefore, agreed to set up a special sub-committee of the CID under the Marquess of Salisbury, son of the former Prime Minister, who had established the first Cabinet Defence Committee at the turn of the Century, '*to enquire into the Questions of National and Imperial Defence*'. It was an extraordinarily powerful body. On it were the Chancellor of the Exchequer, the First Lord of the Admiralty, the Secretaries of State for Foreign Affairs, Colonies, War, India, Air, and Lords Balfour and Weir, and with Hankey as its Secretary.

Powerful though it was, the Salisbury Committee did not, in fact, manage to carry the anti-Air Force vendetta between the Admiralty and War Office on the one hand and the Air Ministry on the other much further forward, other than to confirm once more the continuing need for an independent Air Force. Nor did it recommend the formation of a Ministry of Defence as the Geddes Committee had tried to do. It did, however, achieve two things of historic importance: it brought the Chiefs of Staff Committee officially and permanently into being, setting a pattern for strategic co-ordination that was later followed by the United States; and it gave the RAF a target of 52 squadrons for Home Defence, without which the Battle of Britain could not have been won. Moreover, it backed the RAF in the creation of an Air Deterrent.

Trenchard was remarkably lucky in the timing of the Salisbury Committee. As its evidence was being taken, the policy of Air control in Iraq was being put to the test in the Kurdistan campaign that started in March 1923 to protect Mosul in northern Iraq from Kemal's nationalists. Bonar Law, supported by much of the Press, had been minded to abandon Iraq, and while the Government dithered, Air Marshal Sir John Salmond acted decisively and with Trenchard's full support. In a masterly three month campaign in the Kurdish mountains, fought by the RAF in support of two columns of British, Indian and Iraqi troops on the ground, Salmond forced the Turks to give up their attempts to take Mosul. No one could deny the RAF's success, which strengthened Trenchard's hand immeasurably at a crucial time in the Salisbury Committee deliberations.

The Committee's reaffirmation of the need for an independent Air Force read:

> The most important result of this part of the enquiry was to confirm the vital need for a great increase in our air forces, which had been established in previous enquiries.[16]

The key sentence in their report, regularising the Chiefs of Staff Committee ran:

> . . . each of the three Chiefs of Staff will have an individual and collective responsibility for advising on defence policy as a whole, the three constituting, as it were, a Super-Chief of a War Staff in Commission.[17]

The Chiefs were charged with the responsibility of keeping:

> the defence situation as a whole constantly under review so as to ensure that defence preparations and plans and the expenditure thereupon are co-ordinated and framed to meet policy, that full information as to the changing naval, military and air situation may always be available to the Committee of Imperial Defence, and that resolutions as to the requisite action thereupon may be submitted for its consideration.[18]

Under Hankey's inimitable guidance as its Secretary, the Chiefs of Staff (COS) Sub-Committee, as it was officially designated, became the heart of the CID, spawning its own sub-committees, and so by usage the 'sub' was soon dropped from the title of the main committee, which became known simply as the Chiefs of Staff Committee. Although the Prime Minister and his Deputy (either the Lord President or the Lord Privy Seal) were the titular President and Chairman of the Committee respectively, the Chiefs normally met alone, chaired by one of the three, nominated by the Prime Minister and not necessarily on a rotational or seniority basis.

The COS Committee met formally for the first time on 17 July 1923. The inclusion of the thorny issues of responsibility for Naval Aviation and Aircraft Carriers on the agenda of the meeting did not give the new committee a propitious start. Each Chief was still very much the representative and chief executive of his own Service Board, briefed by his own Service staff, and expected by his Service to fight its corner. As a creature of his own Service, to which he had given his life's work, it was but human nature to look to its interests first before trying to reach a corporate view with his colleagues on the advice that they should tender collectively to the Government on how best to fight the King's enemies.

By 1926, doubts had sprung up amongst Ministers and in Parliament as to whether the Chiefs were indeed paying much attention to their collective as opposed to single service responsibilities. Baldwin, therefore, started the practice giving each Chief a warrant couched in the stately language of a bygone age and signed by the Prime Minister himself, spelling out the importance of their collective responsibilities for tendering strategic advice to the Government of the day. A copy of the first warrant issued to Beatty, Milne, who had

by that time taken over from Cavan, and Trenchard is reproduced at
Appendix B.

In the same year, the Joint Planning Sub-Committee was formed,
consisting initially of the Admiralty Director of Plans and the War
Office and Air Ministry Deputy Directors of Operations. The last
two were replaced by Army and Air Directors of Plans when these
posts had been established. The addition of the Joint Intelligence
Sub-Committee, consisting of the Directors of Intelligence and
chaired by a Foreign Office representative, was not established until
1936. Its formation, when coupled with the Joint Planning Sub-
Committee, gave the Chiefs the support of the equivalent of a much
needed Great General Staff or Joint War Staff.

The story of the creation of the RAF's Home Defence Force (later
called the Metropolitan Air Force) had started in October 1921 when
Lord Balfour, as Chairman of the CID, had addressed the question
of the vulnerability of the United Kingdom to attack by the vastly
superior French Air Force. The threat was examined by the specially
constituted Continental Air Menace Sub-Committee of the CID,
which was spurred on by worsening of Anglo-French relations caused
by the French occupation of the Ruhr in January 1923. Bonar Law
directed the Salisbury Committee to define 'the strength of the Air
Force for purposes of Home and Imperial Defence'.

The Committee concluded that, like the Navy, the RAF's size
should be defined to a 'One Power' standard. It said:

> . . . British air power must include a Home Defence Air Force of sufficient
> strength to protect us against air attack by the strongest air force within striking
> distance of this country.[19]

It recommended that the force of 52 squadrons should be 'created
with as little delay as possible'. The Air Ministry hoped to complete
the necessary expansion over a five year period, giving a front line
strength of 394 bombers and 204 fighters by 1928–29[20].

In the middle and late 1920s, confidence in the continuous pursuit
of disarmament and in the validity of the Ten Year Rule, pervaded
the corridors of power in Westminster and Whitehall. The covert rise
of a vengeful Germany went unrecognised by the general public, and
the overt ambitions of Italy and Japan were thought to be contain-
able by sensible and sympathetic negotiation. The peace of Europe
seemed to have been secured by the 1925 Treaty of Locarno, which
guaranteed the French and Belgium frontiers with Germany from
aggression by either side; and the maintenance of the demilitarisation

of the Rhineland added to security, making disarmament all the more attractive to all political parties.

Peace abroad, however, was not matched by social harmony and economic wellbeing at home. The 1926 General Strike and the 1929 Wall Street crash concentrated the electorate's attention, and hence the Government's efforts, on social reform and economic retrenchment rather than national security; and the modest successes of the 1927 Geneva Naval Disarmament Conference and the 1930 London Naval Treaty encouraged the plethora of political idealists to redouble their efforts towards world disarmament with a blind faith in the effectiveness of the League of Nations. So it was hardly a happy period in which to be one of the Chiefs, and certainly not a time for attempting to break the Treasury's Ten Year Rule.

Some measure of harmony was engendered amongst the Chiefs and a modest start was made in developing their collective voice by the institution of the Chiefs of Staff Annual Review. In their 1926 Review, they spelt out, for the Government's benefit, their assessment of Britain's strategic commitments and highlighted the pathetic inadequacy of the available forces to meet them. A pattern of argument was established that is still relevant today. The Chiefs can and must list priorities, match commitments to resources and argue for appropriate force levels to meet priorities, but none of this is to any avail if their deliberations are not picked up and endorsed by their political masters. In the 1920s, the Chiefs consistently warned the Cabinet of the mismatch between commitments and resources, but the greater importance of short term domestic issues and a tendency of ministers to put their heads in the sands of idealism, verging on pacifism, left their warnings unheeded.

The fault was not entirely that of ministers. The age old controversy between the maritime and continental streams of British strategic thought re-emerged. The Chiefs might have been expected to claim additional resources to rebuild an Expeditionary Force to discharge Britain's Locarno Treaty obligation to intervene on the Continent if either France or Germany was the victim of aggression, but they did quite the reverse. While they did not contest the Foreign Office view that the more the nations of Europe became convinced of Britain's readiness to fulfil her guarantee, the less likely it was that she would be called upon to do so, they concluded that the peaceful international situation in general, and the stabilising influence of the Locarno Treaty in particular, had so simplified Britain's security problems in Europe that they could reduce the overall size of the

Territorial Army, transfer coast and anti-aircraft ground defences to it, and thereby release money and regular manpower for Imperial Defence.

Next year the Cabinet went even further towards Britain's traditional maritime policy. When accepting the 1927 Review they amplified the Ten Year Rule with the words:

> . . . and that the immediate plans of the Army should be based upon preparedness for an extra-European War.[21]

Surprising though it may seem, the Chiefs did not oppose Churchill's reinforcement of the Ten Year Rule in 1928. The Defence deficiencies were so great that they could only be accepted on grounds that no foreseeable threat existed, and yet could only be remedied by an equally unforeseeable programme of expenditure. Nonetheless, they did utter a timely warning:

> We feel bound, however, to impress on the Committee of Imperial Defence how great a responsibility this places on those charged with the day to day conduct of foreign affairs to warn . . . of the first hint of a less satisfactory state of affairs, in order that the necessary adjustments in our defensive arrangements may be considered, the requisite preparations for which would require a period of some years to bring into effective operation.[22]

In refusing to challenge the Ten Year Rule, they were intent upon avoiding the charge that they were exceeding their proper functions by straying into the realms of political policy, but they grossly overestimated the speed with which a democracy can change course when expenditure upon distasteful or unpopular measures is needed.

There were no Henry Wilsons on the General Staff to fight for a new BEF, and the Naval and Air Staffs had no intention of building up the Army's case for expansion, which would have been at their expense. Indeed, the three Services were split over whom they saw as their most likely future enemy. The Navy was worrying about Japan and to a lesser extent about American rivalry. The principal naval problem was how to move the Fleet to the Far East in an emergency without denuding the maritime defences of the British Isles. The development of Singapore as the Far Eastern Fleet base was high on its list of priorities. The RAF was concentrating its thinking on the defeat of French rather than German air attacks on London. And the Army still viewed Russian expansionist aims in Afghanistan and the consequential threat to India as its principal concern.

General Sir George Milne (later Field Marshal Lord Milne), who had commanded the British Salonika Force (1916–18) and the British Army of the Black Sea (1919–20), relieved Cavan as CIGS in

February 1926. 'Uncle George', as he was affectionately known in the Army, was not the Government's first choice for the post. Lord Rawlinson, C-in-C India, was to have succeeded Cavan, but he died in 1925 at the early age of 61.

Milne, a Gunner, had, like his predecessor, no experience of policy-making in Whitehall, but he started off impressively. He showed a sound grasp of strategic principles in the Chiefs of Staff Committee, and, egged on by his Military Assistant, the contro-versial Colonel 'Boney' Fuller, seemed determined to modernise the Army during his tenure as CIGS. In his memoirs, Fuller recalls Milne's conversation with one of the War Office directors, who was telling him what the General Staff wanted him to do. Uncle George snapped out *'Who is the General Staff?'* and answered himself by saying *'I am the General Staff'* – a sentiment that many of his successors would echo when frustrated by the in-built checks and balances of Whitehall bureaucracy.[23]

Milne was a realist, but he accepted rather too easily the Whitehall constraints and need to work within the financial limits imposed by the Government. He never quite had the courage of his convictions, and was not prepared to challenge Treasury interpret-ations of the Ten Year Rule. Nevertheless, Fuller was certainly over critical when he wrote of him:

> Napoleon once said . . . 'The whole art of war consists in a well reasoned and extremely circumspect defensive, followed by rapid and audacious attack.' Because of some curious twist in his mental outfit, Sir George Milne inverted this saying, and so completely that he would invariably start audaciously and end cautiously. Could one have turned him mentally upside down, what a superb CIGS he would have made![24]

Disappointing though Milne's performance may have been in the eyes of ambitous junior officers like G Le Q Martel, 'Hobo' Hobart, Charles Broad, 'Boney' Fuller and the self-ordained military guru, Liddell Hart, all of whom were pressing for the mechanisation of the Army and the development of armoured forces, there was much to be said in his favour. It would have taken a Marlborough or Kitchener and an obvious threat to the country's security to prize open the Treasury grip on military expenditure in the mid-1920s. Milne did encourage thinking throughout the Army about future tactics, orga-nisation and equipment, although he was unable to provide adequate resources for experimental purposes. He sowed the seeds of new ideas that were to germinate when money became more readily available in the mid-1930s.

Milne's initiatives did lead to the creation of the Experimental Mechanised Force and the Armoured Force in the latter half of the 1920s, and to the expansion of the Royal Tank Corps and the formation of the first Tank Brigade in 1931, but it was all on too small a scale to validate battle-winning tactical doctrines and technological policies; or, for that matter, to wean the majority of the Army away from its mistress, the horse, and from what it saw as 'real soldiering' in and around the Empire.

Milne had also to contend with the credible argument, strongly advocated by the Treasury at the time, that it would be foolish to go into mass production of armoured vehicles, self-propelled guns and other mechanised equipment until the Army had made up its mind what it needed. If it went into production too soon, it might be left with a lot of obsolescent equipment. The official CID view was that the Ten Year Rule '*would not in any way hamper the development of ideas but would check mass production until the situation demanded it*'.[25] This was wishful thinking: ideas rarely blossom without the heat of necessity to force them into bloom.

Unfortunately, the financial crisis, which followed the Wall Street crash of 1929, made further worthwhile trials impracticable in the latter half of Milne's tenure, stultifying the growth of tactical ideas. Milne's first priority had to be the preservation of the basic structure of the Army – its traditional regiments – which could only be achieved by cutting almost everything else.

Milne's tenure as CIGS was extended twice. This was largely due to the need for continuity in the long run-up to the Geneva Disarmament Conference, which did not begin until 1932. There is, however, the apocryphal story of Milne's conversation with the Prime Minister on reaching the end of his first tenure. When asked who should succeed him, he is said to have replied '*I have searched far and wide, but I can't find anyone worthy to succeed me*', which perhaps had some justification when we consider the abilities of his successor.

Milne's selection of Sir Archibald Montgomery-Massingberd, another Gunner, had the whiff of an 'old boy net' about it. Sir Archibald, a Lincolnshire landowner, was an experienced staff officer, who had been Chief of Staff to Rawlinson's 4th Army in Flanders. However, while sensibly orthodox in his views, he lacked the military imagination and type of personality needed to energise the War Office. He was complacent to a fault and damped out enthusiasm for modernisation. Soon after taking over in February 1933, he said in a speech '*I will venture to say that the Army is not likely to be used for a big war in Europe for many years to come*.[26] The horse was to continue to hold pride of place in the Army during his time as CIGS.

Beatty's last years as First Sea Lord were spent in opposing the machinations of the United States Navy's Anglophobes in their quest for American naval supremacy via the disarmament conferences. The blinkered Admiral William Benson had been succeeded as US Chief of Naval Operations by more open minded men, but then in 1925 Admiral Hilary P Jones, an alter ego of Benson's and one of the most difficult characters with whom Beatty had ever had to deal, became the principal United States naval adviser at the disarmament conferences. Anglo-American naval relations had sunk to their lowest ebb by the time Beatty retired in 1927.

Beatty was far more successful than Milne in fighting successive Conservative and Labour administrations over cruiser replacement programmes, in spite of Treasury opposition. He was less so in maintaining unrelenting pressure upon Trenchard for the return of Naval Aviation to the Admiralty's budget and control. The Colwyn Committee on Service Expenditure, set up at the end of 1925, again came down on the side of the Air Ministry, and, for the fourth time since 1919, Baldwin reaffirmed the integrity of the RAF in the House of Commons, on 25 February 1927.

Unlike the War Office, with its four year tenures in Council appointments, the Admiralty limit for Board members was seven years. Beatty was suggested for the Governor-Generalship of Canada, but Leopold Amery, First Lord (1922–24), commented to Baldwin that *'he has no manners and an impossible American wife'*[27]. Lord Bridgeman, the First Lord at the time, was reluctant to dispense with his services during the Geneva Naval Disarmament Conference and extended his tenure for nine months, which was just long enough for him to see the Conference break down over the American refusal, prompted by Hilary Jones, to accept any gun smaller than 8-inch for their new cruisers.

By today's standards, Beatty's character was flawed with snobbery and arrogance, but he fought for and created the foundations for a Navy that was still second to none at the outbreak of the Second World War. The United States Congress had been just as reluctant to finance new warship construction as the House of Commons. Stephen Roskill ends his biography of the great naval earl with the words that Beatty wrote in the Duchess of Sutherland's 'Treasure Book': *'To achieve great happiness: work hard, fight hard, play hard, love hard.'*[28] Beatty did all four.

At the end of July 1927, he handed over to Admiral Sir Charles Madden, who had been Jellicoe's Chief of Staff at Jutland and had succeeded Beatty as C-in-C of the Grand Fleet in 1919. Madden's selection owed much to Beatty's wish to heal the rift between the Beatty and the Jellicoe factions over the Jutland controversy. Nevertheless, he was intellectually well qualified for the post and up to handling naval affairs in Whitehall. He was highly experienced in operational command, but he was unlucky to be First Sea Lord in the worst period of economic depression that the country has ever experienced. Even another Beatty could not have made much constructive headway.

When Madden was due to retire, the front runner for the post of First Sea Lord was Sir Roger Keyes of Zeebrugge fame. He was rejected by the then Labour Government as too controversial and a potential political liability. Admiral Sir Frederick Field, one of the most colourless and ineffectual officers to hold the post in this century was appointed in his stead in July 1930. After the Invergordon Mutiny in 1931, King George V is said to have suggested that Field and the other Sea Lords should have been forced to resign for their incompetent handling of the affair.

Trenchard was the only Chief to enjoy a 'bull' market in the latter half of the 1920s after the Salisbury Committee's recommendation of a 52 squadron Metropolitan Air Force. By 1924, when Hindenburg became President of Germany, the RAF's childhood was over: Trenchard hoped that he could start putting muscle onto its well-formed bones, but the process took far longer than he hoped. The 1925 Treaty of Locarno, which seemed to guarantee the peace of Europe, brought political pressure – particularly from Churchill, the new Chancellor of the Exchequer in Baldwin's second Conservative Administration – for an air limitation agreement with France and a delay in the planned completion date of the 52 squadron programme from 1928–9 to 1935–6 for economic as well as political reasons. The Wall street crash then forced a further postponement until 1938–9.

Trenchard retired after eleven years as CAS in December 1929 at the age of 56, and became a great reforming Commissioner of the Metropolitan Police. He left 'a last will and testament' for his successor, Sir John Salmond, demanding an increase of fifteen squadrons to take over Naval and Army tasks overseas, which he believed could be carried out more efficiently by the RAF. This did not endear him to his Naval and Army colleagues, or to Hankey, who believed his action was 'off-side' under Chiefs of Staff Committee rules.

Trenchard's biographers are generally agreed that seeking to strengthen the RAF at the expense of the other two Services at a time of deep financial depression was an unacceptably naive gambit.

Sir John Salmond – known throughout the RAF as 'Tails Up', his favourite expression – had been his obvious successor for some time. He was a faithful disciple of Trenchard and impressively dynamic and resolute in fighting the Air's case. After his successful command in the Middle East, he had held the post of AOC-in-C, Air Defence of Great Britain, for five years and then became Air Member for Personnel on the Air Council. He succeeded to the post of Chief of Air Staff at the remarkably young age of 49. His philosophy did not differ materially from Trenchard's and he was a dedicated apostle of Air Power, though he was rather more circumspect in applying abrasive Air doctrines. In a lecture to senior officers given just before he became CAS, he stated his basic philosophy:

> We must seek our salvation by committing the weight of our forces to the attack. The problem resolves itself into two heads – the close protection of our own vital centres with minimum force compatible with a certain degree of security, and distant bombing of those of the enemy with the greatest force available.[29]

The Chiefs of Staff Committee took some years to settle down and to develop into the successful organisation it became in the Second World War. Lord Ismay, who was one of its first Assistant Secretaries, records:

> For the first few years of their existence, the Chiefs of Staff were not exactly a band of brothers. Inter-Service co-operation had never come their way, and each of them was intent on fighting his own corner. I have a vivid recollection of a meeting at which I was acting for Hankey, when tempers got so heated and language so unrestrained, that I thought it discreet for a mere major to withdraw.[30]

The COS Committee had one glaring fault in its early days. The 'Defence Trinity' was only regarded as authoritative in Whitehall if it spoke with one voice. Under Hankey's guidance, unanimity became the accepted principle for tendering advice to the CID – 'dog did not eat dog' in public! Laudable though this may have been in some respects, it meant that a number of controversial issues that cried out for resolution were left to fester, and were not brought to the Cabinet's attention until events highlighted them in some brutal fashion.

Unanimity was, indeed, almost impossible to achieve after Churchill became Chancellor of the Exchequer at the end of 1924. Despite his great experience in Defence affairs and his clarion calls to arms in the mid-1930s, he tightened the Ten Year Rule remorselessly for the sake of the economy until it became the permanent rolling assumption in Defence estimates from 1928 until it was reluctantly dismantled by Ramsay Macdonald's National Government under the pressure of world events in 1933.

While each 'Chief' was having to fight against the dictatorial policies of Churchill and the Treasury for the lion's share of the meagre resources allocated to Defence, there could be little of the constructive thinking and mutual trust envisaged by the Salisbury Committee. Friction became the permanent ingredient of COS Committee meetings with Beatty, its first Chairman, and Milne resenting the grasping but justifiable acquisitiveness of Trenchard, whose battle cry of 'economy through the substitution of air for naval and military power' had just too much truth in it for comfort.

One of the most controversial issues of the 1920s that suffered from COS disagreements was the Admiralty plan to develop Singapore as a major naval base for the defence of British imperial interests in the Far East and the Antipodes. It had first been put forward by Jellicoe after his post-war mission to Commonwealth navies on behalf of the Admiralty in 1919. Although the plan was cold-shouldered by Wemyss at the time, it was resurrected after the abrogation of the Anglo-Japanese Alliance in December 1921 and given momentum by Churchill's strong support when he was evaluating the Geddes Committee proposals. The advent of the first Labour Government in 1924 led to the project being shelved again because it went against the spirit of disarmament and unbounding faith in the League of Nations. On Baldwin's return to office at the end of 1924, the project was revived once more. It came before the COS Committee early in 1925, where it was debated with increasing acrimony for the next eighteen months.

The cause of the disharmony amongst the Chiefs over the Singapore plan was, as usual, Trenchard's objections not so much as to the cost of the base but to what he saw as Beatty's and Milne's outdated views on its defence. He believed that torpedo bombers rather than 15-inch guns should form the core of the defence. In effect, he was reopening the battleship versus bomber debate that he had lost in the Bonar Law Committee of 1920. In putting his case, he said:

I fail to see the necessity of taking a decision now as to spending a large sum on installing six 15-inch guns which may very conceivably be out of date when the future need arises. In a very few year's time the whole air situation in the East may have been transformed; any change that occurs will strengthen and not diminish the potentialities of air-power for the defence of Singapore and the Far East, and I would urge that no precipitate step be taken now that may involve the locking up of money in fixed defences whose function can so admirably be fulfilled at less cost by utilising the mobility of aircraft.[31]

He was not, however, in a strong position to carry the argument because the air route to the Far East was still being pioneered.

As the Chiefs were divided on the issue, Baldwin, with Churchill's full support, deferred any decision and the debate went on. In July 1926, Trenchard, for the sake of COS harmony, accepted the compromise of emplacing three of the six 15-inch guns as a temporary measure until the air reinforcement route to the Far East was fully established. There the matter rested until the Japanese invaded Manchuria in 1931 and the alarm bells began to ring in Whitehall, heralding the coming end of the Ten Year Rule. Even then, there was a continuing refusal to accept Trenchard's views, although air reinforcement of Singapore was already possible. Baldwin chaired a special committee on the subject in May 1932, and concluded that the coast defences should be organised on a tri-Service basis with the gun retaining its place as the main deterrent to naval attack.

The years between Churchill's conversion of the Ten Year Rule into a rolling assumption in 1928 and its abandonment in 1933 were times of declining hope of world peace through disarmament and faith in the League; and the growing discrepancy between military commitments and resources available to meet then continued to be the repetitive theme of the Chiefs of Staff. In their annual review for 1930, they felt bound to point out that many countries were increasing rather than decreasing their military budgets. In their view, Britain was in a far less favourable position to fulfil her Locarno treaty obligations to go to the aid of France than she had been in 1914. They also remarked that, in their opinion, the strategic centre of gravity was shifting from Europe eastwards to the Middle East and on towards the Far East, where Japan was becoming increasingly restive.

The Foreign Office supported these warnings, but, in view of the world economic depression, the Foreign Secretary was not prepared to propose more than a review of the Ten Year Rule in the light of whatever results were achieved at the 1932 Geneva Disarmament

Conference. The Chiefs, however, were becoming so concerned about the inadequacies of manpower and equipment reserves of the three Services that they now began to challenge the continuing validity of the Ten Year Rule.

In their 1932 review, written in the wake of the Japanese invasion of Manchuria in September 1931, they ventured off military ground altogether and questioned the fundamental political assumptions upon which defence policy was then based. They warned the Government, in a most sombre document, and in terms of unprecedented seriousness, of the weaknesses of the Empire's defences, particularly in the Far East. They said that instead of *'no war for ten years, war might actually begin tomorrow'*.[32] The Ten Year Rule, in their view, had been responsible not only for the slow wasting away of the country's military forces but of its armament industry as well. They recommended the cancellation of the noxious rule; a start to defensive measures with priority accorded to the Far East; and no further waiting for results from the Geneva Disarmament Conference.

The 1932 Review was considered by the CID on 22 March that year. No one disagreed with the Chiefs' conclusions. Their recommendations were accepted in principle and passed to the Cabinet where two near fatal provisos – no doubt drafted by the Treasury – were added. First, that acceptance of the report must not be taken to justify increased Defence spending without regard to the serious financial predicament of the country. And secondly, the close connection with disarmament 'required further exploration'. These two caveats were to delay Britain's rearmament for a full eighteen months. By the end of 1933, the Ten Year Rule had been abandoned. This was certainly a triumph for the Chiefs and fully justified their attack on the Government's political assumptions.

When the COS Committee came to write their review for 1933, there were three new Chiefs in office. Sir Ernle Chatfield, Beatty's Flag Captain during the War and the man that he had always hoped would succeed him, replaced the feckless Field, who was, in any case, in poor health, as First Sea Lord in January 1933. Quiet though Chatfield was in manner, he possessed intellectual powers that probably exceeded Beatty's and a determination which brooked no frustrations or setbacks. He had commanded both the Atlantic and Mediterranean Fleets, and was just the right man to rearm the Fleet and bring it up to the standards needed for war. In his four years as professional head of the Navy, he did much to restore the morale of the Fleet, which had been so damaged by the Invergordon Mutiny, before becoming Minister of Defence Co-ordination in the run-up to the Second World War.

In direct contrast, Montgomery-Massingberd, who succeeded Milne in February, was just as much the wrong type of man to provide the War Office with the imaginative policies needed for the Army's modernisation. Sound and sensible though his contributions were in the Chiefs of Staff Committee, he did not measure up to the needs of the times.

Finally, in March, the admirable and still youthful Sir John Salmond retired from the post of CAS to allow his brother Geoffrey to have his turn as professional head of the RAF. Sadly, Geoffrey died within three weeks of assuming the appointment. Sir Edward Ellington became CAS at the end of April 1933. Trenchard from his position as Commissioner of the Metropolitan Police had little confidence in Ellington, seeing him as a *'man who knew no better than to knuckle under and obey the self-denying rules of what Trenchard thought of as "Hankey's Parlour Game" in the Chiefs of Staff Committee'.*[33] This was unfair: Ellington had an acute mind, a remarkable memory and the ability to grasp and implement new ideas. With the help of subordinates like Sir Hugh Dowding and Sir Cyril Newall, he was to do more than anyone else to turn the RAF into a modern Air Force.

Before the CID considered the Chief's Review for 1933 on 9 November, the Germans and Japanese had stormed out of the Geneva Disarmament Conference and the League of Nations. The CID recommended to the Cabinet that

> the Chiefs of Staff Sub-Committee, with representatives of the Treasury and the Foreign Office, and the Secretary of the CID, should prepare a programme for meeting our worst deficiencies for transmission to the Cabinet.[34]

Thus the Defence Requirements Sub-Committee (the DRC) was born to set in train the assessment and management of Britain's rearmament in the 1930s. It was hoped to reconcile the competing claims of the three Services for what was still to be a limited amount of money, and to develop a co-ordinated national and imperial defence plan. But little had really changed. The Chiefs were still to be faced with what Churchill has called the 'Locust Years' from 1933 to 1938, during which they failed to build a more compelling case for earlier and swifter rearmament. Their failure is well illustrated by a comparison of British and German military spending in terms of percentages of gross national product. In 1932 Britain was spending 3 per cent to Germany's meagre 1 per cent; in 1933 both spent 3 per cent; but thereafter the figures make Churchill's point for him:

	Britain	*Germany*	
1932	3%	1%	
1933	3%	3%	
1934	3%	6%	
1935	3%	8%	The
1936	4%	13%	Locust
1937	6%	13%	Years
1938	7%	17%	
1939	18%	23%	
1940	46%	38%	

1 Comparison of British and German Defence Expenditure between 1932–40, as a percentage of GNP[35]

Chronology
FOR CHAPTER SIX

1934

Feb   First Defence Requirements Committee Report.

Mar   Baldwin promises Air Parity.

               RAF Expansion Scheme 'A'.

Aug   Hitler becomes Head of the German State on the death of Hindenburg.

Dec   Japan denounces the Washington Naval Treaty.

1935

Feb   Stresa Front (Britain, France and Italy) formed.

March   France extends conscription to two years.

               Germany introduces conscription.

               Hitler reveals Luftwaffe strength.

May   Baldwin confesses loss of Air Parity.

               RAF Expansion Scheme 'C'.

June   Baldwin becomes Prime Minister.

               Anglo-German Naval Treaty.

July   Second Defence Requirements Committee Report.

Oct   Italy invades Abyssinia – non-oil sanctions imposed.

1936

Feb   RAF Expansion Scheme 'F'.

March   Hitler reoccupies the Rhineland.

               Third Defence Requirements Committee Report.

               Inskip appointed Minister for the Co-ordination of Defence.

April   Deverell replaces Montgomery-Massingberd as CIGS.

July   Spanish Civil War begins.

| Nov | Rome-Berlin Axis and Anti-Comintern Pact announced. |

1937

Jan	Anglo-Italian Naval 'Gentleman's Agreement'.
	RAF Expansion Scheme 'H'.
May	Chamberlain becomes Prime Minister.
	First Treasury Review of Rearmament Programmes.
Aug	Japanese aggression in China resumed.
	Newall replaces Ellington as CAS.
Oct	Visit of General Milch to London.
	RAF Expansion Scheme 'J'.
Dec	First Treasury Report Accepted (Appeasement Policy).
	Gort replaces Deverell as CIGS.

1938

Feb	Second Treasury Review of Rearmament Programmes.
	COS warning of situation 'Fraught with greater risks than at any time in living memory'.
March	Austro-German *Anschluss*.
	'Business as Usual' policy scrapped.
	RAF Expansion Scheme 'L'.
July	Hankey replaced by Bridges and Ismay in Cabinet Office.
Sep	Munich Agreement.
	Backhouse replaces Chatfield as First Sea Lord.
Nov	Final RAF Expansion Scheme 'M'.

1939

	German threat to Holland seen as *casus belli*.
	COS recommend fully equipped BEF.
Feb	Chatfield, Minister for the Co-ordination of Defence.
	COS European War Appreciation.
	Continental scale BEF authorised.
March	Germans occupy Prague.
	British guarantee to Poland.
	Territorial Army establishment doubled.
April	Italy invades Albania.
	Conscription introduced in Britain.
	British guarantees to Greece and Roumania.
May	Fleet Air Arm transferred to Admiralty.
June	Anglo-French War Plans agreed.

	Pound replaces Backhouse as First Sea Lord.
August	Ribbentrop-Molotov Pact signed.
Sep	Germany invades Poland.
	Britain declares war on Germany.

6

APPEASEMENT AND THE DRIFT TO WAR

The Chiefs versus the Treasury: 1934–1939

First Sea Lords		Chiefs of the Imperial General Staff	
Sir Ernle Chatfield		Sir Archibald Montgomery-Massingberd	
Sir Roger Backhouse	1938	Sir Cyril Deverell	1936
Sir Dudley Pound	1939	Viscount Gort	1937

Chiefs of Air Staff	
Sir Edward Ellington	
Sir Cyril Newall	1937

'. . . it was Mr Chamberlain's views that really mattered. It was he, who more than anyone else, stressed the need to limit defence spending in the long-term interests of economic strength, to strengthen spending on the Royal Air Force at the expense of the Army, and to concentrate the attention of the Royal Navy on Germany rather than Japan.'

Professor Norman Gibbs's summing up on the inter-war period in *Grand Strategy* Vol 1[1]

The three new Chiefs – Chatfield, Montgomery-Massingberd, and Ellington – who had taken over in 1933, found it easier than some of their predecessors to act as the Salisbury Commission had intended – as '*a Super-Chief of a War Staff in Commission*'. In the first place, they did not carry the same burden of wartime reputations which had to be protected. And second, they were less abrasively extrovert – '*that amenable trio*' – as Vansittart, the Permanent Head of the Foreign Office, called them in 1934, and so were better able to work together as a team under the able chairmanship of Ernle Chatfield[2].

But what really drew them together was the growing external threat posed by Nazi Germany, Fascist Italy and Imperial Japan, which helped them in their arguments with their common internal enemy, the Treasury. The collective responsibility for offering corporate advice to the Government on Defence policy began to assume equal, though rarely greater, importance in their minds than the narrower interests of their own Services. They could still be accused of ducking the most controversial inter-Service issues whenever they could not achieve the unanimity demanded by their Secretary, Maurice Hankey, but as the threat grew, so did their confidence and the quality of their advice to the Government. By the time war was declared in September 1939, the Chiefs of Staff Committee with its Secretariat, Joint Planning Staff and Joint Intelligence Sub-Committee had become the British Great General Staff in all but name.

The Treasury was – and still is – cast by the Services, sometimes justifiably but more often unthinkingly, as the ultimate enemy. Doctor G C Peden in the Introduction to his *British Rearmament and the Treasury, 1932–1939* quotes a senior Treasury official in the 1930s remarking that if he had been given a penny for every time the Treasury was damned, he would have been a very rich man; and his estate would be richer still if it had been able to collect pennies off historians of the period, who have continued to do so![3] The Treasury officials were, however, just as much the guardians of the country's solvency and economic well-being as the Chiefs were of its security.

In the 1930s, the Treasury had to advise the Government on the critical balance to be struck between spending too much, thereby undermining the economy and bringing about another 1931 style depression, and the danger of not being ready for war if and when it came. The balance itself had to be struck by the Government: the Treasury mandarins were but the executives of Ministerial decisions as, of course, were the Chiefs in their own field of responsibility. However, in presenting the hard facts about the economy generally, and about industrial capacity in particular, they forced Ministers and the Chiefs to face up to crucial decisions on priorities.

There was another important factor in the change of attitudes in the Chiefs of Staff Committee. They had an outstanding chairman in Admiral Chatfield, whose primary aim was

> . . . the unity of the three Services, and, through that unity, the strengthening of the committee in their task of rebuilding of the Fighting Services, which by 1933 had been reduced to such a state of unreadiness for war.[4]

And in this he was undoubtedly successful. At the same time, he was quietly determined to curb the ambitions of the Air Staff, and to quell its claims that the expansion of air power was the cheapest and most effective way of defending the country and its overseas interests. As one of the convinced 'Big Gun' sailors, he was determined to win the battleship versus bomber argument; and as a former Third Sea Lord and Controller of the Navy, who had been involved in the bitter controversy with the Air Ministry over the Fleet Air Arm in the 1920s, he was equally determined to reopen the dispute and win it while he was First Sea Lord.

In tendering balanced professional military advice to the Government in the 1930s, the Chiefs still had to swim against two powerful adverse tides: the electorate's fear of another world war and the Treasury demand for economic stringency. Despite the rise of raucous nationalism in Europe and the Far East, political consensus in favour of disarmament and toothless collective security was slow to dissipate. The League of Nations did lose some credibility after the fiasco of trying to impose sanctions upon Mussolini during his rape of Abyssinia, but the ghosts of the Somme and Passchendaele still haunted British minds, making the avoidance of war at almost any cost an article of faith to many people. Rearmament was viewed as a regrettable necessity, but the possibility of having to use those arms was anathema. And fear of war was not lessened by the obvious vulnerability of London to air attack. It was, indeed, increased by the publication of novels like H G Well's, *The Shape of Things to Come*, the film of which opened with a scene in Trafalgar Square of the steeple of St Martin-in-the-Fields crashing down upon terrified crowds within minutes of an outbreak of war.

From the economic point of view, there was a justifiable reluctance to open Treasury coffers for rearmament until the economy had recovered from the 1931 depression. The Chiefs recognised the need for financial caution until there were some signs of returning prosperity, but when recovery did begin, they found themselves faced with the Treasury view that the damage likely to be done to the economy by rearmament posed a greater threat to the country's security than the hypothetical ambitions of the three predator powers. The more obvious the economic strength of Britain and her Empire, the greater would be the deterrent to aggression. Increased armaments could only lead to a financially crippling and politically objectionable arms race.

In his memoirs, *It Might Happen Again*, Chatfield expresses the frustration, which the Chiefs have often felt before and since the

1930s over what they saw as the Treasury's abuse of its executive position:

> Overpowering everything, was the immense power of the Treasury. That power was to be found everywhere. Its proper function of avoiding waste and extravagance, was extended until it ruled as an autocrat in Whitehall, a veritable tyrant. It possessed innumerable officials whose duty it was to be ready to counter the demands of the fighting departments; and in those departments themselves it had its familiars who could, if they used their power, oppose, or delay, all action involving the spending of money. It was a power that was greatly abused.[5]

The Chiefs had also to contend with the usual peacetime mismatch between commitments undertaken by the Foreign Office in its efforts to deter predators and available military resources. Even after rearmament had been accepted as inevitable in 1936, the Treasury demanded that there should be no interference in the country's industrial and mercantile creation of wealth. 'Business as usual', and adherence to the much prized 'voluntary system' in all things, were Government policy until the Munich Crisis in 1938. Normal peacetime contractual methods were enforced; no direction of labour was allowed; and demands for conscription were resisted. Unforgivable delays occurred in making good Services deficiencies, and in overcoming the depredations of the Locust Years.

The drift to war that gathered momentum from 1934 onwards fell into three distinct periods as far as the Chiefs were concerned.

From March 1934 to March 1936, three successive reports by the Defence Requirements Committee, on which they played the dominant role, set the parameters for rearmament from the politico-military point of view.

From April 1936 to September 1938, the Treasury brought the realities of industrial capacity and financial constraints to bear in its endeavours to make the rearmament programmes practicable without putting the economy onto a war footing.

And from October 1938 to September 1939, desperate measures had to be employed to make up the ground lost through political wishful thinking and economic misjudgement in the 1920s and early '30s, which had so reduced the country's military-industrial base that the Services could not spend all the money voted to them when the rush to rearm started.

One man remained at the country's helm throughout the drift to war – Neville Chamberlain. As Chancellor of the Exchequer, he was by far the most powerful personality in Ramsay MacDonald's and

Baldwin's Governments, and it was his views rather than those of the Prime Ministers that really mattered in Whitehall. It was his policy, as we will see, to limit Defence spending for the benefit of the longer-term interests of the economy; to strengthen the Air Force at the expense of the Army; and to concentrate the attention of the Navy on Germany rather than Italy or Japan. When he became Prime Minister in 1937, he supported Sir John Simon, his successor as Chancellor, in maintaining the Treasury grip on expenditure.

With their rearmament programmes delayed and incomplete, and uncertain whether the necessary manpower could be recruited, the Chiefs, when it came to the crunch, had no option but to recommend appeasement, first of Japan, then of Italy and finally of Germany. Indeed, they would have been irresponsible not to have done so. Too much damage had been done by the Ten Year Rule, which had dissipated much of the country's armament manufacturing capacity, and too little time was left after its scrapping in 1933 for Britain to fight over Czechoslovakia in 1938: she was barely ready to defend herself, let alone attack, by 1939.

The Defence Requirements Committee (DRC), which had been set up in November 1933, was an 'Official' as opposed to a 'Minister-ial' committee; and was to be reproduced much later, albeit only for a short time, as the Defence and Overseas Policy (Official) Committee after the Mountbatten reforms in 1964. It consisted of the three Chiefs of Staff, together with Sir Robert Vansittart, rep-resenting the Foreign Office, and Sir Warren Fisher, the Permanent Under-Secretary at the Treasury. By common consent of all the members, Hankey was elected to be its neutral chairman. It was tasked to prepare a programme for meeting the Services *worst* defi-ciencies. France, Italy and the United States were to be taken as friendly. The areas for which preparations were to be considered were the Far East, India, and Europe – in that order – with particu-lar reference to the potential hostility of Japan and Germany. Proposals were to be limited to making good deficiencies that had accumulated during the period of the Ten Year Rule and the abor-tive quest for disarmament. It was the Government's avowed inten-tion to avoid launching a new armaments race.

The DRC first had to clear its collective mind on the threat. Even though Japanese military action in China had been the initial cause of the Chiefs of Staff alarm about the future, it was agreed that Germany presented the longer-term and most dangerous threat. While the most glaring deficiencies in the Far East should be put right, priority should be given to meeting the German threat, and every effort should be made to resume cordial relations with Japan. Warren Fisher went as far as saying *'the worst of our deficiencies is our entanglement with the United States'*. He recommended that Britain should sacrifice American friendship, including making preparations for hostilities with her, in order to regain the more valuable alliance with Japan! The Committee, however, felt that this was going too far[6].

With Germany placed at the top of the list of potential enemies, assessments had to be made of how quickly Hitler could, in fact, rearm; and at what rate British forces could be re-equipped without putting the country on a war footing or upsetting economic recovery. Five years was taken as a reasonable estimate on which to build up the 'Deficiency Programme'. This was nothing more than an educated guess in 1934, but proved remarkably accurate as events unfolded.

The DRC completed its First Report in February 1934. It could not recommend a major capital shipbuilding programme for the Navy because the Washington Naval Treaty limitations would still be in force until 1936. Instead it gave priority to modernisation of existing ships and naval bases, particularly Singapore, work on which it was hoped would be completed by 1938. With Germany as the ultimate enemy, the Committee foresaw the need for an expeditionary force to help in the defence of the Low Countries, which they believed would be vital to the United Kingdom's air defence. They envisaged a force of four infantry divisions, a cavalry division, a tank brigade and two anti-aircraft brigades to be mobilised in one month. It would be supported by an air component of 19 squadrons. In addition, the Army was to be responsible for supplementing the RAF's fighter defences with guns and searchlights. The Air Staff was to complete its 1923 programme of 52 squadrons for Home Defence, which had been cut back during the economic depression and was still 10 squadrons short of establishment. The Fleet Air Arm was also to be expanded to match the naval modernisation programme, and another 10 RAF squadrons were to be raised for use mainly overseas.

The DRC estimated the cost of the First Deficiency Programme as £75m over the five years. They recommended it to the CID as a well balanced, financially practicable and militarily sound programme. They then argued that the worst deficiency in the country's defences lay in the nation's 'moral disarmament', which was outside their remit. It would be up to the Cabinet to decide how to present this very modest programme to the electorate. The omens were not good. At the East Fulham by-election in October 1933, the Labour candidate, advocating continued disarmament and support for collective security, had turned a Tory majority of 14,000 into a deficit of 4,000! There can be little doubt that this reflected the mood of the country.

The Air lobbies in Parliament and in the Press were not slow to suggest once more that air power could solve the country's military and economic problems. Lord Rothermere made amends for this unseemly treatment of Trenchard in 1918. He launched with him a very effective press campaign that played on both the electorate's fear of air attack and Trenchard's well known claim that the RAF could protect the country more efficiently and cheaply than the other two Services. The views expressed coincided with those of Neville Chamberlain, who was tasked by Baldwin to head a ministerial committee to examine the DRC report from the Treasury point of view.

Chamberlain made three assumptions: the Deficiency Programme was too big a burden for the economy to bear, so priorities must be more closely defined; the public's anxieties were about Germany's rearmament and not about Japanese ambitions; and the chief danger was from German air attack. The best immediate defence was a powerful air force based in Britain; and, in the longer term, an Army capable of providing greater depth by helping in the defence of the Low Countries, but which would mobilise more slowly than the DRC envisaged and would be deployed on the Continent at a more leisurely pace while the initial air battles were being fought. He proposed increasing the Home Defence Force by 38 squadrons.

The Chiefs took this political intervention in strategic policy more calmly than might have been expected, and managed to maintain a more or less united front, because Ellington and the Air Staff did not try to make capital out of the RAF's windfall, and they rebutted Chamberlain's proposals as unsound. The Air Staff pointed out that inadequate provision was made for reserve aircraft, without which the scheme was mere window-dressing, designed to placate public opinion and to produce a deterrent facade, which they were convinced would not fool the Germans. Furthermore, they had grave doubts as to whether the RAF's training organisation would be able to provide the air crew and manpower reserves for so large an expansion. A compromise was reached with the Treasury whereby the force would be increased by a more realistic figure of 23 squadrons from 52 to 75 squadrons by 1939, and their reserve backing would be provided between 1939 and 1942. This plan became known as Air Expansion Scheme 'A' – the first of thirteen numbered 'A' to 'M' – and envisaged a first-line strength for the Metropolitan Air Force of 1,252 aircraft.

Amongst the Chiefs themselves, there was continued scepticism about the Government's decision to give so high a priority to air defence. Ellington still doubted the soundness and practicability of Scheme 'A'. Montgomery-Massingberd was not convinced of the air threat to London. From evidence at his disposal, he thought, quite rightly as it turned out, that the *Luftwaffe's* main effort would be deployed in the tactical support of the *Wehrmacht*. He and Chatfield both questioned the Trenchard philosophy of offensive air operations as a war-winning weapon, and whether bombing of open towns was a legitimate method of waging war. With London so vulnerable, it seemed to them unwise to initiate bombing of non-military targets. This uncertainty in 1934 about the wisdom of an offensive air policy was to grow in the minds of British and French political and military leaders.

To pay for the air increases, the Cabinet halved the DRC estimates for the Army by lengthening its re-equipment programme and questioning the need for a BEF; and the Navy's programme was delayed until the outcome of the forthcoming Naval Disarmament Conference, due in June 1935, was known. The Official Historian, Professor Norman Gibbs, summed up the outcome of the First DRC Report:

> The balanced programme of £75m had been amended to one of only two thirds that size, and so altered in distribution that the air gained at the expense of the other two arms for reasons far from convincing on military grounds alone, however much they appealed to the general public.[7]

Such validity as the Government's decisions on the DRC's first report may have had in 1934 did not last long. Hitler became Head of the German State on the death of Hindenburg in August; Japan denounced the Washington Naval Treaty in December; and by the early months of 1935, German rearmament became too blatant to be ignored. France, Italy and Britain came together in February 1935 to form the Stresa Front to contain Germany. The French increased conscription to two years on 15 March, and on the following day Hitler responded by announcing the start of conscription in Germany. At the end of March, Hitler boasted to Sir John Simon and Anthony Eden, during their talks with him in Berlin, that

Germany had already achieved air parity with Britain and was aiming for parity with France's first-line strength of 1,500 aircraft. Intelligence sources revealed that the *Wehrmacht*, which had been restricted to 100,000 men by the Treaty of Versailles, was already 300,000 strong, with 21 infantry and 3 cavalry divisions in being and 2 mechanised divisions in the process of formation; manpower reserves were being created by giving military training to the SS, SA and Reich Labour Service; and the German Navy was well advanced in its modernisation and capital ship construction programmes.

The Air Staff initially questioned Hitler's claim to air parity, but Baldwin, who in March 1934, as Lord President of the Council, had assured the House of Commons that the Government would maintain the RAF's superiority over any other air force within striking distance of the United Kingdom, was forced to confess in May 1935 that parity might have been lost, and announced that a new, enlarged, air expansion plan was in preparation. Behind the scenes, the DRC had been directed to review its first report. It worked quickly. A new Air Expansion Scheme 'C', with a target of 1,512 aircraft for the Metropolitan Air Force by 1937, was accepted by the Cabinet within the month. And the DRC recommended in its Second Deficiency Report at the end of July that the whole Deficiency Programme should be reassessed.

> . . . on the assumption that by the end of the financial year 1938–39 each service should have advanced its state of readiness to the widest necessary extent in relation to the military needs of national defence and within the limits of practicability.[8]

In other words, the true defence requirements were to be assessed free from financial constraint. The only limitation was to be the practicability of carrying through the proposed programmes. It looked to the Chiefs almost too good to be true, and so it proved. The Treasury did not give up easily; the definition of practicability still lay in their hands!

While the DRC worked on its Third Deficiency Report, the international situation continued to deteriorate. The Abyssinian crisis came to a head and burst with Mussolini's invasion in October. The Mediterranean Fleet and British garrisons in Malta, Egypt and Aden were reinforced, but collective security again showed itself to be a mirage. Worse still, the British Government, in its endeavours to make good the popular demand for effective action by the League of Nations, damaged its own strategic interests by alienating Italy, thus endangering its lines of communication through the

Mediterranean to the Far East. The only helpful event, though disliked intensely by France, had been the signing of the Anglo-German
Naval Treaty in June by which Germany accepted limitation to 35
per cent of British Naval strength.

Two new and dynamic personalities had arrived in the Air
Ministry. Lord Swinton had taken over from Lord Londonderry as
Secretary of State when Baldwin became Prime Minister in June
1935, and Group Captain Arthur Harris, the future wartime commander of Bomber Command, had become Deputy Director of Air
Plans. Ellington had so far been reluctant to accept too rapid an
expansion of the RAF because air technology was galloping ahead,
and new aircraft such as the Hurricane and Spitfire fighters and the
Wellington bombers were being developed. He did not wish his
Service to be saddled with too many obsolescent aircraft, and he
continued to object to political window-dressing of the first-line without proper scales of reserves. Swinton and Harris took a more positive line. Under their ebullient influence, the Air Staff cashed in on
the Abyssinian crisis and made the case for a more ambitious and
better balanced expansion plan: Scheme 'F', with a Metropolitan Air
Force Target of 1,736 first-line aircraft and properly balanced reserves by 1939. This was approved by the Cabinet in February 1936,
ahead of the DRC's Third Deficiency Report, which was not finalised
until March, after Hitler had reoccupied the Rhineland.

The Third Deficiency Report was by far the most important of the
DRC reports. The crucial importance of the close relationship between Foreign and Defence policy was underlined, the Committee
stating that it should be:

> . . . a cardinal requirement of our national and imperial security that our
> foreign policy should be so conducted as to avoid the possible development of a
> situation in which we might be confronted with the hostility, open or veiled, of
> Japan in the Far East, Germany in the West, and any Power on the main line of
> communication between the two.[9]

The Chiefs were henceforth to warn the Government at frequent
intervals of the dangers of being faced with war on three fronts. It
was, in their opinion, the greatest danger against which the Foreign
Office should guard. Accommodating Japan was vital, and it was
important to stay closely aligned with France in the Mediterranean,
since it would not be practicable to prepare for war with Italy as well
as Germany in the time scale of the Deficiency Programme.

In recommending the measures that should be taken, they stressed that they were no longer dealing with 'worst deficiencies', but with measures of rearmament to bring the Services up to readiness for war by 1939 – a very different matter. Indeed, they were presenting the Government with the bill for the country's years of idealism since 1918; a bill so big that Baldwin and his Cabinet Colleagues were to find it difficult to present to the electorate.

As far as the Navy was concerned, the DRC concluded that the One-Power Standard must be replaced with a modified Two-Power Standard – the so called DRC Standard – that would enable a large enough fleet to be dispatched East of Suez to deter the Japanese while leaving an adequate force in Home waters for war with Germany. A full Two-Power Standard would have meant creating an offensive capability against both Germany and Japan, which was beyond the bounds of practicability by 1939. As it was, the DRC Standard would require the replacement of seven capital ships in the years 1936 to 1939; five new cruisers per year in the same period; four new aircraft-carriers by 1942; and accelerated building of destroyers and escorts.

The DRC was equally robust about the needs of the Army. It was seen as having three tasks, which in order of priority were: maintaining overseas garrisons in support of the civil power in the Colonial Empire; providing its share of Home Defence, including anti-aircraft defences; and enabling Britain to dispatch a Field Force overseas with adequate equipment and reserves to give it reasonable endurance. They pointed to the probable use of the Field Force in the defence of the Low Countries since their retention in friendly hands was vital to the successful air as well as naval defence of the United Kingdom. The DRC proposed a BEF of five divisions and an air component for movement to the Continent within a fortnight, which would be followed by four Territorial divisions in four months, another four in six months, and a final four two months later. They pointed out that the regular Field Force would lack endurance, as it had done in 1914, if it was not backed up by the Territorial Army as they proposed.

The DRC supported the Air Ministry's Scheme 'F', because, in their view, the previous schemes lacked a proper balance between first-line and reserves. They called also for an acceleration of the establishment of 'shadow' factories for the rapid expansion of aircraft production, if and when, the Government was forced to abandon its 'business as usual' policy.

The Cabinet studied the DRC's Third Deficiency Report at the end of February 1936. The main recommendations were accepted in principle, but again hedged with limitations in practice. As far as the Navy was concerned, there was to be no public announcement of the change from the naval One-Power to the DRC Two-Power Standard; only two replacement capital ships would be laid down in the 1936 programme; and the whole programme was to be considered provisional until the battleship versus bomber controversy had been resolved. The Army came off much worse. The establishment of a five division Field Force with its air component was accepted, but not the Territorial Army follow-up, on the grounds that it was not practical to re-equip both the regular formations and the twelve TA divisions in the time-scale. The TA would only be equipped with training scales of modern weapons, and no plans would be made for their dispatch to the Continent. Only the Air Force recommendations were left unscathed.

Once Hitler had reoccupied the Rhineland, all the alarm bells should then have sounded in Westminster and Whitehall. Some did, of course, but the general consensus was that Hitler was only putting to rights the wrongs of Versailles. Once Germany was re-established as a member of the European community of nations, Hitler's ambitions would be fulfilled and he would become easier to handle. The wish was father to the thought, especially in the Treasury, where the Services were suspected of using the crisis to grab an unfair share of national resources.

The Treasury was, however, on firmer ground in objecting to the piecemeal nature of the rearmament programmes, and it was not alone in its criticisms. The naval, air, and, to a lesser extent, army lobbies in Parliament and the Press were unhappy about the treatment of their adopted Service. The Navy's allocation of cash was said to be too large; the Air Force share too small; and no one seemed to care much about the Army, which was less well represented and still apparently happy to get on with 'real soldiering' around the Colonial Empire. Indeed, there was quite a body of opinion in the Army, including several eminent generals, and encouraged by Liddell Hart, who believed that sending an expeditionary force to the Continent was asking for trouble. It would be too small to make a significant contribution to the land battle, and so Britain's continental commitment should be confined to RAF operations, while the Army was kept for imperial defence.

In these debates about defence policy, the old demand for a Ministry of Defence broke surface once more. The Chiefs were accused of continuous in-fighting, of shelving difficult inter-Service problems, and of needing an independent chairman, who could adjudicate between them, all of which was no longer true under Chatfield's chairmanship. Nevertheless, on Hankey's advice, Baldwin chose to appoint a Minister for the Co-ordination of Defence, primarily to relieve himself of some of the growing burden of formulating Defence policy and to help shape the disparate rearmament programmes in a coherent and financially practical manner. Both Baldwin and Hankey were opposed to the creation of a Ministry of Defence: the former because its Secretary of State could become a serious rival to the Prime Minister; and the latter because he saw that it would undermine his own authority.

Baldwin had some difficulty in filling the post. Sir Austen Chamberlain refused it; Churchill was considered too much of a warmonger; and Sir Samuel Hoare was still under a political cloud for the Hoare-Laval peace plan for ending the Abyssinian crisis. Eventually the choice fell on Sir Thomas Inskip, a former Attorney-General. Baldwin seems to have chosen him for the clarity of his legal mind and mastery of complex briefs. Neville Chamberlain did not see him as an ideal choice, but accepted that he was nonetheless 'strong and sound' and would 'make no friction with either the Chiefs of Staff or the Service Ministers'.[10] Churchill was less charitable, describing the choice as 'the strangest appointment since Caligula made his horse a consul'. But while Inskip may not have had the dynamic qualities needed in a Minister of Defence, he was well suited to the more limited role of a co-ordinator. Regrettably, from the Chiefs' point of view, he was to become the willing tool of the Treasury, and there was an increasing risk that, if the Chiefs could not agree a common doctrine, they would have one imposed upon them by politicians and civil servants, who might subordinate military considerations to financial and economic requirements.

With the Cabinet acceptance in principle of the DRC's Third Report and with Inskip's appointment as Minister for the Co-ordination of Defence in March 1936, the period of defining the Defence parameters ended and rearmament began, but the world did not stand still, nor did the threat posed by the three expansionist powers diminish. The Treasury, however, had grave and realistic doubts about the practicability of the DRC's programmes.

In July 1936, the Spanish Civil War began. Britain was drawn once again into the imbroglio of abortive League of Nations' peace-keeping efforts, which gave Hitler and Mussolini further opportuni-

ties to flex their military muscles. In November, the Rome-Berlin
Axis was formed and the Anti-Comintern Pact was announced between Germany, Italy and Japan, which was to make it much more
difficult for the Foreign Office to placate one, let alone two, of
Britain's potential enemies. It was with some relief, therefore, that
the Chiefs welcomed the Anglo-Italian 'Gentlemen's Agreement' to
respect each others interests in the Mediterranean, which was signed
in January 1937.

But there was no other relief for the hard pressed Chiefs in either
the Far East, where the Japanese were renewing their attacks in
China, or in Europe, where Intelligence sources were providing evidence of acceleration in the *Luftwaffe's* expansion, which was by then
aimed at giving Germany air parity with the large Soviet Air Force.
The Air Ministry, acting on the Government's promise to maintain
parity with any air force within striking distance of the United
Kingdom, introduced Scheme 'H' to raise the first-line strength of
the Metropolitan Air Force up to 2,422 aircraft. Much of the expansion was to be in bombers, but there had to be some pruning of
reserves to make the air-frame and engine requirements match production. Training air crew and maintenance personnel was by then
becoming the most critical factor in the successive expansion schemes
brought in to match the *Luftwaffe's* growth.

In the first few months of Inskip's tenure in charge of the rearmament programmes, Chatfield persuaded ministers to remove some of
the uncertainties about the naval programme by questioning the Air
Ministry's contention that money should be spent on bombers and
not on 'outmoded' capital ships. Chatfield won the battle on the
grounds of whole-life costing, and the need to maintain a 'belt and
braces' policy until the vulnerability arguments were proved one way
or the other by war. Lay lobbyists suggested that a thousand
bombers could be bought for the cost of one battleship. When the
Admiralty professionals did comparative whole-life costings, they
concluded that one battleship equated to forty-five medium bombers.
The Air Ministry experts, much to their own surprise, came up with
a figure of thirty-seven bombers for one battleship![11] Ministers were
convinced of the need to retain the battleship not by these costings,
but by Chatfield's argument that:

> If we rebuild the battle-fleet and spend many millions in doing so, and then war
> comes and the airmen are right, and all our battleships are rapidly destroyed by
> air attack, our money will largely have been thrown away. But if we do not
> rebuild it and war comes, and the airman is wrong and our airmen cannot

destroy the enemy's capital ships, and they are left at large with impunity on the world's oceans and destroy our convoys, then we shall lose the British Empire.[12]

Chatfield was almost as successful when he reopened the Fleet Air Arm argument in July 1936. Such had been the public and ministerial pressure to insure air parity for the Metropolitan Air Force that the Air Ministry had been forced to give naval aviation a lower priority than the Admiralty deemed necessary to meet the operational requirements of the Fleet. Conditions had also changed since Balfour rejected the naval case in 1923 in favour of maintaining a 'Unified Air Force'. The Fleet Air Arm now represented only a fraction of the country's total air strength; interchangeability of flying personnel was accepted by both sides as impracticable; and the operation of aircraft at sea had become too specialised for there to be much commonality between the two environments.

Baldwin did not accept Chatfield's persistent demands for a new enquiry until March 1937, two months before he resigned as Prime Minister. As a preliminary step, he asked Inskip to discuss the vexed problem with the Chiefs of Staff before putting it to a ministerial committee. The committee never met because Inskip produced an acceptable compromise. He questioned the validity of the Air Ministry's argument about the need for 'maximum flexibility' on the one hand, and the Admiralty's demand for 'specialisation' on the other. The Air Ministry had, in his view, a strong case for controlling all shore-based aircraft to give flexibility in air operations; and he found the Admiralty's argument, that carrier and other warship-borne aircraft were an integral part of the Navy's armament, equally telling. The solution that he proposed was elegantly simple: shore based aircraft should remain under the RAF, while ship-borne aircraft should pass to Admiralty control. Chatfield clinched the deal by accepting centralised procurement of all aircraft.

The Cabinet confirmed the agreed compromise in July 1937, but it took almost two years to unravel the existing organisation. The Fleet Air Arm did not pass to Admiralty control until May 1939.

While these Naval/Air arguments were being resolved, there was a change of CIGS. Montgomery-Massingberd handed over to Sir Cyril Deverell at the end of his tenure in April 1936. His contributions to the Chiefs of Staff and DRC debates had been sensible and constructive, but his task had not been easy, with Army requirements accorded lowest priority by the Government. Chatfield was remarkably sympathetic: the Army, he saw, was entering a phase of techno-

logical revolution similar to the Navy's in Jackie Fisher's day before
the First World War. In his memoirs he comments:

> But Lord Fisher, at his best, could not have rebuilt the Navy without money.
> Nor could the Army emerge from its great past into a new future, when the
> Army Estimates were cut to the bone. . . . Plans were laid by the Supply Board
> to increase army production, to equip factories, and to increase material sup-
> plies when the bell struck. But the bell never struck, and plans remained on
> paper, because the money was withheld, for few wanted an expensive Army if it
> could possibly be avoided.[13]

Deverell was a Guernsey man, who had been commissioned into
the West Yorkshire Regiment in 1895. He had shown outstanding
command abilities in the First World War as a Divisional
Commander, and had then served in India, becoming its
Quartermaster-General (QMG) in 1927 before returning to England
to command Western and then Eastern commands in the early
1930s. He was 63 when appointed CIGS and promoted field marshal, but his tenure was only to last eighteen months. When
Chamberlain became Prime Minister in May 1937, he appointed the
ambitious showman Hore Belisha in place of the able but idle Duff
Cooper as Secretary of State for War. Deverell was anathema to the
new Secretary of State, who found him obstructive and lacking in the
dynamism that he and his self-appointed unofficial adviser, Liddell
Hart, deemed necessary for the belated modernisation of the Army.

By the beginning of 1937, Chamberlain had become increasingly
worried about the strain being placed on the economy by rearmament. He was also coming under increasing pressure from within the
Treasury to establish priorities and to set a ceiling on Defence expenditure. When he became Prime Minister in May, he kept Inskip on
as Minister for Co-ordination of Defence, although he had made little
impact so far upon Defence policy. Inskip, however, came into his
own when Chamberlain set in hand the first of two major Treasury
reviews of the effects of the rearmament programmes upon the economy which started work that month. In these reviews, the Treasury
was not unreasonably trying to turn the DRC's requirements into
economically and industrially practical programmes.

Chamberlain, Simon and Inskip had much in common in their
thinking and methods of working, but it was Chamberlain who
provided the lead and forced his long held views upon the Review
Committee and the Cabinet: '*priority for the Royal Air Force, if not
always in the shape that the Air Staff wanted; a strong Navy, but directed
against Germany and not designed to fight two major naval enemies at once; and*

an Army designed for imperial policing and small wars, not for "Continental adventures".[14] Inskip became his principal agent for imposing these views and Simon's financial policies upon the Chiefs.

A process very similar to a modern Defence Review was set in train: the Treasury set the financial ceiling; the Service departments presented costings of their programmes for five years instead of today's ten; the Chiefs under Inskip's chairmanship determined priorities from their points of view; and the Cabinet was left to accept or reject the strategic implications. The Treasury maintained that the most that the economy would be able to bear over five years was £1,500m, of which £1,100m would come from revenue and £400m from War Loan.

By October 1937, the Service ministries had done their sums based upon the Third DRC Report. Their total for the three costings came to £1,605m, but before the ink was dry on the Air estimate, the *Luftwaffe's* General Erhard Milch, on a visit to London, revealed some startling increases in German air strength, which induced the Air Ministry to propose a new Scheme 'J', some 25 per cent larger and faster than Scheme 'F'. Scheme 'J', if approved, would raise the overall financial requirement to £1,884m, and it could not be carried out at the speed required on a 'business as usual' basis. Priority would have to be accorded to aircraft production; materials in short supply would need to be rationed; and there might have to be direction of skilled labour.

Inskip worked with the Chiefs to provide the Cabinet with an interim report by December, in which he set out the general principles that he advocated. The problem was not so much money, but manpower, productive capacity, financial confidence and the general balance of trade. The maintenance of economic stability should be treated, he said, as *'a fourth arm in defence, alongside the three Defence Services'*.[15] Germany could best be deterred by establishing the conviction in Hitler's mind that he could not win with a quick knockout, and that Germany would be faced with a long war which she was unlikely to be able to survive against the combined resources of the British Empire once they were fully mobilised. Not only must Britain be strong enough to withstand an attempted knock-out, but she must be seen to be strong enough to sustain a long war as well. The converse was true: if the aggressor powers detected any signs of economic strain, the deterrent effect of high peacetime defence expenditure would be lost. The Cabinet must balance the size of military forces considered necessary by the Chiefs of Staff for deterrence against the need to re-establish a strong economy. His most telling conclusion was:

> Nothing operates more strongly to deter a potential aggressor from attacking this country than our stability, and the power which this nation has so often shown of overcoming its difficulties without violent change, and without damage to its inherent strength.[16]

When the Cabinet discussed Inskip's paper in December 1937, many of the points had echoes in the post-war Defence reviews: the accelerating cost of equipment development due to galloping technology; the need to avoid 'gold plated' weapon systems; the inevitability of cost over-runs; and the need to reassess priorities to make ends meet. The Chiefs were given new strategic guidelines. Their priorities were to be: the defence of the United Kingdom as the hub of the Empire; the protection of the sea routes; the defence of overseas territories; and, only after these had been catered for, the support of any allies Britain might gather in war. The continental liability, calling for an expeditionary force, had suddenly all but vanished.

The Cabinet accepted that in order to bring spending down to the £1,500m the Navy must certainly be restricted to the DRC and not the full Two-Power Standard; the Army should concentrate on anti-aircraft defence largely provided by the TA at home, and on imperial commitments abroad for which its Field Force would be equipped on 'colonial scales' for use most probably in Egypt, the vital focal point on the line of communication to the Far East; and the RAF should increase the fighter strength of the Metropolitan Air Force at the expense of slower and more expensive bomber production, and of its overseas squadrons.

In fact, the switch from bomber to fighter aircraft production was not due to any new tactical thinking by the Air Staff: on the contrary, Newall had circulated a letter to RAF commands, informing them that there was no weakening of the Air Staff's belief in an offensive policy based on bomber forces. The initiative came from Treasury officials, who argued that Britain did not possess the industrial capacity to overtake German bomber production; it was logical, therefore, that a switch should be made to more quickly produced and cheaper defensive fighter aircraft. The Foreign Office suggested that it might also be possible to negotiate some limitation on the size of bomber forces on the lines of the Anglo-German Naval Agreement if concessions were made to assuage Hitler's colonial ambitions.

Lord Halifax, Lord President of the Council, who became Foreign

Secretary after Eden's resignation over appeasement in February 1938, was due to meet Hitler shortly. The Cabinet decided that he should offer a deal of this kind. In the end, no agreement was reached with Hitler over the limitation of bomber forces, but ironically it was the Treasury-inspired switch from bomber to fighter production, taken on industrial and economic grounds, that was to save Britain in 1940.

The Chiefs were given until February 1938 to reassess their programmes on the basis of the new guidelines. However, by then commitments and costs had escalated and the new sum needed was £2,000m, with every chance that it would go on creeping up. The Treasury calculated that £1,650m was the most that could be spent without giving up the 'business as usual' policy. Inskip, reflecting the views of the Chiefs of Staff, concluded bleakly:

> ... the burden in peace-time of taking the steps which we are advised – I believe rightly – are prudent and indeed necessary in present circumstances, is too great for us. I therefore repeat with fresh emphasis the opinion which I have already expressed as to the importance of reducing the scale of our commitments and the number of our potential enemies.[17]

No minister disagreed with Chamberlain's summing up that the alternatives facing the country were either expense on a scale which carried its own dangers, or an improvement of relations with potential enemies however difficult it might be to find a proper compromise.[18] This was shorthand for appeasement.

The Chiefs had naturally been watching the Cabinet debate on the Treasury Review with acute anxiety, and had put in hand their own review of strategy, which led to their COS paper, which gave the famous warning that the military situation was:

> ... fraught with greater risk than at any time in living memory, apart from the war years.[19]

They went on to recommend that the Government should take powers to control industry and manpower to eliminate delays that were being experienced in the current programmes, and to implement even larger programmes if necessary.

The Chiefs did not need to argue their case. Hitler did it for them. In March, the Austrian Anschluss took place, and Czechoslovakia became embarrassingly vulnerable from the Western Powers' point of view. The Cabinet sought the Chiefs' views on what could be done. They were not encouraging. They reported:

> ... no pressure that we and our possible allies can bring to bear, either by sea,

on land, or in the air, could prevent Germany from invading and over-running Bohemia and from inflicting a decisive defeat on the Czechoslovakian Army. We should then be faced with the necessity of undertaking a war against Germany for the purpose of restoring Czechoslovakia's lost integrity and this object would only be achieved by the defeat of Germany and as the outcome of a long struggle.[20]

They put the position more succinctly when they wrote:

We can do nothing to prevent the dog getting the bone, and we have no means of making him give it up, except by killing him by a slow process of attrition and starvation.[21]

On 24 March 1938, Chamberlain announced in the Commons:

In order to bring about the progress which we feel to be necessary, men and materials will be required, and rearmament work must have first priority in the nation's effort. The full and rapid equipment of the nation for self-defence must be its primary aim.[22]

'Business as usual' was at last cancelled; Air Expansion Scheme 'L' was authorised with fighters given an even higher priority than in Scheme 'J'; but the Army remained for the time being the Cinderella of the rearmament ball. The Cabinet, the Chiefs and the electorate were still determined to avoid a continental commitment. Staff talks with France were opened at Military Attaché level on a very restricted basis. It was to be made clear to the French that only two divisions would be available on 'colonial' scales of equipment at the outbreak of war, and that there was no commitment to send them to the Continent. There was no double-talk as there had been in 1914: the French were told to expect no support on land.

During these crucial debates there had been two changes amongst the Chiefs. Ellington had been succeeded by Sir Cyril Newall (later Lord Newall) in September 1937 after four and a half years in the post, during which the series of escalating Air Expansion Programmes from 'A' to 'J' had been implemented; the Hurricane, Spitfire, Wellington and the forerunners of the Lancaster had been developed; and Radar had been brought to a state of operational usefulness. These were no mean feats, and are a testament to Ellington's abilities as a staff officer. By objecting to the political window-dressing of a showy first-line strength without adequate reserves, and by insisting on a balanced expansion of the RAF, he laid the foundations not only for victory in the Battle of Britain, but for the Combined Bomber Offensive at the climax of the War. He had many critics, who accused him of being misanthropic and politically naive in that he maintained that politics were the concern of his

Secretary of State and not his. And in the Chiefs of Staff Committee he was less forceful and more prepared to compromise than his predecessors had been. He did not laud the priority accorded to the RAF by the Cabinet and the electorate in their discussions, and he supported Chatfield in his determination that the Chiefs should always present balanced inter-Service views and recommendations to the CID and Cabinet.

Newall took over at a time when the Air Staff were smarting over the loss of the Fleet Air Arm argument, and were hoping for a return to a more forceful 'Air Force über alles' type of leadership. They were to be somewhat disappointed. Sir John Slessor, who was Deputy Director (effectively Director) of Air Plans at the time gives a pen-picture of Newall in his memoirs, *Central Blue*: outwardly self-confident in manner, but reserved and difficult to get to know; a more forceful character than he appeared to be, and the last man to claim intellectual abilities; and a sound, level-headed decision-maker, who stuck to his policies. In appearance he was not unlike Anthony Eden: always well groomed, with a clipped moustache, and his hat set at the 'Beatty' angle. Slessor commented '*I have never met a man who was so good for one's morale as Newall; when times were at their worst I would come out of his office feeling as though I'd just had a stiff whisky and soda*'[23].

One unfortunate aspect of Newall's selection as CAS in 1937 was that he was a bomber man at a time when fighters were being given priority. He had commanded the RAF's earliest strategic bomber force based in France in 1917, and he was an advocate of the offensive use of bombers as the best form of air defence. However, he did not appreciate fully that Bomber Command in 1938–9 was not capable of delivering the knockout blow that his great supporter, Trenchard, had envisaged. Its aircraft did not have the range or bomb-load needed; there were too few of them; their navigational instruments and bombing aids were inadequate; and their crews were not properly trained for the role. Sir Edgar Ludlow-Hewitt, who took over Bomber Command at the time Newall became CAS, reported that his new command was:

> entirely unprepared for war, unable to operate except in fair weather, and extremely vulnerable in the air and on the ground.[24]

The weapon for a counter-air offensive upon which Newall and his Air Planners were counting in 1937, had not, as yet, been forged.

Three months after Newall took over, Deverell, the CIGS, had finally succumbed to Hore Belisha's determination to be rid of what he saw as the moribund old guard on the Army Council. His dismissal by the Secretary of State was typical and discourteous in the extreme. Deverell arrived in his office one morning to find a letter on his desk sacking him! Hore Belisha was keen to appoint an expert in mechanised warfare to command the new Mobile Division, in which a number of cavalry regiments had to exchange their horses for armoured cars and light tanks. Deverell had wanted the job given to a cavalryman, Major-General Blakiston Houston, the Inspector of Cavalry, to ease the psychologically awkward transition for the regiments concerned. The Army Council compromised by appointing Major-General Alan Brooke, a forward looking artilleryman and a good horseman, who was to become Churchill's great wartime CIGS. The fact that Deverell should have tried to insist on a cavalryman for Britain's only mechanised force indicated an attitude of mind that Hore Belisha, strongly influenced by Liddell Hart and the young Turks of the Army, deplored.

But this was only the last straw in the unhappy saga of Hore Belisha's crusade to modernise the Army. He had already written to the Prime Minister setting out the aims of his reformation as the elimination of: the 1914–18 mentality and preparing for the last war; refusal by the Army Council to divert funds to mechanisation and anti-aircraft defences; the Army's obsession with India; its attachment to the policy of 'Buggins' turn next'; the inclination not to give the go-ahead in weapon development until perfection had been achieved; and the complacency and the stagnant atmosphere of the War Office. Chamberlain, when faced with the choice of losing the CIGS and most of the Army Council, or his energetic, publicity seeking Secretary of State for War, perhaps rightly, chose to keep the latter[25].

Selecting a successor for Deverell was not easy. Sir John Dill, the GOC-in-C, Aldershot Command and Field Force Commander (designate), was the obvious choice, but he had had a serious riding accident and was unfit. Sir Edmund Ironside, GOC-in-C, Eastern Command, had never served in Whitehall and was openly critical of politicians and all their works. Sir Archibald Wavell, GOC-in-C, Palestine, was considered by Hore Belisha to be too inarticulate and over-demanding. With Liddell Hart at his elbow, he chose the Military Secretary, the Viscount Gort, VC, whom he had only recently brought into this important post from the Staff College in his search for new blood.

Hore Belisha had already dipped down the Army List once to promote Gort over the heads of other excellent officers to make him the Military Secretary. He did so again to promote him CIGS. Gort had got on with him tolerably well in the business of selecting senior commanders and staff officers, which is the Military Secretary's primary function, but he was soon to find that Gort was not his man any more than Deverell had been. He had not been keen to take on the responsibilities of the Army's Chief in the first place, and, indeed, it was not the right job for him and he knew it. He was essentially a commander with a pronounced tactical flare and an ambition to lead the Army in the field if war came. He was too straightforward and lacking in political guile to be successful in fighting for the Army in the jungles of Whitehall, and he was certainly not the man to work with so devious a politician as Hore Belisha. Their relationship could only deteriorate, and this it did as the last two hectic years of peace raced by[26].

During 1938, the year of the Munich crisis, there were two further changes in the Chiefs of Staff Committee. Maurice Hankey retired in July and Chatfield did so in September. It is easiest to breach chronology here to consider these changes before dealing with the Munich débâcle.

Hankey had been Cabinet Secretary for some twenty years and Secretary of the CID for over quarter of a century. The combination of the two jobs had been possible not only because he had helped to create them and had grown up with them, but, more importantly, because his abilities were unique. The *Times* commented at the time of his retirement: '*Hankey's versatility cannot become a heritable organisation*'.[27] Nor was it. After he left, his responsibilities were split into two separate, though closely associated, organisations within the Cabinet Office structure. Sir Edward Bridges, from the Treasury, took over as Cabinet Secretary; and Colonel 'Pug' Ismay (later Lord Ismay), one of Hankey's military assistant secretaries, whom we met earlier disputing the RAF's account of their successes during the 'Mad Mullah' campaign in Somaliland in 1920, inherited the secretaryship of the CID and Chiefs of Staff Committee.

The nickname 'Pug' aptly described Ismay's appearance and determination. Shortish, square faced with dark prominent eyebrows and a boxer style nose, he had as incisive a brain as Hankey; the ability to anticipate the Chiefs' requirements and to articulate in the minutes their less well expressed views and sometimes confused discussions; and the happy knack of never appearing to intrude on their deliberations, but always being ready to help smooth out their differences by working unobtrusively behind the scenes with their personal staffs to clear up misunderstandings. The jingle often ascribed to one of his team, and written at the time of the Casablanca Conference in January 1943, describes his task admirably:

> When the great ones depart and go for their dinner,
> The Secretary stays getting thinner and thinner,
> Trying to recall from his notes and his head,
> All that they hoped that they really had said.

Chatfield retired two months later, just after the Munich Crisis in September 1938. Newall succeeded him as Chairman of the Chiefs of Staff Committee. There were no problems about Chatfield's successor as First Sea Lord. He had been grooming Sir Roger Backhouse for the job for some time. Backhouse had followed Chatfield as Third Sea Lord and Controller of the Navy, and had been C-in-C Home Fleet since 1935. The only other possible candidate was Sir Dudley Pound, the C-in-C Mediterranean Fleet. Backhouse was a striking man, six foot four inches tall, with great strength of character and a winning personality, who was unswervingly devoted to the Navy; but, like Jellicoe and other great sailors before him, he found decentralisation difficult and tended to overwork. He was not in good health when he took over. Sadly he had to relinquish his duties as the Navy's Chief in May 1939, and died in July. Dudley Pound succeeded him.

Chamberlain's appeasement of Hitler during the Munich crisis of September 1938, which was supported by the Chiefs at the time because Britain was so unready for war, was the tragic denouement of the Ten Year Rule, the inadequate Deficiency Programmes, and the Treasury tendency to over-emphasise economic stability at the expense of security when rearmament at last got under way in 1936. If the economic philosophy of 'Business as Usual' had been replaced by 'Business for War' at the time of Hitler's march into the Rhineland, more might then have been achieved in overcoming the country's defenceless state, caused by its earlier near-pacifist idealism. But even in the months after Munich, when every day counted in Britain's desperate efforts to make ready for war, lower level Treasury control was maintained in an unreasoning way more by force of habit than by deliberate policy.

But after Munich, the Chiefs of Staff and the Foreign Office almost, but not quite, ousted the Treasury as the dominant advisers to the Cabinet. The financially inclined Inskip was replaced as Minister for the Co-ordination of Defence in February 1939 by the alert and busness like Admiral Lord Chatfield (raised to the peerage in 1937), who brought soundly based military views into Cabinet discussions. And when Hitler swallowed the rump of Czechoslovakia in March, appeasement efforts slackened as ministers concluded that the Dictators would have to be curbed whatever the cost to the economy.

As crisis after crisis unfolded, the Chiefs of Staff Committee provided the Cabinet with a series of well argued and prescient papers on the strategy that they advocated if war were to come in Europe, in the Mediterranean and Middle East, or in the Far East. The Chiefs themselves were working well together as a team, and were supported by strong and efficient Joint Planning and Joint Intelligence Committees. Few British Cabinets had ever been better briefed by its professional military advisers in the run-up to a war.

Munich changed the perceptions of both the Cabinet and the Chiefs in a number of interconnected ways. The dread of a commitment to intervene on land in Europe was slowly transformed – but only slowly – into a fear that the weak and disunited French Government might seek an accommodation with Hitler and leave Britain to face her three enemies alone if France was not given the fullest British military support. The accepted British strategic policy of intervening on the Continent with only Naval and Air Forces while the Army looked after the Middle East, India and British imperial interests, was seen in France as the usual action of 'Perfidious Albion' intent on fighting to the last drop of French blood. Even from the British point of view, the validity of that policy was becoming increasingly doubtful. The potential of a British naval blockade of Germany had been weakened by Hitler's successes in Eastern Europe, which, if exploited, would give him access to ample alternative sources of supply. And the idea of Bomber Command attacking critical economic targets in Germany no longer looked so attractive with London and Paris lying within easy reach of the now vastly superior bomber forces of the *Luftwaffe*, while Berlin lay beyond the effective reach of the British and French Air Forces.

Views of the RAF's capabilities also changed as Munich demonstrated how near to war the country might be. Despite all the RAF expansion schemes, parity with the *Luftwaffe* had not been regained. The Trenchard Doctrine of offensive counter-air operations had to give way to the deterrent philosophy of the C-in-C Fighter Command, Sir Hugh Dowding, based upon 'Fear of the Fighter'. Dowding wrote:

The best defence of the country is the Fear of the Fighter. If we are strong in fighters we should probably never be attacked in force. If we are moderately strong we shall probably be attacked and the attacks will be gradually brought to a standstill. During this period considerable damage will have been caused. If we are weak in fighter strength, the attacks will not be brought to a standstill and the productive capacity of the country will be virtually destroyed. The other components of the Metropolitan Air Force will then become wasting assets and preservation of their numbers at the present time will prove to have been a fruitless sacrifice . . .[28]

With Air Defence of London standing firmly top of the Cabinet's strategic priorities, a change in Air policy came more easily and quickly than an acceptance of a need for a fully equipped British Expeditionary Force. A new and, as it turned out, final revised Air Expansion Plan 'M' was endorsed in November 1938, giving the highest priority to fighter production and training of fighter pilots. By February 1939, the output of fighters was 25 per cent up on forecasts with some 470 fighters coming off the production lines per month. By the end of June, Fighter Command had 200 reserve aircraft in stock. The turning point in aircraft production as a whole had been reached, but this had been achieved at a price. It would be many, many months before fighter could give way once more to bomber production, and the Trenchard Doctrine of offensive air-warfare could be re-established[29].

Gort and Hore Belisha had a much more difficult row to hoe in creating a consensus in favour of giving the Army increased priority in case the provision of a fully equipped BEF became necessary to preserve the Anglo-French collaboration in the containment of Germany. Despite their personal animosity, they both fought well together on the Army's behalf in the autumn of 1938. It was not, however, until the end of the year that the Chiefs of Staff Committee started their examination of the War Office proposals to equip four regular infantry divisions and two mobile divisions on 'European' warfare scales, two divisions in the Middle East to 'Colonial' scales, and to provide war equipment and reserves for the first four TA divisions. The rest of the TA were to be given only training scales of modern equipment for the time being.

The Chiefs were divided on the continental issue. Newall, their new Chairman, was bitterly opposed to any suggestion of making it possible to support the French on land with more than the token force of the two regular divisions already tentatively agreed. It has been suggested that his opposition was due to his fear that cash would be drawn away from the Air Force programmes, but this was not so. He saw that if the Cabinet succumbed to French political pressure for British intervention on land, the commitment would act as a suction pump and would draw off Army and Air resources needed to protect the United Kingdom from attack by Germany and British imperial interests from Italian and Japanese depredations. With Dowding leaning over his shoulder, he could not but argue that provision of an Air component for the BEF, the lowest priority in British strategy, would seriously weaken the Air Defence of the British Isles, the highest priority.

Backhouse was also opposed initially to the War Office plan because he too disliked unlimited commitments, and because he believed the country did not possess the manpower or industrial capacity to build up all three Services. The decision to avoid a continental commitment for the Army, in his view, should not be changed. Gort, however, stood his ground, recalling Kitchener's farsightedness in1914 and his words that no country could ever wage 'a little war'. The limited liability policy being pursued by the Government could well turn out to be a dangerous myth. The defence of the Low Countries for air defence reasons alone, and quite apart from the danger of France succumbing to Hitler's ambitious political plans for a new German dominated Europe, could well necessitate British intervention on land.

Newall overplayed his hand as far as the Navy was concerned. He belittled the importance of the Channel ports and adjacent airfields, and was roundly condemned by Backhouse, who swung the debate in Gort's favour. The Chiefs then tried to have their cake and eat it. Their paper to the CID was not considered by the Cabinet until the beginning of February, such was the lack of real urgency still prevailing in Whitehall. It started by disclaiming any intention of overturning agreed Government policy, but recommended that it would be prudent to accept the War Office proposals. Chamberlain, Sir John Simon the Chancellor, and Sir Samuel Hoare, the Home Secretary – the inner circle – objected to the plan on the old argument that overspending on defence would destroy the country that it was designed to protect. Halifax, the Foreign Secretary, supported Hore Belisha, declaring that he would prefer bankruptcy to defeat and domination by Germany. The Cabinet procrastinated, and then only authorised the provision of training scales of modern equipment for the TA. The rest of the War Office plan was deferred for further examination by the Treasury, and by Chatfield as the new Minister for Co-ordination of Defence.

Some sense of urgency was created by intelligence reports of German plans to occupy the Low Countries. At the end of February, Chamberlain accepted 'with the greatest reluctance' that there was no alternative to the Army re-equipment plans. Munich had given Hitler what he wanted in the East; he was now free to concentrate much larger forces against France and the Low Countries in the West. It was, therefore, necessary in his view to give up the concept of one general purpose army equipped for service anywhere and to replace it with two armies: one for use in Europe and the other for service elsewhere. But this did not mean that the Government would be accepting the continental commitment: it would merely be taking prudent precautions. The War Office was, at long last, able to start its expansion and re-equipment plans for the Army, but it was starting four years behind the *Wehrmacht*!

The Spring of 1939 was almost a repeat of 1938 as far as the Chiefs' strategic appreciations were concerned. They had just completed their 'European Appreciation for 1939–40', when Hitler gobbled up the rump of Czechoslovakia in March, outdating it just as decisively as his Austrian *Anschluss* had done in 1938. Nevertheless, it was a masterpiece in forward thinking that set out the probable course of the coming war with remarkable accuracy. The Chiefs saw the war being fought in three phases: a grim defensive first phase while Germany and Italy sought a quick victory; a long recovery and build-up second phase while the resources of the British and French Empires were mobilised, and while political and economic warfare, naval blockade and air operations reduced the German and Italian peoples' will to resist; and a final offensive phase which they felt was too far ahead even for speculation. Any opportunities for offensive operations that presented themselves would be seized at any time, and the elimination of Italy was seen as the first step in the final offensive phase. It was hoped the Japan's expansionist tendencies would be curbed by the United States, though the Americans were not expected to desert their isolationist policies until they were forced by threats to their vital interests in the Western Hemisphere to do so. The Chiefs again reiterated their warning of the need to avoid a war on three fronts through diplomatic action.

Hitler's occupation of Prague had a dramatic effect on Chamberlain. Speaking at Birmingham two days later, he refused to recant over Munich, but made it plain that appeasement was over. Desperate last minute attempts to rally Europe in opposition to Hitler resulted in British guarantees being given to Poland, Roumania and Greece – the last being threatened by Mussolini's invasion of Albania – without any deep consideration being given to these diplomatic moves by the Chiefs of Staff. Nor was there any debate when Chamberlain agreed to Hore Belisha's 'off the cuff' proposal to double the establishment of the Territorial Army. Neither Gort nor the General Staff were consulted before the public announcement was made. National Service was introduced a few weeks later at the end of April as a fairer way of manning Britain's defences than the voluntary system which was proving totally inadequate, particularly for manning the anti-aircraft and civil defence organisations.

The Chiefs were, however, deeply involved in the Anglo-French Staff talks, which were reopened at Director of Plans level at the end of March 1939. They were carried forward in two phases: the establishment of a common strategic policy in April; and filling out operational detail, including conferences between local theatre and force commanders, in May. Final approval by both governments was given at the end of June.

The strategic policy agreed upon was a refined and slightly less defensive version of the Chief's recent 'European Appreciation for 1939–40': the first phase was to be mainly defensive and directed towards maintaining the integrity of the British and French Empires, during which no opportunity would be lost for reducing the Italian will to fight; then a second phase directed towards holding Germany and dealing decisively with Italy; and a final phase of bringing about the defeat of Germany by offensive action.

In the detailed planning, the despatch of a second BEF to France was worked out in as much detail as it had been in 1914. Somewhat surprisingly, it was agreed without much opposition and certainly with Gort's support that, unlike 1914, the Commander of the BEF should come under the operational direction of General Gamelin, the French C-in-C, with, of course, the usual right of appeal to the British Government. Co-ordinated plans for the Atlantic and Mediterranean were also agreed.

One major difficulty, which did worry the British side, was the probable French attitude to strategic bombing, which the Air Staff were by then convinced should not be started until the unfavourable balance of air power had been redressed because of the vulnerability of London to retaliatory attack. Their fears, however, proved groundless: the French were even more worried about Paris. It was agreed, therefore, that strategic bombing was to be restricted to clearly defined and obvious military targets, which would not give the

Germans an excuse to attack the Allies' capital cities.

The drift to war gathered pace throughout the spring and summer of 1939. The diplomatic efforts to contain Nazi Germany were brought to nothing, and the flimsy European balance of power was upset by the Ribbentrop-Molotov Pact, which was to prove Hitler's greatest coup, but the breach of which in June 1941 was to prove his worst – indeed fatal – mistake. Only in the Mediterranean was there a grain of diplomatic success. The Anglo-Italian 'Gentleman's Agreement' had not been revoked by Mussolini.

When war broke out, Britain was far from ready, but readier than she would have been if Chamberlain had not appeased Hitler at Munich and had gained an extra year for preparation. Appeasement was the price Britain had to pay for allowing the Treasury view of industrial and economic practicability on a 'business as usual' basis to prevail for too long over the Chiefs of Staff advice on defence requirements.

But the Treasury view would not have prevailed for so long had it not also been the view of Chamberlain, first, as Chancellor of the Exchequer, and then as Prime Minister. Further damage was done by Chamberlain's insistence on giving undue priority to Air Force expansion at the expense of Naval and Military rearmament. The Chiefs consistently advocated a more balanced approach because the unexpected always occurs in war.

But, again, this approach was too expensive for the Government to contemplate after the economic depression of the early 1930s. The pressing need for Air Defence, the calls for continuing naval supremacy in defence of the Empire, and the need for garrisons, left no money for a continental expeditionary force, even if the country had called for one before Munich. With the memories of the Somme and Passchendaele still fresh in the electorate's mind, such a call was not even contemplated until it was clear that our only real ally, France, might collapse unless supported by British forces on land as well as in the air and at sea.

The Chiefs of Staff responsibility for tendering military advice to the Government and the Treasury's duty to ensure financially and industrially sound programmes are the two sides of the defence policy-making coin. Between them lies political leadership. However efficient the Chiefs of Staff and Treasury planning machinery may be, the end result depends on political judgement. Churchill, or indeed Margaret Thatcher, would not have tamely accepted the appeasement policies of Chamberlain: 'business as usual' would have been ended much sooner.

THE FIRST CHIEFS OF STAFF COMMITTEE

17. 4th Marquis of Salisbury, the founder of the Chiefs of Staff Committee. *(Hulton Picture Company)*

18. Admiral of the Fleet Earl Beatty. *(IWM)*

19. Marshal of the Royal Air Force Lord Trenchard. *(RAF Museum)*

20. Field Marshal the Earl of Cavan. *(IWM)*

SOME CHIEFS IN THE INTER-WAR YEARS, 1918–39

21. Field Marshal Lord Milne. *(IWM)*

22. Marshal of the Royal Air Force Sir John Salmond. *(RAF Museum)*

23. Marshal of the Royal Air Force Sir Edward Ellington. *(RAF Museum)*

24. Admiral of the Fleet Lord Chatfield. *(IWM)*

THE CHIEFS AT THE OUTBREAK OF WAR, 1939

25. (Left to right) General Sir Edmund Ironside, Air Chief Marshal Sir Cyril Newall, and Admiral Sir Dudley Pound. *(IWM)*

CHURCHILL'S FINAL TEAM

26. (Left to right) Marshal of the Royal Air Force Viscount Portal, Field Marshal Viscount Alanbrooke, Sir Winston Churchill and Admiral of the Fleet Viscount Cunningham. *(IWM)*

27. General George Marshall (left) and General Sir Alan Brooke (later Field Marshal Viscount Alanbrooke). *(IWM)*

28. The Combined Chiefs of Staff and their principal advisers at Casablanca in 1943.
Left of conference table (foreground): Admiral E J King, C in C US Navy. General Marshal, Chief of Staff, US Army. Lieutenant General Arnold, Commanding US Army Air Force. Right of conference table (foreground): Field Marshal Sir John Dill. Air Chief Marshal Sir Charles Portal. General Sir Alan Brooke. Admiral Sir Dudley Pound. Vice Admiral Lord Louis Mountbatten. *(IWM)*

Chronology
FOR CHAPTER SEVEN

1939

1 Sep	German invasion of Poland
3	Ironside replaces Gort as CIGS.
30 Nov	Soviet invasion of Finland.

1940

20 March	Soviet-Finnish armistice.
9 April	German invasion of Norway.
2 May	Evacuation of central Norway.
10	Churchill becomes Prime Minister.
10	German invasion of France and the Low Countries.
27	Dill replaces Ironside as CIGS.
3 June	Evacuation of BEF from Dunkirk completed.
7	Narvik evacuated.
11	Italy declares war.
22	France capitulates.
3 July	Mers-el-Kebir.
10	Battle of Britain begins.
13 Sep	Italian invasion of Egypt.
17	German invasion of Britain postponed.
25 Oct	Portal succeeds Newall as CAS.
28	Italian invasion of Greece.
31	Battle of Britain ends.
11 Nov	Taranto.
9 Dec	British counter-offensive in Egypt begins.

1941

| 4 Jan | British invasion of Italian East Africa. |
| 5 | Bardia taken. |

12	The *Luftwaffe* arrives in Sicily.
22	Tobruk taken.
24	First Anglo-US Staff talks in Washington.
7 Feb	Beda Fomm; Italian Army surrenders.
11 March	Lend-Lease Act passed by US Congress.
28	Matapan.
30	Rommel's First Offensive begins.
3 April	Rashid Ali rebellion in Iraq begins.
6	German invasion of Greece and Yugoslavia.
11	Western Hemisphere Security Zone extended by Roosevelt to 26° West in the Atlantic.
6 May	Habbanyia relieved.
12	*Tiger* Convoy reaches Alexandria.
16	Duke of Aosta surrenders at Amba Alagi.
27	Crete evacuated.
27	*Bismarck* sunk.
8 June	Anglo-Free French invasion of Syria.
17	'Battleaxe' fails in the Western Desert.
22	German invasion of Russia.
1 July	Auchinleck replaces Wavell.
14	Syrian armistice.
23	Freezing of Japanese assets.
14 Aug	Atlantic Charter signed at Placentia Bay, Newfoundland.
18 Oct	General Togo becomes Prime Minister of Japan.
18 Nov	'Crusader' offensive begins in the Western Desert.
7 Dec	Pearl Harbour.
10	Tobruk relieved.
22	'Arcadia' Conference in Washington.
25	Brooke replaces Dill as CIGS.

7

CHURCHILL'S CHIEFS

Containing the Threat:
September 1939 – December 1941

First Sea Lords	Chiefs of the
Sir Dudley Pound	**Imperial General Staff**
	Sir Edmund Ironside Sep 1939
	Sir John Dill May 1940

Chiefs of Air Staff
Sir Cyril Newall
Sir Charles Portal   Oct 1940

'I cannot say that we never differed among ourselves even at home, but a kind of understanding grew up between me and the British Chiefs of Staff that we should convince and persuade rather than try to overrule each other. This was of course helped by the fact that we spoke the same technical language and possessed a common body of military doctrine and war experience. In this ever-changing scene we moved as one, and the War Cabinet clothed us with ever more discretion, and sustained us with unwearied and unflinching constancy.'

Winston Churchill,
The Second World War, Vol II.[1]

It is not strictly true to say, as the heading of this chapter suggests, that the Chiefs of Staff at the outbreak of war were Churchill's Chiefs. He did not become Prime Minister, nor did he appoint himself Minister of Defence, until 10th May 1940 – the day that Hitler opened his offensive in the West. Nevertheless, as soon as Chamberlain appointed him to the Admiralty when war was declared, he became the dominant personality in the development of British strategic policy. Chamberlain's credibility had been severely damaged by Hitler's cynical disregard for the Munich agreement, whereas Churchill's reputation had been enhanced as the man who could justifiably claim 'I told you so'.

Command organisations set up in peacetime, as the Chiefs of Staff Committee had been in 1923, rarely withstand the test of war, and there are always doubts anyway about waging war by committee. The remarkable thing about the Salisbury Committee's concept of a 'War Staff in Commission' was that it worked as well as it did almost immediately, and needed so little modification under the stresses and strains imposed upon it by the conflict.

This did not seem so at first; indeed, if the question 'Did it work?' had been asked in 1940, the answer would have been an emphatic 'No'! The initial disasters – the defeat of Poland, the futile air operations of the 'Phoney' War, the Norwegian fiasco and the collapse of France – did not flatter the Chiefs, but nor did they destroy Salisbury's concept. Its early faults lay, as we will see, in the political direction from above and in the command structure below, rather than in the Chiefs of Staff Committee system *per se*. The first was righted by Churchill's assumption of power in May, and the second by the creation of the Combined Operations Command system in July 1940.

Sadly it never pays to be a British Chief at the outbreak of a major war. The Chiefs in office when war is declared become scapegoats, who must carry on their backs into the wilderness not only the sins of past governments, but also the peacetime misjudgements of their predecessors. Most of the worst mistakes made by the British in the early years of the Second World War were caused by peacetime misappreciation of the uses and misuses of air power, and of its likely impact upon the war at sea and on land. The German appreciation of its potential was initially, at least, more soundly based.

There were, of course, two important differences between the commanders of the First and the Second World Wars. With only twenty years separating the two conflicts, most of the senior officers in 1939 were highly experienced fighting men. They had been successful Naval captains, Army brigadiers, or Air Force group captains in 1918. They did know what war was all about, and were determined not to allow a repetition of the attritional battles of the Western Front. They sought to use fire power rather than men's lives to win their battles.

The financial stringency in the 1920s and '30s, however, had put the British Second World War commanders at a grave disadvantage. Compared with their German opponents, they had been given little opportunity to develop and test out new ideas; nor did they have the intense political motivation of the Germans in applying the latest advances in weapon technology until it was past the 'eleventh hour'. It is true that the Navy did produce the Asdic for submarine detection in the war at sea, and the RAF was given Radar just in time for the air war, but there was total failure between the Army and Air Force to see the advantages in marrying tanks and close support aircraft together in the land battle. Even if the Army had had the financial resources to develop a *Blitzkrieg* philosophy, there was little chance of the Air Staff being able to find the necessary aircraft to put theory into practice. They were prevented from even trying to do so by the Trenchard doctrine of the indivisibility of air power, and of concentration upon winning the air battle, and hence the war, without the Army needing more than minimal close air support.

The second difference between the two wars was the absence of bitterness between 'Brass' and 'Frocks'. Churchill, as Prime Minister, was leader of the 'Frocks', but he was also the acknowledged head of the 'Brass' as Minister of Defence. He questioned and bullied his Chiefs unmercifully, but he rarely overrode their professional judgements and advice. They were oftfen irked by his impatience and constant quest for offensive action when they were trying to conserve and build up resources, but the only clash in the early years of the war that resembled the strategic disagreements of 1914–18 was over the priority to be accorded to meeting the hypothetical Japanese threat. Churchill took the pragmatic view of first things first and hence accepted greater risks in the Far East than his Chiefs considered wise. Churchill had his way, with unhappy consequences.

The Chiefs themselves were, of course, united in their dedication to winning the war. But though the Treasury had ceased to be their *bête noire*, disputes over allocation of resources persisted, and were more often than not centred upon the handling of air resources. The First Sea Lord and CIGS had two particular causes for dissatisfaction: lack of air cover for Naval and Army operations; and irritation with the Air Staff's continuing tendency to suggest that it could win the war quicker and more cheaply single handed, if the RAF was given the necessary priority to do so. The problem was that the Air Staff could not prove their case, nor could the Naval and General Staffs disprove it. The only evidence available was the undoubted success of the German *Blitzkrieg*. The First Sea Lord and CIGS would have been less than human if they had not succumbed to demands from their own services for separate air forces. The Air Staff's belief that winning the air battle was the best way to help the Navy and Army was vindicated in the end, but it did not endear the airmen to the sailors and soldiers, who had to fight without air cover under the murderous attacks by the *Luftwaffe*, and later the Japanese air force.

All successful teams take time to settle down, and this was certainly true of the Chiefs at the outbreak of war. Only Pound, the veteran First Sea Lord, was to survive long enough to become one of Churchill's trusted Chiefs. He and Newall, the CAS, were already well established in office when war broke out; and Newall had been acting as the Chairman of the Chiefs of Staff Committee since Chatfield left in 1938.

Pound, who took over when Backhouse died, did not have the humanity of Jellicoe, nor the intellectual power and confidence of Chatfield, but he had the trust of the Navy and was seen in the Admiralty as the man who could and would stand up to Churchill. He achieved the well nigh impossible feat of curbing Churchill without losing his confidence, and of forging a partnership with him that was never broken until overwork killed him. He appeared rather reserved, and this was accentuated by growing deafness. Moreover, he suffered from painful osteo-arthritis, which added to his burdens of fighting the war at sea and keeping the Navy's end up in Whitehall. He was not a good committee man and was sparing in his contributions to the Chiefs' debates, tending to confine himself primarily to naval affairs.

There is one aspect of the responsibilities of the Chief of Naval Staff that should not be overlooked. Unlike the CIGS and CAS, he exercised control of ships at sea, using operational intelligence that was only immediately available within the Admiralty. Thus Pound bore the double burden of advising on strategy as the Naval Chief and of personally conducting the war at sea. Like many of his predecessors, he was not a good delegator. Indeed, for the first two years of the war, he would not agree to the resuscitation of the First World War post of Deputy Chief of Naval Staff to assist him.

Newall did not enjoy such a high level of confidence either in the Air Force or in Churchill's mind. There were too many much stronger characters amongst the senior air commanders to make his tenure as CAS an entirely happy one. It was also generally known that he was something of a stopgap, holding the appointment until Sir Charles Portal reached the required seniority to take over in a year's time. He, like Pound, tended to concentrate on issues affecting his own Service, leaving grand strategy to the Army's Chief.

Unfortunately, the Army was not represented by a strategist –

indeed, it was not well represented at all. It changed its Chief as the whistle blew for the 'match' to begin. Hore Belisha, whose relationship with Gort had been deteriorating steadily for some months, saw the dispatch of the BEF to France as a god-sent opportunity for getting rid of him. He had already half promised the command of the BEF to Sir Edmund Ironside, whom he had recently brought back from Gibraltar in anticipation. But there was also Sir John Dill to be considered. He was GOC-in-C, Aldershot Command, a post which was seen in the Army as Commander (Designate) of the BEF. Unhappily, Hore Belisha, on Liddell Hart's advice, gave the command of the BEF to Gort; and instead of replacing him with Dill, the obvious and most suitable choice, he compounded his error by taking Ironside as his CIGS. The choice of Gort for the BEF was reasonable enough in that he was more of a fighting soldier than a staff officer, and it was the job he had always wanted, but to pick Ironside, another commander without staff pretensions, was obtuse. The abler and – to the publicity conscious Hore Belisha – less newsworthy Dill went loyally to France as Commander, 1st Corps, under Gort, his junior.

'Tiny' Ironside was a great bull of a man with a commanding personality but few other qualifications for the job. He was a Gunner, who had made his name in Russia in 1918/19. He had never served in Whitehall and had no wish to do so. Professor J R M Butler sums him up in the Official History, saying:

> General Ironside did not find his new post congenial, and the appointment failed to prove a satisfactory one.[2]

Chamberlain started the war with a system of government not very different from Lloyd George's administration of 1918. He set up a rather larger War Cabinet of nine, which included the three Service Ministers because he wanted Churchill's support and could not have the First Lord of the Admiralty in the Cabinet without taking in Hore Belisha (War) and Sir Kingsley Wood (Air) as well. The CID died, this time for ever. In it's place came the 'Ministerial' Committee for Military Co-ordination under Lord Chatfield's chairmanship, backed by the Chiefs of Staff Committee as its 'Official' counterpart. The Chiefs used to meet at 10 o'clock each morning before the War Cabinet meeting at 11.30, which they also attended more often than not.

In Nazi Germany there was no War Cabinet, nor a Chiefs of Staff Committee. The nearest equivalent was the *Oberkommando der*

Wehrmacht (OKW), which combined the roles of Hitler's Military Headquarters, Ministry of Defence and Great General Staff. Its staff was drawn from the three armed forces and other government departments, but they owed no allegiance to their parent organisations, nor were they advised and backed by them as the British Chiefs were. OKW was, thus, one of those dangerous headquarters that had power of decision without the countervailing discipline of responsibility for execution. The strength of the British Chiefs of Staff system was that the men who made the decisions were also the heads of the staffs responsible for executing them. This may have made them cautious, but power was never divorced from responsibility as it was in Nazi Germany.

The Second World War started very much where its predecessor had ended in 1918. The reopening of the U-Boat campaign was dramatically signalled by the sinking of the passenger liner *Athenia* without warning and with heavy loss of life on the first day. A mine barrage was relaid across the Straits of Dover; the Home Fleet sailed to its war stations in northern waters; the naval blockade was reimposed upon Germany; the convoy system was reintroduced; the first echelons of the BEF crossed the Channel and started preparing First World War style defences, reinforced with anti-tank ditches and concrete pillboxes, on its sector of the Franco-German frontier just north of Lille; and Bomber Command set out on its first abortive attempts to attack the German Navy in its home ports.

But times had changed. Only the war at sea was fought much as expected. The German magnetic mines were a nasty surprise; catching commerce raiders on passage out into the Atlantic proved as difficult as bringing on a general fleet action had been in 1914–18; and through over-confidence in the Asdic, the Admiralty surprisingly reverted to trying to catch the U-boats on passage rather than around the convoys, which could serve as baited traps. There was, however, no 'Phoney War' at sea: the Navy was at full stretch from the first day onwards and there was to be no respite for it or for Pound.

The BEF set about its task determined to do as well, if not better, than its predecessor, but its higher command was not a happy, united team. Gort's two Corps Commanders, Dill and Brooke – themselves both future Chiefs – had little confidence in him. Fine fighting soldier and charming, self-effacing man that he was, he was out of his depth in the international environment that engulfed him. He had accepted, while he was still CIGS, the subordination of the

BEF to the French Supreme Command, and he had neither the desire nor the intellectual capacity to challenge French military policy. He immersed himself in detail and ignored the strategic issues that so alarmed Dill and Brooke. He had his orders from the French High Command, and, convinced of the need for Allied unity, he believed that it was his duty to lead, inspire and fight much as he had always done in the past. Ironside, despite his fluency in French, was no more willing as CIGS than Gort as C-in-C to challenge the French concepts, which were anathema to Dill and Brooke.

Alan Brooke, although from an Anglo-Irish family, had been brought up by his mother in southern France. He was also fluent in French and German, and loved France and the French people. He had fought throughout the First World War on the Western Front as an artilleryman, and is credited with much of the early British development work on rolling-barrage techniques. He had seen a lot of the French *poilu* in the fighting around Verdun in 1916, and was aghast at the deterioration in their morale when he saw them again in 1939. David Fraser, his biographer, quotes from his diary entry after taking the salute with General Corap, Commander of the French 9th Army, after a wreath-laying ceremony:

> I can see those troops now. Seldom have I seen anything more slovenly and more badly turned out. Men unshaven, horses ungroomed, clothes and saddlery that did not fit, vehicles dirty, and complete lack of pride in themselves or their units. What shook me most, however, was the look on the men's faces, disgruntled and insubordinate looks, and although ordered to give 'eyes left' hardly a man bothered to do so.[3]

Perhaps even Brooke did not appreciate at the time that Corap's men reflected the malaise of the French nation, which was as reluctant to fight the Germans as the British had been to furnish an expeditionary force to help them to do so.

The main bone of contention between Gort and Ironside on the one hand and Dill and Brooke on the other was Gamelin's Plan 'D'. This envisaged the BEF, flanked by the 1st and 7th French Armies, pivoting on Corap's 9th Army in an advance to the line of the River Dyle in Belgium, if and when the Germans attacked through the Low Countries. Gamelin's strategy might have been practicable if the Belgium Government had allowed staff talks and had been prepared to construct adequate defences on the Dyle; and if Corap's 9th Army had been strong enough to provide a firm pivot for Gamelin's wheel. But like the other small European states, Belgium was unwilling to antagonise Hitler, and Corap's 9th Army turned out to be little more than a hotch-potch of reservist formations, incapable of offering serious resistance to the German *Blitzkrieg*.

Dill and Brooke disliked Plan 'D' because, although it shortened the Allied front very substantially, the BEF could be caught in a mobile encounter battle, for which it was inadequately equipped and trained. What they did not know, and Ironside and Gort did not try to find out, was anything about the French General Reserves – where they were, how strong they were and what counter-attack tasks they had been given. Gort and Ironside believed in the near infallibility of the French Supreme Command, and felt that the smallness of the British contribution to the continental land battle precluded them from any right to question the soundness of French policy. If Dill and Brooke had realised the inadequacy of the French reserves, they would have been even more worried.

Dill was tactful enough not to reveal his misgivings, but Brooke was not. Gort, who found him difficult and over-pessimistic, contemplated sacking him. Brooke was, in truth, only being himself: mercilessly realistic. But he never allowed his doubts to affect the handling of his Corps, which he trained with great professionalism. His square figure, determined face, rapid staccato voice, decisiveness and imperturbability impressed everyone who met him.

There was similar controversy over Air policy in the first weeks of the war. The *Luftwaffe's* impressive performance in support of the *Wehrmacht* in Poland, and Bomber Command's equally unimpressive attacks on German naval ports, brought the adequacy of air support for the BEF and of the Air Staff's cherished offensive bombing policy into question at Chiefs of Staff level. The first raid on Wilhelmshaven had been a costly fiasco. Three of the 500 pound bombs, which did hit their target, bounced off the armoured deck of the *Admiral Scheer* and into the sea without exploding; and a quarter of the Blenheim bombers that took part in the raid were lost. The results of subsequent raids were, if anything, even more discouraging. Daylight raids, whether escorted by fighters or not, were found to be too expensive to be continued.

Ironside was the first Chief to demand a change in Air policy, but his diaries show that he did so in a rather naive way without appreciating, or showing that he understood, the Air Staff's problems. He wanted substantial reinforcement of the thirteen squadrons that had accompanied the BEF to France as its Air Component. This was reasonable enough, but he and the War Office overplayed their hand by demanding an extra 250 aircraft for close support of the Army by

June 1940, and the formation of an Army Air Force. Newall countered by pointing out that this would almost halve Bomber Command's striking force, and that a British aircraft to rival the German *Stuka* did not exist because the War Office had not stated an operational requirement for it during the Air rearmament programmes.

Chamberlain gave Chatfield the task of adjudicating on the Army/ Air issue. There could be no question of creating an Army Air Force until air superiority had been achieved – and that looked a very long way off in 1939. All that could be done was to combine the thirteen squadrons of the BEF's Air Component with the ten squadrons of Bomber Command's Advanced Air Striking Force stationed in France in order to form a new force, called the British Air Forces in France (BAFF), which was to be under Gort's operational direction and could only be tasked by Bomber Command in special circumstances and then only with War Cabinet authority. This palliative soothed but did not cure the incipient ulcer that was starting to grow in Army/Air relations.

The controversy over bombing policy was less easy to resolve because it was international. The British and French Governments had already agreed that bombing should be confined to strictly military targets partly to be 'on the side of the angels', but more especially to avoid giving the Germans an excuse for bombing London and Paris. In drawing up plans to counter a German offensive in the West, Newall took up a Trenchard-like position, advocating attacks on synthetic oil production in the Ruhr as the surest way of halting German offensive operations in the West instead of trying to attack more difficult and well defended troop concentrations and advancing columns in the battle area. Newall calculated that Bomber Command's 450 operational aircraft could drop

'some 28 tons on the Ruhr's synthetic oil plants, marshalling yards and other key installations' and that 'at this rate we should theoretically be able to destroy the objective in 11–18 days'![4]

The French would have none of it. Their Air Force was too weak to protect Paris, and they rightly doubted the impact that Bomber Command's attacks were likely to have upon *Wehrmacht* operations. The British Government agreed reluctantly 'not to take the gloves off first'. The *Luftwaffe* had just under 2,000 bombers in the autumn of 1939!

The French veto on strategic bombing led to Bomber Command showering Germany by night with 'Nickels' – propaganda leaflets –

which Churchill quipped were 'to raise the Germans to a higher morality', and the future 'Bomber' Harris dubbed 'supplying the continent's requirements of toilet paper'[5]! The Nickel raids, however, did give Bomber Command the opportunity to develop its night navigation equipment and skills, and to assess the German air defences. By the time Portal took over the Command from Ludlow-Hewitt in April 1940, night bombing had, perforce, become its chosen mode of operation.

After the fall of Poland, the Chiefs were uncertain where Hitler would strike next. There was every indication that German divisions were returning to the West, but there was a strong possibility that this was a feint and that he might adopt the easier option of exploiting his successes in Eastern Europe by driving south-eastwards into the Balkans, thereby reducing the effectiveness of the Anglo-French naval blockade before mounting an offensive in the West. After a number of false alarms about attacks in the West during the autumn, the Chiefs persuaded the War Cabinet to build up a general reserve of nine divisions and twenty-two RAF squadrons in the Middle East, and to endeavour to create an anti-German front in the Balkans by diplomatic means.

As in the First World War, the Chiefs hoped for useful dividends from their investment in the naval blockade. They were encouraged by the over-sanguine estimates made by the Ministry of Economic Warfare of its likely longer term effects upon the German war economy. Oil, industrial labour force morale, and iron ore were seen to be the weak points in Hitler's ability to sustain a long war. The first two could not be attacked until Bomber Command was allowed, and indeed was able to open a strategic air offensive. Most of Germany's iron ore, however, came from the Kirkuna and Gallivare mines in northern Sweden. In winter, when the Gulf of Bothnia was frozen, the ore was railed into Norway and shipped out through Narvik. It was carried southwards in German ships sailing within Norwegian territorial waters for most of their passage to the German Baltic ports. The easiest way to stop this traffic was to mine Norwegian waters, thus forcing the ships out into the North Sea where the Royal Navy could intercept them. Mining would need the tacit agreement of the Norwegians, who were as reluctant as the Belgians to give Hitler any excuse to invade.

Matters came to a head when Russia attacked Finland in November 1939, and the Finns put up such a spirited resistance that there was a political outcry in Britain and France for aid to be sent to them. The easiest route for sending help to the Finns, which was thought to be out of German reach, was via the iron ore railway line from Narvik to Kirkuna and thence to the Finnish frontier at Kemi. An Allied landing at Narvik would kill two birds with one stone – stop Germany's ore supplies and open a route to Finland – provided the Norwegians and Swedes could be persuaded to co-operate. Incidentally, the railway was a narrow gauge, electric and owned by Sweden; and there was no road from Narvik to Kirkuna. The Swedes could abort the whole project by cutting the power supplies to the railway if British diplomatic efforts failed to secure their co-operation.

The whole impracticable scheme would have foundered had it not been for Churchill's determination to find some way of hurting the Germans by offensive action. It was the Dardanelles all over again: the First Lord using the Admiralty to drive the project forward because there was no tri-Service command structure available to do so; nor was there anyone else in the War Cabinet able to give dynamic political direction to the Chiefs. Ironside, who never did understand how Whitehall worked and was out of his depth in the political wrangling that went on during the 'Phoney War' period, noted in his diary:

> We had a dreadful Cabinet. Everybody had a different idea upon how much force we would have to use at Narvik. . . . A more unmilitary show I have never seen. The Prime Minister began peering at a chart of Narvik and when he had finished asked me what scale it was on![6]

It has to be said that the Chiefs' machinery failed its first test in the conduct of active operations largely because of the lack of a dynamic Prime Minister. Nevertheless, a number of gross errors of military judgement were made in assessing the requirements for the operation: that the German Navy would not risk major naval operations as far north as Narvik; that only relatively small forces would be needed and that these could be found without detriment to the BEF; that adequate air cover could be given from Scotland, provided that Stavanger airfield on the southern Norwegian coast was destroyed by a raiding force; and that the whole operation could be controlled from Whitehall. No overall commander was appointed, nor was a combined headquarters envisaged, let alone established. Each Service ministry issued separate orders to its own appointed commanders without a positive effort being made by the Chiefs to co-ordinate them.

The first attempt to mount the operation was aborted by the Finns accepting Soviet terms for an armistice on 20 March 1940, but it was revived a week later by French pressure at the Allied Supreme War Council for something to be done to raise Allied morale and to draw off German forces from the Western Front. By this time German Intelligence had become aware of what was afoot. Hitler gave the task of mounting a pre-emptive strike to General von Falkenhorst, and, unlike the British, provided him with a special inter-Service headquarters for the planning and execution of *Fall Weserübung* (Weser Exercise).

Surprise and overwhelming force were the key features of von Falkenhorst's plan. Unlike the Allies, the Germans had no qualms about infringing Scandinavian neutrality. All the modern ships of the German Navy, one thousand aircraft (half of them troop transports), and six divisions, including the specially trained 3rd Mountain Division, were placed at von Falkenhorst's disposal, while the Allies were shilly-shallying about with brigade-size forces amounting to less than two divisions. The German assault troops were to be carried in warships or air-landed, and their heavier equipment was to be sailed in fast merchant ships that would set out from German ports some days before the operation was due to start.

On 5th April, the Allied Supreme War Council at last warned Scandinavian Governments that Norwegian territorial waters would be mined within three days. On the evening of 9th April, the Allies were surprised to learn that the Germans were already in occupation of Copenhagen, Oslo, Stavanger, Bergen, Trondheim and, most surprising of all, Narvik. They were caught off balance and never recovered. The Germans held the initiative throughout this totally mismanaged campaign.

Although the Home Fleet failed to intercept the invasion forces, the German fleet paid a heavy price for von Falkenhorst's success. By the end of the campaign, it had no major units fit for sea. It was, however, the *Luftwaffe* that won the campaign for him. With only three to four hours of darkness, as the arctic summer approached, there was not enough time for the Allied troops to unload guns and other heavy equipment at the small Norwegian ports before the store-ships had to put to sea again to avoid being sunk at the jetties by German bombers. Air support from Scottish airfields proved ludicrously inadequate; and the futile attempt to provide a modicum of local air cover by landing a Gladiator squadron on a frozen lake was abruptly ended when the ice was broken up by German bombs.

The Chiefs – particularly Ironside and Newall – cannot be exonerated for their military misjudgements and impracticable command arrangements, although the root causes of the fiasco were political: governmental vacillation and lack of a war-competent Prime Minister. Chatfield had resigned on 3rd April because he felt that as the Minister for the Co-ordination of Defence without executive powers, he had become a 'fifth wheel of the coach'. Churchill had taken over the chairmanship of the Military Co-ordination Committee, but, unfettered by the constraints of final responsibility, he was like a rogue elephant. His drive to get things done created confusion and could never make up for Chamberlain's deficiencies as a war leader. As Asquith and Lloyd George found, the Prime Minister cannot delegate the ultimate direction of military affairs in war.

The Official Historians' summing up on the Norwegian Campaign expresses what all those who fought in it thought at the time:

> It can hardly be denied that the principle of maintaining the aim was flouted: there were too many changes of plan, and the changed plans did not allow time for corresponding changes to be made in preparations at a lower level. The result was chaos . . . Commanders on land, with hardly an exception, felt that there had been a total lack of realistic planning, especially on the administrative side.
>
> Besides these blunders, there was sheer miscalculation or failure of imagination: the likelihood of the Germans using their heavy ships as they did was not foreseen; the mobility of British and French troops unaccustomed to Arctic conditions was exaggerated; while the daring and performance of the Germans of all three Services were underestimated, and in particular the shattering effect of the Luftwaffe when means of defence were lacking.[7]

The House of Commons was in no doubt where the real fault lay. The debate on 7 and 8 May brought home to Chamberlain the inadequacies of his Government as a wartime administration and of the need for a National Government. It was also clear to him that the Labour and Liberal Parties would not serve under his leadership. At 6 o'clock in the evening of 10 May the King asked Churchill to form an all-party government. Earlier that morning, the long awaited German offensive in the West had started; Gamelin had ordered the execution of Plan 'D'; and the BEF had started on its fateful advance to the Dyle.

Churchill's grasp on the reins of government came too late to save the day in France, but had he not been in power when France capitulated, Britain might have sought an armistice as well. Only his pugnacious leadership saved Britain from that humiliation. Amongst his first actions were cutting down the War Cabinet to five; appointing himself, with the King's approval, as Minister of Defence; and making the Chiefs of Staff Committee, with its highly developed planning and intelligence staffs, his executive for the conduct of the war. Orders to Cs-in-C, and later to Theatre Commanders, were based upon a single strategic plan and issued on behalf of the Chiefs of Staff Committee as the supreme executive body. 'Pug' Ismay, promoted major-general, became Churchill's Personal Staff Officer with a seat on the Chiefs of Staff Committee, and the Secretary-ship was taken over by Colonel Leslie Hollis (later General Sir Leslie).

One thing that Churchill did not do was to provide himself with a Ministry of Defence. All that he needed was what he called a 'hand-ling machine'. The Cabinet Secretariat's Military Wing under Ismay, assisted by Lieutenant-Colonel Ian Jacob (later Lieutenant-General Sir Ian, who became Director-General of the BBC after the War) was just what he wanted, and so it was renamed the Office of the Minister of Defence and stayed within the Cabinet Office. The Military Co-ordination Committee was replaced by a Defence Committee, headed by the Prime Minister, with two panels, one for operations and the other for supply. Whenever vital but intractable problems arose, Churchill would call together special sub-committees to work with him in finding solutions to them. The Atlantic Committee, the Tank Parliament, and the Night Air Defence Committee were examples of these *ad hoc* bodies which he spawned and disbanded when their work was done.

Ismay records in his memoirs:

> It might seem on the face of it that these innovations made little change in existing arrangements: but the practical effects were revolutionary. Henceforward the Prime Minister himself, with all the powers and authority attached to that office, exercised a personal, direct, ubiquitous and continuous supervision, not only over the formulation of military policy at every stage, but also over the general conduct of military operations. There was a remarkable intensification of national effort in every field.[8]

On 13 May, the Commons gave Churchill a unanimous vote of confidence. In reply he uttered the famous words:

> I have nothing to offer but blood, toil, tears and sweat. . . .[9]

In the next five days, the Battle for France was lost, while de-cisions were taken that led to victory in the Battle of Britain. On 14 May Corap's 9th Army collapsed. Next day, Paul Reynaud, the French Prime Minister, rang Churchill, crying *'We are defeated; we have lost the battle.'* Churchill flew to Paris to breathe fresh life into the Reynaud Government, but before leaving he held a crucial War Cabinet meeting. There were two key items on the agenda: should French requests for more fighter aircraft be met; and should Bomber Command attack the Ruhr rather than the German Army. All the Chiefs and their Vice-Chiefs were present as was Dowding, C-in-C, Fighter Command.

On the fighter issue, both Newall and Dowding opposed the dispatch of six extra squadrons to France, and the War Cabinet agreed that they should not be sent 'for the present'. On bombers, Newall pointed to the heavy losses that the BAFF had already suffered trying to slow the German advance with daylight attacks on targets called for by the British and French Armies. They both reiterated the strongly held Air Staff view that:

> the attack on the oil refineries would unquestionably have the effect of retarding the land operations for which the Germans required large quantities of petrol for their mechanised forces.[10]

All the airmen present and the First Sea Lord agreed. Ironside showed himself to be a spent force by not speaking up for the Army. He asked rather lamely for marshalling yards to be attacked as well as oil installations. He recalls in his diary the reaction of the air marshals when Churchill agreed to open the Strategic Air Offensive with attacks on the Ruhr:

> I never saw anything so light up as the faces of the RAF when they heard that they were to be allowed to bomb the oil-refineries in the Ruhr. It did one good to see it. . . . I am wondering what the result in the way of reprisals [on London] is going to be. Shall we get it as soon as tomorrow night in return?[11]

Ironside's worries about reprisals, and the airmen's enthusiasm of bombing the Ruhr, were both totally misplaced. London was not bombed. 99 bombers took part in the first raid on the Ruhr; 16 failed to find their target areas; and only 24 claimed to have hit theirs; but only one Wellington was lost. The damage to the oil-refineries was so negligible that no reprisals were even thought of in Berlin. The *Panzer* divisions rolled on unhindered, and no German fighters or anti-aircraft guns were withdrawn from the front to protect the Ruhr against further RAF attacks. And yet the Air Staff remained convinced that it would only take a few more days to produce decisive results!

Churchill arrived in Paris that afternoon accompanied by Ismay and Dill, who had been brought back from 1st Corps at the beginning of the Norwegian Campaign to become Vice-Chief of the Imperial General Staff in order to ease the load on Ironside's shoulders and to give intellectual depth to the General Staff. There followed the oft described meeting at the Quai d'Orsay, at which Gamelin set forth the bleakness of the prospect and when asked by Churchill where his general reserves were, replied '*Aucune!*' (there are none). Churchill, who had not as yet given up all hope of saving the situation, cabled London, recommending that the six fighter squadrons, discussed that morning, should be sent to France at once. Fortunately, it was found that they could not be accommodated on French airfields and so they operated over France from England instead.

Dowding had every right to be concerned that this was just the beginning of a fatal haemorrhage of Fighter Command's life blood. On 16 May he penned his protest to the Air Ministry:

1. I have the honour to refer to the very serious calls which have recently been made on the Home Defence Fighter Units in an attempt to stem the German invasion on the Continent.
2. I hope and believe that our Armies may yet be victorious in France and Belgium, but we have to face the possibility that they may be defeated.
3. In this case I presume that there is no one who will deny that England should fight on, even though the remainder of the Continent of Europe is dominated by the Germans.
4. For this purpose it is necessary to retain some minimum fighter strength in this country and I must request that the Air Council will inform me what they consider this minimum strength to be, in order that I may make my dispositions accordingly.
5. I would remind the Air Council that the last estimate which they made as to the force necessary to defend this country was fifty-two squadrons, and my strength has now been reduced to the equivalent of thirty-six squadrons . . .[12]

Newall 'saw the light' and at least temporarily became a fighter man, supporting Dowding to the full. He presented Dowding's protest to the Chiefs on 17 May, urging that no more fighters should be sent to France. A few more squadrons would not save France, but they could make all the difference between victory and defeat in the skies over Britain. On 19 May, as the German tanks were approaching the Channel coast at Abbeville, Churchill gave his agreement. Newall had won a vital decision.

On the same day, 19 May, Gort warned the War Office that he might have to retreat on Dunkirk. The BEF had repulsed all German attacks, but the collapse of the French to the south and the Belgians to the north left him with no other option. Ironside, judging the situation over-optimistically, persuaded the War Cabinet that Gort should strike southwards across the German armoured penetration to re-establish the front with the French on the Somme. He flew to Gort's headquarters while Churchill and Dill went to Paris to do what they could to salvage something from the wreck. It was all in vain. Ironside accepted Gort's view and the retreat to Dunkirk began. Churchill momentarily saw some hope in Weygand's plan for a counter-offensive, but nothing came of it as the French collapse gathered momentum, and the BEF returned to England, disarmed but not annihilated.

During those fateful days, Churchill's confidence in Ironside collapsed. It had never been particularly high, and had been reduced by his inept handling of the Army's part in the Norwegian Campaign. Churchill had been accompanied by Dill during his many flying visits to France, and had been impressed by his 'abilities and strategic knowledge'[13]. With a German invasion of England increasingly probable, it was time to apppoint a strong commander as C-in-C Home Forces to defend the British Isles. Ironside, sensing Churchill's loss of confidence in him and feeling that he could make a greater contribution preparing the country's defences, volunteered for the job. Dill became the Army's Chief on 27th May 1940, three years later than he should have done if Hore Belisha had not chosen Gort as CIGS in 1937.

Once any great battle is joined, it is the task of the Supreme Command to look ahead to the likely outcome, and to set action in train either to exploit success or to limit damage. As early as 19 May, the Chiefs were examining a Joint Planning Staff paper on '*British Strategy in a Certain Eventuality*' – the collapse of France. The Directors of Plans assumed that Italy would soon enter the war to grab her share of the spoils; that French North Africa would be accessible to the Germans; and that Spain, Portugal and all the Balkan countries except Turkey would be under some form of German control. On the other hand, Britain could count on the full economic and financial support of the United States, which might possibly extend to active intervention against Germany; and Russia might become frightened enough of Germany to change sides. They posed two questions for the Chiefs: could Britain hold out until the mobilisation of her Imperial resources and American aid made themselves felt; and could Britain eventually bring sufficient economic pressure to bear upon Germany to encompass her defeat?[14]

In answering the first question, the Chiefs saw Germany adopting three modes of attack: unrestricted air attack to break civilian morale; blockade by the destruction of shipping and ports; and actual invasion. The crux of the matter was winning air superiority over the British Isles. Unless the Germans could knock out the RAF and the British aircraft industry, they were unlikely to succeed militarily. All would depend upon the British people's will to resist. The Chiefs concluded more in faith than logic:

> . . . *prima facie*, Germany has most of the cards; but the real test is whether the morale of our fighting personnel and civil population will counterbalance the numerical and material advantages which Germany enjoys. We believe it will.[15]

In answering the second question, the Chiefs were equally forthright. Germany could be defeated by a combination of naval blockade, air attack on economic targets and civilian morale, and the generation of widespread revolt in occupied territories. They saw oil and focal points in the German transportation system as the best targets for air attack. And they gave emphasis to the expansion of Fighter and Bomber Commands, and to naval construction, but said nothing whatsoever about the possibility of the Army playing a decisive role in the future.

Italy did declare war on 11 June; France capitulated on 22nd; the French Fleet at Mers-el-Kebir was destroyed by Admiral Somerville's Force H on 3 July, embittering Anglo-French relations still further; and on 10 July, the Battle of Britain began in the skies over Kent. Newall's and Dowding's efforts to preserve Fighter Command were to be fully vindicated, as was the fortuitous Treasury-imposed switch from bomber to fighter production in 1937/8.

The growing efficiency of the Chiefs of Staff machinery under Churchill's leadership was soon evident. He and the Chiefs were soon looking far beyond the immediate air battles and threat of invasion. His restless imagination, however, would not allow him to accept the orthodoxy of the Joint Planners. At the end of August, he decreed that he would task them himself in future, though they were still to put their papers through the Chiefs of Staff Committee. This was fine in theory, but as the Directors of Plans were also members of the Naval, General and Air Staffs they continued to reflect the views of their Chiefs. All that happened was that they had to look at rather more of Churchill's less practicable ideas than they would have done otherwise.

The Prime Minister was particularly concerned about the effects of Italy's entry into the war on Britain's position in the Middle East. He had never met Wavell, so he invited him home at the beginning of August to take his measure. The meeting resulted in one of the boldest decisions ever taken by Churchill and the Chiefs. Despite the threat of invasion, 150 tanks out of the meagre 400 available to Ironside for Home Defence, were to be shipped to Egypt. Churchill wanted to send them direct through the Mediterranean in a fast convoy, but Pound and Admiral Sir Andrew Cunningham, Naval C-in-C, Mediterranean, supported by Dill and Wavell, objected. The Italians were showing little inclination to invade Egypt, and it would only take three weeks longer to send the tanks round the Cape. In their view, the risk of losing one third of Britain's available armour to save so short a time could not be justified.

Churchill accepted his professional advisers' views, as he usually did in the end, but with great reluctance. He felt that both Wavell and Cunningham needed prodding, which was as unwarranted as it was unfair to both these able commanders. Cunningham reacted resentfully to the Churchillian goad; Wavell, in his taciturn way, just refused to be rushed into an unsound strategy. Wavell's accomplishment with his pen was not matched by coherence in debate, and he was worsted by Churchill, who recorded:

> While not in full agreement with General Wavell's use of the resources at his disposal, I thought it best to leave him in command.[16]

Soon after Wavell's visit, the Chiefs turned their attention to the Far East, and found themselves in total disagreement with the Prime Minister. Dill recommended that the 7th Australian Division should be deployed as a mobile force in northern Malaya, but Churchill declined to approve his proposal. He insisted that the defence of Singapore must depend upon the Fleet: one division would, in his view, be wasted in a jungle country the size of England. Each of the Chiefs disagreed with him although for different reasons: Pound argued that a fleet could not be provided without stripping the Mediterranean; Dill rightly saw the need to hold northern Malaya to block the land approach to Singapore; and Newall wanted the RAF's airfields there, which were under construction at the time, protected. Churchill remained unconvinced and countered that risks had to be taken somewhere; war with Japan was not a foregone conclusion; and the more immediate dangers lay at home and in the Mediterranean. On this occasion, the Chiefs were overruled, and 7th Australian Division was disembarked in the Middle East.

Towards the end of August, when the Battle of Britain was at its height, the Americans sent a tri-Service team of senior staff officers to London under the cover name of 'The Standardisation of Arms

Committee', headed by Admiral Robert Ghormley. Their primary duty was to report to the President on the likelihood of Britain holding out, but they were prepared to discuss the future without commitment. Newall, as Chairman of the Chiefs of Staff Committee, briefed them, using an early draft of a Joint Planners Review of Strategy which was to be presented to the Chiefs on 4 September. He reiterated the view that Germany could only hope to break British resistance by unrestricted air attack, by the destruction of shipping and ports, or by invasion. The last was unlikely to succeed in view of the *Luftwaffe's* failure to crush Fighter Command, but Hitler could intensify his bombing and U-boat campaigns. When Ghormley asked whether there were any plans for failure to withstand invasion, Newall's reply was sanguine:

> Our whole strategy was based on the assumption that we should withstand attack, and it was the fixed determination of the whole nation to do so.[17]

But over-optimistically he suggested that by the summer of 1941 German morale would be sagging, her oil reserves expended and her operations curbed by lack of fuel. This favourable state of affairs would be brought about by relentless air attacks by Bomber Command while British resources were accumulated for offensive operations. The elimination of Italy was the first objective. Success in the Mediterranean would make the economic blockade of Germany more effective, and would free resources for use in deterring Japan. Support of the American Fleet in the Far East would transform the situation there, but United States economic and industrial help was more important still.

When the final version of the Review was sent to the War Cabinet, the Chiefs added a further gloss:

> It was not our policy' [they said] 'to raise, and land on the Continent, an army comparable in size with that of Germany. We should aim, nevertheless, as soon as the blockade and air offensive had secured conditions when numerically inferior forces could be employed with good chance of success, to re-establish a striking force on the Continent with which we could enter Germany and impose our terms.[18]

It was a remarkable act of faith on the part of the Chiefs to conclude this Review in the autumn of 1940 with the words:

> . . . our strategy during 1941 must be one of attrition. . . . But the general aim should . . . be to pass to the general offensive in all spheres and all theatres with the utmost possible strength in the spring of 1942.[19]

They were only six months out in their estimate. The Battle of El Alamein – the turning point of the war as far as the British were concerned – started on 23 October 1942!

By the end of September 1940, the months of supreme crisis were over. Hitler had postponed his invasion of England; the Italians had invaded Egypt but had ground to a halt at Sidi Barrani, having run out of determination and supplies; neither Spain nor Vichy France had entered the war; the Battle of the Atlantic had neither been won nor lost; and the RAF had the measure of their opponents by day.

With the Battle of Britain over, the Prime Minister felt that the Air Ministry plan to replace Newall at the end of his tenure as CAS with Sir Charles Portal, the C-in-C, Bomber Command, should go ahead. It was not that Newall had failed – though he had shown some feebleness in handling his more forceful and quarrelsome 'fighter barons' during the Battle of Britain – but because Churchill was building a command team of his own choice, and his eyes had already fallen on Portal as the man whom he wanted as his principal Air adviser. He had admired Portal's aggressive bombing of the invasion barges assembled in the heavily defended Channel Ports; and he was enthralled by Portal's attack on Berlin on the night after the first bombs fell on London on 21 August. The 81 bombers that Portal sent on the raid did little material damage but the feat was heartening to Winston and the British people, and could hardly have been encouraging to Hitler and the Nazi Party.

Newall went out to New Zealand as Governor General, and proved himself a very happy choice. Churchill's choice of Portal to join the Chiefs was equally happy. He was well known to and liked by Dill and Pound, the latter replacing Newall as Chairman of the Chiefs. Tall, dark haired with a beakish nose and deep facial lines, his very appearance reflected his intellectual capabilities, integrity and moral courage. Moreover, he had the strength of character to handle Churchill, and the physical stamina to match his exacting routine. He did have a quiet charm and pleasant sense of humour, but subordinates found him reserved and not easy to get to know well. Perhaps his greatest attribute was his ability to stand back from the detail and to concentrate upon the critical issues.

At Portal's request, Air Chief Marshal Sir Wilfrid Freeman, who had been responsible for aircraft development in the 1930s and is often referred to as the 'father' of the heavy bomber force, was appointed his Vice Chief of Air Staff. Freeman, who was renowned for his outspokenness, looked after the day to day management of the

RAF, while Portal concentrated on Chiefs of Staff business and on international summit conferences, which increased in frequency as the war went on.

Portal took over on 25 October 1940, and was immediately engulfed in a minor but distasteful issue and a major strategic controversy. The Admiralty, as we have seen, were never happy about Coastal Command belonging to the RAF, and felt that it was being starved of the aircraft it needed in the Battle of the Atlantic. Much to Pound's annoyance, and without his backing, the First Lord, A V Alexander, and the Minister of Aircraft Production, Lord Beaverbrook, proposed the transfer of Coastal Command to the Admiralty. Churchill had his doubts, but decided that he must support his old friend, the 'Beaver', and ordered an inquiry. Pound and Portal closed ranks against this unwarranted political intrusion, and worked out a mutually acceptable plan for strengthening Coastal Command squadrons. Political face was saved by placing the Command officially under the Admiralty's operational, but not administrative, control, which was the case in practice anyway, though this had never been formally acknowledged by the Air Ministry.

The major controversy was over strategic bombing policy, which was a crucial issue in the conduct of the war. Portal soon found himself at one with the Prime Minister, whose view was that

> The Navy can lose us the war, but only the Air Force can win it. Therefore our supreme effort must be to gain overwhelming mastery of the air. The Fighters are our salvation, but the Bombers alone provide the means of victory. We must therefore develop the power to carry an ever increasing volume of explosives to Germany, so as to pulverise the entire industry and scientific structure on which the war effort and economic life of the enemy depend.[20]

But there were other claimants for bomber support. The Navy wanted bomber help in disabling German surface raiders and U-boats in their base ports, and in mining their approaches; the Army wanted more bombers in the Middle East; and the civilian population was calling for bomber retaliation on German cities. Only a man with a clear view of strategic priorities and the determination to maintain them would have been able to stop the dispersion of bomber effort in ineffective 'penny-packeting'.

Portal's first directive to Bomber Command after assuming the duties of CAS gave 'Oil and Enemy Morale' as its primary targets. Both were to prove harder to damage than he or the Prime Minister expected: oil because its installations were more difficult to hit than to repair; and morale because the Germans 'could take it' just as staunchly as Londoners. 'Transportation' was added later to 'Oil', and 'Attacks on Morale' became 'Area Bombing' after it was found that, with existing equipment, Bomber Command could not hit anything much smaller than a medium sized German industrial town! Only about 35 per cent of the crews were reaching their target areas and half their bombs were falling in the open countryside![21] This problem would persist until the arrival of new navigational and target finding aids, in the shape of Gee and Oboe, at the end of 1942.

There are parallels to be drawn between Haig's offensives on the Western Front in 1916–17 and Portal's Strategic Bomber Offensive of 1941–45. Both were compelled by the absence of any other practicable way of wearing down the German will to resist; and both resulted in heavy loss of valuable life. By the end of the war Bomber Command had lost some 47,000 aircrew on operations out of the RAF'S total loss of just over 70,000 all ranks. As aircrew were all leaders or potential leaders, their loss was the equivalent to the junior leadership (officers and sergeants) of around a thousand battalions! It is perhaps not too unfair to equate the single-mindedness of Robertson and Haig with the absolute conviction of Portal, the Air Staff and 'Bomber' Harris that they could produce equally decisive results without much help from the two older Services.

While the winter Blitz darkened the skies over England, a false dawn broke in the Mediterranean. The Fleet Air Arm crippled the Italian Fleet at Taranto on 11th November 1940. General Richard O'Connor surprised the Italian 10th Army at Sidi Barrani on 9th December, and sent it reeling back past Bardia, Tobruk and Benghazi to its complete destruction at Beda Fomm on 7th February 1941. Generals Platt and Cunningham started their invasion of the Italian East African Empire from the Sudan and Kenya, which resulted in the surrender of the Duke of Aosta, the Italian Viceroy of Abyssinia, at Amba Alagi on 16 May 1941. The decision to reinforce the Middle East at the height of the Battle of Britain had paid off, and Churchill had been given every reason to douse his doubts about Wavell – at least for a short time.

This period also saw the dawn, which was by no means false, of close Anglo-American military collaboration. Admiral Ghormley returned to the United States in November. After his debriefing, Admiral Stark, Chief of US Naval Operations, with the concurrence of General George Marshall, the United States Army Chief of Staff, reported to the President:

I believe that the continued existence of the British Empire, combined with building up a strong protection in our home areas, will do most to assure the *status quo* in the Western Hemisphere, and to promote our principal national interests. . . .[22]

Stark advised Roosevelt to authorise secret, formal staff talks. A British Tri-Service delegation set out for Washington on 12 January 1941 under the cover name of 'Advisers to the British Supply Council in North America'. From this small acorn grew the great oak of the Anglo-American Combined Chiefs of Staff organisation, which we will be meeting in the next chapter.

Unfortunately, the old adage that success leads to success did not come true in the Mediterranean. The British victories in the Western Desert and East Africa goaded Hitler to go to the aid of his feckless Italian ally in the Balkans and the Western Desert. His thrust south-eastwards, which the Chiefs had half-expected after the fall of Poland a year earlier, led the principal members of the British Supreme Command concerned with the Middle East – Churchill, Eden, Dill and Wavell – once again into a gross under-estimation of the power and reach of the *Luftwaffe* and *Wehrmacht*. Yugoslavia and Greece were quickly devoured in April 1941; the British Expeditionary Force to Greece – largely Australian and New Zealand troops – was forced into another well-conducted, but nevertheless ignominious with-drawal; Rommel drove the weakened Western Desert Force back to Egypt, avenging Beda Fomm by capturing Generals O'Connor and Neame; Crete was lost in May; and by June, German forces were established in the Mediterranean as a direct threat to the Suez Canal. The only British successes were in crushing the German inspired rebellion of Rashid Ali in Iraq in May, the defeat of the Vichy French in Syria in June–July and holding on to the fortress of Tobruk.

Churchill was not to be deterred by these defeats. At the height of the crisis in April, he, personally, chaired a crucial meeting of the Chiefs of Staff Committee at which it was decided that '*the re-establishment of a front in Cyrenaica should have the priority in the resources of all three Services in the Middle East*'[23]. Portal considered that the need for fighters was now greater in the Middle East than at home and agreed to dispatch six extra squadrons of Hurricanes to Egypt, in addition to the steady stream of new aircraft already being flown there across Central Africa over the Takoradi air reinforcement route from Accra in the Gold Coast. Dill and Pound, however, had doubts about Churchill's renewed suggestion that tank reinforcements should be sent to Wavell in a fast convoy through the Mediterranean instead of round the Cape. Dill questioned the wisdom of weakening the United Kingdom's defences when there was renewed evidence of German invasion planning; and Pound was worried about the serious naval losses that might result from running the convoy past Sicily where the *Luftwaffe* had been established since December 1940, and had recently crippled the new aircraft-carrier *Illustrious* off Malta.

Neither Dill nor Pound sustained their objections, and so Churchill had his way. The 'Tiger' convoy, carrying 238 tanks, which Churchill christened his 'Tiger Cubs', and 41 Hurricanes, reached Alexandria safely with the loss of only one ship on 12th May, thanks to the strenuous efforts of Admirals Somerville and Cunningham, operating from the opposite ends of the Mediterranean. Churchill, blinded by his well known lack of appreciation of logistic problems, expected his 'Tiger Cubs' to be in action in a matter of days rather than weeks after their arrival. His disappointment led to the beginning of his loss of faith in Dill and to his penultimate clashes with Wavell.

Dill's doubts about Churchill's obsession with the Middle East drove him to act in respect of tanks much as Dowding had done over fighters in May 1940, but with less fortunate results. On 6th May 1941 he presented the Prime Minister with a closely argued paper, setting out his views and those of Alan Brooke, who had succeeded Ironside in July 1940 as GOC-in-C, Home Forces. He pointed out that the threat of invasion had not receded; the Germans could reconcentrate in the West in six to eight weeks after their operations in the Balkans were completed; their invasions of Poland, Norway, France, the Balkans and Libya had been achieved through close co-operation between armour and air power; the Chiefs of Staff had already agreed that six armoured divisions were needed for the successful defence of the British Isles; but, by June, only three would be available. It was dangerous, he stressed, to discount the German ability to mount a successful invasion. Their capacity to overcome military difficulties had invariably been under-estimated. The loss of Egypt would be a calamity, but it would not end the war, whereas a successful invasion of Britain would do so almost certainly. Egypt was not even second in the agreed strategic priorities: Singapore had been given a higher priority and yet was being starved of resources. Risks must, of course, be taken somewhere, but they should be calculated risks. He believed that the Chiefs had gone to the limit, if not beyond, in reinforcing Wavell. Further dispatch of reinforcements should be confined to replacements, and even this would strain available shipping.[24]

The Prime Minister was taken aback by Dill's paper, and took a week to reply:

> . . . I gather you would be prepared to face the loss of Egypt and the Nile Valley, together with the surrender or ruin of the Army of half a million men we have concentrated there, rather than lose Singapore. I do not take that view . . . I have already given you the political data upon which the military arrangements for the defence of Singapore should be based, namely, that should Japan enter the war, the United States will in all probability come in on our side; and in any case, Japan would not be likely to besiege Singapore at the outset, as this would be an operation far more dangerous to her and less harmful to us than spreading her cruisers and battle-cruisers on the Eastern trade routes.[25]

Many governments, Churchill maintained, would have wilted before so grave a pronouncement by the highest professional authority, but Pound, Portal and the War Cabinet did not support Dill's *démarche*. Having made his protest, Dill wisely let the matter rest, but henceforth Churchill had his doubts about him as he did about Wavell.

Churchill-Wavell antagonism resurfaced over the Rashid Ali rebellion in Iraq. Wavell was reluctant to send forces from Egypt to deal with the rebellion, but Auchinleck, C-in-C India, reacted with, in Churchill's eyes, creditable speed, and was largely responsible for ending the affair. Then came the crisis over the proposed invasion of Syria. Wavell believed that this was largely inspired by Free French chicanery, and that Whitehall was asking him to mount something like a Jameson raid on de Gaulle's behalf. Dill defended Wavell, suggesting that he should be allowed to handle the affair in his own way or be relieved of his command. Dill won, and Wavell mounted a properly organised and successful campaign, forcing an armistice on Vichy by mid-July.

Churchill's final breach with Wavell as C-in-C, Middle East, came over the use of the 'Tiger Cubs'. Wavell was not prepared to attack Rommel on the Egyptian frontier until they had been modified in workshops for desert warfare, and the crews had had time to train with them. Churchill wanted him to attack in May before the Germans could recover from the heavy losses that they had suffered in Crete at the hands of Freyberg's New Zealanders, and before Rommel's supply position, which 'Ultra' radio intercepts suggested was causing him difficulties, could be improved. Wavell, supported by Dill, was not prepared to launch his 'Battleaxe' offensive to relieve

Tobruk until 15 June; and when it was launched it proved a costly failure in terms of tanks lost. Rommel's ingenious use of his 88 mm anti-aircraft guns as anti-tank weapons came as a nasty surprise to the Western Desert Force, as did his aggressive handling of the two panzer divisions of the Afrika Korps.

Churchill was deeply hurt by the apparent misuse of his precious 'Tiger Cubs', and he was even more upset by Wavell reporting that he could not try again for at least three months. Dill tried to protect Wavell, but realising that the Prime Minister had lost confidence in him, acquiesced in a change of command. Wavell did not complain. Using a cricketing metaphor, he agreed, that '*he had had a few sixes knocked off him recently, and that it was time to change the bowling*'.

Auchinleck and Wavell changed places at the end of June, Wavell becoming C-in-C India and Churchill snidely quipping that he could enjoy a well earned rest dispensing justice under the banyan tree. Auchinleck, whom Churchill had never met, was very much on trial in his new post. His helpful reaction to the Rashid Ali rebellion told in his favour, but his caution when in command at Narvik during the Norwegian campaign made him suspect in the Prime Minister's estimation.

The Air Force commanders in the Middle East did not escape Churchill's criticism either. He insisted on the dismissal of the AOC-in-C, Sir Arthur Longmore, for 'belly-aching' too much about lack of resources. He was replaced by his deputy, Sir Arthur Tedder, but Churchill was soon 'belly-aching' about him, saying that he was '*a nut and bolt administrator, lacking strategic and tactical flare*' – but events were to disprove this early judgement of Tedder.

Since the Battle of Britain had been won, each of the Chiefs had had his own cross to bear. Dill had struggled under the load of disasters in the Balkans and Middle East. Portal had anxieties about being able to generate an effective strategic bomber offensive whilst countering the German Blitz on Britain. But Pound had by far the heaviest burden of all: the long, fraught Battle of the Atlantic. After postponing his invasion of England, Hitler intensified his U-boat, surface raider and air blockade of the British Isles. By the beginning of 1941, shipping losses were escalating at an alarming rate: January 326,000 tons, February 402,000 tons, March 537,000 tons and April 654,000 tons. The writing was on the wall, and although the fight was being waged by many hands on both sides of the Atlantic, and not least by the drive and dynamism of the Prime Minister, it was Dudley Pound who led the Admiralty team to eventual success.

One of Pound's key decisions was to appoint Admiral Sir Percy Noble as C-in-C Western Approaches and to move his headquarters to Liverpool where it was established close to that of Air Chief Marshal Sir Frederick Bowhill's Coastal Command. These two commanders worked closely together with their supporting scientists to devise new equipment and tactics for the battle. Thanks to Canadian efforts in providing escorts on their side of the Atlantic, the U-boats were forced to operate further and further out in the Atlantic. Discussions between the Admiralty team in Washington and the United States Navy Department, which were directed by Pound from London, led to Churchill's correspondence with the President over 'the mid-Atlantic gap'. On 11th April 1941, Roosevelt extended the Western Hemisphere Security zone out to longitude 26 degrees West and authorised the establishment of American air bases in Greenland and Iceland, thus reducing the awkward gap in escort cover.

The Battle of the Atlantic was far from won, but in May the sinkings had dropped back to 500,000 tons and to 431,000 tons in June. Thanks to acceleration in ship repair and new construction under the generous American Lend-Lease programmes passed by Congress in March, the nett loss was progressively reduced by the arrival of new and repaired tonnage. The destruction of the *Bismarck* by the Royal Navy, and the damage inflicted on the *Scharnhorst* and *Gneisenau* in Brest by Bomber Command, helped to lighten Pound's anxieties.

The British Supreme Command had every reason to rejoice when Hitler invaded Russia on 22 June 1941, but there were two sides to this welcome diversion. On the positive side, Hitler's 'entanglement with the Bear', as Churchill delighted to call the struggle in the East, produced immediate relief from the Blitz as the *Luftwaffe* flew off eastwards to support the *Wehrmacht*; the threat of invasion declined; and Axis pressure in the Mediterranean and Middle East was eased; but in the Atlantic there was no respite, because Hitler directed the German Navy to concentrate on bringing Britain to her knees by starvation, while its sister Services conquered Russia.

On the negative side of the Russian coin, the Chiefs doubted whether the 'Bear' could survive long enough for rescue by 'General Winter' as had happened in 1812. Their doubts grew as the *panzer* spearheads thrust deeper and deeper into Russia, and massive surrenders of encircled Russian armies were reported. By autumn, the understandable, but irritatingly raucous Soviet demands for help were beginning to suggest that Russia might become more of a liability than an asset. The Chiefs appreciated, however, that, if meeting Stalin's demands would stop him following France's example by making peace with Hitler, some sacrifice of American Lend-Lease weapons and equipment destined for Britain would be worthwhile.

In such a changed situation, it was imperative that the President and Prime Minister should meet. Roosevelt's special envoy and adviser on Lend-Lease, Harry Hopkins, arrived in London in July to make preliminary arrangements for the Atlantic Meeting which was to be held in the battleships *Augusta* and *Prince of Wales* at Placentia Bay, Newfoundland. He was also on his way to meet Stalin in Moscow to assess Russia's chances of survival and the best ways of helping her continued resistance. While in London, he revealed, much to Churchill's alarm, that Admiral Ghormley's 'Standardisation Team' was reporting adversely on what they considered to be a British waste of resources in the Middle East. In the team's view, British priorities for Lend-Lease supplies should be: defence of the United Kingdom, the Battle of the Atlantic, and defence of Singapore and Australasia. They did not deem operations in the Middle East important enough to warrant Lend-Lease help. In reporting thus, they were probably echoing Dill's views, which they would have gleaned from their lower level contacts in the War Office.

Churchill was determined to scotch these ideas before they could do any real damage to his Mediterranean policies. He invited Harry Hopkins, Averell Harriman, who was Hopkins's Lend-Lease deputy in London, and Ghormley's team to a briefing by the Chiefs on British strategic policy. Portal pointed to the increased strength of both Fighter and Bomber Commands since the Battle of Britain, suggesting that the United Kingdom was now secure against invasion. Pound was equally confident that this was so, and that naval effort must be concentrated on winning the Battle of the Atlantic. And Dill loyally, but without eating any of his words in his 6 May paper, gave a powerful presentation of why Britain must continue to defend her position in the Middle East. Churchill left the meeting confident that the Americans had been convinced – he misjudged them!

Churchill crossed the Atlantic in *Prince of Wales*, accompanied by Pound, Dill, Freeman (deputising for Portal, who was left behind to 'mind the shop') and Ismay, and by powerful Foreign Office and Cabinet Secretariat teams. Drafting the Atlantic Charter took priority, but need not concern us here. More important from the Chiefs' point of view was their first meeting with their American counterparts: Admiral Harold Stark and General George Marshall – there was no independent United States Air Force, Stark and Marshall being responsible for United States Naval and Army Aviation.

In the amicable military discussions, the British Chiefs soon found that the Americans were not thinking much beyond the problems of the defence of the Western Hemisphere, Marshall going as far as to suggest that the United States might have to occupy Columbia, Venezuela and Brazil to protect the Panama Canal. He seemed more preoccupied with the possibility of a pro-Nazi coup in Brazil than with events in Europe.

As the military discussions proceeded, it also became clear that the Americans had little liking for the British concept of holding the ring around Germany while weakening her through blockade, peripheral attacks and intense air bombardment. They regarded such a strategy as a waste of time and a negative policy. They had an instinctive urge to use America's great wealth, industrial capacity and manpower resources to finish the war quickly with a direct thrust to the heart of Nazi Germany. Any operations, like those in the Middle East, which did not contribute to this primary aim, were suspect and deemed diversionary. Thus, the seeds were sown of a renewed Easterner-Westerner controversy, reminiscent of the First World War. The British took the Easterner view, advocating the indirect approach as the only practicable way of breaking the German will to resist with the resources actually available. The Americans were the new Westerners, determined upon the concentration of effort on the shortest, though most heavily defended, route to victory. They were blithely confident that this was the best way to use their vast resources once they were mobilised. The British wondered how long this would take. At this stage of the war, the American Army had scarcely begun to gear itself up to meet the demands of the modern battlefield nor had it any trained formations worthy of the name. As we shall see in Chapter 8, at national level they still lacked the machinery to staff and co-ordinate, let alone execute, major plans.

The germination of these seeds of inter-allied strategic dispute still lay in the future. As far as current policies were concerned, the most disturbing revelation was American scepticism about Portal's bombing policy, and the growing demands of the expanding United States Army Air Force for a larger share of available American bomber production, which the British were warned might halve the planned flow of United States-built bombers to the RAF. The Americans also confirmed their dislike for British Middle East policy, and their belief that the reinforcement of Singapore was more important than the Western Desert. Surprisingly, they seemed to have only the sketchiest plans for reinforcing their own forces in the Philippines. They were sending a mere fifty fighters and one squadron of Flying Fortress bombers to Manila. Regrettably, they were falling into the same trap that had already ensnared the British in 1940–41 of overestimating their own power to deter their principal enemy, the Japanese, and underestimating the Japanese determination to establish an Asian Co-prosperity Sphere in the Far East.

Three weeks before the Atlantic Meeting, the situation in the Far East had taken a marked turn for the worse. The Japanese extorted an agreement from the Vichy French for stationing Japanese troops and aircraft in Indo-China. Realising that if this move was not resisted, the Japanese would go on to occupy Siam, the State Department reacted sharply and froze all Japanese assets within the United States' control. The British and Dutch Governments followed suit, and for a time it looked as if the Japanese had accepted this rebuff because they agreed to open negotiations with Washington for a general settlement of Far Eastern problems. Churchill was not impressed, and advocated warning Tokyo that any infringement of Siamese sovereignty would be seen by the three Western Governments as a *casus belli*. He thought that he had persuaded the President to do so during the Atlantic Meeting, but when Roosevelt returned to Washington, the State Department watered down Churchill's draft and issued a much weaker version that did not impress the extremists in Tokyo.

Until Britain could settle her affairs in the Middle East, she could not find the resources with which to oppose Japan in the Far East. The Chiefs hoped that Roosevelt would delay a showdown with the Japanese until Auchinleck had defeated Rommel in the Western Desert, and it had been possible to send air and naval reinforcements to the Far East. Much to their chagrin, Auchinleck was no more prepared to attack Rommel until he was ready than Wavell had been, and this would not be before November at the earliest.

Churchill, as usual, would brook no such delay. The second and perhaps decisive phase of Hitler's operations in Russia had begun. Unless Auchinleck attacked by September, he might find himself faced with Rommel's Afrika Korps reinforced with troops released from Russia, or with a German force appearing in his rear through the Caucasus or Anatolia, or perhaps all three. Auchinleck was obdurate and would not agree to bring forward the date of the 'Crusader' offensive. He was summoned home for consultations as Wavell had been. Tedder accompanied him.

Churchill summed up the outcome of the 'Auk's' visit:

> . . . General Auchinleck's unquestioned abilities, his powers of exposition, his high, dignified, and commanding personality, gave me the feelng that he might be right, and that, even if wrong, he was still the best man. I therefore yielded to the November date for the offensive, and turned my energies to making it a success.[26]

Tedder did not escape his share of Prime Ministerial criticism. After returning to Cairo, he sent a cable to London suggesting that the Axis would probably enjoy 'numerical superiority' – he did not say 'air superiority'. Churchill's former doubts about Tedder resurfaced, and he insisted on a very senior officer being sent out to enquire what had been happening to all the aircraft sent to the Middle East at the expense of the bomber offensive and the defence of Singapore.

Portal sent out his Vice Chief, Wilfrid Freeman, but before Freeman could report back, Churchill was demanding Tedder's head. Portal persuaded Sir Archibald Sinclair, the Secretary of State for Air, to resign with him if the Prime Minister forced the issue, but first he cabled Freeman, asking two questions: should Tedder be relieved, and, if so, would Freeman be prepared to take his place? The answer was a firm 'No' to both. Auchinleck supported Freeman's view, stressing that Tedder had made great strides in restoring the Army's and Navy's confidence in the RAF, which had been so badly shaken by lack of air cover during the recent disasters in Greece, Crete, the Western Desert and at sea in the Mediterranean. Freeman reframed the statistics of relative air strengths to satisfy the Prime Minister, who minuted later, when it was suggested to him that the two sets of figures were not all that far apart:

> It is only the kind of difference between plus and minus, or black and white.[27]

Nonetheless, Tedder survived and was to win Churchill's confidence before long. Auchinleck was to be less fortunate but such is the price of dynamic Prime Ministerial leadership.

During the pause before 'Crusader' was launched on 18 November 1941, US-Japanese relations continued to deteriorate in a downward spiral. A month earlier, Prince Konoye had been replaced as Prime Minister of Japan by General Togo, who was more susceptible to pressures from the military extremists. Although it was not known in Washington or London, the Japanese Army and Navy Chiefs had set a deadline of 25 November for a satisfactory settlement or war.

The defence of Singapore was primarily a naval and air problem, and not, as is so often made out, of the big guns on Singapore Island facing in the wrong direction. The Chiefs recognised that a successful defence of Singapore depended upon command of the sea; and this, in turn, needed shore-based and carrier borne air cover. They had decided as long ago as August 1940 to entrust the defence of Malaya, from which shore-based air cover was to be provided, to the Royal Air Force with a Far Eastern establishment of 336 first-line aircraft. The principal role of the Army was to defend the Malayan airfields, built for this size of force. There was no intention of defending the long, undeveloped and jungle covered east coast of the Malay Peninsula.

In the autumn of 1941 there were only 158 largely obsolescent aircraft in Malaya, as opposed to almost one thousand modern first-line machines in the Middle East. To make matters worse, the Far East had been low on the priority list for Radar, and so far no effective early-warning system had been established for Malaya or Singapore.

At the time of the Atlantic Meeting, the Joint Planners had recommended the dispatch to the Far East of one battleship from the Mediterranean, which would be followed by four recently modernised R Class battleships as soon as they were worked up. The aircraft-carrier *Eagle* would also be sent as soon as she was ready. By March 1942, it was planned to have a Far Eastern Fleet of some seven capital ships, a carrier, ten cruisers, and twenty-four destroyers based upon Singapore. If the Americans had spun out their negotiations with the Japanese, making concessions to buy time if need be, the combined United States, British and Dutch fleets would have had a fair chance of maintaining command of the Asiatic seas.

Churchill did not like the Planners' proposals. Recalling the way in which the threat of a foray into the Atlantic by the *Bismarck* had tied down most of the Navy's capital ships, he insisted on the dispatch of a small force of modern ships instead of the four R Class. Pound could not agree. He did not believe that effective deterrent action could be taken in the Far East until a balanced fleet could be despatched there in the spring of 1942. In his view, British and American foreign policy should be developed with this time factor in mind. The War Cabinet overruled him and insisted on the inevitable compromise: while the Naval Staff plan should go ahead as the longer term deployment, *Repulse* and *Prince of Wales* should be sent at once via the Cape as a short term deterrent to the Japanese. The carrier *Indomitable* was to have accompanied them but was delayed by mechanical defects.

As *Prince of Wales*, wearing the flag of Admiral Sir Tom Phillips, the former Vice Chief of Naval Staff, left Cape Town, Auchinleck opened his 'Crusader' offensive on 18 November. After a month's hard fighting, with fortunes swaying up and down the Desert between the Egyptian frontier and Tobruk, and in which epic actions like First and Second Sidi Rezegh, Rommel's 'dash for the frontier wire', *Totensonntag*, Trigh Capuzzo and Bir el Gubi opened the history of the newly created British 8th Army, Rommel was forced to lift the siege of Tobruk and to withdraw temporarily from Cyrenaica into Tripolitania. But Auchinleck's hard won success was to prove but a pyrrhic victory. He had felt obliged to replace his Army Commander in the middle of the battle. The inbred cavalry spirit of the British Army was still too much alive for sound armoured tactics to be evolved without pain and grief. 8th Army's tank losses were so crippling that Auchinleck could not continue operations to drive Rommel out of Africa. The Germans were to remain unbeatable in the Desert until Montgomery showed how armour should be handled in the Battle of Alam Halfa at the end of August 1942.

Tobruk was, in fact, relieved on 8 December, the day after Pearl Harbour, and Rommel was disengaging two days later as both the *Repulse* and *Prince of Wales* were sunk off the Malayan coast. Rommel was soon back on the offensive and sent 8th Army reeling back to the Gazala Line in January 1942. Churchill's and the Chiefs' hopes of being able to transfer resources to the Far East after 'Crusader' were sadly diminished.

There has never been a satisfactory explanation of why Washington foreclosed negotiations with Tokyo so soon and so abruptly on 26 November 1941 by presenting the Japanese with impossible terms. The Japanese reserve negotiating position, Plan 'B', was not all that different from the American draft *Modus Vivendi* proposals. The gap between the two sides could have been bridged, at least temporarily and for long enough to allow British and American precautionary measures to be taken. Cordell Hull, the American Secretary of State, seems to have totally misjudged the Japanese negotiating position. The American cryptographers had broken the Japanese Diplomatic code 'Purple' and so the State

Department was reading its opponent's communications. But even so, Washington remained in a curiously unrealistic mood of half expecting the Japanese to return to the negotiating table after the definitive Japanese rejection of the American terms. The Navy Department did warn its Cs-in-C of the termination of the talks, but the State Department did not bother to inform London, and the President went off for a short holiday at Warm Springs!

Tragic though events were that flowed from the Japanese surprise attack on Pearl Harbor, the United States was at last in the war. Churchill lost no time in inviting himself and his Chiefs of Staff to Washington to concert war plans with the Americans. He left for the United States with a large staff in the battleship *Duke of York* on 14 December 1941. His team differed in two important respects from the one that he took to the Atlantic Meeting. Portal replaced Freeman, which was to be expected, but Dill did not cross the Atlantic as CIGS, but as Churchill's and the British Chiefs' representative (designate) with the United States Chiefs. Alan Brooke was to be the new CIGS, and stayed behind in London to be briefed and to read himself into the job while the 'Arcadia' conference, as these second Churchill-Roosevelt talks were called, was going on in Washington.

Churchill's decision to change the Army's Chief had been long in maturing. One difference of opinion after another, especially over the relative scales of reinforcement of the Middle and Far East, had progressively clouded Dill's relationship with the Prime Minister. He was, perforce, the principal strategist amongst the Chiefs. Pound and Portal tended to concentrate on their own Service problems, leaving Dill to take Churchill's pounding on grand strategy, which, although essentially maritime and peripheral, was largely dictated by the actions of Hitler and the *Wehrmacht* on land. Dill became haunted by the anxiety lest the nation would be rushed into premature offensive operations, which might not only fail in themselves, but would also prejudice the future by squandering resources that should have been garnered, as was the agreed strategy, for the final offensive phases of the war.

Churchill began to feel that, sound strategist though Dill most certainly was, he suffered from over-caution and lacked imaginative inspiration. The truth is that although Dill was highly respected by the Army, he never managed to get on terms with the Prime Minister as Pound and Portal had done. He gradually became the weakest member of the Chiefs' team from Churchill's point of view. He was rarely able to carry an argument with Churchill as he felt that he should have been able to do. His health too was not robust enough, and he lacked the necessary psychological toughness for the hurly-burly of Churchill's way of conducting affairs. Dill lived on his nerves, and he was not helped by the death of his first wife in 1940. He became a much happier man after he remarried in October 1941, but it was too late to re-establish Churchill's confidence in him. On 18 November, the day 'Crusader' was launched, his coming replacement by Brooke was announced with 25 December as the effective date.

Churchill rewarded Dill with his Field Marshal's baton, and had offered him the Governorship of Bombay. Pearl Harbour changed all that. His intimate knowledge of British strategy, of the workings of Whitehall, of its leading personalities, and of the innermost secrets of the Chiefs, made him an ideal choice as their representative in Washington as Head of the British Joint Staff Mission that was to be established in the wake of 'Arcadia'.

Brooke was not Churchill's first choice as Dill's replacement. He was first drawn towards Lieutenant-General Sir Archibald Nye, the Vice Chief of the Imperial General Staff, whom Beaverbrook favoured as another 'Wully' Robertson, in that he too had risen from the ranks and hence would be a popular choice in Britain's increasingly egalitarian society. The 'Beaver' also favoured Sir Frederick ('Tim') Pile, the GOC-in-C, Anti-Aircraft Command, but no one else did. Dill, himself, recommended Brooke not only as his own choice but as the man in whom the Army had greatest confidence. The Prime Minister hesitated. He had already had a passage of arms with Brooke and had lost. After Dunkirk, Brooke had been sent back to France to command the Second BEF, which was being landed in France through Cherbourg. As the French collapse gathered momentum, Brooke advised pulling out before it was too late. Churchill came on the phone and argued that the force must stay 'to make the French feel that we were supporting them'. Brooke's sharp reply was that *'it was impossible to make a corpse feel; the French Army was to all intents and purposes dead!'* After half an hour's argument over the phone, Churchill gave way and allowed the withdrawal. Few of Hitler's generals would have been allowed to get away with such strategic commonsense. Brooke, however, survived Churchill's chagrin, and took over Southern Command on his return to England.[28]

The next Churchill-Brooke meeting was more amicable. The Prime Minister visited Brooke's headquarters and toured units with him during the hectic anti-invasion preparations in the summer of

1940. Brooke's handling of Southern Command so impressed Churchill that three days later he was appointed C-in-C Home Forces in place of Ironside, whom he had decided was too old at 60 to give the dynamic leadership needed to repel an invasion attempt. Brooke had plenty of opportunity to study Winston at close quarters and vice versa in the underground Cabinet War Room where the C-in-C Home Forces had an office relatively close to the Prime Minister's. Both men were far from sure that they would get on, Churchill remarking to Nye, with whom he discussed Dill's recommendation of Brooke:

> When I thump the table and push my face towards him what does he do? Thumps the table harder and glares back at me – I know these Brookes – stiff-necked Ulstermen and there's no one worse to deal with than that![29]

At first neither Pound nor Portal liked the idea of Brooke joining them as their Army colleague. They felt that he was too abrupt, over-forceful, and tactless. The general consensus in Whitehall and in the Army, however, favoured Brooke as the only senior Army officer mentally large enough, physically tough enough, and politically impartial enough for the job. Churchill was wracked with doubt; '*I don't think we will get on*' he had said, but later confided to Eden that '*Brooke was the right man – the only man.*'[30]

Brooke was a scion of the Brookes of Colebrooke in County Fermanagh. Like Milne and Ironside, he was a Gunner; but unlike them he had gained much experience in the workings of Whitehall, first, as Director of Military Training in the War Office in 1936; then working close to the corridors of power as Commander of the experimental Mobile Division in 1938, and of Anti-Aircraft Command later that year; and finally as C-in-C Home Forces, the key Army command in 1940/41. His battle experience in the First World War on the Western Front was the foundation of his military judgement, and it was sharpened and brought up to date by his brilliant handling of 1st Corps in the face of the German *Blitzkrieg* in France in 1940.

Brooke was soon to prove himself a master of grand strategy, and a match for the Prime Minister in strategic thinking. His precise mind could filter essentials from complex detail, and he could discern the pattern of events as they unfolded with perceptive clarity. Paradoxically, his great strength of conviction and intellectual integrity were matched by remarkable flexibility of mind. He would hammer his points home relentlessly in his clipped, staccato mode of speaking, but he was always prepared to accept valid opposing arguments and to modify his policies accordingly. He was devoid of all pomposity and self interest, and yet he was not an easy man with whom to deal. His mind moved too fast to suffer fools gladly, and he was impatient to a fault, outdoing even Churchill in this respect. Churchill's imagination needed no stimulation, only discipline: Brooke provided that discipline.

Pound, Portal and now Brooke were men of the same ilk, who could stand up to Churchill without losing his confidence. Amongst themselves they would argue through professional disagreements without losing their deep personal respect for each other. In short, the Chiefs' team at the beginning of 1942 was a match for Churchill, and it was to be one of the country's greatest assets in the 'Coalition War', as the Americans call the period from 1942 to 1945.

Chronology
FOR CHAPTER EIGHT

1942

17 Jan	'Arcadia' Conference ends in Washington.
21	Rommel counter-attacks in the Western Desert.
1 Feb	New U-boat 4th wheel Enigma coding introduced, British convoy code broken by Germans.
11 Feb	*Scharnhorst* and *Gneisenau* escape up the Channel.
15	Fall of Singapore.
8 March	Fall of Rangoon.
9	Brooke becomes Chairman of the COS Committee.
28	Bombing of Lubeck.
1 April	Marshall Memorandum presented to the President.
5	Japanese Fleet bombardment of Colombo.
8	Marshall and Hopkins arrive in London.
8 May	Battle of the Coral Sea.
20	Burma evacuated.
26	Rommel attacks at Gazala.
30	First 'Millennium' (1,000 bomber) raid – on Cologne.
4–7 June	Battle of Midway.
17–21	Churchill visits Washington.
21	Fall of Tobruk.
4 July	Loss of Arctic Convoy PQ 17.
18	Marshall, King and Hopkins arrive in London.
24	CCS agree strategy for 1942/43 (CCS 94).
7–8 Aug	Changes of command in the Middle East.
12–16	Churchill in Moscow.
19 Sep	Dieppe raid.
23 Oct	Battle of El Alamein.
2 Nov	Russians counter-offensive starts at Stalingrad.
7–8	'Torch' Landings in French North Africa begin.

1 Dec   U-boat 4th wheel Enigma codes broken.

1943
14–24 Jan Casablanca Conference (Symbol).
23   Capture of Tripoli.
2 Feb   German surrender at Stalingrad.
7 May   Capture of Tunis.
11–27   Second Washington Conference (Trident).
2 June   'Pointblank' Directive Offensive issued.
10   Invasion of Sicily.
25   Fall of Mussolini.
5 July   Battle of Kursk.
27   Clandestine Italian armistice negotiations begin.
14–25 Aug 1st Quebec Conference (Quadrant).
3 Sep   8th Army crosses Straits of Messina.
8   Salerno landing and Italian armistice.
1 Oct   Capture of Naples.
14   Air Battle of Schweinfurt.
21   Death of Pound; Cunningham becomes CNS.
22–28 Nov Cairo Conference (Sextant), 1st Stage.
28–1 Dec Tehran Conference (Eureka).
3–7   Cairo Conference (Sextant), 2nd Stage.

1944
22 Jan   Anzio Landings – First Battle for Rome begins.
12 Feb   First Battle of Cassino.
16   Second Battle of Cassino.
25   CCS approve priority for Italy over 'Anvil'.
15–23 Mar Third Battle of Cassino.
24   'Anvil' postponed to July.
30   Battles of Imphal and Kohima begin.
10 April CCS deadlocked on 'Anvil' directive to Wilson.
11 May   'Diadem', the Second Battle for Rome opens.
22   Japanese withdrawal starts from Imphal.
4 June   Capture of Rome.
6   'Overlord' landings in Normandy begin.
10–15   CCS meet in London.
19   Channel storm jeopardises Allied build-up.
2 July   'Anvil' fixed for 15th August as 'Dragoon'.
20   Hitler assassination attempt fails.
13 Aug   Battle of Falaise begins.

15	'Anvil/Dragoon' landings in South of France.
19	Allies enter Paris.
8 Sep	Assault on the Gothic Line in Italy opens.
12–16	Second Quebec Conference (Octagon).
17	Battle of Arnhem begins.
1 Oct	14th Army offensive in Burma begins.
15	Liberation of Athens.
23–6	Battle of Leyte Gulf.
4 Nov	Dill dies in Washington.
3 Dec	Communist rebellion in Athens.
16–25	German Ardennes counter-offensive.

1945	
9 Jan	US landing on Luzon.
17	Russians enter Warsaw.
30	Malta Conference (Argonaut).
4–11 Feb	Yalta Conference (Argonaut).
8 March	Negotiations for German surrender in Italy open.
22–24	Crossing of the Rhine.
9 April	Final offensive opens in Italy.
2 May	German surrender in Italy.
9	VE Day.
17 June	Potsdam Conference (Terminal) begins.
6 Aug	First Atomic bomb dropped on Japan.
2 Sep	VJ Day.

8
THE TRIUMPH OF THE COMBINED CHIEFS OF STAFF
The Coalition War: 1942–1945

First Sea Lords	Chiefs of the Imperial General Staff
Sir Dudley Pound*	Sir Alan Brooke
Sir Andrew Cunningham Oct 1943	Dec 1941

Chief of Air Staff
Sir Charles Portal

'It may well be thought by future historians that the most valuable and lasting result of our first Washington conference – "Arcadia", as it was code-named – was the setting up of the now famous "Combined Chiefs of Staff Committee" . . . There was never a failure to reach effective agreement for action, or to send clear instructions to the commanders in every theatre. Every executive officer knew that the orders he received bore with them the combined conception and expert authority of both Governments. There never was a more serviceable war machinery established among allies, and I rejoice that in fact, if not in form, it continues to this day.'

Winston Churchill
The Second World War, Vol III.[1]

Churchill and the British Chiefs of Staff used their passage in the *Duke of York* across the wintery North Atlantic just before Christmas 1941 to distil and rehearse their proposals for Anglo-US grand strategy that they would put to their American colleagues when they met them for the first post-Pearl Harbor summit – code-named 'Arcadia' – in Washington on 22nd December. Churchill had led the debates during the voyage by tabling three remarkable papers of his own, which set out the policy that, in the end, did win the war: concentrating against Germany first; drawing the ring around her while she was weakened by bombing, blockade, subversion and losses on the

---

* Died in office.

Russian front; clearing the North African coast and approaching Nazi occupied Europe, initially via its soft Mediterranean under-belly with the aim of knocking Italy out of the war, and of drawing German strength southwards and away from North West Europe; and delivering the *coup de grâce* across the English Channel, hopefully in 1943.

By the end of the voyage, the British Joint Planners had cast this policy in the form of a Chiefs of Staff paper ready for presentation to the Americans. It was, in essence, the traditional peripheral, mari-time strategy which the British cherish when facing Continental opponents, and which had been given even greater credibility in their minds by the 1914–18 slaughter on the Western Front, and by the French débâcle in 1940, leading to Dunkirk. In the view of the British Chiefs, there could be no return to the Continent until Germany had been very seriously weakened, like a bull in a Spanish bull-fight. The immediate problem was to decide how the weakening process should be carried out, and how the efforts of the Anglo-American picadors should be co-ordinated.

The Americans were far from ready to take major strategic de-cisions so soon after Pearl Harbor, and their outlook was fundamen-tally different, if not diametrically opposed, to that of the British. They were not ready, first, because they were still struggling to contain the effects of the Japanese assault; and, secondly, because they did not, as yet, possess the staff machinery needed for strategic planning. When it came to discussing the British Chiefs of Staff Paper – given the title WW 1 – they allowed it to go through almost on the nod for want of anything better to put in its place. This was unfortunate in that it gave a greater semblance of agreement than existed between the two sides.

'Arcadia's' importance lay more in the establishment of the co-ordinating machinery needed for coalition warfare than in the premature attempt to reach agreement on strategy. The American system for developing national defence policies was about where the British had been before the days of the Committee of Imperial Defence. In 1941, the United States Army and Navy were further apart and less amicably disposed towards one another than the British Services, but they had the advantage of having no indepen-dent United States Air Force to muddy their inter-Service relation-ships, and so there had been less pressure to establish a Chiefs of Staff Committee system. The long standing Joint Army-Navy Board and the Joint Ammunition Board were the only pieces of formal co-ordination machinery considered necessary. Inter-Service co-operation depended, as it had done in Britain, on personal contact and correspondence between the Secretaries for the Army and Navy, and between their professional advisers in their Departments.

With British and American missions established in each other's capitals since early 1941, there had been ample exchange of views on command and staff systems, but, with America still theoretically neutral, little had been done to align them until 'Arcadia'. General Ismay records how *'the President, after discussing the British arrangements with the Prime Minister, decided to set up a Chiefs of Staff Organisation on the British model'*.[2] At the same time, they agreed to establish the Combined Chiefs of Staff Committee, consisting of the British and American Chiefs and supported by a Combined Secretariat, and Combined Planning and Intelligence Staffs. In order to distinguish between national and combined staffs, 'Joint' prefixed the former and 'Combined' signified the latter. Thus, the American Chiefs became the Joint Chiefs of Staff (JCS) to distinguish them from the Combined Chiefs of Staff (CCS), but the British, as the founders of the system, never added 'Joint' to their title, keeping their short title as COS.

As it was impracticable for the Chiefs of either country to be away from their own headquarters for long, Washington was chosen as the permanent location of the CCS. It was the capital of the major partner; it was safe from German bombardment; and, as the British Joint Staff Mission in Washington pointed out, *'co-ordination can only take place in Washington, as we consider it unlikely that the US Chiefs of Staff would delegate sufficient responsibility to their representatives in London'*.[3]

In Washington, the British Chiefs of Staff were represented on the Combined Chiefs of Staff Committee by Field Marshal Sir John Dill as the Head of the British Joint Staff Mission and three senior Naval, General and Air Staff representatives, who collectively and individually transmitted the British Chiefs of Staff Committee's views to the JCS and vice versa. The Joint Staff Mission also included staffs to work with the Americans to form the CCS Secretariat, Combined Planning Staff and Combined Intelligence Committee.

Dill was an excellent, if fortuitous, choice as Head of the British Joint Staff Mission. He was well known to and liked by the Washington establishment. Initially, Churchill kept him there on a temporary basis, while the CCS system was developing. He did not make up his mind to cancel Dill's appointment as Governor of Bombay, which he had described to Dill, when sugaring the pill of his dismissal from the post of CIGS, as '*a position of great honour, followed by a bodyguard of lancers*', until pressed to do so by the President and Harry Hopkins. But then Churchill gave him the additional responsibility of representing him in Washington in his capacity as British Minister of Defence with authority to correspond directly with him.

The only times when the British Chiefs themselves sat down together with their American colleagues were at the ten Roosevelt-Churchill Summits and on three other lesser occasions. Otherwise, it was Dill who led the British team at CCS meetings and was their principal spokesman. The first senior members of Mission were: Admiral Sir Charles Little, Lieutenant-General Sir Colville Wemyss and Air Marshal 'Bomber' Harris. Harris was soon to be recalled to take over Bomber Command.

The CCS system, so elegantly simple in concept and yet immensely complex in practice, could never have worked with the success that it did if it had not been for the constructive personal chemistry of the principal members of this extraordinary Anglo-American Supreme Command, which was to prove itself so superior to anything set up in the First World War, and in any other previous war involving alliances. The CCS did have the advantage of the common Anglo-Saxon language and heritage, and of an unusual measure of good-will on both sides that flowed downwards from the President and Prime Minister. Nevertheless, latent national rivalries would have wrought havoc, as they usually do in alliances, if it had not been for two specific personal relationships: the respect that Roosevelt and Churchill had for each other; and the close friendship that grew up between General George Marshall and Sir John Dill, whose ability to translate the intentions of both sets of Chiefs to each other made his appointment one of the happiest pieces of Anglo-US casting.

One major difference remained between the British and American systems. The British COS Committee was a sub-committee of the War Cabinet, which had no parallel in Washington. The American JCS reported direct to the President as C-in-C of the United States Army and Navy. Thus Roosevelt could, in theory at least, have wielded greater direct power than Churchll in the direction of national military strategy. In practice, this was far from the case. Churchill's position as Prime Minister and Minister of Defence made him the British warlord, and his unrivalled military experience in war and the direction of war, gave him an influence in strategic affairs that Roosevelt could never match. American presidents did not begin to enjoy the full benefits of the British War Cabinet system until 1947 when the National Security Council was established.

In one respect, however, the Americans moved ahead of the British when setting up their Joint Chiefs of Staff Committee, which met for the first time on 9 February 1942. Such was the depth of suspicion that permeated United States Army/Navy relations that Roosevelt decided in July 1942 to appoint a neutral chairman – Fleet Admiral William D Leahy, who had been United States Ambassador to the Vichy Government in France – instead of rotating the chairmanship between the Chiefs, as was the British practice. Admiral Leahy's post was named Chief of Staff to the C-in-C, i.e. to the President. It was to take the British another decade and a half to follow suit, when Anthony Eden appointed Marshal of the Royal Air Force Sir William Dickson as Chief Staff Officer to the Minister of Defence and neutral Chairman of the Chiefs of Staff Committee in 1955.

The original members of the JCS were Admiral Leahy, General Marshall, Admiral Ernest J King, Chief of United States Naval Operations, and General H H ('Hap') Arnold, Commanding General of the United States Army Air Force. We are indebted to General Ismay, who saw them in action at most of the great summit meetings, for the assessments of them in his *Memoirs*. Of Marshall he says:

> He was a big man in every sense of the word, and utterly selfless. It was impossible to imagine his doing anything petty or mean, or shrinking from any duty, however distasteful. He carried himself with great dignity. At first he seemed somewhat cold and aloof; he never used nicknames or Christian names. Eisenhower was never Ike; Dill was never Jack . . . His integrity was unshakable, and anything in the nature of intrigue or special pleading was anathema . . . As a picker of men he was remarkably successful. His selection of Eisenhower, a recently promoted brigadier-general, to command all the American troops in Europe was a stroke of genius; and nearly all his appointments to high command were vindicated by results.[4]

Marshall is generally accepted as 'the Organiser of Victory' as Churchill called him: the man who expanded the United States Army from 200,000 to eight million, organising, equipping and training it for decisive operations directed at the heart of Germany. However, Alan Brooke, rather surprisingly, thought little of his mental ability and even less of his strategic ideas.[5] In both respects, he was certainly unfair to his great American colleague and strategic opponent. Brooke was quicker in debate and more incisive, but Marshall with his organisational brain was no less able and a massively stabilising influence in Allied councils. Brooke's antipathy to him as a strategist stemmed from differences in national outlook and upbringing. Marshall reflected traditional Continent-style thinking, based on American experience in their great Civil War. He prized the principle of concentration of effort at the decisive point, whereas Brooke was, perforce, bound to pursue the indirect approach due to lack of adequate resources to do otherwise.

King was the antithesis of Marshall. Ismay's description of him runs:

> He was tough as old nails and carried himself as stiffly as a poker. He was blunt and stand-offish, almost to the point of rudeness. At the start, he was intolerant of all things British, especially the Royal Navy; but he was almost equally intolerant and suspicious of the American Army. War against Japan was the problem to which he had devoted the study of a lifetime, and he resented the idea of American resources being used for any other purpose than to destroy Japanese. He mistrusted Churchill's power of advocacy, and was apprehensive that he would wheedle President Roosevelt into neglecting the war in the Pacific. Like Marshall, King was a great organiser.[6]

What Ismay did not say was that King had been one of the controversial figures in the United States Navy in the inter-war years. He was an outstanding seaman, aviator and commander, but he was one of those men who shine in war and cause infinite trouble in peace: a hard drinker, to the verge of alcoholism; a womaniser, despite having a happy family life with six daughters and a son; tactless, petty and parochial; and a hot-tempered and rigid disciplinarian. He had ambitions to become Chief of Naval Operations in 1939, but Admiral Harold Stark was given the job. The promotion did Stark little good: he became the scapegoat for Pearl Harbor. Roosevelt looked for a dynamic figure to re-establish the United States Navy's confidence. King was the obvious choice. He was appointed not only Chief of Naval Operations but also to the newly created wartime post of C-in-C of the US Navy. He wielded the greatest power at sea ever enjoyed by an admiral in the world's history.

'Hap' Arnold was a mellower personality, and was in a weaker position than Marshall and King since there was no independent United States Air Force and he was one of Marshall's subordinates. In consequence he spoke very little at CCS meetings. Ismay describes him as

> a veteran airman, with an unlimited belief in air power. But he did splendid work behind the scenes, and the friendship and confidence between him and Portal enabled many difficulties to be ironed out. He was always cheerful and smiling. His nickname "Hap" was a natural. But he could be tough when

occasion required, notably when he fought, and won, his battle for the day bomber.[7]

Arnold was an outstanding publicist in the cause of air power. His enthusiasm led to some lack of realism and balance in his pursuit of his policy of daylight precision bombing, undertaken against the advice of his British colleagues, which resulted in his pyrrhic victory in the skies over Schweinfurt. On 14 October 1943, just under 300 Flying Fortresses of the United States 8th Air Force did considerable damage to the ball-bearing factories around the city in a major daylight raid beyond the range of their fighter escorts, but German defenders shot down 60 Fortresses and damaged a further 117. 'Hap' was not deterred. A crash programme of long range fighter escorts enabled the United States Army Air Force to carry on the daylight half of the Combined Bomber Offensive with precision attacks, while the RAF continued its area bombing by night. The enormous contribution made by the American Army Air Force to the defeat of Germany and Japan was to enable 'Hap' to win independence for it after the war, and to become its first five star General.

Admiral William Leahy, who joined the JCS team later, had been Chief of Naval Operations (1937–39) before going to Vichy in 1940. He was a highly respected father figure, a close and trusted friend of Roosevelt, an experienced diplomat and a conciliator by temperament. He became Chairman of the JCS by virtue of his status as the President's Chief of Staff and through his seniority in the United States Services. Such was his reputation for balanced commonsense and sound judgement that he was elected unanimously by the British and American Chiefs as Chairman of the Combined Chiefs of Staff Committee.

The fascination of the story of the Chiefs during the second and coalition phase of the War lies in the ebb and flow of the debates at the ten great code-named summit meetings of the President and Prime Minister at which their Chiefs hammered out modifications to the agreed combined grand strategy for their approval. The British team had dominated the 'Arcadia' meeting at which WW 1 had been very tentatively agreed by the Americans. They continued to do so at the second and third meetings – 'Symbol' at Casablanca in January 1943 and 'Trident' at Washington in May. At 'Quadrant', the first Quebec meeting in August 1943, and at 'Sextant' in Cairo and 'Eureka' in Tehran in December 1943, the two sides were equally matched. Thereafter, the British team were increasingly less successful in gaining their ends as their resources as a proportion of the

Anglo-American effort declined and victory loomed ahead. Thoughts and ambitions about the shape of the post-war world began to drive wedges between the two teams, and, indeed, fanned differences between Churchill and his own Chiefs, particularly over Mediterranean strategy.

Throughout 1943, the British team had the experience and the forces in being to dominate the debates. They did know what war was all about and, in the primary European theatre, British forces were doing the lion's share of the fighting. American strength in the early debates lay in their ability to provide the resources without which the war could not be won, and they had it in their power to divert those resources to the Pacific if they were not persuaded that the right strategy was being pursued by the British. The two men who had to be convinced were Marshall and King: the former committed to the European theatre, but not to the British policy of the indirect approach; and the latter determined to seize every opportunity to divert resources to the Pacific theatre, where his heart and those of many of the American electorate lay.

The disasters that befell the Allies in the first three months of 1942 did not invalidate the 'Arcadia' WW 1 strategy, but they put it temporarily 'on the back burner' as the Americans say. The Japanese surge of invasion forces drew all readily available American and British forces into South East Asia and the Pacific to check their onrush. Rommel counter-attacked in the Western Desert on 21 January, four days after 'Arcadia' ended, and drove the 8th Army back to the Gazala Line, covering Tobruk. The British reverse had been largely due to diverting troops and aircraft from the Middle East to the Far East, but, with Rommel back in the ascendant, there was little possibility of the Vichy French in North Africa being willing to change sides, as had been hoped. Auchinleck's failure reinforced the strongly-held American view that operations in North Africa and the Middle East were a waste of resources. Much to Marshall's satisfaction, British-inspired plans to start clearing the North African shores with an Anglo-American landing in Morocco were cancelled by the CCS on 3rd March, and he was able to direct his planning staff under Brigadier-General 'Ike' Eisenhower to start a detailed study of the options for a direct attack towards the heart of Germany once the Japanese had been checked.

The war at sea was going equally badly. Dudley Pound found himself faced with a deteriorating situation on three fronts: Atlantic, Arctic and Indian Ocean. In the Battle of the Atlantic, the U-boats were again gaining the upper hand for three good reasons: the un-readiness of the United States Navy to operate a convoy system off the east coast of America and in the Caribbean turned the Western Atlantic into a U-boat paradise; on 1 February, the Germans intro-duced a fourth wheel into their U-boat Enigma coding machines, which defeated the cryptologists at Bletchley Park for almost the whole of 1942; and at around the same time their German counter-parts broke the Allied convoy control code. Allied shipping losses doubled between January and May 1942. In the Arctic, the supply convoys to Russia were coming under increasing attack from German aircraft, U-boats and surface ships based in northern Norway. In the Indian Ocean, the Japanese Navy was pressing westwards towards Ceylon and threatening the convoy route round the Cape to Suez. Sensibly, Pound realised that he could not go on carrying the burden of the chairmanship of the Chiefs as well as directing the crucial war at sea. On 5 March, he wrote to the Prime Minister:

> As you are aware, the Admiralty have to exercise general operational control over naval forces and from time to time have immediate situations to deal with which require my undivided attention.
>
> As Chairman of the COS Committee, I am naturally even more reluctant to absent myself from their meetings than I should be if I were not Chairman.
>
> This alone would not have moved me to ask that I should be relieved of the Chairmanship of the COS Committee, but, taken in combination with the fact that I have been Chairman for nearly a year and a half, I would like to suggest that the Chairmanship should be taken over by one of the other Services. As the Army have not held the Chairmanship during the war, it would seem appropri-ate that they should have a turn.[8]

Churchill accepted Pound's proposal and Brooke became Chairman on 9 March 1942. He was an excellent choice. Churchill and Brooke were to make a formidable and well balanced team. Moreover, it was a good moment to change chairmen: the war had reached the stage when, despite the disasters in the Far East, the time had come to plan the final defeat of Germany. The Naval and Air picadors were beginning to weaken the German bull: it was, indeed, appropriate that the Army matador should take over lead in planning Germany's final defeat. Brooke was also ten years older than Portal, and a harder man with the wider experience which was needed in dealing with Churchill, but less of a diplomat when work-ing with the Americans – Portal was the man, who usually stepped in to cool Anglo-American arguments when they became overheated.

Churchill took one specific and controversial step to strengthen the British Chiefs in planning the future assault on Western Europe.

Mountbatten had replaced the elderly Admiral of the Fleet Sir Roger Keyes as 'Adviser' on Combined Operations in October 1941. With the development of amphibious warfare equipment and techniques gaining in importance, and with the practicability of their mounting becoming crucial in the Anglo-American strategic debate, Churchill promoted him Chief of Combined Operations in March 1942. He then went on to make him a member of the Chiefs of Staff Committee with the rank of Vice Admiral and the equivalent honorary ranks in the Army and RAF. This was not welcomed by the Chiefs with much enthusiasm.

The war in the air was going no better than at sea or on land. The expansion of Bomber Command was lagging behind schedule, and the results being achieved were disappointing. Matters came to a head with the examination of the results of raids carried out by 400 bombers on the night 7–8 November 1941. The targets stretched from Boulogne to Berlin; almost 10 per cent of the aircraft were lost; and minimal damage was done. Portal decided that a change of leadership was needed. 'Bomber' Harris took over the command on 22 February 1942 and stamped his ruthless personality upon it straight away. Bomber Command henceforth was in no doubt that it had a commander with finite policies that its officers and men could understand.

Harris took over at a time when the RAF's monopoly of British offensive capability was on the wane. America's entry into the war made a land campaign in Europe a certainty, and a reduction in Bomber Command's high priority in the allocation of British resources an ominous probability as far as Portal and Harris were concerned. Throughout the rest of 1942, the two men fought to maintain the integrity of the Bomber offensive as the primary means of defeating Germany. In this they had some success using strategic and tactical concentration of effort.

At strategic level, they resisted pressure to divert bombers to help the Navy and Coastal Command in the Battle of the Atlantic, and only reluctantly accepted the need to bomb German occupied French Atlantic ports and to harass U-boats operating from them on transit through the Bay of Biscay. And at tactical level, they developed the Path Finder force and their fire-raising and saturation bombing techniques, which enabled them to concentrate enough weight of bombs on German industrial towns to do real damage. Lübeck, with its oxygen manufacturing capacity for U-boats, went up in flames on 28–29 March; and Rostock, with its Heinkel and Ardo works, suffered a similar fate in April. Harris made his point most forcibly on 30 May by concentrating every available bomber in his command, together with aircraft from operational training units to mount his 'Millennium' raid on Cologne with a thousand bombers. It did more damage to Cologne in 90 minutes than 70 previous raids had done. 'Millennium' was repeated over Essen on 1st June. Losses over Lübeck, Rostock, Cologne and Essen were all under 5 per cent.

Harris could not sustain such attacks, but he had demonstrated to both Churchill and the Chiefs what should be possible when Bomber Command's expansion was further advanced, and when 'Hap' Arnold's Americans joined in with their daylight precision bombing, if the latter proved practicable. Unfortunately, and this was not known at the time, Harris's successes were greater in the minds of the beholders than on the ground in Germany. Such was the extraordinary resilience and improvising capabilities of the German people that the effects of the raids were short lived and industrial production was restored in a matter of days.

After the Cologne attack, Harris made his bid for overriding priority for his bomber offensive. In a memorandum to Churchill on 17 June he declared it to be:

> imperative if we hope to win the war to abandon the disastrous policy of military intervention in the land campaigns of Europe, and to concentrate our air power against the enemy's weakest spots.[9]

These sentiments were echoed by Trenchard, who wrote to the Prime Minister, as was his wont, saying:

> For the country to get mixed up this year or next in land warfare on the Continent of Europe is to play Germany's game – it is to revert to 1914–1918 . . .[10]

Pound and Brooke rebutted Portal and Harris's claims throughout the summer, but in the autumn the Prime Minister came down on the Air side and decreed the expansion of Bomber Command from 32 to 50 squadrons by the end of 1942. Portal estimated that with this force he could drop $1^{1}/_{4}$ million tons of bombs on Germany in 1943–44, which would unhouse three quarters of the populations of all German towns with over 50,000 inhabitants, and destroy a third of German industry. It was virtually a policy of mass murder, but one from which no one from Churchill down to the bomber crews flinched in this total war against Nazi tyranny, which had engulfed all Europe. Had aircrew been asked to use flame throwers on the ground against civilians, which amounted to almost the same thing as dropping incendiaries, their reaction would have been very different. Doing so from 20,000 feet made the task utterly impersonal and so somehow psychologically acceptable as an act of war. Besides, it was seen quite clearly as the only way that the Western Allies could take the war to Germany at that time, and British cities had already received similar treatment.

In Washington, the initial rush to send ships, troops and aircraft to the Pacific was over by early March. It was not only time to take WW 1 off the back burner, it was essential to do so if the Pacific was not to drain off United States resources that should under WW 1 have been sent to Europe. Eisenhower was quite blunt when reporting the United States Planners' view to Marshall on where the first major Allied offensive should be mounted. There must, he said, be a target on which to fix Washington's and London's sights. Unless the British were prepared to make a cross-Channel invasion of Europe the Allies' primary objective,

> . . . we must turn our backs upon the Eastern Atlantic and go, full out, as quickly as possible, against Japan![11]

In the last week of March, the Combined Planners were given their first major challenge – reconciling British and American views on when and how to invade Western Europe – and they failed. Although the British Joint Planners had advocated, before 'Arcadia', a return to the Continent in 1942, their subsequent studies had convinced them that shortages of assault shipping and landing craft made it unlikely that it could be mounted before the early summer of 1943, and then only if Germany had been seriously weakened by the Combined Bomber Offensive and by losses sustained in Russia: a more practicable route into Europe might open up in the Mediterranean. The Americans believed, on the contrary, that a cross-Channel operation was the only sound, and certainly the quickest way to defeat Germany through concentration of British and American air, land and naval forces at the decisive point. Any suggestion of a Mediterranean approach was anathema to them. In any case, diversionary landing in Western Europe in the summer of 1942 might well become a vital necessity if Russia was to be kept in the war. The actual cross-channel invasion of Europe should be carried out not later than the spring of 1943, if it was to be any help to Russia.

The Combined Planners work highlighted the points of agreement and difference between the United States JCS and the British COS.

Both accepted the need to plan for a return to the Continent in 1943, but saw diametrically opposite reasons for being ready to do so in 1942. The Americans looked upon it as a diversionary operation to help a desperate Russia. The British saw it as a sacrificial effort, which they were not prepared to make with memories of their losses in trying to rescue Greece in similar circumstances in April 1941. They only envisaged a 1942 cross-Channel operation to exploit an imminent German political, economic or military collapse. Until Germany had been seriously weakened, their preferred approach was through the Mediterranean, or perhaps, as Churchill at times demanded but was rebuffed by his own Chiefs, through Norway.

There were, however, deeper differences that lay hidden beneath the surface of the Alliance. From bitter experience, the British knew that war never moves on prescribed lines. They wished to retain the advantages of a flexible strategy as long as possible and not be forced into final decisions until the last moment. The Americans, with their vast resources and a massive onslaught on the Continent in mind, needed a fixed plan and a firm date to which their complex production, training and administrative machinery could work. They liked agreements in black and white; and British failures so far in the war did not suggest an outstanding strategic ability that they should copy.

Having, as yet, little faith in the novel and embryonic Combined Chiefs of Staff machinery, Marshall decided to approach the President direct for approval in principle of plans prepared by Eisenhower for the invasion of Europe in 1943, together with provision for emergency landing in 1942, if Russia looked like collapsing. At a White House lunch party attended by Harry Hopkins and the American Chiefs, Marshall presented the Eisenhower plan informally and was given the green light. At Hopkins' suggestion, it was agreed that he and Marshall should short-circuit the British members of the CCS and take the plan, re-named the 'Marshall Memorandum', direct to London for discussion 'at the highest political level'.

Hopkins and Marshall arrived in London on 8 April. It was the first time that the American 'organiser of victory' and Churchill's 'principal strategic adviser' – Marshall and Brooke – had met. It cannot be said that the two men took to each other straight away. Both had powerful personalities and had been brought up in the very different traditions of the British and American Armies. Brooke records in his diary:

After lunch I had Marshall for nearly two hours in my office . . . He is, I should think, a good general at raising armies and at providing the necessary link between the military and political worlds, but his strategical ability does not impress me at all. In fact, in many respects he is a very dangerous man whilst being a very charming one.

He went on to explain in later notes:

My conversation with Marshall that afternoon was an eye-opener. I discovered that he had not studied any of the strategic implications of a cross-Channel operation. He argued that the main difficulty would be to achieve a landing. I granted that this would certainly present grave difficulties, but that our real troubles would start after landing. We should be operating with forces initially weaker than the enemy, and, in addition, his rate of build-up would be at least twice as fast as ours . . . His formations were fully trained and inured to war whilst ours were raw and inexperienced. I asked him to imagine that his landing had been safely carried out, and asked him what his plans would then be . . . I found he had not begun to form any plan of action or to visualise the problems that would face an army after landing . . .[12]

Thanks to Dill's perceptive interpretation of the American motive for requiring a British commitment to a cross-Channel operation as the basis for the build-up of United States troops and aircraft in the United Kingdom – Plan 'Bolero' – and of the British doubts about the operational practicability of either the 1942 emergency operation, 'Sledgehammer' or the full scale invasion of the Continent in 1943, 'Round-up', Churchill and the British Chiefs accepted the Marshall proposals purely for logistic and movement planning purposes, although they did not spell this out. At 'Arcadia' the Americans had let WW 1 go through on the nod because they had not had time to give it full consideration: the British let the Marshall Memorandum stand because they saw no point in arguing, provided 'Bolero' went ahead. Marshall and Hopkins returned to Washington as elated as Churchill and his team had been after 'Arcadia', with just as little real cause for satisfaction.

Soon after their arrival back in Washington, Marshall demonstrated his commitment to 'Bolero' by appointing Eisenhower as Commander of the European Theatre of Operations, US Army (ETOUSA), and General Carl Spaatz as the United States Army Air Force Commander, Europe, with their Headquarters in London.

With the Combined staffs working closely together on both sides of the Atlantic, it was not long before the Americans became aware that the British had concluded, after exhaustive examination by nominated force commanders and by Mountbatten's Combined Operations Headquarters, that 'Sledgehammer' was not an operation of war. Scarcity of landing craft would limit the scale of the initial assault to about a brigade group, and a follow-up force of six divisions, which was the most that could be made available from British sources, was hardly likely to survive in the face of the 44 German divisions garrisoning Western Europe. Nevertheless, the War Cabinet agreed that 'Sledgehammer' and 'Round-up' planning should go ahead on two conditions:

> No substantial landing in France in 1942 unless we are going to stay;
>
> No substantial landing in France unless the Germans are demoralised by failure in Russia.[13]

There was, thus, to be no sacrificial landing to help Russia as far as the British were concerned.

The Americans became convinced, understandably but quite incorrectly, that 'Perfidious Albion' was up to her old tricks and was using plausible but unsound arguments to renege on her agreements. Churchill flew with a team to Washington in the third week of June to assure the President that this was not so, and to revive the idea of invading French North Africa as a preliminary to clearing the whole of the North African coast, which would be the quickest and most practical way of achieving three things: bringing American troops into action in the European Theatre; saving Allied shipping by opening the Mediterranean; and helping Russia by drawing German forces away to counter the new threat of an Allied invasion of Europe from the south.

In disgust at this apparent failure on the part of the British to maintain the principle of concentration of effort, the United States Chiefs advised the President that the United States should assume the defensive against Germany, except for air operations, and give priority to the Pacific. The President, however, would not go that far, commenting that such a course would be ill-adapted to the purpose of securing the '*full, wholehearted collaboration of the leader of a proud people*', Winston Churchill.[14] Instead, he dispatched Hopkins, Marshall and King to London in mid-July to hammer out a compromise with the instruction:

> It is of the highest importance that the US ground troops be brought into action against the enemy in 1942.[15]

While Churchill was in Washington, his position had been weakened by the fall of Tobruk on 21st June. Paradoxically, the genuine sympathy and generous reaction of Roosevelt and Marshall in send-

ing 300 Sherman tanks and 100 self-propelled guns, which had
already been allocated to the United States Army, to the Middle
East to help re-equip 8th Army before the Battle of El Alamein, laid
the foundations of their friendship with Churchill and Brooke that
endured throughout the war despite many strategic disagreements.

During the Hopkins/Marshall/King July visit to London, Dill
acted once more as the interpreter and go-between. He cabled the
reasons why Marshall, King and the American staffs disliked the
invasion of French North Africa so much: it was diversionary and
detracted from the main aim of direct cross-Channel assault; it would
draw American aircraft carriers away from the Pacific where they
were most needed; a new and hazardous convoy route would have to
be established across the Central Atlantic, giving the U-boats extra
targets and overstretching available escorts; Casablanca and Algiers
were unsatisfactory landing areas and communications inland
through the Atlas mountains were primitive; and, most crucial of all,
if the Germans intervened, a French North African campaign would
so drain Allied resources that 'Round-up' might become impossible
in 1943. In an aside for Churchill's benefit, he reported that both
Marshall and King had been reading 'Wully' Robertson's *Soldiers and
Statesmen*, condemning Churchill's Dardanelles campaign for very
similar reasons. The Prime Minister was quick to reply:

> I am glad our friends are coming. Soldiers and statesmen here are in complete
> agreement.[16]

In a subsequent cable Dill was able to tell Churchill that the
President had refused to allow the visitors to play the ace of trumps –
switch of United States resources to the Pacific. The home team held
the king – 'Sledgehammer' had to be a British operation since there
would not be enough American troops and aircraft available in the
United Kingdom to mount the operation before autumn weather in
the Channel killed 'Sledgehammer 1942' anyway.

The President's emissaries arrived in London on 18 July, determined not to meet Churchill, 'the great diversionist' until they had
sought the views of the American commanders and staffs in London.
Eisenhower, quite naturally as the original author of 'Sledgehammer
1942' and 'Round-up 1943', and 'Tooey' Spaatz were still strongly in
favour of both, although Admiral Stark was less so. Eisenhower
suggested that 'Sledgehammer' should be aimed at taking and holding Cherbourg in 1942 as a bridgehead from which 'Round-up' could
be developed in the spring of 1943. This plan jumped the first British

hurdle of intention to stay, but it failed to clear the second, the pre-condition of a weakened German Army. The Germans had opened their 1942 offensive and were once again sweeping all before them in their thrust towards the oil fields of the Caucasus with no sign of demoralisation. Stalingrad was still only an inconsequential name on the map of southern Russia.

After three days of friendly, yet tense, debate with the British Chiefs, the American team accepted that they were not going to win the argument and cabled Washington for the President's instructions. Roosevelt authorised them to settle for any practicable operation that would bring United States troops into action in 1942. 'Torch', the Allied invasion of French North Africa, was agreed and the decision recorded in a Combined Chiefs of Staff document, CCS 94. Churchill's and Brooke's policy of developing the indirect approach through the Mediterranean seemed to have been accepted by the American Chiefs, but, in truth, they had in no way been converted to the British indirect approach. They had bowed to Roosevelt's political expediency, and were still as determined as ever to return to the true faith of concentration of effort on a cross-Channel thrust to the German heartland. In the light of the disastrous Dieppe raid three weeks later, and of the scale of effort eventually needed to break into Normandy in 1944, there can be little doubt that the British Chiefs were right in 1942.

Unfortunately, the CCS 94 agreement's weasel-wording was subject to differing interpretations in London and Washington. Its crucial fourth paragraph read:

> (4) That it is understood that a commitment to this operation (Torch) renders 'Round up' in all probability impracticable of successful execution in 1943 and therefore we have definitely accepted a defensive, encircling line of action for the Continental European theatre, except as to air operations and blockade; but that the organisation, planning, and training, for eventual entry in the Continent should continue so that this operation can be staged should a marked deterioration in German military strength become apparent, and the resources of the United Nations, available after meeting other commitments so permit.[17]

To the British, this paragraph seemed to provide everything they had fought for, but some policy makers in Washington – particularly King's Naval staffs – interpreted it as acceptance of a shift of priority in favour of the Pacific. This seemed to be confirmed in a later paragraph that authorised the transfer to the Pacific of a divisions's lift of shipping and fifteen United States Army Air Force groups. Dill had to point out ruefully to Marshall that:

At present our Chiefs of Staff quote WW 1 as 'The' Bible whereas some of your
people, I think, look upon CCS 94 as the Revised Version.[18]

The CCS 94 agreement to start the process of clearing the North
African shore from the west with 'Torch' needed a complementary
effort by Auchinleck's forces in the Western Desert to throw Rommel
back from El Alamein where he was threatening Cairo and the Suez
Canal, and to lift the Axis siege of Malta. It also needed someone to
tell Stalin that there would be no Second Front in 1942. These two
birds were killed with the stone of Churchill's and Brooke's August
visit to Cairo and then Moscow. It did not of itself turn the tide of
war in the Allies' favour, but it marked the moment when their
strategy started to reap some reward.

Their visit to Cairo could not have come at a more propitious
moment. In the Pacific the United States naval victories in the
battles of the Coral Sea in May and Midway in June had halted the
Japanese. In Russia, the Germans had failed to destroy the Russian
armies west of the Don; their thrust towards the Caucasus had been
halted in the foothills short of the oil fields; and the first moves in the
Russian counter-offensive, which was to lead to the German defeat at
Stalingrad, were taking shape.

Churchill's decision in Cairo to replace Auchinleck with Alexander
as C-in-C in the Middle East, and to appoint Montgomery to command 8th Army in the Western Desert, was to lead to the decisive
battles of Alam Halfa at the end of August and El Alamein at the end
of October, and to 8th Army's clearance of the North African shore
westwards towards Tunis. 'Torch' was a success in that the Anglo-
American forces established themselves ashore and could threaten
Tunis from the west. By the turn of the year, the CCS were faced
with the question: 'Where next?' Would Tunis fall in time to allow
them to withdraw enough troops, aircraft and assault shipping back
to England to mount 'Round-up' in the summer of 1943 as the
American Chiefs still hoped, or should they develop a thrust north-
eastwards across the Mediterranean as their British colleagues believed was the only practicable strategy?

These questions were to be resolved at the second wartime summit, the 'Symbol' Conference at Casablanca, which opened on 14
January 1943. The debating power of the British Chiefs might have
been seriously weakened if Churchill had done what he originally
intended when choosing the new Middle East command team. He
had first offered the post of C-in-C to Brooke instead of Alexander.
Brooke recorded in his diary:

... he wanted me to take over ... with Montgomery as my Eighth Army Commander. This made my heart race very fast! ... However, I told him without waiting that I was quite certain it would be wrong to move me. ...

He continued:

I could not put the real reasons to Winston. ... I had discovered the perils of his impetuous nature. I was now familiar with his method of suddenly arriving at some decision as it were by intuition without any kind of logical examination of the problem. ... I knew that it would take at least six months for any successor, taking over from me, to become familiar with him and his ways. During that six months anything might happen.[19]

What he did not say was that the carefully devised British strategy of not attacking across the Channel until the *Wehrmacht* had been fatally weakened by bombing, losses in Russia, and the defeat of Hitler's Italian ally in the Mediterranean, might be overturned by the Americans if he was not at Churchill's side.

Casablanca has often been portrayed as a British walk-over. Indeed, many of Marshall's staff believed that this was so. General Albert C Wedemeyer, Marshall's chief planner, commented bitterly, '*We came, we listened and we were conquered!*'[20] Most great summits are, in reality, gatherings to finalise policies already thrashed out in pre-conference preparatory work, but at Casablanca this was far from so. There were still differences, which did not run entirely on national lines, and which could only be settled by the President and Prime Minister. Churchill was initially nearer to Marshall than to his own Chiefs in that he still believed that 'Round-up' might be possible in 1943; Portal and Arnold were allied against everyone else in seeking exclusive priority for their Combined Bomber Offensive against Germany; and Pound and King were united as far as the Atlantic was concerned; but King was also playing a lone hand as champion of the Pacific Theatre.

The British peripheral strategy did prevail for one very important reason: it had been thrashed out between the Prime Minister and his Chiefs with Churchill as head of and very much part of the British team. On the American side, Roosevelt stood back from the military debate and confined his interventions to using his political instincts when decisions were required of him. With little love lost between the Departments of the Army and Navy in Washington, friction was increased by Marshall being seen to represent the needs of the European Theatre and King those of the Pacific. In consequence, the

Americans arrived at Casablanca without a fully agreed negotiating position.

Superficially, it appeared to the Americans that the British success was based on the much larger staffs which they brought to the conference, backed up with clerical and cypher facilities in their amphibious warfare headquarters ship, HMS *Bulolo*, berthed at Casablanca. This feeling was to have repercussions, as we will see, at the next summit.

In the British strategic debate that had raged throughout November and December 1942 in the run-up to Casablanca, Churchill had been at odds with his Chiefs. During his visit to Moscow in August, he had personally promised Stalin that the Second Front would be mounted in the summer of 1943, and he had no wish to renege on that promise despite his Chiefs' arguments, pointing to its impracticability. Brooke fought him every inch of the way until the idea dawned on him that he could save face with Stalin by using the analogy of attacking the soft underbelly of the Axis crocodile in the Mediterranean before attacking its snout with a subsequent crossing-Channel assault. With this worry put aside in Churchill's mind, the British team arrived at Casablanca united, although Brooke still feared that Marshall might yet swing the argument, with Churchill's support, back to closing down Mediterranean operations prematurely in order to mount 'Round-up, 1943'.

The Casablanca Conference opened with an attempt to define the level of resources that should be devoted to holding the Japanese in check until Germany had been defeated. King remained totally intransigent for the first four days about the level of forces that he required in the Pacific. Two things mellowed him: first, Churchill gave a categorical assurance that Britain would concentrate all her resources on the defeat of Japan once Germany had been defeated – after all, Britain had more to regain from the Japanese than the United States; and secondly, Portal intervened with a form of words devised by Air Marshal Slessor, which, in effect, allowed King to keep all forces already allocated to him in the Pacific. King's mood changed: he had won his battle for resources for the Pacific, and he had less to fear from the 'Europe First' policy. He collaborated wholeheartedly for the rest of the conference in the search for an agreed European strategy. He went as far as to promise American assault shipping for the British plan 'Anakim', the re-entry of Burma with the capture of Rangoon from the sea as its objective.

In the debates on the European strategy, Brooke showed himself at his very best, reflecting all the skills that he had developed during weeks of argument with his tough and suspicious Prime Minister. The Germans, he said, were now on the defensive both in Russia and North Africa; their allies were faltering; their manpower was shrinking; and they were running short of oil. Victory in Europe in 1943 was by no means impossible. The best way to achieve this was to give Russia maximum support; to exploit the Combined Bomber Offensive; and to launch amphibious operations. For these, points of entry should be selected where the enemy would have the greatest difficulty in bringing large forces to bear, as opposed to Marshall's philosophy of selecting the area where the Allies were best able to concentrate for their assault.

European geography, Brooke pointed out, favoured his policy. Good east-west communications in Europe would allow the Germans to transfer divisions relatively easily from Russia to France, but the poor north-south communications would hamstring their efforts to meet Allied threats in the Mediterranean. They would also have to disperse their forces to cover the many options open to the Allies in the Mediterranean: Sardinia, Sicily, the Balkans, Greece and the Aegean islands would all be vulnerable, and Hitler would probably have to prop up Mussolini when the Allied threat became apparent to the Italian people. And a Mediterranean strategy, he argued, would do more to help Russia than any premature landing in France before the *Wehrmacht* had been decisively weakened.

King and Pound supported Brooke because opening the Mediterranean would save the shipping; Arnold and Portal were enthusiastic about establishing air bases from which they could attack Germany and the Roumanian oilfields from the south; and Eisenhower, who was asked to give his views, stated that, in the light of his experience with the 'Torch' landings, his earlier estimates of troops and assault shipping needed for the cross-Channel operation were far too low. He doubted whether the necessary resources could be built up in England in time to make 'Round-up' practicable in 1943.

Marshall gave in without rancour. He saw that by the time the Axis forces had been expelled from Africa, there would be a large concentration of battle-experienced troops in the Mediterranean, who would be better employed there rather than being kept out of battle in the United Kingdom while the airmen and the Russians weakened Germany, and while landing-craft were being produced in the numbers now deemed necessary for 'Round-up'. The possibility of eliminating Italy from the war, which would force Hitler to take over the Italian commitments in the Mediterranean, was an added bonus.

The only decision then to be taken was whether to invade Sardinia or Sicily. The former was perhaps the easiest and would provide air bases straight away, but would not necessarily open the Mediterranean for Allied convoys. Taking the latter would certainly do so, and it would create a more direct threat to Italy and provide bomber bases within range of the Roumanian oil fields. The CCS chose Sicily, which was to be attacked in the favourable period of the July moon. Plans, however, were also to be made for an invasion of Sardinia in case Sicily was found to have been heavily reinforced wth German troops.

Plans for the Combined Bomber Offensive were agreed without acrimony, but with considerable scepticism on the British side. While the RAF would continue to burn and blast German industrial towns by night, the United States Army Air Force would carry out precision attacks on specific targets by day. It was agreed that Portal would direct the offensive (codenamed 'Pointblank'), but the Americans would be responsible for their own tactical decisions. Only time would tell if the American daylight operations were practicable: Portal and Harris had their doubts, as we have seen.

At Casablanca, both Churchill and Brooke made it clear that they were firmly committed to mounting 'Round-up' at the earliest practicable date – probably the spring of 1944 – but nothing would convince the American staffs that British hearts were really in it. They believed that Brooke's Mediterranean policy was a subtle formula for putting off, if not avoiding altogether, the evil day when the Channel might run red with British blood. The Mediterranean operations were, in the American view, too open ended, and would, if not checked, drain away 'Round-up's' lifeblood. At every decision point after Casablanca they tried with increasing success, as their resources and experience grew, to limit the Mediterranean 'diversion', while Churchill, and to a lesser extent the more realistic Brooke, saw new strategic opportunities beckoning to them in the Mediterranean, if only their American colleagues would see the advantages of keeping resources there for just a bit longer.

In the first five months of 1943, the tide did finally turn in the Allies' favour. Tripoli fell to Montgomery in January; von Paulus surrendered at Stalingrad in February; Rommel was compelled to leave Africa a sick man after his defeats in southern Tunisia in

March; Montgomery breached the defences of Wadi Akarit in April; and Tunis fell in May, leaving over quarter of a million Axis prisoners in Allied hands. The euphoria of these events suggested that another summit would be timely. The President invited Churchill and the British Chiefs to Washington for the 'Trident' Conference at the beginning of May.

'Trident' was the most difficult and acrimonious of all the summits. The Americans were playing on their home ground and were determined not to be out-manoeuvred again. Churchill was recovering from one of his bouts of pneumonia and was advised not to fly, so he and his large British team crossed the Atlantic in the *Queen Mary*, using every moment of the voyage to refine their position. When the conference opened on 11 May it was like a centre court tennis match at Wimbledon with tiers of supporting staff seated behind their principles. Although the Combined Chiefs cannot be accused of playing to the gallery, their freedom to compromise was inhibited by the presence of staffs dedicated to specific policies. The British Official Historian, Michael Howard comments:

> Moreover Washington did not provide a setting as helpfully tranquil as had been that of Casablanca. The American participants could not escape from their day to day duties, nor, more important, from domestic political pressures. The British found themselves almost equally loaded with inescapable social commitments, and these, on top of three if not four full meetings a day, added appreciably to their work.[21]

The British team made two unfortunate tactical errors in presenting their case for the continuation of offensive operations in Mediterranean throughout 1943 in preparation for 'Round-up' in 1944. Instead of starting the debate with a forthright declaration of intent to cross the Channel in the spring of 1944, which would have reassured the Americans, Brooke started with the British Chiefs' vision of the opportunities opening up before the Allies in the Mediterranean.

Brooke made out a very strong case. The critical factor in mounting 'Round-up' would be the relative speeds of build-up which the two sides could achieve in and around the beachhead. The Allies would be limited by the availability of assault shipping, and calculations showed that unless enough German divisions were pinned down by the Russians on the Eastern Front and by the Allies in the Mediterranean, 'Round-up' could fail. The maximum number of Allied divisions which could be used in the shipping likely to be available, could be concentrated in England by 1944 without drawing upon the Mediterranean. The forces there would be best employed driving Italy out of the war and drawing the greatest number of German divisions away from Western Europe and the Russian front. The seizure of airfields ever closer to the German heartland was a further factor favouring keeping up the pressure on the underbelly of Hitler's European fortress.

But then he made his second tactical error. In presenting the spectrum of opportunities for drawing German divisions southwards into the Mediterranean after Sicily had been taken, he ranged from taking Sardinia and Corsica in the west to Greece and the Aegean islands in the east. He stressed the advantages of concentrating on Italy as a stepping-stone into the Balkans. This was nearly fatal: any operations east of the toe of Italy were seen by the Americans as furthering British post-war ambitions in the Eastern Mediterranean and Middle East in which they wished to play no part. Brooke's Mediterranean strategy became totally suspect in their eyes.

The American Chiefs argued that operations invariably act as a suction pump, drawing in more resources than planned. To land troops in Italy would create just such a pump, which could reduce 'Round-up' to little more than a 'Sledgehammer' type operation. If this was what the British wanted, then the United States would switch priorities to the Pacific. The severity of the fighting in the Solomons was showing that rooting the Japanese out of the Pacific islands was going to be very costly, and a substantial body of American political, military and public opinion had turned in favour of concentrating upon the defeat of Japan.

Marshall had an additional important point to make, which led to an agreement on future operations. 'Round-up' would need battle-hardened troops from the Mediterranean, who were already experienced in amphibious operations. Brooke accepted this as a valid requirement, although, in the event, the divisions brought back from the Mediterranean did not fight in Normandy as well as the unblooded divisions – the veterans feeling that they had done their fair share of fighting already. It was agreed, nonetheless, that whatever happened in the coming months, three British and four United States divisions and the bulk of the assault shipping would be withdrawn from the Mediterranean by 1 November 1943 to return to England to prepare for 'Round-up' in the spring of 1944. This gave Marshall the power to limit the Mediterranean commitment and some assurance of the British commitment to 'Round-up'.

Nevertheless, no final conclusion could be reached until the

Combined Chiefs met in private session, free from the pressures of their supporting staffs. The British Chiefs again largely had their way, but within stricter limits than hitherto. The target date for 'Round-up' was fixed for 1 May 1944 with an assault force of nine divisions, seven of which would come from the Mediterranean, and a subsequent build-up to 29 divisions. Mediterranean operations were to continue for as long as possible in order to maintain pressure on the Axis and to make full use of the Allied forces already in action there. The decision as to what should happen after the invasion of Sicily was left for Eisenhower to recommend in the light of operational developments. He was instructed to exploit success with such operations

> . . . as are best calculated to eliminate Italy from the war and to contain the maximum number of German forces. Each specific operation will be subject to approval of the Combined Chiefs of Staff.[22]

The United States forces in the European Theatre were still inferior in numbers and experience to the British, but the gap was rapidly narrowing in both respects. It would not be long before the British influence in CCS decisions began its decline, but in the spring and summer of 1943 it was at its zenith in the Mediterranean with the three principal force commanders under Eisenhower all being British – Cunningham (Sea), Alexander (Land) and Tedder (Air).

Churchill, with the full support of his Chiefs, put his weight behind the task of ensuring that Italy would be the next target. In his romantic mind, he began to see himself marching in the footsteps of his great ancestor, Marlborough, to the Danube, this time from the south via Italy, primarily with British forces and with Vienna as their objective. It was a dream that was always in the back of his mind, and was to strain his relations with Brooke in the later phases of the war.

After 'Trident', Churchill persuaded Roosevelt to allow Marshall to accompany Brooke and himself to Algiers to speed up the decision making, and, of course, to influence Eisenhower in favour of invading Italy rather than Sardinia. Marshall and Eisenhower, however, resisted his plea that

> . . . the alternative between Southern Italy and Sardinia involved the difference between a glorious campaign and a mere convenience.[23]

Marshall objected to the choice of Italy on grounds of shortage of shipping for a prolonged campaign. Churchill countered by declaring that he was prepared to cut British rations to make enough shipping available.

Eisenhower set his staff to draw up two alternative sets of post-Sicily plans: one set for Sardinia, and the other for very modest operations across the Strait of Messina and landings on the toe of Italy. The Prime Minister minuted his Chiefs after his return to London:

> The question arises why we should crawl up the leg like a harvest-bug from ankle upwards. Let us strike at the knee . . .

> Once we have established our Air power in the Catania plain [in Sicily] and have occupied Messina, etc . . ., why should we not use sea and air power to land as high up Italy as air fighter cover from Catania warrants?[24]

The Bay of Salerno, just south of Naples, was just in range from Catania. With Marshall's agreement, planning for a major landing at Salerno, Operation 'Avalanche', was added to Eisenhower's responsibilities.

With the invasion of Sicily on 10 June, events in the Mediterranean began to gallop. Despite reinforcement of the Italian garrison with two German divisions, the landings, though fraught, were successful. Italian resistance collapsed; Mussolini was ousted; the Germans in Sicily were forced back to a bridgehead around Mount Etna in the north-east corner of the island, covering the Strait of Messina; and a steady stream of German divisions started flowing into Italy just as Brooke had hoped they would. His policy of drawing German strength southwards away from the Eastern Front and Western Europe was already bearing fruit. And in the Ukraine, the greatest tank battles ever fought raged around Kursk with the Russians emerging as the victors. Kursk, added to Stalingrad, removed any allied fears that Russia might collapse.

These events, far from helping to resolve Anglo-US strategic disagreement, exacerbated them. The British Chiefs, acting with no more than what they saw as opportunistic common sense, cabled the United States Joint Chiefs, recommending that all resources likely to be needed by Eisenhower to exploit the probable collapse of Italy should be left in the Mediterranean for the time being, regardless of the effect on other theatres. Without waiting for an American response, Pound issued a 'stand-still' order stopping all shipping movements out of the Mediterranean. The United States Chiefs were furious: believing that the British were about to abrogate unilaterally the recently agreed strategy, they replied in a curt and forceful cable that the Mediterranean commanders must make do with their allocated resources. Marshall had every reason to fear similar British demands as success beckoned in the Mediterranean. He suspected that even 'Round-up' might be endangered.

With Allied plans thrown into flux by victory in Sicily and by Mussolini's fall, another summit was needed to restore harmony. The President's medical advisers were against him flying to London for a return match, but the Canadians were more than willing to host a summit in Quebec, which was chosen as a congenial meeting place where the Combined Chiefs of Staff would be free from day to day business and be able to concentrate upon repairing the tears in their grand strategy. Both sides, indeed, approached this fourth wartime summit, code-named 'Quadrant', in an exasperated mood, verging upon outright mistrust of each other.

There was another reason for a summit in August. General Sir Frederick Morgan, who had been appointed Chief of Staff to the, as yet, unnamed Supreme Allied Commander (COSSAC) for 'Round-up' was ready to present his plans for the operation, which had been renamed 'Overlord'.

Churchill and his Chiefs again crossed the Atlantic in the *Queen Mary* for what was to be a less fraught meeting than either side expected, thanks largely to the sagacity of Dill. During the voyage the first real signs of strain began to appear in Brooke's relationship with Churchill, whose enthusiasm for the cross-Channel invasion, so high before Casablanca, had begun to wane as the possibility of a brilliant British campaign in the Mediterranean started to warp his thinking. He began to have genuine doubts about the practicability of 'Overlord' with the assault shipping likely to be available in the spring of 1944. During the Atlantic crossing, he advocated the alternative of advancing northwards through Italy as far as the Po valley. The Allies would then have the option of turning westwards into southern France, or north-eastwards through Venetia and the Ljubljana gap in the Julian Alps towards Vienna. Simultaneously, they could help the resistance forces in the Balkans to expel the Germans from Yugoslavia and Greece. In case 'Overlord' did prove impracticable, plans should also be polished up for his favourite Operation 'Jupiter' – the invasion of Norway.

Brooke and Dill realised that the Prime Minister's proposals would result in the Americans turning their backs on Europe, and King getting everything he dreamed of for the Pacific. They managed to persuade him that the real case for continued operations in the Mediterranean was the paramount need to draw, pin down and destroy German divisions in the Mediterranean throughout the autumn and winter to give 'Overlord' the greatest possible chance of success in the spring. Churchill reluctantly acquiesced and agreed to allow Brooke to make the sternly practical, as opposed to the politically emotional, case for maintaining pressure on the Axis in the Mediterranean while preparations for 'Overlord' went ahead.

The conference, which opened on 14 August, started on a sour note with the Americans tabling what amounted to an ultimatum, demanding a reaffirmation of the 'Trident' decision to mount 'Overlord' with the assigned forces, including the seven divisions from the Mediterranean by 1 May 1944. Opportunism in the Mediterranean must stop. Their paper went on to say:

> The United States Chiefs of Staff believe that the acceptance of this decision must be without conditions and without mental reservations.[25]

Brooke had no easy task in convincing the United States Chiefs that the British did accept 'Overlord' in both letter and in spirit, while, at the same time, winning their acceptance of the need to go on fighting the Germans in the Mediterranean to make 'Overlord' practicable. He was helped by two interconnected ways. First, Morgan's detailed plan, when he presented it to the conference, showed the need for a substantial cut in *Luftwaffe* fighter forces in the West, a halving of the number of first quality German army divisions in France and the Low Countries, and a reduction in Hitler's ability to rush troops to Normandy from the Russian Front. Everything possible would have to be done to destroy German fighters and army divisions in the months before 'Overlord': merely drawing them into the Mediterranean would not be enough. And secondly, Portal and Arnold came out strongly in Brooke's support. Deploying their strategic bombers on Italian airfields would bring within their range all southern Germany, 60 per cent of German fighter production, and the main German East-West communications. But more important still, it would double the commitments of the German fighter forces. In Portal's words:

> If we could base a strong force of Heavy and Medium Bombers there [in Italy] in the near future, Germany would be faced with a problem that seems insoluble.[26]

One of the strengths, but also a problem, of the Combined Chiefs of Staff system, was the close interlocking nature of the staffs at all levels. Few secrets could be kept within either team: every nuance of opinion was known to both sides. Brooke made little impact on his American colleagues during the plenary sessions. They seemed to ignore his arguments without attempting to rebut them, since they were convinced that they were nothing more than diplomatic window-dressing to conceal a basic unwillingness to undertake 'Overlord'. As at 'Trident', no progress could be made until the conference room was cleared of supporting staffs and blunt speaking could begin.

No record of the closed session exists but Brooke's diary records:

> Our talk was pretty frank. I opened by telling them that the root of the matter was that we were not trusting each other. They doubted our real intentions to put our full hearts into the cross-Channel operation next spring and we had not full confidence that they would not in future insist on our carrying out previous agreements irrespective of changed strategic conditions . . . In the end I think our arguments did have some effect on Marshall. . . . We finished our conference at 5.30 p m, having been three hours at it . . .[27]

Brooke had, in fact, succeeded better than he thought. Agreement was reached next day, 17 August, which spelt out the Mediterranean task as:

> . . . the maintenance of unremitting pressure on German forces in Northern Italy and the creation, with available Mediterranean forces, of conditions required for 'Overlord', and a situation favourable for the eventual entry of our forces, including the bulk of the re-equipped French Army and Air Force, into Southern France.[28]

The passing reference to the entry into Southern France (Operation 'Anvil', later rechristened 'Dragoon') was to cause another Anglo-American rift, but that still lay in the future.

Brooke's success was marred by personal disappointment. He knew that the Prime Minister was intent on persuading the President to give him the Supreme Command of 'Overlord'. When Churchill approached Roosevelt about the appointment before 'Quadrant' opened, he was rebuffed. The United States Secretary of the Army, Henry Stimson, had got in first. He had submitted a memorandum to the President, pointing out that, as British hearts were not in 'Overlord', a British Supreme Commander would not provide the vigorous leadership needed. Marshall and not Brooke was the right man for the job. Moreover, once 'Overlord' was launched, the number of American troops would far exceed the British contribution. The American public would demand an American commander. As a sop, Roosevelt suggested to Churchill, quite sensibly, that the Mediterranean should become a British command – it was there Churchill's ambitions really lay; and that Mountbatten should become Supreme Commander South East Asia.

Brooke recorded his deep disappointment:

> I had voluntarily given up the opportunity of taking over the North African Command. . . . because I felt at that time I could probably serve a more useful purpose by remaining with Winston. But now when the strategy of the war had been guided through to the final stage – the stage when the real triumph of victory was to be gathered – I felt no longer necessarily tied to Winston and free to assume the Supreme Command which he had already promised me on three separate occasions. It was a crushing blow to hear from him that he was now handing over this appointment to the Americans, and had in exchange received the agreement of the President to Mountbatten's appointment as Supreme Commander for South East Asia. Not for one moment did he realise what this meant to me. He offered no sympathy, no regrets at having had to change his mind, and dealt with the matter as if it were one of minor importance . . .[29]

After that, Brooke's relations with Churchill were never quite as close as they had been up to 'Quadrant'. Sadly also, Dudley Pound suffered the first of the strokes in Quebec which were to kill him two months later. He died on Trafalgar Day, 21 October 1943, knowing that the Battle of the Atlantic had been won. Churchill's tribute to him that he was *'my trusted naval friend'* is an appropriate epitaph.[30]

Pound's obvious successor was Admiral Sir Andrew Cunningham – ABC as he was known – the victor of many Mediterranean naval engagements and currently the Allied Naval Commander in the Mediterranean, but Churchill did not want so strong a character as First Sea Lord, fearing that he might turn out to be another Jackie Fisher. A V Alexander, the First Lord, pressed ABC's claims and won, with Churchill grumbling:

> All right, you can have your Cunningham, but if the Admiralty do not do as they are told, I will bring down the Board in ruins even if it means my coming down with it.[31]

Churchill had every reason to fear ABC. He had imposed his will upon both Churchill and the Italian Navy from the very beginning of the war at sea in the Mediterranean. He was one of the few Service commanders, who could and did withstand Churchill's constant nagging and probing, and he had proved himself unsackable. Eisenhower aptly described him as a Nelsonian type of Admiral, and King likened him to Jervis, Earl of St Vincent. Like Nelson, he was a smallish man with sparkling blue eyes, not particularly robust physically, but with a will of iron and no respecter of persons. He was loved by the Fleet, and, indeed, he was seen in the Navy as Nelson's true successor. Two of his famous signals deserve to rank with Nelson's *'England expects . . .'*:

Stick it out. The Navy must not let the Army down,[32]

made during the evacuation of Crete, and

> Be it pleased to inform their Lordships that the Italian Fleet now lies at anchor under the guns of the fortress of Malta.[33]

Unlike many First Sea Lords, he could both inspire a staff and delegate responsibility to subordinates. He brought good sea sense to the Chiefs of Staff Committee, where his forthright attitudes matched those of Brooke and Portal. Brooke recorded:

> Andrew Cunningham's arrival was indeed a happy event for me. I found him first and foremost one of the most attractive of friends, a charming associate to work with and the staunchest of companions when it came to supporting a policy agreed amongst ourselves, no matter what inclement winds might blow.[34]

One of the most far reaching accords at 'Quadrant', which, for security reasons, found no place in the conference records, and was known only to a handful of people on either side of the Atlantic, was the Anglo-US-Canadian 'Quebec Agreement' on the joint development of the Atomic Bomb.

'Quadrant' had, as the Americans intended, finalised the grand strategy which, in the end, did win the war. After Cunningham took over Pound's place in the British team, the Combined Chiefs of Staff remained unchanged until victory over Germany and Japan was won. Arguments, often heated, usually complex and sometimes exasperating to one side or the other, still went on in the process of refining and directing that strategy as events unfolded, but, in this story of the Chiefs, they need only be briefly sketched. The positions taken up by each of the Combined Chiefs, and the attitudes of their political masters, did not change; the COS system was not altered in any way; and there was only one real strategic crunch when the Americans, in sheer exasperation, used their weight to impose a policy upon their British colleagues to which they had deeply rooted objections. This *cause célèbre* was over the launching of the 'Anvil' attack on southern France in August 1944, which emasculated Alexander's Italian campaign after the fall of Rome in June.

While 'Quadrant' was still in session, the clandestine negotiations for Italy's surrender were in progress. The final announcement of the armistice was made on the evening of 8 September 1943 as the Allied assault ships entered the Bay of Salerno and the 'Avalanche' landings began. The Germans showed at once how hazardous either a 'Sledgehammer' or a 'Round-up' would have been in 1943, and how hard fought 'Overlord' would be in 1944. Not only did Kesselring's handful of German divisions manage to disarm the Italian Army over the next ten days, but they also came near to driving the Allies back into the sea.

At first all went well for the Allies after the battles at Salerno had ultimately been won. Uncharacteristically, Hitler ordered Kesselring to fall back slowly to the Northern Apennines along which Rommel was preparing the formidable Gothic Line to defend the Po Valley and the southern approaches to the Reich. Naples fell on 1st October and the airfields in the plain of Foggia were taken into use by the Allied bombers. Then the autumn weather broke and with its help Kesselring managed to slow the Allied advance to a crawl in country that gives all its favours to the defender. Hitler seized the opportunity to reimpose his 'no withdrawal' policy, which had already lost him quarter of a million men at Stalingrad and then in Tunisia, and was to lose him the war. By mid-November, the Allied Armies were stalled in front of the hastily prepared Gustav Line, running East and West through Cassino only 70 miles south of Rome.

Churchill saw Rome as a crock of political gold, tantalisingly just out of reach; Brooke looked upon the Italian capital as bait to draw German forces into Italy; and Marshall believed that all his worst fears of the Mediterranean acting as a suction pump were being confirmed. Nevertheless, it was expected that Rome would fall in a matter of weeks and that, by the time 'Overlord' was launched, the Allies would be up against the defence and natural strength of Rommel's Gothic Line in the Northern Apennines, where the Germans would have all the advantages. But where else could the Allies strike to keep the Mediterranean pot boiling before, during and after 'Overlord': eastwards from Italy into the Balkans to help Russia directly, or northwards from Egypt into the Aegean to induce Turkey to enter the war on the Allied side as the British suggested; or westwards with the proposed 'Anvil' landing in southern France as the Americans insisted? The decision was left until Stalin could express his views at the next summit which was in two parts: 'Sextant' in Cairo from 22 to 28 November 1943, which included Generalissimo Chiang Kai Shek and his charming but formidable wife; and 'Eureka' in Tehran with Stalin from the 29 November to 1 December. There was a short four-day Anglo-US 'wash-up' back in Cairo before the Combined Chiefs left for home on 8th December.

So far the summits had been predominantly military debates, but from 'Sextant' onwards, their political content steadily increased. The critical factor at 'Sextant' and 'Eureka' was the availability of assault shipping, which had to be juggled between the two sacrosanct operations, Marshall's 'Overlord' and King's offensives in the Pacific, and a number of subsidiary operations, each of which had its own supporters and detractors. At 'Eureka', Stalin, much to every-one's surprise, showed himself strongly in favour of the 'Anvil' land-ings in southern France to help 'Overlord', rather than operations in the Balkans and Aegean, which it was thought would have a greater impact upon the Russian front. Stalin, however, had no wish to see Anglo-US forces in an area of future Soviet influence. Churchill welcomed leaving the necessary assault shipping in the Mediter-ranean with enthusiasm, not because he liked the idea of 'Anvil', which the British Chiefs thought was a futile waste of resources, but because, as he said in Cairo:

> Overlord remains top of the bill but should not be such a tyrant as to rule out every other activity in the Mediterranean.[35]

He saw that the 'Anvil' shipping could be used in the meantime for a landing at Anzio (Operation 'Shingle') to accelerate the capture of Rome. The CCS agreed that 'Shingle' should be launched at once, and 'Anvil' a short time before 'Overlord'.

During 'Eureka', Stalin made it plain that he would not believe that his Western allies were in earnest about 'Overlord' until they announced the name of its commander, but he was assured that he would be told the name soon after the conference was over. Roosevelt prevaricated for a time and then decided that he could not spare Marshall and substituted Eisenhower in his stead.

Nothing went right for Churchill in the Mediterranean that winter, but Hitler played into Brooke's hands and enabled him to bring about the required conditions for 'Overlord' that had been specified by Morgan at 'Quadrant'. The landings at Anzio were a disaster, Churchill moaning that he had hoped

> we were hurling a wild cat on the shore, but all we got was a stranded whale.[36]

Hitler's reaction to the landing could not have been better for Brooke's purposes. Speaking to General Warlimont in OKW he said:

> If we succeed in dealing with this business down there [at Anzio] there will be no further landings anywhere.[37]

He reinforced Kesselring with von Mackensen's 14th Army, which was rushed down from Germany with some of the best panzer, panzer-grenadier and parachute divisions in the German Army to destroy the Allied beachhead, while von Vietinghoff's hardened 10th Army held the Gustav Line. The bitter battles of Anzio and Cassino, which constituted the First Battle for Rome, raged throughout February and March, inflicting severe losses on the continuous stream of first class German divisions thrown almost heedlessly by Hitler into the Italian cauldron.

The need to keep the Anzio beachhead supplied absorbed 'Anvil's' assault shipping and put paid to it as a curtain raising diversion for 'Overlord'. The American Chiefs had no option but to agree to its postponement until July. The actual prelude to 'Overlord' was Alexander's highly successful 'Diadem' offensive – the Second Battle for Rome – which opened on 11 May 1944 and led to his capture of the city on 4 June, two days before Eisenhower's invasion of Normandy began. The timing could not have been bettered, and the results fully justified the British Chiefs' determination not to launch 'Overlord' until the *Wehrmacht's* strength in Western Europe had been decisively weakened, despite all the pressure from the American Chiefs and from the rowdy 'Second Front Now' lobbies that were so intense throughout 1942 and 1943.

The regrettable crunch in the CCS over 'Anvil' came in June, when the American Chiefs visited Europe to see the situation for themselves at first hand. Alexander cabled to London:

> My object is to complete the destruction of the German armed forces in Italy, and in the process to force the enemy to draw to the maximum on his reserves, whereby I shall be rendering the greatest assistance to the Western invasion of which my armies are capable.

He went on:

> I now have two highly organised and skilled armies capable of carrying out large scale attacks and mobile operations in the closest co-operation. Morale is irresistibly high as a result of recent successes and the whole forms one closely articulated machine capable of carrying out assaults and rapid exploitation in the most difficult terrain. Neither the Apennines nor even the Alps should prove an obstacle to their enthusiasm and skill.[38]

Alexander and his Chief of Staff, General Sir John Harding (later Field Marshal Lord Harding, CIGS in the mid-1950s) saw the opportunity to make Churchill's dream of an advance on Vienna come true. Their plan was to rush the Gothic Line in the Northern Apennines before the Germans could consolidate its defence; cross the Po; and then thrust north-eastwards across the Venetian plain to the Ljubljana Gap and on to Vienna ahead of the Russians. What made this plan most attractive to Churchill was that it would be largely a British and British Commonwealth campaign – the glorious fulfilment of his and Brooke's Mediterranean strategy.

Brooke, however, had few illusions about the impracticability of Alexander's plan and opposed the Prime Minister over the issue. He saw the value of threatening the valuable industrial resources of Northern Italy and of establishing Allied air bases in the Po Valley, which he saw as a more effective way of keeping German reserves away from Normandy than a landing in southern France. Moreover, he knew that the idea of advancing on Vienna would be a red rag to the bull as far as Marshall and the United States Chiefs were concerned – it would be dispersion of effort with a vengeance.

Marshall, as Brooke expected, would have none of it. 'Anvil' had been promised to Stalin at the Tehran conference, and Roosevelt was committed to landing the re-equipped French Mediterranean forces back in France as soon as it was practicable to do so. 'Anvil' was ideal for this purpose. Marshall also argued that Hitler would not be foolish enough to fight south of the Po. He would pull back to the Alps if pushed too hard and be able thereby to save troops for use in Normandy. He did accept, however, that 'Anvil' should be further delayed until Kesselring's armies had been destroyed or at least driven back into the Gothic Line.

So far, so good, but Hitler then played the 'wild card' of heavily reinforcing Kesselring, in spite of the major battles raging in Normandy and on the Russian Front. Alexander's advance slowed, and in Normandy worries about a possible stalemate arose as the great Channel storm of 19 June swept away the American Mulberry harbour and severely damaged the British Mulberry at Arromanches, slowing down the Allied build-up. It was not surprising, therefore that Eisenhower pressed for 'Anvil' both to divert German divisions from Normandy and as a quicker way of landing more American and French troops in France.

In the bitter debates about 'Anvil' in the last week of June, American patience broke. This might not have happened if Dill had not been taken terminally ill at that time. He spent June, July and August in hospital and although he seemed fit enough to take part in 'Octagon' he died on 4 November. Such was the American esteem for his great services to the Alliance that he was buried in Arlington Military Cemetery, and is the only British soldier to have a memorial erected to his memory there. Had he been fit enough to work during the 'Anvil' crisis, his great diplomatic skills would have been invaluable in reducing its bitterness.

Against the wishes of the British Chiefs, 'Anvil' (re-named 'Dragoon') was ordered for 15 August, using almost entirely American and French resources, and withdrawing General Juin's highly successful French Expeditionary Corps from Alexander's command to take a leading part in landings. The British Official History comments sadly:

The debate on 'Anvil' had ended most unpleasantly. The views of the United States Chiefs of Staff and of the British Chiefs of Staff on the correct strategy for the Italian campaign and for the Mediterranean Theatre differed irreconcilably. The President and Prime Minister each supported his own Chiefs of Staff, and when the American view prevailed, Mr Churchill protested in the name of His Majesty's Government.[39]

Protest was in vain; the United States was now the predominant partner in the Alliance with forces to spare, while Britain's were declining fast, bringing the need to disband divisions as manpower reserves neared exhaustion.

The withdrawal of Juin's French troops from Italy was fatal to the Vienna plan. Alexander had intended to break the centre of the Gothic Line with the French mountain-trained troops, as he had none of his own. Instead, he was forced to move the 'armour heavy' 8th Army secretly across the Apennines to the Adriatic coast in order to breach the German defences in the less mountainous east coast sector. The switch cost him three weeks of summer weather, and although he did breach the Gothic Line, the autumn rains broke before his armies could reach the Po Valley. They spent a debilitating winter in the Apennines, fighting from ridge to ridge and river to river in an attritional struggle to hold as many German troops as possible in Italy. Again, Hitler played into the Allies' hands by maintaining his no withdrawal policy, despite the obvious advantages of slipping back over the Po to the Alps as Marshall feared he would do. Vienna stayed a Churchillian dream, but the Italian campaign fulfilled all Brooke's expectations by holding German troops away from North West Europe and the Russian Front, and giving incalculable advantages to Portal and Arnold in their Combined Bomber Offensive.

Churchill watched the 'Dragoon' landings from the sea. Cabling Eisenhower to congratulate him on the destruction of von Kluge's troops in the Falaise pocket, he commented sarcastically:

> You have certainly amongst other things effected a very important diversion for our attack at 'Dragoon'![40]

By the time the final wartime summits took place – 'Octagon', for the second time at Quebec in September 1944, and 'Argonaut', in Malta and Yalta in January and February 1945 – the end of the war was in sight and post-war considerations were assuming greater importance than grand strategy. There might have been quicker ways of winning the war at theatre command level, but the Combined Chiefs could look back with justifiable satisfaction to their achievements and to the creation of the staff machinery that brought victory over both Germany and Japan in 1945.

One important decision, the dropping of the atomic bombs on Japan, was not taken by the Combined Chiefs, nor were the British Chiefs formally consulted. The technical planning was in the hands of a small team in the United States, of which Doctor (later Sir William) Penney was a key member. Operational planning and execution were confined to the United States Chiefs since the bombs could not be ready in time for use in Europe and so would be used, if at all, in the Pacific Theatre, where the writ of the British Chiefs did not run. However, the terms of the Anglo-US Quebec Agreement on collaboration in atomic weapon development was fulfilled by Churchill giving the British Government's assent through the Joint Staff Mission in Washington.

As far as the British Chiefs were concerned, three factors made for the success of the Chiefs of Staff system: the combination of the functions of Prime Minister and Minister of Defence in one man, who had the exceptional experience, driving personality and abilities to fulfil both roles in an outstanding way; the combination of strategic policy-making and executive responsibility in the hands of the three Chiefs; and the successful selection of exceptional Chiefs, who had the confidence of the Prime Minister and of their own Services.

Two issues were soon to arise when the war was over: would a Ministry of Defence be needed in peacetime when the Prime Minister could no longer devote so much time to defence questions; and would it be necessary to introduce a neutral chairman for the peacetime Chiefs of Staff Committee when unity compelled by the enemy threat was replaced by the disunity caused by the return of financial constraints?

The combination of the offices of Prime Minister and Minister of Defence was practical and, indeed, essential in wartime, but would not be so in peace, when defence policy no longer dominated national decision-making. Clearly, the Prime Minister would need either a deputy to deal with Defence policy as Balfour and Asquith had before the First World War; or a Minister for Co-ordination of Defence as Baldwin and Chamberlain found necessary in the inter-war years. But would this suffice? Would not a Minister of Defence in the Cabinet and with a fully fledged ministry behind him be needed? The Services hoped not, believing that such a ministry would merely add an extra tier to governmental decision-making machinery, and, worse still, reduce their independence.

The introduction of a neutral chairman for the Chiefs of Staff Committee had been mooted in Parliament and the Press in the early days of the war when disaster was more prevalent than victory. The suggestion, however, was steadfastly opposed by the wartime Chiefs because it breached the principle that those who proposed policies should bear the responsibility for carrying them out. This was an eminently sound position to take as long as the Chiefs had the unifying aim of winning the war, but, as the inter-war years had already shown, peacetime financial pressures made rivals of the best of men, and reinforced the case for a neutral chairman provided, of course, that a man with sufficient breadth of experience could be found to occupy the chair and maintain the confidence of the three Chiefs.

The American Joint Chiefs of Staff did have Admiral Leahy as Chairman in his capacity as President's Chief of Staff. This was necessary because Roosevelt took less part in the actual formulation of military policy than Churchill. Ismay, Churchill's Chief Staff Officer, acted as a go-between and interpreter of the Chiefs to the Prime Minister and vice versa. Although he was a member of the Chiefs of Staff Committee, he took great pains never to assume the status of a Chief.

Apart from this major difference, the fact that the Americans adopted and adapted the British Chief of Staff system, and that the Combined Chiefs of Staff system worked as well as it did, reflects great credit on its founding fathers, the Salisbury Committee of the 1920s. The success of the system cannot be better put than in Churchill's own words quoted at the head of this chapter, and his tribute to the Chiefs themselves was no less heartfelt:

> And here is the moment when I pay my personal tribute to three British Chiefs of Staff, with whom I have worked in the closest intimacy throughout these heavy, stormy years. There have been very few changes in this small, powerful, and capable body of men, who, sinking all Service differences and judging the problems of the war as a whole, have worked together in perfect harmony with each other. In Field Marshal Brooke, in Admiral Pound, succeeded on his death by Admiral Andrew Cunningham, and Marshal of the Royal Air Force Portal, a team was formed who deserved the highest honour in the direction of the whole British war strategy and in its relations with that of our Allies.[41]

When the atomic bombs dropped on Japan and the war ended on 2 September 1945, no one could tell what future development of the system lay ahead of it on either side of the Atlantic. Neither country had, as yet, created a Ministry of Defence. In Britain the Committee of Imperial Defence no longer existed, and in the States the National Security Council was yet to be born.

But Churchill foresaw the need to maintain the close Anglo-American military partnership after the war. In the same passage in which he paid his tribute to his own Chiefs, he went on to say with great prescience:

> It may well be said that our strategy was conducted so that the best combination, the closest concert, were imparted into the operations by the combined Staffs of Britain and the United States. . . . Some people say, 'Well what would you expect, if both nations speak the same language, have the same laws, have a great part of their history in common, and have very much the same outlook on life, with all its hopes and glory?' And others may say, 'It would be an ill day for all the world and for the pair of them if they did not go on working together and marching together and sailing together and flying together, whenever something has to be done for the sake of freedom and fair play all over the world.' That is the great hope for the future.[42]

It was, indeed, a sad day when they fell out over Suez in 1956, but happily they were working, marching, sailing and flying together again in the Persian Gulf in 1990–91.

THE WARRING CHIEFS

29. Marshal of the Royal Air Force
Lord Tedder. *(IWM)*

30. Field Marshal Viscount
Montgomery. *(IWM)*

31. Admiral of the Fleet Sir John
Cunningham. *(IWM)*

32. A.V. Alexander. *(Hulton Picture
Company)*

THE KOREAN CHIEFS

33. Admiral of the Fleet Lord Fraser.
(IWM)

34. Field Marshal Viscount Slim.
(IWM)

35. Marshal of the Royal Air Force Sir
John Slessor. *(RAF Museum)*

36. Admiral of the Fleet Sir
Rhoderick McGrigor. *(IWM)*

THE SUEZ CHIEFS

37. Marshal of the Royal Air Force Sir William Dickson. *(RAF Museum)*

38. Admiral of the Fleet Earl Mountbatten. *(IWM)*

39. Field Marshal Sir Gerald Templer. *(IWM)*

40. Marshal of the Royal Air Force Sir Dermot Boyle. *(IWM)*

DEFENCE REORGANISATION, 1964

41. (Left to right) Admiral of the Fleet Earl Mountbatten (CDSO), Peter Thorneycroft (S of S), Sir Henry Hardman (PUS), and Air Marshal Sir John Lapsley (Secretary of the Chiefs of Staff Committee). *(IWM)*

MOUNTBATTEN'S FAREWELL, 1965

42. (Behind Mountbatten on top step, left to right) Field Marshal Sir Richard Hull, Admiral (later Admiral of the Fleet) Sir David Luce, General (later Field Marshal) Sir James Cassels, Air Chief Marshal Sir Charles Elworthy (later Marshal of the Royal Air Force Lord Elworthy). *(IWM)*

Chronology
FOR CHAPTER NINE

1945

Sep   VJ Day.
             US Congress ends Lend-Lease.
Oct   Jewish Revolt in Palestine begins.
Dec   American Loan Agreement signed.

1946

Jan   Tedder succeeds Portal as CAS.
March Churchill's *Iron Curtain* speech at Fulton, Missouri.
June   John succeeds Andrew Cunningham as First Sea Lord.
             Montgomery succeeds Brooke as CIGS.
Aug   MacMahon Act passed by US Congress.
Sep   Montgomery's *Sequoia* Meeting with the US JCS.
Dec   A V Alexander becomes Minister of Defence.

1947

Jan   Attlee authorises atomic bomb production.
March Truman Doctrine accepted by US Congress.
May   US takes over Greek commitment from Britain.
June   Marshall Plan for Europe.
Aug   India granted Independence.
Nov   Withdrawal from Palestine begins.

1948

Feb   Communist Coup in Czechoslovakia.
March Brussels Treaty signed.
June   Berlin Blockade begins.
             State of Emergency declared in Malaya.
Sep   Fraser succeeds John Cunningham as First Sea Lord.

Nov   Montgomery becomes Chairman of the Western
European COS.
Slim succeeds Montgomery as CIGS.

1949
April   North Atlantic Treaty signed: birth of NATO.
US Mutual Defence Aid Programme passed by
Congress.
Aug   Soviet atomic bomb tested.
Sep   Devaluation of Sterling.
Oct   Chinese People's Republic proclaimed.

1950
Jan   Slessor succeeds Tedder as CAS.
Feb   Attlee wins his second General Election.
Emanuel Shinwell becomes Minister of Defence.
June   Korean War begins.
Rearmament programme begins.
Dec   First V Bombers ordered.

1951
April   Eisenhower becomes SACEUR with Montgomery as
Deputy.
May   Abadan oil crisis.
Oct   Churchill Prime Minister and Minister of Defence.
Dec   McGrigor succeeds Fraser as First Sea Lord.

1952
Jan   Rearmament programme slowed.
March   Field Marshal Alexander becomes Minister of Defence.
April   Chiefs of Staff Global Strategy Review at Greenwich.
July   King Farouk overthrown.
Oct   British atomic bomb tested at Monte Bello.
Mau Mau Rebellion starts in Kenya.
Nov   Harding succeeds Slim as CIGS.
US hydrogen bomb tested at Bikini Atoll.
Dec   Decision to develop a British hydrogen bomb.

1953
Jan   1st 'Radical Review' of Defence policy.
Dickson succeeds Slessor as CAS.

March	Stalin dies.
June	Alexander/Duncan Sandys 'Three Categories'.
	Churchill's stroke.
July	Korean War ends.
Aug	Soviet hydrogen bomb tested.

1954

Feb	McGrigor/Dickson Carrier Agreement.
	Fall of Dien Bien Phu.
April	Second 'Radical Review' of Defence policy.
May	Formation of SEATO.
July	Cabinet decision to build British hydrogen bomb.
Oct	Anglo-Egyptian Treaty signed.
	Germany accedes to Brussels Treaty.
	Macmillan replaces Alexander as Minister of Defence.

1955

Feb	Baghdad Pact signed.
April	Eden becomes Prime Minister.
	Selwyn Lloyd becomes Minister of Defence.
	EOKA terrorist campaign begins in Cyprus.
	Mountbatten succeeds McGrigor as First Sea Lord.
May	Eden wins General Election.
Sep	Templer succeeds Harding as CIGS.
Oct	Soviet-Egyptian arms deal announced.
	Dickson becomes Chairman of the COS Committee.
	Boyle succeeds Dickson as CAS.
Dec	Walter Monckton becomes Minister of Defence.

1956

June	Last British troops leave Egypt.
July	Nasser nationalises the Suez Canal.
Oct	Anthony Head becomes Minister of Defence.
	Anglo-French landings at Port Said.

9

TOWARDS
A MINISTRY OF DEFENCE

Victory over Japan to
Disaster at Suez: 1945–1956

Ministers of Defence

Clement Attlee	1945
A V Alexander	1946
Emanuel Shinwell	1950
Winston Churchill	1951
Earl Alexander of Tunis	1952
Harold Macmillan	1954
Selwyn Lloyd	1955
Sir Walter Monckton	1955
Anthony Head	1956

First Sea Lords

Viscount Cunningham	
Sir John Cunningham	1946
Lord Fraser	1948
Sir Rhoderick McGrigor	1951
Earl Mountbatten	1955

Chiefs of the Imperial General Staff

Viscount Alanbrooke	
Viscount Montgomery	1946
Sir William Slim	1948
Sir John Harding	1952
Sir Gerald Templer	1955

Chiefs of Air Staff

Viscount Portal	
Lord Tedder	1946
Sir John Slessor	1950
Sir William Dickson	1953
Sir Dermot Boyle	1955

'For the Service Ministries, historic corporations with their own strong traditions, dedicated to the interests of the Services they administered, with their own links to the Treasury, the Foreign office, their procurement agencies and if need be with Downing Street, the Ministry of Defence at Storey's Gate was at best a useful tool for their own purposes, at worst an irrelevance.'

Michael Howard, *The Central Organisation of Defence*[1]

When the Second World War ended in September 1945, the prestige of the Chiefs of Staff had never stood higher. They had been able to articulate strategic policy with Churchill on equal terms and, despite strong American opposition, had formulated the war-winning strategy. They had done more: they had established a relationship of mutual respect between their own professionalism and responsibility for executive action on the one hand with the Prime Minister's power to deliver Parliament and the British people on the other, without whose support the Armed Forces of the Crown cannot wage war effectively.

It is hardly surprising, therefore, that there was initially no great pressure for change: only a need to institutionalise the system that had grown up since 1923, and to make such modifications as were deemed necessary to meet the needs of what it was hoped would be a long period of peace after three successive German wars – 1870, 1914–18 and 1939–45.

But as 1945 swept to its close, the system, which had worked so well in wartime, was beginning to come under altogether different pressures. When the enemy had been at the gates, the three Chiefs had been able to hammer out agreed policies; and when they could not do so for valid differences over principles, they had been able to refer the dissected and exposed problems for decision by a single all-powerful personality, who not only held the offices of Prime Minister and Minister of Defence, but also had a life-long experience in the arts of war, and, through the combination of his two offices, was in daily contact with the conduct of the war and the developing strategy of the Alliance. Furthermore, in Brooke, they had had, from 1941 onwards, an outstanding chairman to whom they willingly deferred, and who could concentrate his mind on grand strategy because he was prepared to delegate much of his day to day responsibility for the Army to his Vice-Chief.

By June 1946 all this was changing: the imperatives of conflict had gone; Churchill had gone; the three wartime Chiefs, Brooke, Cunningham and Portal, who had got on so well together, and were now Viscounts, had all retired: the Chairmanship of the Chiefs was strictly rotational again; and finally Clement Attlee, understandably pulling back from Churchill's autocratic style of government, was indulging in greater Cabinet consensus, albeit with firm chairmanship. The *ambience* of the Chiefs was undergoing a sea change.

In the first post-war team of Chiefs, Montgomery and Tedder almost selected themselves as Brooke's and Portal's successors through their wartime triumphs. Montgomery was neither Churchill's nor Brooke's choice as CIGS. His professional military abilities were undeniable, but his lack of political finesse made him suspect. Alexander was preferred and, indeed, attended the Potsdam Conference as CIGS (Designate). By then, however, Churchill had persuaded Brooke to extend his tenure for a year until June 1946, and Alexander was asked for by the Canadian Government as their next Governor General. This left Montgomery with a strong claim to the succession, which Cunningham and Portal, much to the future regret of their successors, did not oppose when it was discussed at a Chiefs meeting in August 1945.[2] Brooke might have been wiser to have pressed the claims of General Sir Archibald Nye, his long serving VCIGS, who, though less well known to the public, had been the Army's chief executive through-out Brooke's tenure as CIGS and knew how to handle the Chiefs and Whitehall with a lightness of touch that Montgomery did not possess. There was also General Sir William Slim, commander of the victorious Fourteenth Army in Burma, but, as a member of the Indian Army, he was not thought to be a serious contender in 1946.

There was less doubt about Tedder, who had both the command ability, demonstrated so well in the Mediterranean, and political dexterity, shown equally clearly as the Overlord Deputy Supreme Allied Commander under Eisenhower. Unfortunately, he and Montgomery were bitter enemies, stemming from Tedder's un-edifying and abortive 'Plot' to have Montgomery sacked when stale-mate threatened to engulf the Normandy beachhead in July 1944.[3] Tedder was Portal's choice, and when Portal retired in January 1946, Tedder became the first of the new team to take over. It was the Air's turn to inherit the chairmanship of the Chiefs from Brooke, and so Tedder became Chairman (Designate).

The equally obvious, but unaccepted, choice for First Sea Lord was Admiral Lord Fraser of North Cape, C-in-C, Home Fleet, dur-ing the second half of the war against Germany, and then C-in-C, Pacific Fleet, co-operating with the Americans in the closing stages of the war against Japan. After consultations within the Navy, Cunningham recommended his namesake, Admiral Sir John Cunningham, who was not related to him, for the post. He was three years older than Fraser, who would be available to take over later. The two Cunninghams could not have been more different: 'ABC' fiery, aggressive, intolerant and inclined to schoolboyish boastful-

ness, but a highly successful naval commander; John rather dour
with an acid tongue, intellectually inclined and with a far better
brain, but an unlucky operational commander with the experience of
defeats in Norway, Dakar and the Dodecanese, which gave him a
cautious and cynical outlook. Nevertheless, as Stephen Roskill, the
naval historian who knew the three men well, points out, John was
better suited to fighting for the Navy in Whitehall in the immediate
aftermath of the war than either 'ABC' or Fraser.[4]

The greatest change faced by the new Chiefs was the substitution
of Attlee, with his consensus style of leadership, for the autocratic
Churchill as Prime Minister and, for the first eighteen months, as
Minister of Defence as well. Although Attlee had the experience of
being a member of the War Cabinet throughout the war, and was a
tough disciplinarian within his own post-war Cabinet, he lacked
strategic vision and imagination. Sir George Mallaby, a Cabinet
Secretary remarked:

> Cabinet Committee meetings were usually orderly and brisk . . . Meetings
> ended on time . . . But there was nothing very constructive about all this . . .
> He was like a schoolmaster who kept order very well but did not really teach
> you very much.[5]

Attlee was happy to go along with the proposals for the post-war
Defence structure put forward by officials, who had themselves
worked the war-time system so successfully and saw no reason to
dismantle it. The Committee of Imperial Defence was not resuscitated. The Defence Committee of the Cabinet, chaired by the Prime
Minister, was to remain in being, and a separate Minister of Defence
was to be appointed with much the same imprecise co-ordinating
and non-executive functions of the pre-war Minister for Co-
ordination of Defence. He was, however, to be given a small ministerial staff of only some 50 military officers and administrative grade
civil servants in the Storey's Gate offices to harmonise Service
administration, and to administer Joint Service establishments.

These changes did not affect the working of the Chiefs of Staff
Committee, the Joint Planning Staff and Joint Intelligence
Committee, which were deemed to be part of the Ministry of
Defence; nor was there to be any diminution of the executive and
financial independence of the three powerful Service Ministries. The
Chiefs retained their corporate responsibility as the Government's
professional advisers for preparing strategic plans and for submitting
them to the Defence Committee. They were expected to discuss such

plans with the Minister of Defence first, but this in no way implied submission through him. The Minister of Defence, however, was the sole representative of the Services in Cabinet, although the three Service Ministers were invited to attend when Defence matters were on the agenda, and they remained responsible to Parliament for their respective Services.

The fuzziness of these arrangements weakened central direction and leadership over a wide range of urgent Defence issues, and correspondingly strengthened the influence of the single Service lobbies. The linkage of the Chiefs' collective responsibilities for the development of strategic policies with their executive responsibilities was unimpaired, but, as the wartime emphasis on the former declined, the Admiralty, War Office and Air Ministry, each with its own Secretary of State, again became the dominant forces in Defence affairs. The Minister of Defence with no real department of his own, and with only a shadow of Churchill's wartime powers, was hardly well equipped to prevent a return to the disagreeable and unproductive aspects of pre-war inter-Service wrangling.

The proposed changes were set out in a 1946 White Paper, titled *Central Organisation for Defence*. Its authors were at pains to discredit any suggestion of the formation of a 'Combined Great General Staff'. They stressed the importance of avoiding what they saw as the fatal defects of Hitler's OKW:

> The German system failed because the Planning Staffs of the OKW were not drawn from the headquarters of the three Services. The plans had later to be handed to those headquarters for execution, and were often found to be unrealistic. The cleavage between planning and execution set up dangerous antagonisms, and entirely nullified the theoretical advantages of the German system.[6]

The eminent military historian, Michael Howard, in his 1970 study, *The Central Organisation of Defence*, damns the analogy as 'curiously inept' because it was based upon the evidence of German generals captured on the Western Front, whose knowledge was partial and who had axes to grind of their own. Subsequent evidence, he suggests, does not sustain its aptness.[7] Whether this was so or not, avoiding a divorce of policy from execution was seen in the late 1940s and the 1950s to be a cardinal principle governing the post-war crawl towards a fully fledged Ministry of Defence and Defence Staff. Great care was taken in 1946 to ensure that the new Minister of Defence, A V Alexander, who took up his appointment on 20 December 1946, could not infringe the powers and responsibilities of the Chiefs and the three Service Ministries.

There were many similarities between the situations faced by the first group of post-war Chiefs – John Cunningham, Montgomery and Tedder – and their First World War predecessors – Beatty, Wilson and Trenchard – in 1919. The country was again near bankruptcy, and brought nearer to the brink by the United States Congress ending Lend Lease as soon as Japan surrendered and imposing the harshest competitive terms for the first post-war United States Loan to Britain. Anglo-American relations were further damaged by the MacMahon Act of August 1946, which reduced collaboration in atomic research and development to minimal levels; and by the generally anti-colonial bias of American post-war foreign policy.

The Anglo-American 'Special Relationship' almost collapsed for other reasons. Americans looked upon the British not only as poor relations, ignoring the causes of their poverty, but as dangerous ones as well. British Socialism, so alien to their way of life, seemed but a short step away from Communism, which they feared would engulf the whole of Europe. Attlee was politely received by Truman, but there was no meeting of minds between the two men or between their administrations. Doors in Washington, which used to open so readily and cordially to British knocks when Roosevelt and Churchill were in power, stayed obstinately closed in the Truman/Attlee era. In the all important atomic field, the American view was that the British Isles were too exposed to Soviet attack to risk production or minimal stockpiling of atomic weapons on British soil; and British security was too suspect to allow the free passage of secret atomic information. The uncovering of the British scientists, Alan Nunn May, Klaus Fuchs and Bruno Pontecorvo as Soviet spies confirmed their worst fears about Britain.

There were, of course, important differences too between 1918 and 1945. The British were not as impoverished psychologically as they had been in 1919: standing alone in 1940–41, and bearing the brunt of the fighting in the Mediterranean, Middle East and Western Europe until mid-1944, had given them an immense pride in achievement. Post-war military commitments were even greater than in 1918: British troops were in occupation of the Italian, French and Dutch Empires, and were in the process of re-establishing sovereignty over British territories occupied by the Japanese. While demobilisation and financial retrenchment were once again the order of the day, there was a general determination to rebuild the British Empire on Commonwealth lines, and to avoid the military mistakes of the 1920s and 1930s, the consequences of which new Chiefs fully appreciated from first-hand experience. They were determined not to allow a repetition of the demobilisation shambles of 1918–19; the lack of coherent strategic planning; and the re-imposition of the Ten Year Rule.

Demobilisation was certainly carried out more fairly, using the carefully devised points system based on age and length of service at home and abroad. The 'Three Pillars' of British strategy were re-established as: defence of the United Kingdom base, which included the defence of Western Europe; defence of sea communications; and a firm hold on the Middle East as the crossroads of empire and the main source of sterling oil supplies. The Ten Year Rule *per se* was not reimposed, although the rapid advances in weapon technology, particularly in the atomic and missile fields, did provide an excellent excuse for delaying re-equipment programmes. Such caution was quite out of place in the face of the growing threat of Communist aggression linked with Afro-Asian nationalism.

Attlee soon came under intense pressure from Hugh Dalton, the Chancellor of the Exchequer, to reimpose the Ten Year Rule, but the most that he would do was to insist that the Chiefs should plan on no major war in the next two to three years. The Treasury kept up the pressure, demanding that men and manufacturing capacity must be released to enable the country to rebuild its export trade and regain a measure of financial solvency before the American loans ran out. By May 1947, an agreement was reached in the Defence Committee that plans should be based on a two-phased and fixed ten-year time frame, which would not be rolled forward each year as had been the case in the 1920s. The Chiefs' paper on 'Future Defence Policy', agreed by the Defence Committee that month, read:

> Planning should proceed on the assumption that the likelihood of war in the next five years was small. The risk will then increase gradually in the following five years and increase steeply after ten years. The risk of war at any time will be comparably decreased to the extent that we and our potential allies show strength.[8]

Subsequent assessments of Soviet capabilities and intentions refined the date of readiness for major war as 1957. Thus the pre-war rolling Ten Year rule became the fixed dated 'Five plus Five Year' assumption.

These assumptions were not established through the unity and persuasive powers of the Chiefs. On the contrary, they were achieved in spite of their regrettable disunity. At no period before or since has there been such bitterness and personal animosity in the Chiefs of

Staff Committee. The root cause of all the antagonism was not arguments over retrenchment, which were to be expected in a period of sharp budgetary decline, but Tedder's and John Cunningham's personal and professional dislike of 'Monty'. Brigadier Nigel Poett (later General Sir Nigel), who was Army's Director of Plans at the time, described the antipathy, mimicking Monty's style of speech:

> Monty couldn't stand Tedder; had declared war on Tedder at an earlier stage [Normandy]. John Cunningham was very clever; Monty did not like his style of cleverness; didn't like him at all. John Cunningham didn't like Monty; Tedder did not like Monty so it was not a very happy organisation – with Cunningham and Tedder ganging up on Monty.[9]

Personal jealousy played a part in the antagonism. In 1946, Montgomery's popularity with the press and public exceeded that of the ousted Churchill. Tedder was barely known outside Service circles, and John Cunningham was little known, even in the Navy. Monty not only was a national figure; he saw to it that he remained one and that everyone knew it!

This disunity was all the more regrettable because there was so much to be done. The workload of the Chiefs was intense, necessitating at least three meetings a week, either by them or their Vice Chiefs. At these meetings, each Chief would arrive bowed down with copious written briefs, all flagged up with alphabetical tags to give him easy access to key papers, facts and figures. Thus armed, he was expected to 'fight his corner' and achieve what the various echelons of his department judged to be in the best interests of his Service, and, *ipso facto*, of the country as well. It was, and still is, a point of honour amongst the junior staff officers to get their briefs through the many staff levels unchanged and unamended, and to win the solution that *they* thought right for their Service.

There was, of course, two-way traffic in the preparation of briefs with direction and ideas coming down from above as well as advice being thrust up from below. However much a Chief believed in his own personal ideas, he would always be afraid of letting his Service down by overlooking some crucial factor, by compromising too soon, or by failing to master his brief and just returning to his staff empty handed. For most of the time, sheer pressure of work compelled the top men to accept their briefs without too much questioning or ordering their 'briefers' back to the 'drawing board'.

In such circumstances, agreement was not easy to achieve. Montgomery recalled in his waspish way that almost the only occasion on which there was unanimous agreement in the Chiefs of Staff

Committee was when he put forward a proposal that the Chiefs should ask the Prime Minister for a new Minister of Defence in place of A V Alexander.[10]

Montgomery was his own worst enemy. Supremely self-confident after his wartime victories, he saw himself as a military Messiah, sent to ensure that the faults of the inter-war years were not repeated for a second time. No CIGS has ever entered office with more careful self-preparation behind him. In his inimitable way, he had thought through and over-simplified all the problems he could foresee, so that he should never be caught off balance in Whitehall battles any more than he would have allowed himself to have been on the battlefield. He did not believe in committees and made little attempt to conceal his dislike for the Chiefs of Staff Committee.

He had an equal contempt for the Cabinet system, especially under what he saw as the 'very wet' and indecisive leadership of Attlee. 'They haven't got a plan', he would say, 'you must have a plan, which everyone understands. There must be no "bellyaching".' He always did have a plan, and what annoyed his colleagues – military and political – was the way in which he was so often proved right by events.

His global tours and discussions with world leaders became apocryphal. He used his renown to solicit invitations to visit all the great men of the day, and paid scant attention to official briefings on the line he should take or the speeches and Press announcements that he should make while abroad. He irritated Attlee and Ernest Bevin, the Foreign Secretary – one of the few members of the Cabinet for whom he had any time – by cabling them with gratuitous advice during his tours; and he caused deep resentment on his return to London by telling his fellow Chiefs what should be done about most intractable international political and military problems. Tedder's antipathy burgeoned at what he saw as Monty's drive to take over the Chairmanship of the Chiefs.

Montgomery can and should be blamed for making little or no attempt to ease the tension between himself and Tedder and John Cunningham, or to meet them half-way. Pettiness ensued on both sides, which nearly brought about the disintegration of the Chiefs while the Attlee Government was deciding to jettison India, Palestine and Greece in the hope of easing the burden on the economy and ending wartime conscription.

He must, however, be given full credit for his exploitation of Churchill's *Iron Curtain* speech at Fulton, Missouri, of March 1946, which led, in the end, to the creation of NATO. Disguising his true purpose, he persuaded the Canadian Government to invite him to Canada for a good-will visit. He then wrote to Eisenhower, who had succeeded Marshall as Chief of United States Army Staff, suggesting that he should return from Canada via Washington so that they could meet to discuss mutual military problems.

He crossed the Atlantic in the *Mauritania* in the latter half of August 1946 with instructions from his colleagues not to attempt to meet Canadian and American politicians ringing in his ears, but with every intention of engineering and then accepting such invitations as a matter of courtesy. Both Mackenzie King, the Prime Minister of Canada, and Harry Truman, the United States President, did invite him. The former was soon persuaded of the need to face up to Soviet hostility and to let Monty speak for Canada in Washington. The latter gave approval for what amounted to a resuscitation of the Combined Chiefs of Staff to examine the way ahead and to devise a counter-Communist strategy. Monty reported to General Sir Frank Simpson, his VCIGS in London:

> The present situation is as follows: the Heads of State of Canada and America have both expressed their wish that we should cease being on merely friendly terms, but should get down to full and frank discussions on all defence matters. The opportunity is there for us to grasp. No further comment from me is necessary.[11]

He added:

> . . . take the necessary action in London with the Chiefs of Staff who will probably decide the best method of approach to the Prime Minister . . .[12]

Attlee was appalled; he had authorised no such approach. He would have difficulty in carrying the Cabinet with him if he tried to pick up the torch of an anti-Soviet crusade being thrust into his hands by Monty; and there would certainly be trouble with the Left wing of the Labour Party if any details of Monty's secret talks in Ottawa and Washington were to leak into the public domain. Any Chief other than Monty would have been sacked for such an unauthorised excursion into international politics, but to retire him would have been to give him the freedom to speak his mind in the House of Lords. With Truman's approval, and with Attlee's warning on secrecy and the avoidance of specific commitment, Montgomery met and discussed measures to counter the Soviet threat with the United States Joint Chiefs on 16 September in the yacht *Sequoia* under the guise of a social cruise down the Potomac. Thus began the sequence of secret military and political talks from which the Western

European Union (WEU) and then NATO eventually sprang, thanks to Montogomery's almost single-handed efforts and his dedication to the cause of Western European defence.

Tedder and John Cunningham were no less appalled than Attlee. History was repeating itself: for the third time in the 20th Century, Britain was being cajoled by the War Office into accepting a continental commitment, this time with forces permanently stationed in Europe. Such a policy would mean abandoning Britain's traditional and more flexible maritime strategy and would give primacy to the Army at the Navy's, though not necessarily the Air Force's, expense.

Success usually leads to success, but not in Monty's case: it created increased resentment and obstruction throughout Whitehall. Armies must be commanded, but Monty failed to realise that Whitehall cannot be treated in that way – consensus must be built if new policies are to gain acceptance in its corridors of power and those of the Palace of Westminster. Instead of doing his utmost to carry the other members of the Chiefs of Staff Committee with him, he alienated them, often refusing to attend meetings, especially those chaired by Tedder – the VCIGS went instead.

One of Montgomery's most unseemly clashes with his colleagues occurred when he demanded that they should back him in pressing for eighteen months instead of a year's compulsory service in the National Service Act that was being placed before Parliament in the summer of 1948. They refused, but that did not stop him going behind their backs to Attlee and fighting the measure through the Defence Committee and Cabinet single-handed. He won a thankless victory, which added most of the Cabinet to his list of enemies.

Thus Monty's military rake's progress went on with him acting more and more as a law unto himself. It came as some relief all round, when at the end of 1948, after only two and a half years in post, he was packed off by Attlee to put his European defence ideas into practice and to exercise his military paternalism, first as Chairman of the Western European Union Chiefs of Staff Committee and then as Deputy Supreme Allied Commander in the new North Atlantic Treaty Organisation; and later still, under the auspices of the *Times*, to visit his 'very good friends', the Pope, Tito, and Mao Tse Tung.

Brooke's period as Chairman of the Chiefs had demonstrated the strength of the system. He, Pound, Andrew Cunningham and Portal had been determined to act as a united team bent only upon the best interests of the country. Policies were developed in frank, honest and often heated arguments, which never became personal or in any way affected their cordial relationships and respect for each other. Tedder's period as Chairman started to reveal the system's two major defects: its vulnerability to personality clashes, which is a fault inherent in most corporate organisations; and its lack of strong central tri-Service direction, which was to become more blatant as the nuclear era dawned and weapon technology not only galloped off up an exponential curve of performance and cost, but also increased the need for the Services to get their act together.

The selection of a Chief cannot be based solely upon his command ability and acceptability as the professional head of his own Service; nor can it be judged on his intellectual talents, political sensitivity and ability to handle the Whitehall bureaucracy. Both these sides of the high command coin must be balanced in his personality. Montgomery had everything required of a great Chief except political feel and the ability to work in a team. He believed that a headless and largely leaderless Chiefs of Staff Committee was no way to advise the Government and to run the Armed Forces in peacetime. Privately, he urged the replacement of the Chiefs by a Supremo to act as an independent adviser to the Minister of Defence, but, as with so much else, he was ahead of his time and a voice crying in the wilderness.

There is no evidence that Monty had himself in mind or courted the appointment, although this must be an assumption. Unsuited though he was to working in Whitehall in peace or war, he was the one man who might have been able to straddle the three environments successfully at that time. He would have thrown himself enthusiastically into the job, pontificating on and over-simplifying naval and air warfare with much the same sureness of touch that he displayed in land warfare, but no-one was prepared to offer him the job. Nonetheless, he did, as we will see, accelerate the advance towards the appointment of a Chief of Defence Staff and the establishment of a more powerful Ministry of Defence before his active days were over.

There was one area of Defence policy where there was no disunity amongst the Chiefs: the paramount need for a British atomic bomb to be carried by the RAF as Britain's ultimate weapon. They stated their operational requirement for the weapon as early as January 1946. Portal, on his retirement as CAS, was persuaded to take on the job of Controller of Atomic Energy in the Ministry of Supply and, by the autumn of 1946, British preparations to manufacture atomic bombs were far enough advanced for him to seek a mandate from the Prime Minister to start production.

The passage of the MacMahon Act through the United States Congress in August 1946 was only a contributory factor in Attlee's decision, taken in January 1947, to authorise Portal to go ahead. The Chiefs argued that Britain, as a great power (the term superpower was not yet current), could not leave her security in the hands of the Americans, who, however friendly, could veer so unpredictably from generous international collaboration to self-centred isolationism, as their precipitate cancellation of Lend-Lease had shown so recently. Attlee, for his part, was not prepared to be bullied by anyone, least of all the Americans, whom he recognised were trying to gain an atomic weapon monopoly. Portal received his full support, enabling Britain to go it alone until the MacMahon Act was amended in her favour.

The struggle for financial resources did not become as tough a bone of contention amongst the Chiefs in the immediate post-war years as might have been expected. This was largely due to the re-emergence of a major threat to security posed by the Kremlin's ambitions, which kept demands for military retrenchment at bay. American assumption of world leadership in 1947, with Congress's acceptance in March of the Truman Doctrine of the containment of Communism, and of the Marshal Plan, in June, for economic aid to Europe, helped to reduce British military commitments to manageable levels. However, there were still more than enough emergencies to be dealt with to keep the Services fully stretched. The new Ministry of Defence had neither the power nor the staff to intervene in the Services' budgetary negotiations, which were undertaken almost exclusively between the sovereign Service departments and the Treasury. Neither A V Alexander nor 'Manny' Shinwell, the first two Ministers of Defence, carried enough political clout to do more than seek compromises that would make individual Service demands more palatable to the Cabinet as the Communist threat to Western interests in general, and to British colonial territories in particular, grew in intensity.

1948 was the year in which any residual doubts about the virulence of the Communist threat – Russian and Chinese – were quashed by events. The Soviet coup in Czechoslovakia took place in February; the Brussels Treaty was signed in March; the Berlin Blockade started in June; and in the same month, the Chinese terrorist campaign opened in Malaya. Meanwhile the next generation of British Chiefs started to take over and were soon facing the possi-

bility of the Cold War turning hot at any time. Admiral Lord Fraser
of North Cape became First Sea Lord in September; General Sir
William Slim (later Field Marshal, the Viscount), whom Attlee
brought back from his retirement job as chairman of the recently
nationalised British Railways, succeeded Montgomery, albeit against
the latter's wishes, in November; and Air Marshal Sir John Slessor
took over from Tedder but not until the beginning of 1950, when the
latter was appointed to head the British Joint Services Mission in
Washington during the run-up to the Korean War.

The new team, all of whom were outstanding in their own ways,
got on well together and did much to restore confidence in the Chiefs
of Staff system. Slim was a large man in every sense of the word, who
was unusually acceptable both as head of the Army and of the
General Staff in spite of his Indian Army background: a great leader
of men, who gave confidence in adversity and stability in periods of
chaos, as his campaigns in Burma had shown; intellectually articulate, as the many readers of his best seller, *Defeat into Victory*, can
vouch; and possessed of a sureness of political touch, which helped
him in Whitehall and later as Governor General of Australia. There
was nothing petty about Slim; nor was there about Fraser, who was
respected throughout the Navy as a very able 'old sea-dog'; and,
although his intellect was considered by some critics too limited for
real success in Whitehall, his judgement in naval and national policy
was always sound and, like Slim's, well balanced.

Slessor, who joined the team a year later, complemented it in that
whereas Slim and Fraser were commanders first and chiefs of staff
second, Slessor was the reverse. He made his name as Portal's
Assistant Chief of Air Staff (Policy) at the Casablanca Conference,
where he drafted the compromise formula which broke the deadlock
in the Anglo-American debate on strategy. Later, he showed himself
to be an able C-in-C of Coastal Command during the Battle of the
Atlantic in 1943 and as AOC-in-C, Mediterranean and Middle East,
in 1944. His great strength lay in his ability to argue a case – and
herein lay the rub. He was a devotee of the Trenchard theory that
the RAF could fight wars more effectively and cheaply than the older
Services, and of the doctrine of centralisation of air power, which led
him to clash with Fraser over carriers and naval aviation.

1949 was a 'curate's egg' of a year. On the positive side, the North
Atlantic Treaty was signed in April, and the United States Congress
passed the complementary Mutual Defence Aid Programme to start
building up Western European military forces to counter the Soviet

threat. On the negative side, the Russians tested their first atomic bomb in August and Mao Tse Tung proclaimed the establishment of the Chinese People's Republic in October, reaping the fruits of the Communist conquest of the Chinese mainland.

In Britain, financial bankruptcy was again a threatening possibility. Sir Stafford Cripps had become Chancellor of the Exchequer after Hugh Dalton's unfortunate budget-leak and started to demand further major reductions in all Government expenditure. Had the new Chiefs not recovered unity of purpose by the time Sterling was devalued in September 1949, the Service votes would have suffered more damaging cuts than they did. Nevertheless, retrenchment was severe enough to bring the continued existence of battleships into question and for doubts to be expressed about Britain's ability to afford large fleet carriers. The first shots were soon being fired by Slessor in the long running carrier battle that was to rage in Whitehall throughout the 1950s and most of the 1960s.

Attlee only just won the February 1950 General Election. In his Cabinet reshuffle, he replaced the ineffective A V Alexander as Minister of Defence with 'Manny' Shinwell, who had been Secretary of State for War. Attlee, himself had always been sceptical about the Navy's case for large ships, saying 'who is there to fight at sea?' At that time, there was no evidence of the Soviet naval expansion which was to start in earnest in the 1960s. Shinwell was equally sceptical about naval costs, and was made all the more so by the Admiralty's requirement for specialised high performance aircraft for its carriers. One cynic summed up the general feeling in Whitehall on the large fleet carriers:

> Ministry of Defence recommend them out; Admiralty want them retained. General opinion: we cannot afford them.[13]

Slessor stepped in with a radical proposal for merging his former Coastal Command with Naval Aviation to form a joint Maritime Air Force, which Fraser could never have accepted and still remained as First Sea Lord. The Chiefs wisely tried to settle the issue with an internal study of the thorny problems caused by the overlaps between sea and air power. General Sir Gerald Templer (later to become CIGS and Field Marshal) was appointed as a neutral, but dynamic personality to chair the committee of inquiry, composed of four Admiralty and four Air Ministry representatives. Fortunately for the Navy, the Korean War broke out, and the Fleet was able to display the versatility of its larger existing carriers. Templer came down in their favour: the Navy had won the first round of the great carrier battle.

The outbreak of the Korean War was fortuitous in another way as far as the Chiefs were concerned. The growing tensions were relieved between themselves and the Chancellor, and amongst themselves, as the Exchequer coffers were prized open and rearmament began. The Attlee Government loyally supported the American-led United Nations war effort in the common resolve not to let an aggressor get away with it, and dispatched British forces from Hong Kong to the aid of South Korea. This loyalty was not to be repaid five years later during the Suez crisis!

Allied intelligence assessments suggested that the Communist offensive in Korea was but a preliminary skirmish to draw Anglo-American forces to the Far East, and to hold them there while Soviet Forces destabilised the politically shaky states of Western Europe. In 1950, the Communist parties in Italy and France were large and active enough to substantiate this fear. The chances of the Third World War breaking out by 1953 instead of 1957 as previously predicted were deemed too high for any complacency in Western capitals.

In Washington, the Combined Chiefs of Staff machinery was reactivated, with Tedder taking the part of Dill in planning the rearmament and war effort of both countries; and later in giving valuable support to the President and Joint Chiefs of Staff under the chairmanship of General Omar Bradley in opposing General McArthur's attempt to widen the conflict to the Chinese mainland. The British rearmament programme proposed by the Combined Chiefs was to cost £6,000m over three years, to which the United States would make an undefined contribution. This figure represented a rise in Defence expenditure from just over 6 per cent to about 12 per cent of the British Gross Domestic Product (GDP). Subsequent Cabinet and Service Department screening in Whitehall reduced the figure to £4,700m or 10 per cent GDP, which was the most that the Treasury believed could be sustained without putting the economy onto a war footing. The British electorate, conscious of the lessons of pre-war appeasement, accepted the burden as reasonable.

The rearmament programme killed the Five plus Five Year rule, and led to crash production programmes at the expense of the previous policy of giving priority to research and development. The V Bomber programme was hurried forward, the first production order for the Valiant being placed in December 1950; the Hunter and Swift fighters were produced as stop-gaps until the Lightning could be produced; and the building of Beverley and Britannia air transports was begun. Unlike the failure to collaborate in the atomic field, an Anglo-US Missile Agreement had been signed in February 1950, which allowed unfettered interchange of missile technology, and enabled Britain to make rapid progress in the development of the Blue Streak 2,500 mile strategic ballistic missile, the Blue Water tactical missile, and a family of anti-aircraft missiles – the Navy's Sea Slug, the Army's Thunderbird, and the RAF's Bloodhound. The question as to whether missiles would oust bombers and fighters was an open one in the early 1950s, and, like the carrier battle, was to cause dissension between the fledgling Ministry of Defence and the next generation of Chiefs.

The scale of the rearmament programme soon proved too ambitious for Britain's fragile economy, and fatal to Attlee's Government. The balance of payments crisis of 1951 was caused by the Iranian nationalisation of the Anglo-Persian Oil Company in May, which forced Britain to buy oil for American dollars; and by American stockpiling of strategic raw materials, which not only increased world prices, but also enabled British colonies to spend newly earned dollars on their own development, causing a major out-flow of sterling. Attlee might have ridden the crisis had it not been for the internal rift within the Labour Party brought about by Aneurin Bevan's claim that the imposition of National Health prescription charges was the direct result of financial strains caused by the rearmament programme. Attlee went to the country over the issue in October 1951 and lost the General Election. Churchill became Prime Minister again and, for a time, reassumed the Defence portfolio. He recalled Lieutenant General Sir Ian Jacob temporarily from the Director Generalship of the BBC to undertake Lord Ismay's former role of his personal Chief of Staff and link man with the Chiefs.

Changes in Defence policy rarely occur overnight. There has to be a convergence of ideas or pressures before a consensus for change builds up in Whitehall and Westminster. It often takes a specific event to focus the image of the change that is needed. Churchill's return to power in 1951 drew together the disparate factors of the country's economic needs, the deterrent potential of atomic weapons, and the NATO demands for larger conventional forces in the defence of Western Europe.

When Churchill's Chancellor of the Exchequer, R A Butler, opened the Treasury books on assuming office, he was aghast at what he found. It was clear to him that the rearmament programme, as it stood, was more than the British economy could bear. His initial reaction was to spread it over an extra year, but by the beginning of 1952 a new Sterling crisis loomed, forcing him to demand cuts as well, which the Chiefs could not accept as long as they were committed to the war in Korea; the Malayan campaign; holding the Canal Zone in Egypt; garrisoning the fortress colonies – Gibraltar, Malta, Aden, Singapore and Hong Kong – on the lines of communication to the Far East and Australasia; maintaining a naval presence in the Atlantic and Mediterranean, and on other British sea-borne trade routes; and building up Rhine Army to the Brussels Treaty requirement of four divisions plus supporting air forces.

Churchill paid his first post-election visit to Washington in January 1952. Doors that had remained firmly shut in Attlee's days began to reopen. He was briefed in depth on the United States Strategic Air Plan, and quickly grasped the implications of what he heard. The briefing convinced him that a combination of atomic weapons and air power would swing the world balance of power firmly in the Western Alliance's favour for the foreseeable future.

A month later, the NATO Council, meeting in Lisbon, set conventional force goals for the Alliance, which took no account of American atomic capabilities. Britain's target was set by the Council initially at nine to ten regular and territorial divisions; and later this was increased to an even more impracticable figure of nine of each within a month of mobilisation. These plans made no sense to Churchill. Why superimpose a conventional force plan upon what should have been an atomic based strategy? Surely major savings in conventional forces should be practicable?

On his return from America, Churchill realised that at his age he could not carry the dual load of Prime Minister and Minister of Defence. His old favourite, Field Marshal Alexander, was about to return from Canada at the end of his tenure as Governor General and seemed an excellent choice for Minister of Defence: apolitical, with sound military judgement and well able to speak to the Chiefs in their own language. Alexander had qualms about accepting the job but did so out of duty to the country and loyalty to Winston. He was not the right man to put the Defence case in Cabinet or in the hurly-burly of Westminster.

Templer, who was summoned to Canada to see Churchill before he was appointed Supremo in Malaya, was staying in Government House, Ottawa, when Alexander told him that Churchill had asked him to become Minister of Defence. Templer was taken aback and said,

> But, Alex, for heaven's sake don't. You'll make a most imperial nonsense of it. You'll get mixed up with politicians!

Alex's naive reply was:

> Oh no, I won't: I'll be in the House of Lords![14]

Templer was right in that Alexander was not a natural public speaker or at home in debate; nor did he ever fathom the true nature and personal motives of politicians; and he was temperamentally unsuited to and disliked politics. In distinguishing between A V Alexander, who was by then in the Lords as well, Churchill quipped, *'not the one that runs co-ops, the one that wins battles'*.[15]

Churchill gave 'Alex' the task of examining with the Chiefs ways of discharging Britain's military commitments more economically with fewer men, less use of steel and fewer American dollars. The Chiefs, at Slessor's suggestion, decided that the task was of such fundamental importance that they should take the unusual step of leaving Whitehall for a few days in order to thrash out a new strategy free from the day to day distractions of their offices. Admiral Sir Rhoderick McGrigor, who had recently taken over from Lord Fraser as First Sea Lord in December 1951, offered the Royal Naval College, Greenwich, as the venue for the discussions, no doubt feeling that in such an historic naval setting it would be all the harder to write off the Navy as having no future in the Atomic Era.

'The Wee Mac', as McGrigor was affectionately known in the Navy, hosted the Greenwich meeting. As the new boy, he might have been out-ranged by the formidable guns of Slim and Slessor, but he was quite capable of looking after himself and the interests of his Service in such company. He had no mean intellect, but like Fraser before him, his talents were more suited to the bridge of a flagship in battle than to an office in Whitehall. Paradoxically, he preferred arguing a case on paper, and, as a torpedo specialist, he was more technically orientated than Slim or Slessor. Although modest and rather shy, like many small men he possessed unbounded energy, which he could use to telling effect if he felt that the Navy was being unfairly treated.

This special Greenwich Chiefs conference, away from the day-to-day hubbub of Whitehall, lasted from 28 April to 2 May with Slim in the chair and with their principal technological and scientific advisers readily available. Ian Jacob attended as Chief Staff Officer to the Minister of Defence, and to give the Chiefs the benefit of his wartime experience in drafting strategy papers for the Cabinet, which proved very necessary. The first draft of their 'Global Strategy Paper' emerged as a patchwork of uneasy compromises between the three Services' views, and lacked coherence. May and June were spent in refining it with the help of Jacob and Sir Frederick Brundrett, their trusted scientific adviser, and with inputs from Sir Pierson Dixon of the Foreign Office.

In its final version, the 'Global Strategy Paper' set out three tasks for the Services: protecting Britain's worldwide interests in the Cold War; building up Britain's share of NATO forces; and making 'reasonable' preparations for a hot war should one break out. There was nothing controversial about the first two tasks: it was on the third that it was difficult to reach acceptable conclusions without prejudicing the vital interests of one Service or another. The paper postulated that a hot war would begin with a short period of high intensity operations in which atomic weapons would be used. This phase could only last a matter of weeks if not days. If one side or the other did not collapse, then an indefinite period of 'broken-backed' warfare would ensue in which the two sides tried to rebuild their forces for a further all-out effort.

The main deterrent to hot war was seen as the atomic threat posed by the United States Strategic Air Force, but the Chiefs believed that Britain needed her own atomic strike force for two sound, and one not so sound, reasons: first, to ensure that targets vital to Britain, which were not high enough on the American's target list, would be struck; secondly, as a hedge against a return to American isolationism; and thirdly and less plausibly, as a matter of great power prestige – Britain still deemed herself to be in that league in 1952.

The idea of fighting an atomic war and of a 'broken-backed' phase was thought to be credible in 1952, since the power of the atomic bomb and the numbers of weapons available were limited. The detonation of the American hydrogen bomb in November 1952 was to change all that, but the implications for the continued existence of mankind posed by the use of nuclear, as opposed to atomic weapons, still lay in the clouded crystal of the future.

Slessor had every reason to be content with the Chiefs' assessment of strategic requirements. The three principal RAF Commands had the security of important roles. By the end of 1953, Bomber Command would be manning Britain's strategic deterrent, using its V Bombers and British atomic bombs, which were to be tested at

Monte Bello Island off the north-west coast of Australia in October 1952, five months after the Greenwich meeting. Fighter Command would remain a vital component in Britain's and NATO's hot war air defences, and Transport Command would be expanded, to give the Army strategic and tactical mobility in Cold War operations and to enable overseas garrisons to be reduced once emergency air rein-forcement and routine air trooping proved practicable.

Slim could also be satisfied. As far as the Army was concerned, the problem was not how to build up a case for its continued existence, but how to reduce overstretch, which was to get worse as successive governments tried to follow the responsible colonial policy of only granting independence to overseas territories when they were politi-cally, economically and militarily ready, in HMG's view, to stand on their own feet. Nationalist liberation movements wanted a faster rate of change and had to be kept in check by British garrisons.

Concurrently with the presentation of the Global Strategy Paper in Cabinet, Anthony Eden, the Foreign Secretary, tabled a paper giving the Foreign Office point of view. After setting out an impressive list of commitments, ranging from the defence of Western Europe to the maintenance of garrisons in the fortress colonies around the world, he declined to recommend liquidating any of them. The nearest that he came to doing so was when he wrote:

> A very minor commitment which we could endeavour to dispose of to the United States is the Falkland Island Dependencies. I do not advise such action, for public admission of inability to maintain these traditional possessions would cause loss of prestige wholly out of proportion to the saving of money obtained.[16]

In considering the Cold War problems, both the Chiefs and the Foreign Office misjudged the threat. They expected Chinese Communist subversion to create increasing instability in the Far East, and to prevent any reduction of force levels East of Suez, whereas a successful outcome of the current renegotiation of the Anglo-Egyptian Treaty was confidently expected to lead to a sub-stantial saving of troops in the Middle East. King Farouk of Egypt was de-throned a few weeks after this assessment was made!

McGrigor was the Chief whose Service was under greatest threat. There was no question of abandoning Britain's traditional long term faith in sea power, but, in the arguments about relative priorities in the shorter term, the Admiralty's case had some glaring weaknesses. The main threat was from two land powers, Soviet Russia and Communist China, hence the Army and Air were bound to take precedence in resource allocation. At best, the Navy could be seen as having a subsidiary role in the Cold War; not much more in the first short, sharp phase of a hot war; and a significant part to play only in the 'broken-backed' phase when the safe passage of re-supply convoys across the Atlantic would be vital to Britain's survival. For none of these tasks was there a clear requirement for more than escort carriers, destroyers and frigates. The usefulness of the heavy ships – battleships, fleet carriers and cruisers – could be and were questioned, and demanding funds for their modernisation and replacement was seen as the Admiralty's Achilles heel.

The Global Strategy Paper pleased Churchill, but not Butler, the Chancellor, or his principal Treasury advisers. History repeated itself: the two Treasury Reviews of the pre-war rearmament programme in 1937 and 1938 had almost exact parallels in two 'Radical Reviews' of the post-war rearmament programmes, which Butler, with Churchill's full support, forced upon the Government and the Chiefs in 1953 and 1954, and for much the same reasons as Chamberlain had done in the inter-war years – a flourishing economy was seen as the foundation of a sound defence. In Butler's view, the Global Strategy Review conclusions would not reign back rearmament costs significantly: the expenditure needed to implement the Chief's policy could only be met at the political price of reducing standards of living. Furthermore, the key to correcting Britain's balance of payments deficits lay in increasing export of metal based products in direct competition with the Navy's modernization and building programmes. He demanded a review that would marry the Chiefs' views on strategic requirements with the Treasury's assessment of the economic facts of life.

The First 'Radical Review' began under Sir Norman Brook, Secretary to the Cabinet, in January 1953. Its conclusions confirmed the Global Strategy Paper's conclusions and gave the Navy some solace in that it said that *'the first aim of the rearmament programmes should be to insure national survival in the initial attack and to safeguard sea communications in the second phase'*[17]. Contrary to political expectations, Brook recommended a slight increase rather than a decrease in expenditure, which met with no approval in Cabinet. Despite Churchill's long experience in the Admiralty and his love for the Royal Navy, he became highly critical, if not actually hostile, to Naval Staff plans, believing, as he had always tended to do, that inflated shore establishments were being kept at the expense of ships in commission.

It was, however, his son-in-law, Duncan Sandys, the Minister of

Supply, who launched the most damaging two-pronged attack, first, on the Chiefs, and, secondly on the Naval Staff. From the Chiefs, he demanded that the conclusions of the Global Strategy Paper should be more starkly defined: only forces that contributed to Britain's position as a world power in the Cold War and were relevant to *the first six weeks* of a hot war should be maintained. Much to the Chief's annoyance, Alexander, as Minister of Defence and no doubt reflecting Churchill's own views, devised a compromise whereby all combat forces were placed in one of three categories: Category I, those needed for Cold War commitments; Category II, those for survival in the first six weeks of a hot war; and Category III, 'broken-back' phase requirements in which he included most of the Navy.

Churchill suffered his first stroke in June that year, leaving Butler and the Treasury in the ascendant, and Sandys unchecked. Sandys immediately launched the second prong of his attack, this time with the support of Lord De L'Isle, Minister for Air, and Slessor, on the Navy's carrier and cruiser programmes. He argued that the country could no longer afford continued duplication in maritime warfare, which, in his view, could be waged more cost-effectively by placing greater reliance upon shore-based aircraft. He insisted that savings so made should be spent on strengthening strategic bomber and air defence fighter forces within the limited Defence budget.

So concerned did McGrigor become about these unsolicited attacks that he sent the VCNS, Admiral Sir Guy Grantham, and the Director of Naval Intelligence, Admiral Sir Anthony Buzzard, to give Sandys a personal briefing on the Navy's case. They spent three hours with him, but to little avail. Sandys remained critical, conceding only that carriers and cruisers could be categorised as 'desirable', but as such could not be afforded. He held to his view that the Air share of the Defence vote should be increased at the expense of the Navy.

Over the next six months, McGrigor fought back with great tenacity, and, as had happened so often in the past and was to do so again in the 1980s, the Navy was saved by world events. A number of new factors emerged. The Soviet naval threat increased with the commissioning of the powerful *Sverdlov* class of commerce-raiding cruisers, which could only be countered effectively by strike aircraft launched from carriers. Then intelligence of Soviet air defences began to suggest that the high level V Bombers might become dangerously vulnerable to Russian surface-to-air missiles. Carrier-borne low level strike aircraft, armed with atomic weapons, would be a sensible precautionary supplement to the British deterrent. And to cap the Navy's good fortune, the NATO force planners required three carrier groups in the North East Atlantic, which could only be provided by the Royal Navy in the initial phases of a war at sea because the American carriers could not arrive until about $D + 15$ (ie: 15 days after war had been declared).

McGrigor was not slow to make the point that providing three carrier groups was just as important in maintaining influence in NATO's naval command structure as the V-Bombers were in the case of the United States Strategic Air Command. The Naval Staff had, in fact, already anticipated the requirement and had plans for 50,000 ton carriers equipped with a new naval strike aircraft to be developed as a dual purpose *Sverdlov* killer and low level strike bomber – the controversial NA 39, of which much more was to be heard during the TSR 2 controversy of the mid-1960s.

By January 1953, the tide of opinion in Whitehall was beginning to turn in the Navy's favour. Personalities played an important part in the change of atmosphere. Churchill returned to office after his stroke, but was clearly failing and was becoming increasingly irrelevant in opposing naval plans. Amongst the Chiefs, General Sir John Harding (later Field Marshal Lord Harding) replaced Slim in November 1952 before the latter went out to Australia as Governor General; and Slessor was succeeded on completion of his tenure in office by Air Marshal Sir William ('Dickie') Dickson two months later in January 1953. McGrigor, Harding and Dickson, a diminutive trio in physical stature, were to become a powerfully united team.

Harding had been Alexander's highly respected Chief of Staff for most of the Italian Campaign. Brooke had once criticised him as a strategist because he gave strong support to Churchill's and Alexander's proposals for the advance on Vienna instead of the American inspired landings in Southern France in 1944. But Harding was, in fact, every bit as sound and balanced as Slim, and very much respected by the Army and in Whitehall. The Army, at that time, was not as yet a target for cuts because continuing Cold War operations and the build up of BAOR to Brussels Treaty requirements were still stretching it to the limits. Harding, like Slim, could therefore act as 'honest broker' in the continuing Naval/Air battles.

Dickson, from the point of view of improved relations amongst the Chiefs, was good news. His early years in the Services had given him an unusually wide perspective of inter-Service relations. Although he was no less devoted to his own Service, he was not so wedded to the 'RAF über alles' syndrome of many of his predecessors. He was commissioned originally into the Royal Naval Air Service during the First World War, and landed the first Sopwith Pup on the improvised landing deck fitted to HMS *Furious* in 1917. He transferred to the RAF in 1922, but continued with Naval Aviation as Fleet Aviation Officer in HMS *Queen Elizabeth*. He gained his experience of Army problems when commanding the Desert Air Force in 1944 during the Italian Campaign, and further widened his tri-Service understanding as AOC-in-C Mediterranean and Middle East after the war.

Dickson had a nimble intelligence and a charm of manner, which helped to ease some of the inter-Service tensions built up by the First Radical Review. This was shown soon after he took over as CAS. He and McGrigor came to an informal agreement which served as a basis of an Air Ministry/Admiralty truce. If the Air Force would cease its attacks on the Navy's new Carrier Strike Force concept, the Navy would not reopen its offensive for the transfer of Coastal Command to Admiralty control, which would be a sensible operational and psychological *quid pro quo* if the Navy were to lose its fleet carriers.

Then the Navy's prayers must have been answered: Sandys was taken ill as the Cabinet started its final round of debates on the First Radical Review. McGrigor's submission, 'The Navy of the Future', was a prescient document. In it he forecast the introduction of strategic ballistic missiles, carrying nuclear warheads; atomic powered submarines and surface ships; the replacement of gun armed battleships and cruisers with missile equipped destroyers and frigates; and the design of smaller carriers with vertical take-off strike aircraft and air defence missiles. The Navy in ten years time would be slimmer, but would pack a greater punch than it could in 1954 when the First Radical Review was wound up.

The Chiefs were soon wrong-footed by events, which made a mockery of their Global Strategy Paper assumption that reductions in force levels would not be possible in the Far East, but should come about in the Middle East. British successes in the Malayan jungles contrasted sharply with French failure in Indo-China (Dien Bien Phu fell in May 1954); and Anthony Eden's diplomacy led to the Indo-China settlement at Geneva in July that year, giving some hope that withdrawal of troops from South East Asia would soon be feasible. In the Middle East, the opposite occurred. The rise of

Colonel Nasser, as dictator of Egypt and leader of Arab Nationalism, extinguished any such hopes. He drove a much harder bargain than King Farouk's ministers, and the British negotiating position was weakened by the American diplomats in Cairo, who covertly supported and advised Nasser, and by the machinations of American oil companies operating in the Middle East. Reinforcement of the Middle East garrisons became necessary as alternative bases were rapidly established in Cyprus and Aden as precautionary measures. It all added up to yet another example of the unexpected happening in military affairs: something that governments find difficult to accept, and the Treasury to budget for.

It was not, however, Cold War problems that induced the Second Radical Review, which began in April 1954. The recognition of the overwhelming power of the hydrogen bomb affected the Cabinet in two ways. Churchill saw that Britain could not stay amongst the great powers without it; and he and Butler saw it as a means of reducing Defence expenditure on conventional forces still further to help the economy. Development work of the British nuclear bomb ('nuclear' replaced 'atomic' in weapon jargon after the testing of the American H-Bomb) was at the stage when decisions on actual production were needed. The final Cabinet decision to build 'thermonuclear' weapons was taken in the spring in parallel with another Global Strategy Review by the Chiefs and the Second Radical Review by a Defence Expenditure Review Committee briefed to prune the Defence votes yet again.

The Chiefs recognised that while the atomic bomb could be considered an enhancement of conventional weapon power, the devastating effects of thermonuclear weapons fundamentally changed the whole nature of war. As long as the United States held nuclear superiority, the Third World War was unlikely, but the Cold War waged by the Communist powers through subversion and supply of arms to proxy third powers was likely to go on indefinitely. Priority should be given to the build-up of British nuclear forces, with a shield of conventional land and air forces in Western Europe. Naval forces were still needed for protection of Allied sea communications, but were a supplement to the main deterrent.

The Navy were soon in trouble again. Sandys and De L'Isle set about exploiting the Chiefs' conclusion by complaining that the inter-Service shares of the reduced Defence 'cake' did not, in their view, match the Chiefs' strategy. Lord Swinton, the Colonial Secretary and a former Secretary of State for Air, was given the task of looking into priorities with a small group of ministers, including Sandys but not the Service Ministers! Once again the cost-effectiveness of carriers and naval aviation was questioned. Swinton's conclusion was damaging to the Navy's case:

> The cost of the Fleet Air Arm.. . . appears to impose a burden disproportionate to the results. Moreover, the role of the aircraft carrier is already restricted through the ever increasing range of shore based aircraft.[18]

McGrigor fought back once more with all the sound and familiar naval arguments about the need for carriers to carry out the tasks allotted to the Navy in the Chiefs' and NATO's grand strategy. Once again, events and changes of personalities saved the day for the Admiralty.

Churchill's last administration, like himself, was failing. In the Cabinet reshuffle designed to breath new life into it, and in preparation for Eden's eventual takeover – Churchill would be 80 in November – Alexander was allowed to resign the portfolio of Minister of Defence, which he was finding increasingly uncongenial. He was replaced by Harold Macmillan in October 1954. Duncan Sandys was packed off to be Minister for Housing in Macmillan's place.

Macmillan, with his feel for Service sensibilities, which he had acquired when he was British political adviser to the Supreme Allied Commanders, Mediterranean – Eisenhower, Wilson and Alexander – saw Sandys' attack on the fleet carriers as futile. The savings in the Defence vote through their scrapping before their useful lives were over would be only marginal and eaten up by consequential increases in the RAF's maritime air capability. As the decision on building the next generation of carriers need not be taken until 1959, he allowed the Admiralty to find the savings called for in the Second Radical Review from elsewhere in its votes. McGrigor chose to sacrifice the minesweeper programme on the grounds that the threat to British ports was now nuclear attack and not mining.

Macmillan's entry into the Ministry of Defence was a milestone in the development of the Chiefs of Staff system, not so much for what he did during the short six months that he was there before becoming Eden's Chancellor of the Exchequer in April 1955, but for the impression he gained at first hand of the weaknesses developing in the Defence policy-making structure in Whitehall, and with which he was to grapple during Eden's and his own administrations.

Those weaknesses had existed since the turn of the century when the Committee of Imperial Defence was formed to improve the co-ordination of naval and military strategy and inter-Service allocation of resources. The need had grown more pressing with the formation of the RAF after the First World War, and had resulted in the creation of the Chiefs of Staff system by the Salisbury Committee, which accepted the near impossibility, in those day, of finding men with sufficient depth of knowledge and breadth of experience to control the armed forces as a single entity. But by 1954, closer inter-Service co-operation and management was no longer just desirable, it was essential in the nuclear and missile age. The right men and ways to carry it out still had to be discovered.

Creating the men with the necessary qualifications had begun with the establishment of the Imperial Defence College for senior policy-makers in the inter-war years, and had been carried down to lower staff levels when the Joint Services Staff College was set up after the Second World War (its inspiring charter, signed by John Cunningham, Montgomery and Tedder, is at Appendix C). But only time and learning from experience could provide the men with sufficient width of vision to take further steps towards greater centralisation of policy-making and the closer integration of the three Services. What could be done, however, was to provide the organisational means for faster evolutionary development.

In 1954, when Macmillan took over as Minister of Defence, the problem was not seen in this way. There were two extreme schools of thought, with many gradations in thinking between them: those who wanted to rush towards a unified Defence Service, which was the course the Canadians took and have regretted ever since; and those who held what could be called the 'anti-OKW' view. Macmillan merely perceived the need for stronger central direction of Defence. In his memoirs he recalls:

> This new Ministry of mine is a queer kind of affair. I have no power; yet I am responsible for everything – especially if it goes wrong. The PM is always busy about defence affairs – on Wednesday the Defence Committee sat under his chairmanship for nearly six hours. (It is true that it could all have been done in 20 minutes.) When I ask for a small meeting with the Service Ministers, about 40 to 50 people turn up![19]

With Alexander gone, Montgomery started to lobby the new Minister of Defence from his position as Deputy Supreme Allied Commander Europe (D/SACEUR) for the changes that he had been advocating ever since his days as CIGS:

> . . . I am more than ever convinced that our nation will not get the best defence for the most economic expenditure so long as we adhere to the present set-up –

nor will we ever get it until the Service empires are broken down, and each Service chief ceases to fight for his own corner.[20]

Monty persisted in his attacks on the Chiefs of Staff system until change did come, half-heartedly under Eden, and more convincingly under Macmillan, when he had found his feet as Prime Minister after Suez, as we will see in the next chapter.

1955 was a year of change in Government and amongst the Chiefs. In April, Churchill handed over to Eden; Selwyn Lloyd became Minister of Defence; and Mountbatten took over as First Sea Lord from McGrigor. In September, General Sir Gerald Templer succeeded Harding as CIGS; and in December, Air Marshal Sir Dermot Boyle was due to take over from Dickson as CAS.

The new team of Chiefs, who were to guide British strategy through the earliest years of the nuclear era, were not quite as united as their immediate predecessors, but were far more so than the Tedder-Monty-John Cunningham team. The principal cause for their disunity was distrust of Mountbatten, whose deviousness marred his well known abilities, and made him an awkward member of any team unless it was 'his' team.

Gerald Templer had his faults too, but deviousness was not one of them. A martinet in appearance and frank in manner, his displeasure and even his appearance were intimidating. After a successful war, he became Director of the British Military Government of Germany and had the doubtful distinction of being the man who sacked Conrad Adenauer, the then *Burgomeister* of Cologne! He went from Germany to become Director of Military Intelligence in the War Office before succeeding General Sir Frank Simpson as Montgomery's VCIGS. He was suddenly picked by Churchill, on Slim's advice, to go out to Malaya to combine the political role of British High Commissioner with the military responsibilities of Director of Operations against the Communist terrorists. The amalgam of his clear perceptive mind, resilient energy and politico-military charisma led to the development of decisive policies that won the battle for the hearts and minds of the people of Malaya, and, after his time, eliminated the Chinese Communist gangs. At heart, he was an imperialist and a dedicated infantryman with little interest in European defence and a dislike of alliances. He regarded Britain's withdrawal from Empire and the reductions in the infantry order of battle that flowed from it with extreme distaste.

Dermot Boyle was a highly experienced air commander and staff officer with balanced orthodox views on strategy and the needs of his

Service. He served in Bomber Command during the War and was no
stranger to the Chiefs of Staff Committee, as he had served in its
Secretariat in 1941. He was C-in-C Fighter Command before succeeding Dickson as CAS. He was, perhaps, more wedded to fighting
the RAF corner than Dickson had been, because he was by nature an
air commander first and a staff officer second. He was no match for
Mountbatten's wiles, nor for Templer's irascibility, although he and
Templer got on well together and tended to gang-up on
Mountbatten.

Eden, as the new broom, egged on by Macmillan as his
Chancellor, decided to make a concerted effort, after he had won the
General Election in May, to reduce the damaging effect of heavy
defence expenditure upon the balance of payments by making full
use of the revolutionary changes in warfare heralded by the advent of
thermonuclear weapons (preparations for Britain's first H-Bomb test
on Christmas Island in 1957 were already under way).

Eden himself wrote the guidelines for Selwyn Lloyd's 1955 Defence
Review, carried out by a small Cabinet sub-committee, the key
paragraph reading:

> The main threat to our position and influence in the world is now political and
> economic rather than military. . . . Effort must be transferred from military
> preparations to the maintenance and improvement of our political and econ-
> omic position.[21]

The result of Selwyn Lloyd's work was not earth-shattering. It
was as if he were a 'John the Baptist' to the 'Messiah' Duncan
Sandys, who was to become Macmillan's Minister of Defence after
the Suez fiasco ended Eden's tenure as Prime Minister. The probable
effects of nuclear warfare were spelt out. The Services were seen as
having four roles: contributing to the Allied deterrent; playing their
part in the Cold War; dealing with outbreaks of limited war; and
fighting in a global war if Western nuclear deterrence failed.[22] The
Navy was to be a general purpose force, supporting British influence
and interests world wide. The Army was to be organised primarily
for cold and limited war. And the RAF was to continue to have
pride of place in manning Britain's nuclear deterrent, be it with the
super-sonic successor to the V-Bombers, the AVRO 730, or the
strategic missile, Blue Streak – which was yet to be decided.[23] Service
manpower was pruned down from about 900,000 to 800,000,
but the real 'nuclear dividend' – the ending of National Service –
was not yet demanded. Selwyn Lloyd had earlier suggested that the
best way to save money was to prune back National Service

from two years to eighteen months and later to a year, but Harding, and subsequently Templer, had successfully countered his arguments by pointing out that cutting length of service would not reduce the expensive training organisation significantly, and would only make the use of national servicemen East of Suez uneconomic. The Services did, however, benefit from the debate in that pay and conditions for regulars were improved as a stepping-stone to all-regular Services.

Eden had accepted that the time was not ripe for the abolition of conscription and had not mentioned its possibility in his guidelines. In his election speeches, he was at pains to give no hostages to fortune on the issue. Furthermore, it was not mentioned in the 1956 Defence White Paper either, for two good reasons. First of all, there were currently three Cold War campaigns in progress – Malaya, Kenya and Cyprus – requiring every available man. The only glimmer of hope in reducing Army over-stretch flickered in Egypt, where the withdrawal of British troops from the Canal Zone was completed on schedule in June 1956, in accordance with the recently signed Anglo-Egyptian Treaty. There seemed little possibility of making manpower savings unless Eden was prepared to prune back overseas commitments, which, as an imperialist of the old school, he would not do for fear of lowering British prestige throughout the world.

The second reason for hesitancy was well-founded doubts about the practicability of recruiting enough regulars in the conditions of over-employment that existed in the country in the 1950s. Nevertheless, behind the closed doors of the War Office, General Sir Richard Hull (later Field Marshal and successively CIGS and CDS) was chairing a committee tasked to draw up plans for an all regular Army if and when ending National Service became practicable. Thus it came about that, while the operational staffs of the three Services were grappling with the Suez crisis in the summer of 1956, which required the call-up of large numbers of reservists, they were also being bombarded with questions from the Hull Committee on how to halve the strength of the Army in the early 1960s. This schizophrenia was to be repeated during the Gulf crisis nearly 35 years later.

Eden, however, did take some preliminary steps in the autumn of 1955 that were to help Macmillan when he became Prime Minister. Listening to his views on the powerlessness of the Minister of Defence; to the promptings of Montgomery, who was wont to declare 'The Minister has no power and the Chiefs need a professional head'; and to the urgings of Mountbatten, whose experience as Supreme

Allied Commander, South East Asia, made him an enthusiast for unification of command at the highest levels, Eden decided that he must take steps to improve Defence decision-making by increasing the powers of the Minister of Defence to cover the formulation of strategic policy, and to give him a Chief of Staff of his own, who would join the Chiefs and be their independent chairman.

Mountbatten, who probably put the proposal of a new supra-Chief forward in the first place with an eye to the future, was naturally in favour of independent chairmanship. Templer was adamantly opposed, fearing a dilution of the Chiefs' corporate responsibilities and infringement of Single Service sovereignty. He saw also a chance of the Chairman becoming a political appointee, which could be dangerous in the event of an extreme left wing government coming to power. Dickson havered: he was in an invidious position. He was the current rotational chairman; he was senior in post; and he was about to hand over as CAS to Boyle, and so was an immediately available, if not obvious choice as first incumbent of the proposed post.

Matters were brought to a head with the drafting of terms of reference for the new post. Eden and Selwyn Lloyd wanted the Chairman to be 'Chief Military Adviser to the Government', but Templer would have none of it, and was prepared to resign over the breach in the principle of corporate responsibility that this would entail. In the end, Templer won the argument and, with Dickson, proposed that the post should be called 'The Chairman of the Chiefs of Staff Committee and Chief of Staff to the Minister of Defence'. This was accepted, although Pug Ismay's old post of Chief Staff Officer to the Minister of Defence was retained for the time being. As a safeguard, it was also agreed that the incumbent of the new post should always be chosen from amongst the Chiefs. There was to be no question of him doing more than representing the corporate views of the Chiefs to the Minister of Defence and in the Defence Committee, nor was he given more than a small personal briefing staff of his own, which left him, in effect, with little power and no executive responsibility. He could make himself useful as far as the Chiefs were concerned by representing them in time-consuming international fora like the Military Committees of NATO, SEATO and later CENTO.

Increasing the powers of the Minister of Defence to cover the formulation of strategic policy was less controversial since it was generally accepted that Prime Ministers did not have the time to handle the details of peacetime Defence policy. Nor was there much opposition to the Minister of Defence being given a rather vague responsibility for the overall composition and balance of the Armed Forces, and requiring him to concern himself with the content as well as the costs of Service programmes. His staff remained much as it had been in 1946, which allowed him to do little more than massage proposals put forward by the all-powerful Service Ministries. Sir Walter Monckton, who took over as Minister of Defence when Selwyn Lloyd went to the Foreign Office in Eden's Cabinet reshuffle of December 1955, found his sole means of exerting pressure on the Service hierarchies was through close alliance with the Treasury, whose 'poodle' all Ministers of Defence, apart from Churchill, had been since pre-war days.

'Dickie' Dickson did become the first independent Chairman of the Chiefs. He had the breadth of outlook, and Eden felt his appointment particularly appropriate since he came from the Service that was in the process of picking up Britain's ultimate weapon – the nuclear deterrent. Eden may also have seen him as a stop-gap until Mountbatten, with his experience and obvious qualifications for the post, became available at the end of his tenure as First Sea Lord. The choice of Dickson, however, turned out to be unfortunate in that he was in poor health, which made him something of a liability during the Suez crisis that was about to burst on the Chiefs when Nasser nationalised the Canal on 26 July 1956.

Indeed, no sooner were the new arrangements in place than they were to be sorely tested by the Suez débâcle, which was to demote Britain and France from great to middle power status, and give world recognition of the superpower dominance of the United States and the Soviet Union. Furthermore, it was to form a watershed in the development of British post-war foreign, colonial and defence policy between the immediate post-war period, in which efforts had been directed towards converting Empire into Commonwealth at a responsible pace, and the post-Suez period of precipitate shedding of colonial responsibilities.

The summer and autumn of 1956 were undoubtedly most unhappy and frustrating months for the Chiefs. They themselves were as emotionally and temperamentally divided on the Suez issues, as were the Cabinet, the British electorate, and the old and new dominions of the Commonwealth. Templer was, initially at any rate, amongst the 'hawks', believing with Eden that Nasser must be unseated. Mountbatten, with his experiences as the last Viceroy of India in the forefront of his mind, favoured the 'doves' in that he saw, correctly as

events were to prove, the dangers of confronting Third World nationalism without the backing of world opinion; Boyle was undecided
and 'played a straight professional bat'; and Dickson was away sick
at crucial times, leaving Mountbatten temporarily in the chair.

As the crisis developed, all the Chiefs became concerned, if not
actually embittered by the confused political and foreign policy aims
against which the military operations had to be planned, mounted
and conducted. They became unhappier still when secret Franco-
Israeli collusion was thrust upon them to provide an internationally
implausible *casus belli*.

Five cardinal errors and misjudgements were made from which all
else flowed: two by the Chiefs at the beginning of the crisis, and three
by the Cabinet towards its end. In the first place, the Chiefs misjudged the Joint Intelligence Committee's assessments of the opposition likely to be met in using military force against Egypt. Russia
had been rearming Egypt since mid-1955, when the United States
had rejected Nasser's request for American arms because they would
be used against Israel. Although it was appreciated that the
Egyptians were most unlikely to be able to make best use of their new
Soviet aircraft, tanks and guns, there was known to be a high risk
that key weapons systems, particularly aircraft, would be manned by
Eastern Bloc 'volunteers'. A properly prepared and supported operation was, therefore, deemed necessary – indeed, a mini-Normandy
style invasion was planned.

The second error of judgement by the Chiefs lay in their over-
emphasis on the avoidance of military risk and their underestimate of
the speed of military reaction needed in the post-war world of mass
communication, in which the media can influence public opinion so
quickly. They and their generation of senior British commanders had
all experienced disasters during the Second World War through
underestimating opponents, and they had learnt the principles of war
the hard way. Templer, in particular, was at pains to reiterate the
dangers of doing so. The Chiefs' Suez plan was militarily sound
within the orthodoxy of their generation; and was, in any case,
largely dictated by the facts of Mediterranean geography, and by the
dearth of airborne and amphibious forces and the means by which to
deploy them, but it was flawed politically because it was too slow.

A quickly mounted *coup de main* operation to retake the Canal from
both ends with the parachute and naval amphibious forces which
happened to be in the Mediterranean and Red Sea when the crisis
broke, was proposed by Mountbatten and the French, but was

deemed too hazardous in the face of the assessed Eastern Bloc opposition. Hindsight suggests that such operations might have been just
as successful as the recapture of the Falklands twenty-six years later,
if they had been mounted at once without allowing time for world
opinion to muster to support the Afro-Asian underdog.

The initial landings, when they were eventually carried out, were
successful; and there were sufficient forces waiting behind them to
ensure the overthrow of Nasser and the reoccupation of Egypt until
an acceptable Middle East settlement could be achieved. In most of
Britain's military campaigns, a battalion is sent to do a brigade's job
and is given a 'bloody nose'; the rest of its brigade is then sent to join
it with equally dire consequences; and, in the end, adequate forces at
divisional or corps strength have to be mustered for success. In the
case of Suez, the equivalent of four divisions – two British and two
French – were assembled for the assault and immediate follow-up,
and logistic arrangements were made to move further British divisions from BAOR and French divisions from Metropolitan France
through Toulon and Marseilles if they were needed for the occupation phase of the operation.

There was, in fact, little wrong with the Chiefs' plan once the
opportunity for a *coup de main* operation had been allowed to pass.
The critical differences between the Suez and Falklands operations
lay in the Cabinet's subsequent errors: failure to win and hold the
support of the British electorate and American Government;
choosing an incredible *casus belli*; and calling a halt before achieving
the primary objective of reoccupying the Canal Zone. The extent of
these misjudgements were revealed all too clearly as events unfolded.

At first all went well in politico-military planning. There were two
possible landing areas, Alexandria or Port Said, for a force dispatched to topple Nasser, as Garnet Wolseley had done to Arabi
Pasha in 1882 after the Battle of Tel el Kebir in the early days of the
Canal. There was not much to choose between them politically if the
aim was to unseat Nasser rather than simply reoccupying the Canal
Zone, but militarily Alexandria had two major advantages. It was a
deep-water port able to discharge ocean-going ships quickly, and the
exits from the city could not be easily blocked. Port Said was only a
shallow, lighter operated roadstead, which would make any landing
there slow and tedious, and its exits could easily be blocked by the
demolition of key bridges over the many waterways in the area.

The contingency plan – Operation Musketeer – for re-entry into
Egypt if the negotiations with Nasser failed, was therefore based on

landings at Alexandria, although Eden was far from happy about the
choice. Preparations could not be completed for a D-day much before
17 September, and then only if the Cabinet gave the order to sail the
invasion fleets from Malta and Algiers six days earlier. 10th
Armoured Division would advance on Alexandria across the Western
Desert from Libya; the British and French airmen would start sub-
duing the Egyptian Air Force two days before the landings; Anglo-
French parachute and commando units would secure the port for the
sea-borne follow up; and a 20th Century equivalent of the Battle of
Tel el Kebir would probably be fought on the road to Cairo about a
week later.

As the tortuous negotiations, led by John Foster Dulles, the United
States Secretary of State, within the Suez Canal Users' Association
developed, Nasser, helped with covert advice from the American
Embassy, never put a foot wrong, and studiously avoided giving any
excuse for Anglo-French military intervention. The same sure-
footedness cannot be ascribed to the British Cabinet. Doubts began
to grow about the political credibility of landing at Alexandria when
the *casus belli* was Nasser's illegal seizure of the Canal; and the
Cabinet, Chiefs and country became more and more divided within
themselves about the wisdom and morality of using force to settle the
issue.

Mountbatten had never been sanguine about the operation on
political rather than military grounds. Philip Ziegler, his official
biographer, quotes a riposte he made in the Chiefs of Staff
Committee when Templer called for more resolute action:

> If we were fighting a visible enemy who was trying to dominate the Middle East
> by force of arms, I should back you to the limit. . . . But there is no such enemy.
> . . . The Middle East conflict is about ideas, emotions, loyalties. You and I
> belong to a people which will not have ideas which we don't believe in thrust
> down our throats by bayonets. Why should we assume that this process will
> work with other people?[24]

Dickson tended to side with Mountbatten, and Boyle with
Templer, who felt, like Eden, that they were seeing Hitler's 1936
March into the Rhineland being repeated by Nasser exactly twenty
years later. By the end of August, Mountbatten had written his letter
of resignation as First Sea Lord, but was persuaded by the First
Lord, Viscount Cilcennin, to withdraw it on the grounds that a Chief
could not be seen to refuse a Government order to go to war.
Cilcennin resigned soon after giving him this advice, and was replaced at the Admiralty by Lord Hailsham, who, though a strong

supporter of Eden in his determination to make Nasser disgorge his Canal loot, was distressed when he realised the extent of the civilian casualties likely to result from an attack on either Alexandria or Port Said.

In the first week of September, events and all the many doubts within Eden's Cabinet welled up and forced the cancellation of the first version of Musketeer. The Suez Canal Users' Association's mission to Cairo, led by Sir Robert Menzies, the Prime Minister of Australia, failed, largely due to lack of American diplomatic support. The Egyptians, annoyingly, managed to keep the Canal traffic flowing after the British and French pilots had been deliberately withdrawn in the hopes of using the ensuing breakdown as a reason for intervention. The feeling of repugnance grew within the Cabinet as the likelihood of heavy Egyptian civilian casualties due to naval and air bombardment dawned upon its members. The credibility of attacking Alexandria was weakend as the issues at stake were narrowed down to safeguarding the integrity of the Canal as an international waterway rather than the earlier assumption that toppling Nasser would solve everything. And there was the public outcry, led by the Labour Party and the TUC, which burst forth as people came to realise that Britain, of all countries, was preparing to use force without the sanction of the United Nations. Even the hawkish Templer was by this time clear that there could be no prolonged occupation of Egypt:

> We could probably beat the Egyptians with one brigade, but to hold Egypt would take eight divisions and five hundred Military Government officers.[25]

On 7 September the Chiefs were instructed by Eden to look for an alternative means of bringing force to bear without such damaging political risks. Dickson, back in office for a short time, and Boyle advocated, à la Trenchard, the substitution of air action, coupled with diplomatic pressure, to replace the amphibious assault. The Musketeer forces would still be needed to back up the threat, and for follow-up purposes. They could, however, be landed at Port Said instead of Alexandria since speed of landing would no longer be crucial.

The new plan – Musketeer Revise – was based on an eight day aero-diplomatic campaign to break the Egyptian will to resist. It had obvious political attractions: careful selection of targets would reduce civilian casualties; the weight of attack could be orchestrated to respond to diplomatic requirements and Egyptian reactions; and the

Musketeer forces might be able to land unopposed. The Foreign Office had high hopes that the Egyptians would settle as soon as the first bomb was dropped. Others in the Cabinet, like Walter Monckton whose resignation and replacement by Antony Head as Minister of Defence was announced on 18 October, were less certain about the morality of even this circumscribed use of force, and about its outcome.

There was one military advantage to offset the frustrations inherent in this major change of plan. The Navy had been worried about the assault convoys coming within range of the Egyptian Iluyshin bombers before the Egyptian air force had been neutralised. Under the new concept they need not be sailed until the week's air action had begun. There was to be no change in the original air plan to destroy the Egyptian air force in the first 48 hours, but thereafter the Anglo-French air forces would turn to politically important and economically critical targets like the 'Voice of the Arabs' radio transmitters outside Cairo, and to the highly vulnerable oil pipe-line from Suez upon which the life of capital depended.

As 'a belt and braces' measure, the actual Musketeer Force was re-tasked for an assault landing at Port Said. The target date for the operation was put back to 8 October, but this did not allow enough time to reload the ships for landing at a lighter-operated port. The force commanders would have to improvise as best they could if an opposed landing was, in the event, required.

October brought the Anglo-French appeal to the Security Council and further rambling political debates in which the Americans continued to play an unhelpful part. With autumn weather approaching, and the practicability and probability of launching Musketeer declining, Templer and the War Office staff became anxious about maintaining the high state of readiness of the large force that they had mustered. Reservists were pressing for release to return to their civilian jobs. Shipping companies were anxious to get their requisitioned vessels back into commercial operation. And tanks and vehicles, particularly their batteries, were deteriorating in the ships' holds, despite the best efforts of the maintenance crews on board each ship. It seemed an opportune moment to transfer equipment and supplies from requisitioned to 'Grey Funnel' shipping, which had been taken out of mothballs during the summer, and to place the Musketeer forces at ten days notice for the winter. Templer's plea was accepted by the Cabinet, but barely had reloading started than the unexpected occurred. A stand-fast order was given, and the shutters came down in Whitehall with only those close to the inner Cabinet being fully aware of what was happening.

The French, who had felt increasingly frustrated by the Anglo-American led negotiations and with cautious British military planning, had begun to look for their own alternatives, and to exploit their close links with Israel. The possibility of an Israeli winter offensive to clear the constant Egyptian threat to their southern borders had been evident for some time, but it was not until mid-September that joint Franco-Israeli planning for such an offensive started, in which the French agreed to provide naval and air support, and to take Port Said as a bargaining counter. General Beaufre, the commander of the French Musketeer force, claims that he was the first to suggest the ploy of an Anglo-French intervention force acting on behalf of the United Nations to safeguard the Canal after an act of aggression by Israel. In an appreciation for General Ely, Templer's French opposite number, he wrote:

> This solution would turn us into a UNO advance guard and might lead with equal certainty to the political results at which we aim.[26]

How privy the Chiefs were to Anglo-French-Israeli political collusion will not be known until the Chiefs of Staff records for the period are opened to historians. At secret meetings between British and French ministers and officials at a villa at Sèvres on 22 and 24 October the final plot was hatched. Israel would attack on 19 October; the British and French Governments would appeal for a ceasefire next day and for a withdrawal by both sides to lines 10 miles back from the Canal to allow Anglo-French forces to ensure its continued operation as an international waterway; and, if either side refused, the Musketeer forces would attack to clear it.

Eden thought he had found a credible reason for military intervention and was determined to go ahead with the ultimatum as a pretext for taking back the Canal by force if need be. Macmillan, who was advising him on likely American reaction, from his experience of working closely with Eisenhower in Algiers during the war, was convinced that they would protest vigorously in public, but in private would be relieved that the decision had been taken out of their hands without involving them directly in the conflict. Both men had made misjudgements that were to have the direst consequences.

Israel attacked on 29 October. The Anglo-French ultimatum was issued next day as planned. It was accepted by the Israelis, who had already defeated the Egyptians in Sinai and were approaching the

Canal. Nasser, with Soviet backing, rejected it, and at 4.15 pm on 31 October RAF Valiant and Canberra bombers took off from Cyprus to start the neutralisation of the Egyptian air force. The timings envisaged were: occupation of Port Said on 6 November, Ismailia on the 11th and Suez next day. Under normal circumstances, six days of increasing military pressure would have allowed ample time for decisive diplomatic action. But the circumstances were far from normal. The high-handedness of the Anglo-French international 'police action' smacked too much of nineteenth century gunboat diplomacy, and it united most of the world and half of Britain against Eden and his closest colleagues.

It was soon evident that the Egyptians would resist any attempt to land at Port Said and were sinking concrete filled block-ships in the Canal itself. Mountbatten made one last plea to Eden not to go ahead with the assault on Port Said:

> I am writing to appeal to you to accept the resolution of the overwhelming majority of the United Nations to cease military operations and to beg you to turn back the assault convoy before it is too late, as I feel that the actual landing of troops can only spread the war with untold misery and world wide repercussions.
>
> You can imagine how hard it is for me to break with all service custom and write to you direct in this way, but I feel so desperate about what is happening that my conscience would not allow me to do otherwise.[27]

His démarche was to no avail, and so he turned to Hailsham, the First Lord:

> However repugnant the task the Navy will carry out its orders. Nevertheless, as its professional head, I must register the strongest possible protest at this use of my Service, and would ask you as the responsible Minister to convey that protest to the Prime Minister.[28]

It is often suggested that Mountbatten, with his great personal standing, and perhaps the other Chiefs, should have resigned rather than allow Musketeer to go ahead. It has to be realised, however, that he and they were faced with one of the classic dilemmas of democratic government. Refusal by officials, for that is what the Chiefs are, to implement the policy of elected leaders would be both unconstitutional and an abuse of power. For the country's military leaders to do so when war was imminent, or had actually begun, would have amounted to dereliction of duty. This was all the more so after Eden had flared up and made it abundantly clear to the Chiefs, when discussing one of their more critical papers as late as 25 October, that he would not tolerate any military interference in political matters. Resignation would only have been appropriate if they had been ordered to do something militarily impossible, unconstitutional or criminal. In the case of Musketeer, none of these epithets applied.

The Musketeer landings, which were hurried forward to 5 November, started with the parachute attacks by the British on Gamil airfield and by the French on Port Fuad. There was significant opposition but it was swept aside in time for the amphibious landings next day. One important feature of the operations, which was to prove important in Defence politics in a few years time, was the use made of the controversial aircraft carriers: the larger fleet carriers provided much of the close air support for the troops on shore; and the smaller carriers, *Ocean* and *Theseus*, were used for the first time by any power in war as assault carriers, landing 45th Commando by helicopter near the de Lesseps statue.

In the five days since the RAF bombers started their operations, intolerable internal and external pressures built up against Eden and his determination to avoid another Munich. Internally, the country was split asunder between those who found the use of force without the sanction of the United Nations intolerable, and those who were equally sure that Eden was right not to follow Chamberlain's appeasement policy. Externally, the Commonwealth divided on ethnic lines, the old dominions generally supporting Britain and the new following Nehru's India in Afro-Asian opposition. The United States opposed the former colonial powers at almost every point.

5 and 6 November were days requiring strong nerves, not so much in Port Said as in London. Egyptian resistance crumbled, despite the efforts of Cairo's Soviet Ambassador to prolong it, and the build-up of Anglo-French forces ashore was progressing well in the face of the anticipated port operating difficulties. On the 5th, Eden, together with the French and Israeli prime ministers, received Bulganin's letter threatening to intervene with 'volunteers' and, if need be, atomic weapons. This blatant threat to start the Third World War frightened Washington more than it did London, where it was seen for what it was: a cynical attempt to widen the rift between the Americans and their NATO allies; to further Soviet penetration of the Middle East; and to divert attention away from the concurrent Soviet military repression of the anti-Communist revolt in Hungary.

Early on the morning of the 6th, Eisenhower, who was about to be re-elected President on his 'Man of Peace' ticket, phoned Eden and presented him with the brutally phrased ultimatum: cease-fire or forfeit Anglo-American friendship and solidarity. With an American orchestrated run on the pound threatening Britain's currency reserves, Macmillan, the Chancellor, reported to Cabinet that the real American terms were a cease-fire by midnight in return for an International Monetary Fund loan to prop up the pound. Eden bowed to *force majeure* and ordered the cease-fire for midnight 6 November, much to the fury of the French and the amazement of the world.

The three cardinal political mistakes made by the Cabinet in 1956 contrast starkly with the handling of the Falklands crisis in 1982. Eden was under just as much pressure to do something positive about Nasser's nationalisation of the Canal as Margaret Thatcher was to recover the Falklands from the Argentines. But she, as will be seen in Chapter 13, did secure the unity of the country, her Cabinet and the Chiefs; American support was won and held; and there was no loss of political nerve when naval losses mounted. However sound the Chiefs' planning and advice may be, they cannot succeed militarily without the dynamic inspiration of the Prime Minister of the day. Under Churchill and Margaret Thatcher, disaster could be ridden out until success was achieved; under Eden, a sick man and vacillating prime minister, potential military success was turned into political disaster.

Much of the political vacillation on both sides of the Atlantic could to some extent be accounted for by the ill-health of the three Anglo-American principals in the Suez drama: Eisenhower was suffering medically from ileitis and politically from electionitis; Foster Dulles, the American Secretary of State and villain of the piece in British eyes, had cancer; and Eden, on whose judgement success or failure depended, had a recurrence of the abdominal obstruction that had laid him low in 1953.

And although the Suez fiasco was not primarily, still less exclusively, the fault of the Chiefs, it did produce a strong political and, to a lesser extent, informed military reaction against the Services. Politically, the dangers of Britain trying 'to go it alone' in the postwar world had been made abundantly clear; the size, ponderousness and even relevance of National Service based forces was questioned; the ability of Britain to maintain her responsible and premeditated rate of withdrawal from empire in the face of Communist backed nationalism was seriously undermined; and uncertainty about the impact of nuclear weapons on the organisation of the Services was highlighted by Bulganin's threat to use them. Militarily, the startling successes achieved so quickly by the Israelis in Sinai, and the clear French superiority in air-mobile operations in Algiers and at Port Fuad, did not flatter the Chiefs' Second World War type of approach to war in the latter half of the 20th Century!

Improving speed of reaction was seen as an immediate post-Suez military requirement, but it needed the introduction of expensive air mobility and amphibious warfare equipments – helicopters, transport aircraft and assault shipping – which could not be provided as long as the high costs of National Service both in cash and in the absorption of regulars in the large training organisation had to be borne within the limits of a declining Defence budget. Budgetary problems were also being exacerbated by the need to finance research, development and production in the nuclear and missile fields in which the three Services were rivals for funding.

When Macmillan took over from Eden in January 1957, the time was ripe for pursuing three objectives: a further strengthening of the Ministry of Defence and the Chiefs' system to bring about the closer integration of Defence policy in the increasingly complex and expensive nuclear and missile era; the abolition of National Service; and the acceleration of the withdrawal from empire. The first two were to be nettles grasped immediately by Duncan Sandys, who became Macmillan's first Minister of Defence; and the third was tackled rather later by Iain McLeod, his future Colonial Secretary, who inspired his 'Wind of Change' speech in Cape Town in 1960.

The conflict that was to arise between Sandys and the Chiefs, and the great influence wielded by Mountbatten in the post-Suez reformation of both Defence policy and organisation is the burden of the next chapter.

Chronology
FOR CHAPTER TEN

1957
Jan   Macmillan replaces Eden as Prime Minister.
March   Treaty of Rome Signed.
            Eisenhower/Macmillan Bermuda meeting.
April   Sandys 1957 Defence White Paper published.
May   British hydrogen bomb tested on Christmas Island.
            Naval 'Fairlead' presentation at Greenwich.
June   Mountbatten/Rickover nuclear submarine agreement.
July   Dhofar campaign in the Oman begins.
Oct   Soviet *Sputnik* I launched.
            Eisenhower/Macmillan meeting in Washington.
Nov   Soviet *Sputnik* II launched.

1958
Jan   CND formed.
April   Unified Command established in Aden.
            RAF 'Prosper' presentation.
July   Iraqi Hashemite dynasty overthown in Baghdad.
            Anglo-US interventions in Jordan and Lebanon.
            US McMahon Act amended by Congress.
            Sandys' White Paper, *The Central Organisation of Defence*, published.

1959
Jan   Zurich Agreement on Cyprus signed.
June   SSN *Dreadnought* laid down.
July   Mountbatten becomes CDS.
Aug   CENTO established.
Oct   Macmillan wins his Second Term.

Harold Watkinson becomes Minister of Defence.

1960

Feb	Macmillan's 'Wind of Change' speech in Cape Town. French test their atomic bomb.
March	Camp David meeting on Skybolt, Polaris and Holy Loch. First CND Aldermaston march.
April	Cancellation of Blue Streak announced.
June	Skybolt agreement signed with US.
Sep	TUC votes for unilateralism.
Oct	'Fight and fight again' speech by Gaitskell.

1961

March	Macmillan/Kennedy meeting at Key West.
July	British intervention in Kuwait.
Aug	British application to join the EEC.
Sep	Design work on Carrier CVA 01 begins.

1962

July	Thorneycroft becomes Minister of Defence.
Aug	Cancellation of Blue Water.
Oct	Cuban missile crisis. Nasser inspired revolution in the Yemen.
Nov	Unified Command established in the Far East. Skybolt cancelled by US.
Dec	Macmillan/Kennedy Nassau meeting: Polaris agreement. British intervention in Brunei revolt.

1963

Jan	First EEC application vetoed by de Gaulle.
April	'Confrontation' with Indonesia begins.
May	Last National Serviceman leaves the Forces.
July	Carrier CVA 01 ordered. White Paper on Unified Ministry of Defence published.
Oct	Douglas Home becomes Prime Minister.
Dec	State of Emergency declared in Aden.

1964

Jan	East African Mutinies quelled.
	Radfan campaign starts in the Aden Protectorate.
April	Unified Ministry of Defence established.
July	Independence for South Arabia by 1968 announced.
Sep	First flight of the TSR 2.
Oct	Harold Wilson wins the 1964 General Election.

10
THE MOUNTBATTEN ERA

Duncan Sandys to a Unified Ministry of Defence: 1957–64

Ministers of Defence		Chiefs of Defence Staff	
Duncan Sandys	1957	Sir William Dickson*	1957
Harold Watkinson	1959	Earl Mountbatten	1959
Peter Thorneycroft	1962		

First Sea Lords		Chiefs of the Imperial General Staff	
Earl Mountbatten			
Sir Charles Lambe	1959	Sir Gerald Templer	
Sir Caspar John	1960	Sir Francis Festing	1958
Sir David Luce	1963	Sir Richard Hull	1961

Chiefs of Air Staff	
Sir Dermot Boyle	
Sir Thomas Pike	1960
Sir Charles Elworthy	1963

'Mountbatten was only the second Chief of the Defence Staff, and he was resolved that the office would be vastly different when he left it to what it was when he took it over. What he envisaged was an overhaul of the whole structure of defence in which the machinery in Whitehall would be radically reorganised and the relationship between the three Services reconsidered.'

Philip Ziegler's opening of his chapter on the Defence Staff.[1]

It may seem a misnomer to head this chapter, which covers the years 1957 to 1964, '*The Mountbatten Era*' since he did not become Chief of Defence Staff until July 1959, a third of the way through the period. Nevertheless, as First Sea Lord in the earlier years, he wielded the greatest influence, if not power, amongst the Chiefs. His secret opposition to Eden's Suez policy did not detract from the respect in which

---

* Chairman of Chiefs of Staff since 1955.

he was held in Whitehall, where it was generally known; nor, of course, in the country at large or in the Services, where it was not. On the contrary, he emerged from the débâcle with his reputation enhanced as the most powerful figure in the Defence establishment. His position was further strengthened by the general assumption that he would almost certainly inherit the chairmanship of the Chiefs of Staff Committee when Dickson retired.

Harold Macmillan had three primary objectives in mind when he took over as Prime Minister from Anthony Eden in January 1957: to salvage the economy; to repair ravaged Anglo-American relationships; and to restore the fortunes of the Tory Party. With the next general election not due until May 1960, he had over three years in which to establish himself, provided he could ride through the political fall-out of Suez.

The need for radical changes in Defence policy lay at the root of Macmillan's aspirations. Improving standards of living demanded swingeing cuts in Defence spending to release skilled manpower into the economy; closer collaboration with the United States could reduce weapon development costs; and an imaginative Defence policy, which was perceived as providing adequate security at much lower cost, could help his Party's electoral image.

Macmillan's hopes of devising a sound, yet cheaper, Defence policy rested upon judgements as how best to grasp the possibilities offered by nuclear weapons and missile systems. There was, as yet, no significant revulsion in the electorate against the idea of their use to save military manpower; indeed, it was seen as one of the benefits that should flow from Britain's scientific expertise. Ending National Service through exploiting the nuclear armoury was looked upon as a political prize of some worth. If the Tories did not manage to carry it off, Labour, in those pre-CND days, would almost certainly win votes by doing so.

Macmillan decided on a two-handed approach. With one hand, he would try to mend fences with the United States by using his own personal friendship with Eisenhower and other members of the United States Administration and Joint Chiefs of Staff. With the other hand, he would exploit the nuclear defence philosophy first sketched out by the Chiefs in their 'Global Strategy' paper written at Greenwich in 1952. As a former Minister of Defence, Foreign Secretary, and Chancellor of the Exchequer, he was all too familiar with the difficulties of implementing new Defence policies. He was convinced that no major changes in the *status quo* would be negotiable unless the Minister of Defence was given the power to overrule the special pleadings of the Admiralty, War Office and Air Ministry. The vigour with which changes were imposed would help to create public confidence in his Administration; and a measure of ruthlessness would be needed to overcome the Chiefs' conservatism. What he needed was a minister with the strength of character, reforming zeal and enough technological understanding to push through the changes that he had in mind to help consolidate his political power.

Duncan Sandys was the obvious, and to the Chiefs, much feared choice as that 'hatchet man'. He had the drive, determination and abrasiveness for the part, and his time in the Ministry of Supply had given him experience in, and a fascination for, advanced weapon systems. He was unlikely to brook any opposition from the entrenched hierarchies and bureaucracies of the Service ministries. He had, in theory at least, no Service allegiances, and he had enjoyed challenging them singly or in concert when Minister of Supply. His support of the Air Ministry in the earlier carrier arguments, however, did not give the Board of Admiralty much confidence in his impartiality. Fortunately, from their point of view, they had in Mountbatten, as First Sea Lord, an even more powerful personality with comparable technological awareness.

Macmillan appreciated, perhaps more clearly than Eden had done, that the powers of the Minister of Defence were still too limited to enforce radical change. In giving Sandys his remit, he made him responsible for:

> deciding all questions on the size, shape, organisation and disposition of the forces, as well as their equipment and supply, their pay and conditions of service.[2]

Service Ministers and the Chiefs were, in future, to submit all papers for the Defence Committee and the Cabinet through Sandys. For a trial period of eighteen months Dickson, as Chairman of the Chiefs of Staff Committee, would subsume the responsibilities of the Chief Staff Officer to the Minister of Defence (Ismay's former job) to remove any ambiguity as to whom the Minister should turn for military advice, but there was, as yet, no suggestion of calling him Chief of Defence Staff.

Soon after taking up his appointment, Sandys went off to Washington to update himself on the latest American operational thinking and advances in weapon technology. His friendly reception there confirmed suggestions, gleaned through diplomatic channels, that the Americans were anxious to heal the wounds of Suez. In order to reinforce the British nuclear deterrent while the RAF's V-Force was being built up, they offered to supply their nuclear-tipped Thor intermediate-range ballistic missiles for deployment in Britain, which would be manned by the RAF but controlled by a dual key system. They also agreed to help in speeding up Britain's ballistic missile development by providing American Atlas rocket engines and inertial guidance systems for Blue Streak, thus cutting British development costs as Macmillan hoped.

There was, of course, American self-interest in this generosity: they obtained missile sites in England relatively cheaply when compared with the incalculable risks run by Britain in having Thors sited in her crowded islands, even though the possibility of the Soviets being able to counter with similar missiles of their own was discounted as 'remote' by the Chiefs in January 1957.

A more significant outcome of Sandys' visit to Washington was the arrangement for Eisenhower and Macmillan to meet at Bermuda in March to put Suez behind them, and to enable Macmillan to give the President an insight into changes in British defence policy before they were announced in Parliament.

On his return from Washington, Sandys dived into drafting sessions with Dickson and the principal civil servants in the Ministry of Defence to produce his revolutionary 1957 Defence White Paper, which he presented to Parliament on 4 April, only eleven weeks after assuming office, setting out a five year programme of reforms! Such meetings as he had with the Chiefs were acrimonious and confirmed their worst forebodings about the part he was going to play in their affairs. It was not so much the scant attention that he paid to their views in committee that riled them, but the unconstitutional way in which he disregarded their corporate responsibilities for advising the Cabinet on strategic policy. He took such advice as he needed from his own small group of advisers at Storey's Gate, whom he allowed to usurp the proper functions of the Chiefs.

Sandys's five year programme was a dogmatic document built around the premise that National Service was to be abolished by increasing dependence upon nuclear weapons and missile systems. He concentrated on the needs for global war, acknowledged the possibility of limited war, and paid little attention to counter-insurgency, which he treated as just a good way of keeping the Army trained in peacetime. The Chiefs did not deny the need to get rid of National Service, but they believed that his views on substituting nuclear weapons for conventional forces were flawed. They also saw that he was concentrating on the wrong issues. Suez had shown the irrelevance of nuclear weapons in the type of operations that Britain was likely to face in the latter half of the 20th Century. What was needed most was the development of quick-reaction forces, equipped with the necessary transport aircraft, helicopters and amphibious shipping so that trouble could be quickly snuffed out by centrally held reserves, thus reducing the need for large overseas garrisons and enabling National Service to be phased out with less risk to national interests.

The Chiefs were also united in opposing Sandys as much by their dislike of him personally as by his methods. Each had his own cross to bear. Mountbatten was warned by 'Wee' McGrigor – not that he needed any warning – what to expect from Sandys, based on his own experience of arguing with him over the carriers in the early 1950s. The views that he ascribed to Sandys, epitomised naval frustration at the time:

a. In war very little of a Navy is necessary as everything will be finally decided by the H-Bomb.
b. In peace, foreign stations are unnecessary. We can always warn trouble makers that if they don't stop it, the RAF will deal with them.
c. Cruisers are not needed and should be scrapped.
d. Aircraft Carriers and Naval Aircraft are unnecessary. The RAF can do it all and it is their job.
e. Other types of ships should be drastically reduced.
In fact the Navy is no longer needed and it is a luxury the country cannot afford.[3]

Sandys, in truth, did not see any role for the Navy in nuclear war, which he assumed would be over in a matter of days. Mountbatten, like McGrigor before him, fought back with every weapon in his very considerable armoury of influential contacts at home and abroad. Under his leadership, the Board of Admiralty switched from nuclear war scenarios, which they left to the RAF, and argued their case for a balanced carrier-based fleet upon the requirements for limited war and counter-insurgency operations. It was a shift of emphasis which was to pay dividends in the years to come.

Mountbatten's arguments in favour of carriers won the unanimous agreement of the Chiefs at a meeting in February. Even the Chief of Air Staff could not deny their usefulness, which had been so recently demonstrated at Port Said. Sandys accepted the Chiefs' surprising unanimity on the issue, and in his White Paper gave the Navy the ill-defined role of 'bringing power rapidly to bear in peacetime emergencies and *limited war*, in which carrier task forces would play an important role, particularly East of Suez.[4]

Mountbatten was initially less successful over naval aircraft. The Admiralty wanted to continue the development of the NA 39 (later called the Buccaneer), which had a low level strike capacity below enemy radar cover. Sandys, with his technological hat pulled firmly down over his ears, would have none of it, and insisted that the Navy and RAF must use the same airframe for strike purposes. The RAF wanted the heavier and more expensive TSR 2 as their 'capital' aircraft of the future and were not prepared to compromise on their own operational requirements for such a key aircraft in order to meet the more limited requirements of the Navy. It took Mountbatten another nine months of constant pressure to win the argument. Sandys did eventually give in, and the NA 39 and TSR 2 projects went ahead separately.

Templer and the Army Council were ambivalent about ending National Service, which affected the Army more than the Navy and RAF. They were delighted at the prospect of being rid of the tread-mill of training national servicemen, and of getting back to pro-fessional soldiering, but they looked askance at the amalgamation or disbandment of some 51 major fighting units, 17 of which were long established infantry regiments with battle honours stretching back over the centuries. Even with the help of air mobility, of which the War Office doubted the Air Ministry's willingness to provide at the expense of combat aircraft, Templer could not see how the Army could meet its operational commitments with only 165,000 regular soldiers – the upper limit of the demographic estimate of regular recruiting. He pressed for a system of selective service to be kept until it was possible to judge whether regular recruiting could be raised by improving pay and conditions, and to what extent the Sandys' poli-cies would reduce Army commitments. Sandys, rightly from the political point of view, would not recommend selective service to the Cabinet, but he allowed the Army to plan on reaching a ceiling of 185,000 through an intensified recruiting campaign, thus saving, or at least delaying, some regimental disbandments.

Templer and Mountbatten found common cause in objecting to Sandys' conviction that nuclear weapons could actually be used. They were both ahead of their time in arguing that while nuclear deterrence was the right policy for preventing a Third World War breaking out in Europe, it had little relevance elsewhere. Wars would still be fought outside Europe with conventional weapons, unless a nuclear power's vital interests were threatened. Even in Europe, the actual use of nuclear weapons, as opposed to the threat of their use, would amount to national suicide. Sandys rebutted their arguments, treating them as special pleading in the parochial interests of their own Services.

Boyle and the Air Staff, as the beneficiaries of the Sandys' doctrine, had little to complain about in the short term. Their worries lay in Sandys' firm conviction that the days of the manned combat aircraft were numbered: missiles would take the place of the V-Bombers, and the Lightning, then in development, would be the last British air defence fighter. They failed to dissuade him from cancelling the AVRO 730, super-sonic bomber, and closing down future fighter development – both grave misjudgements that the British aircraft industry and the RAF were to live to regret.

When Sandys' 1957 Defence White Paper was published, after thirteen 'final drafts' and further amendment as it went to the printers, it received a surprisingly warm reception in the Press and Parliament where Service opposition was, as usual, pilloried as the reaction of antediluvian brass-hats. The Labour opposition showed some chagrin that the Tories had stolen a march by abolishing National Service, but even Aneurin Bevan, the shadow Foreign Secretary and a unilateralist at heart, accepted Sandys' nuclear thesis, making his oft quoted remark that for Britain to abandon her nuclear deterrent would be to 'send a British Foreign Secretary, whoever he might be, naked to the conference table'.

Publishing his revolutionary White Paper was one thing; sustaining his revolution against opposition from the Chiefs was to prove much more difficult. Mountbatten, realising that the very future of the Navy was at stake, took the unusual, and some would say improper, step of 'going public' to win support amongst the opinion-makers, politicians, industrialists and Commonwealth representatives in London. He staged a major presentation of Naval policy at the Royal Naval College, Greenwich, appropriately called Exercise 'Fairlead', in May 1957. Not to be outdone, Boyle staged a similar exercise rather later, called 'Prospect'. In his summing up, Boyle made the RAF's opposition to Sandys' policies unambiguous:

> We in the Royal Air Force, if you ask for our professional advice, are convinced that we will require manned aircraft as far as we can see to supplement the missile in both the offensive and defensive roles.[5]

Sandys found selling his policy of substituting nuclear weapons for manpower to the NATO allies and the Commonwealth just as difficult. The French were the first to object to his proposals to reduce the strength of BAOR: they still had qualms about a rearmed Germany. The Germans too objected: they had no wish to take over more of 1st British Corps' front. It took all the very considerable skills of Macmillan and the British ambassadors in Washington, Brussels, Paris and Bonn to win acceptance of Sandys' theory that 45,000 British regular troops with tactical nuclear weapons were of more value to the Alliance than 75,000 National Servicemen with only conventional artillery and air support.

During tours that Sandys made to the Middle East and Africa in July, and to the Far East in August, opposition was unrelenting. Governors, High Commissioners, Cs-in-C and local political leaders sang the same tune: nuclear weapons stored at V-Bomber bases in England were no substitute for the presence of soldiers stationed in areas of potential instability. The proposed reduction in overseas garrisons proclaimed publicly in the 1957 Defence White Paper was doing immense damage. It confirmed in the minds of anti-colonial agitators that the decline in British power was terminal. There could, however, be no going back on the decision to end National Service. Templer and the General Staff were left with the unenviable task of seeking ways to deploy a much smaller Army to meet a rising threat of instability in British dependent territories.

Sandys had been helped to some extent by Macmillan's success in re-establishing the Anglo-American 'special relationship' during his meeting with Eisenhower in Bermuda in March 1957. In the aftermath of the meeting, goodwill surged to and fro across the Atlantic. The British H-Bomb was tested on Christmas Island in the Pacific in May 1957, increasing American respect for Britain as a partner in the Cold War, and giving credibility to Sandys' drive to establish a viable British nuclear deterrent. It also enabled Mountbatten to pull off a coup that perhaps only he could have done.

He had made friends with Admiral Hyman Rickover, '*the introvert iconoclast from the Ukraine*', who was the father and all-powerful master of the United States Navy's nuclear submarine programme, and who had '*fallen under the spell and aura of Queen Victoria's grandson*' during a visit to London in 1956.[6] Rickover had been blocking the transfer of information on nuclear propulsion to the Royal Navy under a strict interpretation of the McMahon Act, and because of his contempt for all things British. The successful Christmas Island H-Bomb test, however, enabled Mountbatten to convince Rickover that Britain had the scientific know-how, and that it was in America's best interests to help the Royal Navy to short cut development processes by providing the propulsion unit for the Navy's first nuclear submarine *Dreadnought*. Not only did Rickover agree to do so, but he authorised the provision of the latest second generation unit.

It would be no exaggeration to say that it was Mountbatten's charisma that enabled the Navy to enter the nuclear submarine club so quickly and relatively cheaply. But it did more than that: British naval staffs working in the States were made aware of American progress in developing two mobile strategic missiles: the United States Air Force's bomber-launched Skybolt, and the United States Navy's nuclear submarine-launched Polaris. Sandys saw no need for either system: he was satisfied that Blue Streak would replace the V-Bombers in due course.

In this wave of American goodwill there was, in the wake of Suez, an undercurrent of condescension until the Russians upset the world's strategic balance by launching their *Sputniks* in the autumn of 1957. The Western Hemisphere would soon be in range of and vulnerable to Soviet intercontinental ballistic missiles, carrying megaton warheads. The United States' nuclear umbrella over Western Europe became less certain, and hence the British independent nuclear deterrent more important to British security. Moreover, the Americans appreciated that their supposed technological superiority over the Russians was an illusion. They needed British and Western European support more than they had been prepared to admit in public. Self-interest, if nothing else, killed condescension and brought in its place a genuine desire to establish closer reltions with Britain.

Macmillan crossed the Atlantic in October to consolidate the newly re-formed 'special relationship'. The window-dressing outcome of his talks was the 'Declaration of Common Purpose': the substance lay in the amendment of the McMahon Act by Congress in July 1958, which was so drafted that only a power, like Britain, with a well developed nuclear capability, could benefit from the exchange of nuclear know-how which it allowed. Thus the costly developments of Britain's H-Bomb had paid off handsomely. Henceforth, Britain would be able to update her nuclear deterrent at much lower cost in research and development funds.

Relationships between Sandys and the Chiefs did not improve as he tried to convert the policies, outlined in his 1957 Defence White Paper, into executive action. Dickson found himself in an impossible position: as Chairman of the Chiefs of Staff Committee he was

responsible for representing the views of the Chiefs to Sandys; and as
his Chief of Staff he had to implement policies with which the Chiefs
did not agree. Believing that their constitutional responsibilities were
being ignored or emasculated, Templer and Boyle treated Dickson,
as Sandys' agent, with minimal courtesy and co-operation. Had it
not been for the conciliatory efforts of Mountbatten, who appreciated
Dickson's difficulties and knew that he would almost certainly inherit
them, the Chiefs of Staff Committee system might well have broken
down.[7]

In the ensuing wrangle over Dickson's powers, Templer and Boyle
had most of the senior Whitehall officials – civil and military –
behind them, but Mountbatten, as much by conviction as with an
eye to the main chance, sided with Macmillan and Sandys in their
determination to increase the powers of the 'Centre' rather than
revert to single Service domination of decision-making. Templer and
Boyle lost the battle, but not the war. In July 1958, Sandys published
his White Paper on 'The Central Organisation of Defence' with the
Cabinet's full support, but it had been given such a rough passage by
the Chiefs and the majority of senior Whitehall officials during its
preparation that it proved something of a damp squib.

In this White Paper, the increased powers given to the Minister
of Defence by Macmillan in 1957 were confirmed; and, in addition,
he was made ministerially responsible to the Prime Minister for
military operations. A new Defence Board was set up under his
chairmanship analogous with the Board of Admiralty, the Army
Council and Air Council but at Defence level, consisting of the
Service Ministers, the Chiefs of Staff, the Permanent Under
Secretary of State of the Ministry of Defence and the Chief
Scientific Adviser (CSA); and to increase the standing of Dickson's
post as Chairman of the Chiefs of Staff Committee, it was retitled
Chief of Defence Staff (CDS).

These changes amounted to a very limited victory for Sandys,
Dickson and Mountbatten. The Service Ministries still held the real
power, with their sovereignty under Parliament still unimpaired; and
the Ministers, though no longer in the Cabinet, still had seats on the
Defence Committee of the Cabinet. The Defence Board was too
unwieldy, rarely met and died on the vine. And Dickson found that
his title had an improved ring about it, but little else. He was still not
given an executive staff of his own and had to rely on a small
personal briefing staff. The Joint Planning Staff (JPS) was responsible to him only as Chairman of the Chiefs of Staff Committee and

not as CDS. He could not direct them; the terms of reference for their papers had to be cleared by the Chiefs in Committee; and each Director of Plans worked for, was supported by, and was loyal to his own Chief and Service Ministry. That loyalty was powerfully reinforced by their confidential reports, on which their future careers depended, being written within their own Ministries and not in Storey's Gate.

Nor could the new CDS and his colleague, the Permanent Under-Secretary of the Ministry of Defence, make much impact upon the size and shape of the Forces or upon the allocation of resources: they did not have the staff to do more than give Service budgets cursory examinations. For instance, the Assistant Under-Secretary responsible for drawing up overall resource allocations had no authority over his opposite numbers in the Service Ministries, no access to their files, and a lack of specialised knowledge to dissect and analyse them properly anyway. The power of the Service Ministries to preserve their empires and to decide the balance of their forces was, in practice, as great as ever. Michael Howard concluded:

> The historian must wonder how far the care taken to limit this officer's [the CDS's] powers was due to the hazy and incorrect memories of the OKW, which were still stressed in public debate, and how far the realisation that the next incumbent, on the retirement of the tactful and self-effacing Marshal of the Royal Air Force Sir William Dickson, was virtually certain to be the First Sea Lord, Admiral Earl Mountbatten of Burma: a man who had exercised supreme triphibious command fifteen years earlier and who did not conceal his dislike for the reversion to separate service responsibilities which had taken place since the Second World War.[8]

Sandys did, however, have one notable, if only partial, success. Like Mountbatten, he favoured the unification of the three Services, and wanted to set this in train as part of his revolutionary period in office. Macmillan saw that the amalgamation of the Service Ministries, if carried out concurrently with the sweeping changes in Defence policy, would be more than the Defence establishment could take. He had no objection, nevertheless, to experimental steps being taken at a lower level. The opportunity for doing so came in the Middle East. After the evacuation of the Canal Zone, GHQ Middle East had been set up in Cyprus, but the Arab air/sea barrier between the Mediterranean and Indian Ocean, imposed after Suez, made it easier to command Aden and East Africa direct from London rather than from Cyprus. The Cyprus headquarters was renamed GHQ Near East, and Sandys was instrumental in establishing a co-located, though not as yet unified, tri-Service headquarters in Aden. The RAF remained in overall command, as it had done since pre-war days, but the foundations for unification were laid by setting up Naval and Army HQs in the same complex. He made an attempt to do the same thing for the Far East in Singapore, but determined Naval opposition thwarted him.

The battles in Whitehall overshadowed, but did not stop, British military operations overseas. The rebellion in the Oman in July 1957 involved British troops and aircraft in its successful suppression; the Nasser-inspired overthrow of the Hashemite dynasty in Iraq led to the Anglo-American pre-emptive interventions in Jordan and Lebanon in July 1958; and military success in Cyprus against EOKA brought about the Zurich Agreement in January 1959.

Back in the United Kingdom, the first positive political opposition to the philosophy of nuclear deterrence, upon which Sandys' policies depended, began to crystallise with the formation of the Committee for Nuclear Disarmament in January 1958. 'Rather Red than Dead' was its slogan; marching from Aldermaston to Westminster became a way of life for many church-goers, left-wing intellectuals, pacifists and liberal moralists; and the schism in the Labour Party between multi- and unilateralists began to open up. The Chiefs, henceforth, had to take unilateralism seriously in their assessments of future political trends.

Macmillan went to the country in October 1959, and won the General Election with the electorate generally agreeing with his slogan 'You've never had it so good'. He had achieved the three objectives that he set himself on taking over from Eden: the economy was flourishing; the 'Special Relationship' was restored and strengthened; and the hundred seat majority in the Commons showed that the Tory Party's fortunes had been revived.

But these successes had been bought at a military price, which had to be paid for in his second term and by his successors. The premature ending of National Service meant the acceleration of withdrawal from empire and retreat into middle power status. The general consensus in Whitehall was that Sandys had tried to go too far too fast. He contributed to his own lack of success through failing to inspire Service loyalty and support, and had greatly overestimated, from ulterior financial and political motives, the utility of nuclear weapons. No man, even such a determined minister as Sandys or a strong Chief like Mountbatten, can force Whitehall to accept more that it collectively sees as reasonable. Sandys' efforts were generally ridiculed, and no more so than by General Sir John Cowley, Controller of Munitions, who concluded a lecture at the Royal United Services Institute by adding four lines to Lewis Caroll's verse about the old man on the gate:

> I also have a plan to spend a million pounds,
> To buy some guided missiles and to hide them in the
> ground.
> And then to clearly paint on each 'These things must not
> be used'.
> No wonder that our citizens are getting so confused.

He ended by saying:

> I believe that in a 100 years people will look back on the middle of the twentieth
> century as a nightmare period when mankind suddenly discovered the means to
> destroy itself, and was seriously considering this as a preferable alternative to
> reconciling differing political views.[9]

Macmillan was not unaware of the stresses and strains caused in the Defence establishment by Sandys' abrasiveness; nor of the lack of confidence that had grown up between him and the Chiefs. In the post-election Cabinet reshuffle, he was packed off to use his undoubted talents and energies in creating the much needed Ministry of Aviation. He was replaced by the able, and much less flamboyant industrialist, Harold Watkinson, who was a sound administrator and better suited to the task of restoring military balance.

In the same Cabinet changes, Iain Mcleod, a far-sighted minister with the confidence of his own convictions, became Colonial Secretary and was faced with the need to match overseas political commitments to reduced military capabilities. He was in no doubt that the grants of independence to dependent territories must be accelerated: Britain no longer had the resources, nor the resolution, to dictate the pace of advance from Colonial to Commonwealth status.

The Chiefs team was changing too. On the Army side, the intense, belligerent but human, experienced and at times brilliant, Templer went first in September 1958. He was pressed to succeed Montgomery as Deputy SACEUR, but felt that it was a 'non-job' and refused. The Governorship of Kenya was then suggested to him, but he had done his stint in that type of job in Malaya and so it did not attract him. He was finally offered the Commissioner-Generalship of South East Asia. He thought a lot about it, and was clearly tempted, but it would have meant dealing with politicians and he had had enough of them as CIGS. In truth, he was simply played out. He had over-worked in Malaya where he contracted amoebic dysentery. Its recurrence from time to time, and the pain from injuries to his back, caused by a mine explosion when he was commanding 6th Armoured Division in Italy in 1944, sapped his strength, though not his vitality. Besides serving on a number of important Government committees and inquiries after his retirement, he put his heart and soul into establishing the magnificent National Army Museum next to the Royal Hospital in Chelsea as a memorial to the British Army, which he so loved and had served so well. He also followed Alexander and Alanbrooke as Her Majesty's Lord Lieutenant of London.

Templer was succeeded by General Sir Francis Festing, whom Sandys appointed in preference to the one-armed airborne gunner, Sir Geoffrey Bourne, who had succeeded Templer in Malaya and had, indeed, accelerated the military defeat of the Communist terrorist gangs in the jungle. Bourne was given the consolation of a peerage.

'Frankie' Festing was a large, untidy and unruly Rifleman with an excellent brain, plenty of personality but a propensity for idleness, whose métier was soldiering in the field and not in the jungles of Whitehall. Office work, toiling in the London atmosphere, conforming to dress conventions, and being on time, were abhorrent to him. His sparse experience in the War Office was a handicap, but his down to earth commonsense was just what was needed for his principal task of converting the Army back into an all-regular force. Moreover, he had a greater rapport with Mountbatten than Templer ever had. Mountbatten had known him as the highly successful commander of 36th Indian Division in Burma, and had a genuine affection for him. He found also that Festing was less hostile to strengthening the 'Centre', as Storey's Gate was now known, and unworried about possible encroachments into the Chiefs' corporate responsibilities. Indeed, Festing, who showed a marked propensity to deviate from the briefs provided by his own staff, felt that some reform was both necessary and desirable to bring the Services closer together.

Mountbatten became CDS three months before the October 1959 General Election. The choice of his successor as First Sea Lord lay between Sir Guy Grantham, an Admiral in the Andrew Cunningham tradition, or Sir Charles Lambe, the Second Sea Lord, who was an exceptionally gifted and broad-minded sailor, renowned for the soundness of his judgement. Mountbatten did not like the former, who was too intense and humourless for his liking. The latter had been his friend and confidant for many years, but he also had other sound reasons for recommending him to Sandys:

> Grantham is a fine sea-going sailor, whom I would put in command of a Fleet before Charles Lambe. I think he would just win a popularity poll in the Fleet – but that is his limit. The whole Navy would have confidence in Charles Lambe because they would feel he would be able to look after the interests of the Navy in Whitehall.[10]

Mountbatten was also influenced in his choice in the knowledge that it had been Lambe who had been instrumental at staff level in winning the earlier carrier battles against Sandys and De L'Isle. He was a supporter too of Mountbatten's crusade to strengthen the Centre. Sadly Lambe had a serious heart attack six months after taking over as First Sea Lord and had to retire in May 1960, dying three months later.

Lambe was replaced by Sir Caspar John, son of the great painter Augustus John, who inherited his father's fiery temper, brusque approach and outspokenness. When asked by a tiresome lady if he also painted, he is purported to have replied, 'No madam, I leave all that to Daddy'. He was as straightforward in his handling of men and affairs as Mountbatten was devious. He was also the first naval aviator to become the professional head of the Navy, which made him just as acceptable to the carrier-conscious Naval Staff as Lambe had been. On matters of Naval policy, he and Mountbatten usually saw eye to eye, but on methods of implementing those policies they were poles apart, Caspar disparaging Mountbatten's theatricality and critical of what he saw as downright dishonesty in many of his dissembling ploys. Nor were these differences helped by a lack of warmth between these two strong personalities.

Dermot Boyle's tenure as CAS came to an end three months after the General Election. In his place came Sir Thomas Pike, whose elder brother was VCIGS. Tom Pike was as honest and straightforward as Caspar John, but less colourful. His views were always carefully thought through and firmly stated, but his less well informed critics felt him unassertive. This was unfair to Pike: little did they know what a weak hand he was dealt by the fates in the politically fraught and technologically complex Blue Streak/Skybolt/Polaris controversy, which was to lead to the RAF losing its primacy as the wielder of the British nuclear deterrent. His relations with the Admiralty were also soured by the vexed issue of TSR 2 versus NA

39 (Buccaneer) as the strike aircraft of the future, in which he was much more successful in defending the RAF's interests. Despite these naval/air issues, Mountbatten hoped, initially at least, that Pike would be easier to work with than Boyle, particularly over strengthening the Centre. He was to be disappointed: Pike no more trusted the CDS's impartiality than Boyle had done.

The holders of two other posts in the Ministry of Defence began to play increasingly important parts in the story of the Chiefs as Mountbatten took over as CDS and started looking for levers of power. They were the Permanent Under-Secretary (PUS), the newly appointed Sir Edward Playfair, and the Chief Scientific Adviser (CSA), Sir Solly Zuckerman. CDS, PUS and CSA were the triumvirate of co-equal advisers to the Minister of Defence. As such they were feared by the single-Service Ministries as an inner cabal. Playfair's impartiality and good sense were unquestioned. Zuckerman, who had been an old ally of Mountbatten during his days as wartime Chief of Combined Operations, did not enjoy the same confidence. Though accepted as an eminent scientist, he was also seen as an iconoclastic political manipulator with a dangerously brilliant analytical brain and sceptical outlook. He was, nonetheless, an admirable foil for Mountbatten, feeding him ideas and curbing some of his excessive enthusiasms. Naturally the 'Zuk-Batten' axis was deeply suspect amongst the Chiefs.

Mountbatten would have liked to have pursued his own ideas for unification of Service Ministries and of the Services as soon as Macmillan's new administration was in place, but he found no immediate enthusiasm in Westminster or Whitehall for yet another wave of revolutionary change. Watkinson rebuffed him because he believed that his task was to restore Service stability and strategic balance after the excesses of Sandys' revolution. He felt also that the new CDS structure should be allowed to evolve. Macmillan too, although still convinced of the need for further change, was pragmatically disinclined to risk further damaging battles with the Chiefs. His success in ending National Service was enough for the time being.

So, in spite of Mountbatten finding himself at the head of a new team of Chiefs, who seemed to him, at least, somewhat more responsive to his unification ideas, he had to be content, for the moment, with strengthening his own powers as CDS. His first step in this direction was to reinforce his personal briefing staff with men of his own choosing, a measure to which no one could object, but it was quite another matter when he proposed that the CDS should have his own Director of Plans, who would chair Joint Planning Staff Committee meetings, thus reflecting CDS's chairmanship of the Chiefs and ensuring that his views were fully reflected in their work. He won in the end against intense opposition from his colleagues, who felt 'Here we go again: more power to Dickie!'

Baulked in his unification ambitions, Mountbatten turned his sights onto the higher command structure outside Whitehall, aiming to build on Sandys' experimental collocation of the Naval, Army and Air Headquarters at Aden. He won agreement to setting up unified commands overseas as part of an evolutionary approach to integration of command at all levels, including Whitehall, once experience had been gained in the working of tri-Service headquarters. Headquarters British Forces were established on a tri-Service basis in Cyprus in 1960; in Aden in 1961; and in Singapore in 1962 in the face of determined local Service opposition led by the GOC-in-C, Dick Hull, who told Mountbatten bluntly that there was no place for supreme commanders in peacetime. This attitude was to sour relations between the two men, Hull remarking *'From then on Mountbatten knew that he had an opponent in me'*.[11]

Admiral Sir David Luce became the first Commander-in-Chief British Forces, Far East, just in time to handle the Brunei Revolt and the Confrontation with Indonesia, which started in December 1962.

The birth of these three tri-Service overseas commands necessitated setting up a small 'Operational Executive' at Storey's Gate to communicate with them and to give them operational direction – another modest increment to the Centre's power.

By the time these steps had been completed, Peter Thorneycroft had taken over as Minister of Defence from Harold Watkinson, who fell in Macmillan's 'Night of the Long Knives' in July 1962; and the atmosphere in Whitehall had again become more conducive to radical change at the Centre. Before we examine the Thorneycroft/Mountbatten reforms we must, however, look at other more crucial problems that faced the Chiefs during Watkinson's two and three-quarters years as Mountbatten's political master.

The first task that Watkinson set himself was to re-establish better relations with the Chiefs. This was not difficult because the three single-Service Chiefs welcomed his evolutionary approach, and there was general agreement that Sandys had overstepped the fine line between sensibly constructive and imprudently radical change. It was time to shift the emphasis from the nuclear end of the spectrum of war back to a more balanced central position. Watkinson records in his memoirs:

> I was more interested in the need to achieve a reorganisation of Britain's conventional forces under firm businesslike direction, coupled with a policy which would speed up their reaction time and create a mobile force with a poised capacity to operate from land or sea bases. This seemed to me a more important priority in 1959 than overmuch argument about nuclear philosophical heresies of one kind or another.[12]

This was the line that the Chiefs had felt should have been taken by the Government after Suez, but unfortunately, as soon as Watkinson started on his quest for strategically mobile forces, the Blue Streak/Skybolt/Polaris issues forced nuclear affairs to his and the Chiefs' attention.

One of the planks in Sandys' policy had been the replacement of the V-Bombers by the Blue Streak ballistic missile. By the autumn of 1959, it was clear to the Chiefs that Blue Streak, with its unprotected launch system and slow reaction time, due to its use of liquid fuel propellant, would be far too vulnerable to Soviet pre-emptive strikes in the *Sputnik* age. Placing the missiles in hardened silos would be prohibitively expensive, and, in any case, installing any static system in the crowded British Isles would neither be militarily wise nor politically sensible. Macmillan and Sandys, as Minister of Aviation, fought hard to prevent Blue Streak's cancellation, but Watkinson and the Chiefs had an unimpeachable case against it. In February 1960, the Cabinet agreed to write off the £60m already spent and to seek an alternative vehicle for Britain's strategic nuclear deterrent.

Mountbatten and Zuckerman had visited the United States in the autumn of 1959, and had been shown the massive underground silos of the Titan inter-continental ballistic missiles. They had concluded that Britain had neither the resources nor the need to enter into the land-based ICBM league. Her nuclear delivery system's invulnerability would have to be sought in airborne or submarine mobility.

There were three airborne solutions: the United States Air Force's Skybolt, modified to fit the V-Bombers; a simpler British ram-jet alternative, called Pandora, for the TSR 2; or the continued development of the RAF's Blue Steel stand-off bomb, which had been stopped by Sandys. Submarine solutions were more limited: the United States Navy's solid fuel Polaris missile could be bought complete with American submarines, or fitted into British built hulls.

The debate on these options was one sided. Pike quite naturally wanted to maintain the RAF's hold on the deterrent role, as his predecessor, Dermot Boyle, had done, and Caspar John was not yet ready to make a bid. The Admiralty doubted the continued viability of a British independent nuclear deterrent, and they feared that the financial burden of Polaris on the Navy's budget could adversely affect the build-up of the carrier-based fleet and squeeze out Naval Staff plans for the new fleet carrier, CVA 01. Mountbatten, who would have liked to have won Polaris for the Navy, for once maintained the impartiality expected of a CDS and supported Pike in his bid for Skybolt, which the Air Staff deemed the best of the air options.

Surprisingly, debates in the Chiefs of Staff Committee on nuclear issues tended to be more peripheral than was generally supposed or thought desirable. Political considerations so dominated thinking about Britain's nuclear posture that many decisions were taken, and would continue to be taken, on political judgements that flowed from the advice of senior policy-making Civil Servants without the military implications being fully explored by the Chiefs.

Mountbatten tried to correct this by pressing for papers on these very complex and controversial issues to be placed on the Chiefs' agenda without any lasting success. He himself was horrified by the catastrophic potentialities of nuclear weapons, their multiplicity and the over-kill inherent in the balance of terror being developed by the two superpowers. He was sceptical about the value and usability of tactical nuclear weapons, and he had some doubts about Britain's Independent Nuclear Deterrent. Although he reluctantly accepted that nuclear weapons provided a unique constraint on major wars, and, having been invented, had to be held in sufficient numbers to deter war, he never saw them as usable weapons, and only as a contribution to reductions in armaments generally.

Mountbatten wanted to stimulate nuclear discussion and argument, even to the extent of airing heretical views himself in order to do so. The single-Service Chiefs, on the other hand, were suspicious of his somewhat emotional ideas and felt it right, in strictly military terms, to abide by the straightforward and generally accepted view that Britain had to have its own nuclear weapons if others had them. They were vital to the security of the British Isles; and while contributing to the NATO deterrent as a whole, they could still be used by HMG *in extremis*.

In March 1960, Macmillan flew to Washington, primarily to discuss the proposed Nuclear Test Ban Treaty. He came back with an exchange of letters, in which Eisenhower agreed that Britain could

buy Skybolt; and, in return, the Americans could use Holy Loch in
Scotland as a United States nuclear submarine base. No formal
undertaking was given by Eisenhower to provide Polaris if the
Skybolt development were to fail, but Macmillan felt confident that
the Americans would be willing to do so in that event.

At home there was a hue and cry in all political parties when the
substitution of Skybolt for Blue Streak was announced in April.
Tories were upset, because it confirmed what many people feared
about Britain slipping behind the superpowers in weapon technology
and being in danger of losing a measure of sovereignty by having to
buy key weapon systems from the United States. Labour multilatera-
lists were discomforted by the undermining of Britain's independence
in foreign policy; and the unilateralists were boosted by the belief
that their case was being made for them. It was no coincidence that
the first CND march from Aldermaston to Trafalgar Square took
place that Easter weekend; nor that the TUC, under Frank Cousins'
leadership, came out strongly for unilateralism at its annual conference in September. Hugh Gaitskell was forced to make his famous
'fight and fight and fight again' speech to prevent a unilateralist
victory in the Labour Party Conference in October.

It is one of the unhappy paradoxes of Whitehall that its establishment reacts to the goad of a strong, abrasive minister like Duncan
Sandys, whose revolutionary ideas it detests, and yet it is slow to
implement the more balanced and evolutionary policies of the
Watkinsons of this world for which it craves! Events, however, like
actions, speak louder than words in the Whitehall market place.
Watkinson could thank Iraq's General Kassim for bringing strategic
mobility requirements back onto the Chiefs' agenda by threatening
Kuwait with tank forces as Saddam Hussein was to do in August
1990. In 1961, however, Britain had a Defence Agreement with
Kuwait's ruler, which she honoured.

The crisis broke at the end of June and was to provide the first test
for the new Operations Executive at Storey's Gate, and for the
Tri-Service command headquarters in Aden and Cyprus. At the time
there were three British frigates and the Amphibious Squadron in the
Gulf, carrying half a squadron of tanks: the other half squadron's
worth was already stockpiled in Kuwait itself. The Commando-
Carrier *Bulwark* with 42 Commando embarked was at Karachi doing
hot weather trials, and 45 Commando was in Aden. The Aircraft-
Carrier *Centaur* was in the Indian Ocean with her escorts, and the
24th Infantry Brigade of the Strategic Reserve was in Kenya.

The nearest parachute battalions were in Cyprus, which was also important as an air staging post on the way to the Gulf.

Well judged anticipatory moves, advised by the Chiefs of Staff before the Ruler actually called for British military assistance, led to *Centaur* joining *Bulwark* in the Gulf; the Amphibious Squadron being stationed over the horizon off Kuwait; a Canberra squadron from Germany arriving at Bahrain, where Hunters and Shackletons from Aden were also concentrated; and 24th Infantry Brigade, and 45 Commando being ready to fly into Kuwait as soon as the airfield had been secured by 42 Commando, flown off *Bulwark* in helicopters.

The Ruler's request came on 30 June. By next evening, (1 July), Brigadier Horsfield, commanding 24th Infantry Brigade had the equivalent of half a brigade with tank and air support on the Mutlah Ridge, blocking the direct route to Kuwait city, and by the end of the week he had a force of five battalions with tank, artillery, air and naval gunfire support ready to oppose the Iraqis. Thus, an effective force had been assembled in a very short time, and the Government, advised by the Chiefs under Mountbatten's leadership, had taken the right political and military decisions.

Kassim, unlike Saddam Hussein, did not attack. Nor was this first British attempt to use quick-reaction forces without its difficulties. 'Many useful lessons' were learnt as usual! For instance, the operation room facilities in Storey's Gate proved quite inadequate: they had not been modernised since Churchill used them in the Second World War and looked more like a railway waiting-room than the focal point for the control of operations. Mountbatten was seen at the beginning of the crisis with an armful of maps and a handful of drawing pins, shouting for the 'Duty Captain' and looking for wall space to set up a proper situation map! A purpose-built Operations Centre was not provided until the present Ministry of Defence Main Building was occupied in 1964.

The Kuwait intervention demonstrated, if demonstration was necessary, the effectiveness of quickly mounted amphibious and air-transported forces, and provided Watkinson with the precedents he needed to swing the balance back into the centre of the spectrum of war. Whitehall's doubts about the practicability and usefulness of such forces were softened, and projects with an East of Suez flavour became fashionable. The vertical take-off ground-attack fighter, the P 1127, which turned into the famous Harrier, was given its initial boost at this time; and the Air Staff started to laud the TSR 2, operating from island bases, as a more cost-effective answer to the

Indian Ocean strike requirements than the expensive CVA 01, carrying Buccaneers.

In his last Defence White Paper, published in February 1962, Watkinson was able to point the moral:

> Our policy of deterring war has been severely tested in the past twelve months . . . If we had nothing but nuclear forces, this would not be credible. A balance must be maintained, therefore, between conventional and nuclear strength.[13]

Frankie Festing retired in September 1961 and was succeeded by Sir Richard Hull, a cavalryman, who had first come to prominence commanding Blade Force in the abortive thrust for Tunis after the Allied landings in French North Africa in November/December 1942. He was an extraordinarily able staff officer, but an unlucky commander: his 1st Armoured Division suffered severe losses at Coriano and Ceriano, trying to break into the Po Valley in the autumn of 1944 during the Italian campaign. He was militarily orthodox in his approach, but such were his perceived abilities that the Army were grooming him as a potential successor to Mountbatten after he had served his time as its Chief. It would be an understatement to say that he was no admirer of Mountbatten: the two men loathed each other. Hull, an upright English gentleman, steeped in traditional values, found Mountbatten's urbane vanities and dissemblings intolerable. Their respective ADCs used to observe their clashes with amusement mingled with horror. It was hardly surprising that Dick Hull joined Caspar John and Tom Pike in their bitter opposition to Mountbatten's coming reforms.

By the time the more politically ambitious Peter Thorneycroft took over from the self-effacing Watkinson in July 1962, pressures were again building up for another step towards unification of the Service Ministries. The success of the Kuwait intervention was a feather in the cap of the tri-Service command structure overseas and of the Operational Executive in London, and it had shown up the inherent inefficiencies in mounting quick reaction operations through the Admiralty, War Office and Air Ministry. Irritating inadequacies were also emerging in the weapon procurement field where the existence of these three separate ministries, each with a somewhat different perception of conflict, was complicating already over-complex scientific and technological decision-making.

Thorneycroft's triumvirate of advisers in the Ministry of Defence – Mountbatten, Sir Robert Scott, who had succeeded Playfair as PUS, and Zuckerman – all felt it was time to launch a new unification assault: Mountbatten, because he was coming to the end of his tenure as CDS and wanted to go down in history as the man who won the final battle; Scott, because he saw it as the sensible administrative thing to do; and Zuckerman, because, as a clear headed scientist, he saw the over-laps between sea, land and air warfare were by the 1960s becoming too great for efficient handling by four different ministries.

The time was, indeed, so ripe for the change that it took little to whet Thorneycroft's ambitions, or to persuade Macmillan that further change was necessary to produce a more economic and responsive Defence organisation. The obvious man to master-mind unification and to force it through was Mountbatten, although his three year tenure was nearing its end, and so, under the normal rules, he would not be available to do the job while still CDS.

Normal rules had never been applicable to Mountbatten! Macmillan seems to have toyed with the idea of making him a non-political Minister of Defence, but the precedents of Chatfield and Alexander were not encouraging. Instead, he took the easier option of extending Mountbatten's tenure to five years to enable him to undertake the task. Countess Mountbatten had died in February 1960, leaving him a lonely man, so he accepted this new and final military challenge of his long career with alacrity and undisguised enthusiasm.

Two problems presented themselves immediately: how sweeping should his reforms be; and how should they be launched? Paradoxically, Mountbatten, while being the generator of the unification proposals, was also the main obstacle to their acceptance. The suspicion with which he was regarded by the single-Service Chiefs – Caspar John, Dick Hull and Tom Pike – ran so deep that any radical suggestions would be rigorously opposed if they were seen to have originated with him. In the eyes of his colleagues on the Chiefs of Staff Committee, three principles were sacrosanct and not matters for negotiation: corporate responsibility; independent single-Service management; and a firm linkage between power to advise and responsibility for implementation.

Mountbatten needed firm Cabinet backing if he were to recommend denting, let alone, breaching these hallowed principles, but Macmillan rightly felt that the Cabinet must be clear about what he had in mind before giving direction on the extent of the reforms he was to propose. He was, therefore, asked to submit a memorandum through Thorneycroft, setting out his personal views on the future organisation.

Mountbatten took two months to write his paper, which he only discussed with Scott and Zuckerman outside his personal staff. He was determined that he would not have his proposals attacked by the single-Service Chiefs before he was ready, and that he would put in a tough and realistic paper:

> . . . however much Chief of Air Staff, the old Blimps and the Civil Service may hate it. Both the PM and the Minister approve my preparation of such a paper and no one can expect me to put up a half baked wishy-washy compromise. I would sooner have a brave, drastic and "correct" paper turned down than a weak compromise accepted.[14]

He started his paper with a rehearsal of the weaknesses of the current organisation: how the formulation of broad defence policy was frustrated by narrower single-Service interests; how this exacerbated the already difficult budgetary situation; and how it divided the loyalties of Service Ministers, the Chiefs and their staffs. He then swept quickly to his main conclusion and the key to the rest of his paper. Nothing short of the abolition of the Service Ministries and the creation of a single Ministry of Defence would eradicate the deepseated weakness of the defence organisation as it stood.

For the time being he discarded, as premature, the concept of a unified defence force on Canadian lines, although that was what he believed should be the ultimate solution. He hoped the establishment of a single ministry would bring sailors, soldiers and airmen closer together, and help the process of unification in the longer term.

His paper then went on to give a broad outline of his new-style unified ministry. There would be one Secretary of State assisted by Ministers of State with functional rather than single-Service responsibilities. The Naval, General and Air Staffs would be integrated into a Defence Staff responsible to the CDS, who would be advised by the single-Service Chiefs of Staff on sea, land and air matters as the heads of their sections of the overall Defence Staff. The CDS would have clear paramountcy over them, not just as their chairman, but in his own right; and the Service Chiefs would lose their status as the professional heads of their Services, which would be taken over by three Commanders-in-Chief or Inspectors General of the Navy, Army and Air Force, who would act as the Principal Personnel Officers of their own Services, responsible for their general 'wellbeing', taken to mean their management, training, morale and operational efficiency.

Mountbatten undoubtedly proposed these drastic changes in the

Chiefs' roles in order to rid them of parochial single-Service pre-occupations and to encourage them to think nationally across the board. It was a near fatal error: he was overturning the three principles, which the single-Service Chiefs deemed non-negotiable, and he was undermining the very foundations of the Chiefs of Staff system.

Thorneycroft treated his paper with benign interest and Macmillan welcomed it, but the single-Service Chiefs received their copies with anger, alarm and varying degrees of personal animosity towards Mountbatten himself. In their near hysterical reaction to this assault on the fundamental principles of their position, they found ready support from retired Chiefs like Harding, Slessor and Portal, the last resurrecting the specious OKW analogy.

The single-Service Chiefs counter-attacked with a paper of their own, which accepted the principle of unified commands overseas, and agreed to the strengthening of the Central Staffs shown to be necessary by the recent intervention in Kuwait and by technological problems over nuclear delivery systems, but they were adamantly opposed to any downgrading of their corporate responsibilities as military advisers to the Government, or as the professional heads of their own Services.

Faced with this vitriolic reaction, Macmillan took the usual course in such circumstances of commissioning an independent inquiry on the Cabinet's behalf into this conflict of views. He chose as his inquisitors Lord Ismay and Sir Ian Jacob, Churchill's trusted war-time staff officers. Jacob had also been the author of the 1946 White Paper on the Central Organisation of Defence, and more recently the Chiefs' adviser during the Global Strategy meeting at Greenwich in 1952. It was an authoritative and impressive team, and a master stroke by Macmillan, which was strongly approved by Mountbatten, who realised that this would take the heat off his own paper. Ismay and Jacob would be reporting direct to the Cabinet, thus making it constitutionally difficult to muster support against their conclusions, and he had every confidence that their judgements would vindicate his proposals.

Jacob took the lead in writing their report, which he completed in the remarkably short time of six weeks. It was highly critical of the existing system, and put forward three alternative solutions for Cabinet consideration.

The first option amounted to little more than tinkering with the existing structure. They did not recommend it because it did not go

far enough in tackling fundamental weaknesses, but they did stress
the importance of strengthening the CDS's position and ensuring
that the best man was selected for the job irrespective of 'Buggin's
turn'.

The second option was the collocation of Ministry of Defence,
Admiralty, War Office and Air Ministry in one building, if a large
enough one could be found. A Secretary of State for Defence would
be in overall charge with the Service Ministries reduced in status to
that of Departments of the new super Ministry of Defence, each
under its own junior minister. The Board of Admiralty, Army
Council and Air Council would be downgraded and subordinated to
a new Defence Council, becoming the Admiralty, Army and Air
Boards. There would be some strengthening of the Central Staffs, but
the Chiefs would retain their corporate responsibilities and remain
the professional heads of their Services.

The third option was a fully integrated and functional ministry
with all officers of two-star rank and above merged into an Armed
Forces Staff and wearing a common uniform. Service identity would
be retained at one-star level and below.

Ismay and Jacob held the third option to be premature, but
thought it worthy of consideration as a longer term objective. They
envisaged the Navy, Army and Air Force remaining as far as fighting
units were concerned with regiments revering their battle honours,
and the Navy and Air Force continuing to honour their own great
traditions. Serving officers would, however, be encouraged and
trained to adopt a tri-Service outlook, and to hold a wider range of
appointments on the basis of the best man for the job, irrespective of
Service. In this way, it was hoped to build up a body of senior
officers fully capable of handling military policy and decision-making
at Defence level.

In recommending the middle course to the Cabinet, they did so
not only on its intrinsic merits, but also as a stepping-stone to the
third option. The Prime Minister and his colleagues recoiled from
the idea of complete Service integration with 'mud coloured' uni-
forms for senior officers, and from degrading healthy British triba-
lism in what they saw as an un-British ultimate solution. In the light
of the Canadian experience, who would deny the political soundness
of their instincts? They accepted the second option with enthusiasm
as an elegant and eminently sensible solution, which breached none
of the Chiefs' sacrosanct principles, but would bring the Services
much closer together; and they ordered it to be implemented with

full collocation by the spring of 1964.

Mountbatten was delighted with the Cabinet decision to accept the second option, describing the Ismay/Jacob Report as a remarkable document, even though it did not go quite as far as he had proposed. He was greatly encouraged by the decision on collocation and the creation of one Ministry of Defence, thus abolishing, at a stroke, the Admiralty, War Office and Air Ministry. He set about the process of implementation with all his very considerable energy, powers of persuasion and occasional subterfuge to win as much power for the CDS and degree of functionalization for the new Ministry as he could extract from the broad principles laid down by the Cabinet.

The single-Service Chiefs, while relieved that their own positions were intact and Service management was still decentralised and not functionalised within the unified Ministry of Defence, were equally determined that Mountbatten should not be allowed to use the thin ends of any wedges to achieve his covert aims. The trouble was that there was enough scope for different interpretations of the concept to assuage the prejudices of both sides. Mountbatten was convinced that the Cabinet decisions gave him authority to go a bit further than Ismay/Jacob Option 2, and the Service Chiefs were equally certain that it gave them the opportunity to retain more than he did of the *status quo*.

In the wrangling over the interpretation of Option 2, Mountbatten was never averse to outflanking the Chiefs by going behind their backs to Ministers, or by taking the Queen's name in vain. '*I was staying at Windsor last weekend*' he would say benignly at the start of a Chiefs' meeting, '*and she said how glad she was that we were going to do so and so. . . .*'. The fact that the particular subject was of such complexity or triviality that the Queen could not be expected to have an opinion or interest in it, destroyed the story's credibility, but that seemed to concern him very little. On other occasions, he would give his colleagues the impression that he supported their views and would lead them, as a body, to see Thorneycroft. When the moment came to do so, he would excuse himself from attending the meeting on grounds of 'doctor's orders', having written to Thorneycroft advising him not to agree to what they were proposing!

These dubious methods naturally infuriated Mountbatten's colleagues, who became increasingly frustrated, often accusing him to his face of deceptions of one kind or another. He remained unperturbed and unrepentant, shrugging off attacks with the justification that he was right and his critics were wrong; and that, in any case, the end justified the means.

On one important issue he was partially defeated. Most of the new Ministry was to be organised on a 'Joint' rather than on an 'Integrated' or 'Functional' basis as he wanted. That is to say, sections of the Naval, Army and Air Staffs with similar responsibilities remained separate within their own Departments, but were brought together in joint committees. Cynics talked about doing in four places what had previously been done in three! This co-ordinating work was largely done by the civil servants of the PUS's Defence Secretariat, which acted as the nerve-system of the whole Ministry. However, four new integrated staffs were created: the Defence Operations Executive for crisis management; the Defence Operational Requirements Staff for weapon specification; the Defence Signals Staff; and the Defence Intelligence Staff. Their establishment gave Mountbatten some hope that they would set the pattern for the future as the tri-Service overseas commands had done.

In this story of the Chiefs, it would be tedious to discuss all the intricate reorganisations that had to be engineered in the personnel, logistic, scientific, equipment procurement and financial corridors of power to make the new Ministry a reality. Suffice it to say that the battles fought in these fields between those favouring joint staff systems and the integrationists were no less fierce than amongst the Defence policy and operational staffs.

The Cabinet's decision was announced in early March 1963, but the White Paper was not published until July. Those three months saw intense activity and much emotion generated as the various committees worked under Mountbatten's strong direction to put flesh on the Ismay/Jacob skeleton. It was a mammoth task in which a certain Lieutenant-Colonel Edwin Bramall played a leading part as one of Mountbatten's reorganisation team, and was to be CDS himself some 20 years later when a further reorganisation was set in train – a case of *déjà vu* as far as he was concerned.

A large enough Whitehall building was found to accommodate the policy staffs of the Centre and the three Services Departments as they now became. On All Fools' Day 1964 – a point not lost on critics of the reorganisation – the Service Ministries closed down, and the staffs moved on schedule into the present Ministry of Defence Main Building. This had previously housed the Air Staff at the Parliament end and the Board of Trade at the Charing Cross end. The building was sliced like a layered cake. The vertical slices were by Service: Air

Staff at their original end; Army and Central Staffs in the middle; and the Naval Staff at the Charing Cross end. The horizontal layers were by function. The sixth floor was the principle floor, housing Ministers, the Chiefs, the senior Civil Servants, the Chief Scientist, and their personal staffs; the seventh floor was for personnel and logistic policy staffs; the fifth for operational staffs, including the new Joint Operations Centre; the fourth for Intelligence; and so on. A residue of non-policy staffs was left in what were to be called the 'Old' Admiralty and 'Old' War Office buildings, which were refilled on a tri-Service basis to prevent any reversion to single-Service usage!

Incidentally, one sad but belated change was made on vesting day. The 'Imperial' was dropped from the title of the Army's Chief, who henceforth became just Chief of General Staff (CGS).

Mountbatten held his first Chiefs of Staff meeting on 7 April 1964 in the specially appointed Chiefs of Staff Conference Room described in the Prologue to this book. It was situated on the fifth floor and fitted with the most modern communications and display facilities. He took his seat in the new high-backed, black leather swivel chair, emblazoned with the insignia of the Order of the Garter, his showmanship as impeccable as ever. He had every right to be pleased with his accomplishment. He had achieved as near a victory for his point of view as he could ever have hoped. No one else could have pulled it off against such opposition.

Was the reorganisation worth all the acrimonious argument and the subsequent turmoil of the move. The answer is most certainly, 'Yes'. It was the logical next step in the evolution of Defence policy-making and of the Chiefs of Staff system. Co-location, alone turned out to be an enormous asset and streamlined the way work was done. The Chiefs and their staffs could, and increasingly did, walk into each others offices' to settle issues by direct contact instead of over the telephone or by interminable correspondence. The national Defence effort was now under one Secretary of State, responsible to Parliament, making the allocation of resources within a tight budget much more positive. The position of the CDS had been strengthened without weakening the managerial powers of the Service Chiefs; and decision-making at all levels was improved by the inter-departmental co-ordination of the PUS's unified Defence Secretariat. In the case of CDS, the strengthening was not as great as Mountbatten would have wished, in that his enhanced powers stemmed only from his position as Chairman of the Chiefs of Staff Committee, and not in his own right. This hidden flaw would require remedial action in the years ahead.

Nor were the worst fears so freely bandied about at the time, not least by the Chiefs themselves, borne out in practice. The reorganisation did not lead to an inflated bureaucracy; both military and civilian staff numbers declined, and significant savings were made in the integrated staffs and through the rationalisation of administrative and logistic services. Once the Services had got over their initial qualms that their individualities and tribal customs were going to be submerged into an amorphous mass, they welcomed the new arrangements as a constructive and dynamic approach to the real problems facing them. Nevertheless, there was an equally strong feeling that any greater centralisation of power might lead to the Services having compromise policies and weapon systems foisted upon them, in which tri-Service economy rather than battle winning performance could be the most important criteria. The professional advice of the single-Service Chiefs could be progressively degraded if the powers of the Centre were not firmly circumscribed. These fears were to re-emerge later when the time was again ripe for another step to be taken towards total unification.

The reforms, in reality, went as far as the perceived wisdom of Whitehall and the Defence establishment would allow, and were to survive virtually intact for the next 20 years, evolving all the time as each new generation of Chiefs brought its own lifetime of experience and ideas to bear on the crises of the day. Michael Howard in his historical study of the Central Organisation of Defence summed up:

> On paper these reforms appeared extraordinarily impressive and far-reaching. The Services, it is true, were left intact, administered by their own Boards and led by their own Chiefs, who retained ultimate responsibility for all operations they might be required to undertake. They had only to mourn the passing of certain historic titles. . . . The degree to which the Services were left intact, indeed, was seen by several critics as a major obstacle in the path of the Secretary of State in the exercise of his new responsibilities. But the erosion of the independence of the Service Ministries, and the drastic reduction in status of the Service Ministers, the budgeting powers placed in the hands of the Permanent Under-Secretary, and the increase in the controlling apparatus at the disposal of the Chief Scientific Adviser added up to an administrative revolution unparalleled since the days of Cardwell.[15]

Neither the world nor British Defence policy stood still while the unification debates went on. Macmillan was pursuing a two-handed foreign policy: building up a relationship with the new Kennedy Administration in Washington; and trying to persuade de Gaulle of the genuineness of Britain's first application to join the EEC. He had little success with the latter, but he established an elder-statesman relationship with the young Jack Kennedy, helped by British support of the United States during the Cuban Missile crisis of October 1962, which did much to overcome the problems presented to Thorneycroft and the Chiefs by McNamara's cancellation of Skybolt in November of that year.

The first official intimation that Skybolt was becoming increasingly expensive and might fail in development, reached London as early as October 1960, only four months after the original Skybolt Agreement was signed. Mountbatten, as CDS, advised Macmillan and Watkinson that it would be better to spend the money on Polaris missiles, and the Admiralty set up a 'Polaris Executive' on American lines to prepare contingency plans for their purchase. Pike and the Air Staff, perhaps goaded by the expectation of Mountbatten siding with his own Service, reacted strongly to the possible loss of the RAF's prime role with vigorous anti-Polaris lobbying. A Tri-Service Scientific Committee was set up to examine the Skybolt replacement options, but such was the intense partisanship of the Naval and Air Staff representatives that the Committee could only agree that whatever system was chosen must have mobility and instant readiness.

The controversy went on into 1962, with the RAF claiming lower capital expenditure for Skybolt because the V-Bombers, which were to carry the missiles, already existed. The Navy countered with very much lower running costs for Polaris submarines and their longer life expectancy. Skybolt's problems did prove terminal as far as McNamara was concerned, but the Pentagon was prepared to continue the project for the RAF's benefit if Britain paid half the costs. With the RAF's primary role in jeopardy, Pike fought hard to save the project, but the cards were stacked too heavily against him. When the vulnerability factor was taken into account, submarines clearly had the edge over air-delivered systems; and there was no guarantee that throwing more money at Skybolt, Pandora or any other air-launched missile would be successful.

Ironically, Naval fears about the budgetary effects of taking over the nuclear deterrent upon the size and shape of the Fleet were allayed by the increased centralisation of the Defence votes, which Pike and Templer had opposed so bitterly. The nuclear deterrent under the new Ministry's accounting system was transferred from the Naval to Central Staff costings. Lord Carrington, then First Lord, persuaded the Cabinet that the Admiralty could, should and was now willing to build British Polaris hulls if the Americans would allow the purchase of the missiles. There was, of course, no guarantee that the Kennedy Administration would honour Eisenhower's informal agreement to do so: American thinking about Europe was known to be in the process of change. Macmillan, nevertheless, made up his mind to go for the best solution, Polaris, and not be fobbed off with anything else.

Macmillan met Kennedy at Nassau in December 1962, just after his abortive visit to de Gaulle at Rambouillet. Their meeting has been described as '*one of the greatest confrontations in the history of Anglo-American relations*'.[16] The Skybolt/Polaris issue swept all else off the agenda. The United States State Department and Pentagon officials were adamantly against supplying Polaris to Britain for three good reasons that proved to be well founded: it would fuel de Gaulle's prejudices against NATO, as indeed it did; it would single out Britain for special treatment and make her entry into Europe more difficult, which it did as well; and it would jeopardise their pet, but impracticable, scheme for building up a mixed-manned European nuclear force, and this it killed indirectly!

But the two politicians were their own men. Macmillan played on Kennedy's political instincts by suggesting that failure to honour Eisenhower's unwritten pledge to supply Polaris missiles, if Skybolt failed, could sink the Macmillan Government and lead to the election of an anti-American alternative – Tory or Labour. Virulent anti-Americanism in the post-Suez era was not confined to either major British political party. If there must be a parting, he said, Britain would continue to honour her side of the Anglo-American nuclear understandings: the Holy Loch base and Fylingdales early warning station would remain available to American forces; RAF air bases would still house United States bombers; and Britain would continue to shoulder the risks of nuclear attack that these United States privileges entailed. She would not ask for any further exchange of nuclear information, but she must be released from her obligation not to use the knowledge that she already had in seeking collaboration with other partners – France for instance.

Though some of the President's men wished to drive Britain out of the nuclear deterrent business altogether, Kennedy assessed the political and strategic costs of doing so to be too high. He insisted on a formula being found that would allow Britain to buy Polaris missiles without prejudicing the chances of the proposed multinational nuclear force. A compromise was reached by the British side agreeing to assign their Polaris force, V-Bombers and tactical nuclear weapons to SACEUR, subject to the usual overriding proviso '*except where Her Majesty's Government may decide that the supreme national interests are at stake*'.

Thus it came about that the RAF lost primacy in British Defence priorities that it had enjoyed in varying forms since Hitler came to power in the early 1930s. Pike and the Air Staff felt outmanoeuvred, detecting the hand of Mountbatten at work behind the scenes, but in hindsight it cannot be said the decision was wrong. They were not slow to switch RAF priorities to limited and counter-insurgency scenarios as the Naval staff had done when faced with Duncan Sandys' refusal to recognise any real role for the Navy in nuclear war. This was to bring the Navy and Air Departments back into renewed confrontation over carriers, since both Services would be trying to show that their future capital equipments – CVA 01 and the TSR2 – were the most cost-effective east of Suez.

Eight months after the Polaris deal had been struck at Nassau, Caspar John, who had steered the Naval Staff so successfully through the Skybolt/Polaris minefields, retired at the end of his tenure. He was replaced in August 1963 by Sir David Luce, a mild man in comparison with Caspar John. He had been the first tri-Service C-in-C, Far East, and had handled the early phases of the operations in Borneo with a sureness of touch, winning the confidence of such 'turbulent priests' as Major-General Walter Walker (later General Sir Walter), the Director of Operations. Both Mountbatten and John had every confidence in him when he was appointed, but that confidence drained away when he failed to fight the final carrier battles in 1965–6 with the robustness that they would have liked. Mountbatten's acid comment was, '*though loyal, he has not the character or perception; the job is above his head*'.[17]

The all-regular Army, which Dick Hull had helped to design in his Hull Committee at the time of Suez, and of which he was now the professional head, was in being by the end of 1962, although the last National Serviceman did not leave until May 1963. It was more overstretched than even he had envisaged, in spite of regular recruiting going better than expected. Its strength was nearing 180,000 men instead of the 165,000 predicted by the demographers. This was just as well because the effects of Macmillan's 'Wind of Change' speech in Cape Town in 1960 were beginning to make an impact on Army commitments.

Nationalist leaders in dependent territories came to realise that

their claims to inherit British power depended on their local creden-
tials as men who fought for independence. Revolts in the Aden
Protectorates and in Aden itself began in 1962; the Brunei revolt,
which was to lead to 'Confrontation' with Indonesia, started at the
end of that year; Archbishop Makarios had to call for British help in
Cyprus in 1963, involving the dispatch of 3rd Division, from the
Strategic Reserve – the division was soon to don the blue berets of
the United Nations and come under its command; and at the beginning of 1964, the military mutinies in newly independent Tanzania,
Kenya and Uganda were successfully quelled by Commandos landed
from the carrier *Centaur* and troops from the Strategic Reserve in
Kenya.

In the Far East, Confrontation with Indonesia was handled by
Mountbatten and the Chiefs with exemplary crisis management from
Whitehall, and it was fought with equal skill, economy of force and
patience in the Borneo jungles, which prevented it escalating into all-
out war. Under Luce's successor, Admiral Sir Varyl Begg, force
levels were gradually increased to some 17,000 troops, including
Australians and New Zealanders, supported by a hundred helicopters manned by both the Navy and the RAF – a very small force
with which to defend one thousand miles of jungle-covered frontier.
Air and Naval power as such was not used, but RAF V-Bombers and
major units of the Royal Navy, including carriers, were deployed to
Singapore and had the necessary deterrent effect on Sukarno's government, which disintegrated in 1965, due to internal fighting between its Communist and anti-Communist factions. The whole
campaign was an excellent example of the intelligent use of force,
contributing to the establishment of the stability in South East Asia,
which still endures in the 1990s. Denis Healey summed up the
Services' achievements in the Commons when he said:

> When the House thinks of the tragedy that could have fallen on a whole corner
> of a Continent if we had not been able to hold the situation and bring it to a
> successful termination, it will appreciate that in history books it will be recorded
> as one of the most efficient uses of military force in the history of the world.[18]

In Aden and its Protectorates, it was a very different story. The
emergency was triggered and sustained by three events: the artifici-
ally engineered marriage of convenience between Aden Colony and
its hinterland to form the Federation of South Arabia, which was
consummated with great reluctance in the autumn of 1962; the
Nasser inspired coup in the Yemen, which encouraged the Arab

Nationalist rebellion in Aden itself at the end of 1963; and the announcement by Duncan Sandys, then the Colonial Secretary, of HMG's intention to grant the Federation its independence not later than 1968. Unlike the Borneo campaign, military operations in South Arabia, though fought on behalf of the Federal Government and in conjunction with the Federal Regular Army, were without the support of the local people, who were Nasser supporters almost to a man but divided amongst themselves in the struggle for power in the wake of the British announcement of withdrawal by 1968.

In all these overseas operations, the new Tri-Service Headquarters British Forces in Cyprus, Aden and Singapore responded quickly and effectively to the directions of the Operations Executive in the new Ministry of Defence and proved their worth. It was all a far cry from the cumbersome days of Suez less than a decade earlier, and from the improvisations of the Kuwait intervention. With Queen's enemies to be defeated or restrained, the Chiefs had no difficulty in co-operating whole-heartedly; and with Mountbatten in the Chair, ministers received clear and emphatic advice, and their decisions were swiftly implemented by the new command machinery.

The most significant world event in the early 1960s was the outbreak of the Vietnam War, which was to cause considerable heartsearching amongst the Chiefs: could the Americans be helped, and if so, how? With the Kremlin smarting over its Cuban missile debacle, reductions in BAOR could not be risked, and with counterinsurgency in the Mediterranean, Middle East and South East Asia at a peak, even a token force would have been hard to find if the Government decided that it must show Anglo-American solidarity.

It was not, however, Vietnam but plain budgetary problems that provided Thorneycroft and the Chiefs in the new Ministry of Defence with their first major challenge. The financial savings from ending National Service had been whittled away by escalating equipment costs, which far exceeded the rate of inflation. New technologies were providing more efficient weapons but at prices that were increasing exponentially. In order to find room in the Defence costings for CVA 01, which had been ordered in mid-1963, Polaris, TSR 2, the prototype of which first flew in September 1964, and the Army's Blue Water tactical missile, were in danger of joining Blue Streak on the scrap heap. And despite the Army's over-stretch, plans were being made at the time of the Brunei revolt to reduce the Brigade of Gurkhas rather than cut any more British infantry battalions to save money.

Solving these financial problems, however, was soon to be bequeathed to the Labour Party, which just managed to win the October 1964 General Election after Macmillan had resigned through ill-health and Alec Douglas Home had succeeded him as Prime Minister. Before the General Election, Thorneycroft had insisted that Mountbatten's tenure as CDS should be extended one more year to July 1965, making six years in all, to enable him to see the new organisation through its early teething troubles, and to prevent any sliding back to the old system. This was a far from popular decision. Philip Ziegler is correct in his assessment of the reasons for this:

> But the real cause for disquiet was the fact that Mountbatten was so patently pre-eminent among the Chiefs of Staff, and yet disagreed with them on so many issues, that discussion tended to be unbalanced and opposition overridden. He was, in effect, too big for the job; a circumstance which, it was felt, both impaired the present running of affairs and would make life uncommonly difficult for his successor.[19]

It must also be remembered that he was blocking his chosen successor, Dick Hull, who, in consequence of the extension, had his tenure shortened by a year to maintain the retiring age of senior officers at 60.

The Mountbatten era ended, in effect, when Denis Healey took over as Minister of Defence in the first Wilson Administration. Although he served on for the remaining nine months of his over-long six year tenure, a new era in the history of the Chiefs had begun – the era of Defence Reviews, enforced by Britain's economic decline and by equipment cost inflation.

Mountbatten's achievements should not be underestimated. His personal stature alone enabled him to force through radical and very necessary reforms that would have defeated lesser men. He did not endear himself to his colleagues; nor was his concept of them giving him advice free from single-Service prejudice practicable in the face of their determination to maintain the collective responsibility so dear to the British mode of decision-making. But he did focus and strengthen the power of the military voice in Whitehall as no one else could have done, and from this the whole Chiefs of Staff organisation benefited. His successors were to remember the level of authority that he achieved and tried to emulate it. He brought a wide ranging and experienced mind to bear on the complexities of defence policy, and never allowed the human aspects of war to be overlooked. With all his faults and whatever his methods, he was more often right than wrong, and he must be numbered amongst the most significant British military figures of the century.

The last words of Philip Ziegler's *Mountbatten* seem appropriate here:

> '*He flared brilliantly across the face of the twentieth century; the meteor is extinguished but its glow lingers on in the mind's eye.*'[20]

Chronology
FOR CHAPTER ELEVEN

1964

Oct   Harold Wilson becomes Prime Minister.
Denis Healey becomes S of S for Defence.
Chinese Atomic Bomb tested.

Nov   Sterling crisis (US and IMF loans).
Healey's Defence Review begins.

Dec   First Wilson/Johnson meeting in Washington.

1965

Feb   Cancellation of P1154 and HS681.
US bombing of North Vietnam starts.
Cassels succeeds Hull as CGS.

April   Cancellation of TSR 2.

May   Aircraft-Carrier Working Party set up.

July   Decision to create TA & VR.
Hull succeeds Mountbatten as CDS.

Aug   Gulf of Tongkin incident.

Sep   Indo-Pakistan War over Kashmir.

Nov   Rhodesian UDI.

1966

Jan   RAF win the Carrier debate.

Feb   Healey's first Defence White Paper.
Begg succeeds Luce as First Sea Lord.

March   Second Wilson Government elected.
French withdraw from NATO military command.
Seamen's strike.

July   Sterling crisis.
First Revision of Healey's Defence Review.

Aug	Confrontation with Indonesia ends.

1967

March	Aden's independence brought forward to November.
April	Second Revision of Healey's Defence Review.
	Grandy succeeds Elworthy as CAS.
May	Second application to join the EEC tabled.
June	Arab-Israeli Six Day War.
July	Withdrawal from East of Suez by mid-1970s announced.
Aug	Elworthy succeeds Hull as CDS.
Oct	Dock and Rail strikes.
Nov	Devaluation of Sterling.
	Third Revision of Healey's Defence Review.
	Withdrawal from Aden completed.
Dec	De Gaulle vetoes second EEC Application.

1968

Jan	NATO 'Massive Retaliation' replaced by 'Flexible Response'.
	Withdrawal from East of Suez by end of 1971 announced.
	F 111 order cancelled.
Mar	Baker succeeds Cassels as CGS.
July	Supplementary Statement on Defence (Concentration of Forces in Europe).
	MRCA Project started with Germany, Holland and Italy.
Aug	Soviet invasion of Czechoslovakia.
	Le Fanu succeeds Begg as First Sea Lord.
Sep	NATO Eurogroup formed.

1969

April	De Gaulle resigns.
Aug	British troops intervene in Ulster.
Sep	Gadaffi seizes power in Libya.
Dec	Harrier enters service with the RAF.

1970

June	Heath becomes Prime Minister.
	Carrington becomes S of S for Defence.
July	Dhofar Campaign starts in the Oman.

Hill-Norton becomes First Sea Lord on resignation of
Le Fanu due to ill health.

Nov | Death of de Gaulle.
Death of Le Fanu.

1971

Mar | Pollock succeeds Hill-Norton as First Sea Lord.

April | Hill-Norton succeeds Elworthy as CDS.
Carver succeeds Baker as CGS.
Spotswood succeeds Grandy as CAS.

Aug | Polaris improvement programme approved.
Internment without trial in Ulster.

Oct | China admitted to UN.

Dec | Indo-Pakistan War over East Bengal.

1972

Jan | SALT 1 Agreement.

July | Operation 'Motorman' in Ulster.

1973

Jan | Britain enters EEC.
Withdrawal of US forces from Vietnam begins.

April | *Invincible* ordered.

July | Hunt succeeds Carver as CGS.

Oct | Arab-Israeli Yom Kippur War.
Carver succeeds Hill-Norton as CDS.

Dec | Miners' strike.
Sunningdale Conference on Ulster.

1974

Jan | Three Day Week

March | Ian Gilmour becomes S of S for Defence.
Wilson returns as Prime Minister.
Roy Mason becomes S of S for Defence.
Ashmore succeeds Pollock as First Sea Lord.

Aug | Humphrey succeeds Spotswood as CAS.

Oct | Wilson wins second 1974 General Election.

1975

Feb | Mason Defence Review decisions announced.

July | End of internment without trial in Ulster.

Oct   Healey cuts back Defence Vote.

1976

Feb   Sterling crisis.

Independent European Programme Group established.

March   Callaghan succeeds Wilson as Prime Minister.

April   Last British forces leave South East Asia.

June   Group of Ten loan.

July   Gibbs succeeds Hunt as CGS.

Aug   Cameron succeeds Humphrey as CAS.

Sep   Fred Mulley becomes S of S for Defence.

Oct   Humphrey succeeds Carver as CDS.

Dec   IMF loan.

1977

Jan   Humphrey dies in post of CDS, and is temporarily replaced by Ashmore.

Feb   Lewin succeeds Ashmore as First Sea Lord.

May   NATO 3% increase in Defence spending accepted.

Aug   Beetham succeeds Cameron as CAS.

Cameron succeeds Ashmore as CDS.

Nov   Firemen's strike.

Nuclear submarine sent to Falklands as deterrent to Argentina.

1978

April   First Stage in restoration of Service pay comparability.

Dec   Chiefs recommend Polaris replacement.

1979

Jan   Guadaloupe meeting of Western leaders.

Fall of Shah of Iran.

May   Margaret Thatcher wins 1979 General Election.

11
ECONOMIC DECLINE AND DEFENCE RETRENCHMENT
Labour's Defence Reviews: 1965 to 1979

Secretaries of State		Chiefs of Defence Staff	
Denis Healey	1964	Earl Mountbatten	
Lord Carrington	1970	Sir Richard Hull	1965
Sir Ian Gilmour	Jan 1974	Sir Charles Elworthy	1967
Roy Mason	March 1974	Sir Peter Hill-Norton	1971
Fred Mulley	1976	Sir Michael Carver	1973
		Sir Andrew Humphrey*	1976
		Sir Edward Ashmore	Feb 1977
		Sir Neil Cameron	Aug 1977

First Sea Lords		Chiefs of General Staff	
Sir David Luce		Sir Richard Hull	
Sir Varyl Begg	1966	Sir James Cassels	1965
Sir Michael Le Fanu	1968	Sir George Baker	1968
Sir Peter Hill-Norton	1970	Sir Michael Carver	1971
Sir Michael Pollock	1971	Sir Peter Hunt	1973
Sir Edward Ashmore	1974	Sir Roland Gibbs	1976
Sir Terence Lewin	1977		

Chiefs of Air Staff	
Sir Charles Elworthy	
Sir John Grandy	1967
Sir Dennis Spotswood	1971
Sir Andrew Humphrey	1974
Sir Neil Cameron	1976
Sir Michael Beetham	1977

'I sometimes felt that I had learnt nothing about politics until I met the Chiefs of Staff. Each felt his prime duty was to protect the interests and traditions of his own Service.'

Denis Healey in his Memoirs.[1]

* Died in Office.

The new unified Ministry of Defence had barely time to settle in before the October 1964 General Elections brought the first Wilson Government into office with a wafer thin overall majority of four seats. Denis Healey became Secretary of State for Defence, and the Chiefs, although they could not know it at the time, were about to endure the final traumatic spasm in Britain's metamorphosis from an Imperial into a European power. Its pangs were to last for fifteen painful years, but the process was never quite completed: the Thatcher era and the Falklands Campaign came just in time to save Britain's world-wide maritime capability from extinction.

In those fifteen years, which covered the two Wilson Administrations, divided by the Heath interlude and brought to an end by the fall of James Callaghan's Government in 1979, the Chiefs' influence was weakened – at least in relative terms – by the appearance of two new centres of power within the new Ministry of Defence that developed in the wake of unification.

The first was the PUS's unified Defence Secretariat, which at last acquired the staff, machinery and expertise not only to establish some real control over the allocation of resources, but also to take the lead in politico-military affairs such as nuclear weapons policy, and in establishing positions to be taken by British representatives at international fora like NATO, CENTO, SEATO and the United Nations. This was all part of the strengthening of the Centre, but its effects went wider than that: it weakened the ability of the Service Departments to fight their corners. In the old style Service Ministries, the staff officers and civil servants had worked in close-knit teams loyal to their particular Service's interests. The former provided the operational experience and judgement, and the latter the forensic skills and continuity. In the new unified ministry, the civil servants' loyalties were primarily to the Centre, and so the responsibility for arguing the Naval, Army and Air cases fell more heavily on the Service officers' shoulders than hitherto.

This change hit the Navy Department hardest. Unlike the Army and Air Force, the Navy used to pay scant attention to staff training, which was not part of Naval culture nor an important factor in the selection and promotion of its officers. The Admiralty depended upon complimenting the sea-going experience of the Naval Staff with the disciplined minds and bureaucratic skills of the Admiralty Secretariat, the traditions of which stretched back to the days of Samuel Pepys. In the new Ministry of Defence, overdeveloped single-Service loyalties were at a discount amongst the abler and more ambitious civil servants; and so the Naval Staff was left to construct its own arguments, which it was ill-prepared to do during the first few years of unification.

In contrast, the Air Force had always accepted the need for staff training, not only to handle the galloping technological problems of the complex air-warfare environment, but also to provide a cadre of able men with the debating and propagandist skills to help it in the many battles for survival that it had waged since Trenchard's day. In the mid-1960s, it was further helped by the fortuitous appearance in its most senior ranks of officers who had joined the RAF from the legal profession just before the war and had stayed on afterwards. Sir Charles Elworthy, a New Zealander with legal training, had taken over as Chief of Air Staff from Sir Thomas Pike in September 1963, and was more than a match for the reticent First Sea Lord, Sir David Luce. Just as charming and straightforward as Luce, 'Sam' Elworthy had the determination and clarity of mind to overrun the Naval Staff in the gruelling debates that were to engulf the Chiefs during the Healey period. He was ably supported by Air Vice-Marshal Peter Fletcher, the Assistant Chief of Air Staff (Policy), who was also legally trained.

The Army Department policy-making machinery lay somewhere between the two. The Army had been the first to emulate the German General Staff system in the early years of the century, and staff training was a fundamental requirement for selection to higher command. The General Staff, however, tended to look upon its civil servants as agents of the Treasury: indeed, in Kitchener's day, there was often open conflict between the two sides in the War Office. After the Second World War, a General Staff Secretariat was formed, but it never acquired the power and influence of the Admiralty and Air Staff Secretariats, and Army staff officers were far less dependent on, if not, in some instances, actually hostile to, their civilian colleagues. Fortunately, the Army had usually been in a neutral position between the warring factions of admirals and air marshals, and tended to umpire rather than enter their disputes. War Office battles were fought over entirely different issues illustrated by the old adage that the Navy and Air Force manned equipment – and increasingly expensive equipment at that – whereas the Army equipped men, making manpower more important than weapons, although this was changing by the mid-1960s as the Army was slowly becoming more capital intensive.

The second centre of power in the unified Ministry was the Chief

Scientific Adviser's growing weapons and equipment empire, built up by Sir Solly Zuckerman, the executive centre of which was the powerful Weapons Development Committee, whose endorsement was needed at every stage from a weapon's conception to its birth. Although the WDC was tasked by the Operational Requirements Committee, which was, in theory at least, responsible to the Chiefs of Staff, it and its numerous sub-committees became a law unto themselves and something of a no-go area for technological laymen like the Chiefs. As the sophistication and soaring cost of weapons began to devour an increasing percentage of the Defence vote, the Chief Scientific Adviser's influence grew in the *Troika* of principal advisers (CDS, PUS and CSA) to the Secretary of State.

Zuckerman divided his time between being Chief Scientific Adviser to the Ministry of Defence and adviser to Harold Wilson. Healey, however, found him as devious as Mountbatten to work with and engineered his 'elevation' to being Chief Scientific Adviser to the Government only. His duties were divided between his two immediate subordinates, Sir William Cook and Sir Alan Cottrell. Cook had been in the Atomic Energy Authority before joining the Ministry of Defence in 1964. His title was changed to Chief Adviser (Projects and Research). Cottrell became Chief Adviser (Studies). Asked to describe his job, Bill Cook replied '*to see that the programme we undertake on equipment in the Ministry of Defence represents good value for money.*'[2] This was no mean task since the equipment programmes provided the most fruitful search areas in the quest for the Whitehall's Holy Grail – more defence for less money – during the fifteen years of retrenchment in Defence funding.

But these new centres of power made less impact upon the Chiefs – Mountbatten, Luce, Hull and Elworthy – than Denis Healey's appointment as Secretary of State. He arrived in office with the force of personality and intellectual ability to run the new Ministry as its un-disputed master. He had done his homework as a shadow minister in Defence and Foreign Affairs during Labour's long years in opposition. He knew the principle defence policy-makers in the United States as well as in Britain, and he had a close rapport with Robert McNamara, the United States Secretary of Defense, whose industrial cost-analysis methods were in keeping with his own analytical turn of mind. Moreover, his experiences as a Sapper officer in the Mediterranean Theatre during the Second World War gave him a feel for military practicality. But above all, he was able to couple a grasp of technological detail with mastery of wider issues – he did, in truth, see the wood for the trees!

In happier economic times – if such times ever exist – he and the Chiefs would have made a powerful team. As it was, the need for massive retrenchment led, at times, to confrontations between them as the country struggled to divest itself of the trappings of Empire and to become an off-shore island of Europe or perhaps of America if the French veto remained in force.

At the same time, despite Mountbatten's urgings, Healey was not prepared to carry out any further reorganisation of his ministry, preferring to work it as he found it. In his Memoirs, he says:

> The one issue on which Mountbatten and I were always at odds was his determination to get rid of the separate Service Chiefs of Staff and establish single central organisations to carry out the administrative functions of the three Services. . . .
>
> Throughout my six years as Defence Secretary, we were coping with massive reductions in our defence capability and commitments; I did not think it made sense to carry out an appendix operation on a man while he was lifting a grand piano. . . .
>
> I suspected, too, that behind Mountbatten's obsession with integrating the Services was the desire to establish central control of defence policy and operations under himself as Chief of Defence Staff. In my opinion, it was the Secretary of State's job to control defence policy, as an elected member of the British Cabinet, and I was determined to carry it out. Experience in many fields has convinced me that abstract arguments for one form of organisation or another count for little compared with the personal qualities of the individuals available for the key jobs.[3]

Hull, who had disliked many of the Mountbatten reforms, encouraged Healey in this view. When he eventually took over from Mountbatten as CDS in July 1965, he tended to allow power to drift back to the Service Departments, confining himself to acting strictly as Chairman of the Chiefs. He sought consensus and eschewed the role of supremo that Mountbatten coveted; and he accepted the general view that there had been enough change for the time being, and that there should be no further moves towards functionalisation unless a very strong case could be made for it in specific fields.

Some modest organisational changes were, however, made in Healey's time, spurred on no doubt by pressure from Labour colleagues to build on Mountbatten's reforming zeal. 1969 brought a strengthening of the Centre in the Personnel and Logistics fields; and in 1970, a report by Derek Rayner (now Lord Rayner) of Marks & Spencer led to the establishment of the Procurement Executive directly responsible to the Secretary of State, which consolidated the

weapons and equipment centre of power as a quasi-autonomous
body with Rayner himself as its first Chief Executive. In 1977, well
after Healey's period in office, the PUS's power base was reinforced
by the creation of the Financial Planning and Management Group
under his chairmanship and with the Chiefs as members. This was a
significant move in linking policy and management. It was designed
to match the programmes put forward by Service Departments to the
resources available as expressed in the Long Term Costings (LTC),
and it did, in fact, provide machinery for cutting many a Gordian
knot caused by inter-Service rivalry.

The advent of the Wilson Government did not alarm the Chiefs
unduly. They had anxieties about the Labour Party's split mentality
over nuclear weapons; about its harping upon wasteful 'prestige'
projects and 'sacred cows'; and about its constant reference to the
need to switch resources from Defence to the Social Services. But on
the credit side, there seemed to be an encouraging emphasis on
conventional forces, with a chance of burying the Sandys philosophy
with its nuclear bias once and for all; on the need to cut commitments to reduce the Services' overstretch; and on the need to improve their equipment. Mountbatten, for one, welcomed the return of
a Labour Government with equanimity if not enthusiasm: he could
hardly do otherwise after his close association with Attlee in bringing
independence to India, and his opposition to Eden over Suez.

The Chiefs' guarded optimism was not un-justified. Wilson,
Gordon Walker (Foreign Secretary) and Healey saw themselves as
the heirs to Attlee, Bevin and Shinwell, and were just as determined
as they had been to retain Britain's world-wide influence, and to
maintain a military presence East of Suez together with the British
nuclear deterrent, which they accepted was not truly independent.
They believed, as the Attlee Cabinet had done in the late 1940s, that
an economic plan based on sound socialist principles could restore
the country's prosperity and power, provided the incubus of Defence
spending could be lightened by more efficient management, which
Healey was confident he could provide.

Healey did, in fact, provide the better management needed, but his
side of the equation was repeatedly undermined by the failure of the
economy to respond to George Brown's much heralded but rushed
National Economic Plan; to Frank Cousin's efforts in the new
Ministry of Technology; and to James Callaghan's financial administration as Chancellor of the Exchequer. The Healey Defence Review,
which started almost as soon as he took office, became a rolling

programme of studies with three major revisions – all downwards as far as the Defence Vote was concerned.

Healey and his ministerial team (his two functional Ministers – one for the armed forces as a whole and the other for equipment policy – and the three Under-Secretaries of State for the Navy, Army and Air Force) had barely time to absorb their initial briefings by officials before two immediate problems reared up in front of them. The sterling crisis of the autumn of 1964, largely caused by loss of confidence in the world's money markets by Labour's election victory, forced immediate action to stem the financial haemorrhage. And at the same time, the Americans resumed their pressure for London's approval of the NATO Multilateral Nuclear Force (MNF) so that Bonn's agreement could be sought before the forthcoming German elections. Both issues involved Healey's team and the Chiefs. Righting the economy required, as ever, cuts in the Defence spending; and the nuclear force argument was important because it could lead to 'renegotiating' the Nassau Agreement on Polaris, which Wilson had promised during the election campaign.

The two issues – economy and defence – were thrashed out at Chequers, with all the Chiefs in attendance, over the weekend of 20–22 November 1964, known for obvious reasons as the 'Crunch' meeting. Callaghan managed to impose a £2,000m ceiling (at 1964 prices) on Defence spending, which was £400m or 20 per cent off the former government's Defence estimates. But as pay, allowances and pensions absorb more than half the Defence Vote and cannot produce short-term savings, it was the equipment programmes that had to suffer a swingeing 40 per cent cut, which could only be met by abandoning major projects. The Treasury had its eyes on the Fleet Carrier CVA 01 and on the TSR 2, which it saw as the sacred cows of the Navy and Air Departments, but which Luce and Elworthy believed were the 'capital ships' upon which the future fighting efficiency of their Services would depend.

There could be no question of cancelling either CVA 01 or TSR 2 without the full-dress Defence Review, which Healey had already in mind. Immediate savings came from the cancellation of the P1154, the supersonic version of the Harrier, and the HS681, the medium range transport aircraft, and their replacement by cheaper, more efficient and readily available American Phantoms and Hercules. Delays and rising development costs in both British projects had, in truth, been embarrassing Elworthy and the Air Staff, who saw the American buy as sensible. They had, in fact, suggested to Ministers

before the change of government that it might be more cost-effective
to order the US TFX, which became the F-111, rather than continue
with the TSR 2.

The nuclear issue was much more difficult. Before deciding
whether to support the American Multilateral Force (MLF), the
Cabinet had to decide whether to stay in the nuclear deterrent
business at all. As a Shadow Cabinet, they had favoured accepting
an American nuclear monopoly on behalf of the West, provided a
way could be found of giving British governments, present and
future, an effective voice in the control of the Western deterrent. At
the 'Crunch' meeting there were advocates for phasing out Polaris,
but the majority of the Cabinet were swayed by the recent Chinese
atomic bomb test, which had taken place while they had been fighting the General Election. Healey, with the Chiefs' support, clinched
the argument by accepting four instead of the proposed five Polaris
submarines as a viable force.

With Polaris secure, at least for the time being, Healey went on to
propose the replacement of the American MLF plan with what he
called an Atlantic Nuclear Force (ANF), to which Britain would
assign her Polaris boats and her V Bombers, as long as the United
States and, perhaps, France would make comparable contributions.
The non-nuclear NATO powers could help to crew land-based missiles and aircraft if they so wished. When Wilson put the proposal to
the newly elected President Johnson during his first visit to
Washington as British Prime Minister in December, Johnson agreed
to study the idea and gave Wilson the job of selling it to Bonn. Bonn
had already gone cold on the MLF, but would not accept the ANF
idea, enabling Franz Josef Strauss to quip that this was the first time
in history that a fleet, not yet created, had torpedoed another fleet,
which did not exist!

Despite the lack of personal rapport between Johnson and Wilson,
and American suspicion of the Labour Party, the new United States
Administration agreed to support Britain financially. It was in
American interests to keep British forces in Europe and East of Suez,
with the possibility of sending troops to help in Vietnam, and to
encourage the buying of American equipment, not only for the economic benefit of the United States, but also as a route towards the
standardisation of NATO armaments. Broad hints were dropped
that, in return for Britain abandoning such costly prestige projects as
Concorde and TSR 2, dollar offset agreements might be possible to
ease the purchase of alternative American equipments.

Wilson baulked at Johnson's request for a British contingent in Vietnam in spite of the precedent of the Korean War. Seeing himself donning Eden's mantle as co-chairman of a Geneva style conference to settle the conflict through negotiation with Moscow and Peking, Wilson was reluctant to compromise his neutrality. In this he had the support of the Chiefs for two much sounder reasons. The Army was already overstretched with 50,000 men East of Suez and fighting still going on in Borneo and in the Aden Protectorate; and the Chiefs themselves were convinced that Western powers could no longer impose political solutions in Asia by military means at a cost acceptable to their electorates.

Buying American was far from unpopular amongst the Chiefs. A general consensus had been building up in Whitehall for some time that Britain could no longer go it alone in major advanced armament projects. It was not that she lacked the technology or productive capacity to do so, but research and development costs were becoming uneconomic unless spread over larger production runs than British requirements and potential export markets could support. International collaboration was essential, and, as yet, the European armament industry was not far enough advanced to provide a real alternative to collaboration with America.

Ministry of Defence/Pentagon relationships were as warm as those between Downing Street and the White House were cold. The Chiefs on both sides of the Atlantic were still men who had fought together during the war and respected each other; and Healey and McNamara were able to speak frankly to each other, both being convinced of the merits of operational and cost-effectiveness analysis as a means of slaughtering military sacred cows. Healey, who had accompanied Wilson on his first Washington visit in December 1964, soon established the close Healey/McNamara partnership through which Anglo-American systems were improved for pooling research and development work, and for negotiating financial offset arrangements to enable Britain to buy US equipment when it was militarily and economically sensible to do so. It was only to be a matter of weeks, however, before the effectiveness of their collaboration was to be tested.

As soon as Healey returned to London, he set in train the preliminary studies for the Defence Review agreed at the Chequers 'Crunch' meeting. Unlike the Sandys' Defence Review, he was not at loggerheads with the Chiefs, who understood the need for retrenchment and were only concerned that whatever measures were agreed upon would be militarily sound and balanced in the light of the country's dire economic circumstances. Nor did he act as an opinionated one-man band as Sandys had done; every proposal was carefully examined and argued through with the Chiefs, the PUS and the Chief Adviser (Projects and Research).

This first review had three aims: reducing the strain on the nation's economy; lessening operational over-stretch; and shaping a new Defence policy for the 1970s. The Ministry of Defence was to concentrate upon pruning the Defence budget, and determining the optimum mix of forces that could be sustained within the £2,000m ceiling. Concurrently, the political departments were to seek ways of reducing overseas military commitments. The two strands of the review were closely interconnected and reacted upon one another as the work went forward. They were woven together by the Defence and Overseas Policy Committee, but such was the power of Healey's personal contributions that it became known as his review.

The political assumptions for the review were set out in the 1965 Defence White Paper, and made interesting reading some 25 years later when events had turned full circle. The threat to Western Europe, and hence to the United Kingdom, was deemed to be low, thanks to mutual nuclear deterrence between East and West. Greater threats to British interests lay in the instability of areas of the world beyond NATO's boundaries. Furthermore, Britain had obligations to go to the aid of newly independent Commonwealth countries and former protectorates if they were threatened by local predators.

What the White Paper did not spell out was the Wilson Cabinet's determination not to abandon Britain's world role, nor to renege on Commonwealth and other defence agreements. Speaking in the Commons in December 1964, he had said:

> I want to make it quite clear that whatever we do in the field of cost effectiveness, value for money, and a stringent review of expenditure, we cannot afford to relinquish our world role which for shorthand purposes is sometimes called our 'East of Suez' role.[4]

Before the new size and shape of the Forces could be looked at, two major decisions had to be studied, debated and decided: the futures of the TSR 2 and CVA 01, which were interconnected in that both the Air and Naval Staffs were building their case for them on the East of Suez role. Healey decided to tackle the TSR 2 problem first.

Since the TSR 2's inception in 1957 as a replacement for the Canberra, the Air Staff had demanded optimum performance in what they saw as their future 'capital' aircraft once the V-Bombers were phased out; and the Defence scientists had tried to meet the Air Staff requirements by exploiting technology up to, and in some respects beyond, its current frontiers, but without adopting the Barns Wallace swing-wing, which the Americans were exploiting in their rival, the F-111. The specifications were complicated by a decision in 1963, in the wake of the Nassau Polaris Agreement, to give the aircraft a nuclear delivery capability. This entailed adding a low-level terrain-following capability to penetrate below the Soviet radar defences.

The British aircraft industry, quite naturally, aided and abetted this gilding of the TSR 2 lily. It enjoyed the challenge as much as the scientists, and, of course, it benefited from the research and development funds poured into the project by the Air Department. Efforts to attract other customers, however, like the Royal Australian Air Force, failed in the face of American competition and salesmanship, lauding their swing-wing F-111 as better and cheaper. The estimated production cost of TSR 2 per aircraft soared to a point where the loss of a single aircraft could have been seen as a near national disaster.

Healey was not the only one to decide enough was enough. Mountbatten had always been against the TSR 2, ever since his days as First Sea Lord when both Duncan Sandys and Harold Watkinson had failed to insist on the Air Ministry collaborating with the Admiralty in the development of the highly successful NA 39, the Buccaneer. He did more than anyone else, and much to Elworthy's fury, to hammer the nails into the TSR 2's coffin by discouraging, perhaps inadvertently, the Australians from buying it through his advocacy of the Buccaneer. Solly Zuckerman had always had doubts not only about the technical feasibility of the TSR 2, but also of the operational concept of preparing to fight a nuclear war instead of deterring it with strategic weapons like Polaris. Luce and Hull were both anti-TSR 2, not for operational reasons but because it was absorbing too great a slice of the Defence Vote: its demise would help to deflect the Healey axe from their own equipment projects. Even some members of the Air Staff had come to realise that the Buccaneer had been the right answer all along, but cancellation of TSR 2 would leave the RAF without a modern aircraft when the Russians were re-equipping with MIGs and the French with Mirages.

Healey demonstrated his decisiveness by recommending the cancellation of TSR 2, the prototype of which had first flown in September 1964, on grounds of cost-effectiveness. The courage of that decision should not be under-estimated. So much British political capital, as well as £400m, already sunk in TSR 2 would be wasted, and with the earlier axing of the P1154 and HS 681, the future of the British aircraft industry would be placed in jeopardy. Wilson was so worried by the political implications that he insisted on the cancellation announcement being made by the Chancellor of the Exchequer amongst the austerity measures presented to the Commons in April 1965 rather than as part of the Defence Review.

The pill was sugared for the RAF by the promise to buy fifty of the supposedly cheaper American F 111s as a stop-gap until an Anglo-French 'Variable Geometry' aircraft could be brought into service in the late 1970s. With hindsight it is now possible to see that both the British and American solutions to the tactical strike/reconnaissance requirement were flawed. The fixed-wing TSR 2 was ahead of its time, but much of the experience gained in developing it went eventually into the European collaborative Multi-Role Combat Aircraft – the MRCA, later called the Tornado. The swing-wing F 111 proved very much more difficult and expensive to produce than the Americans expected. Swing-wing technology became dated: new light-weight materials, not available in the 1960s, have made the fixed delta-wing the preferred option in the 1990s.

The battle of the TSR 2 had been a one-sided affair, with the Air Staff and Air Industry, with their backs to the wall, against the rest. The Carrier battle, which opened shortly afterwards, was a brutal gladiatorial contest in which the Navy and Air Force were fighting each other for their lives. The Air Staff, used to battles for survival, was experienced in such contests, and its leaders, Sam Elworthy and Peter Fletcher with their legal training, had the edge over Luce and the Naval Staff. Mountbatten, who might perhaps have swayed the issue in the Navy's favour, was in the last few months of his tenure as CDS and had been diverted by Harold Wilson to head a commission, touring the Commonwealth, to devise new immigration policies.

In grappling with the carrier problem, Healey adopted the usual Whitehall ploy of setting up a working party to establish the facts, which were shrouded in specious arguments and special pleading. The question was: could the RAF, using American F 111s, which had not yet flown, let alone been bought, support the Army in operations East of Suez, using island airfields, which had not yet been built in the Indian Ocean, more cheaply than the Navy using carriers, which the country was unlikely to be able to afford anyway?

Healey could not have been fairer to the Navy in that he appointed as its chairman the Deputy Chief of Naval Staff, the blunt, irascible, experienced aviator, Vice-Admiral Sir Frank Hopkins. The Admiralty Board, however, had learnt little or nothing from the demise of TSR 2, and seemed unable to appreciate fully the bleakness of the economic climate. They were not prepared to lower their sights to smaller carriers, like today's *Invincible* class, nor to emulate the Air Department's buy of F 111s by purchasing the smallish American *Essex* class carriers that were available at the time for a fraction of the cost of the CVA 01 class. Having previously beaten Duncan Sandys and Thorneycroft over the carrier issue, they were over-confident in the strength of their subjective case, based upon Naval judgement, which did not impress Healey nearly as much as the Air Department's objective reasoning that relied on cost-analysis.

The Hopkins working party studied a wide spectrum of scenarios, but the initial results were equivocal: land based aircraft could undertake many of the carrier's tasks but not all of them. The argument was carried on in the Chiefs of Staff Committee, sometimes with the Prime Minister present. New scenarios were studied, in which the Navy has always claimed that the Indian Ocean island of Aldabra was shifted 600 miles to suit the shore-based aircraft case! Whether this was so or not, the Navy made one fatal error: it based its case primarily on supporting amphibious operations East of Suez without making enough play with the use of carriers in anti-submarine warfare in the North Atlantic and Norwegian Sea. In consequence, the Air Staff could show that carriers were a prohibitively expensive way of supporting the Army in the comparatively few extreme scenarios when shore-based aircraft could not reach a potential trouble spot East of Suez. The Falklands were not mentioned!

Hopkins was not helped by the ambivalence within his own department. The Air Staff opposed CVA 01 because, in their view, it was un-affordable and should be killed. Luce, on the other hand, took a placatory stance. Diplomatic by nature and a submariner by profession, he lacked the personal commitment to naval aviation to lead an effective counter-offensive. He felt that Mountbatten had tended to alienate the Air Staff unnecessarily, and he preferred a more statesmanlike approach. He argued that the F 111s and carriers were complimentary, and that means had to be found to fund them both. The Admiralty defence was further weakened by it being known that some of the Naval Staff feared the retention of the carriers would force reductions in other ships and submarines, and the Second Sea Lord's staff, with its responsibility for personnel, doubted whether the carriers could be fully manned anyway.

Before the final decision on carriers was taken, Hull had succeeded Mountbatten as CDS. He was impressed by the operational as well as cost-effectiveness arguments. With three carriers in commission, there could only be one stationed East of Suez; it would only be able to deliver a punch equivalent to three F 111s; and it would take days rather than hours to reach an operational area. To make military sense, five carriers would be needed and this was far beyond the realms of practical politics.

Zuckerman was only pro-carrier to the extent that he believed that if the operational case was proved for them, the surplus American *Essex* carriers should be bought on the favourable terms being offered by McNamara. In Healey's view the operational case was not proven. In his memoirs, he concludes:

> I commissioned innumerable studies to find out whether it was possible to perform the carrier's function with the existing RAF aircraft. The answer was that, in most places which concerned us, we could support land operations more cheaply and effectively with land-based aircraft. Moreover, our political commitments would not be affected if we renounced the option of landing or withdrawing troops against sophisticated air opposition, outside the range of friendly land-based aircraft.[5]

Healey advised the Cabinet to cancel CVA 01, but he was sufficiently impressed with the arguments for the use of carriers East of Suez, certainly until the necessary island airfields had been built on Diego Garcia or Aldabra, to agree to an expensive refit for *Ark Royal*, and to run on the lives of *Victorious*, *Eagle* and *Hermes* into the mid-1970s.

In the meantime, the Army had not been left unscathed. The Regular Army was certainly overstretched and its re-equipment programme, started by Harold Watkinson, was virtually complete, so there were no obvious savings to be made there, but the large Territorial Army was an anachronism in the nuclear era. With war in Europe, if it occurred, only likely to last a matter of weeks rather than months, there would be no time to give the Territorial divisions – the heirs of the trained-bands of London and yeomanry and militia of the shires – the training that they would need before being dispatched to the Continent. Only troops ready, trained and equipped, would be of much use to BAOR on mobilization. A root and branch reorganisation of the TA was certainly needed, but Hull's successor as CGS, General Sir James Cassels (later Field Marshal), was hardly the man to tackle such an emotionally fraught task.

Cassels was well cast as the professional head of the Army and was liked and respected as a first class front-line soldier, but he was a most reluctant head of the General Staff. His father had been C-in-C, India, and he himself had commanded successfully three different divisions in three separate wars: the Highland Division in the Rhineland battles towards the end of the Second World War; the 6th Airborne Division in Palestine in 1946/7; and the Commonwealth Division in Korea. Before taking over as CGS, he had been Adjutant-General, one of the few jobs behind a desk that he found congenial because it enabled him to improve conditions of service and quality of life in the Army, but it had also added to his disenchantment with Whitehall. By the time he became CIGS, he was a spent force, and did not have the stomach to slaughter the many historic, but redundant, regiments of the outdated TA.

There were, however, two men in the Army Department who saw the need for change and had the ruthlessness to carry it through in the face of determined opposition from Lords-Lieutenant, Colonels of Regiments and the TA's many supportive lobbies throughout the country: General Sir John (Shan) Hackett, the Deputy Chief of General Staff, and Major-General Michael Carver (later Field Marshal Lord Carver, a future CGS and CDS), the Director of Staff Duties, responsible for the organisation of the Army. They jointly became known in TA circles as 'Shackett and Carver', and a tie with crossed hatchets and carvers was produced in their honour! They amalgamated the TA with the Army Emergency Reserve to form the much smaller Territorial Army and Volunteer Reserve (TA & VR), designed to provide immediate reinforcements for BAOR and for Home Defence. The old TA just had to go, however much it might symbolize the volunteer spirit of the nation.

The review of commitments undertaken by the political departments lagged behind the work of the Ministry of Defence, lacking, as it did, the driving force and intellectual inspiration of Healey. Events rather than constructive forward thinking produced the few new policies that did emerge. Aden was clearly becoming untenable as a base in the face of hostile Arab nationalism, whereas Singapore welcomed the British presence as a stabilising influence in South East Asia. The Vietnam war was going from bad to worse, confirming the soundness of the Chiefs' view that the West could no longer use force in Asia to gain its own ends. And the Wilson Government was embarrassed by Ian Smith's declaration of UDI in November 1965. Labour's slender majority in the Commons precluded any idea of using military force against the rebel régime, and made political and economic pressures the only acceptable, but abortive, counter-measures.

Three political conclusions were drawn from these events, which were enshrined in the Defence Review, published in February 1966 as the annual Defence White Paper. The first principle was not new and had been generally accepted as axiomatic since Suez: Britain would not undertake major military operations except in co-operation with allies. The second stemmed from the coming demise of the carriers: obligations to help other countries would not be undertaken by Britain unless the states concerned were prepared to provide the facilities to make assistance effective – seizing points of entry for an intervention force was to be avoided, as was any oper-ation outside land-based air cover. And the third was directly appli-cable to Aden and Singapore: there would be no attempt to maintain defence facilities in an independent country against its wishes.[6]

There would be a general pruning of overseas garrisons, and a complementary strengthening of intervention forces held in the United Kingdom – the Army's Strategic Reserve, the RAF's Transport Command and the Navy's amphibious forces. The Aden base would be abandoned when South Arabia became independent in 1968; but the Singapore base would be retained for as long as the Malaysian and Singapore Governments agreed to its retention on acceptable terms. Exploratory talks were begun to see whether it would be practicable to establish an alternative East of Suez base in Australia.

The Wilson Government had satisfied the Johnson Administration in Washington by staying for the time being East of Suez, but in the subsequent Parliamentary debates, an increasing number of voices expressed doubts about the practicability and usefulness of doing so. Both the First Sea Lord and his political master, the First Lord, Christopher Mayhew, resigned for different but interconnected reasons. Luce felt compelled to do so over the carrier issue, and Mayhew because he believed that the country could not afford to stay East of Suez, but that if the Cabinet decided to do so, a new generation of carriers would be essential. Their resignations caused scarcely a ripple in Westminster, confirming that if the Chiefs ever wished to obtain political advantage by threat or actual resignation, it would have to be a unanimous and collective act.

Luce's successor was Sir Varyl Begg, who had succeeded him as C-in-C British Forces Far East in 1963 and was C-in-C Portsmouth at the time Luce resigned. He was a far tougher personality, an outstanding naval commander, and well versed in the ways of Whitehall. As VCNS, he had accompanied Solly Zuckerman to Washington to put the flesh on the bare bones of the Nassau Agreement on Polaris. He was pragmatic and realistic in his approach, and he set himself the task of repairing the damage done to the morale of the Fleet by the cancellation of CVA 01, which had been central to the Navy's plans for its future and its self-image. He believed that the carrier decision had come two decades too early, but that their demise, in the longer term, was inevitable in the light of aircraft and missile developments.

The debate was curtailed by the General Election of March 1966, which was won by Harold Wilson, this time with a handsome majority of almost a hundred seats. During the election campaign, a sea-change in the public's view of Britain's position and role in the world became evident: imperial nostalgia was giving way to a reluctant realisation that the country's future might lie in Europe. There was also growing pro-European enthusiasm amongst economists and industrialists, not stemming from any new-found love for Europe, but from the fear of exclusion from such a large and potentially lucrative market on Britain's doorstep. There was unjustified confidence that the country's feather-bedded work-force and overmanned industry could compete successfully in Europe's regenerated economy; and that if this did not prove to be the case, the harsh winds of competition would blow Britain's industrial cobwebs away.

The election result showed approval of Labour's policies so far, but this confidence was not reflected in the international financial markets nor in the banking world; and their jaundiced view of George Brown's National Economic Plan was not helped by the short-sighted policies of the British Trades Unions. All the savings made by Defence in 1965 were squandered in the series of damaging industrial strikes that marred the second Wilson administration, and turned Healey's original Defence Review into a rolling programme of retrenchment.

The election result had another less obvious effect with which the Chiefs had to contend for the rest of the 1960s and most of the 1970s. In Wilson's first administration, the Left Wing was muzzled by Labour's dangerously small majority. The new margin of 96 seats enabled Labour backbenchers to voice their disquiet about the Government's determination to maintain Britain's world-wide role and about its retention of what they saw as a Tory nuclear weapons policy. It also encouraged anti-nuclear lobbyists outside Parliament, like CND, to reinforce their attacks on defence policy.

Healey was forced into three major revisions of his original 1965/6 Defence Review. Just two months after the 1966 General Election, Wilson had to fight off a Parliamentary Labour Party resolution, deploring Britain's continued presence East of Suez. Much more damaging was the Seamen's Strike which started in March and led to the Sterling crisis of July. The Treasury demanded a £100m cut in overseas expenditure, most of which had to come from Defence as it was the principal spender of hard currency. This time, it so happened that the Chiefs could find the savings demanded relatively painlessly because the Borneo Campaign was fizzling out and would release sizeable forces before long. They were also helped by the increasing range and carrying capacity of RAF Transport Command, which would enable them to reduce overseas garrisons still further and depend on meeting commitments East of Suez from the Strategic Reserve in the United Kingdom.

But this first and relatively painless revision of the Defence Review did not satisfy the Labour Left wing, the Tory pro-European lobbyists or the Treasury. So while Harold Wilson and George Brown set off on their tour round Western European capitals to gather support for a second application to join the Common Market, Healey tasked the Chiefs to look into the practicability of disengaging completely from East of Suez as his critics demanded, thus starting the second revision of his Defence Review.

The Chiefs, wisely as it turned out, concluded that such a disengagement made military as well as political sense, and that a phased withdrawal could be carried out, halving the forces East of Suez by 1971 and withdrawing all but a small residual force, based largely in Australia, and backed by the Strategic Reserve in the United Kingdom by the mid-1970s. In spite of Foreign Office protests, the Cabinet accepted the plan in April 1967, subject to negotiations with Washington and Britain's SEATO allies. The decision was by no means unanimous: for instance, Barbara Castle and Richard Crossman, reflecting the feelings of the Left, argued for a swifter withdrawal. The American and Commonwealth Governments, when consulted, did quite the opposite, demanding reconsideration of the decision and a slowing down of Britain's departure from South East Asia.

The Arab/Israeli Six Day War in June 1967 clinched the matter by showing how little power Britain still had to influence affairs in the Middle East, and by inflicting further damage to the ailing

British economy through the closure of the Suez Canal, which forced Britain to buy oil from expensive American sources in dollars. In July, the 1967 Supplementary Statement on Defence announced withdrawal from East of Suez by the mid-1970s, thus ending the second Defence Review revision. The Army was to bear the brunt of the cuts, starting a run-down, which, by 1971, would have taken its strength down from over 200,000 to around the figure of 165,000, set by Duncan Sandys 14 years earlier. 17 major fighting units were to go – four armoured, four artillery, one engineer and eight infantry – by the time the withdrawal was complete. In his concluding paragraph Healey gave a hostage to fortune:

> We have been working continuously for almost three years on a major review of defence, revising Britain's overseas policy, formulating the role of military power to support it, and planning the forces to carry out this role. This statement marks the end of the process.[7]

But all withdrawals tend to snowball once they have begun, and Britain's from East of Suez was no exception.

During 1967 and 1968 there were a number of changes amongst the Chiefs. In April 1967, Sir John Grandy, a Battle of Britain fighter squadron commander, who had been a sound and respected tri-Service C-in-C in the Far East since 1965, became CAS to free Sam Elworthy to take over from Dick Hull as CDS in August. In March 1968, Jim Cassels was relieved as CGS by Sir George Baker, a most likeable Gunner and an extremely able soldier, who had made his name as Director of Operations in Cyprus under John Harding. And in August that year, Sir Michael Le Fanu, the C-in-C, Middle East, succeeded Varyl Begg as First Sea Lord after successfully completing the withdrawal from Aden in November 1967. Le Fanu was the Navy's choice to be Elworthy's successor as CDS in three years time. Begg went out to Gibraltar as Governor and C-in-C in 1969, just as Franco had slammed the frontier gates shut and started the long 15th Siege of the Rock in retaliation for Britain granting the Gibraltarians internal self-government.

Healey described Le Fanu as '*a ginger-haired practical joker sometimes introducing himself as the Chinese Admiral Le Fan Yew*'.[8] He was certainly a most unusual and colourful naval officer: an exceptional leader and administrator with an exhilarating lightness of touch; widely read and with many interests outside service life; witty, with a talent for pithy verse; and an aptitude for putting his point of view over to politicians. One of his most endearing characteristics was his great love for his wife, who had been crippled by polio in her youth. He would take her everywhere in her wheeled chair, and carry her himself up gangways for social functions with the Fleet. Sadly he died of leukaemia before he could succeed Elworthy as CDS.[9]

The new team of Chiefs, who, under Elworthy's chairmanship, worked extremely well together, was to implement the third, final and even more traumatic revision of Healey's Defence Review. In October 1967, the crippling Dock and Rail Strikes, coming on top of the closure of the Suez Canal, forced the devaluation of Sterling upon the reluctant Wilson Government in November, and, thus, the third revision of the Defence Review upon Healey. The speed with which further savings had to be made in all departments of Government drove Healey to turn and swim with the tide of opinion, which welled up in Whitehall for an acceleration of the withdrawal from East of Suez with the final departure date brought forward to the end of 1971. The Chiefs had no option but to follow, each playing his cards so as to reduce the impact upon his own Service by finding new roles for its endangered units in the European defence environment.

Each Chief had his own calvary. Grandy, the CAS, was forced to accept the cancellation of the F 111 order to save dollars, and cuts in the RAF Transport force to save pounds. Ironically, the long running carrier battle, which had been waged so savagely since the end of the Second World War, had thus ended in both gladiators losing their 'capital' ships and aircraft. Baker, the CGS, was faced with the loss a further nine major fighting units, six of them infantry battalions, and with the halving of the Brigade of Gurkhas. And Le Fanu, the First Sea Lord, was presented with the daunting task of reshaping the Navy for a primarily North Atlantic role without carriers, which were to be phased out when the withdrawal was complete, and with a reduced naval construction programme. The Polaris programme remained unscathed: at a mere £20m per annum, it was deemed value for money.

The carrier battle was not in fact over. On taking office as First Sea Lord in 1966, Begg had established a 'Future Fleet Working Party' under Rear Admiral J H Adams, the Assistant Chief of Naval Staff. Adams recommended that the new capital ship of the Navy should be a 'Command Cruiser' with the capability of operating Navy manned helocopters and RAF vertical take-off aircraft for three strictly naval purposes: airborne early warning, investigation of contacts, and anti-submarine search and strike. Begg, however, had been adamant that he would not countenance any resurrection of carriers by the back door. Adams was retired, but several of his working party went on to become Board members with the Command Cruiser firmly implanted in their minds.

Le Fanu's arrival as First Sea Lord in 1968 removed Begg's constraints, and allowed the operational requirement for a Command Cruiser to be drawn up in two alternative configurations – cruiser-shaped with a step down amidships where the helicopter hangar doors would be, or 'through deck'. The choice of which it should be was not made until the Heath Government won the 1970 General Election. Air Department opposition in the Operational Requirements Committee was as strong as ever, particularly over who should pay for and man the Sea Harriers that *Invincible*, the first of class, would carry.

Paradoxically, at the very moment when Britain was calling her legions home and reinforcing NATO with those for whom a new task could be found, de Gaulle was vetoing her second application to join the EEC on the grounds that she still had too many overseas interests to be truly European. He was quite right in that the British electorate was far from certain how European they wished to be. Economic circumstance, rather than conviction, was driving Britain closer to Europe. Nevertheless, Healey and the Chiefs set about realigning British strategy and seeking to give NATO a more credible nuclear policy. It was largely through their joint efforts that the strategy of 'Massive Nuclear Retaliation' was replaced by 'Flexible Response'; that the NATO Nuclear Planning Group was set up to give European governments a greater say in planning that response; and that the Eurogroup was formed to articulate the European view of NATO policy and to generate European collaboration in weapon development.

During the whole of the 1970s, the Chiefs found themselves without a truly British strategy. Their strategy amounted to the agreed NATO strategy; weapons policy was dominated by quests for collaborative European partners; and the Treasury refused to countenance any new expenditure unless it could be shown to heighten the NATO deterrent significantly, and then only if compensating reductions in expenditure could be made elsewhere in the Defence budget. The power of the Chiefs of Staff Committee declined perceptibly within the Ministry of Defence relative to the PUS's Programmes and Budget staff, and to the Chief Adviser's weapons research, development and procurement committees, which were grappling with not just technological change but an accelerating rate of change. International collaboration, with all its political and military implications and pitfalls, could no longer be avoided. The quest for value for money dominated military policy-making more than ever before.

The 1970s were also a period of continuing national decline. The Navy, Army and Air Force were lucky to have the rising Soviet threat to Western Europe, after the rape of Czechoslovakia in August 1968, as a sheet anchor to slow, if not halt, their own decline. The Navy could hold onto the extraordinary rise in Russian naval power; and the Army and RAF had the increased threat to NATO's Central front to secure their orders of battle. Sad though it was to see Northern Ireland collapse into sectarian violence in 1969, it did provide the Army with a new challenge to sharpen its training; and it helped to save the infantry battalions from further reduction at a time when BAOR's tank forces were attracting most of the limited money available to the Army. And the RAF saw its dreams of a new 'capital' aircraft come closer with the start of the European collaborative project to develop the Multi-Role Combat Aircraft (MRCA).

The worst violence in Northern Ireland occurred in the 1970s, but did not affect the Chiefs in their collective capacity because it was generally accepted that military planning, command and supervision of operations in the province were matters for direct contact between the GOC Northern Ireland and the newly established Secretary of State for Northern Ireland. The CGS alone was responsible for advising the Secretary of State for Defence and the Government on military policy for Ulster, reporting from time to time to CDS and the other Chiefs. This was particularly significant in the period 1970–72, which included internment, 'Bloody Sunday' and Operation 'Motorman', designed to break open the so-called 'No Go' areas established by both Republican and Loyalist gangs. Force levels in Ulster were raised to 27 battalions with a total force strength of 21,000 men.

When Edward Heath unexpectedly won the 1970 General Election, there was a brief pause in Defence retrenchment as Lord Carrington took over from Denis Healey. The lives of the carriers were extended marginally, but crippling naval manpower shortages killed any question of their reprieve. Much to the Navy's delight, however, the first of the new Command Cruisers, which were to prove so crucial during the Falklands campaign nine years later, was ordered in April 1973 in the 'through-deck' configuration, although the arguments over who should buy and man her Sea Harriers was still unresolved. The Army saw the reprieve of four of its infantry battalions, including the controversial Argyll and Sutherland Highlanders; retention of five Gurkha battalions, one of which was to be stationed for the first time in England; and a minor comeback East of Suez with the opening of the Dhofar campaign in the support of the Sultan of Oman with loan service personnel.

De Gaulle's departure from office towards the end of the 1970s, enabled Heath to take Britain into the EEC, but his failure to set the economy to rights, the Arab oil price hype caused by the Arab/Israeli Yom Kippur War in October 1973, and his abortive confrontation with the Unions, leading to the Miners Strike and the Three Day Week in the winter of 1973/4, brought Wilson back into power with Healey as Chancellor of the Exchequer and Roy Mason as Secretary of State for Defence.

By the time Wilson returned to Downing Street, two generations of Chiefs had held office. The tragedy of Le Fanu's early retirement in July 1970, and subsequent death in November, brought the sharp and incisive Sir Peter Hill-Norton into the office of First Sea Lord for nine months before taking over from Elworthy as CDS in the place of Le Fanu. The First Sea Lord's job was taken over by Sir Michael Pollock, Flag Officer Submarines in March 1971. He benefited from the Indian summer of Anthony Barber's short-lived reflation of the economy, in which the naval construction programmes were accelerated to help mop up unemployment. Sir Edward Ashmore, the first C-in-C Fleet – the title given to the single fleet command after the withdrawal from East of Suez – succeeded Pollock in March 1974.

On the Army side, there were rather fewer changes of CGS. The iconoclastic and highly intelligent Sir Michael Carver, who had returned home after closing down the Far East Command to become GOC-in-C Southern Command and C-in-C (Designate) United Kingdom Land Forces (UKLF), relieved Baker as CGS in April 1971, and was appointed CDS in October 1973, just before the change of Government. His predecessor as CDS, Hill-Norton, went on to be Chairman of the NATO Military Committee and was given a life peerage in 1979. Carver's place as CGS was taken by Sir Peter Hunt, a sound and very likeable Scottish infantryman and former Commander of the Gurkha Division in Malaya and Borneo, who had recently been C-in-C Northern Army Group and BAOR.

In the Air Department, the equally sound and likeable Grandy held office as CAS for the four years throughout the withdrawal from East of Suez, and was relieved in April 1971 by Sir Denis Spotswood, the C-in-C Strike Command. Spotswood was CAS throughout the rest of the Heath Administration. He handed over to his successor in Strike Command, Sir Andrew Humphrey, who was being groomed as the RAF's choice for CDS after Carver.

The Chiefs in office when Roy Mason took over the reins as Secretary of State for Defence had all worked together before as the principal operational Cs-in-C: Ashmore with the Fleet; Carver with Southern Command; Hunt in Germany; and Humphrey at Strike Command. More importantly, they had all been in senior command and staff appointments during Healey's rolling Defence Reviews and were well aware of the pitfalls of reviews that were financially rather than strategically driven. And apart from Hunt, they had all been members of their Service Boards and were experienced in Whitehall lore.

No government – Tory or Labour – could have left Defence unscathed in the political and economic chaos that engulfed the country in the spring of 1974. Roy Mason, a sturdy Yorkshire miner and a no-nonsense patriot, was in the unenviable position of having Denis Healey breathing down his neck as Chancellor of the Exchequer. But he was fortunate to have the razor-sharp, determined and operationally experienced Carver as CDS and Ashmore, Hunt and Humphrey as a well-balanced and able team of Chiefs to help him argue through another Defence Review, which was thrust upon him by the Labour Cabinet within days of taking office.

Healey, as Chancellor, took the initiative and proposed that studies should be made of the effects of reducing Defence spending from the then 5.5 per cent to 4.5 per cent or 4.0 per cent of the Gross Domestic Product over a ten year period, thus bringing British expenditure more into line with that of her NATO partners. The Chiefs under Carver's forthright leadership would not tolerate another Treasury dominated and resource-led review, and they insisted that reduction of commitments and revision of strategy should be undertaken first. Carver, in his memoirs, explains:

> We appreciated, from experience of previous exercises of this kind, that this [the Treasury] approach would prove highly unsatisfactory. It would lead to a 'shopping list' of reductions, and the mere fact that items were listed at all would qualify them in other people's eyes for reduction. The end result would then probably be, as happened in most negotiations with the Treasury, a bargain between the best and the worst figure. It was impossible to make military sense by this approach. The Chiefs of Staff therefore decided at a fairly early stage to establish what we described as the 'critical level of forces', defining it as the level below which the resultant reduction in our contribution

to NATO would call into question our support for the alliance, and thus put at risk the cohesion of the alliance itself.[10]

There were three immutable commitments, which were not subject to much debate: the Brussels Treaty obligation to maintain BAOR and RAF Germany, on the Continent for the defence of the Central Front; the Navy's contribution to NATO naval forces in the Eastern Atlantic and Channel, 70 per cent of which was British; and the defence of the British Isles and their approaches. There were, however, three questionable commitments, which might or might not lie within the Critical Level: the British nuclear deterrent; the British contribution to the defence of the Northern Flank in Scandinavia; and the British naval presence in the Mediterranean, stretching back to Nelson's day and beyond.

The future of the Polaris force was the most politically sensitive issue, but the easiest to resolve, even though Carver, the CDS, had personal reservations about its credibility. There was no need as yet to consider its replacement and there were few financial savings to be had from disbanding it prematurely. Despite Left wing opposition, the Cabinet decided to retain it on the grounds that it:

> ... provides a unique European contribution to NATO's strategic nuclear capability out of all proportion to the small fraction of our defence budget which it costs to maintain. We shall maintain its effectiveness. We do not intend to move to a new generation of strategic nuclear weapons.[11]

As discussions about the Northern Flank developed, the British contribution to its defence was raised from desirable to vital because of the obvious threat that would be posed to the security of the United Kingdom, if Soviet air forces were able to operate from Norway. Ashmore also wanted to retain credible operational 'pegs' for the Navy's amphibious forces, which the Northern Flank provided. Hunt and Humphrey supported the Naval case.

Regrettably, by no stretch of imagination could the Southern Flank be deemed vital to the defence of the United Kingdom. The White Ensign was to cease flying in the Central Mediterranean when the Malta Military Facilities Agreement expired in 1979. The only world-wide commitments to be retained were the garrisons of the residual dependent territories of Gibraltar, Hong Kong, the Falklands and Belize, together with the Cyprus Sovereign Base Areas. The last of these were to play an important intelligence-gathering role in forewarning of impending troubles in the Middle East, and as a spring-board for peace-keeping tasks in the area. No forces would be assigned to CENTO or SEATO.

In the outcome of the Mason/Carver Review, Ashmore came off best, saving the Navy's amphibious forces and only suffering marginal pruning of its construction programmes. Humphrey came off worst because there was no escape from a savage cut in transport aircraft now that world-wide reinforcement requirements were so reduced, but the RAF could look forward to the MRCA coming into service in the early 1980s as its 'capital' aircraft. The outcome for Hunt was somewhere between the two. The Army's order of battle was secured by the Brussels Treaty commitment and the Northern Ireland requirement. It lost no units, and met the reductions in manpower required of it by pruning its command structure and logistic support. He felt, however, that it had suffered unduly by what he saw as his failure to fight his corner strongly enough, and so he refused promotion to Field Marshal at the end of his tenure, much to the sorrow and yet admiration of the Army.

The Chiefs, nevertheless, could derive some satisfaction from having held the overall reduction in resources to about 4 per cent spread over ten years, and from having kept Britain's contribution to NATO virtually unscathed.

If the Mason/Carver Review had been the end of the story of Britain recognising herself as a European power, the Services might have accepted their new roles as the inevitable consequence of the historical trends set in train by Suez. Unfortunately, the Chiefs were soon faced with the consequences of the Wilson Government's continuing failure to arrest the country's economic decline in spite of its entry into the EEC. Thanks to Wilson's personal worries about the impact of further Defence cuts upon Britain's allies, Healey let Defence off fairly lightly in his austerity measures of October 1975. This infuriated Left-wing Labour MPs, thirty-seven of whom voted against the Government when the House divided on the issue. Nonetheless, the Chiefs had to find another £534m in short-term savings over the next three years.

Since the Services were already at or below the 'Critical Level', savings could only be found by deliberately cutting back military activity generally and delaying the placing of new contracts. Fuel was rationed, training ammunition reduced, purchase of spares limited to essentials, and ship sea time, tank track mileage and pilot flying hours were all cut back. The Chiefs made it quite clear to Ministers that these draconian measures would do irreparable damage to the Services if they were maintained for long, but worse was soon to come.

The Sterling crisis of 1976 began in February when the Bank of England, with Healey's concurrence, allowed the pound to edge down from its over-priced US $2.00 level. The currency markets, as is their wont, took control out of the Bank's hands and the pound went into free-fall. Harold Wilson resigned in March, and Jim Callaghan became Prime Minister without a general election being called. The pound stabilised monetarily at US $1.70 when the Group of Ten provided a short-term loan in June while Healey negotiated the longer term IMF loan. The PUS quite rightly kept the Chiefs in touch with these events on the Treasury side of Whitehall, but the crisis could not have come at a worse time for them as they were in the throes of one of their triennial change-overs.

The first change was in CGS: Sir Roland Gibbs, the C-in-C UKLF, took over from Hunt in July 1976. Like Cassels, he was well cast as the professional head of the Army with a very fine operational record both as a Green Jacket and as a Parachute commander, with a capacity for wise Olympian judgements when he was forced to give them; and one Secretary of State is on record as saying that Gibbs was the Chief that he would choose to go to war with. But he, too, was a reluctant CGS with little experience of working in Whitehall.

The next change was in CAS: Sir Neil Cameron, the Air Member for Personnel, took over from Humphrey as CAS in August so that the latter could relieve Carver as CDS in October. Cameron had a lowly start in life, the son of a Sergeant-Major in the Cameron Highlanders, a holder of a First World War DCM, who died when Cameron was only three weeks old, leaving him to be brought up by his grandfather, the superintendent of the Poor House in Perth. Nevertheless, like 'Wully' Robertson some sixty years earlier, he drew strength from that background and rose to the top of his profession as a progressive thinker and highly articulate advocate. He had had an exceptional career in the RAF, and was deeply imbued with Whitehall lore and tri-Service attitudes, having been a member of Healey's 'think-tank', the Programmes Evaluation Group, during the 1960s.

To complicate the 1976 changes in the Ministry of Defence hierarchy, Roy Mason was transferred in September to the Northern Ireland Office, and his place was taken in Defence by Fred Mulley, who had been Army Minister in Wilson's first Administration. A month later Humphrey took over from Carver as CDS.

The genuine and down-to-earth Fred Mulley had the Armed

Forces very much at heart and would have liked to have been able to improve their lot. He had been a sergeant in the Worcestershire Regiment when taken prisoner at Dunkirk, and while a POW had worked for a degree, subsequently getting a 'First'. Notwithstanding his support however, the new team of Chiefs was still faced with the prospect of further major cuts in equipment programmes being imposed on top of reduced activity levels. The outlook was so serious that Humphrey decided that they must pre-empt events by exercising their constitutional right to approach the Prime Minister directly on the issues involved. Their visit served warning that any further surgery would result in the resignation of the Government's four most senior military advisers. To a government without an overall majority in the Commons, this was a lethal and hence successful threat. The cut in the Defence votes was held down to £3000m over three years, which proved just manageable without another Defence review, and was small compared with the cut-back of £1.5 bn in total government expenditure demanded by the IMF.

Manageable though these successive cuts might seem to the PUS's Programmes and Budget staffs, the worst fears of the Chiefs were soon confirmed. The number of applications for premature release from engagements – a true indicator of Service morale – climbed remorselessly in all three Services. The invaluable skilled officers and men were leaving since it was they who could find alternative employment relatively easily in the over-manned public and private sectors of the economy. Acute shortages of pilots developed in the RAF; the Army had to withdraw tanks and guns into reserve in BAOR because there were not enough trained crews to man them; and the number of ships the Navy could crew sank to the lowest level ever experienced in the 20th Century.

Part of the trouble had been caused by the mishandling of the Military Salary. During successive pay freezes, the recommendations of the Armed Forces Pay Review Body, which was tasked to ensure comparability with civilian rates, could not be implemented in full without breaching the government's own pay-restraint guidelines. Service pay fell further and further behind. The other cause was the growing sense of dissatisfaction with the quality of Service life. Morale was depressed by the prolonged cutbacks in activity, equipment failures due to lack of spares, constant cheese-paring, feeling of being on the losing side in the national struggle for resources, and doubts about the Services' status in a society, which seemed to prefer 'banning the bomb' and 'flower power' to sensible Defence policies.

Before the Chiefs could tackle these issues, the 1976 team was stunned by the premature death of the immensely hard-working Andrew Humphrey in January 1977. Ashmore took over temporarily as CDS for six months while the able and determined Sir Michael Beetham, C-in-C, RAF, Germany, was brought home to take over as CAS in order to release Cameron to continue the RAF's turn in the post of CDS. Sir Terence Lewin (later Lord Lewin, a future CDS), C-in-C, Naval Home Command, succeeded Ashmore as First Sea Lord.

The problems of Service pay and quality of life were brought into focus by the Firemen's Strike, which began in November 1977 and did not end until mid-January 1978. At its peak, some 20,000 Servicemen manned emergency fire-tenders, and dealt with almost 40,000 incidents during the strike. The Chiefs made it clear to Ministers that to make a new and improved offer to the firemen without implementing the recommendations of the Armed Forces Pay Review Body would be grossly unfair and destroy what little faith Servicemen had left in the Government.

By March 1978, the Chiefs had been placed in an invidious position by their Ministers expressing grave doubts about any possibility of improving the Service pay award to bridge the yawning comparability gap, which had by then reached 37 per cent. Their loyalty to the Government as Chiefs of Staff was, thus, brought into direct conflict with their responsibilities as the professional heads of their Services for the welfare of their sailors, soldiers and airmen, who, unlike the firemen, had no trades union to fight for them, and amongst whom only a small minority so far supported current Left-wing proposals to introduce them into the Services as had happened on the Continent – proposals that were rejected not only by the Chiefs of Staff but equally vehemently by the Secretary of State himself.

In his unfinished memoirs, published after his death in 1985, Cameron says that regaining pay comparability was the biggest challenge facing him as CDS. His request for the Chiefs to discuss the issue with the Prime Minister before any final decisions were taken could not be met – or so it was said – for genuine programming reasons. However, Cameron did have a private discussion with Callaghan on the subject on 17th March, which was far from encouraging.[12] The Chiefs, therefore, assumed the worst, and that before long the exodus from all ranks of the Services would turn into a flood, and, even worse, that pressure for unionization would grow. Both would have been disastrous, but sadly the Treasury and Civil Service Department were too intent on working out 'a Majority Paper' as a means of preserving the integrity of the pay-freeze, and of preventing what they saw as un-justified special pleading by different Ministries. Unless, as seemed unlikely, the factor of considerable public support for the Services was highlighted in the Treasury paper, the Cabinet could hardly be expected to do more than accept whatever the officials proposed. In these circumstances, the Chiefs felt the need for some manifest expression of public sympathy and support for their case, which they knew existed and would be readily forthcoming; and, like Mountbatten when faced with Duncan Sandys' intransigence in 1958, they decided to go public with a factual off-the-record briefing of the Press.

As so often happens when there is a major conflict of interest in Whitehall, the Press was already probing for a story and pestering the Ministry of Defence Public Relations staff for information about the high rate of premature releases. Some correspondents were seized with the idea of Armed Forces' trade unions. The Vice Chief of Defence Staff (Personnel and Logistics), General Sir Edwin Bramall (later to become CGS and CDS, and a life peer) was deputed to carry out the briefing, using factual information not in dispute and avoiding political comment. The first half of his presentation, dealing with the philosophical aspects of the pay problem, went well, and resulted in an excellent supportive and apolitical leader in the *Times*, headed 'The Queen's Shilling'. The second half, more by accident than design, gave the impression of releasing new statistical information, which was grasped by the media and flashed out as a news item on the 'ticker-tape' just as Callaghan was about to answer questions on the subject in the House of Commons. Callaghan at first described the figures as useful, but under increased needling by the Opposition and the Press, his attitude hardened and he was calling the release malicious. He ordered a leak inquiry, which was soon stopped when the Chiefs accepted full responsibility for their actions.

In the outcome, the Chiefs did achieve their aim: the media pressure made a significant contribution to the eventual phased pay award and the important forward commitment that went with it. These were both favourable enough to help staunch the outflow of skilled men and women from the Services. Moreover, it seems likely that Mulley's bargaining position in Cabinet was actually strengthened by the publicity, although he himself maintained later that the Services lost 1 per cent of the award through the Chiefs' *démarche*.

However, although such an intervention would have been wholly appropriate for a trades union, which is what the Chiefs had been forced to become, it was frowned on in some quarters, and led some Labour Party ministers to use it as an excuse for avoiding taking military staffs into their confidence. On a lighter note, the whole incident was amusingly portrayed in Mac's cartoon in the *Daily Mail*, showing the Chiefs doing extra fatigues, or 'Jankers', under the steely eyes of Fred Mulley.

Another issue, which might have alienated the Chiefs from any Labour government, was the need to start consideration of the next generation of strategic nuclear weapons to replace Polaris. The determining factor was the life of the submarine hulls, assessed as 25–30 years. The need to replace the boats would provide an opportunity to update the missiles. Callaghan was personally in favour of missile updating, but had to tread cautiously in view of his government's statement that it had no intention of continuing the nuclear deterrent once Polaris came to the end of its useful life. On the advice of the Chiefs, he authorised a study by Professor Mason (later Sir Ronald), then Chief Scientific Adviser in the Ministry of Defence, and Sir Anthony Duff, Deputy Under-Secetary in the Foreign Office, of the options open, if a future government – Labour or Conservative – decided to reverse the decision not to replace Polaris. They were to answer three questions: did Britain need her own nuclear deterrent? if so, what should it do? and this defined, what should it be?

Mason and Duff where given a year in which to complete their work, but were able to report by December 1978 that, in their view, Polaris should be replaced with Trident submarines and C 4 Missiles. Callaghan decided that he must consult President Carter and the principal NATO allies before putting a change of policy to the Cabinet. The opportunity for doing so came almost at once when the President invited Callaghan, Giscard d'Estaing and Helmut Schmidt to meet him on the Island of Guadaloupe in January 1979 to discuss German worries about the SALT negotiations and the Soviet deployment of their latest highly mobile intermediate-range SS 20 Missiles, targeted on Western Europe from deep inside Russian territory.

Two important trains of events flowed from the Guadaloupe meeting. The first was development of the NATO 'Twin Track' response to the SS 20 Missiles: the deployment of American Cruise Missiles in Western Europe, and the simultaneous quest for the elimination of all intermediate range missiles through negotiations with the

Kremlin. The second train was started by Carter's personal willing-ness to provide Trident on favourable financial terms if a future British government decided to go ahead with the replacement of Polaris. Callaghan was further encouraged by Helmut Schmidt mak-ing it clear that the Federal Republic would not wish to see France as the only nuclear power in Western Europe.[13]

Callaghan, however, was not to be faced with the problem of persuading the Labour Party to accept the deployment of Cruise Missiles in the United Kingdom, nor the replacement of Polaris by Trident. Failure in the Welsh and Scottish devolution referenda led to the fall of his minority Government and to the 1979 General Election, which brought the Conservatives back to power with Margaret Thatcher as Britain's first female Prime Minister. The Chiefs, who had been through a very difficult time over the last decade, were cautionsly optimistic that the pressures for continuing retrenchment in Defence would be eased, if not eliminated, and financially driven Defence reviews would become things of the past under the leadership of the 'Iron Lady'. They were to be right about her leadership, but a further spate of retrenchment and another Defence Review lay only just round the corner.

THE CHIEFS AT THE CORONATION, 1953

43. Sir William Dickson and his fellow Chiefs of Staff, Admiral of the Fleet Sir Rhoderick McGrigor and General Sir John Harding, ready to ride in the Queen's Coronation Procession, 1953. *(Crown Copyright/MOD)*

THE FIFTIETH ANNIVERSARY OF THE CHIEFS

44. The Chiefs of Staff Committee in 1973; (foreground left to right) Admiral Sir Michael Pollock (later Admiral of the Fleet), Air Chief Marshal Sir Dennis Spotswood (later Marshal of the Royal Air Force), Admiral of the Fleet Sir Peter Hill-Norton (later Lord Hill-Norton), General Sir Michael Carver (later Field Marshal Lord Carver), Sir James Dunnett and Sir Michael Carey. *(Crown Copyright/MOD)*

SOME CHIEFS OF DEFENCE STAFF IN THE 1970s

45. Marshal of the Royal Air Force Lord Elworthy. *(Crown Copyright/MOD)*

46. Admiral of the Fleet Lord Hill-Norton. *(IWM)*

47. Field Marshal Lord Carver. *(Crown Copyright/MOD)*

48. Marshal of the Royal Air Force Lord Cameron. *(IWM)*

THE CHIEFS IN POLITICAL DISFAVOUR

49. Mac's 1978 cartoon of the Chiefs 'doing Jankers'. *(Lord Mulley)*

THE FALKLANDS TEAM

50. (Foreground left to right) Admiral of the Fleet Sir Terence Lewin (later Lord Lewin), Admiral (later Admiral of the Fleet) Sir Henry Leach, Air Chief Marshal Sir Michael Beetham (later Marshal of the Royal Air Force), General Sir Edwin Bramall (later Field Marshal Lord Bramall), Sir Frank Cooper. *(Crown Copyright/MOD)*

CDSs OF THE 1980s

51. Admiral of the Fleet Lord Lewin.
(IWM)

52. Field Marshal Lord Bramall.

53. Admiral of the Fleet Lord
Fieldhouse. *(IWM)*

54. Marshal of the Royal Air Force
Lord Craig. *(Crown Copyright/MOD)*

Chronology
FOR CHAPTER TWELVE

1979

May	Margaret Thatcher becomes PM with Pym as S of S for Defence.
June	SALT II signed but not ratified.
July	Leach becomes First Sea Lord.
	Bramall becomes CGS.
Aug	Mountbatten murdered by IRA.
Sep	Lewin becomes CDS.
Dec	Soviet invasion of Afghanistan.
	Outbreak of Iraq/Iran War.
	NATO decision to deploy Cruise missiles.

1980

April	Defence budget overspent.
July	Decision to buy Trident I C4 announced.
Aug	Defence contracts moratorium.

1981

Jan	Nott becomes S of S for Defence.
May	Dismissal of the Minister for the Navy, Keith Speed.
	INF talks open in Geneva.
June	John Nott's *The Way Forward* published.

1982

March	Change to Trident II D5 agreed with the US.
19th	Argentine scrap-metal contractors land on South Georgia without British permission.
29th	SSN *Spartan* sailed for South Atlantic.
31st	Leach report to PM, Naval task force being assembled.

Apr 2nd	Argentine invasion of the Falklands.
5th	Task Force sails from Portsmouth.
25th	South Georgia retaken.
May 1st	First Vulcan strike on Port Stanley airfield.
2nd	Sinking of the *Belgrano*.
4th	Loss of *Sheffield*.
19th	Landing authorised by War Cabinet.
21st	Landing at San Carlos.
25th	Loss of *Atlantic Conveyor*.
28th	Battle of Goose Green.
June 6th	Bluff Cove disaster.
11th	Attack on main Argentine defences begun.
14th	Argentine surrender at Port Stanley.

12
STRATEGIC BALANCE LOST AND REGAINED
John Nott's Review and the Falklands Conflict: May 1979 – June 1982

Secretaries of State		First Sea Lords	
Francis Pym	1979	Sir Terence Lewin	
John Nott	1981	Sir Henry Leach	1979

Chiefs of Defence Staff		Chiefs of General Staff	
Sir Neil Cameron		Sir Roland Gibbs	
Sir Terence Lewin	1979	Sir Edwin Bramall	1979

Chief of Air Staff	
Sir Michael Beetham	

'I have learnt not to rely on scenario planning and can only advise that you may confidently expect only the unexpected. The most serious threat against which we must be prepared is at the same time the least likely actually to require us to take action.'

Admiral of the Fleet Lord Fieldhouse,
speaking to Service Staff Colleges in 1986.[1]

The Chiefs, like most of the country, welcomed the change of government in 1979. Fifteen years of economic decline, retrenchment and Defence Reviews had left their mark. They realised that attitudes of mind and economic malaise could not be reversed over night, but they liked what they heard of Margaret Thatcher's ideas for righting the economy and strengthening security. In those early days of her first administration perhaps neither she, nor the Chiefs, appreciated how incompatible monetarism and strengthening defence would prove to be – certainly in the short term.

Soon after Margaret Thatcher became Leader of the Opposition in 1975, she had said in her 'Iron Lady' speech of January 1976:

This is not a moment when anyone should be talking about cutting our defences. It is a time when we urgently need to strengthen them. Of course, this places a burden on us. But it is one that we must be willing to bear if we want our freedom to survive.[2]

In the Tory General Election manifesto, she was more specific:

While we shall seek value for money in defence expenditure as elsewhere, we will not hesitate to spend what is necessary on our armed forces even while we are cutting public expenditure on other things.[3]

1979 was both an auspicious and inauspicious time to start the Thatcher revolution: the electorate was ready for change and craved for the return of a strong government; but the world economic recession, caused by the OPEC hype of oil prices, was growing deeper, with unemployment rising steeply and inflation galloping. Despite all the economic gloom, the new Prime Minister held to her election promises as far as the Chiefs were concerned, taking four decisions almost immediately: two internal and entirely within her own gift, and two external with the establishment of a sound personal relationship with the Carter Administration in Washington as a prerequisite.

The first internal decision was to stem the run-out of skilled men and women from the Services by authorising the immediate payment of the balance of the phased pay award of 32 per cent agreed by the Callaghan Government after the Firemen's strike. The second was to confirm Callaghan's acceptance of the NATO agreement to raise Defence spending by 3 per cent per year for the next seven years. The first did reduce the outflow from the Services; but the second proved to be a mirage, and a new and bitter cause for confrontation with the Treasury.

The two external decisions flowed from President Carter's Guadaloupe meeting of Western European heads of government held just before the 1979 General Election: the deployment of Cruise missiles in Europe, and the possible replacement of Polaris by Trident I C4. Both issues were interconnected in that a co-operative British attitude on the former would help negotiations on the latter. However, before they were brought nearer to resolution by Mrs Thatcher's first official visit as Prime Minister to Washington in December 1979, a new team of Chiefs had taken over.

In July, Sir Henry Leach came from the combined posts of C-in-C Fleet and Allied Commander Channel and Eastern Atlantic, to take over as First Sea Lord from the popular, powerful and effective Lewin, who succeeded Cameron as CDS in September. Leach was as high principled as he was able, and a charming man, who, like

Lewin, was to serve the country in a most exceptional way when the Falklands crisis broke in 1982.

In July also, Sir Edwin Bramall, who was the Army's choice as next CDS in three years time, took over from Gibbs as CGS. He was no stranger to Whitehall, having been one of Mountbatten's team that set up the unified Ministry of Defence in 1964. Since then, however, he had held only command appointments, albeit important and influential ones, away from Whitehall. Fred Mulley had the good sense to bring him back as Vice-Chief of Defence Staff (Personnel and Logistics) to enable him to regain a feel of the Ministry, which Gibbs had lacked. He was, therefore, well qualified for the tasks that lay ahead of him.

There was no change of CAS. Beetham's tour was extended to October 1982 due to the untimely death of Andrew Humphrey, which had left an awkward gap in the Air Secretary's plans for filling senior Air posts.

Margaret Thatcher's Washington visit in December 1979 took place amidst Western confusion caused by the Soviet invasion of Afghanistan. The Russian demonstration of their willingness to use force outside the NATO area, and the obvious threat that they were posing to Western oil supplies from the Middle East, coupled with their preparations to deploy SS 20 missiles in Eastern Europe, made Western solidarity and modernisation of weapon systems crucially important. But there was a reverse side to the coin of nuclear weapon improvements: anti-nuclear lobbies were gathering momentum throughout Europe; and, at home, CND was generating protests against what they assumed would be a reversal of Callaghan's publicly stated intention to phase out Polaris at the end of its useful life.

During the visit, Mrs Thatcher was able to tell President Carter that Britain would accept Cruise missiles in Britain. The robustness of her decision should not be underestimated: politically, it presented the Opposition parties with a useful platform for the next general election; and, militarily, it gave the Soviets more reason to attack the British Isles in any superpower confrontation. Her decision had no major implications for the Defence budget since the Americans were paying for the missiles and their deployment.

The reverse was the case with the Polaris/Trident decision, the cost of which would certainly affect the Defence Vote, though not as severely as many of its critics on both sides of the political spectrum believed. The Chiefs had to consider three options. The cheapest was to refurbish the existing Polaris boats and missiles, but this was discarded for two good general as well as a number of technical reasons: the US Navy was phasing out Polaris and so no further logistic support would be available; and the submarine hulls would have to be replaced anyway. The second and initially favoured option was the purchase of Trident I C4, and the third was a submarine-launched version of the Cruise missile, which would be cheaper than Trident, needing smaller but many more submarines since each missile could carry only one warhead whereas the C4 could lift eight. When the initial and whole-life costings were done, the Cruise option proved more expensive than Trident I C4. Furthermore, the cost of development and logistic support would fall on Britain, and commonality would be lost with the US Navy.

There was, however, a fourth option, lying just over the horizon, in the shape of Trident II D5, able to carry fourteen warheads per missile, which the Carter Administration had not, as yet, endorsed, and was unlikely to be ready by the time Britain needed to replace her Polaris hulls. The position was to be changed dramatically by Ronald Reagan winning the 1980 Presidential Election. As part of his policy of negotiating from a position of strength with the 'Evil Empire', he accelerated the D5 programme, bringing it into the British time frame as an option. The Thatcher Government opted for D5 and stuck to that decision throughout the Trident debate, which raged in and outside Parliament until the issue was decided finally by the electorate giving Margaret Thatcher her second term in the 1983 General Election, during which nuclear policy was a key issue in the campaign.[4]

While success over pay, Cruise and Trident confirmed the Government's commitment to strengthening Defence, its monetary policies soon caused the Chiefs severe difficulties. It was not that Defence did not do as well, perhaps even relatively better, than the other spending departments, but that its programmes had to be cut back at all when the election had been won with Defence high on the list of Tory priorities, and after Labour had already agreed to project future expenditure on the NATO 3 per cent growth curve.

The Treasury started their calculations of the new cash limits, wrongly in the Chiefs' view, from the low base line of the 1979/80 out-turn of expenditure, which had been depressed by an unusually large underspend that year due to slips in major projects, instead of from the estimated cost of the existing Labour programme. This resulted in the new Government's programme being put on a lower and increasingly divergent level of funding from Labour's projected growth line, reducing the Chiefs' expectations by some £1,400m over a four year period. The Treasury, nonetheless, used their financial 'mirrors' to show that, in NATO terms, Defence expenditure was, in fact, rising at 3.5 per cent per annum. This was cold comfort for the Chiefs when equipment-cost inflation was running 5 per cent above the national inflation level.

And worse was to come: reduction in expectations was followed, in November 1980, by a straight cut of £200m and a further indirect one through the imposition of cash limits significantly lower than Defence inflation. Furthermore, the world economic depression emptied industrial order-books, enabling firms to complete Defence contracts ahead of schedule, and cash-flow problems forcing them to demand earlier payment. By August, it was clear that there would be a major overspend – historically a most unusual occurrence in Defence finance – and an unexpected cash crisis.

Francis Pym, Margaret Thatcher's first Secretary of State for Defence, was awkwardly placed. He had either to take responsibility for short-term overspending, which would not have been popular in the atmosphere prevailing in the Cabinet; or he could take significant weapons projects out of the programme without any real military justification for doing so. The latter course would mean yet another Defence review, for which there was not enough time. Instead, he imposed a three month moratorium on all spending not already committed and a period of severe financial restraint for the rest of the accounting year. These measures imposed another period of reduced training activity at every level, and restarted the run-out of skilled men and women from the Services as they shrugged their shoulders, muttering 'Here we go again! The Tories are no better than Labour!' And in the out-turn, the panic was shown to have been quite un-necessary: the dislocation of programmes was such that the Defence budget was under-spent by as much again as the moratorium had been designed to save.[5]

Much to their disgust, the Chiefs saw their programmes being pilloried by outside economic commentators as a major factor in the apparent failure of the Government's financial strategy. They were so alarmed by events that they exercised their sparingly-used constitu-tional right of appeal direct to the Prime Minister personally. Their démarche was not helped by a civil servant in the Navy department leaking an Admiralty document, showing that the Government's pro-Defence rhetoric was not being matched in practice. Behind the scenes, the Prime Minister and Francis Pym were perhaps becoming frustrated with each other: she, because the incompatibility of her Defence and monetary policies was beginning to show; and he, because of his lack of deep interest in financial management and his loyalty to the Services did little to resolve the conflict of policy. In the Cabinet reshuffle of January 1981, the likeable Pym was 'promoted' Leader of the House of Commons, and in his place came the gaunt, ascetic figure of John Nott, the politically ambitious merchant banker, who had once served with the Gurkhas, and was Secretary for Trade.

John Nott (later Sir John) was tasked to take a tougher line than Pym and to clean up what was seen in Whitehall as a financial Augean Stable within the Ministry of Defence. He fervently believed that, even if the 3 per cent growth was honestly applied by the Treasury, the current force structure of the Services could not be sustained, and a fundamental review was needed. His approach echoed those of both Duncan Sandys and Denis Healey: the reforming zeal of the former and the determination of the latter to be master of 'his' Ministry.

Moreover, he was a man in a political and intellectual hurry. Like Sandys, he set off at once on whirlwind tours of Service establishments and the Ministries of Defence of Britain's principal allies, seeking panaceas. Like Healey, he called for innumerable studies and reports in a twelve week break-neck exercise to clear his mind on the issues at stake in trying to master the acceleration in equipment-cost inflation without impairing the country's security, or embarrassing the Government's monetary policy. And like all new Ministers of Defence, he expected to be able to apply the sharpness of his mind to cutting the waste, extravagance and woolly strategic thinking that he was convinced existed in the Services. But he was also set on imposing radical decisions as well. To help him in this, he wanted all options barred so that he could assess political and military risks in setting new strategic priorities in order to balance the Defence books. He suspected, although at this stage he had not made up his mind, that the answers might lie in concentrating Britain's limited military resources on continental defence, virtually abandoning any maritime pretensions now that most of Britain's residual overseas commitments had been liquidated.

The Chiefs, while not unco-operative, could hardly welcome another root and branch Defence review in the wake of Labour's fifteen years of Defence retrenchment, and so soon after the Mason/Carver review had brought the Services down to the 'Critical Level', in which their four tasks had been defined as: maintaining the nuclear deterrent; defending the British Isles; contributing to the NATO defence of the Central and Northern Fronts; and playing a leading role in the maritime defence of the Channel and Eastern Atlantic. What seemed to irk them most was the belief that they were being short-changed by the Treasury. The promised NATO 3 per cent annual increase in Defence expenditure had been further redefined as 21 per cent over the agreed seven year period, thus avoiding the compounding of the annual increase.

It is hardly surprising, therefore, that the Chiefs were unable to offer many alternative options, nor were they united enough to do so. Bramall and Beetham had the clearly defined NATO force levels onto which they could hook the Army's and RAF's orders of battle, and they had little difficulty in defining their tasks to Nott's satisfaction. The Army did offer a plan for streamlining of Rhine Army, which was rejected on the grounds that it might start an unravelling of the delicately woven political and military fabric of NATO.

Leach and the Naval Staff, on the other hand, were faced with the same awkward looseness in definition of the Navy's tasks in nuclear war that had plagued 'Wee' McGrigor during the Chiefs' Global Strategy conference Greenwich in 1952. The 'broken-back' concept of war after a nuclear exchange, which had given the Navy a role then, had been replaced with helping to maintain trans-Atlantic reinforcement and re-supply routes during the initial conventional phase in the NATO strategy of 'Flexible Response', but there were grave doubts about the survivability of surface vessels in the missile age, and about the continued practicability of the convoy system which was fundamental to the shape and size of the Navy. Leach was reduced to arguing his case on the basis of historic need for Britain, as an island power, to have balanced naval forces in being at all times, which would be able to fulfil NATO roles and react to unexpected emergencies wherever they occurred.

This subjective appeal cut no ice with Nott, who was trying to assess priorities on an objective basis. Eric Grove, the naval historian records:

> To Nott it seemed that the Navy itself was arguing more on grounds of sentiment than anything else, 'The navy is the navy is the navy and you are a fool if you do not understand what it is for'. This was not enough for a minister who was seeking to 'analyse these questions' and who had not got 'enough money to do everything'.[6]

Lewin, as CDS, was in an invidious position. Under the

Mountbatten reforms, the CDS was responsible for tendering the collective advice of the Chiefs to the Secretary of State, and only if there was a divergence of view amongst them could he properly register his own preference. As a recent First Sea Lord, steeped in the naval tradition, he could hardly be expected to ignore the naval case, nor could he expect Bramall and Beetham to give Leach more than qualified support. There was unanimity amongst the Chiefs that there was little operational justification for naval cuts, but, if something had to go, CGS and CAS felt that some trimming in the numbers of vulnerable surface ships was not illogical in a purely NATO context, in which the Navy's primary role was anti-submarine warfare in the Norwegian Sea and Eastern Atlantic.

Wth the Chiefs reluctant to come to any unified conclusion, Nott turned for advice to the two other centres of power in his ministry – the PUS, Sir Frank Cooper, and the Chief Scientific Adviser, Sir Ronald Mason – and to the Foreign Office.

The PUS's Department were realists, who knew that it was no use carping about the Treasury's methods in setting the financial targets because there was, in truth, a fundamental mismatch between the existing weapons programmes and the slice of the national cake likely to be considered reasonable by the electorate for allocation to Defence. The Scientists had sound reasons for doubting the validity of the naval programmes. In their view, too much was being spent on hulls, or platforms as they called them, and too little on the weapon systems to go into them. They also favoured increasing resources devoted to submarines at the expense of surface units; and they believed that the Air Staff were right in their claims that greater use should be made of maritime aircraft in the defence of the Eastern Atlantic.[7] The Foreign Office was clear that Britain was now primarily, if reluctantly, a European power, and that land and air defence of NATO's Central Front should take priority over maritime commitments.

With so much advice outside the Chiefs of Staff Committee pointing the finger at the Naval programmes, Nott, with the courage of his own convictions, made his judgement of Solomon. He gave his personal staff broad guidelines for re-shaping the long term costings with '*The RAF better off, the Army about the same and the Navy considerably worse off*'.[8] In his Defence White Paper, entitled *The Way Forward*, and published in June 1981, he said what many laymen felt and most sailors feared:

Our basic judgement . . . is that for the future the most cost-effective mix – the best balanced operational contribution in our situation – will be one which continues to enhance our maritime-air and submarine effort, but accepts a reduction below current plans in the size of our surface fleet and the scale and sophistication of new ship-building, and breaks away from the practice of costly mid-life modernization.[9]

In his proposals, the four Mason/Carver tasks of the Services remained unaltered, but priorities between them were more closely defined. The nuclear deterrent stayed top of the bill; Home Defence came a close second and was stated to need strengthening; but, in the previously co-equal British contributions to the NATO, the Central Front was given precedence over the Eastern Atlantic.

The Chiefs' reaction to Nott's judgement did much to demonstrate the need for another step to be taken towards the unification of Defence policy-making. As ever, each Chief looked first at the likely impact on his own Service for which he was constitutionally responsible. No unified Defence view could be established because the 'Centre' had neither the staff to formulate one, nor the power to enforce it. The Navy was clearly to be the hardest hit, but the General and Air Staffs were reluctant to lend support to their naval colleagues because they would have to foot the bill for any easing of the Navy's lot, and they believed that they were themselves already underfunded. Lewin could not support the Navy either because to do so from the necessarily impartial post of CDS would have been to show overt naval bias. In consequence, the Chiefs' response to Nott's *The Way Forward* was fragmented and much less positive than he would have liked.

One man emerged with honour from the abortive struggle with Nott. The Minister for the Navy, Keith Speed, who had been a regular naval officer until he retired from the Navy to enter politics, felt '*anger, frustration and growing disillusionment*' in March and April when the internal debate within the Ministry was at its height. He decided it was his duty to warn the country of the probable naval cuts before they were set in Whitehall concrete. In a speech to his constituents in May, he said enough to alert the media to the danger of cutting the Fleet in the face of the fast growing Soviet naval threat. The Prime Minister, at Nott's request, asked for his resignation, but he declined and was dismissed. When he left his office for the last time on 19th May, he was given a rousing farewell by Leach and the Admiralty staff, all of whom appreciated his efforts to save the Navy and his forthright public expression of their views.[10]

Leach did not resign in Speed's support as he had a mind to do. The ineffectiveness of Luce's resignation gesture in 1966 did not encourage such ideas. He realised that it would be far more sensible to stay and fight inside, and if necessary outside the Ministry of Defence, to save not only the Navy but Britain's maritime capability as well. The country and Mrs Thatcher can be grateful that he decided to do so: the Falklands victory and the series of Thatcher governments that followed it might have had different endings if he had resigned – such are the random coincidences of events that make history!

Speed was not replaced. The Prime Minister decided to abolish the posts of the three single-Service ministers, which could provide centres for Service cabals, and to make ministerial control within the Ministry of Defence entirely functional with no separate single-Service responsibilities. There is no doubt that the Service Departments had gradually re-established much of the autonomy that they had lost in the Mountbatten Reforms of 1964. This was most marked in the case of the civil servants, who, though rotated between departments, often became as loyal to their current departments as their predecessors were in the old separate Service ministries. For example, a comment by Michael Power, the Assistant Under-Secretary (Naval Staff) and son of Admiral of the Fleet Sir Arthur Power, that Nott's reduced Fleet was not 'the sort of Navy I would send any son of mine to sea in' has passed into naval legend.[11]

The Chiefs were all present when the Cabinet discussed Nott's proposals. No record has been published as yet of the meeting, but the Nott policy was accepted in principle without major change. The details of the actual cuts were worked out over the next nine months. The Navy's frigates were to be run down from 65 to 'around 50'; the ASW carriers were to be reduced from three to two by disposing of *Hermes* and *Invincible* as soon as *Ark Royal* and *Illustrious* were in commission; the nuclear-powered submarines were scaled down from 20 to 17, although this was seen as strengthening the ratio of submarines to surface ships since the latter had been cut more heavily; and the Chatham and Portsmouth Royal Dockyards were to be closed. The Army lost some 7,000 men but no units. And the RAF was able to improve UK Air Defence with extra Phantom and Hawk squadrons; to buy 60 of the advanced US version of the Harrier; to continue the Tornado programme with its European partners; and to increase its tanker fleet for in-flight refuelling by one third.

Nestling in the small print of the Ministry of Defence's White

Paper, in which these details were published in February 1982, was the decision to withdraw the Antarctic patrol ship *Endurance* from the South Atlantic as an economy measure taken despite strong Foreign Office objections. As she was required to remain for political rather than military reasons, the Ministry of Defence suggested that the Foreign Office should pay for her retention, but acceptance of such a proposal could, in Whitehall logic, have led to the cost of most naval activities being charged to Foreign Office votes as the foreign policy executive! *Endurance* remained under sentence of withdrawal if not scrapping.

Nott was obliged to rescind some of his measures before the Falklands crisis broke, but the overall impact of his review was to reduce the real growth in Defence expenditure to about 7 per cent over the three years since the general election. This rose to 8 per cent the following year instead of the 12 per cent hoped for under the NATO 3 per cent annual growth commitment. The naval cuts were to contribute to the Argentine assumption that Britain was no longer concerned about what might happen outside the NATO area, and certainly not as far away as the South Atlantic.

By the beginning of 1982, there was a more constructive initiative originating on the 6th Floor – the Ministers' and Chiefs' floor – in the Ministry of Defence. Lewin, who still had six months of his tour as CDS to run, has stated that he proposed a further step forward in the evolution of the higher organisation of Defence. Convinced that the Chiefs' failure to come up with a firm Defence view had left a vacuum of military advice, and that their failure was largely due to the constraints imposed on the CDS by his constitutional responsibilities, he proposed to his colleagues that he should recommend to the Secretary of State a strengthening of the powers of the CDS to make him the pre-eminent member of the Chiefs of Staff Committee. Despite the Mountbatten reforms almost two decades earlier, the CDS was still Chief of Defence Staff only in name. He controlled and directed the Defence Staff on behalf of the Chiefs of Staff as a body, and then only after terms of reference had been agreed by all of them. This was time consuming; lacked the dynamic that a CDS could impart; watered down and slowed up constructive work by the Central Staffs; and often resulted in bland compromises to which the three Services could safely subscribe.

In this initiative Lewin was supported with varying degrees of enthusiasm by the other Chiefs. Since the 1964 reforms, they and their staffs had all gained experience in working together in the unified overseas commands and had benefited from the tri-Service training provided by the Joint Services Staff College and the Royal College of Defence Studies. In consequence, they were less afraid than their predecessors would have been of strengthening the hand of the CDS and giving him the staff to generate a unified professional military view to counter-balance the influence of the centrally organised financial and weapons procurement empires within the Ministry. Bramall had, of course, been a member of Mountbatten's team and had been privy to his inner thoughts on unification in 1963/4, and as front-runner to be the next CDS, he was far from antagonistic to strengthening the Centre's military voice, provided there was no weakening of the flow of professional sea, land and air advice in the policy-making process.

The more general Whitehall dissatisfaction with the lack of a 'Defence' voice during the Nott review, had created the climate of opinion that enabled Lewin to win the agreement of his colleagues to five important new principles, which were accepted by Nott and Margaret Thatcher, and implemented in January 1982, just three months before they were to be tested to the full by the Falklands crisis. First, CDS was to be the principal military adviser to the Government in his own right, and not just as Chairman of the Chiefs of Staff Committee. Second, that committee was to be the forum from which he would draw single-Service advice, but it would also lose its collective responsibility for the military advice tendered by CDS to the Government. Third, the Chiefs were to remain the professional heads of their Services, responsible for their efficiency and morale, and for tendering single-Service advice to CDS. Fourth, the Central operational and military policy staffs were made responsible to CDS rather than the Chiefs of Staff Committee. He would take the initiative and give them direction for their studies, the results of which would be put subsequently to his colleagues for endorsement or criticism. This would allow a more positive approach in tendering advice to Ministers and speedier dispatch of operational business. And fifth, a Senior Appointments Committee was to be set up to oversee the promotion and appointments of all three- and four-star officers.

Lewin stopped short, as Mountbatten had done, of full integration of the Naval, General and Air Staffs because he did not have the support of his colleagues to go any further; and because the Services were not as yet ready for a functionally organised Defence Staff, which had been a gleam in many a reformer's eye since the early

1900s. He wisely left that for the future when more experience had been gained; new generations of commanders and staff officers had risen through the Service selection system; and case law and staff procedures had been built up in working the revised system.

The Lewin reforms were soon put to the severest test of all – war; and were to prove their worth under the most extreme political, strategic and geophysical conditions 8,000 miles away in the South Atlantic.

In February 1982, the Foreign Office were expressing concern about the Argentine Junta's reaction to the seemingly constructive series of talks on the future of the Falkland Islands, or the Malvinas as the Argentines insist on calling them. Anticipating increased Argentinian pressure that might possibly involve limited military action by the end of 1982, the Ministry of Defence was asked to reconsider the withdrawal of *Endurance*. The Cabinet was also briefed on the reaction of the Callaghan Government to a similar threat to the islands in 1976/7, when the nuclear submarine *Dreadnought* was dispatched to reinforce *Endurance*, and the Exocet-armed frigates *Alacrity* and *Phoebe* were stationed in the middle of the South Atlantic a thousand miles to the north of the Falklands to provide a reliable communication link to the headquarters of C-in-C Fleet at Northwood on the northern outskirts of London. Rules of engagement were worked out and the decision taken to announce a 50 mile 'identification zone' around the islands, if Argentine aggression seemed imminent. This was, in fact, a preparatory defensive move rather than a deterrent ploy, and was kept secret. It seemed to work as the latter, although there is no evidence that the Argentine Government knew much about it at the time.

On the evening of 19 March 1982, a party of Argentine scrap-metal contractors landed without permission on the British Dependant Territory of South Georgia, some 600 miles east of the Falklands, which were themselves 350 miles from the Argentine mainland. Despite protests from the British Government, the Argentine Junta refused to remove them or regularise their presence, and added insult to injury by landing a small group of their Special Forces to support them. This action placed question marks over their intentions, but as far as the Falkland Islands were concerned the Foreign Office counselled caution. There was little, if any, hard intelligence of the Junta planning an invasion. Certainly none was brought to the attention of the Chiefs of Staff, and the Foreign Office was still under the impression that for the moment negotiations were continuing in good faith.

It was not until 29 March that the Cabinet decided to repeat Callaghan's dispatch of a nuclear submarine to the South Atlantic. A major part of the Fleet was then off Gibraltar, carrying out the annual 'Spring Train' exercises under Flag Officer 1st Flotilla, Rear Admiral Sandy Woodward, a sharp, highly professional and forthright Cornishman with a subtle, if perhaps devious, turn of mind. The SSN *Spartan* was quietly armed with operational torpedoes by the Gibraltar Naval Base and sailed forty-eight hours later on her ten day passage to the Falklands, while the SSNs *Conqueror* and *Splendid* made ready to follow her from Faslane. The First Sea Lord, Sir Henry Leach, was, however, unconvinced that submarines would be a sufficient deterrent if General Galtieri had already decided to divert Argentine internal domestic unrest by embarking on a surprise Falklands adventure as was being suggested in some reports. This was precisely the type of unforeseen emergency, on which he and the Naval Staff had been basing their arguments with Nott over the need to maintain a balanced surface and sub-surface fleet. It seemed as if Neptune was once more coming to the rescue of the hard pressed Royal Navy. Rarely can such far-reaching decisions on the shape and size of Britain's armed forces, as those set out in Nott's *The Way Forward*, been so quickly and brutally overturned by events.

In remarkable anticipation of what was going to happen, Leach warned the C-in-C Fleet, Sir John Fieldhouse, who was in *Glamorgan* observing 'Spring Train', of the possible need to send a balanced naval task force to the South Atlantic direct from Gibraltar. Fieldhouse summoned Woodward to his flagship to discuss plans for meeting such an eventuality, and then flew back to London on 30 March.[12]

On 31 March Leach was visiting naval establishments at Portsmouth when intelligence came in that the Argentine Navy, under the guise of an exercise, was, indeed, intending to invade the islands in a matter of days if not hours. He rushed back to London and met Nott in the Commons to express dissent about a pessimistic briefing that the Secretary of State had just been given by the Central Staff on the options open to HMG. Quite fortuitously he was the only Chief available in Westminster when the Prime Minister was briefed by Nott. Lewin was away on a visit to New Zealand; his deputy, Beetham, the CAS, had not been summoned to the briefing; and the CGS, Bramall, was visiting troops in Northern Ireland. Leach told Margaret Thatcher that a powerful naval task force was being assembled ready to sail in a matter of days if ordered to do so. He made it clear that in his view, if the Argentines did invade, the Navy should and could respond despite all the very real difficulties, which had been set out by the Central Staff.[13] Ironically, this was about the only scenario not studied during the aircraft carrier arguments in Healey's day. Despite the demise of the fleet carriers, Leach judged that the risks of operating so close to the Argentine air bases with only the two ASW carriers to provide air cover should be taken.

This was a courageous judgement, but exactly what the Prime Minister wanted to hear. For as earlier deliberations in the Defence Committee had made clear, neither military action, nor repossession through negotiation, would be possible without a demonstration of Britain's ability to project her power and manifest will to act in the South Atlantic in response to aggression. Moreover, she sensed that the electorate would react with intense anger and shame to the invasion, which took place two days later on 2 April with the capture and subsequent repatriation of the small, 65 strong, token Royal Marine garrison on the islands. Leach alone at this very early stage gave her the confidence to seize the military initiative.

In the dramatic and acrimonious debate in the Commons next day, members on both sides of the House did, indeed, make it clear to the Prime Minister and her Government that not only were they being held responsible for failing to deter the Argentines and allowing the islands to be occupied in the first place, but they would have to expel the invaders quickly by political pressure or force if they were to retain the confidence of the House and electorate. With the country as well as Parliament demanding action to restore the honour, credibility and future status of Britain, the Chiefs were beholden to produce a practicable plan to bring this about – no easy task, for important though the principles at stake might be, the difficulties of achieving repossession by military means alone were clearly going to be immense. The risks would have to be very accurately assessed if humiliating mistakes were to be avoided.

Thanks to Leach's anticipatory action, the Task Force, comprising over a hundred ships, many taken up from the shipping trade, and with 28,000 men embarked, left home ports in an unbelievably short time on 5 April and followed Woodward's ships that had already sailed southwards from Gibraltar. It was by any standards a feat to be proud of, and only made possible by the Prime Minister's determination, and by Leach making it clear to the Navy that all obstacles were to be overcome to re-establish its position as the Senior Service.

Willing support was given by the Army and RAF; by ship-owners whose vessels were taken up; by the dockyard workers who modified them for service; and by the dockers who got the ships away in the Battle of Britain spirit. The United States Government helped by allowing their facilities on the British owned Ascension Island, near the Equator, to be used as a forward operating base where the ships could be topped up with anything left behind in the rush to get away. The RAF soon established a Hercules operated air resupply route via Gibraltar and the Gambia to Ascension, which became known as the 'Motorway', the traffic on it being so heavy and continuous, day and night.

At the core of the Task Force were the ASW carriers *Hermes* and *Invincible* with Sea Harriers embarked, and the assault ships *Fearless* and *Intrepid* – all ships that had been sentenced to death by Nott in his 1982 Defence White Paper! Had the crisis boiled over a year later, they and some of the twelve destroyers and frigates that sailed southwards with them would no longer have been available. It was a close run thing!

With the Task Force sailing southwards to emphasise Britain's determination not to accept Argentine occupation of the islands, intense diplomatic activity was generated through the United Nations and through the energetic auspices of the US Secretary of State, General Alexander Haig. The Chiefs were able to apply themselves to analysing the various tactical options available once the Task Force reached the Falklands area. These included the precise balance of forces needed, and the opportunities and the degrees of risk that might develop as events unfolded. They met once and sometimes twice daily under Lewin, who had returned post-haste from New Zealand. The discussions and arguments ranged forcefully and comprehensively over every aspect of the crisis, and demonstrated that four minds, covering the whole spectrum of professional competence and military judgement, are better than one when properly led and directed, as they certainly were.

Once decisions had been taken on the composition of the Task Force, which had to include enough ground troops to retake the Falklands if negotiations failed, the next major issue discussed was the chain of command. As the initial phases of the operation were likely to be almost entirely naval, command and detailed planning were entrusted to the able and robust Sir John Fieldhouse, C-in-C Fleet, at his joint maritime headquarters at Northwood, where Air advice was available through the integrated 18 Group RAF and

Army advice could be provided when needed. Fieldhouse exercised command – other than over the submarines which would remain commanded from Northwood – through the Task Force Commander, Sandy Woodward, flying his flag in the carrier *Hermes*. If a landing had to be made, Fieldhouse would have a Land Force Commander – the very likeable and experienced Royal Marine Major-General Jeremy Moore – reporting to him as well. Fortuitously all four admirals and the general involved – Lewin, Leach, Fieldhouse, Woodward and Moore – had served together at one time or another and knew each other well.

If there was any criticism to be levelled at these arrangements, it concerned the command of the landing forces, consisting initially of the 3rd Commando Brigade under Brigadier Julian Thompson with its own three Commandos and the 2nd and 3rd Parachute Battalions, embarked in the two assault ships and the P & O cruise-liner Canberra. As any repossession would involve amphibious land-ings, the Navy, quite understandably, insisted upon a senior Royal Marine Officer being appointed to command them and subsequent operations in the Falklands. Moore was an excellent choice in every way, but Fieldhouse needed him at Northwood as his senior Land Force planner and adviser during the initial stages of the deploy-ment. He intended to send him down to the war zone by air to Ascension and then on by sea with the main reserves at a later stage.

There is always merit in delegating the planning of any operation to the man who will eventually execute it, but, as events unfolded, it became increasingly difficult for Moore to do both. There was a crucial 72 hour period after the beachhead was seized at San Carlos when his presence was badly needed ashore to provide impetus and direction, but he was still on his way to join the Task Force. With hindsight, Moore should have handed over at Northwood to another Army or Marine adviser much sooner or travelled south by some faster means. He should have been with Woodward during the final deployment and approach to the landing area, and in command ashore at an earlier stage.

Above Task Force level, there were few grounds for criticism. Lewin first discussed key issues with the Chiefs, who gave him their views on broad strategy and on the implications affecting their own Services. He would then tender his own advice to the Defence Committee (Falklands) – in effect a War Cabinet and often described as such – consisting of the Prime Minister, the Lord President of the Council, the Foreign Secretary, the Defence Secretary and the

Chancellor of the Duchy of Lancaster with the CDS always in attendance. The committee provided a well defined politico-military interface for refining the broad lines of policy and any political constraints within which the military would have to operate. This enabled Lewin to give Fieldhouse his general directions, aims and objectives, and to leave him free to plan and execute the sea and air battles, leading to the repossession of the islands. It all worked smoothly, and commanders in the operational area seldom suffered from an excess of back-seat driving, nor a lack of direction on what they could or could not do in any set of circumstances, although the delayed arrival of Moore did lead to some misunderstandings and delays immediately after the initial beachhead had been secured.

The next issue that the Chiefs had to establish with the War Cabinet was the extent to which Britain was to be considered actually at war with Argentina, and hence the rules of engagement and restraints, which needed to apply. Clear definition was needed to establish early psychological superiority and to seize the initiative, which was all important to success. Although the Argentine Junta had committed a clear act of aggression, they had achieved their aim without inflicting a single British casualty. As long as there was any hope of international political or British military pressure persuading them to withdraw, the British Government was naturally reluctant to start hostilities, or to use any more force under Article 51 of the United Nations' Charter than was absolutely necessary. Taking action in self-defence was perfectly legal under International Law, but in the missile era, when stand-off weapons could inflict crippling damage from considerable distances, it was not easy to define what exactly constituted imminent hostile intent, against which pre-emptive action would be legal in self-defence.

The Task Force would be operating under the most atrocious weather conditions as the Southern Hemisphere winter closed in; supply lines would be stretching back across the Atlantic to Ascension; and the not inconsiderable Argentine naval and air forces were based only 350 miles away. The Argentine carrier, *Veinticinco de Mayo* (the ex-HMS *Venerable*) was capable of embarking the French Super Étendard attack aircraft armed with Exocet, and their two submarines (one ex-American and the other recently German built) could not be ignored. There was, therefore, every incentive, as Leach was quick to point out, to reduce these threats at the earliest opportunity, otherwise the Task Force might well suffer a serious reverse 8,000 miles from home.

The reconciliation of these conflicting factors led to some argument in the Chiefs of Staff Committee, but an agreed formula was soon found, which led to a maritime exclusion zone with a 200 mile radius being declared around the islands, which was to be effective on 12th April. Any warship or auxiliary found inside this zone, the Argentines were told, would be assumed hostile and could be attacked. The zone was initially established by the nuclear submarines, whose presence could not be confirmed with any certainty by the Argentines. On 30 April, as the Task Force came within range of the islands, the Zone would become a Total Exclusion Zone (TEZ) for aircraft as well as ships, and would be patrolled by Harriers from the Task Force.

Just over two weeks after the original exclusion zone was declared, an RAF Vulcan bomber, refuelled no less than seven times by tanker aircraft, hit the centre of Port Stanley airfield with a large bomb on 1 May, rendering it unusable by high performance aircraft such as the Super-Étendard, although short landing and take-off aircraft, like the Hercules, could still use it. This success reduced the threat to the Task Force, and enhanced the effectiveness of the exclusion zone. It also demonstrated the reach of British strike aircraft, a point not lost on Buenos Aires. Thanks to the unremitting efforts of Beetham and the Air Staff, in-flight refuelling enabled the small force of Sea Harriers in *Hermes* and *Invincible* to be reinforced by RAF Harrier GR 3s from England. It also did something to correct the purely professional fears of the RAF that it would miss the campaign altogether, having fought so hard for so long to prove that there was no need for carriers or, indeed, naval aviation!

Once the rules of engagement for operations inside and outside the exclusion zone had been established, it was up to Lewin, Fieldhouse and Woodward to ensure that no captain had any doubt about what was expected of him in any given situation. The rules, as modified from time to time on the authority of the War Cabinet, were strictly observed throughout the campaign.

Perhaps the most important issue to be settled was the concept of operations for the period immediately after the Task Force reached the South Atlantic. What additional land forces would be needed, if diplomatic pressure and the show of force did not persuade the Junta to withdraw, and instead ordered their troops on the islands to offer spirited resistance, fully supported by their Navy and Air Force? And, if the risks of undertaking an opposed landing were assessed as too great, what alternatives, such as blockade, were available?

One thing the Chiefs and the War Cabinet were very clear about: it would be disastrous for Britain's future status in the world to do a 'Grand Old Duke of York', sailing the Task Force 8,000 miles south and then back again without restoring a government at Port Stanley of the Falkland Islanders' own choice.

The strategy that the Chiefs evolved was elegant in its simplicity and effective in practice. It struck a well judged balance between giving the Task Force protection while not escalating the conflict during the international to-ing and fro-ing to find a solution to the crisis; and it seized the initiative in an admirably subtle way. The Argentines could either run the risk while trying to resupply their garrison of being attacked by the powerful British nuclear submarines to which they had no counter; or they could accept the terms of the exclusion zone and be seen to be driven from the seas around the very islands whose sovereignty they were claiming, as well as having to abandon the re-supply of their troops by ship. They chose the latter with all the loss of face, prestige and initiative that it entailed.

And then the Chiefs had to tackle the thorny problem of South Georgia. Their deliberations revolved around timing and what forces would be needed to ensure success with minimum casualties. Cut off from Argentine air support, the small garrison presented an attractive opportunity to inflict a damaging psychological blow to the Argentines, and to set the tone of subsequent operations, which in turn depended upon the operation being totally and speedily successful. The Navy had already made some provision to divert a small number of ships, led by *Antrim*, with a company of Royal Marines embarked, but this, it was judged, would not be enough to put the issue beyond doubt. Happily the matter was quickly resolved by the discovery that a squadron of the Special Air Service (SAS) had also been embarked in the *Antrim* group of ships, and was ready and eager for the fray. The Chiefs were then satisfied that these two companies of fit and highly trained troops would suffice. With the War Cabinet's concurrence, Lewin directed Fieldhouse to go ahead with the recapture of South Georgia, a task that he completed extremely skilfully on 25th April without any actual casualties, despite a few anxious moments when the helicopter crashed while inserting and withdrawing a reconnaisance party in appalling weather conditions. Britain had scored the all important 'opening goal', and the Prime Minister was moved to declare in a moment of elation in front of 10 Downing Street that the country should rejoice at the success of British arms.

In the last days of April, the Task Force was, however, sailing into more difficult and dangerous waters with Argentine bases coming ever closer, and Britain herself entering a more turbulent international political phase as US-led negotiations within the Organisation of American States reached their acrimonious climax. The first military moves of the campaign had taken place in a phased approach, allowing ample time for political negotiations: sailing south (Phase 1); retaking South Georgia (Phase 2); establishing the TEZ and bombing Port Stanley airfield (Phase 3); and positioning the Task Force within striking range of the TEZ and the Falklands, but out of the effective range of most of the Argentine Air Force (Phase 4). These moves had all been predictable, the risks calculated, and success as certain as anything can be certain in war – so far so good!

The risks were altogether different and manifestly higher after 1 May when President Reagan publicly pledged US support for Britain and after the US Secretary of State Al Haig had failed to persuade Galtieri to back down. The chances of the British show of naval power succeeding without a fight were fading fast; the probability of having to mount an assault landing was becoming more certain; and the Task Force was coming within the range of the Argentine air bases and submarine attack. The military risks were, indeed, very high with less than 40 Harriers to give air cover from the tossing decks of *Hermes* and *Invincible* in the foulest winter weather of the South Atlantic, whereas the Argentine Air Force and Navy had some 200 aircraft with secure and stable land bases only 350 miles away.

Any doubts as to whether the two sides were in earnest, and whether lives would have to be lost before an equitable political solution could be found, were quickly dispelled by the closely linked sinkings of the *Belgrano* and *Sheffield*.

Woodward had started to deploy his ships inside the TEZ, to land and support reconnaissance parties ashore by helicopter, when three Argentine naval Task Groups set out to oppose what they thought was an imminent major landing near Port Stanley with a three pronged operation: TG 97.1, led by the carrier *Veinticinco de Mayo*, on the northern side of the TEZ; TG 97.4 with three French-built and Exocet armed frigates in the centre; and TG 97.3, comprising the cruiser *Belgrano* and two ex-US destroyers also fitted with Exocet, around the southern side of the TEZ. On 1 May, the central and northern groups were recalled when it was discovered that no landing was taking place. The Argentine carrier, shadowed by SSN

Splendid, tried to launch a Super Étendard attack on the Task Force from some 200 miles north of the islands, but the wind across her deck was too light for take-off and her mission was aborted. Two land-based Super Étendard attacks with Exocet failed because the aircraft missed their refuelling tanker aircraft; and an attack by the German built submarine *San Luis* also failed when her homing-torpedo's guidance wire broke. The *Belgrano* Group, shadowed by SSN *Conqueror*, was left to patrol the southern side of the TEZ. The Argentines were certainly not holding their fire.[14]

Woodward, conscious of the multiple threat, quite rightly, requested a change in the Rules of Engagement to allow the SSNs to attack Argentine warships posing an immediate threat to the Task Force even if they were outside the exclusion zone when an opportunity occurred. His signal reached Fieldhouse on 2 May, just as the Chiefs were assembling at Chequers for one of their periodic reviews of the situation with the Prime Minister. Although only the War Cabinet were directly involved in the decision to authorise the submarines to attack the *Belgrano* outside the TEZ, the Chiefs were aware of the situation and it was plain that any other decision would amount to extreme negligence of the safety of Woodward's ships. The fact that the *Belgrano* had turned away from the TEZ by the time the order to attack reached *Conqueror's* captain, Commander C L Wreford Brown, was irrelevant; TG 97.3 was still a serious threat and its change of course could have been tactical. Wreford Brown fired a spread of three Mark VIII torpedoes, two of which sank the *Belgrano*, and the third hit one of her escorts but did not explode.

The sinking of the *Belgrano* with the loss of some 300 lives convinced the world that hostilities had really begun, and that the British forces in the South Altantic were not just dancing a ritualistic minuet with no intention of retaking the islands by force if need be. More importantly, from the military point of view, it ensured that the Argentine Navy never left their own territorial waters again. But it did erode some of Britain's international support and goodwill, and it came at an awkward moment for President Reagan and Al Haig, who had just made it clear that the US Administration had moved away from its neutral stance and was tilting towards Britain. It is to their great credit that they did not pull back.

Criticism of the British action was soon muted by the Argentines' successful Exocet attack by a land-based Super Étendard two days later, 4 May, on *Sheffield*. Casualties (20 killed) were thankfully lighter than might have been expected, but as she was the first ship in the Royal Navy ever to be crippled and eventually sunk by a remotely fired missile, it brought home to the country, as perhaps nothing else could, that the men of the Task Force would be fighting for their lives from then on.

The end of the political road was reached with Peru's failure to find a peaceful way out of the crisis. The Prime Minister and the British people were in no mood for a sell out; and nor was General Galtieri. The War Cabinet had no option but to take the calculated risks, laced with an element of chance, and direct Fieldhouse to retake the islands.

Fieldhouse had, in fact, done much of the outline planning with his commanders at a meeting held in *Hermes* off Ascension Island as far back as 18 April. It was only necessary to make final amendments based on the most up-to-date reconnaissance information and intelligence, and to get his plan approved by the War Cabinet. The arguments and counter-arguments about operational policy surrounding the plan were thoroughly debated by the Chiefs, who would be required to support it, at their daily meetings, and at other informal gatherings in Nott's or Lewin's offices. It helped for the Chiefs to express varying shades of opinion when the balance of advantage and disadvantage was a fine one and capable of differing interpretations.

Before their meetings, each Chief was briefed by his own staff on the exact capabilities and problems of his Service, but at the actual meetings all three acted within their own professional competence, experience and judgement to stray across demarcation lines and to assess each issue on its merits. None of them was proved consistently right, but the collective wisdom of their four minds was rarely at fault. Although Lewin was the only Chief who attended the War Cabinet regularly and held ultimate responsibility, the other Chiefs met the Prime Minister frequently and at all critical times at 10 Downing Street, in her room in the Commons or at Chequers.

This system enabled Lewin to use his drive and personality to produce the most dynamic solutions, tapping the best ideas coming up from the Service Departments through their Chiefs. His proposals were then always tested for realism and practicality in frank debate at Chiefs of Staff meetings, during which the key staff officers, both military and civilian, were in attendance to record the decisions; to turn them and other thoughts into submissions to ministers and for use by CDS in the War Cabinet; and to see that all loose ends were tied up. The staffs concerned, being present during the discussions, were able to appreciate the nuances in the developing situation, and this progressively improved the quality and relevance of work at lower levels, making for sureness of touch in the totality of the team-work needed for success in complex combined amphibious operations.

The completed plan had a ring of Wolfe's expedition, which left England 225 years earlier to sail across the Atlantic and up the St Lawrence River to capture Quebec. The actual Falklands' landing plan was, of course, very different. It was specifically designed to make best use of the physical and electronic shelter of San Carlos Bay on the west side of East Falkland to reduce the risks from weather, from sea-skimming missiles and from submarine attack. The Special Air Service and the Special Boat Service units were to pin-point the Argentine positions, and to attack opportunity targets such as the group of Pucara aircraft on Pebble Island, which they destroyed with a brilliantly executed raid on 15 May. The Commando Brigade's three commandos, reinforced by the two para-chute battalions, would seize a beachhead at San Carlos; and once enough troops, equipment and supplies were ashore, they would advance across the Island to attack the main Argentine forces hold-ing Port Stanley.

For his plan, however, Fieldhouse needed a reserve of brigade size, which could be used for a variety of tasks such as taking over the beachhead to enable the commandos to develop their operations across the island; reinforcing their assault, if need be, on the main Argentine defensive positions in the hills around Port Stanley; and providing the longer term garrison of the island.

The designated Strategic Reserve formation for such tasks was the 5th Brigade at Aldershot, but it had already been denuded of its two parachute battalions to join the Comando Brigade's landing force, leaving only its Gurkha battalion. Moreover, due to the financial stringency of the 1970s and the concentration on Continental defence, the 5th Brigade was not a fully established formation. Its headquarters was skeletal, and it lacked most of the necessary sup-porting and logistic units needed for the scale of operations envis-aged. These deficiencies had to be made good, two new battalions found for it, and the whole brigade group given a crash period of intensive training together. The two most readily available battalions were 1st Welsh and 2nd Scots Guards, both first-class battalions with recent service in Ulster, but they were at the time on ceremonial Public Duties in London, and they too needed a period of concentrated battlefield training. These problems were solved by giving the brigade its intense training in Wales and then dispatching the whole reserve force in one lift in the great cruise liner, Queen Elizabeth II, to the South Atlantic in time to back Fieldhouse's landing operations.

In the various internal discussions between the Chiefs, and between CDS's staff and Fleet Headquarters, the General Staff felt that San Carlos was uncomfortably far from the key high ground just west of Stanley. There was a risk that, if the Argentines fought well, the advance could bog down half way across the island in deteriorating winter weather, and with international pressure building up for a cease-fire. After going, at the CDS's instigation, to see Fieldhouse and discussing it with him, Bramall became personally convinced that the protection of the ships in the landing phase, when they would be most at risk from sea-skimming Exocet attack and low-level bombing, was more important than shortening the advance on Stanley. There were no other well protected landing areas further east, and the beaches near Stanley were known to be heavily mined. Once ashore the dangers of a damaging air attack on the land forces would diminish as they dispersed and moved inland. The battle would then depend on the ability and willingness of the Argentine conscripts to stand up to the British regular troops. The General Staff, thereafter, gave Fieldhouse's plan their full support.

There was also discussion on what further should be done to reduce the Argentine naval threat. But the national and international reaction to the sinking of the *Belgrano* had shown how delicately balanced opinion was over attacks outside the TEZ. It was, therefore, decided to extend the TEZ closer to Argentine territorial waters so that if, and only if, the Argentine Navy ventured out, its ships could be attacked earlier. In the event, they stayed at home.

Once the *Queen Elizabeth II* with the reserve brigade was approaching South Georgia in the middle of May, and with negotiations accepted by HMG as having virtually broken down, final authorisation by the War Cabinet was sought to allow Woodward to deploy his ships in time for a landing at the optimum moment. On 19 May, it met with the Chiefs in attendance in the Cabinet room of 10 Downing Street. No record of this meeting has been published, but it is generally known that each Chief was required to back his own judgement, and to say how he saw the landing turning out and whether it should be attempted. Even with hindsight it is doubtful if any of them would have changed the views that they expressed. By this time options were few: no solution – military or negotiated – would have been possible unless the Task Force had sailed, and at that time it was not known whether military repossession would be feasible or not; and yet once it arrived there could be little question of its returning empty-handed. For repossession to be abandoned, irrefutable military evidence that landing could not succeed would have been needed. The risks were high, due to the unfavourable air situation, but not high enough for the attempt to be called off, with all the damage to the British prestige that would have resulted if a blockade had to be imposed instead.

Having deployed the Task Force to put pressure on the Argentines to withdraw, it was now necessary, in the light of their refusal to do so, to take matters to their logical conclusion by landing and retaking the islands by force. The Task Force was poised ready to do so, but would need the War Cabinet's immediate approval if the landing was to take place at the optimum moment, which could only be decided by Woodward in the South Atlantic. Provided the preliminary Air and Special Forces operations were allowed to take their toll, the sooner the landing went ahead the better.

The risks of the operation were clearly spelt out. In the absence of air superiority, which had yet to be won, losses from Argentine air attacks in the initial stages were likely to be high, perhaps amounting to a major naval unit and up to half a dozen destroyers/frigates – an estimate that proved remarkably accurate except that the major unit was the container ship *Atlantic Conveyor* instead of a carrier. The possibility of such losses, however, would have to be accepted in the absence of any valid alternative. Whatever happened, and given a reasonable amount of luck, Woodward's men would win through; the vital principle that aggression must not be allowed to pay would be upheld; and Britain's status in the world, and respect for the strength and deterrent credibility of her professional regular forces would be enhanced for many years to come. The operational plan reduced the initial risks to a mimimum, and would be pushed through by all ranks with the greatest resolution, courage and skill. Once the troops were safely ashore, the risks should decrease significantly.

Presented with a united front by the Chiefs, and having had the risks clearly put to them, the Prime Minister and her War Cabinet gave the go-ahead. And so the die was cast. By dint of heroism, skill and quick learning on the part of the Royal Navy, the landing went commendably smoothly. The configuration of the coastline and hills around San Carlos Bay did provide a measure of protection for the ships, and by taking the calculated risk of bringing the great white hull of the liner *Canberra*, carrying the bulk of the immediate follow-up troops, into the sound close behind the assault ships *Fearless* and *Intrepid*, the dangerous first phase of the operation was reduced to the shortest possible time. Some 5,000 troops were landed with scarcely any casualties, and this was repeated just over a week later when 5th Brigade arrived in *QE II*.

The landing was a triumph for Woodward, who had handled his Task Force with consummate skill throughout, and for Fieldhouse who masterminded the whole operation. The subsequent losses once the Argentines had located the landing area and had started to react were indeed high, giving some weight to Nott's argument about the vulnerability of surface ships; and they might have been still higher if the Falklands had been a hundred miles nearer to the mainland, and if two unexpected problems had not beset the Argentine Air Force. Its pilots flew so low in trying to avoid the British Sea Dart, Sea Cat and shore-based Rapier missiles that their bombs, which were equipped with short delay-action fuses to allow the aircraft just enough time to escape the blast of their own bombs, did not have time to arm before hitting their targets. And their low flying resulted in the ingestion of sea spray into their engines, causing, at best, mounting unserviceability, and, at worst, loss of aircraft at sea during the flight home. These problems helped to neutralise the undoubted bravery and skill of the Argentine pilots.

One destroyer and two frigates were sunk in the aftermath of the landing and during the subsequent three week battle, and twelve others were damaged, some seriously, mostly by unexploded bombs. Most of the frigate losses were due to their air defence computers, which were being used for the first time in war, becoming confused or over-loaded. Six Sea Harriers and four RAF Harrier GR 3s were lost, together with 21 naval and three RAF helicopters. The Navy lost 84 killed, while 350 Army casualties occurred in the battles for Goose Green and Port Stanley, including the Welsh Guardsmen lost in the logistic ship *Sir Gallahad* at Bluff Cove.

Despite the early losses in establishing the beachhead, which included the sinking of *Atlantic Conveyor*, carrying vital heavy lift helicopters and stores, by an air-launched Exocet, the most difficult part of the operation was over by 26 May, and the way lay open for the advance on Port Stanley. 25 May had been the Argentine National Day, and their Air Force had put in its final all-out effort to cripple the Task Force. By the end of that day, accumulated losses and unserviceability had put three quarters of the Argentine aircraft out of action; and, although their Air Force had fought well, they had lost air superiority for good. And the Argentine Navy, after losing the *Belgrano*, lay skulking within their own 12 mile limit, unprepared to play any further part in the campaign.

It was at this juncture that the absence of Moore in the beachhead became significant. Brigadier Julian Thompson (later described by Moore as 'the man of the match'), who was commanding the Commando Brigade and all other troops ashore at this stage, undoubtedly had considerable problems due to the loss of *Atlantic Conveyer's* helicopters, which slowed up his logistic build-up and reduced his troop-carrying capacity. Moreover, he was under the impression that his task at this juncture was no more and no less than to secure an adequate beachhead for the arrival of 5th Brigade. Yet his battalions, holding a tight beachhead perimeter and faced, as was well known in London, by virtually no immediate opposition, were achieving nothing except risking casualties from air attacks and suffering the exigencies of the weather.

When the final plan for the landings had been approved by the War Cabinet, the CGS, remembering other amphibious operations, which had floundered after a successful assault landing like Gallipoli in 1915 and Anzio in 1944, was particularly conscious of the importance of the leading brigade, if unopposed, breaking out of the beachhead, establishing contact with the main Argentine positions around Stanley, and generally seizing the initiative. All this was generally agreed policy amongst the Chiefs and at Northwood where it was thought that Moore had also accepted it. Certainly back in Whitehall, with more comprehensive intelligence to hand, and unharassed by battlefield crises and dangers, there was seen to be a clear need to exploit success without delay.

Pressure from Fieldhouse at Northwood and Moore's belated arrival soon overcame the tactical hiatus, and the superbly trained and powerful Commando Brigade then got under way with great style and physical toughness for its 'Yomp' across the island to Stanley. The heroic action of 2nd Parachute Battalion on the flank of the main advance at Goose Green in defeating a force three times their own numbers, and during which their Commanding Officer, Lieutenant Colonel 'H' Jones won his posthumous Victoria Cross, swung the fortunes of the land campaign in Britain's favour from the very start.

By the end of the first week of June, Moore had the Argentines penned into a small area around Stanley and was dominating them from the high ground to the west. Ensuring that full use was made of all available fire support, and carefully co-ordinating fire and movement, he methodically and tenaciously made the Argentine positions untenable.

In the first phase of the final and decisive operations, which began on the night of 11th/12th June, 42 and 45 Commandos, in a superb night attack, stormed Two Sisters and Mount Harriet, and 3rd Parachute Battalion seized Mount Longdon in as tough a fight as 2nd Parachute Battalion had had at Goose Green. These attacks were undoubtedly helped by not publishing the Bluff Cove casualty figures. The Argentines, it was subsequently learnt, thought the losses had been much higher than they were, and that the attack would be delayed for another fortnight.

In the second phase, 2nd Parachute Battalion attacked Wireless Hill immediately north-west of Stanley; the Scots Guards went for Tumbledown held by the Argentine Marines; and the 1st/7th Gurkha Rifles stormed Mount William. These features were well fortified and were expected to be tough positions to crack, but the three assaults won immediate success. Argentine resistance collapsed, and the Gurkhas, with their formidable reputation no doubt preceding them, hardly had to fight at all for Mount William. As the Gurkhas approached, the Argentines turned and fled back to Port Stanley. The leading battalions entered the town with the Argentine conscripts throwing down their arms all around them. The final count of prisoners was about 11,000, mostly from the Stanley area instead of the 6 to 7,000 that it was believed were there.

Britain will always look back with pride on this feat of arms, for which the principal credit must go to the courage, toughness and professionalism of the men on the spot, who fought the battles around and on the Islands against a far from inept enemy, and to the efficiency of the men working the 8,000 miles logistic chain. It was also made possible by the closest inter-Service co-operation from the Chiefs in Whitehall down to the sailors, soldiers and airmen in the Task Force. Although the total casualties in the three Services of 255 killed and 775 wounded was to be greatly regretted and grieved, the operation not only restored the Falklands to British sovereignty, but reinforced respect for British arms.

The campaign also reaffirmed the soundness of the Chiefs of Staff system, and proved the advantages of the most recent step forward in its development, inspired and implemented by Lewin just before the crisis broke. There was a simple and direct chain of responsibility from the War Cabinet downwards, in which a nice balance was struck between the need for decisiveness in command and yet full and detailed examination of possible courses of action, after which the CDS could take a final decision on the advice that he would tender to the War Cabinet, and then give clear directions to the tri-Service C-in-C for the implementation of the Government's decisions. The Naval, General and Air Staffs were still separate entities under CDS's close overall direction, which enabled them to work in unusual harmony during the campaign. How different it all was from the earlier experience at the start of the Norwegian Campaign in 1940!

But the success of any organisation depends on the personalities of those who are managing it, and on the personal chemistry controlling their reactions to one another. There was an excellent direct relationship between the Chiefs and the Prime Minister, which is the first requirement of any democracy in war; and she herself proved an ideal war leader – robust, quick, thoroughly informed and decisive. Lewin, as the CDS with newly enhanced responsibilities, grasped his opportunities brilliantly and was, together with the Prime Minister, a most powerful influence in the War Cabinet throughout the campaign, impressing and even dominating his political colleagues with his confident and emphatic professionalism.

Appropriately, Lewin was also the driving force within the Chiefs of Staff Committee, giving it momentum and providing the C-in-C with clear direction and maximum support. The single-Service Chiefs expressed a variety of opinions at critical moments in the campaign on such issues as forces required, objectives to be achieved, timings, and risks to be faced and accepted, but they were invariably harmonised within the Committee itself. In the event, and bearing in mind that a strong leader attracts resolution, it was always possible to give the War Cabinet unanimous, realistic and firm advice through CDS and sometimes, on crucial occasions, directly. The risks were assessed realistically, but never over-assessed, as they might have been. This harmony greatly strengthened Lewin's hand, and, indeed, made it much easier for the Prime Minister to take difficult decisions.

John Nott too played a well judged and significant part. In war, the position of a Secretary of State for Defence, who is not also Prime Minister, can be anomalous. There has to be a direct relationship between the Prime Minister and the Chiefs. Nott cast himself as something of a devil's advocate in his discussions with the Chiefs within the Ministry of Defence, ensuring that political requirements and military planning were co-ordinated, and that realism always prevailed. Thanks to the part that he played, the Falklands campaign turned out to be one of those rare episodes in history which ended with the politicians and the military enjoying mutual respect for each other's contributions to victory.

And so perhaps the best epitaph for this small epic in British history might be Churchill's words:

> All the great struggles in history have been won by superior willpower wresting victory in the face of odds or upon the narrowest of margins.

For the greatest single factor in the South Atlantic victory was the way in which all ranks of the three Services showed the will to take risks, the will to overcome obstacles and setbacks, and the will, if need be, to make the final sacrifice. But it was also the will to decide and the will to win of the Prime Minister and her Government, as advised by the Chiefs, that created the conditions for all ranks to give of their best.

Chronology
FOR CHAPTER THIRTEEN

1982

Aug   Stanier succeeds Bramall as CGS.

Oct   Bramall succeeds Lewin as CDS.
              Williamson succeeds Beetham as CAS.

Dec   *Falklands Lessons* published.
              Fieldhouse succeeds Leach as First Sea Lord.

1983

Jan   Heseltine becomes S of S for Defence.

June   Thatcher wins second term.

Oct   US intervention in Grenada.

Dec   Geneva INF talks begin.

1984

Jan   Cruise Missile deployment in UK begins.

April   Heseltine proposals for Ministry of Defence reform.

July   Chiefs' meeting with Prime Minister on the reforms.

Oct   IRA bombing of Grand Hotel in Brighton.

1985

Jan   Reorganisation of the Ministry of Defence.

Mar   Gorbachev becomes Soviet Head of State.

Aug   Staveley succeeds Fieldhouse as First Sea Lord.
              Bagnall succeeds Stanier as CGS.

Oct   Craig succeeds Williamson as CAS.

Nov   Reagan/Gorbachev Geneva Summit.
              Anglo-Irish Agreement signed.
              Fieldhouse succeeds Bramall as CDS.

1986
Jan   Heseltine resigns over the Westland affair.
               Younger becomes S of S for Defence.
               Britannia evacuates British refugees from Aden.
April   US bombing of Libya.
               NATO 3 per cent annual budget increases end.
Sep   Keel of first British Trident submarine laid down.
Oct   Reagan/Gorbachev Reykjavik Summit.

1987
June   Thatcher wins third term.
Dec   Reagan/Gorbachev Washington Summit: INF Treaty
               signed.

1988
April   US/Soviet agreement on withdrawal from Afghanistan.
June   Reagan/Gorbachev Moscow Summit.
Aug   Iran/Iraq Armistice signed.
Oct   Fieldhouse retires as CDS.

13
HESELTINE
MAKES HIS MARK

From Victory in the Falklands to the Collapse of the Berlin Wall: July 1982 – October 1989

Secretary of State		Chiefs of Defence Staff	
John Nott		Sir Edwin Bramall	1982
Michael Heseltine	1983	Sir John Fieldhouse	1985
George Younger	1986		
		Chiefs of General Staff	
First Sea Lords		Sir John Stanier	1982
Sir John Fieldhouse	1982	Sir Nigel Bagnall	1985
Sir William Staveley	1985		

Chiefs of Air Staff	
Sir Keith Williamson	1982
Sir David Craig	1985

'The Falklands Campaign was in many respects unique. We must be cautious, therefore, in deciding which lessons of the campaign are relevant to the United Kingdom's main defence priority – our role within NATO against the threat from the Soviet Union and her allies.'
John Nott's *The Falklands: The Lessons*.[1]

It was not just John Nott's thinking that was dented by the South Atlantic Campaign. It had demonstrated a basic fallacy in Whitehall's strategic thinking in the post-Suez era. From Duncan Sandys onwards, there had been a progressive drift away from Britain's traditional maritime strategy towards a virtually exclusive continental commitment, which amounted to an over-emphasis on the potentially greatest threat to the United Kingdom at the expense of the more likely danger to British interests outside the NATO area.

Successive British governments had misread the lessons of the Suez débâcle, and had insisted that Britain would never again go it

alone or get heavily involved in any military action beyond NATO's
boundaries. In truth, the fault with Suez had lain more in inept
political stage-management than with military capability and performance. Economic decline had forced stark choices upon them, and
in a search for ways of cutting defence with least risk, they had
jettisoned the principle of maintaining balanced forces ready and
able to meet the unexpected in favour of single-minded concentration
on European defence. Nott's decision to cut the surface fleet was but
the dénouement of Whitehall's post-Suez thinking.

Since the early 1960s, when the United Nations' debates and
resolutions on de-colonisation had breathed new life into the
Argentine claim to the Falklands and Spain's to Gibraltar, there had
been a political unwillingness to face up to the former. The Falkland
Islands, unlike the Rock, were considered by the Ministry of Defence
to be of little strategic importance, and by the Foreign Office as an
unfortunate legacy of Britain's colonial past. Their seizure by the
Argentines in 1982 demonstrated, if indeed demonstration was
needed, the unpredictability of military events, and the need to retain
reserves against the unforeseen.

All the Chiefs of Staff of the post-Suez years must share some of
the blame for not resisting more strongly Treasury insistence on only
funding projects needed primarily for NATO purposes. It is always
easier to justify force levels against fixed commitments like the
specific pledges to the North Atlantic Alliance than against the ill-
defined need to react to unexpected or miscalculated threats to
British interests elsewhere, and this remained just as true in the post-
Falklands era.

No great bureaucracy like Whitehall welcomes the invalidation of
its perceived wisdom, and it was all too easy to argue that the South
Atlantic Campaign was an exceptional 'one-off' affair which was
never likely to be repeated, and, therefore, that great care should be
taken not to draw false conclusions. It is to John Nott's great credit
that, as a result of his personal post-Falklands efforts, central contingency funds were set aside for the replacement ships, aircraft and
equipment lost in the fighting; and that Defence expenditure was
allowed to rise to the full NATO 3 per cent growth line in real terms,
thus enabling three ASW carriers and two assault ships to be
retained, and the Commando Brigade and 5th Infantry Brigade to be
fully established under a major-general's headquarters as an intervention force.

Understandably, the other major spending departments in

Whitehall and the Treasury were not slow to put down markers to stop Britain's mini-Pentagon profiting from the 'Falklands Windfall'; and within the Ministry of Defence itself there was no rush to change attitudes and some scepticism about the need for an intervention reserve. Nott's December 1982 Defence White Paper, *The Falklands Campaign: The Lessons*, concluded:

> Following the Falklands Campaign, we shall now be devoting substantially more resources to defence than had previously been planned. In allocating these, we shall be taking measures which will strengthen our general defence capability by increasing the flexibility, mobility and readiness of all three Services for operations in support of NATO and elsewhere.[2]

In October 1982, Lewin, who had handled the Falklands crisis so expertly and had been rewarded with his immediate elevation to the House of Lords, had handed over the post of CDS to Bramall, who inherited a completely new team of post-Falklands Chiefs. Bramall himself had been relieved as CGS by the able, articulate and personable Sir John Stanier in August; Beetham by the more self-effacing but very likeable Sir Keith Williamson as CAS in October; and Leach as First Sea Lord by the C-in-C and victor of the Falklands Campaign, Sir John Fieldhouse. John Nott 'soldiered on' until the run up to the 1983 election. He had become disenchanted with politics and wanted to return to his merchant banking career. After he left, the Chiefs had hoped for a period of consolidation, in which the lessons of the Falklands could be absorbed, new equipment brought into service, and a new strategy developed. This was not to be: the Prime Minister replaced Nott with the flamboyant 'mover of mountains', Michael Heseltine, who three years later was to resign so dramatically over the Westland affair; and, in 1990, was to bring about Mrs Thatcher's downfall.

Bramall, as the Services' new professional head, also inherited Armed Forces and their supporting Defence programmes in much better shape than a few years earlier. The former were immensely respected by the majority of the population both for their fighting qualities and the incredible feat of organisation which had enabled them to win a campaign so far from home. The latter were now large enough to give expectations of restoring operational balance and correcting the most glaring equipment weaknesses by the end of the decade. There was every hope that the financial momentum acquired would provide consistent growth over the next seven years and a high enough plateau of money in the system with which to face a more uncertain future.

Soon after Mrs Thatcher had won the 1983 General Election, in which she had used the Falklands factor to her advantage, the financial alarm bells started to ring out once more. The Treasury demanded a straight cut in Defence spending, but failed to carry the day. The Prime Minister reconfirmed the Falklands cash windfall for equipment replacements, garrisoning the islands and construction of Mount Pleasant airfield; and she accepted the NATO 3 per cent growth rate up to the end of 1986, together with more realistic allowances for Defence cost inflation. Perhaps the most important achievement of the Chiefs and the PUS's Department that year, however, lay in winning Treasury agreement to modest carrying forward of underspends on capital equipment at the end of financial years into subsequent years, making financial planning less of a gamble. The Chiefs had reasonable cause for quiet satisfaction as Michael Heseltine began to feel the reins of office.

All Chiefs of Defence Staff since Mountbatten's day had been faced with a stream of financially driven Defence reviews. But with the Defence programmes in better shape; with the Services held in much higher regard by the country; and with the clear demonstration of the need to reshape Defence policy to take greater account of the possibility of 'out-of-area' operations, Bramall decided that the time was ripe to commission a series of staff studies to form the basis of a Chiefs-driven review of strategy. In so doing, he was trying out the Lewin/Nott system whereby the Defence Staff operated under the firm direction of the CDS, and the other Chiefs were only brought in officially at a late stage to comment and amend if necessary, although, of course, their staffs were fully aware of development of the studies as they progressed.

Michael Heseltine, however, devoted his energies to being a decisive Defence reformer rather than an innovative strategist. Although he noted the Chiefs' conclusions to each of the studies, their work remained a mind clearing exercise within the Defence Staff.

In his studies, Bramall used a two-handed approach: one set of papers covered NATO, and the others analysed the full range of possible commitments beyond NATO's boundaries. Both aimed to ensure that the balance of priorities and the composition of the Forces continued to reflect the country's current and future interests. The conclusions on the former were unexceptional. The Chiefs remained firmly and emphatically of the opinion that the security of the United Kingdom still rested upon NATO's collective defence of Western Europe, and that it was right to continue assigning of 95 per cent of Britain's military resources to the Atlantic Alliance. The four roles of British forces within NATO strategy identified in the 1974 Mason/Carver Defence Review – nuclear deterrence, defence of the home base, land and air contributions to the defence of the Central and Northern Fronts, and naval contribution to the defence of the Eastern Atlantic – remained valid. In their judgement, credible deterrence depended upon the close but not precipitate linkage between conventional and nuclear forces, and it was on the former that studies were largely focussed. The Trident decision was re-endorsed; specific weaknesses in the conventional weapon system for continental warfare were identified; and the mix of sea, land and air forces was judged reasonably well balanced.[3]

In the 'Out-of-Area' studies, emphasis was placed on improving the flexibility and strategic and tactical mobility of the NATO assigned forces stationed in the United Kingdom, so that they could be double-earmarked and could react more quickly to unforeseen crisis like the Falklands. Historical precedent suggested, and this has been confirmed by recent events in the Gulf, that incidents needing British military intervention in some form or other were much more likely to occur outside rather than inside Europe, and that such threats could also endanger the vital interests of the countries of the Atlantic Alliance, particularly their dependence upon Middle East oil supplies.

In the studies of specific geographic areas, the Middle East stood out as by far the most important area strategically from the point of view of maintaining world peace and enhancing British economic interests. With the Iran/Iraq war continuing and the Lebanon in turmoil, there was an obvious coincidence of critical factors in the area: dangers of a widening conflict and superpower confrontation; threats to the West's energy supplies; international competition in arms sales and general trade; and Britain's past and continuing involvement in the area. The Chiefs, therefore, judged that there was national interest as well as international obligation to work for a stable balance of power in the Middle East. This would be best achieved, short of re-establishing troops in the area, for which there was neither political nor military support, by using Britain's historic links in the area to help friends to help themselves.

This concept of indirect military influence was very much Bramall's own philosophy, which he had been developing while he was CGS, and which became known as the 'Fifth Pillar' of British strategy. He pulled together all the unco-ordinated strands of military

assistance to other countries by establishing an Out-of-Area
Co-ordinating Group to give coherent political, military, industrial
and intelligence direction to the many agencies involved: positioning
high quality Service attachés in British Embassies and High
Commissions; provision of loan-service personnel, advisers and military assistance teams; offering training courses in British military
establishments; exchange personnel schemes and VIP visits; judi-
cious arms sales; contributing to United Nations and other peace-
keeping forces; maintaining naval visits and Fleet deployments
world-wide; exercising in friendly overseas territories; and, as a last
resort only, being ready to commit intervention forces, if asked to do
so by a friendly country in trouble.

In their final conclusions, the Chiefs judged that it was timely to
break with the strict tenets of the Mason/Carver 'Critical Level'
philosophy and to acknowledge an out-of-area intervention requirement. This would be achieved by improving strategic mobility and
flexibility; by double earmarking the Commando and 5th Airborne
Brigades under a two-star headquarters (the Army's South East
District) for NATO and out-of-area operations; and by building up
'Fifth Pillar' measures. The dispatch of an armoured brigade to the
Middle East was not envisaged at that time, but the concept of
improved strategic mobility, which included the retention and eventual replacement of the assault ships, and the continuing use of the
Army's logistic ships with tank carrying capacity, covered such an
eventuality.[4]

Michael Heseltine, however, was another Secretary of State for
Defence, like Duncan Sandys and John Nott, in a political hurry. A
rising star in the Tory Party, with an unashamed ambition to become Prime Minister in the not too distant future, he wished to make
his mark before moving on upwards. His chosen weapon was MINIS
(Management Information Service), a system which he had devised
while Secretary of State for the Environment for probing departmental organisation and ways of doing business. For most of 1983, his
first year as Secretary of State for Defence, he probed his new
ministry with innumerable fact-finding MINIS inquisitions. All the
signs pointed to a politically inspired urge to achieve large cuts in
staff numbers, particularly amongst the civil servants.

The fundamental principle upon which the Ministry of Defence
had been set up by Mountbatten in 1964 was the centralisation of
policy and the decentralisation of management, although it was often
difficult to define where one stopped and the other began. But

there were two schools of thought as to how the staffs should be organised. The one which enjoyed most support, particularly amongst the Service officers as opposed to the civil servants, saw overall policy being the responsibility of the 'Centre' while management rested with the Service Departments, the three environments – Sea, Land and Air – being treated as separate entities within the overall system. The opposing school favoured an organisation based on 'function' rather than Service at all levels with greater centralisation and a weakening of the Service Departments.

The organisation that Michael Heseltine set out to probe was still run on Service lines, reflecting the three very different environments in which the Armed Forces live, train and fight, rather than on the less manageable, less assessable and certainly less human functional lines with 'purple' departments for Personnel, Equipment, Supply, Movement, Barracks and so on. It was the task of the four Chief executives – Chief of Defence Staff, Permanent Under-Secretary, Chief Scientific Adviser and Chief of the Procurement Executive – to reconcile the disparate Service points of view, and to cut through the barrage of special pleading from vested Service interests, boasting in General Motors' style that what was good for the Navy, Army or Air Force was good for Britain. Awkward though this might be, it did provide useful checks upon any ill-considered Central Staff policies; the chain of responsibility was clearer than in a functional system; and, above all, the principle of each Chief being responsible for the ultimate execution of the advice that he tendered to the CDS in the Chiefs of Staff Committee was unbreached.

Heseltine, as a compulsive reformer, tended to take the minority functionalisers' point of view. He decided – not unreasonably – to strengthen his own and his successors' control over the ministry, and over its programmes and allocation of resources. He was on reasonably safe ground in that Mountbatten had stopped short of his original unifying aspirations, and the central policy function of the Defence Staff had been gradually eroded since his day by single-Service pressure. There were also elements in the Ismay/Jacob Report and in Mountbatten's own arguments, which could be surrected with some credibility and with the accompanying impression that something was at last being done by reformer Heseltine to bring the full Mountbatten concept to fruition after a lapse of two decades! And there was no dearth of outside experts without direct responsibility, who were prepared to urge him on 'to cut the Service Chiefs down to size'. Taking a knife to the head office of any large organisation is rarely an unpopular exercise, and the Ministry of Defence was often accused of growing while the Armed Forces were steadily contracting.

Heseltine set about his reforms behind closed doors. Without reference to the Chiefs, he produced his own paper, setting out in some detail what he intended to achieve: the functionalisation of the Defence Staff; the weakening of the influence of the Service Departments and particularly the power of the single-Service Chiefs; and the strengthening of his own control over programmes through the creation of a new and largely civilian Office of Management and Budget, reporting direct to him through a 2nd PUS, and responsible for deciding the shape and size of the Forces.

In functionalising the Defence Staff and reducing the power of the single-Service Chiefs, he gave little recognition of recent Lewin/Nott reforms which had strengthened the CDS's powers in relation to his colleagues and had worked so well during the Falklands campaign. In truth, his ideas probably owed as much if not more to what Mountbatten had not achieved than to his own MINIS investigations. Nonetheless, he undoubtedly illuminated a number of anomalies, duplications and over-tiered structures, which might provide opportunities for streamlining to the benefit of the front line.

His proposals centred upon clipping the wings of the single-Service Chiefs by removing their Vice-Chiefs of Staff and cutting down their executive staffs. As much management responsibility as possible was also to be decentralised downwards to the principal Commanders-in-Chief outside Whitehall. The three three-star posts of the Vice-Chiefs would be re-used to head three of four functional sections of the new Defence Staff as Deputy Chiefs of Defence Staff 'Commitments', 'Systems', and 'Programmes and Personnel' (the fourth being 'Policy' under a three-star civil servant). All four were to report to the CDS through a four-star Vice-Chief of Defence Staff with the status of a full member of the Chiefs of Staff Committee. The single-Service Chiefs were left with two-star Assistant Chiefs of Staff advised by one-star directors.

Illogically, the creation of the largely civilian manned Office of Management and Budget cut right across two of Heseltine's stated aims: improving and simplifying chains of responsibility, and welding the civilian and military staffs closer together in the functional staffs to avoid duplication of effort. It brought a new centre of power into existence with its own 'freemasonry', and, far from correcting duplication of civil and military advice, it seemed likely to prove a new and divisive hierarchy in its own right, complicating rather than easing the already over-complex fields of programming, weapon procurement and management generally.

The Chiefs were brought into the debate only on the eve of Heseltine putting his broad outline proposals to his Cabinet colleagues in late April 1984. Their task was to help draw up the detailed blueprint of organisation and working arrangements needed to implement his plan. While there could be no change in his main proposals, his paper was to be treated as a consultative document, and was, indeed, so used in the constructive dialogue that followed in fleshing out the practical details. Moreover, the Chiefs' worst fears were set at rest by there being nothing in his paper that could be construed as infringing the independence of the Services themselves or the responsibility of the Chiefs for their management, morale and fighting efficiency.[5]

The Chiefs were in something of a dilemma. As public servants, they could not take issue with Heseltine's intention to strengthen his position in his own ministry, since this was what Parliament would expect him to do; nor could they reject functionalisation out of hand because there was considerable merit for its extension into some fields like crisis management, long-term concepts, and programme scrutiny and control. If policy had really been slipping too much to the wings – to the Service Departments – as critics maintained, and this had encouraged some of the more disagreeable aspects of inter-Service rivalry, and made decision-making and allocation of tight resources that much harder and more frustrating as a process, then the sooner it was corrected the better.

The CDS, who through his close association with Mountbatten, had experienced Whitehall hostility to any organisational change, was keen that the Chiefs should be as constructive and open-minded as possible. The important thing was to build upon the sound elements of his proposals, and seek to extract maximum safeguards in areas of difficulty. A special Steering Group was set up to carry out the work in two months.

A blueprint was produced towards the end of June. While the scheme had the merits of centralising strategy, allocation of resources and control of operations, it was flawed by the emasculation of the single-Service Chiefs' own staffs. Their ability to discharge their duties as the professional heads of their Services and as CDS's advisers on policies, to be pursued in their very different environments, was bound to be significantly diminished; lines of responsibi-

lity were likely to be blurred, particularly by the introduction of the
Office of Management and Budget; and, worst of all, there was a
danger of policy becoming too far removed from management, as had
happened in Hitler's OKW.

At the heart of the matter lay the degradation of specialist Sea,
Land and Air advice in the formulation of Defence policy and
decision-making. The real fears were not whether the new organisation could be made to work in peacetime – almost any organisation
could be made to do so if staffed by the right people – but what
would happen in war. Instead of the First Sea Lord, for instance,
being listened to with respect and confidence when he told the Prime
Minister at the start of the Falklands crisis that the Navy could sail a
powerful fleet in a matter of days, which could look after itself if
attacked by the Argentines, a future head of the Navy would have to
say that it was no use asking him as neither he nor his predecessors
had had any real say in the size, shape and equipment of the naval
Service. There was merit in some tipping of the organisational balance towards the 'Centre', but soundly based tri-Service professional
dialogue was essential to prevent policy being hijacked by bureaucrats who might be influenced more by political and economic factors
than by the best available professional judgement.

Heseltine made some concessions, allowing the single-Service
Chiefs to keep stronger executive staffs of their own, and the *modus
operandi* of the Office of Management and Budget was made more
acceptable by close collocation with the Central military staffs dealing with the same subjects; but he was not prepared to bring back
the Vice-Chiefs nor to rethink the core issue of single-Service advice.
The Chiefs could live with the further strengthening of the 'Centre',
but not happily with the isolation and distancing of single-
Service Chiefs from policy. The CDS, therefore, at the Secretary of
State's suggestion, exercised the Chiefs' constitutional right of access
to the Prime Minister to ensure that the implications of the new
organisation were fully understood before the die was finally cast in
its favour.

The Prime Minister held two meetings on 4th July 1984: one with
the CDS and Secretary of State, and the other with all the Chiefs
present. It was agreed that the blueprint should be implemented,
subject to review after a year's working. Each Chief was to be left
with an adequate executive staff of his own, and the Prime Minister
is said to have stressed the importance she attached to the Chiefs of
Staff as an institution, both individually and collectively, recalling

how she had brought them all into the advisory and decision-making process during the Falklands. The Prime Minister's regular meetings with the Chiefs which had lapsed in her predecessors' time, were to be revived. And the Chiefs' individual and collective access to the Prime Minister was confirmed.

Fortified by the Prime Minister's very considerable assurances, which provided some safeguards against their longer term fears, the Chiefs set about the complex task of implementing the blueprint by Heseltine's target date of 1 January 1985. On 18 July 1984, the CDS, on behalf of the Chiefs, commended the amended exercise to the senior officers of the three Services.

Only time will tell whether it would have been wiser to build on the Lewin/Nott reorganisation rather than suffer the upheaval of the Heseltine reforms. The Chiefs of Staff Committee remained firmly above the Defence Staff as the final arbiter of advice tendered to the CDS; the single-Service Chiefs of Staff retained just enough power to exert their professional influence, although they sorely missed their Vice-Chiefs; and checks and balances within the organisation had been incorporated to prevent the Office of Management and Budget from adopting bureaucratic solutions which were long on political and economic appeal but short of military judgement and value.

Whether the crucial balances between policy and management, and between power and responsibility, had been wisely struck would probably not be known until some great military crisis occurred. In the meantime it looked as if the Centre would be able to operate more quickly and directly, and with less frustration and impeding vetoes from Service Departments than in the past. At the end of the day, the quality of the people, the decisions that they took and when they took them, were going to be more important than lines on an organisational chart. Thanks to sensible compromises on both sides, the new organisation got off to a reasonable start.

Heseltine's drive as a ruthless administrator, and as a man of radical ideas, did find outlets in two other quite different areas. The first was winning the nuclear debate against the unilateralist and CND lobbies, which had gathered strength and momentum during the anti-Cruise Missile protests that had been sweeping Europe in the mid-1980s. The second was in the search for value for money in the equipment field. In both he made a major contribution in Defence affairs, and could claim considerable success.

In the nuclear debate, he seized the initiative and rallied public support to such an extent that the Labour Party, with its unilateralist leanings, was thrown on the defensive in the run-up to the 1987 General Election. In the quest for value for money, he improved the performance of the Procurement Executive in negotiating competitive contracts; increased the equipment share of the Defence vote by some 15 per cent, mostly at the expense of civilian manpower; and sought and achieved greater collaboration with Western European armament industries, although this brought about his resignation over the Westland Helicopters affair in January 1986.

Bramall handed over to Fieldhouse as CDS in November 1985, two months before the well-liked, sound and more phlegmatic George Younger became Secretary of State for Defence in Heseltine's place. Sir William Staveley, who had been Vice-Chief of Naval Staff at the time of the Falklands and later C-in-C Fleet, had taken over as First Sea Lord the previous August; Sir Nigel Bagnall, a profound and advanced military thinker, who had made a marked impact upon the armoured tactics adopted by NATO on the Central Front, became CGS in the same month; and Sir David Craig, who was the RAF's candidate as the next CDS, was appointed CAS in October.

During his time as CDS, Bramall had achieved his aim of nudging Whitehall into a more open acceptance of the out-of-area role with its need for greater strategic and tactical mobility and organisational flexibility, and he had established the 'Fifth Pillar' of projecting and protecting British overseas interests by indirect military means. Whitehall could not be expected to tolerate a greater change of strategy during a period in which there were no military crises to force more far-reaching change. He left the further consolidation of the concept of more balanced continental-cum-maritime forces able to react quickly to the unforeseen, inside and outside the NATO area, in the capable hands of John Fieldhouse, whom the Prime Minister had selected as CDS although it was not the Navy's turn to provide the next incumbent.

Fieldhouse with the experience of being C-in-C during the Falklands Campaign behind him and with his deeply held conviction that greater emphasis on a maritime out-of-area strategy was good for the Navy and *ipso facto* good for the country, needed no prompting. He saw, as the quote at the head of the last chapter shows, that the Soviet threat, although the most dangerous, was at the same time the least likely to lead to war. He went on to say:

> We will not be able to devote substantially greater resources directly to our out-of-area capability than we do today. We must, therefore, ensure that what we do is best tailored to our needs, and that we engineer flexibility and mobility

into our NATO forces wherever possible so that double earmarking makes sense.[6]

His expression 'engineering flexibility and mobility into our NATO forces' reflected the prescient and growing conviction amongst the Chiefs that the 'heavy army' on the Continent rather than the Fleet was the albatross around their necks long before there was any overt sign of the collapse of Communism in Eastern Europe. Fieldhouse and his team were well ahead of the rest of Whitehall where his grumbles about 'sea-blindness' in the bureaucracy were met with scepticism by the majority of policy-makers, who still believed, despite the Falklands, that Britain's growing links with Europe were turning British sea-power into an anachronism.

The Chiefs' views on the need to maintain balanced forces against the unforeseen started to gain credibility as assessments of the impact of Gorbachev's assumption of power in the Soviet Union began to point to significant changes of attitude in Moscow. The need for a more general purpose balance in British Defence policy was becoming more obvious as established patterns of strategic thinking were brought into question by the course of events in the Communist world. The 1987 Defence White Paper devoted an unusually large section to out-of-area operations, concluding:

> We must, of course, be realistic about what – in political, military and economic terms – we can afford to do. And we must aim to use our defence resources as effectively as we can in support of our interests throughout the world.[7]

After Bramall's period of relatively comfortable budgetary stability, Fieldhouse's new team of Chiefs had to face up to the ending of the NATO 3 per cent growth and the fading away of the Falklands cash windfall. To make matters more difficult, a 5 per cent cut was imposed on the Defence vote on the politically attractive but quite unwarranted assumption that the loss would be compensated for by increased efficiency, stemming from the managerial reforms.[8] The perennial problems of money and manpower returned to haunt the new Chiefs; and they were also faced with the prospect of a general election as Margaret Thatcher's second administration neared its end.

The tapering of the Bull market – the Defence share of the GDP fell from 5.2 per cent in 1984 to 4.3 per cent by 1988 – made equipment procurement decisions increasingly difficult, but the financial crunch, which so many opponents of Trident D5 were predicting would force another defence review, did not occur. The Younger/Fieldhouse team were remarkably successful in arguing the

Defence case in successive Public Expenditure Reviews, but their efforts would have been negated if the Labour Party had won the 1987 General Election, which was again fought and won by Mrs Thatcher largely on Defence issues.

In the event Labour lost, and the Younger/Fieldhouse team not only managed to justify some real growth, albeit from a lower base-line, but also secured agreement that their financial targets over those three years would only be reviewed if there was a significant change in the world situation or in the country's economic prospects, which would necessitate a major change in Defence policy.

Almost as soon as they had achieved this welcome measure of financial stability and had ridden off demands for a new Defence Review, the unexpected did, indeed, start to happen on an un-predictable scale in the Middle East, in China and in Eastern Europe. The Iraq/Iran armistice was signed in August 1988 bringing an end to that long and bloody war, but not restoring stability to the Middle East where the thorn of Israeli existence still festered in the Arab body politic. The Tiananmen Square massacre crushed the life out of the pro-democracy student revolt in Peking in the spring of 1989. The collapse of the Berlin Wall followed that summer, and the reunification of Germany became a disturbing but obvious possi-bility. And interest rates in Britain peaked at 15 per cent without having much immediate effect on rising inflation in the economy. The conditions for a review of Defence spending targets could no longer be resisted: the major Communist threat had all but col-lapsed, and the British economy needed a peace dividend.

Both Younger and Fieldhouse had left office by this time, and it was up to their successors, Tom King and Sir David Craig, to initiate the 'Options for Change' studies, the Tory euphemism for a defence review. But before these could be finalised, the unexpected happened yet again: Saddam Hussein invaded Kuwait.

It is too early to assess how well the Heseltine/Bramall reorganisa-tion has fared in meeting the demands of these traumatic events, for this story of the Chiefs really ends with Fieldhouse's tenure as CDS. But it should surprise no one if it was found necessary to restrengthen the influence of the First Sea Lord, the Chief of General Staff and the Chief of Air Staff as advisers to the Chief of Defence Staff and the Government. The principle of not giving power to those who do not hold responsibility for executive action is still as true in the 1990s as it was in Churchill's and Alanbrooke's day. Four heads, each possessing some forty years of personal and three centuries of inherited experience in the Armed Forces of the Crown, can still be better than one in developing and implementing Britain's grand strategy, and, when men are fighting for their lives, there must never be any blurring of the executive lines of responsibility.

EPILOGUE
Looking Back from the Nineties: One Step Too Far?

The Chiefs of 1990

Secretary of State for Defence	Tom King	1989
Chief of Defence Staff	Sir David Craig	1988
First Sea Lord	Sir Julian Oswald	1989
Chief of General Staff	Sir John Chapple	1988
Chief of Air Staff	Sir Peter Harding	1988
Vice Chief of Defence Staff	Sir Richard Vincent*	1987

'O God! that one might read the book of fate
And see the revolution of the times . . .'
Shakespeare, Henry IV, Part 2

While this story of the Chiefs was being completed, the new team – David Craig, Julian Oswald, John Chapple, Peter Harding and Richard Vincent (VCDS and fifth Chief) – were facing the first real test of the Heseltine re-organisation of the Ministry of Defence: the collapse of the Soviet threat, upon which the shape and size of the Armed forces had been based since the Second World War, leading to the 'Options for Change' studies, the crisis in the Gulf caused by Saddam Hussein's invasion of Kuwait and a full scale, if happily brief, war to turn him out again.

Perhaps Craig's team will never really know quite how well or badly the new system has worked in comparison with the past. It is their successors, at present working down in the engine-room of the central Defence and single-Service staffs, who will be more aware of its strengths and weaknesses. It is always easier to look upwards to see the way an organisation is working; and there is every incentive to do so if you are likely to have to work it yourself one day. It is, however, well worth looking back over the history of the evolution of the Chiefs to consider what the future may hold for them.

---

* to become CDS in 1991.

One requirement stands out above all others in the working of the Defence decision-making system, and that is the need for balance: balance between the politically desirable and the militarily practicable, or vice versa; balance between the needs of the three Services, operating together although in the three very different environments; and balance between central policy-makers, who, as the old adage puts it, tend to know less and less about more and more, and the experts in naval, land and air warfare, who have the opposite skills, knowing more and more about less and less, but who are vital in deciding what is practicable in war and peace.

The quest for balance has taken place over three consecutive periods in the evolution of the Chiefs: 1904–1923; 1923–1964 and 1964 onwards. The ground rules for politico-military balance were evolved by the Committee of Imperial Defence and had been firmly established by 1923 when the Chiefs of Staff Committee was formed. Before that, naval and land warfare had not overlapped enough for special inter-Service co-ordinating machinery to be necessary. It was the formation of the RAF as the third Service at the end of the First World War that impelled the establishment of the Chiefs of Staff Committee in 1923, and began the quest for inter-Service balance. And finally it was Mountbatten's drive for unification of Defence decision-making in the early 1960s that triggered the current search for balance between the Central policy makers and the managers of the Service Departments.

The critical factor common to all three periods has been the span of responsibility that ministers and their professional advisers have been deemed able to handle. Paradoxically, despite the increasing complexity of warfare, which should have enforced decentralisation, advances in communications and electronic command and control systems, have been even more rapid. They have made centralisation ever more practicable and, indeed, more necessary for operational efficiency and economic management.

In the first period, which really began at the end of the 19th Century, the problem was how to achieve naval and military efficiency without surrendering political control. The Admiralty Board and Army Council systems were already in place to provide separate collective professional advice to ministers on sea and land warfare, and for the internal management of the Navy and Army, but there was no governmental machinery for developing national strategy on which the allocation of resources between the two Services could be based. There was some hankering for the appointment of a

Minister of Defence, but the task was considered too great for one man to handle. There were also suggestions that the First Lord of the Admiralty and the Secretary of State for War should be former professional men with seats provided for them in the House of Lords: an idea that was not finally quashed until Kitchener demonstrated during the First World War the incompatibility of the characteristics of the political and military mind.

The development of the Kaiser's German Great General Staff set a precedent which could have been copied had it been as appropriate for a democracy as it was for an absolute monarchy. But, for the British, it smacked too much of dictatorship, and so the more politically acceptable Committee of Imperial Defence, chaired by the Prime Minister, was established in 1904 in traditional British mode with a secretariat, which had to serve as a substitute for a British Great General Staff. Although the CID was replaced by various forms of War Cabinet during the First World War, and its secretariat became the Cabinet Secretariat under the ubiquitous Maurice Hankey, the principles needed for balance in politico-military relations had been firmly established by 1923.

The two most important of these principles were, first, that only the Prime Minister in Cabinet had the mandate to take the major decisions of Defence policy. A deputy, or later a Minister of Defence, could be tasked to carry some of the burden in peace, but the ultimate responsibility for the security of the realm rested with the Prime Minister. And second, that the tasks of the Chiefs were to tender collective and individual military advice to the Government, and, as the professional heads of the Navy and Army, to maintain their battle-winning efficiency and high morale. These principles could well hold good today.

The Navy and Army fought hard during the second period to overturn the 1917 decision to form the RAF as an independent Service, but they could never counter the Trenchard philosophy of the indivisibility and independence of air power. With sea and land warfare straddled by the air, the replacement of the defunct CID by the Chiefs of Staff Committee was the logical outcome of the Salisbury Commission's deliberations, but opinion in Westminster and Whitehall in the 1920s saw the appointment of a Minister of Defence as politically undesirable in that it was still believed to require too wide a remit for one man to handle, and anyway would concentrate too much power in his hands. The possibility of appointing a Chief of Defence Staff was not even considered. If it had been, it would probably have been turned down for the same reasons, and for fear of re-opening the door to the ghost of Cromwell!

The Chiefs of Staff system proved itself under Churchill and Alan Brooke in the Second World War, and it was copied, almost *in toto*, by the Americans with one important exception. With Churchill combining the roles of Prime Minister and Minister of Defence there was no lack of political direction, but doubts were expressed from time to time about the British system of rotating the chairmanship of the Chiefs instead of appointing the equivalent of a Chief of Defence Staff, as the Americans did with Admiral Leahy as the first incumbent. Brooke and his colleagues rejected such an appointment on the sound principle that it is always unwise to divorce military planning from responsibility for execution, or policy from management. Again this principle remains equally sound today, and its breach could spell disaster in war.

The post-war explosion of weapon technology, and the acceleration in the rate of military change with its related Defence costs inflation, enforced the appointment of Ministers of Defence and Chiefs of Defence Staff with stronger supporting staffs, and prepared the ground for the third period starting with the Mountbatten reforms of 1964. Economic decline and the consequential shrinkage in resources available for Defence added to the pressures for greater centralisation of policy to neutralise the intense rivalry, which grew up between the Chiefs as they fought on behalf of their own Services for the lion's share of the smaller Defence cake.

In creating the unified Ministry of Defence in 1964, Mountbatten was stopped well short of the total functionalisation of the ministry and the unification of the Services. The power of the CDS flowed from his chairmanship of the Chiefs of Staff Committee. The only staff that he was allowed in his own right was his personal briefing team: the newly created Defence Staff were responsible to the Chiefs of Staff Committee *per se*. Power still rested with the Chiefs, who, as the managers as well as the policy makers of their Services, could wield the veto in the Chiefs of Staff Committee whose views CDS was constitutionally responsible for representing, rather than tendering advice to the Government in his own right.

The system worked unscathed for almost two decades, but in that time two new centres of power gradually developed within the Ministry of Defence to cater for the explosion in weapon technology and the consequential financial stresses: the Chief Scientific Adviser's staff, and the Permanent Under-Secretary's empire consisting of

Defence Secretariat, which provided the co-ordinating nervous system for the Ministry, and his financial staffs. Both had centralising instincts and motivation. By the beginning of the 1980s, the ground was once again ready for another step towards greater centralisation in the short term and perhaps unification of the Services in the more distant future. The optimum balance between policy and management was still not satisfactorily resolved.

The successive Lewin and Heseltine reforms have strengthened the Centre at the expense of the Service Departments. Advising the Secretary of State and hence the Government, there is now a triumvirate at the highest level: the Chief of Defence Staff, the Permanent Under-Secretary, and the Chief Scientific Adviser, although he is, in fact, subordinate to the Permanent Under-Secretary. The Chiefs in their collective capacity have been reduced to a subordinate advisory level, and in their individual capacities they are now in a lower management tier. If that centralising trend continues, they could become Commanders-in-Chief outside Whitehall, like Wolseley in the 1880s, or even Chief Personnel Officers of their own Service within the Ministry of Defence as has been mooted in some quarters. Divorced from the formulation of Defence policy, and denied their Vice-Chiefs, they could even have difficulty in finding out what is being planned and prepared in the Centre, let alone making an early and significant contribution to the process.

In the actual conduct of the Gulf War – admittedly largely a United States responsibility – the Service Chiefs were kept more on the fringes of operational policy and planning than would have been the case in the past. The CDS alone advised the Government, and although he debriefed the Chiefs after meetings of the War Cabinet, he did not draw on their wider experience or expertise before the event, relying more on the briefing of his own central staff. The Chiefs were confined to planning and organising the deployment of British forces, and to making the complex movement and logistic arrangements involved. This was in marked contrast to the all-British Falklands Campaign eight years earlier when the Prime Minister, at times, drew on the experience and ideas of all the Chiefs, and when the CDS always consulted them before War Cabinet meetings.

The key questions now therefore are: has centralisation been taken too far? Is policy becoming too divorced from management? And are the Chiefs' days numbered? Let us, therefore, look briefly at the Chiefs' strengths and weaknesses.

Since their inception the Chiefs have been, individually, the Chief executives of their own Service, and, collectively, the professional advisers to the Government. Like all human beings they are fallible, though much less so as a collective body than individually. They can never forget that they epitomise the hopes and fears of their own Service; but they have shown themselves capable of both evolution and of operating effectively within the political and financial constraints properly laid upon them by the Cabinet and Parliament; and they have worked in reasonably constructive harmony with their civilian and scientific colleagues. They can certainly claim considerable achievements since the Second World War; and, despite some anti-nuclear sentiment within the electorate, the stock of the Armed Forces has rarely stood higher. Few parents do not feel a pride in seeing sons and daughters serving their Sovereign in the Royal Navy, Army or Royal Air Force. The Chiefs can take some credit for this state of affairs.

The principal criticism levelled at them is that when resources are tight, as they usually are, the Chiefs tend to eye each embryonic change of strategy, organisational initiative or breakthrough in weapon technology from the point of view of its impact on their own Service's programmes, rather than in the wider context of national security. It would certainly be difficult to find a CGS prepared to welcome a major swing away from the Continental commitment to a wholly Maritime strategy, which would drastically reduce the Army's operational units; or a First Sea Lord, who was keen to accept, without question, a rationale for drastically reducing surface escorts, thus breaching the principle of maintaining a balanced Fleet able to react to the unforeseen.

The Chief's collective and individual responsibilities do therefore clash sometimes, and this can lead to divided loyalties, but there is a reverse side to this coin. If the Chiefs were not to make their parochial points, particularly in a climate when there are seldom enough resources in any Service to meet existing commitments let alone the unexpected, and risks have to be taken, critical considerations could go by default. Those who talk glibly about a 'best' Defence solution to which the Chiefs should be ready, loyally and enthusiastically to subscribe, are not necessarily referring to what is best in military terms. They are probably describing the politically most attractive course; or one that conforms to the view of Treasury officials, who, as has so often been said in the past, are better at assessing the cost of things than their relative value to the nation; and who cannot escape responsibility for Britain's military plight in 1939. The political and financial factors are certainly important, and ultimately may have to be overriding, but the military voice must be clearly heard and understood in the corridors of Whitehall, albeit not necessarily in the country at large, where presenting the Defence case must remain the prerogative of Ministers.

Even if there were no inter-Service arguments, there would be others on less easily assessable and manageable lines of antipathy within a functional organisation, such as personnel versus equipment or equipment versus barracks and pay, and so forth. The apparent weakness caused by rivalry within the Chiefs of Staff system can, therefore, be far from unproductive, provided there is the central machinery with the knowledge and determination to cut Gordian knots. This is where the CDS, his Vice-Chief and the Defence Staff play their crucial role, interacting with the PUS's largely civilian manned Office of Management and Budget. The Chiefs still have their right of access to the Prime Minister, who can overrule or support them if the Centre, in some exceptional case, has not been able to resolve the issue within the Ministry.

A study of the Chiefs also shows that they never have been, and probably never can be, particularly innovative. All their background and training, and the professional briefing that they receive from their staffs, tends to make them err on the side of caution both in peace and war as Churchill realised. '*You may take the most gallant sailor, the most intrepid airman, and the most audacious soldier, put them at a table together – and what do you get?*' he used to ask, '*The sum of their fears!*'[1] This was less than generous to Alan Brooke's team, who curbed his less practicable ideas; but he may not have been far wrong. It was the balancing of his restlessly innovative mind by the more cautious professionalism of the Chiefs, who had to weigh the risks and bear the responsibility for executive action, that ensured the coherent and dynamic direction of the Second World War, which contrasted so sharply with the conduct of the First, when the Chiefs of Staff system did not exist.

Certainly, if the Chiefs are to give their best, particularly during active operations, there must be a linkage of mutual respect between their expertise as professional advisers and the drive of a decisive Prime Minister capable of 'delivering' Parliament and the country, without whose support the Armed Forces of the Crown cannot operate efficiently. This was the secret of success in the Second World War, and it was repeated with great advantage during the Falklands

Campaign.

Under purely peacetime conditions, the Chiefs may see themselves too much the guardians of what they believe is worth preserving within their own Services to espouse very willingly some novel proposal from which one Service or another might suffer. They are highly suspicious of politically or financially inspired initiatives, and they dislike reformers like Sandys, Nott and Heseltine with political ambitions, whose tenure in office can often be much shorter lived than the damage that they can inflict. The prime example of the Canadian experiment in unification stands as a warning of what can sometimes happen. The instigator left public life soon afterwards, never to reappear, but the Canadian Forces were stuck with his unsound system for many years.

So perhaps it is hardly surprising that, in return, ministers tend to treat the Chiefs with some wariness, often believing that if they take them into their confidence too early, they may use the time to take up entrenched positions, rally arguments and gather outside support. Ministers feel more secure with a small caucus of civil servants beholden only to them. Michael Heseltine's decision not to take the CDS into his confidence until the eleventh hour before revealing his plans for the 1985 reorganisation of the Ministry of Defence, may have been a case in point. He no doubt thought that if he revealed his plans earlier, the CDS would be in duty bound to inform the other Chiefs and this would make it more difficult for him to achieve what he wanted. On that occasion he may have done the Chiefs less than justice since they showed themselves to be constructive in discussions with him, and they made no attempt to gather outside support against him.

But old habits die hard. There have been many other clashes with ministers in the past and wariness persists. The latest studies, 'Options for Change', have again been carried out largely by the Centre and away from the formal Chiefs of Staff machinery, but in this case there seems to have been no clear ministerial view of the way ahead or of what the Government wanted to do – hence the title!

At the root of the matter lies the fundamental differences between sea, land and air warfare, and in the types of men and women and the equipment they need, which must never be overlooked. Although there has been a growing together in weapon technology, logistic support and general inter-Service co-operation, the three Services still fight under very different operational conditions, which require diverse techniques handed down from one generation to another. It takes a lifetime's experience to master war in one environment. It is only possible in the latter half of an officer's career to achieve a broad understanding of the problems of fighting in the other two environments. Brilliant though a tri-Service commander may prove himself to be, he still needs expert advice on the other Services' capabilities in the same way that a brigade commander would be lost without his gunner and sapper advisers. The same applies to the CDS, who will usually have proved himself already as a tri-Service commander, but is still dependent on the advice of First Sea Lord, CGS and CAS.

So it is in their collective capacity that the Chiefs have the greatest part to play in the development of national security policy and in crisis management. It is they who bring to bear the whole weight of experience accumulated over the centuries in their own Services to ensure a full debate on the complex issues, which are the day to day fare of any ministry of defence. Four minds (or five now the VCDS is a full member of the Chiefs) are invariably better than one in the assessment of military options and their attendant risks. Moreover, whatever may be supposed, and however much the Chiefs may be criticised for lack of unanimity, ministers do not always like to be presented with Hobson's choice; nor do they appreciate their political options being too constrained.

It is, of course, never wise to fight wars by committee, and, indeed operational planning and execution should always be delegated to a C-in-C as was done in the Falklands and in the Gulf. Nevertheless, at Ministry of Defence level, all options, practical difficulties and risks must be exposed and analysed; and when this is being done, there is great advantage in bringing to bear the power of those minds that have the executive responsibility and the depth of knowledge of the capabilities of the three very different Services.

The final argument in favour of curtailing the swing away from the Chiefs of Staff system is that if an effective military voice is to be heard in national affairs, the CDS needs to be seen to be able to call upon the full support of his professional colleagues, each at the head of his Service and with its full weight behind him. The CDS is not there to ride roughshod over them, but rather to provide the central dynamic; clarifying issues, identifying genuinely alternative points of view, giving his own objective thoughts on issues, and stage-managing and presenting the whole spectrum of military advice for political decision. He has to do this with foresight and in a way that ministers understand; and, whenever possible, in a way that harmonises with political objectives. But he may on occasion have to take an opposing line, and then, like any other national leader, he needs a power base if he is not to be ignored. The Chiefs of Staff Committee, as the collective military heads of the Armed Forces, undoubtedly provides the CDS with that base. Without it, the CDS is little more than the head of a purely bureaucratic structure subject to political manipulation. Nor would he have the ability to demonstrate that his advice could only be discarded at national military peril and, hence, political risk.

In this connection, the recent selection of the VCDS as CDS to succeed Craig – the first time that this appointment will have been filled by someone who, although a full member of the Chiefs of Staff Committee, has not been head of his own Service, may be significant. The appointment of this immensely able officer, wise in the ways of Whitehall, has been welcomed in many quarters, but it may suggest a further deliberate strengthening of the Central Staff at the expense of the practical influence of the Service Chiefs; and it would be unfortunate to say the least if, as a result, the post of CDS came to be regarded in political circles as just another senior official divorced from any responsible power base.

For over a quarter of a century, the Chiefs have provided, under the direction of a CDS, the ideal forum for thinking through strategy and other Defence policy issues, and for measuring possible solutions, plans and recommendations against practical reality and manageability; and for establishing a proper dialogue with ministers. Such a forum will be as important as ever in arguing through new strategic policies in response to the dramatic changes in Eastern Europe and events in the Middle East.

Indeed today, the Ministry of Defence is once again in the thick of it, and may be facing a 'sea change' in parliamentary and public attitudes. But the same things were happening when the Salisbury Commission established the Chiefs of Staff Committee sixty-seven years ago, and a mere fifteen before the outbreak of the Second World War. History does not necessarily repeat itself since lessons are learnt and international views on the use of force change. But the world is still a highly dangerous place, in which we have to maintain our security through the astute manipulation of alliances to keep the balance of power in our favour. For this we need balanced military forces with which to back our foreign policy. It is the Chiefs' duty, directly and indirectly, to advise the Government on the shape and size of our Armed Forces, which must be capable of quick expansion in an emergency, be highly mobile and hard-hitting, and above all

confident, contented, fully manned and armed with up to date weapons, tactics and techniques. It is no easy task to fulfil in a climate of
constant financial stringency.

Moreover, the human factor must never be overlooked. Each
Service is a living organism with all the collective strengths and
weaknesses of the men and women who wear its uniform, and who,
like any team, will only give of their best if properly led by a captain
in whom they have trust and confidence. There have been times
when, if it had not been for the leadership of the Chiefs as professional heads of their Services, those organisms would have wilted
and decayed through lack of confidence. They would not have with-
stood the constant salami-slicing of expenditure; the counter-
productive contracts moratoria; the savage reductions in training
activity with depressing restrictions on sea miles steamed, track miles
travelled and flying hours flown; the never ending administrative
cheese paring and reduction of operational reserves; and the frequent
failures to maintain pay comparability. It is the Chiefs, who have
maintained morale and made successes like those in the Falklands
and the Gulf possible, but it has often been a close run thing.
Without the leadership that the Chiefs have provided, the fighting
experience and professional skills of the Services, accumulated over
the centuries, would have been dissipated, and backing for British
foreign policy lost.

Defence is an on-going and ever changing business, requiring high
morale that comes from good leadership. The Chiefs must not be
allowed to wither on the vine through over-pruning their powers and
responsibilities in favour of a bland central staff organisation, and
isolating them from the mainstream of Defence policy. For in spite of
the political character of military operations at the end of the 20th
Century, depth of realism and professional expertise is still vital
when conflict looms. Bureaucrats, working in the interests of expediency, must not be allowed to take over from the doers. The dire
consequences could be a re-run of the 1920s and '30s.

Much will depend upon the selection of successive CDSs. While
the CDS must rightly have the ultimate responsibility for advising
the Government on military policy, it will be to the advantage of his
own authority and to the quality of his advice that he brings the
other Chiefs into his deliberations. He will naturally try for a consensus on policy, which is easy enough when adequate resources are
available, but far less so under the more normal conditions of inadequate funding. When consensus lies beyond his grasp, he should

concentrate on identifying the different points of view and the respective risks for ministerial decision, annotating them with his own hopefully more objective assessments. This is the way the Chiefs have worked in their more successful moments.

There should be little difficulty in developing future Defence policy, provided CDSs, even if chosen from a wider field, are men who can keep their colleagues 'in on the act' while they themselves take the initiative in strategic thinking and give objective advice to ministers. Under such leadership, a proper balance between policy and management should be maintained, and the Defence voice should remain strong in the corridors of power, whatever the future may hold. And it is also vitally important that Service officers should never become identified with any political party. They must continue to serve Her Majesty's constitutionally elected ministers, whatever their politics. It would be a sad day, if, as happens in some other countries, the Chiefs were ever to be chosen more for their political sympathies rather than their professional qualities.

The corporate nature of the Chiefs' system is also, to some extent, a hedge against political nepotism. Another hedge is the much maligned 'Buggin's turn next' in the selection of CDSs, which has been a way of making certain that each Service grooms its brightest officers by giving them the necessary background and experience to join the Chiefs at the appropriate time. In this way each Service has a suitable candidate for the post of CDS when its own turn comes round. Such considerations have to be balanced, of course, against current judgement of the best man for the job; and ministers certainly expect to be able to consider more than one candidate. The long-term nature of the Services' sifting system, however, does take these appointments out of the political arena. This is essential if the quality and integrity of the Chiefs, upon whose judgements the security of the realm primarily depends, is to be ensured.

The Chiefs of Staff Committee is a very British institution, suitable only for Anglo-Saxon style democracy with its abhorrence of dictatorship – the curse of Cromwell – in any shape or form. It provides military efficiency without loss of political control; it gives cohesion in sea, land and air warfare; it maintains the vital linkage between power and responsibility; and it balances policy and management. Perhaps the best description of its functions was given by Field Marshal Lord Alanbrooke, speaking to the Royal Empire Society in 1946. He provides an appropriate tailpiece for this book:

Development of the three Services in time of peace must be co-ordinated and correlated to ensure that we have a closely-knit and well-balanced fighting machine at our disposal. This in itself is not sufficient. Our fighting machine must be closely enmeshed into the gear wheels of Government. Modern defence embraces questions intimately connected with foreign policy, home security, man-power labour, transportation, supply, food, and most of the other matters of Government concern. Defensive plans at all times must be closely interlocked with the activities of all the various Government Departments so as to ensure that from their very inception they are built on the rocks of close co-operation and not on the sands of isolation. Furthermore, the defensive organisation must be so closely integrated with the Government executive as to provide responsible statesmen with that true appreciation of the country's strength and weakness so essential in ensuring a relation between selected policy and the strength required to support it.

We have built up in this country during the last couple of decades the organisation of the Chiefs of Staff Committee, constituting probably the best system that history has produced to date.[2]

Defence policy is not just about the defence of the realm. It is also about the projection and protection of British interests world-wide; about the support of British foreign policy in this unstable world; and about what Britain wishes to be seen by others to be able to do in the development of a new world order. The Chiefs of Staff Committee provides the forum for debate on strategic issues and the dynamic to implement measures needed to ensure that Britain's armed forces are such that they are sought by allies and feared by opponents, not so much for their size, but for the impact that their fighting qualities can make upon balances of power.

Appendix A

THE CHIEFS FROM 1904 TO 1991

CHIEFS OF DEFENCE STAFF

Sir William Dickson*	1957–59 (with no Defence Staff)
Earl Mountbatten	1959–65 (Defence Staff formed in April 1964)
Sir Richard Hull	1965–67
Lord Elworthy	1967–71
Lord Hill-Norton	1971–73
Lord Carver	1973–76
Sir Andrew Humphrey	1976–77 (Died in Office)
Sir Edward Ashmore	1977 (February to August)
Lord Cameron	1977–79
Lord Lewin	1979–82
Lord Bramall	1982–85
Lord Fieldhouse	1985–88
Lord Craig	1988–91

FIRST SEA LORDS

Sir John Fisher	1904–10
Sir Arthur Wilson	1910–11
Sir Francis Bridgeman	1911–12
Prince Louis of Battenberg	1912–14
Lord Fisher	1914–15
Sir Henry Jackson	1915–16
Viscount Jellicoe	1916–18
Sir Rosslyn Wemyss	1918–19
Earl Beatty	1919–27
Sir Charles Madden	1927–30
Sir Frederick Field	1930–33
Lord Chatfield	1933–38

---

* Chairman of the Chiefs of Staff Committee from 1955

Sir Roger Backhouse	1938–39 (Retired in ill-health)
Sir Dudley Pound	1939–43 (Died in Office)
Viscount Cunningham	1943–46
Sir John Cunningham	1946–48
Lord Fraser	1948–51
Sir Rhoderick McGrigor	1951–55
Earl Mountbatten	1955–59
Sir Charles Lambe	1959–60 (Retired in ill-health)
Sir Caspar John	1960–63
Sir David Luce	1963–66 (Resigned)
Sir Varyl Begg	1966–68
Sir Michael Le Fanu	1968–70 (Died in Office)
Lord Hill-Norton	1970–71
Sir Michael Pollock	1971–74
Sir Edward Ashmore	1974–77
Lord Lewin	1977–79
Sir Henry Leach	1979–82
Lord Fieldhouse	1982–85
Sir William Staveley	1985–89
Sir Julian Oswald	1989–

CHIEFS GENERAL STAFF
('IMPERIAL' FROM 1910 TO 1964)

Sir Neville Lyttelton	1904–08
Lord Nicholson	1908–12
Earl French	1912–14
Sir Charles Douglas	1914 (Died in Office)
Sir James Wolfe-Murray	1914–15
Sir Archibald Murray	1915
Sir William Robertson	1915–18
Sir Henry Wilson	1918–22
Earl of Cavan	1922–26
Lord Milne	1926–33
Sir Archibald Montgomery-Massingberd	1933–36
Sir Cyril Deverell	1936–37
Viscount Gort	1937–39
Lord Ironside	1939–40
Sir John Dill	1940–41
Viscount Alanbrooke	1941–46
Viscount Montgomery	1946–48

Viscount Slim	1948–52
Lord Harding	1952–55
Sir Gerald Templer	1955–58
Sir Francis Festing	1958–61
Sir Richard Hull	1961–65
Sir James Cassels	1965–68
Sir Geoffrey Baker	1968–71
Lord Carver	1971–73
Sir Peter Hunt	1973–76
Sir Roland Gibbs	1976–79
Lord Bramall	1979–82
Sir John Stanier	1982–85
Sir Nigel Bagnall	1985–88
Sir John Chapple	1988–

Chiefs of Air Staff

Lord Trenchard	1917–18
Sir Frederick Sykes	1918–19
Lord Trenchard	1919–29
Sir John Salmond	1930–33
Sir Geoffrey Salmond	1933 (Died in Office)
Sir John Salmond	1933 (April–May)
Sir Edward Ellington	1933–37
Lord Newall	1937–40
Viscount Portal	1940–45
Lord Tedder	1945–49
Sir John Slessor	1950–52
Sir William Dickson	1953–55
Sir Dermot Boyle	1955–59
Sir Thomas Pike	1960–63
Lord Elworthy	1963–67
Sir John Grandy	1967–71
Sir Dennis Spotswood	1971–74
Sir Andrew Humphrey	1974–76
Lord Cameron	1976–77
Sir Michael Beetham	1977–82
Sir Keith Williamson	1982–85
Lord Craig	1985–88
Sir Peter Harding	1988–

Appendix B

MEMORANDUM BY PRIME MINISTER
INAUGURATING
THE COMMITTEE OF CHIEFS OF STAFF

3RD AUGUST, 1926

TO

Admiral of the Fleet David, Earl Beatty, Knight Grand Cross of the Most Honourable Order of the Bath, Member of the Order of Merit, Knight Grand Cross of the Royal Victorian Order, Companion of the Distinguished Service Order, First Sea Lord and Chief of the Naval Staff,

General Sir George Francis Milne, Knight Grand Cross of the Most Distinguished Order of Saint Michael and Saint George, Knight Commander of the Most Honourable Order of the Bath, Companion of the Distinguished Service Order, Chief of the Imperial General Staff; and

Air Chief Marshal Sir Hugh Montague Trenchard, Baronet, Knight Grand Cross of the Most Honourable Order of the Bath, Companion of the Distinguished Service Order, Chief of the Air Staff

GREETING.

WHEREAS it has been found to be essential for the defence and safety of the realm that a permanent body should be created and charged with the duty of considering and investigating the question of Imperial Defence as a whole, of co-ordinating the functions and requirements of the Navy, Army, and Air Force, and of the Civil Administration in matters of Imperial Defence, and of advising His Majesty's Government on the matters of general policy arising therefrom;

AND WHEREAS the Committee of Imperial Defence has been appointed for the aforesaid purpose and charged with the aforesaid duties;

AND WHEREAS it is necessary for the due and efficient discharge of the aforesaid duties that the Committee of Imperial Defence should be furnished with expert advice and assistance in regard to the respective functions and requirements of the Navy, Army, and Air Force, and the best method of combining and co-ordinating their efforts for their common object of the defence of the Empire;

NOW THEREFORE, I, the Right Honourable Stanley Baldwin, His Majesty's Prime Minister, one of the Commissioners for executing the office of Lord High Treasurer of the United Kingdom of Great Britain and Ireland, and Chairman of the Committee of Imperial Defence in consultation with the Secretary of State for War, the Secretary of State for Air, and the First Lord of the Admiralty, do by these presents constitute and appoint you the said

David, Earl Beatty, being First Sea Lord and Chief of the Naval Staff; Sir George Francis Milne, being Chief of the Imperial General Staff;
and

Sir Hugh Montague Trenchard, being Chief of the Air Staff to be a standing Sub-Committee of the Imperial Defence, under my direction, to investigate and consider in common all such matters as may from time to time be referred to you by the said Committee of Imperial Defence, and to report thereon for the information of the said Committee to the best of your knowledge and capacity.

AND YOU are to submit to the Chairman of the said Committee of Imperial Defence, for the consideration of the said Committee, any matter relating to Imperial defence on which, in your opinion, further enquiry or investigation is necessary, and to forward copies of all Reports and Minutes of your proceedings to me and to the Secretary of State for War, the Secretary of State for Air, and the First Lord of the Admiralty.

AND YOU are expressly to take notice that in all matters in respect of which you are so required jointly to investigate, consider, deliberate, and advise, each of you is to keep always before his mind the object for which the said Committee of Imperial Defence was created and exists, that is to say, for the consideration of questions of defence as a whole and for the co-ordination of the function of the several arms of His Majesty's Forces, all considerations concerning a single Service being subordinated to the main object of National and

Imperial Defence which the three Services have in common.

GIVEN under my hand at Downing Street, Westminster, this third day of August, 1926.

(*signed*) Stanley Baldwin.

Appendix C

JOINT SERVICE DEFENCE COLLEGE
THE FOUNDATION OF THE COLLEGE

1. The College was established originally in 1947 at Latimer as the Joint Services Staff College (JSSC). The JSSC Course continued until August 1971, when Latimer became the National Defence College. In April 1979, the Joint Warfare Establishment moved from Old Sarum to become the Joint Warfare Wing (JWW) of the College while the National Defence Course came under the aegis of the Defence Studies Wing (DSW). In June 1982 it was decided that the National Defence College would move to the Royal Naval College Greenwich and with effect from 25 April 1983 would be known as the Joint Service Defence College (JSDC). The JWW meanwhile separated from the National Defence College and moved to Wilton and subsequently to Poole.

2. The present concept of the College has a great deal in common with the JSSC and the message received from the Chiefs of Staff in 1947 is equally appropriate today:

'Under the pressure of the late war the fundamental interdependence of the 3 Fighting Services was effectively realised. The combination of forces of sea, land and air, united as never before by common dangers towards a common end, proved irresistible. Our enemies lacked this team spirit. They lost. Nor without it should we have been able to win.

In peace the bow is unbent, the spur of great events no longer presses, and each Fighting Service tends to travel its own particular path and, lacking a common purpose, to wander further apart from the others. This has happened before. The Joint Services Staff College has great responsibilities to ensure that it shall never happen again.

The College has been founded as a centre to nourish and to disseminate amongst the higher commanders of all Services and their staffs that mutual understanding and Inter-Service comradeship-in-arms which, in war, were the very base of our success and without which we should be in poor shape to face a future war.'

Tedder
J H D Cunningham
Montgomery of Alamein

References

Chapter 1 (1868–1899)

Based principally upon F A Johnson's *Defence by Committee*, N A M Rodger's *The Admiralty*, W S Hamer's *The British Army: Civil-Military Relations; 1885–1905*, H Gordon's *The War Office* and the report of the Hartington Commission.

1. Hartington Commission Report, C 5979 of 1890 para 20.
2. Quoted by H Gordon in *The War Office*, p 27.
3. Rodger, *The Admiralty*, p 94.
4. The post of Secretary at War was abolished in 1854, when the Secretary of State for War and Colonies shed his colonial responsibilities and took sole charge of the War Office.
5. Rodger, p 95.
6. Mackay, *Fisher of Kilverston*, p 151.
7. Hamer, *The British Army*, p 8.
8. Johnson, *Defence by Committee*, p 17, quoting Colonial Conference Proceedings 1887, Vol 1, C 5091 p 9 & 16.
9. Johnson, p 27, quoting Hansard Vol 323 of 5 March 1888, col 229.
10. Hartington Commission Report, C 5979 of 1890, p v.
11. *Ibid*, p vi, para 7.
12. *Ibid*, p vi, para 10.
13. Quoted by H Gordon, p 69.
14. Hartington Commission Report, p xxix, last para.
16. *Ibid*, para 40.
17. *Ibid*, p viii, para 20.
18. *Ibid*.
19. *Ibid*, p vii, para 15.
20. Quoted by H Gordon, p 71.
21. Quoted by Maurice and Arthur, *Wolseley*, pp 278–9.

Chapter 2 (1899–1914)

Based on the same works as Chapter 1 together with the Elgin and Esher Reports, Samuel R Williamson's *The Politics of Grand Strategy*, and Nicholas d'Ombrain's *War Machinery and High Policy*.

1. Esher Report (Part I), p 3, para 2.
2. Memorandun by F-M Wolseley; Cd 572 (1901) xxxix 3–4.
3. Hansard Vol 90, 4 March 1901, p 545.
4. Elgin Report, Cd 1789 (1903), terms of reference.
5. Mackay, *Fisher of Kilverston*; p 293.
6. Esher Committee Report; Pt I; Sec 1; para 1.
7. *Ibid*, para 4.
8. *Ibid*, para 2.
9. *Ibid*; Covering Letter; final para.
10. *Ibid*; Sec 1, para 15.
11. *Ibid*; Sec 2; para 5.
12. Hamer; *The British Army*; p 254–5.
13. Cd 2200 of 4 May 1904.
14. D'Ombrain; p 68, quoting Balfour B M Add. MS. 49701.
15. Williamson; p 167.
16. *Ibid*; p 187, quoting Fisher to Mckenna, 20 August 1911.
17. *Ibid*; p 193, quoting Asquith to Haldane 31 August 1911.
18. *Ibid*; p 309, quoting CAB 16/28A of 7 Nov 1913.
19. Callwell; *Wilson*, Vol I, p 154.

Chapter 3 (1914–1916)

Based upon Hankey's *Supreme Command, 1914–1918*; Winston Churchill's *The World Crisis*; Cassar's *Kitchener*; Admiral Bacon's *Life of Lord Fisher of Kilverstone*; Callwell's *Wilson*; Robertson's *Soldiers and Statesmen*; and Marder's *Dreadnought to Scapa Flow*, Vols 2 and 3.

1. Hankey, *Supreme Command, 1914–18*, Vol 1, p 244–5.
2. *Ibid*, p 176 para 1.
3. Robertson, *Soldiers and Statesmen, 1914–18*, Vol 1, p 41–2; and Cassar, *Kitchener*, p 331.
4. Marder, *Dreadnought to Scapa Flow*, Vol 2, p 87.
5. *Ibid*, p 37.
6. Cassar, p 176.
7. Callwell, *Wilson*, Vol 1, p 178.
8. Churchill, *The World Crisis*, p 324–5.
9. Magnus, *Kitchener*, p 322.
10. Churchill, p 329.
11. Marder, p 210.
12. *Ibid*, p 210.
13. Robertson, p 103.
14. Cassar, quoting Kitchener to Birdwood, CAB 19/13.
15. Hamilton, *Gallipoli Diary*, Vol 1, p 2.
16. Marder, p 237, quoting Dardennelles Commission.
17. Marder, p 145.
18. Cassar, p 354–6.
19. Bacon, *Life of Lord Fisher*, p 260.
20. Marder, p 281.
21. *Ibid*, p 285.

22. Churchill, p 360.
23. Cassar, p 402.
24. *Ibid*, p 434–5.
25. *Ibid*, p 436–8.

Chapter 4 (1917–1918)

Based on the same works as Chapter 3 with Malcolm Cooper's *The Birth of Independent Air Power*, David Woodward's *Lloyd George and the Generals*, and Smuts Committee's 2nd Report on *Air Organisation* of 17 August 1917.

1. Hankey, *Supreme Command*, Vol 2, p 650 quoting diary entry of 29 April 1917.
2. Lloyd George, *War Memoirs*, Vol 3, p 1041.
3. Woodward, *Lloyd George and the Generals*, quoting Royal Archives, RA GV Q1078/6.
4. Hankey, Vol 2, p 639.
5. Marder, *Dreadnought to Scapa Flow*, Vol 4, p 159 quoting WC 126, report of PM's visit to Admiralty.
6. *Ibid*, p 161, quoting Churchill's *Thoughts and Adventures*, p 136.
7. Haig, *Private Papers*, p 240–1.
8. Cooper, *The Birth of Independent Air Power*, p 58, quoting Trenchard to Henderson, 21.4.16.
9. Smut's *2nd Report on Air Organisation and Home Defence against Air Raid*, 17 August 1917, GT 1658, para 1.
10. *Ibid*, para 5.
11. Marder, Vol 5, p 4, quoting Beatty to Jellicoe of 27.12.17.
12. Robertson, *Soldiers and Statesmen*, p 287.
13. Cooper, p 122, quoting Trenchard to Rothermere, Trenchard Papers MFC 76/1/19.
14. *Ibid*, p 122, quoting Rothermere to Trenchard, MFC 76/1/19.
15. *Ibid*, p 123, quoting *Daily Mail* of 15.4.18.
16. *Ibid*, p 136, quoting Trenchard Papers, MFC 76/1/32.
17. Hankey, Vol 2, p 792.

Chapter 5 (1919–1933)

Based upon: Gibbs' *Grand Strategy*, Vol 1, Churchill's *The Second World War*, Vol 1, and the Salisbury Committee Report of 1924; Roskill's *Naval Policy between the Wars* and *The Earl Beatty*; Callwell's *Wilson* and Nicol's *Milne*; and Malcolm Smith's *British Air Strategy between the Wars*, Boyle's *Trenchard*, and Laffin's *Sir John Salmond*.

1. Ismay, *Memoirs*, pp 51–52.
2. Terraine, *The Right of the Line*, p 16.
3. Roskill, *Naval Policy between the Wars*, p 45.
4. Jeffery, *Military Correspondence of Henry Wilson*, Letter 74 of 13 June 1919.
5. CD 9230, *Haldane Report*, p 6 para 10 and p 22 para 4.
6. Gibbs, p 3.
7. Boyle, *Trenchard*, p 351.
8. Roskill, *Beatty*, p 303.
9. Gibbs, p 12.

10. Ismay, *Memoirs*, p 35.
11. Boyle, p 383.
12. Roskill, *Naval Policy*, p 366 sub-para 12.
13. Jeffery, p 376.
14. Fuller, *Memoirs*, p 422.
15. Boyle, p 437.
16. Cmd 2029, *Salisbury Committee Report*, p 6 para 12.
17. *Ibid*, p 25 para 1.
18. *Ibid*, pp 17–18 para 7 (iv).
19. *Ibid*, pp 20–21 para 43.
20. Gibbs, p 48.
21. *Ibid*, p 55.
22. *Ibid*, p 60.
23. Fuller, pp 422–3.
24. *Ibid*, pp 433–434.
25. Gibbs, p 61.
26. Liddell Hart, *Memoirs*, Vol 1, p 228.
27. Roskill, *Beatty*, p 355.
28. *Ibid*, *Beatty*, p 375.
29. Laffin, Swifter than Eagles, pp 202–203.
30. Ismay, p 52.
31. Boyle, p 552.
32. Gibbs, p 78.
33. Boyle, p 679.
34. Gibbs, p 87.
35. Peden, *British Rearmament & the Treasury, 1932–39*, p 8.

Chapter 6 (1934–39)

Based upon Gibbs' *Grand Strategy* Vol 1, Churchill's *The Second World War* Vol 1, Roskill's *Naval Policy between the Wars*, Malcolm Smith's *British Air Strategy between the Wars*, and G C Peden's *British Rearmament and the Treasury*; supplemented by Lord Chatfield's *It Might Happen Again*, Roskill's *Hankey, Man of Secrets*, Colville's *Man of Valour*, Slessor's *The Central Blue*, and Terraine's *The Right of the Line*.

1. Gibbs, *Grand Strategy*, Vol 1, p 809.
2. Roskill, *Hankey, Man of Secrets*, p 103.
3. Peden, *British Rearmament and the Treasury*, p 1.
4. Chatfield, *It Might Happen Again*, p 77.
5. *Ibid*, p 198.
6. Gibbs, p 96.
7. *Ibid*, p 127.
8. *Ibid*, p 180.
9. *Ibid*, p 256.
10. *Ibid*, p 276.
11. Chatfield, p 100.
12. *Ibid*, p 99.
13. *Ibid*, p 203.
14. Gibbs, p 277.

15. *Ibid*, p 284, 2nd para.
16 *Ibid*, p 284, 3rd para.
17. *Ibid*, p 293.
18. *Ibid*, p 295.
19. *Ibid*, p 307.
20. *Ibid*, p 313.
21. *Ibid*, p 646.
22. *Ibid*, p 315.
23. Slessor, *The Central Blue*, p 240–1.
24. Terraine, *The Right of the Line*, p 82.
25. Minney, *The Private Papers of Hore Belisha*, p 66.
26. Colville, *Man of Valour*, p 80.
27. Ismay, *Memoirs of Lord Ismay*, p 89.
28. Terraine, p 76.
29. *Ibid*, p 72.

Chapter 7 (1939–41)

Based on *Grand Strategy*, Vols II and III; Churchill's *Second World War*, Vols II and III; Roskill's *War at Sea*; and Terraine's *The Right of the Line*; and supplemented by Ismay's *Memoirs*; Colville's *Man of Valour* (Gort's biography); *The Ironside Diaries*; Richard's *Portal of Hungerford*; and Tedder's *With Prejudice*.

1. Churchill, Vol II, p 20.
2. Butler, *Grand Strategy*, Vol II, p 7.
3. Fraser, *Alanbrooke*, p 137.
4. Butler, p 171.
5. Terraine, *The Right of the Line*, p 107.
6. *Ironside Diaries*, p 227.
7. Butler, p 149.
8. Ismay, *Memoirs*, p 159.
9. Butler, p 181.
10. Terraine, p 141.
11. Ironside, p 309.
12. Terraine, p 151.
13. Churchill, *Second World War*, Vol II, p 64.
14. Butler, p 210.
15. *Ibid*, p 211.
16. Churchill, Vol II, p 376.
17. Butler, p 342.
18. *Ibid*, p 344.
19. *Ibid*.
20. *Ibid*, p 408–9.
21. Terraine, p 267.
22. Butler, p 423.
23. *Ibid*, p 453.
24. Churchill, Vol III, p 373–6.
25. *Ibid*, p 376.
26. *Ibid*, p 361.

27. Tedder, *With Prejudice*, p 184.
28. Fraser, p 168.
29. *Ibid*, p 202.
30. *Ibid*, p 203.

Chapter 8 (1942–45)

Based upon *Grand Strategy* Vols III to VI; the US Department of the Army's Official History, *Strategic Planning for Coalition War* 1941–42 and 1943–44; and Churchill's *Second World War* Vols III to VI; and supplemented by the biographies of the British and American Chiefs.

1. Churchill, *Second World War*, Vol III, p 608–9.
2. Ismay, *Memoirs*, p 243.
3. Gwyer, *Grand Strategy*, Vol III, p 383.
4. Ismay, p 251.
5. Bryant, Vol I, *Turn of the Tide*, p 360.
6. Ismay, p 253.
7. *Ibid*, p 253–4.
8. Public Record Office, Premier 3/119/6, 5 March 1942.
9. Howard, *Grand Strategy*, Vol IV, p 21.
10. *Ibid*, p 23.
11. Matloff & Snell, *Strategic Planning for Coalition War*, 1941–42, p 182.
12. Bryant, Vol I, p 358–9.
13. Matloff & Snell, p 266.
14. *Ibid*, p 276 a.
15. *Ibid*, p 276 b.
16. Gwyer, p 633.
17. *Ibid*, Appx V, para (c), (4).
18. Howard, p 192.
19. Bryant, Vol I, p 444–5.
20. Matloff, *Strategic Planning for Coalition War*, 1943–44, p 106.
21. Howard, p 410.
22. *Ibid*, p 432.
23. *Ibid*, p 498.
24. *Ibid*, p 502.
25. *Ibid*, p 569.
26. *Ibid*, p 568.
27. Bryant, Vol I, 708.
28. Howard, p 570.
29. Bryant, Vol I, p 707.
30. Roskill, *Churchill and the Admirals*, p 236.
31. *Ibid*, p 237.
32. Pack, *Cunningham*, p 1.
33. Molony, *Mediterranean & Middle East Campaigns*, Vol V, p 217.
34. Bryant, *Triumph in the West*, p 62.
35. Churchill, Vol V, p 295.
36. *Ibid*, p 432.
37. Warlimont, *Inside Hitler's Headquarters*.

38. Molony, Vol VI, Pt 1, p 313.
39. *Ibid*, p 313.
40. Churchill, Vol VI, p 86.
41. *Ibid*, Appendix F, p 670
42. *Ibid*, p 671.

Chapter 9 (1945–56)

Based upon the Defence White Papers from 1946 to 1956, Michael Howard's *Central Organisation of Defence*, Eric Grove's *Vanguard to Trident*, Nigel Hamilton's Vol III of *Monty*, Anthony Eden's *Full circle*, Harold Macmillan's Vol III, *The Tides of Fortune, 1945–55* and Vol IV, *Riding the Storm, 1956–59*, and John Cloake's *Templer*. It is supplemented with the *National Biographies* of each Chief of Staff.

1. Howard, *Central Organisation of Defence*; p 8.
2. Hamilton, *Monty*, Vol III; p 579.
3. *Ibid*, Chapter 11.
4. Grove, *Vanguard to Trident*, p 24.
5. Hamilton, Vol III, p 577.
6. Cmd 6923 of 1946, p 5, para 16.
7. Howard, p 8.
8. Grove, p 32–3.
9. Hamilton, Vol III, p 643.
10. Montgomery, *Memoirs*, p 483.
11. Hamilton, Vol III, p 658.
12. *Ibid*, p 658.
13. Grove, p 66.
14. Cloake, *Templer*, p 204.
15. Macmillan, Vol III, p 561.
16. Grove, p 85.
17. *Ibid*, p 91.
18. *Ibid*, p 111.
19. Macmillan, Vol III, p 560.
20. Hamilton, Vol III, p 922.
21. Eden, *Full Circle*, p 371.
22. Cmd. 9691, p 4–5.
23. *Ibid*, p 7.
24. Ziegler, *Mountbatten*, p 539.
25. Cloake, p 348.
26. Beaufre, *The Suez Expedition, 1956*, p 74.
27. Ziegler, p 545.
28. *Ibid*, p 545.

Chapter 10 (1957–64)

Based on the Defence White Papers, 1957–1963, Volumes III and IV of Harold Macmillan's Memoirs, Eric Grove's *Vanguard to Trident*, Philip Ziegler's *Mountbatten*, John Cloake's *Templer*, Harold Watkinson's *Turning Points*, and Michael Howard's *Central Organisation of Defence*.

1. Ziegler, *Mountbatten*, p 578.
2. Macmillan, Volume IV, p 244.

3. Ziegler, p 550.
4. Cmnd 124 of 1957.
5. Wood, *Project Cancelled*, p 160.
6. Ziegler, p 558.
7. *Ibid*, p 562.
8. Howard, *Central Organisation of Defence*, p 10.
9. RUSI Journal, 105/617 of 1960, *Future Trends in Warfare*, by Sir John Cowley.
10. Ziegler, p 564.
11. *Ibid*, p 585.
12. Watkinson, *Turning Points*, p 112.
13. Cmnd 1639 of 1962, p 5, para 8.
14. Ziegler, p 610.
15. Howard, p 18–19.
16. Nunnerley, *President Kennedy and Britain*, 149.
17. Ziegler, p 628.
18. Walker, *How Borneo Was Won*, p 20.
19. *Ibid*, p 622–3.
20. Ziegler, p 702.

Chapter 11 (1965–79)

Based primarily on the Defence White Papers of the period, supplemented by the autobiographies of Harold Wilson, James Callaghan, Denis Healey and Solly Zuckerman, Michael Carver and Neil Cameron, and by Ziegler's *Mountbatten* and Grove's *Vanguard to Trident*.

1. Healey, p 263.
2. Howard, p 28.
3. Healey, p 261.
4. Hansard, 16 Dec 1964, col 423–4.
5. Healey, p 275–6.
6. 1966 Defence White Paper, p 31, para 4.
7. 1967 Supplementary Statement on Defence, p 12, para 1.
8. Healey, p 266.
9. National Biography: 1961–70, p 664–5.
10. Carver, p 448.
11. 1975 Defence White Paper, p 19, para 25 (d).
12. Cameron, p 204.
13. Callaghan, p 555.

Chapter 12 (1979–82)

Based upon Field Marshal Lord Bramall's recollections as the CGS at the time; on John Nott's *The Way Forward*, Keith Speed's *Sea Change*, Eric Grove's *Vanguard to Trident*, and Max Hastings & Simon Jenkins *The Battle for the Falklands*, and on Open Government Documents 80/23 and 82/1.

1. Unpublished lecture notes of Lord Fieldhouse.
2. *Times*, 20 Jan 1976.
3. Conservative Party Manifesto, *The Right Approach*, Chap 12.
4. OGDs 80/23 and 82/1, and Lewin's *British Nuclear Deterrent: A Commentary*.

5. Grove, p 345.
6. *Ibid*, p 346.
7. 1981 Defence White Paper, page 1, para 6.
8. Grove, p 346.
9. Comnd 8288, p 9, para 23.
10. Speed, p 103–7.
11. Grove, p 346.
12. Hastings & Jenkins, *The Battle for the Falklands*, p 61–63.
13. Grove, p 361.
13. *Ibid*, p 365–6.

Chapter 13 (1982–89)

Based on the Defence White Papers of the period, Reports of the House of Commons' Defence Committee, Bramall's recollections, and his own and Fieldhouse's unpublished lecture notes to Service Staff Colleges.

1. Comnd 8758, *The Falklands: The Lessons*, p 15, para 201.
2. *Ibid*, p 35, para 313.
3. Jackson, *Britain's Defence Dilemma*, p 170–2.
4. *Ibid*.
5. HC 584; Defence Committee 3rd Report, 1983–4 Session, paras 47–51; and Ministry of Defence Press Conference on Cmnd 9315.
6. Fieldhouse, unpublished lecture notes of November 1986.
7. 1987 Defence White Paper, p 24, para 7.
8. Jackson, p 178.

Epilogue

1. Harold Macmillan, *The Blast of War*, chap 16.
2. Arthur Bryant, *Triumph in the West*, p 534.

Bibliography

OFFICIAL DOCUMENTS

Comnd. 5979 of 1890; Report of the Hartington Commission of 1888–90.

Cd 1932, 1968, and 1968 of 1904; Esher War Office (Reconstitution) Committee, Parts I, II and III.

Cd. 2200 of 1904; Treasury Minute authorising the Committee of Imperial Defence.

GT. 1658 of 1917; Smuts Committee 2nd Report on Air Reorganisation and Home Defence.

Cd. 9230 of 1918; Haldane Committee Report on Machinery of Government.

Cmd. 2029 of 1924; Salisbury Sub-Committee of CID on National and Imperial Defence.

Cmd. 6923 of 1946; *Central Organisation of Defence.*

Defence White Papers, 1946 to 1990.

Open Government Documents:

   OG-D 80/23: The Future of the UK Nuclear Deterrent Force.

   82/1: The UK Trident Programme.

   OG-D 82/25: Study of Financial Accountability (Ministry of Defence).

House of Commons Reports:

   HC 584: Third Report of Defence Committee, 1983–4 Session.

BRITISH OFFICIAL HISTORIES
First World War

   France & Belgium:
      14 Vols, Brig-Gen Sir James Edmonds.
   Egypt & Palestine:
      2 Vols, Lt-Gen Sir George Macmunn & Captain Cyril Falls.
   Italy, 1915–19:
      1 Vol, Brig-Gen Sir James Edmonds.
   Macedonia:
      2 Vols, Captain Cyril Falls.
   Mesopotamia:
      4 Vols, Brig-Gen F Moberly.

Second World War
   Grand Strategy:

Vol I, N H Gibbs.
Vol II, J R M Butler.
Vol III, J M A Gwyer.
Vol IV, Michael Howard.
Vols V and VI, John Ehrman.
The Campaign in Norway:
One Vol, T K Derry
Mediterranean & Middle East:
Vols I to IV, Maj-Gen I S O Playfair.
Vol V, Brig C J C Molony.
Vol VI, Gen Sir William Jackson.
Victory in the West:
Vols I & II, Major L F Ellis.
The War at Sea:
Three Vols, Captain S W Roskill RN.
The Strategic Bomber Offensive:
Four Vols, Sir Charles Webster & N Frankland.

BIOGRAPHICAL REFERENCES

The National Biography; Oxford University Press.
Who Was Who; A & C Black, London.
Who's Who; A & C Black, London.

OTHER BOOKS & WORKS

Bacon, Admiral Sir Reginald; *The Life of Lord Fisher*; (Hodder & Stoughton, London, 1929)
Beaufre, General, A; *The Suez Expedition, 1956*; (Faber & Faber, 1969)
Black, R; *The Private Papers of Douglas Haig*; (Eyre & Spottiswoode, 1952)
Bond, B; *British Military Policy between the Two World Wars*; (Clarendon Press, Oxford, 1980)
Boyle, A; *Trenchard*; (Collins, London, 1962)
Bradford, Admiral Sir Edward; *Admiral of the Fleet Sir Arthur Wilson*; (John Murray, London, 1923)
Bryant, Arthur; *The Turn of the Tide*; (Collins, London, 1957)
Bryant, Arthur; *Triumph in the West*; (Collins, London, 1959)
Callaghan, James; *Time & Change*; (Collins, London, 1987)
Callwell, General Sir Charles; *Field Marshal Sir Henry Wilson*; Vols I & II; Cassell, London, 1927)
Cameron, M of RAF Lord; *In the Midst of Things*; (Hodder & Stoughton, London, 1986)
Carver, F-M Lord; *Out of Step*; (Hutchinson, London, 1989)
Cassar, G H; *Kitchener: Architect of Victory*; (William Kimber, London, 1977)
Chatfield, Lord; *The Autobiography of*; Vols 1 & 2; (Heinemann, 1942 and 1947)
Churchill, Winston; *The World Crisis; 1911–1918*; one volume edition; (Thornton Butterworth, London, 1931)
Churchill, Winston; *The Second World War*; Vols I to VI; (Cassell, London, 1948 to 1954)
Cloake, J; *Templer*; (Harrap, London, 1985)

Coffey, T M; *Hap*; Biography of US General 'Hap' Arnold (Viking Press, New York, 1982)

Colville, J R; *Man of Valour* (Lord Gort); (Collins, 1972)

Cooper, M; *The Birth of Independent Air Power*; (Allen & Unwin, London, 1986)

Cunningham, A of F, Viscount; *A Sailors Odyssey*; (Hutchinson, London, 1951)

Danchev, A; *Very Special Relationship: Field Marshal Dill and the Anglo-American Alliance 1941-44*; (Brassey's Defence Publishers, London, 1986)

Darby, P; *British Defence Policy East of Suez, 1947-68*; (Oxford University Press, 1973)

Dockrill, M; *British Defence Policy Since 1945*; (Basil Brackwell, London, 1988)

D'Ombrain, N; *War Machinery and High Policy*; (Oxford University Press, 1973)

Eden, Sir Anthony; *Full Circle*; (Cassell, London, 1960)

Ehrman, J; *Cabinet Government and War, 1890-1940*; (Cambridge University Press 1958)

Ferris, J R; *Evolution of British Strategic Policy, 1919-26*; (Macmillan, London, 1989)

Fraser, General Sir David; *Alanbrooke*; (Collins, London, 1983)

French, D; *British Strategy and War Aims; 1914-1916*; (Allen & Unwin, London, 1986)

Fuller, J F C; *Memoirs of an Unconventional Soldier*; (Eyre & Spottiswoode, London, 1936)

Fuller, J F C; *The Decisive Battles of the Western World*; Vol 3; (Eyre & Spottiswoode, London, 1956)

Gooch, J; *The Chiefs of Staff and the Higher Organisation for Defence in Britain, 1904-1984*; Chapter 3 in Hattendorf, J B & Jordan, R S, *Maritime Strategy and the Balance of Power*; (Macmillan, 1989)

Gordon, H; *The War Office*; (Putman, London, 1935)

Grove, E J; *Vanguard to Trident*; (Bodley Head, London, 1987)

Guinn, P; *British Strategy and Politics; 1914-1918*; (Oxford at Clarendon Press; 1965)

Hamer, W S; *The British Army*; (Oxford University Press; London 1970)

Hamilton, General Sir Ian; *Gallipoli Diary*; Vols I & II; (Arnold, London, 1920)

Hamilton, Nigel; *Monty*; 3 Vols; (Hamish Hamilton, London, 1981 to 1986)

Hankey, Lord; *The Supreme Command*; 2 Vols; (Allen & Unwin, London; 1961)

Hankey, Lord; *Government Control in War*; (Cambridge University Press, 1945)

Hannah, W H; *Bobs, Kipling's General*; (Leo Cooper, London, 1972)

Hastings, Max, & Jenkins, Simon; *The Battle for the Falklands*; (Michael Joseph, London, 1983)

Hayes, G P; *The History of the Joint Chiefs of Staff in World War II*; (US Naval Institute, Annapolis, 1953)

Healey, Denis; *The Time of My Life*; (Michael Joseph, London, 1989)

Hodges, Arthur; *Lord Kitchener*; (Thornton Butterworth, London, 1936)

Howard, Michael; *The Central Organisation of Defence*; (RUSI, London, 1970)

Howard, Michael; *The Continental Commitment*; (Temple Smith, London, 1972)

Ismay, General Lord; *The Memoirs of Lord Ismay*; (Heinemann, London, 1960)

Jackson, General Sir William; *Withdrawal from Empire*; (BT Batsford, London, 1986)

Jackson, General Sir William; *Britain's Defence Dilemma*, (BT Batsford, London, 1990)

James, A G T; *The Royal Air Force, The Past 30 Years*; (Macdonald & Jane's, London, 1976)

Jeffery, K; *The Military Correspondence of Field Marshal Sir Henry Wilson, 1918-1922*; (Army Records Society and Bodley Head, London, 1985)

Johnson, F A; *Defence by Committee*; (Oxford University Press, London, 1960)

Laffin, J; *Swifter than Eagles: A Biography of Marshal of the RAF Sir John Salmond*; (Blackwood, London, 1964)

Laqueur, W; *The Second World War*; (Sage Publications, London, 1982)

Lewin, Admiral of the Fleet, Lord; *Britain's Nuclear Deterrent: A Commentary*; written at MOD request for US Defence Journals

Lloyd George; *War Memoirs*; 6 Vols; (Ivor Nicholson & Watson, London, 1934)

Lloyd, Selwyn; *Suez 1956*; (Jonathan Cape, London, 1978)

MacDiarmid, D S; *The Life of Lt-General Sir James Grierson*; (Constable, London, 1923)

MacLeod, Colonel R & Kelley, D; *The Ironside Diaries*; (Constable, London, 1962)

Mackay, R F; *Fisher of Kilverstone*; (Clarendon Press, Oxford, 1973)

Macmillan, H; *Tides of Fortune, 1945–55*; (Macmillan, London, 1969)

Macmillan, H; *Riding the Storm, 1956–59*; (Macmillan, London, 1971)

Magnus, Sir Philip; *Kitchener: Portrait of an Imperialist*; (Murray, London, 1958)

Marder, A J; *From Dreadnought to Scapa Flow*; 5 Vols; (Oxford University Press, 1961–72)

Marder, A J; *Winston is Back*; Supplement 5 of *The English Historical Review*; (Longmans, London, 1972)

Matloff, M; *Strategic Planning for Coalition War, 1943–44*; (Department of the Army, Washington, 1959)

Matloff, M & Smell, E M; *Strategic Planning for Coalition War, 1941–42*; (Department of the Army, Washington, 1953)

Maurice, General Sir Fredrick, and Arthur, Sir George; *The Life of Lord Wolseley*; (Heinemann, London, 1924)

Maurice, General Sir Fredrick; *Haldane, 1856–1915*; (Faber, 1937)

Minney, R J; *Private Papers of Hore-Belisha*; (Collins, 1960)

Morgan, K O; *Lloyd George*; (Weidenfeld & Nicholson, London, 1974)

Mosley, L; *Marshall, Organiser of Victory*; (Methuen, London, 1982)

Nicol, G; *Uncle George: Field Marshall Lord Milne of Salonika and Rubishaw*; (Reedminster Publications, London, 1976)

Pack, S W C; *Cunningham, the Commander*; (Batsford, London, 1974)

Peden, G C; *British Rearmament & the Treasury*; (Scottish Academic Press, Edinburgh, 1979)

Richards, D; *Portal of Hungerford*; (Heinemann, London, 1977)

Robertson, F-M Sir William; *Soldiers and Statesmen*; 2 Vols, (Cassel, London, 1926)

Rodger, N A M; *The Admiralty*; (Terence Dalton, Lavenham, 1979)

Roskill, S; *Churchill and the Admirals*; (Collins, London, 1977)

Roskill, S; *Naval Policy between the Wars*; 2 Vols; (Collins, London, 1968–1976)

Roskill, S; *Hankey; Man of Secrets*; 3 Vols; (Collins, London, 1970–74)

Roskill, S; *Earl Beatty*; (Collins, London, 1980)

Slessor, Marshall of the Royal Air Force Sir John; *The Central Blue*; (Cassell, London, 1956)

Smith, M; *British Air Strategy between the Wars*; (Clarendon Press, Oxford, 1984)

Snyder, W P; *The Politics of British Defence Policy, 1945–62*; (Ernest Benn, London and Ohio State University Press, 1964)

Speed, K; *Sea Change*; (Ashgrove Press, Bath, 1982)

Sydenham, Lord (George Clarke); *Studies of an Imperialist*; (Chapman & Hall,

London, 1928)

Tedder, M of RAF Lord; *With Prejudice*; (Cassell, London, 1966)

Terraine, J; *The Right of the Line*; (Hodder & Stoughton, London, 1985)

Walker, Gen Sir Walter; *How Borneo Was Won*; (Round Table, 1969)

Watkinson, H; *Turning Points*; (Michael Russell, London, 1986)

Williamson, S R; *The Politics of Grand Strategy*; 2 Vols; (Harvard U P, 1969)

Wilson, Harold; *The Labour Government, 1964–1970*; (Weidenfeld & Nicholson, London, 1971)

Wilson, K M; *The Policy of the Entente*; (Cambridge U P, 1985)

Wood, D; *Project Cancelled*; (Macdonald & Jane's, London, 1978)

Woodward, R D; *Lloyd George and the Generals*; (University of Delaware Press, Newark, USA, 1983)

Ziegler, P; *Mountbatten*; (Collins, London, 1985)

INDEX